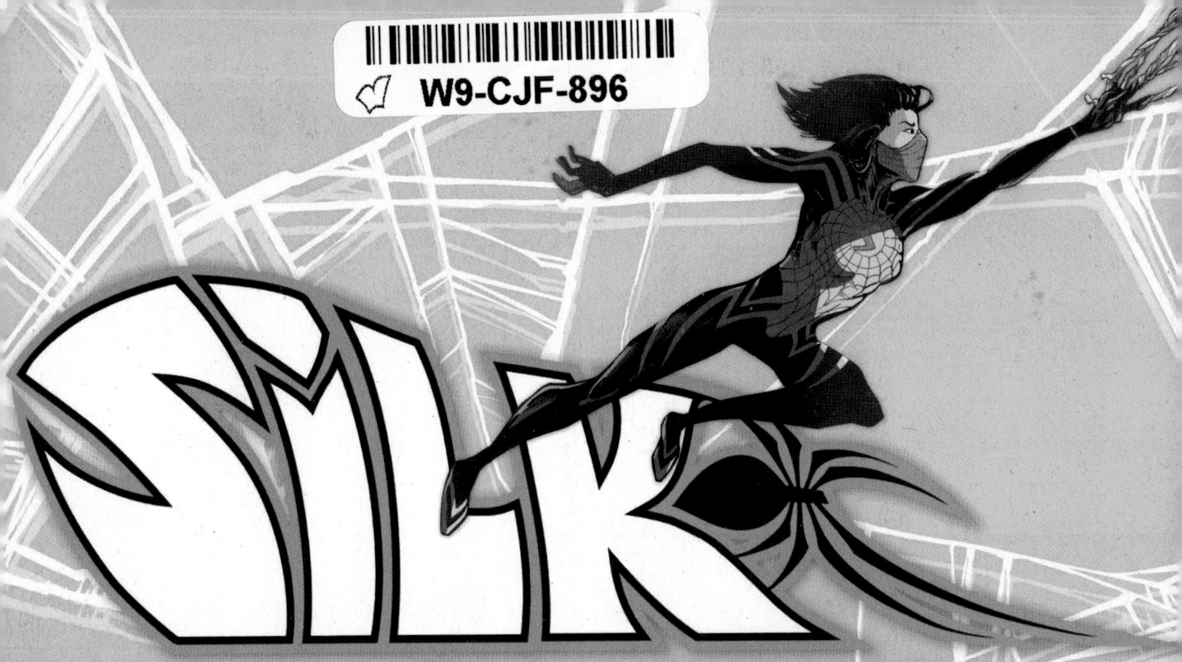

SILK
OUT OF THE SPIDER-VERSE VOL. 1

AMAZING SPIDER-MAN (2014) #4-6

WRITER: Dan Slott
PENCILER: Humberto Ramos
INKER: Victor Olazaba
COLOR ARTIST: Edgar Delgado
LETTERERS: Chris Eliopoulos (#4-5) & VC's Joe Caramagna (#6)
COVER ART: Humberto Ramos & Edgar Delgado

SILK (2015A) #1-7

WRITER: Robbie Thompson
ARTISTS: Stacey Lee (#1-3 & #5-6), Annapaola Martello (#4) & Tana Ford (#7)
COLOR ARTIST: Ian Herring
LETTERER: VC's Travis Lanham
COVER ART: Dave Johnson

AMAZING SPIDER-MAN (2015) #1 "BREAKING BAD"

WRITER: Robbie Thompson
ARTIST: Stacey Lee
COLOR ARTIST: Ian Herring
LETTERER: VC's Travis Lanham
COVER ART: Alex Ross

SILK (2015B) #1-6

WRITER: Robbie Thompson
ARTISTS: Stacey Lee (#1), Tana Ford (#2-3 & #6) & Veronica Fish (#4-5)
COLOR ARTIST: Ian Herring
LETTERER: VC's Travis Lanham
COVER ART: Helen Chen

ASSISTANT EDITOR: Devin Lewis EDITORS: Nick Lowe & Ellie Pyle

COLLECTION EDITOR: Jennifer Grünwald
ASSISTANT EDITOR: Daniel Kirchhoffer
ASSISTANT MANAGING EDITOR: Maia Loy
ASSISTANT MANAGING EDITOR: Lisa Montalbano
ASSOCIATE MANAGER, DIGITAL ASSETS: Joe Hochstein
VP PRODUCTION & SPECIAL PROJECTS: Jeff Youngquist
BOOK DESIGNER: Stacie Zucker
SVP PRINT, SALES & MARKETING: David Gabriel
EDITOR IN CHIEF: C.B. Cebulski

SILK: OUT OF THE SPIDER-VERSE VOL. 1. Contains material originally published in magazine form as AMAZING SPIDER-MAN (2014) #4-6, SILK (2015A) #1-7, SILK (2015B) #1-6 and AMAZING SPIDER-MAN (2015) #1. First printing 2020. ISBN 978-1-302-92873-5. Published by MARVEL WORLDWIDE, INC., a subsidiary of MARVEL ENTERTAINMENT, LLC. OFFICE OF PUBLICATION: 1290 Avenue of the Americas, New York, NY 10104. **Printed in the U.S.A.** KEVIN FEIGE, Chief Creative Officer; DAN BUCKLEY, President, Marvel Entertainment; JOE QUESADA, EVP & Creative Director; DAVID BOGART, Associate Publisher & SVP of Talent Affairs; TOM BREVOORT, VP, Executive Editor; NICK LOWE, Executive Editor, VP of Content, Digital Publishing; DAVID GABRIEL, VP of Print & Digital Publishing; JEFF YOUNGQUIST, VP of Production & Special Projects; ALEX MORALES, Director of Publishing Operations; DAN EDINGTON, Managing Editor; RICKEY PURDIN, Director of Talent Relations; JENNIFER GRÜNWALD, Senior Editor, Special Projects; SUSAN CRESPI, Production Manager; STAN LEE, Chairman Emeritus. For information regarding advertising in Marvel Comics or on Marvel.com, please contact Vit DeBellis, Custom Solutions & Integrated Advertising Manager, at vdebellis@marvel.com. For Marvel subscription inquiries, please call 888-511-5480. **Manufactured between 12/25/2020 and 1/26/2021 by FRY COMMUNICATIONS, MECHANICSBURG, PA, USA.**

10 9 8 7 6 5 4 3 2 1

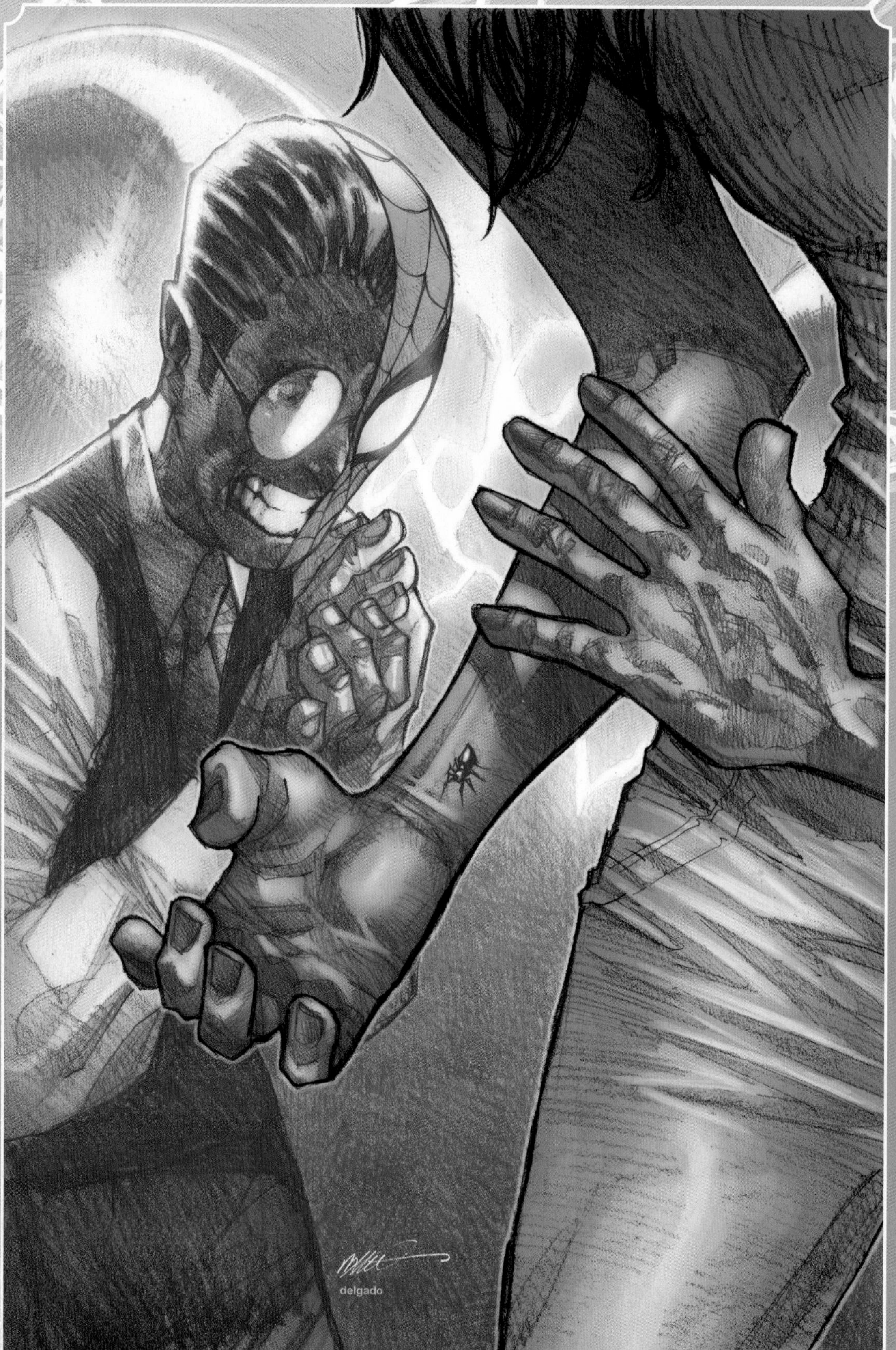
delgado

AMAZING SPIDER-MAN (2014) #4

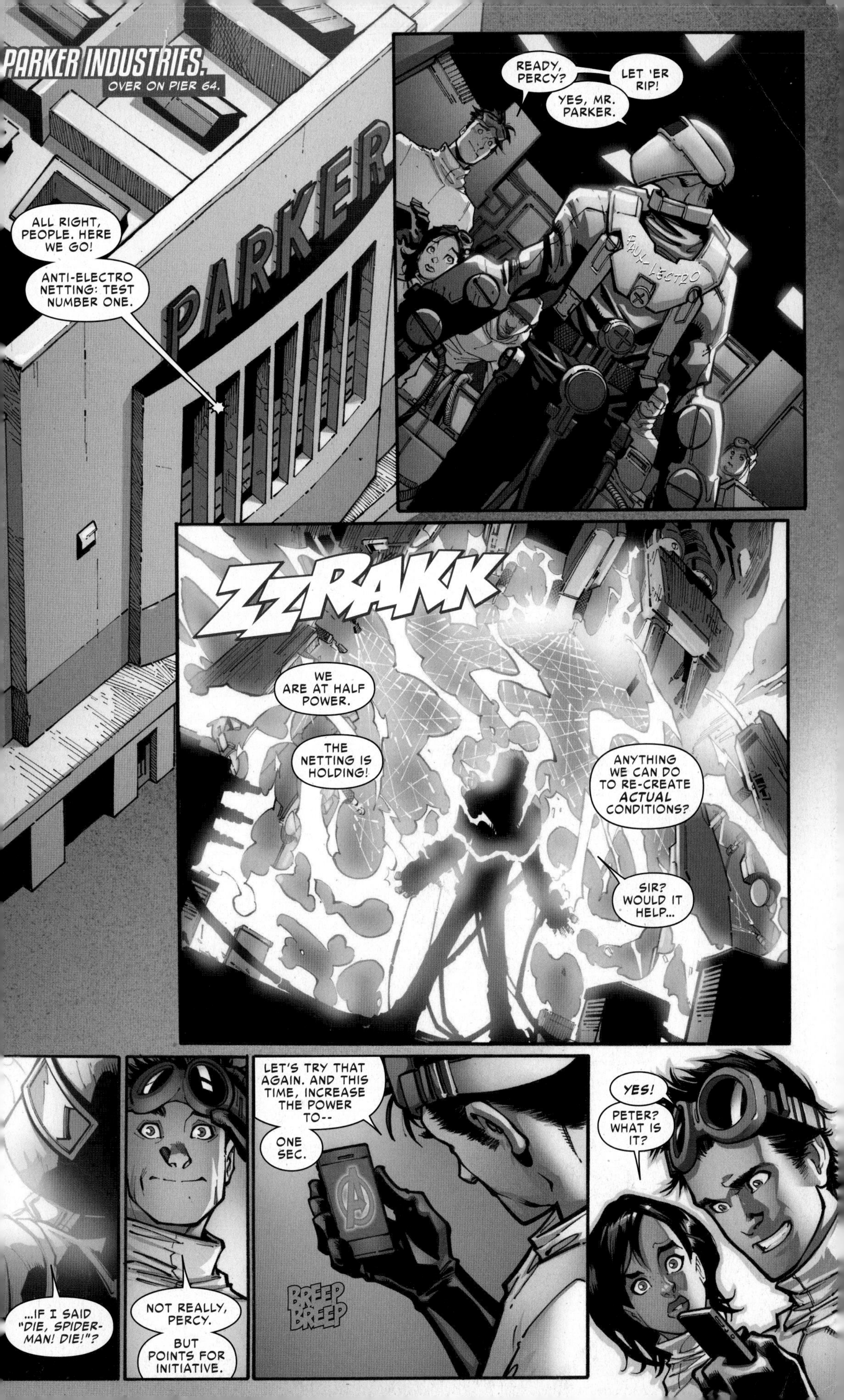
PARKER INDUSTRIES.
OVER ON PIER 64.
PARKER
ALL RIGHT, PEOPLE. HERE WE GO!
ANTI-ELECTRO NETTING: TEST NUMBER ONE.
READY, PERCY?
LET 'ER RIP!
YES, MR. PARKER.
FAUX-LECTRO
ZZRAKK
WE ARE AT HALF POWER.
THE NETTING IS HOLDING!
ANYTHING WE CAN DO TO RE-CREATE ACTUAL CONDITIONS?
SIR? WOULD IT HELP...
...IF I SAID "DIE, SPIDER-MAN! DIE!"?
NOT REALLY, PERCY.
BUT POINTS FOR INITIATIVE.
LET'S TRY THAT AGAIN. AND THIS TIME, INCREASE THE POWER TO--
ONE SEC.
BREEP BREEP
YES!
PETER? WHAT IS IT?

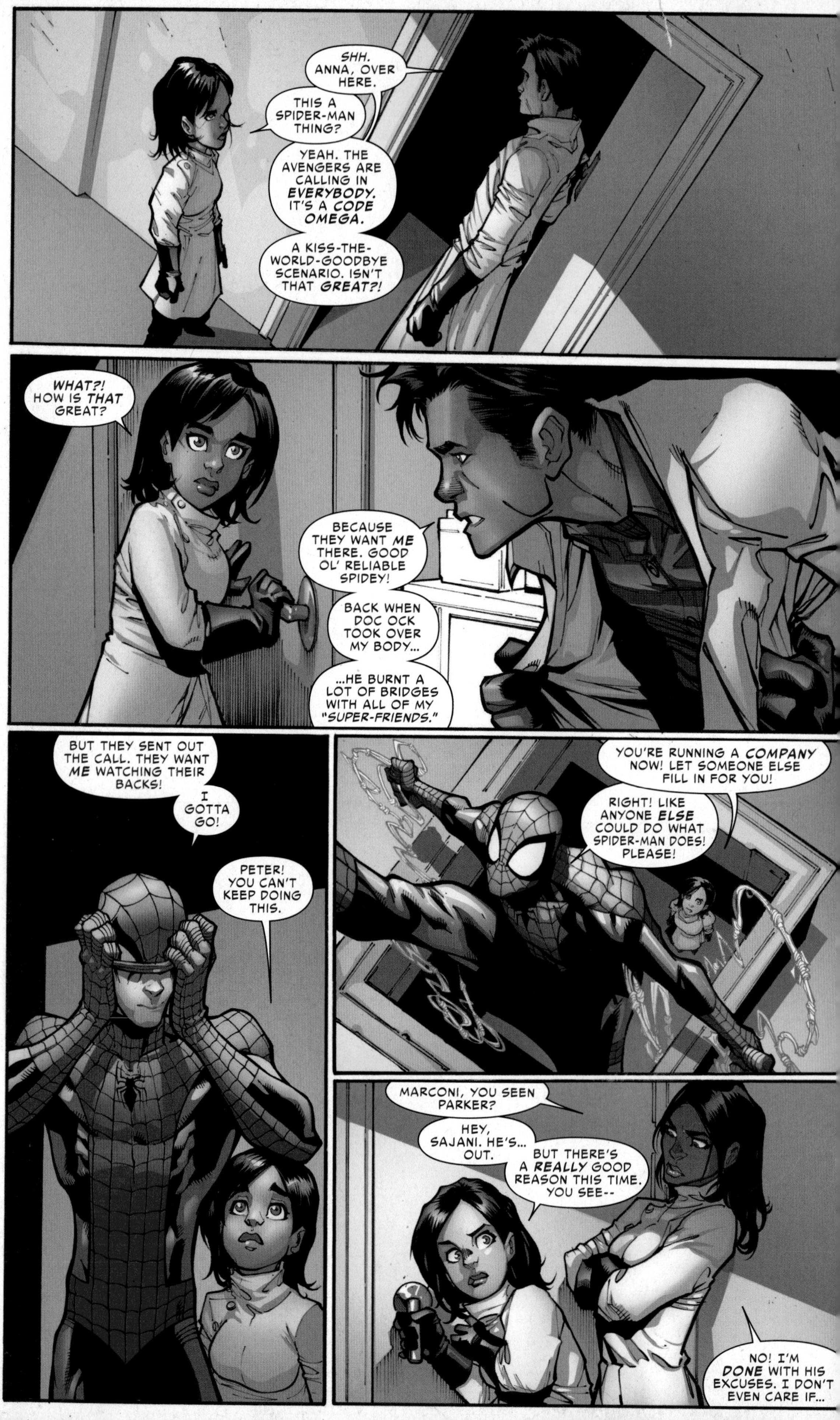
SHH. ANNA, OVER HERE.
THIS A SPIDER-MAN THING?
YEAH. THE AVENGERS ARE CALLING IN EVERYBODY. IT'S A CODE OMEGA.
A KISS-THE-WORLD-GOODBYE SCENARIO. ISN'T THAT GREAT?!
WHAT?! HOW IS THAT GREAT?
BECAUSE THEY WANT ME THERE. GOOD OL' RELIABLE SPIDEY!
BACK WHEN DOC OCK TOOK OVER MY BODY...
...HE BURNT A LOT OF BRIDGES WITH ALL OF MY "SUPER-FRIENDS."
BUT THEY SENT OUT THE CALL. THEY WANT ME WATCHING THEIR BACKS!
I GOTTA GO!
PETER! YOU CAN'T KEEP DOING THIS.
YOU'RE RUNNING A COMPANY NOW! LET SOMEONE ELSE FILL IN FOR YOU!
RIGHT! LIKE ANYONE ELSE COULD DO WHAT SPIDER-MAN DOES! PLEASE!
MARCONI, YOU SEEN PARKER?
HEY, SAJANI. HE'S... OUT.
BUT THERE'S A REALLY GOOD REASON THIS TIME. YOU SEE--
NO! I'M DONE WITH HIS EXCUSES. I DON'T EVEN CARE IF...

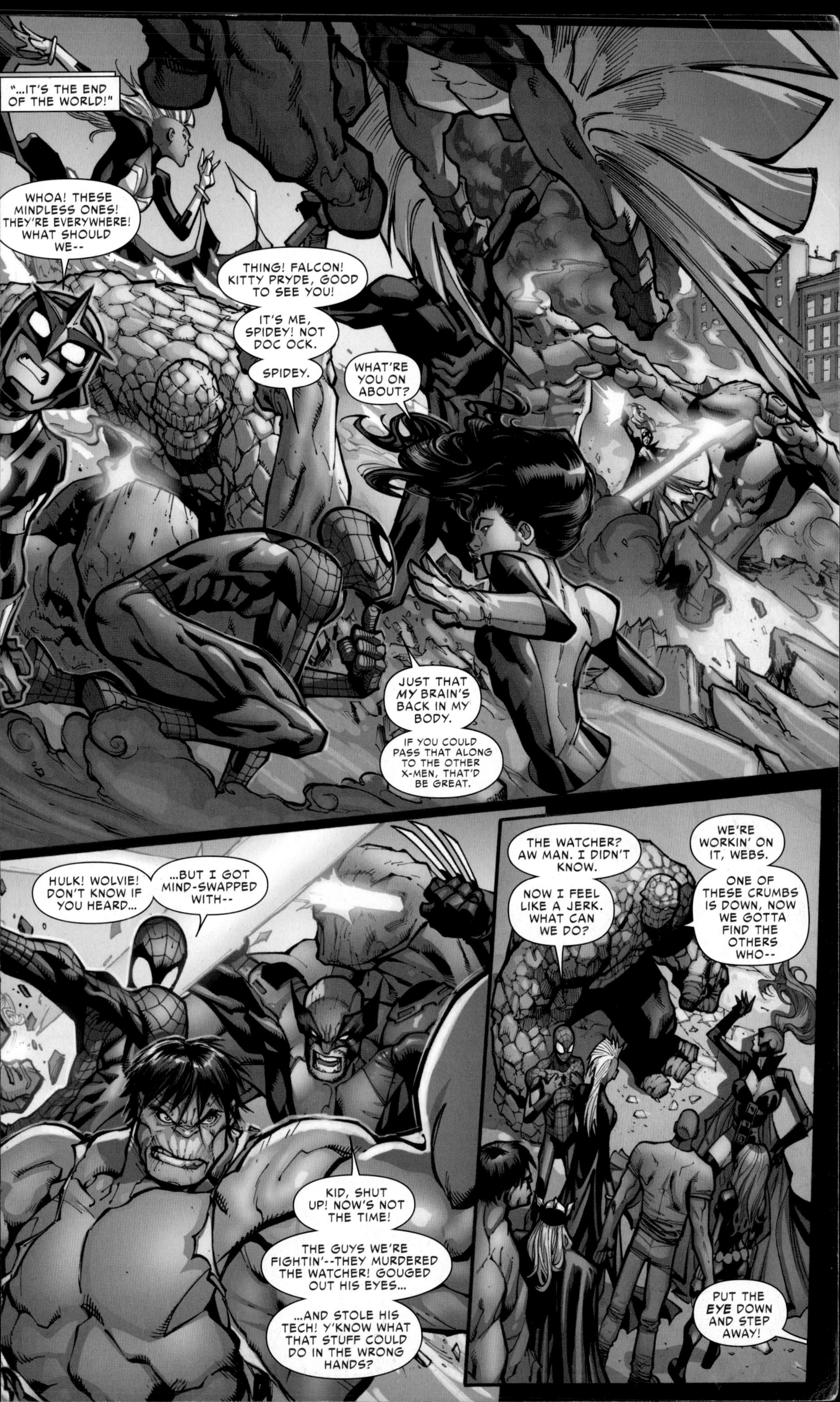
"...IT'S THE END OF THE WORLD!"
WHOA! THESE MINDLESS ONES! THEY'RE EVERYWHERE! WHAT SHOULD WE--
THING! FALCON! KITTY PRYDE, GOOD TO SEE YOU!
IT'S ME, SPIDEY! NOT DOC OCK.
SPIDEY.
WHAT'RE YOU ON ABOUT?
JUST THAT MY BRAIN'S BACK IN MY BODY.
IF YOU COULD PASS THAT ALONG TO THE OTHER X-MEN, THAT'D BE GREAT.
HULK! WOLVIE! DON'T KNOW IF YOU HEARD...
...BUT I GOT MIND-SWAPPED WITH--
KID, SHUT UP! NOW'S NOT THE TIME!
THE GUYS WE'RE FIGHTIN'--THEY MURDERED THE WATCHER! GOUGED OUT HIS EYES...
...AND STOLE HIS TECH! Y'KNOW WHAT THAT STUFF COULD DO IN THE WRONG HANDS?
THE WATCHER? AW MAN. I DIDN'T KNOW.
NOW I FEEL LIKE A JERK. WHAT CAN WE DO?
WE'RE WORKIN' ON IT, WEBS.
ONE OF THESE CRUMBS IS DOWN, NOW WE GOTTA FIND THE OTHERS WHO--
PUT THE EYE DOWN AND STEP AWAY!

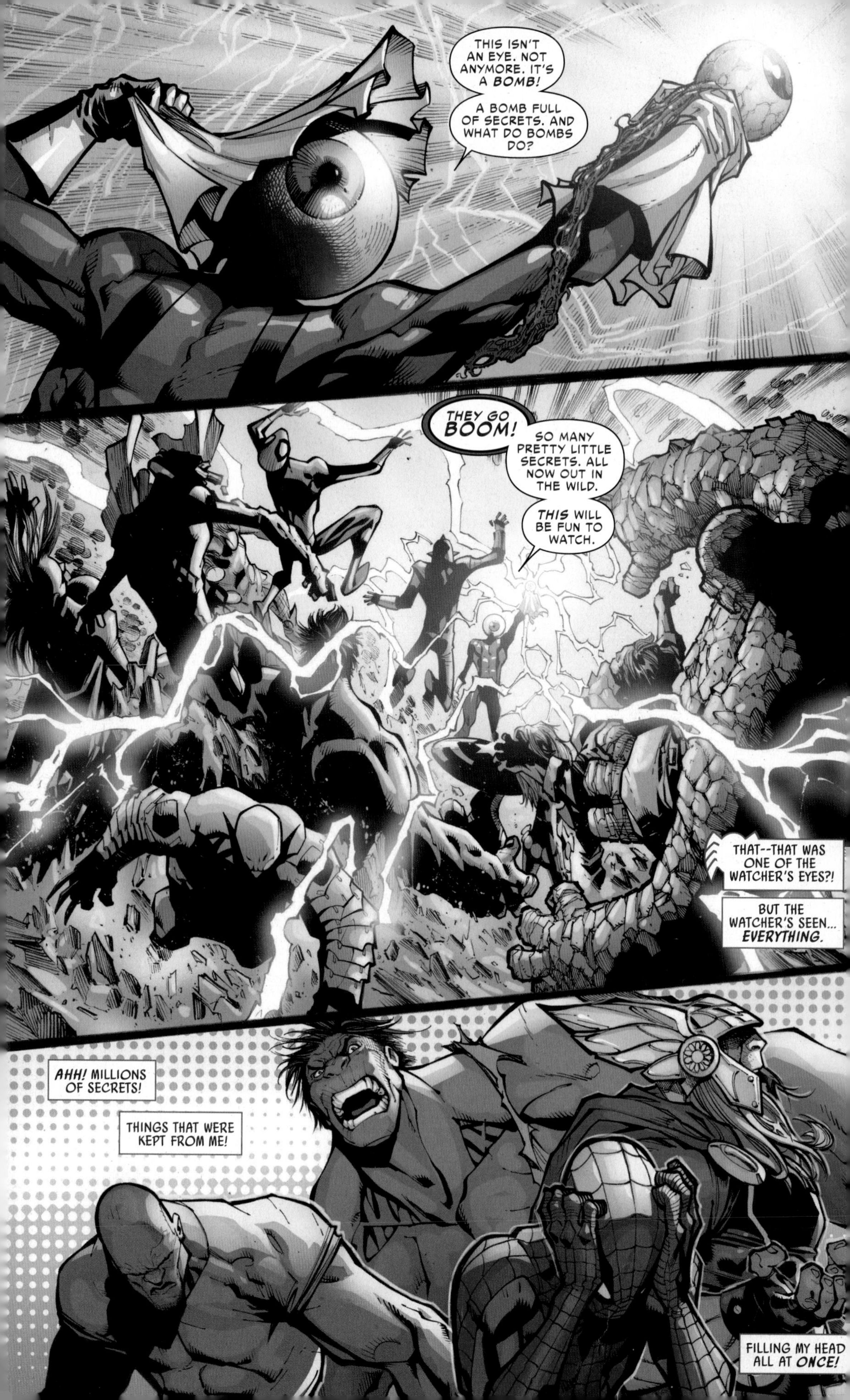
THIS ISN'T AN EYE. NOT ANYMORE. IT'S A BOMB!
A BOMB FULL OF SECRETS. AND WHAT DO BOMBS DO?
THEY GO BOOM!
SO MANY PRETTY LITTLE SECRETS. ALL NOW OUT IN THE WILD.
THIS WILL BE FUN TO WATCH.
THAT--THAT WAS ONE OF THE WATCHER'S EYES?!
BUT THE WATCHER'S SEEN... EVERYTHING.
AHH! MILLIONS OF SECRETS!
THINGS THAT WERE KEPT FROM ME!
FILLING MY HEAD ALL AT ONCE!

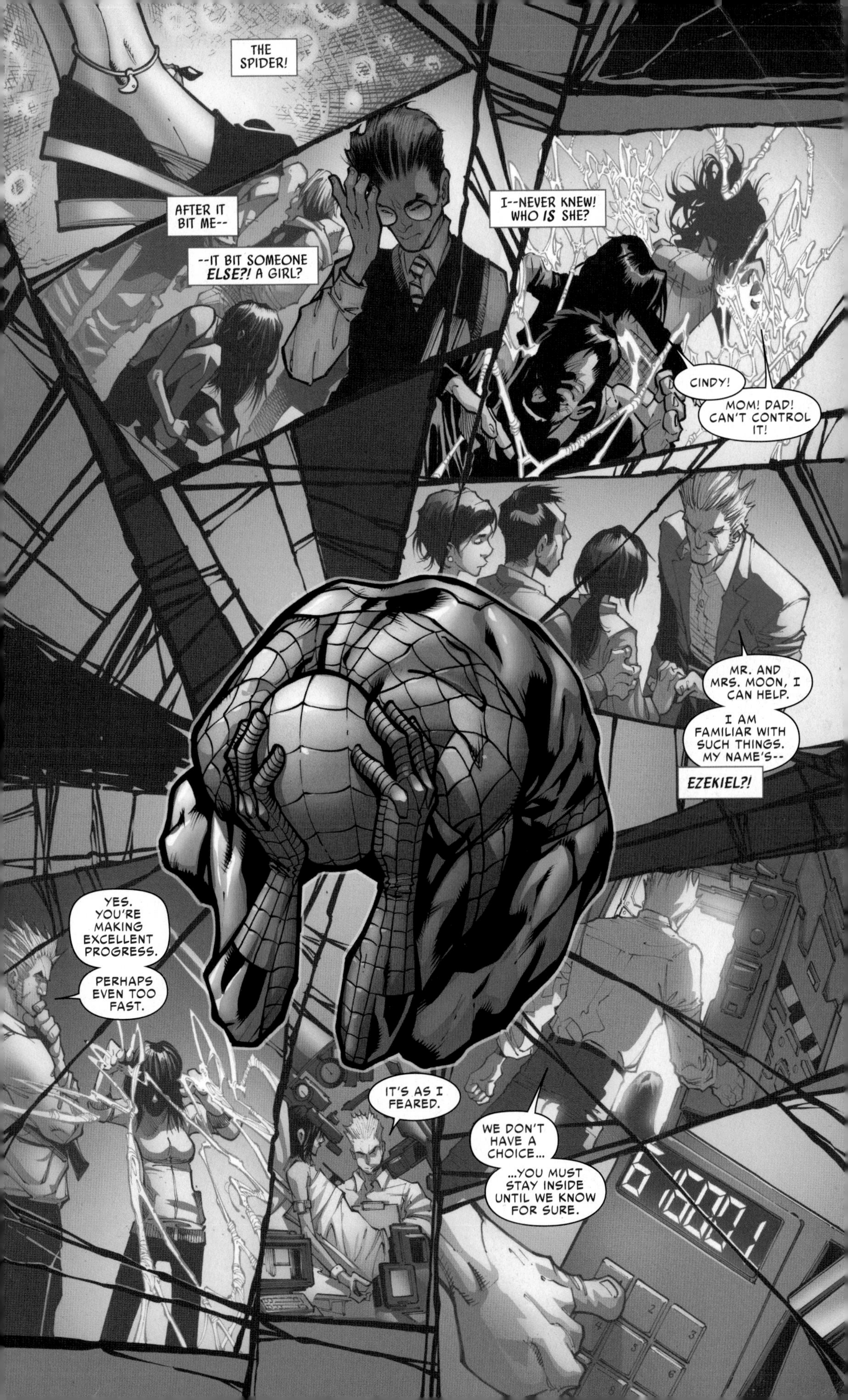

THE SPIDER!
AFTER IT BIT ME--
--IT BIT SOMEONE ELSE?! A GIRL?
I--NEVER KNEW! WHO IS SHE?
CINDY!
MOM! DAD! CAN'T CONTROL IT!
MR. AND MRS. MOON, I CAN HELP.
I AM FAMILIAR WITH SUCH THINGS. MY NAME'S--
EZEKIEL?!
YES. YOU'RE MAKING EXCELLENT PROGRESS.
PERHAPS EVEN TOO FAST.
IT'S AS I FEARED.
WE DON'T HAVE A CHOICE...
...YOU MUST STAY INSIDE UNTIL WE KNOW FOR SURE.

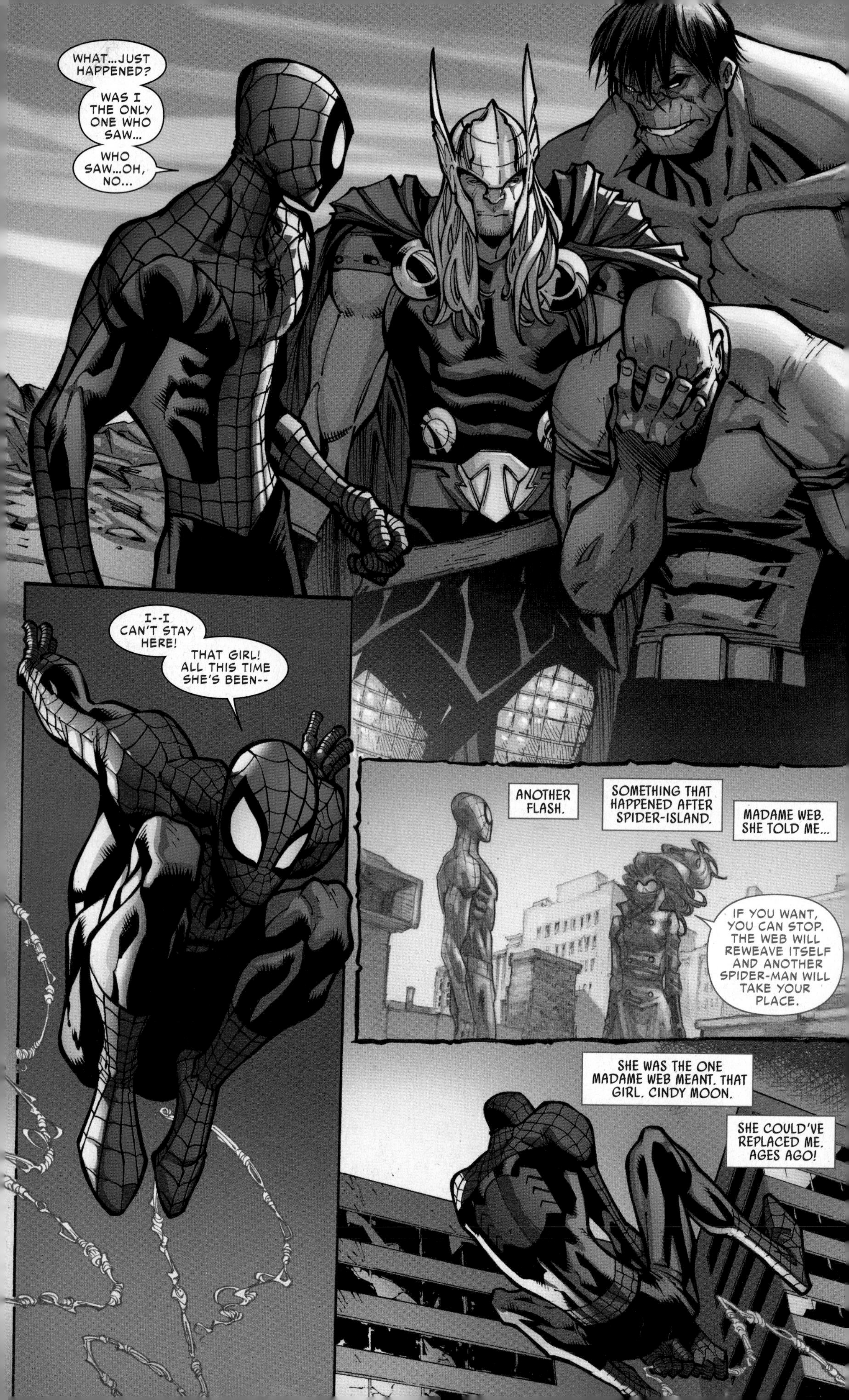
WHAT...JUST HAPPENED?
WAS I THE ONLY ONE WHO SAW...
WHO SAW...OH, NO...
I--I CAN'T STAY HERE!
THAT GIRL! ALL THIS TIME SHE'S BEEN--
ANOTHER FLASH.
SOMETHING THAT HAPPENED AFTER SPIDER-ISLAND.
MADAME WEB. SHE TOLD ME...
IF YOU WANT, YOU CAN STOP. THE WEB WILL REWEAVE ITSELF AND ANOTHER SPIDER-MAN WILL TAKE YOUR PLACE.
SHE WAS THE ONE MADAME WEB MEANT. THAT GIRL. CINDY MOON.
SHE COULD'VE REPLACED ME. AGES AGO!

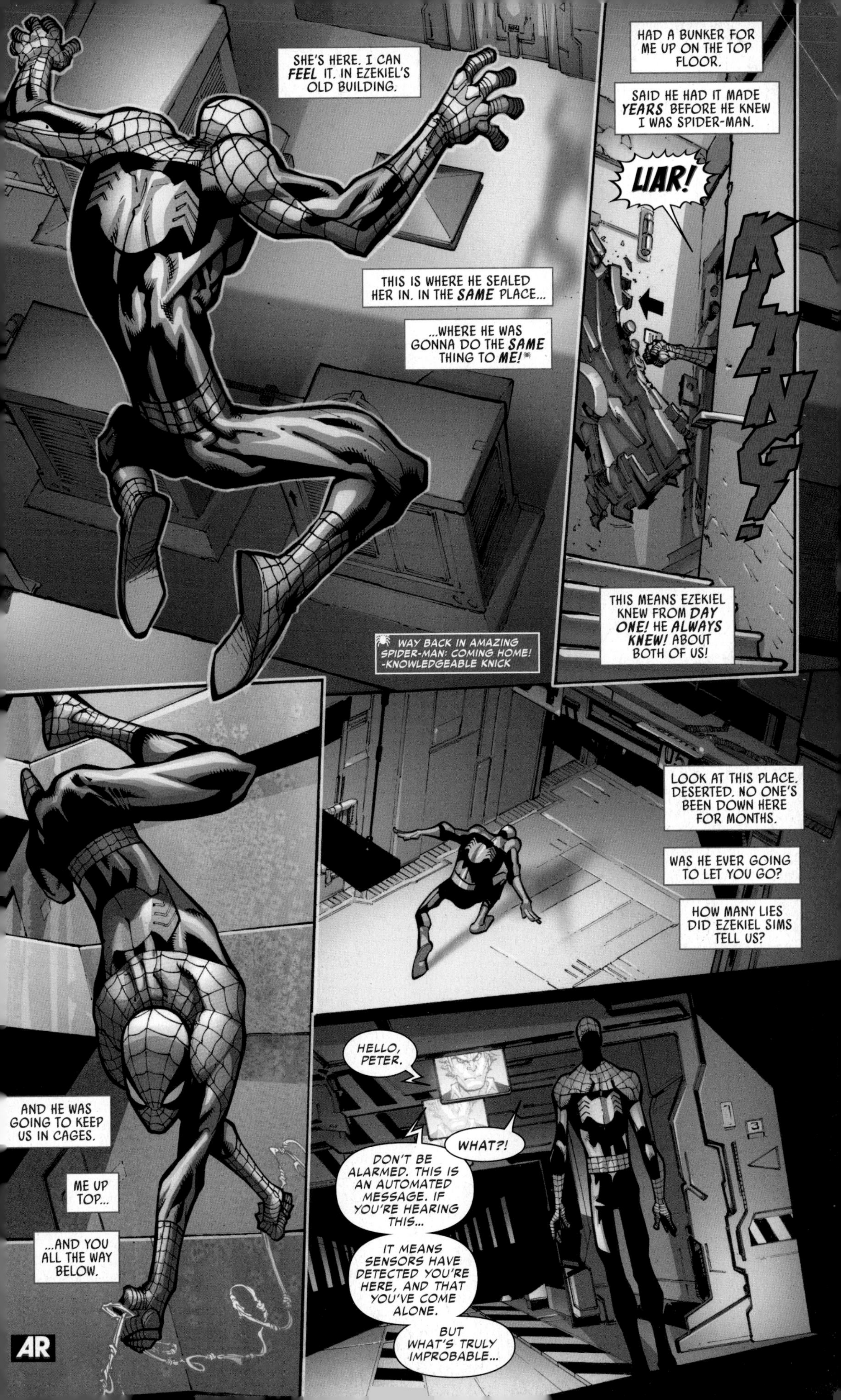

SHE'S HERE. I CAN FEEL IT. IN EZEKIEL'S OLD BUILDING.
THIS IS WHERE HE SEALED HER IN. IN THE SAME PLACE...
...WHERE HE WAS GONNA DO THE SAME THING TO ME!
WAY BACK IN AMAZING SPIDER-MAN: COMING HOME! -KNOWLEDGEABLE KNICK
HAD A BUNKER FOR ME UP ON THE TOP FLOOR.
SAID HE HAD IT MADE YEARS BEFORE HE KNEW I WAS SPIDER-MAN.
LIAR!
KLANG!
THIS MEANS EZEKIEL KNEW FROM DAY ONE! HE ALWAYS KNEW! ABOUT BOTH OF US!
AND HE WAS GOING TO KEEP US IN CAGES.
ME UP TOP...
...AND YOU ALL THE WAY BELOW.
LOOK AT THIS PLACE. DESERTED. NO ONE'S BEEN DOWN HERE FOR MONTHS.
WAS HE EVER GOING TO LET YOU GO?
HOW MANY LIES DID EZEKIEL SIMS TELL US?
HELLO, PETER.
WHAT?!
DON'T BE ALARMED. THIS IS AN AUTOMATED MESSAGE. IF YOU'RE HEARING THIS...
IT MEANS SENSORS HAVE DETECTED YOU'RE HERE, AND THAT YOU'VE COME ALONE.
BUT WHAT'S TRULY IMPROBABLE...
AR

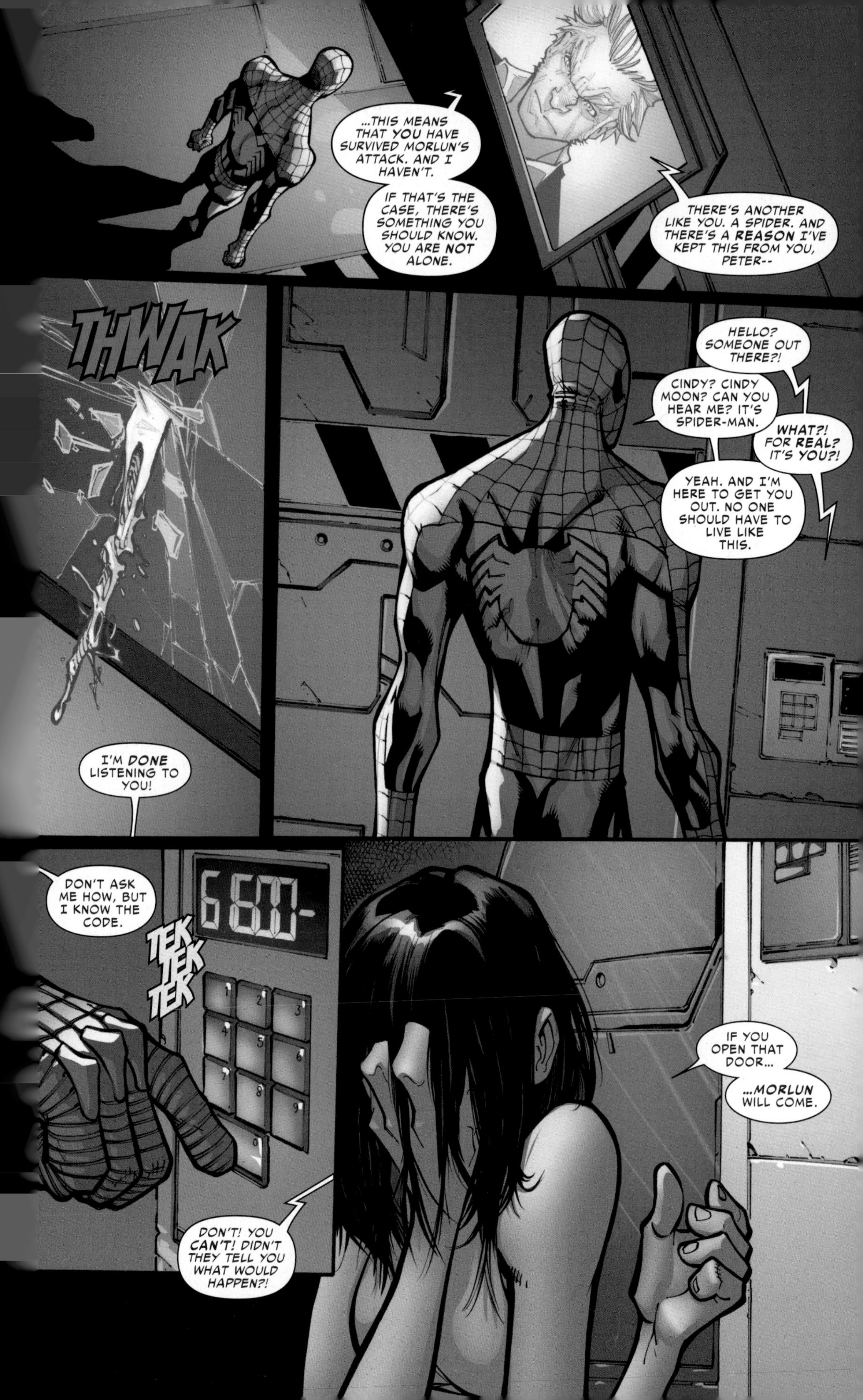

...THIS MEANS THAT YOU HAVE SURVIVED MORLUN'S ATTACK. AND I HAVEN'T.
IF THAT'S THE CASE, THERE'S SOMETHING YOU SHOULD KNOW. YOU ARE NOT ALONE.
THERE'S ANOTHER LIKE YOU. A SPIDER. AND THERE'S A REASON I'VE KEPT THIS FROM YOU, PETER--
THWAK
I'M DONE LISTENING TO YOU!
HELLO? SOMEONE OUT THERE?!
CINDY? CINDY MOON? CAN YOU HEAR ME? IT'S SPIDER-MAN.
WHAT?! FOR REAL? IT'S YOU?!
YEAH. AND I'M HERE TO GET YOU OUT. NO ONE SHOULD HAVE TO LIVE LIKE THIS.
DON'T ASK ME HOW, BUT I KNOW THE CODE.
TEK TEK TEK
DON'T! YOU CAN'T! DIDN'T THEY TELL YOU WHAT WOULD HAPPEN?!
IF YOU OPEN THAT DOOR...
...MORLUN WILL COME.

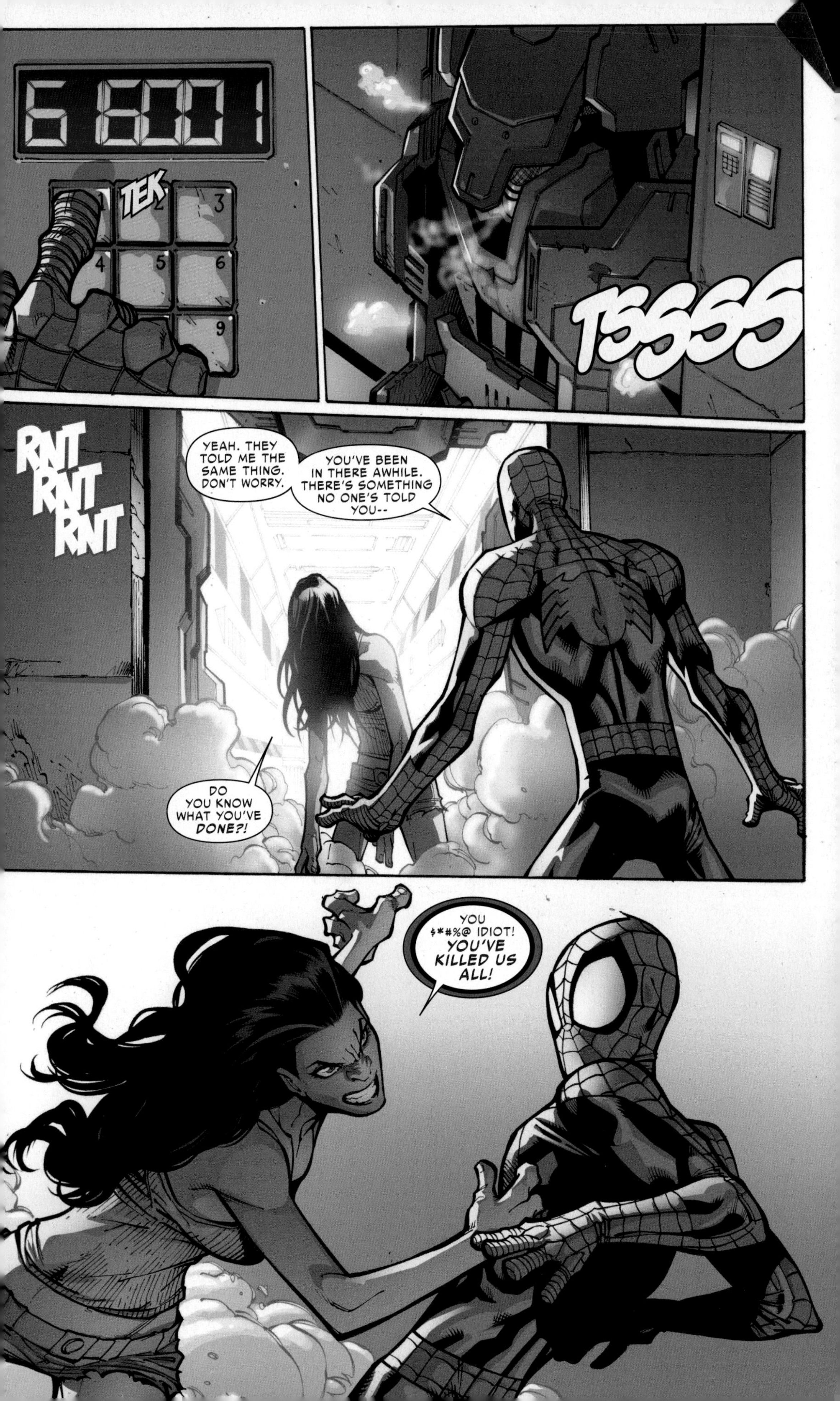
6 6001
TEK
TSSSS
RNT RNT RNT
YEAH. THEY TOLD ME THE SAME THING. DON'T WORRY.
YOU'VE BEEN IN THERE AWHILE. THERE'S SOMETHING NO ONE'S TOLD YOU--
DO YOU KNOW WHAT YOU'VE DONE?!
YOU $*#%@ IDIOT! YOU'VE KILLED US ALL!

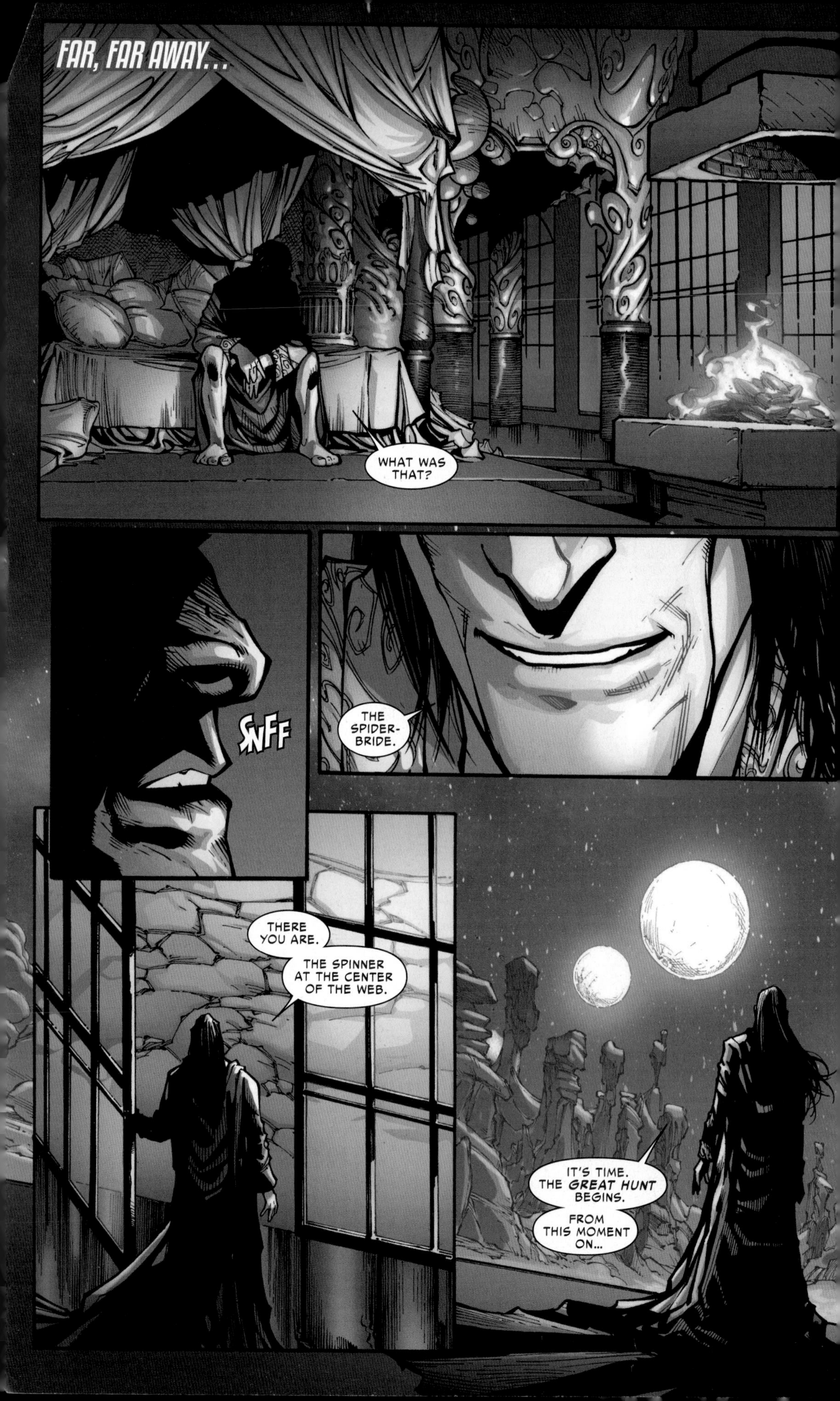
FAR, FAR AWAY...
WHAT WAS THAT?
SNFF
THE SPIDER-BRIDE.
THERE YOU ARE.
THE SPINNER AT THE CENTER OF THE WEB.
IT'S TIME. THE GREAT HUNT BEGINS.
FROM THIS MOMENT ON...

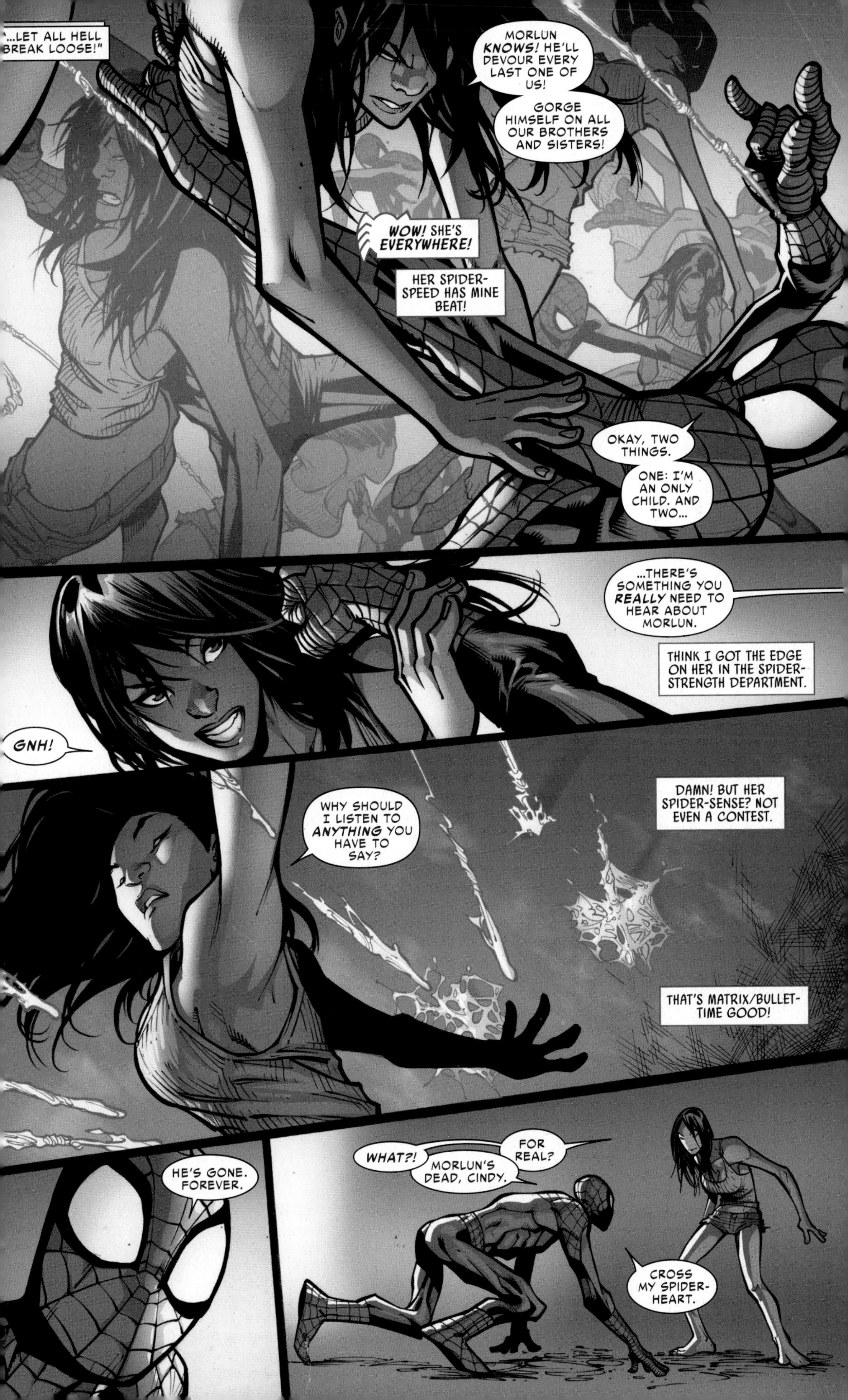
"...LET ALL HELL BREAK LOOSE!"
MORLUN KNOWS! HE'LL DEVOUR EVERY LAST ONE OF US!
GORGE HIMSELF ON ALL OUR BROTHERS AND SISTERS!
WOW! SHE'S EVERYWHERE!
HER SPIDER-SPEED HAS MINE BEAT!
OKAY, TWO THINGS.
ONE: I'M AN ONLY CHILD. AND TWO...
...THERE'S SOMETHING YOU REALLY NEED TO HEAR ABOUT MORLUN.
THINK I GOT THE EDGE ON HER IN THE SPIDER-STRENGTH DEPARTMENT.
GNH!
WHY SHOULD I LISTEN TO ANYTHING YOU HAVE TO SAY?
DAMN! BUT HER SPIDER-SENSE? NOT EVEN A CONTEST.
THAT'S MATRIX/BULLET-TIME GOOD!
HE'S GONE. FOREVER.
WHAT?!
MORLUN'S DEAD, CINDY.
FOR REAL?
CROSS MY SPIDER-HEART.

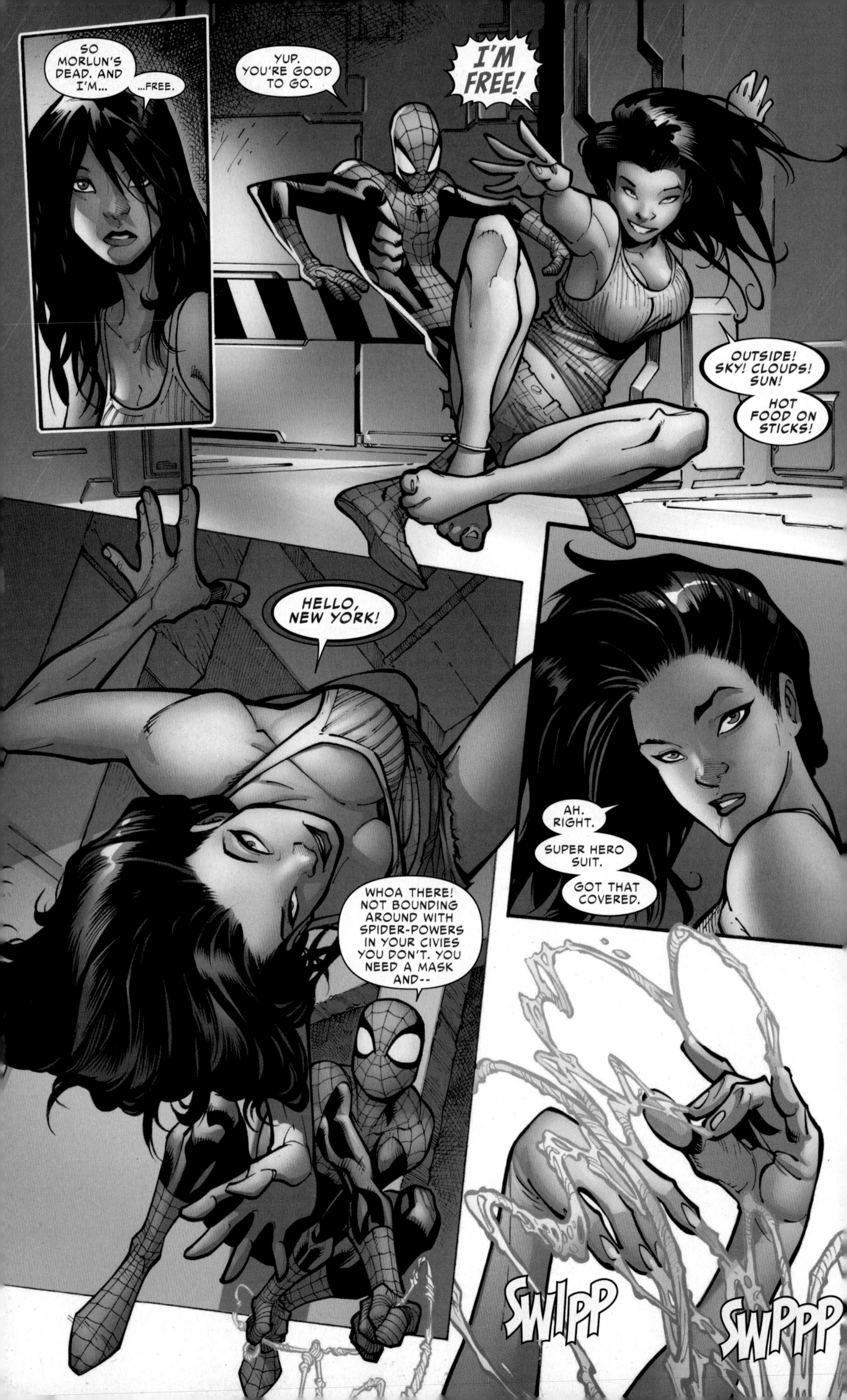
SO MORLUN'S DEAD. AND I'M...
...FREE.
YUP. YOU'RE GOOD TO GO.
I'M FREE!
OUTSIDE! SKY! CLOUDS! SUN!
HOT FOOD ON STICKS!
HELLO, NEW YORK!
WHOA THERE! NOT BOUNDING AROUND WITH SPIDER-POWERS IN YOUR CIVIES YOU DON'T. YOU NEED A MASK AND--
AH. RIGHT.
SUPER HERO SUIT.
GOT THAT COVERED.
SWIPP
SWPPP

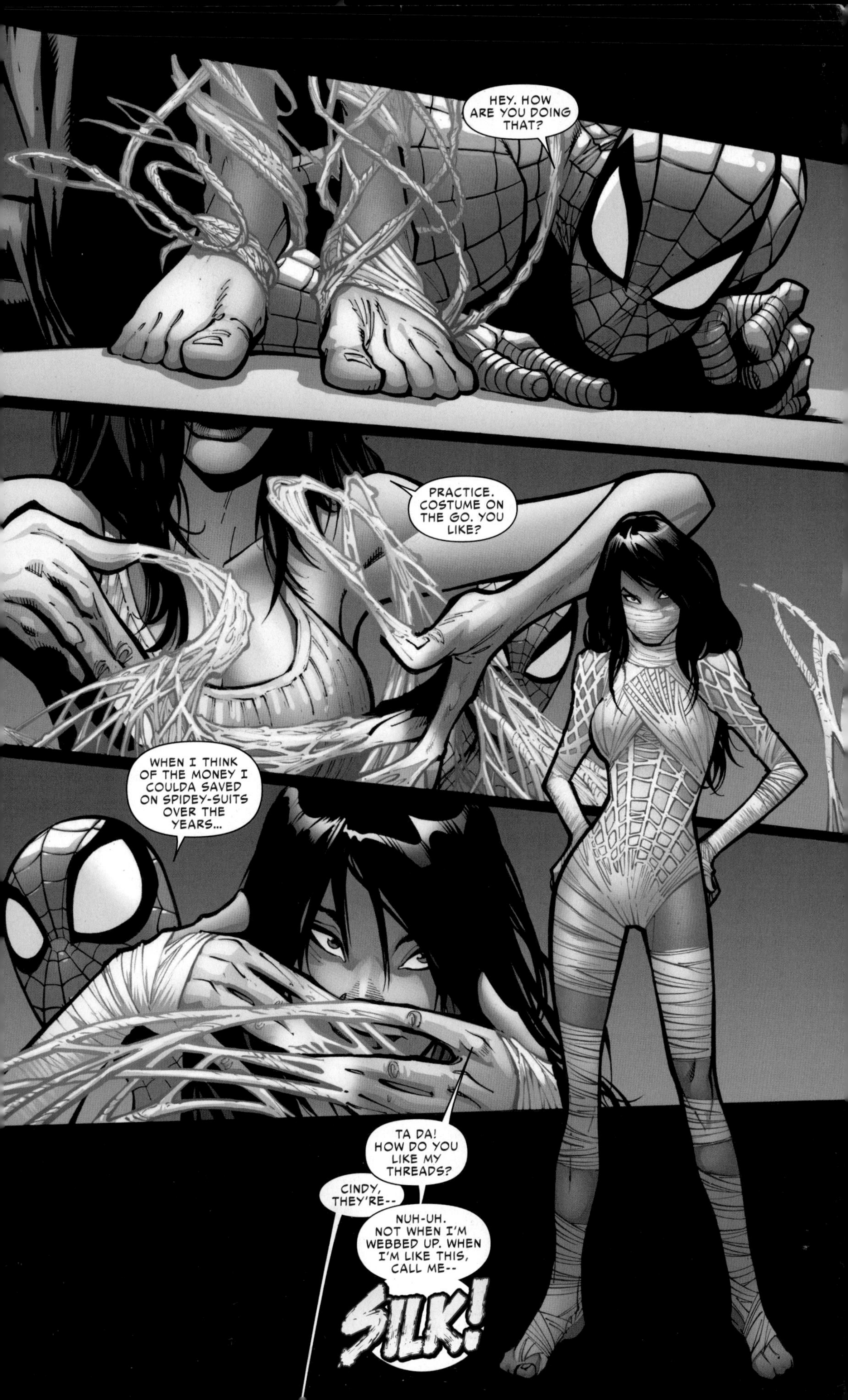
HEY. HOW ARE YOU DOING THAT?
PRACTICE. COSTUME ON THE GO. YOU LIKE?
WHEN I THINK OF THE MONEY I COULDA SAVED ON SPIDEY-SUITS OVER THE YEARS...
TA DA! HOW DO YOU LIKE MY THREADS?
CINDY, THEY'RE--
NUH-UH. NOT WHEN I'M WEBBED UP. WHEN I'M LIKE THIS, CALL ME--
SILK!

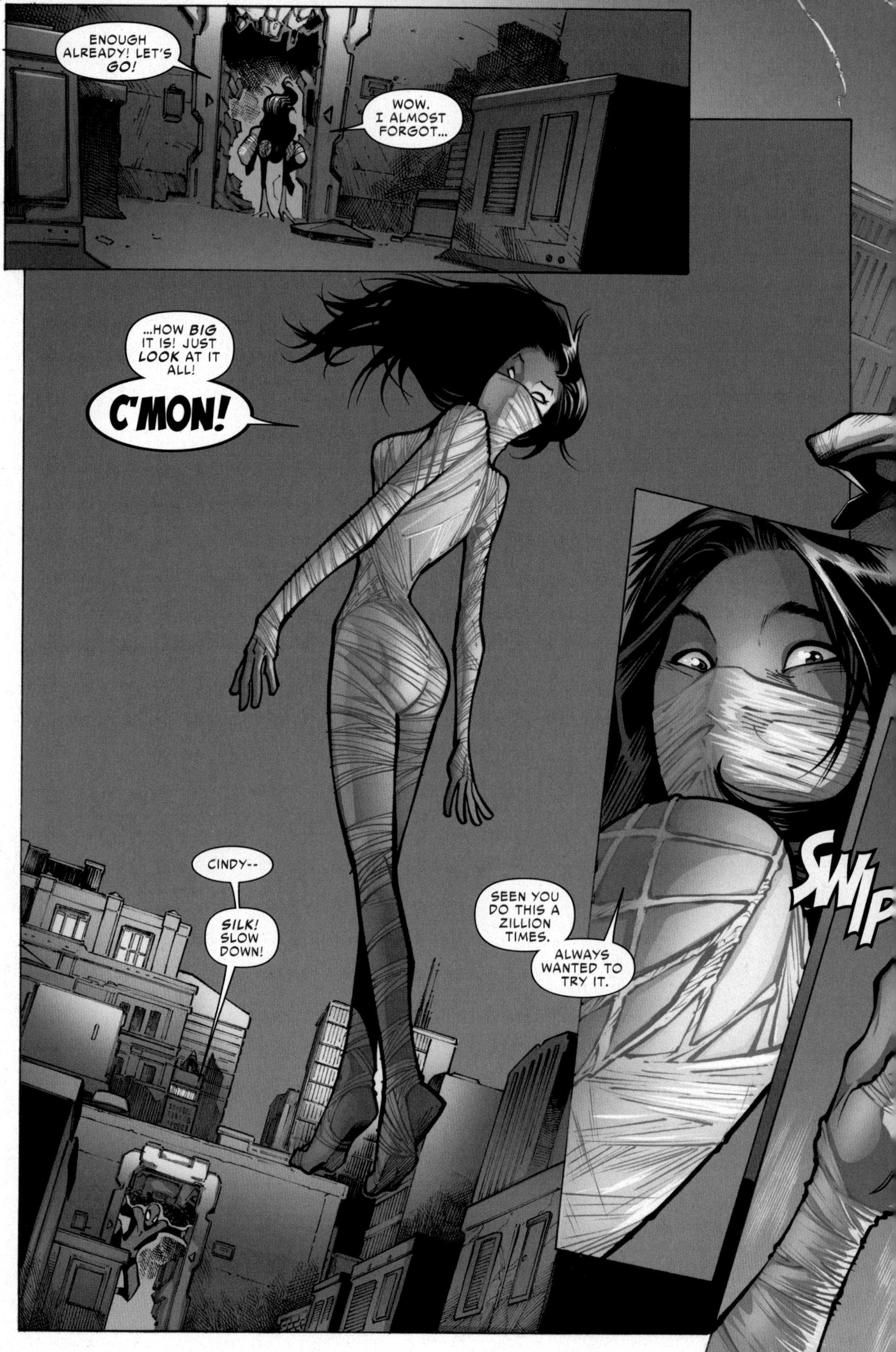
ENOUGH ALREADY! LET'S GO!
WOW. I ALMOST FORGOT...
...HOW BIG IT IS! JUST LOOK AT IT ALL!
C'MON!
CINDY--
SILK! SLOW DOWN!
SEEN YOU DO THIS A ZILLION TIMES.
ALWAYS WANTED TO TRY IT.
SWIP

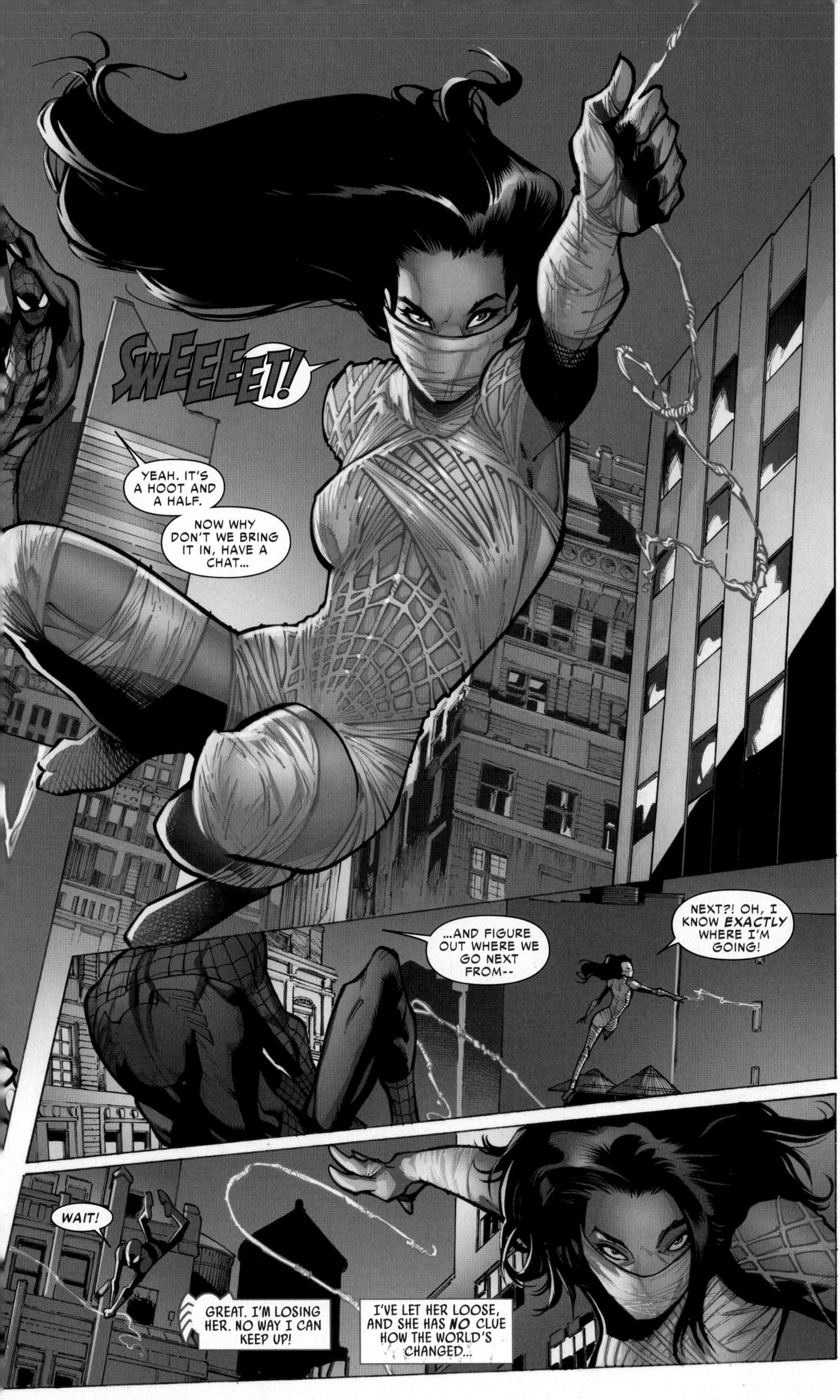
SWEEE-ET!
YEAH. IT'S A HOOT AND A HALF.
NOW WHY DON'T WE BRING IT IN, HAVE A CHAT...
...AND FIGURE OUT WHERE WE GO NEXT FROM--
NEXT?! OH, I KNOW EXACTLY WHERE I'M GOING!
WAIT!
GREAT. I'M LOSING HER. NO WAY I CAN KEEP UP!
I'VE LET HER LOOSE, AND SHE HAS NO CLUE HOW THE WORLD'S CHANGED...

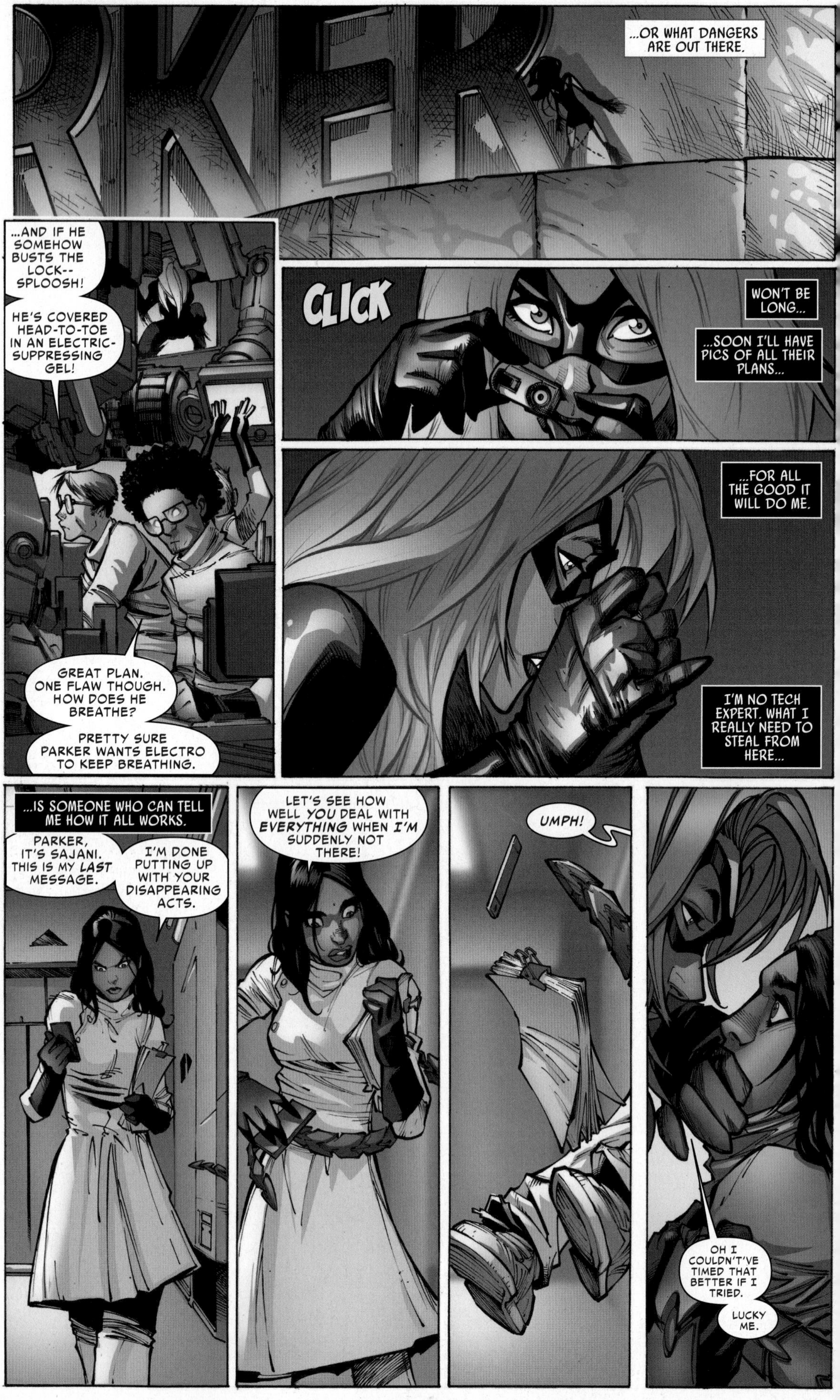
...OR WHAT DANGERS ARE OUT THERE.
...AND IF HE SOMEHOW BUSTS THE LOCK--SPLOOSH!
HE'S COVERED HEAD-TO-TOE IN AN ELECTRIC-SUPPRESSING GEL!
GREAT PLAN. ONE FLAW THOUGH. HOW DOES HE BREATHE?
PRETTY SURE PARKER WANTS ELECTRO TO KEEP BREATHING.
CLICK
WON'T BE LONG...
...SOON I'LL HAVE PICS OF ALL THEIR PLANS...
...FOR ALL THE GOOD IT WILL DO ME.
I'M NO TECH EXPERT. WHAT I REALLY NEED TO STEAL FROM HERE...
...IS SOMEONE WHO CAN TELL ME HOW IT ALL WORKS.
PARKER, IT'S SAJANI. THIS IS MY *LAST* MESSAGE.
I'M DONE PUTTING UP WITH YOUR DISAPPEARING ACTS.
LET'S SEE HOW WELL *YOU* DEAL WITH *EVERYTHING* WHEN *I'M* SUDDENLY NOT THERE!
UMPH!
OH I COULDN'T'VE TIMED THAT BETTER IF I TRIED.
LUCKY ME.

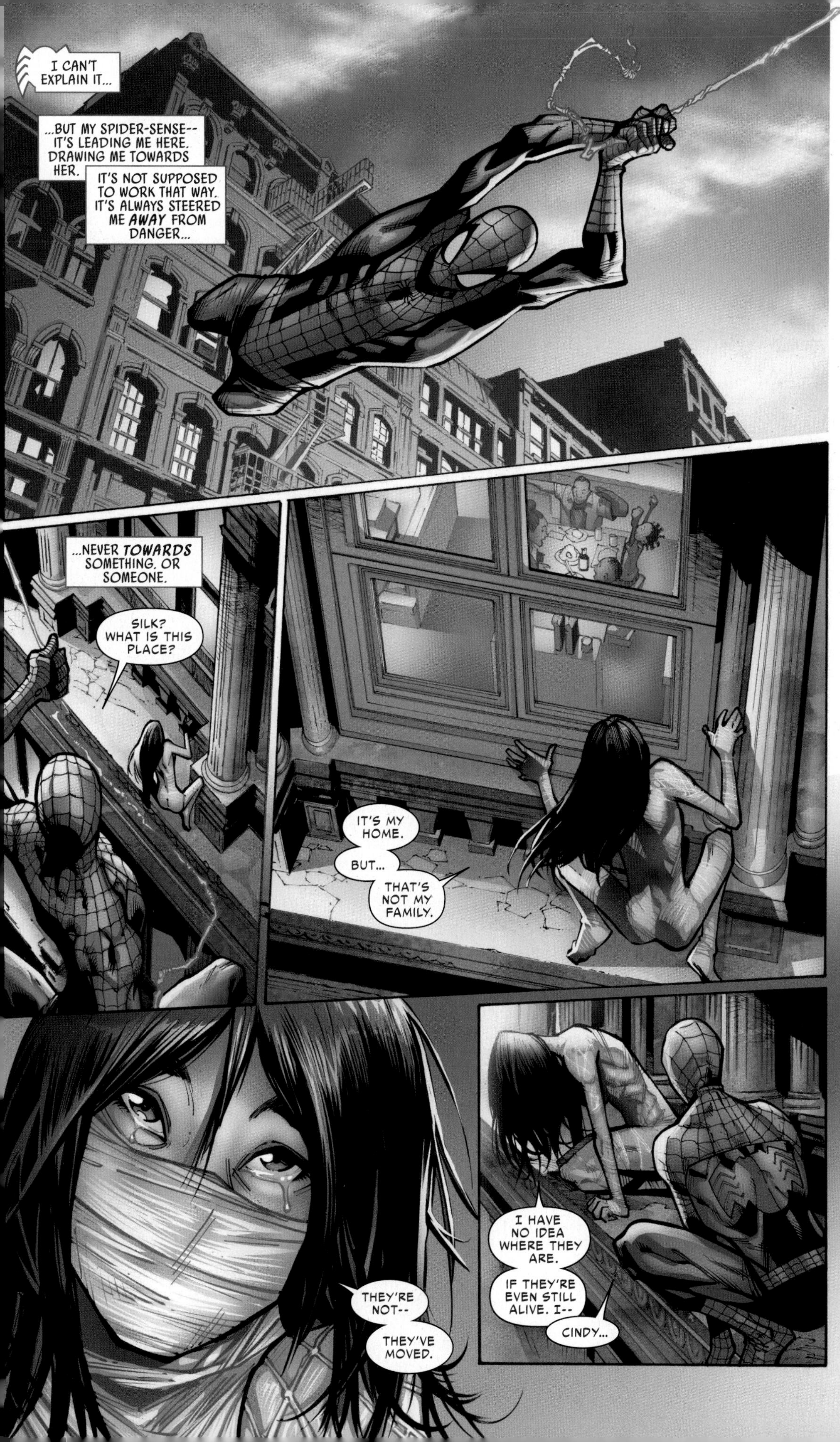

I CAN'T EXPLAIN IT...
...BUT MY SPIDER-SENSE-- IT'S LEADING ME HERE. DRAWING ME TOWARDS HER.
IT'S NOT SUPPOSED TO WORK THAT WAY. IT'S ALWAYS STEERED ME AWAY FROM DANGER...
...NEVER TOWARDS SOMETHING. OR SOMEONE.
SILK? WHAT IS THIS PLACE?
IT'S MY HOME.
BUT...
THAT'S NOT MY FAMILY.
THEY'RE NOT--
THEY'VE MOVED.
I HAVE NO IDEA WHERE THEY ARE.
IF THEY'RE EVEN STILL ALIVE. I--
CINDY...

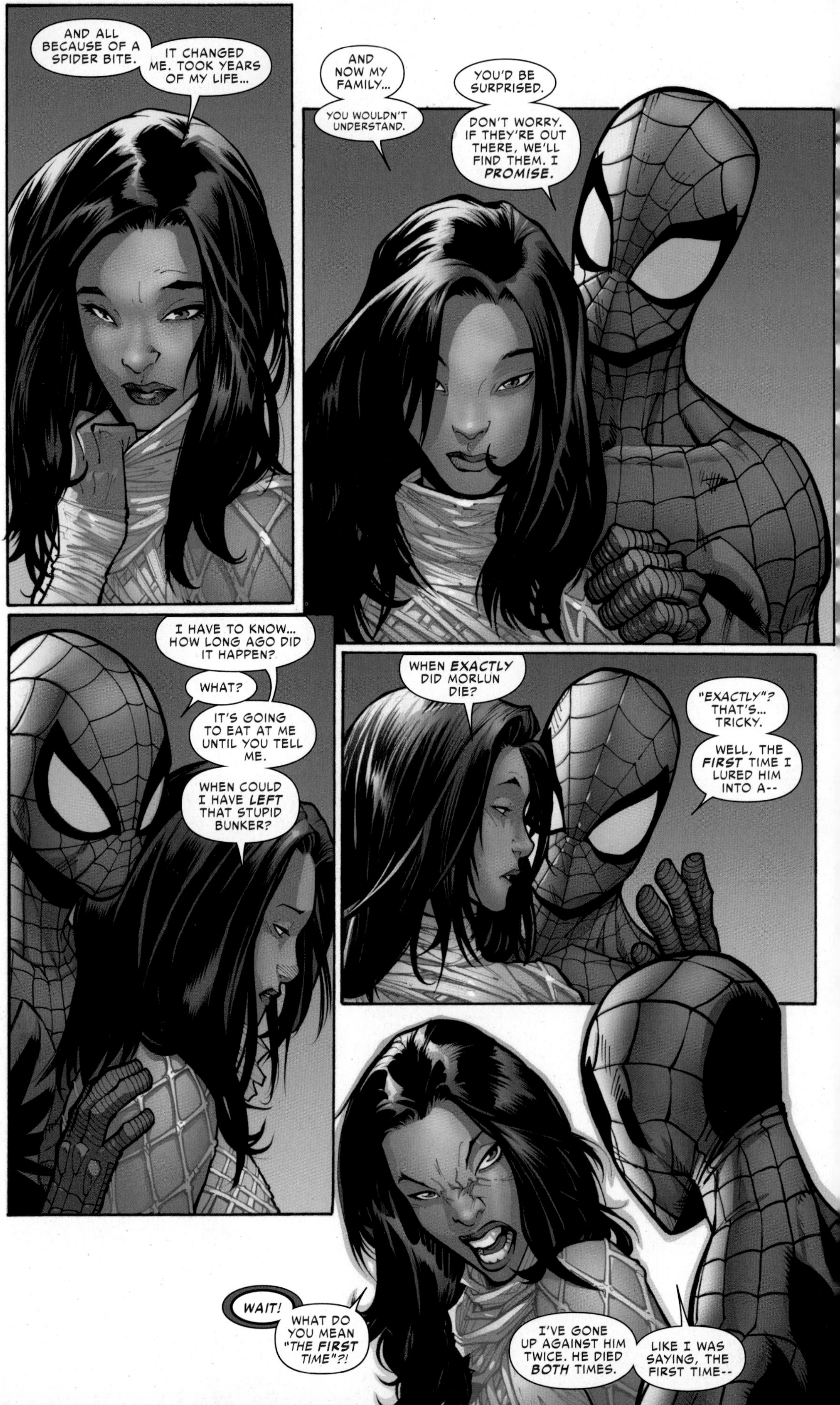

AND ALL BECAUSE OF A SPIDER BITE.
IT CHANGED ME. TOOK YEARS OF MY LIFE...
AND NOW MY FAMILY...
YOU WOULDN'T UNDERSTAND.
YOU'D BE SURPRISED.
DON'T WORRY. IF THEY'RE OUT THERE, WE'LL FIND THEM. I PROMISE.
I HAVE TO KNOW... HOW LONG AGO DID IT HAPPEN?
WHAT?
IT'S GOING TO EAT AT ME UNTIL YOU TELL ME.
WHEN COULD I HAVE LEFT THAT STUPID BUNKER?
WHEN EXACTLY DID MORLUN DIE?
"EXACTLY"? THAT'S... TRICKY.
WELL, THE FIRST TIME I LURED HIM INTO A--
WAIT!
WHAT DO YOU MEAN "THE FIRST TIME"?!
I'VE GONE UP AGAINST HIM TWICE. HE DIED BOTH TIMES.
LIKE I WAS SAYING, THE FIRST TIME--

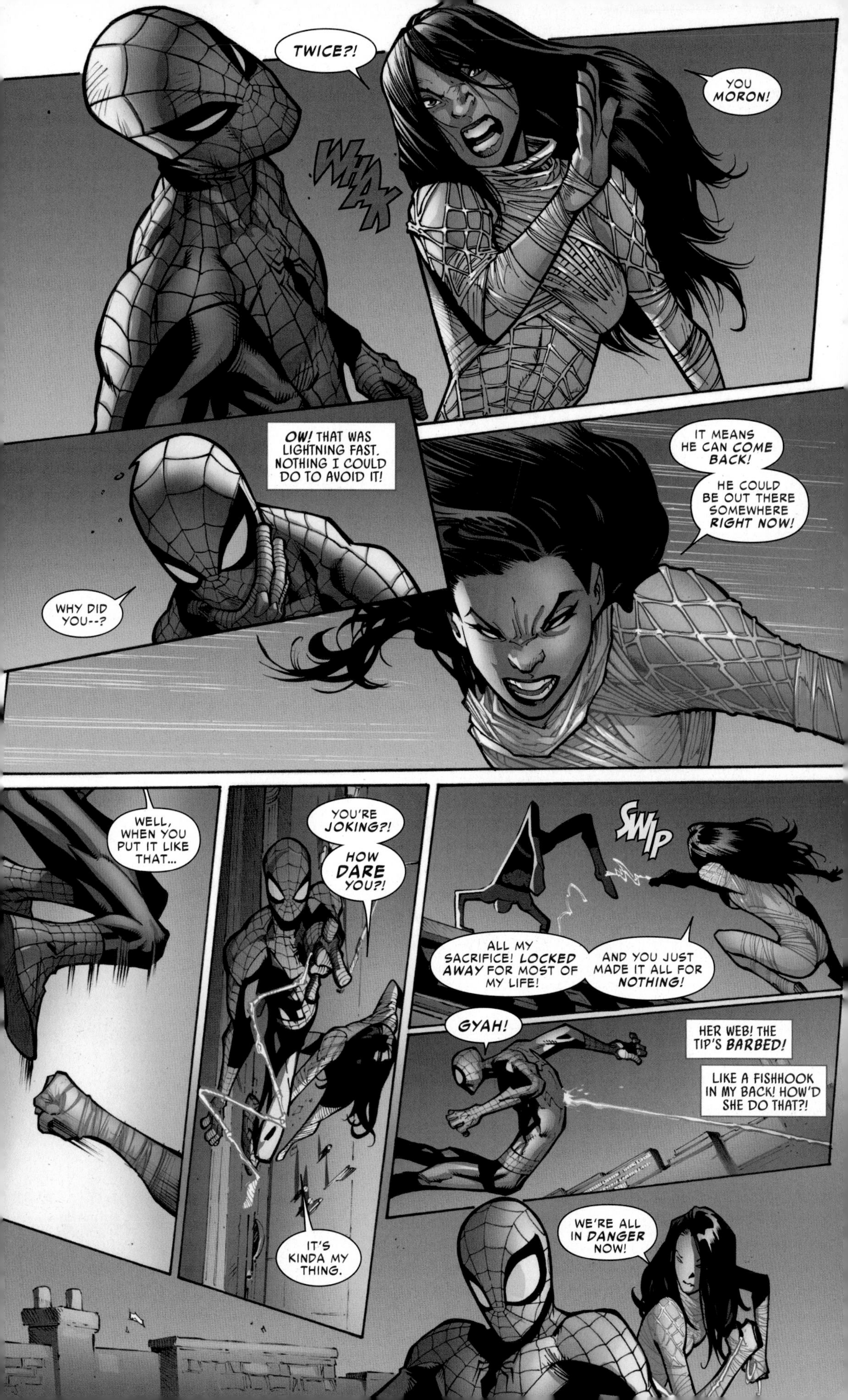
TWICE?!
WHAK
YOU MORON!
OW! THAT WAS LIGHTNING FAST. NOTHING I COULD DO TO AVOID IT!
WHY DID YOU--?
IT MEANS HE CAN COME BACK!
HE COULD BE OUT THERE SOMEWHERE RIGHT NOW!
WELL, WHEN YOU PUT IT LIKE THAT...
YOU'RE JOKING?!
HOW DARE YOU?!
IT'S KINDA MY THING.
SWIP
ALL MY SACRIFICE! LOCKED AWAY FOR MOST OF MY LIFE!
AND YOU JUST MADE IT ALL FOR NOTHING!
GYAH!
HER WEB! THE TIP'S BARBED!
LIKE A FISHHOOK IN MY BACK! HOW'D SHE DO THAT?!
WE'RE ALL IN DANGER NOW!

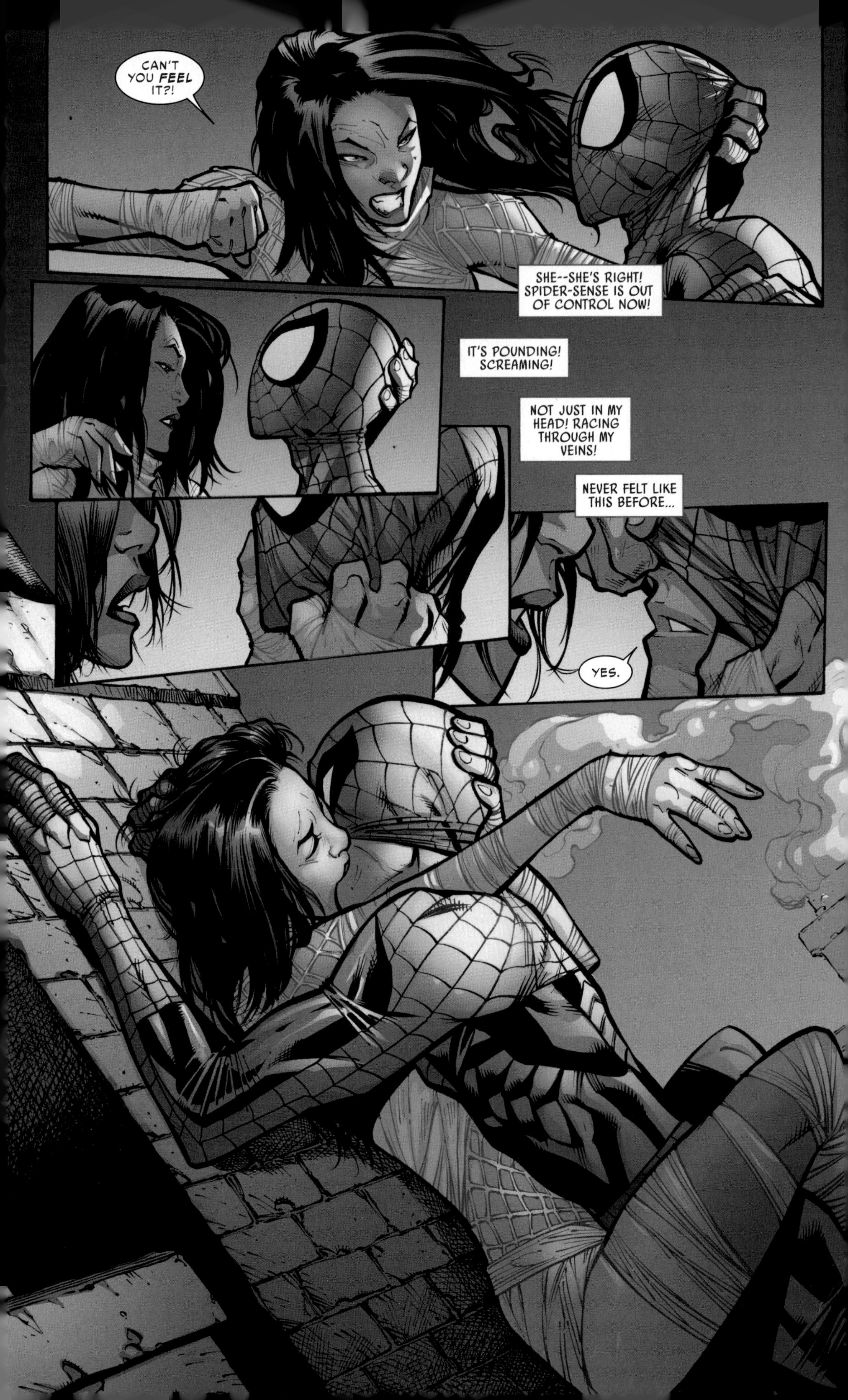
CAN'T YOU FEEL IT?!
SHE--SHE'S RIGHT! SPIDER-SENSE IS OUT OF CONTROL NOW!
IT'S POUNDING! SCREAMING!
NOT JUST IN MY HEAD! RACING THROUGH MY VEINS!
NEVER FELT LIKE THIS BEFORE...
YES.

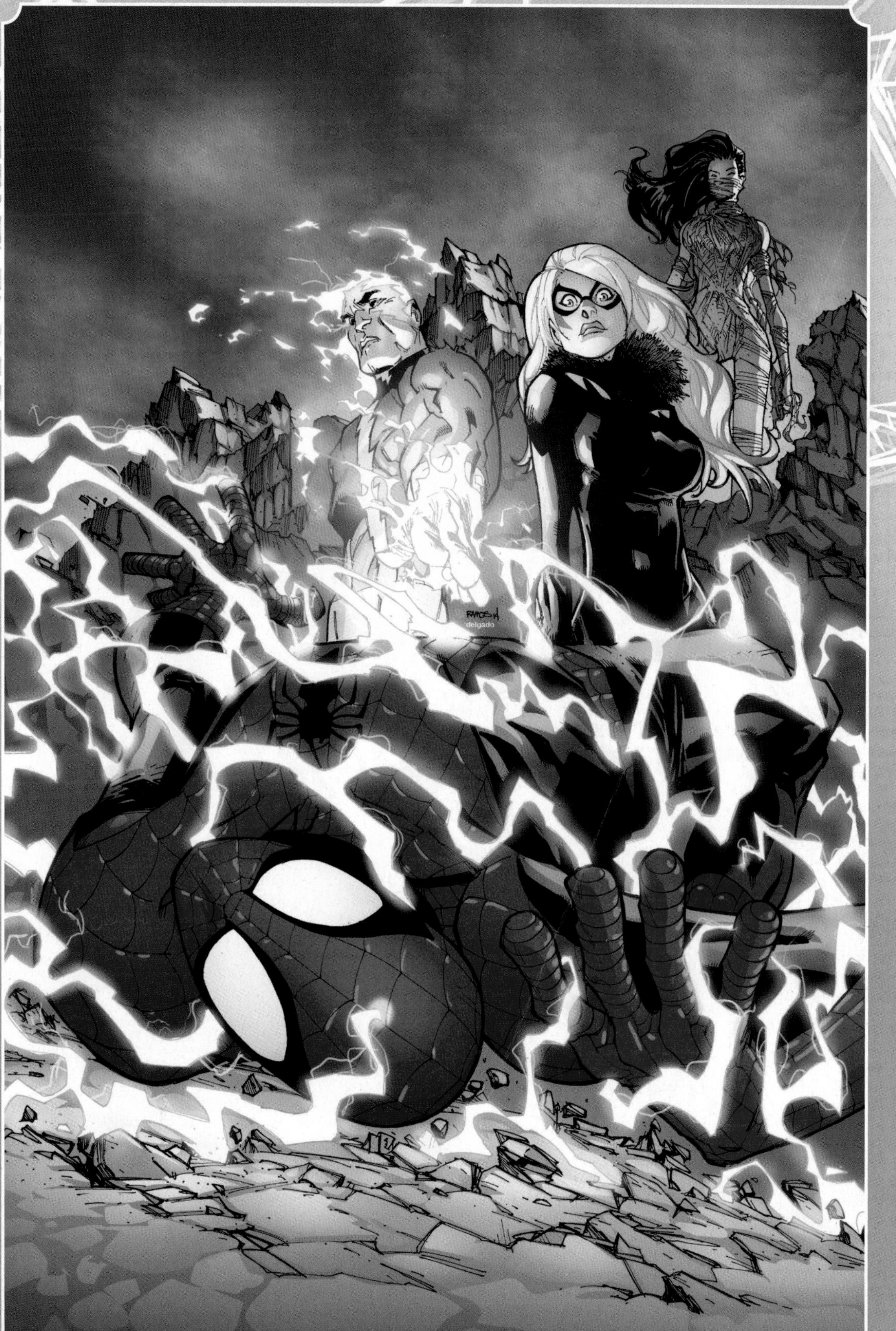

AMAZING SPIDER-MAN (2014) #5

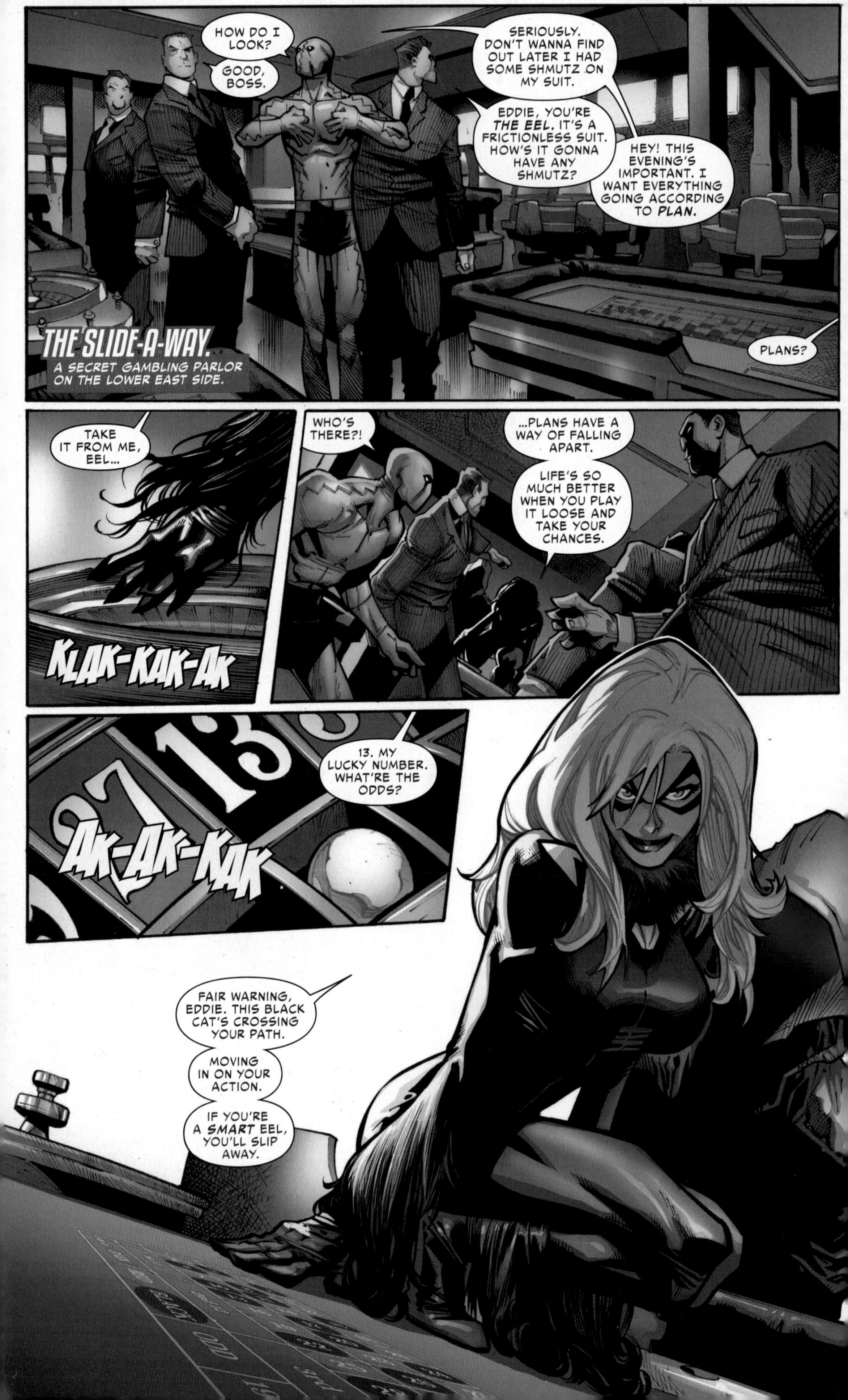
HOW DO I LOOK?
GOOD, BOSS.
SERIOUSLY. DON'T WANNA FIND OUT LATER I HAD SOME SHMUTZ ON MY SUIT.
EDDIE, YOU'RE THE EEL. IT'S A FRICTIONLESS SUIT. HOW'S IT GONNA HAVE ANY SHMUTZ?
HEY! THIS EVENING'S IMPORTANT. I WANT EVERYTHING GOING ACCORDING TO PLAN.
THE SLIDE-A-WAY.
A SECRET GAMBLING PARLOR ON THE LOWER EAST SIDE.
PLANS?
TAKE IT FROM ME, EEL...
KLAK-KAK-AK
WHO'S THERE?!
...PLANS HAVE A WAY OF FALLING APART.
LIFE'S SO MUCH BETTER WHEN YOU PLAY IT LOOSE AND TAKE YOUR CHANCES.
13. MY LUCKY NUMBER. WHAT'RE THE ODDS?
AK-AK-KAK
FAIR WARNING, EDDIE. THIS BLACK CAT'S CROSSING YOUR PATH.
MOVING IN ON YOUR ACTION.
IF YOU'RE A SMART EEL, YOU'LL SLIP AWAY.

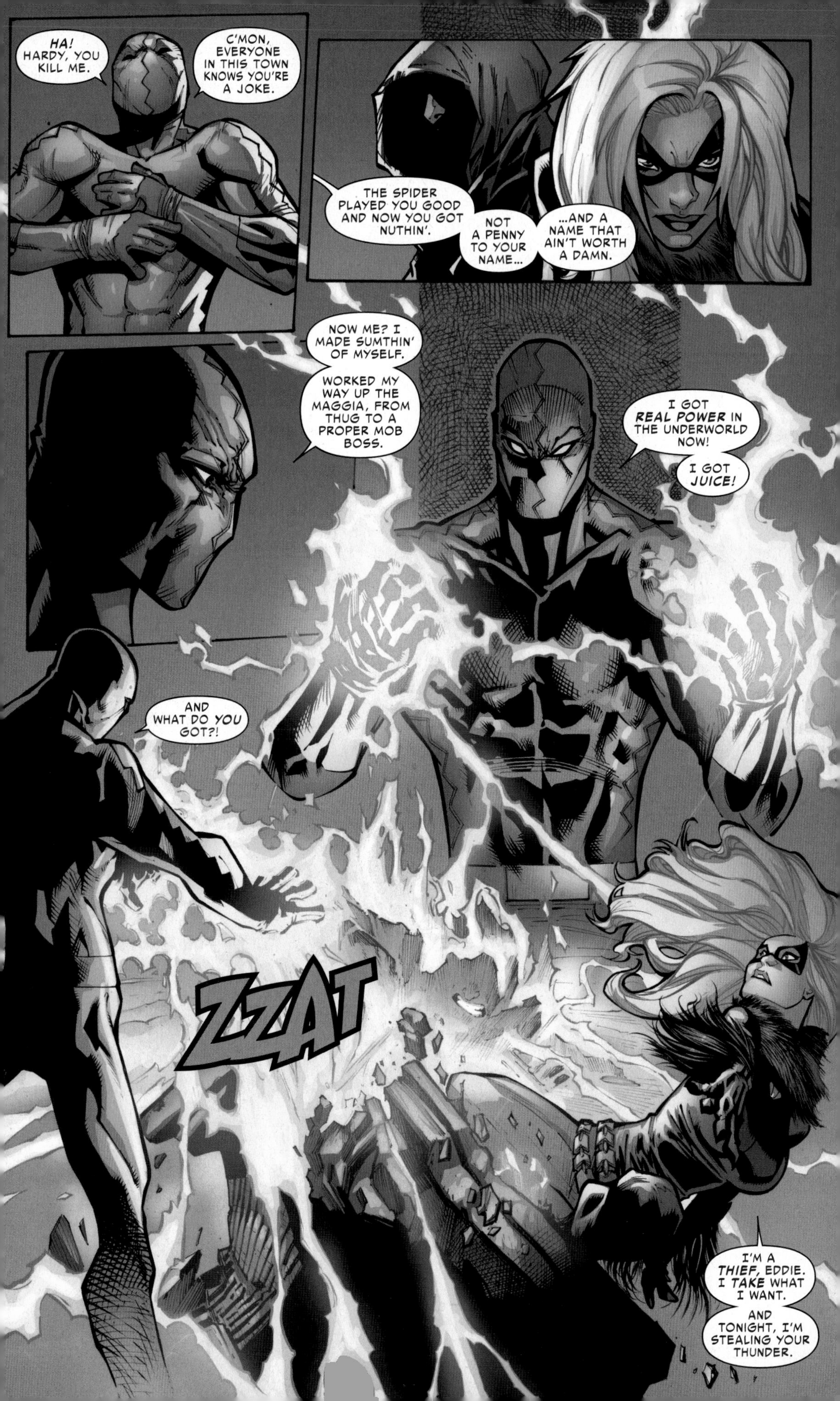
HA! HARDY, YOU KILL ME.
C'MON, EVERYONE IN THIS TOWN KNOWS YOU'RE A JOKE.
THE SPIDER PLAYED YOU GOOD AND NOW YOU GOT NUTHIN'.
NOT A PENNY TO YOUR NAME...
...AND A NAME THAT AIN'T WORTH A DAMN.
NOW ME? I MADE SUMTHIN' OF MYSELF.
WORKED MY WAY UP THE MAGGIA, FROM THUG TO A PROPER MOB BOSS.
I GOT REAL POWER IN THE UNDERWORLD NOW!
I GOT JUICE!
AND WHAT DO YOU GOT?!
ZZAT
I'M A THIEF, EDDIE. I TAKE WHAT I WANT.
AND TONIGHT, I'M STEALING YOUR THUNDER.

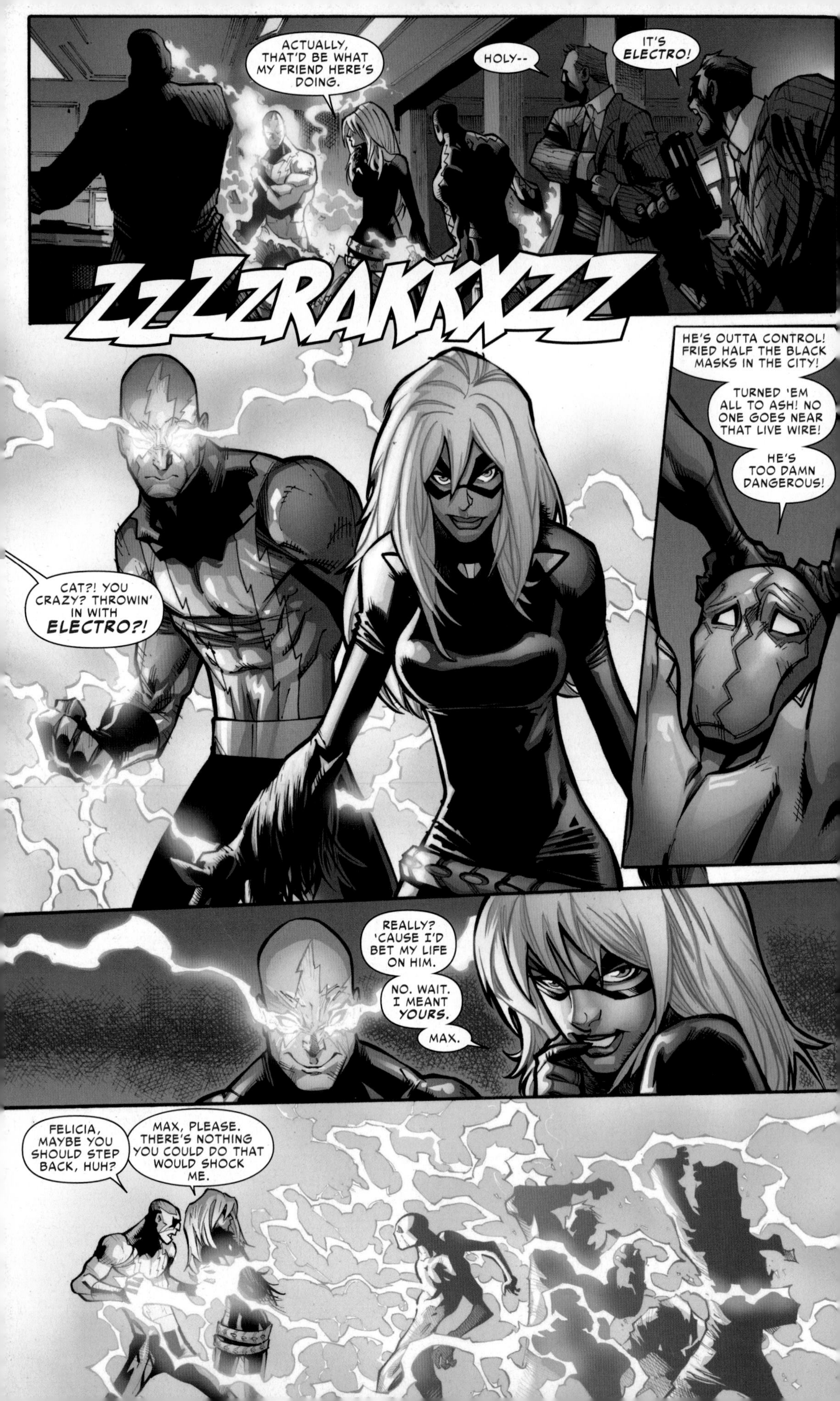
ACTUALLY, THAT'D BE WHAT MY FRIEND HERE'S DOING.
HOLY--
IT'S ELECTRO!
ZZZZRAKKXZZ
HE'S OUTTA CONTROL! FRIED HALF THE BLACK MASKS IN THE CITY!
TURNED 'EM ALL TO ASH! NO ONE GOES NEAR THAT LIVE WIRE!
HE'S TOO DAMN DANGEROUS!
CAT?! YOU CRAZY? THROWIN' IN WITH ELECTRO?!
REALLY? 'CAUSE I'D BET MY LIFE ON HIM.
NO. WAIT. I MEANT YOURS.
MAX.
FELICIA, MAYBE YOU SHOULD STEP BACK, HUH?
MAX, PLEASE. THERE'S NOTHING YOU COULD DO THAT WOULD SHOCK ME.

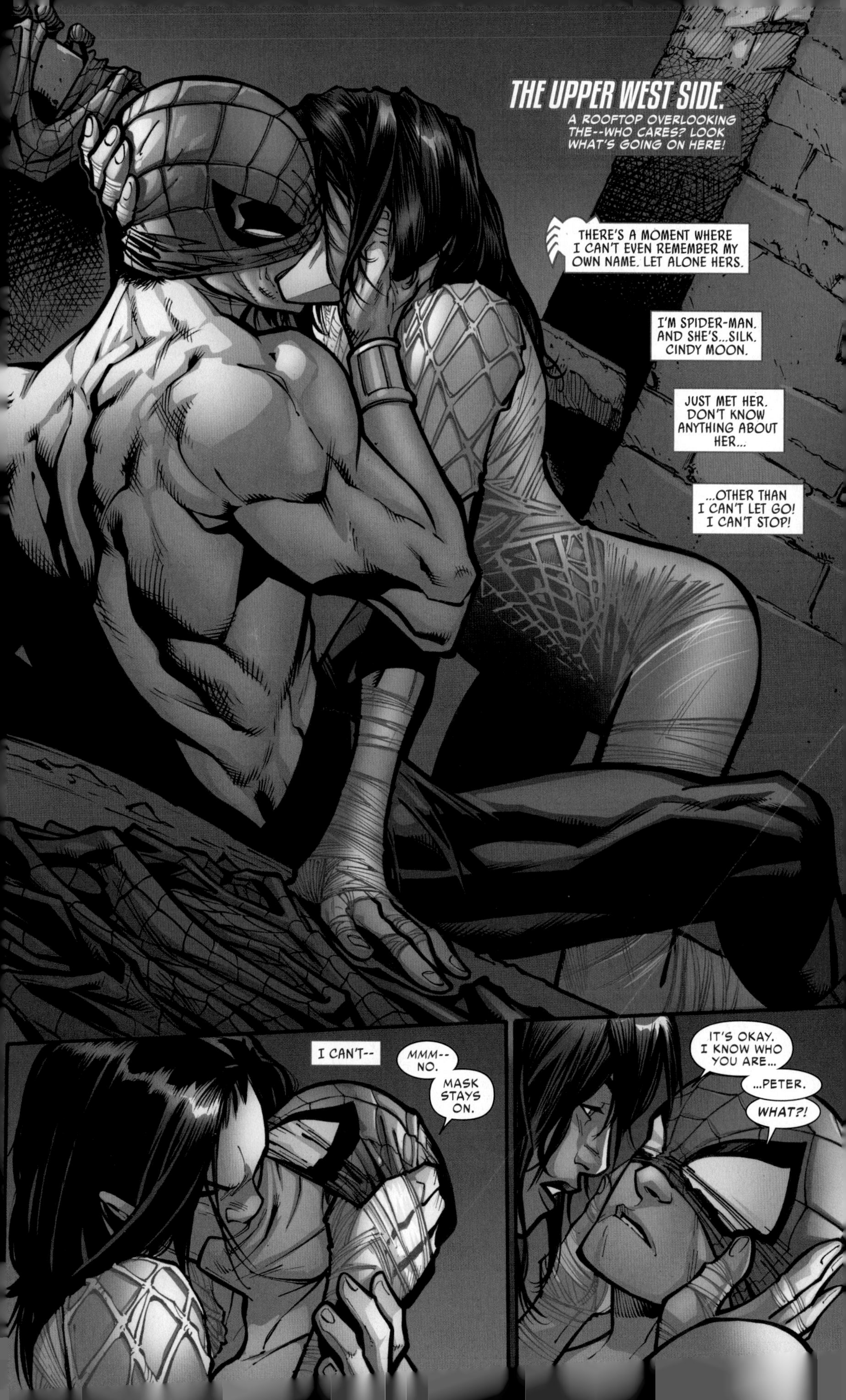

THE UPPER WEST SIDE.
A ROOFTOP OVERLOOKING THE--WHO CARES? LOOK WHAT'S GOING ON HERE!
THERE'S A MOMENT WHERE I CAN'T EVEN REMEMBER MY OWN NAME. LET ALONE HERS.
I'M SPIDER-MAN. AND SHE'S...SILK. CINDY MOON.
JUST MET HER. DON'T KNOW ANYTHING ABOUT HER...
...OTHER THAN I CAN'T LET GO! I CAN'T STOP!
I CAN'T--
MMM--NO.
MASK STAYS ON.
IT'S OKAY. I KNOW WHO YOU ARE...
...PETER.
WHAT?!

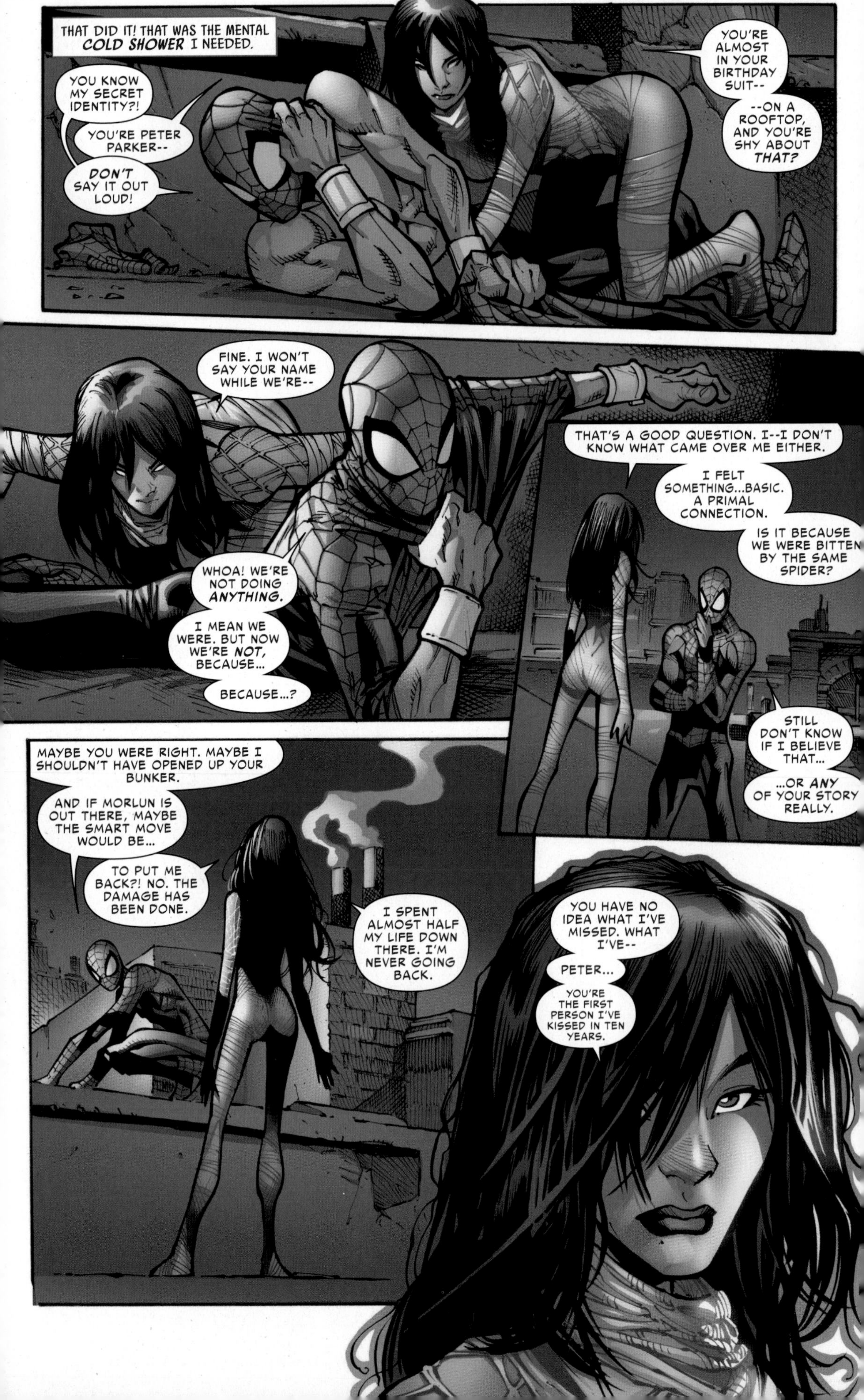
THAT DID IT! THAT WAS THE MENTAL COLD SHOWER I NEEDED.
YOU KNOW MY SECRET IDENTITY?!
YOU'RE PETER PARKER--
DON'T SAY IT OUT LOUD!
YOU'RE ALMOST IN YOUR BIRTHDAY SUIT--
--ON A ROOFTOP, AND YOU'RE SHY ABOUT THAT?
FINE. I WON'T SAY YOUR NAME WHILE WE'RE--
WHOA! WE'RE NOT DOING ANYTHING.
I MEAN WE WERE. BUT NOW WE'RE NOT, BECAUSE...
BECAUSE...?
THAT'S A GOOD QUESTION. I--I DON'T KNOW WHAT CAME OVER ME EITHER.
I FELT SOMETHING...BASIC. A PRIMAL CONNECTION.
IS IT BECAUSE WE WERE BITTEN BY THE SAME SPIDER?
STILL DON'T KNOW IF I BELIEVE THAT...
...OR ANY OF YOUR STORY REALLY.
MAYBE YOU WERE RIGHT. MAYBE I SHOULDN'T HAVE OPENED UP YOUR BUNKER.
AND IF MORLUN IS OUT THERE, MAYBE THE SMART MOVE WOULD BE...
TO PUT ME BACK?! NO. THE DAMAGE HAS BEEN DONE.
I SPENT ALMOST HALF MY LIFE DOWN THERE. I'M NEVER GOING BACK.
YOU HAVE NO IDEA WHAT I'VE MISSED. WHAT I'VE--
PETER...
YOU'RE THE FIRST PERSON I'VE KISSED IN TEN YEARS.

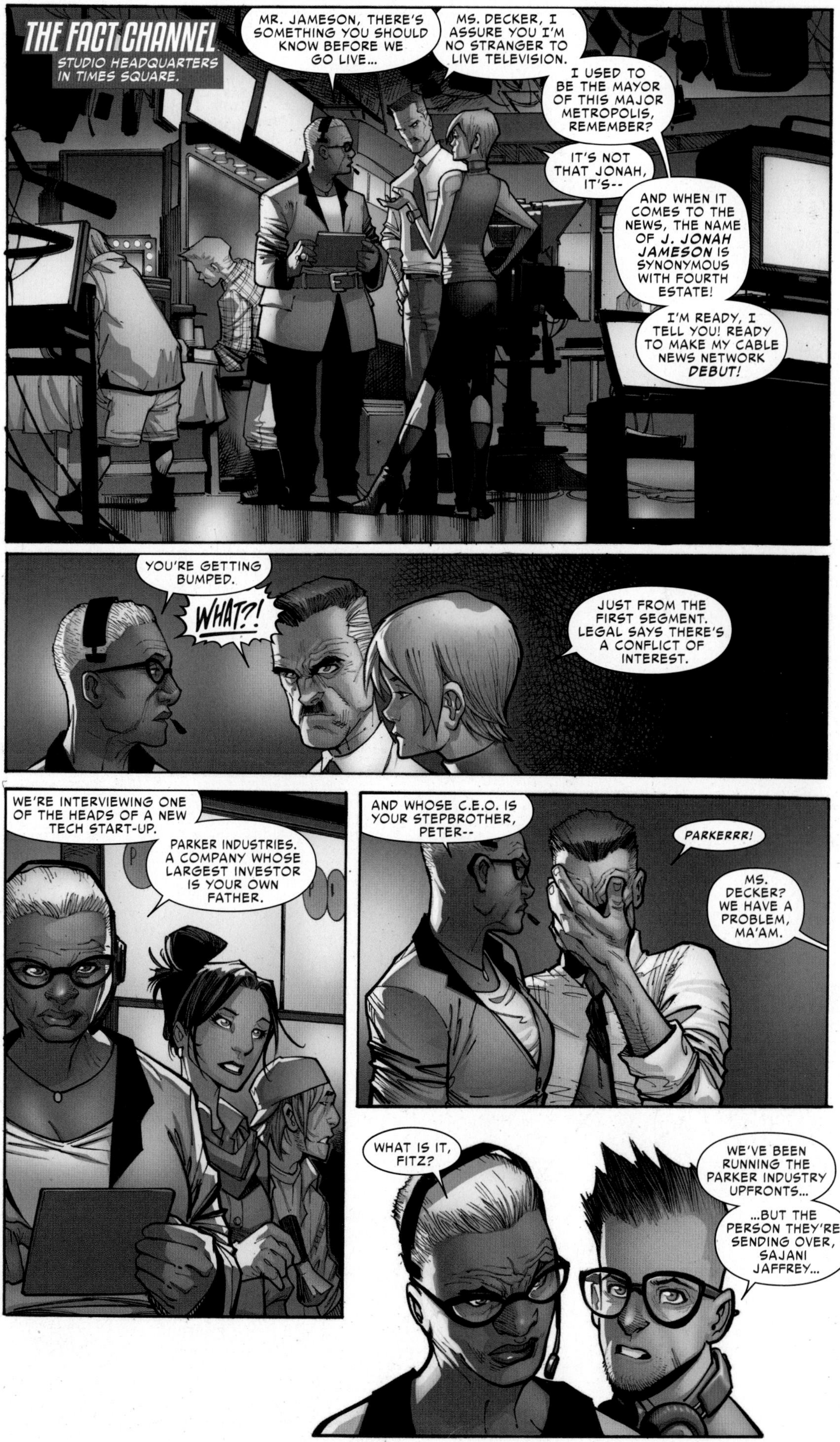
THE FACT CHANNEL
STUDIO HEADQUARTERS IN TIMES SQUARE.
MR. JAMESON, THERE'S SOMETHING YOU SHOULD KNOW BEFORE WE GO LIVE...
MS. DECKER, I ASSURE YOU I'M NO STRANGER TO LIVE TELEVISION.
I USED TO BE THE MAYOR OF THIS MAJOR METROPOLIS, REMEMBER?
IT'S NOT THAT JONAH, IT'S--
AND WHEN IT COMES TO THE NEWS, THE NAME OF J. JONAH JAMESON IS SYNONYMOUS WITH FOURTH ESTATE!
I'M READY, I TELL YOU! READY TO MAKE MY CABLE NEWS NETWORK DEBUT!
YOU'RE GETTING BUMPED.
WHAT?!
JUST FROM THE FIRST SEGMENT. LEGAL SAYS THERE'S A CONFLICT OF INTEREST.
WE'RE INTERVIEWING ONE OF THE HEADS OF A NEW TECH START-UP.
PARKER INDUSTRIES. A COMPANY WHOSE LARGEST INVESTOR IS YOUR OWN FATHER.
AND WHOSE C.E.O. IS YOUR STEPBROTHER, PETER--
PARKERRR!
MS. DECKER? WE HAVE A PROBLEM, MA'AM.
WHAT IS IT, FITZ?
WE'VE BEEN RUNNING THE PARKER INDUSTRY UPFRONTS...
...BUT THE PERSON THEY'RE SENDING OVER, SAJANI JAFFREY...

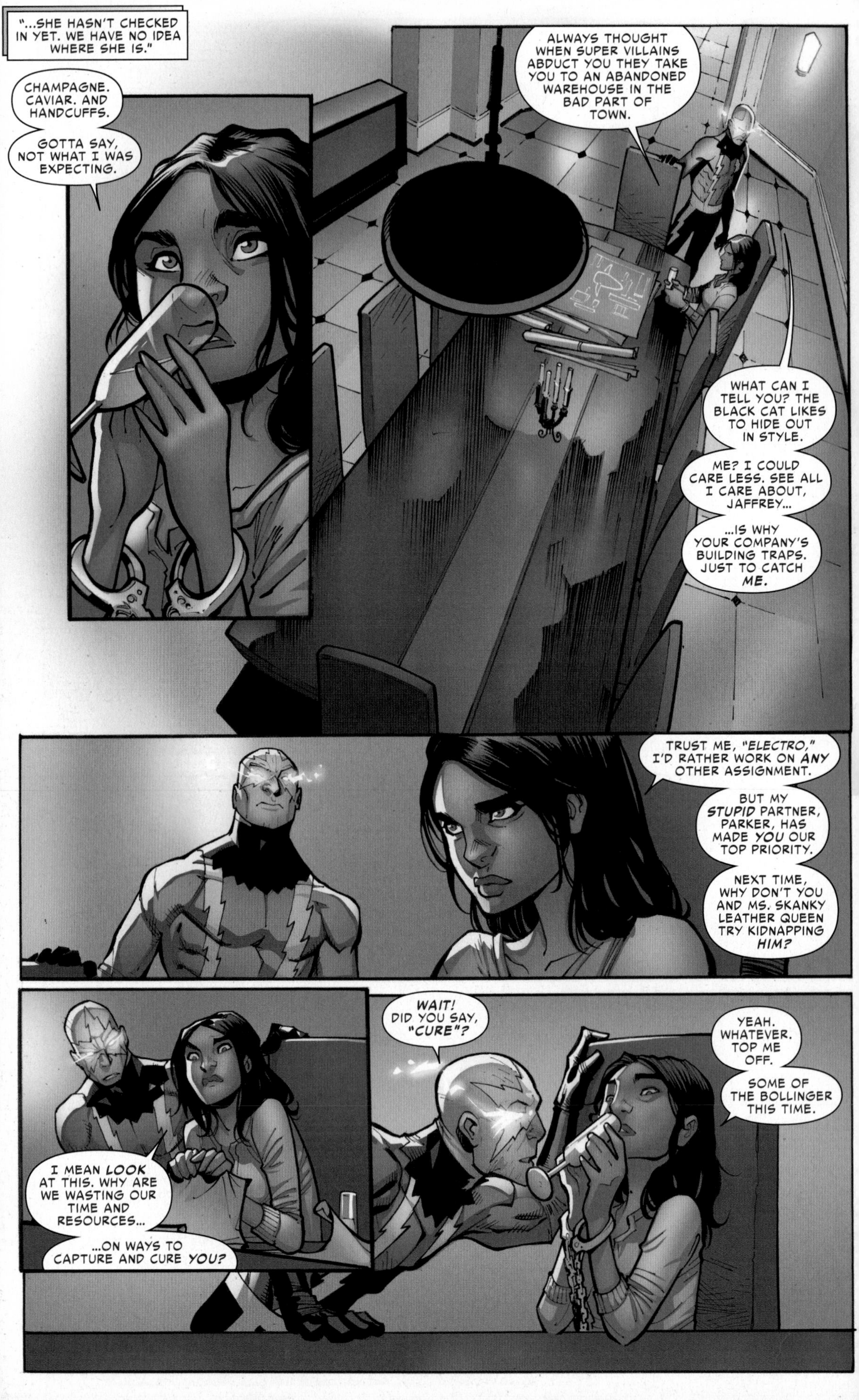

"...SHE HASN'T CHECKED IN YET. WE HAVE NO IDEA WHERE SHE IS."
CHAMPAGNE. CAVIAR. AND HANDCUFFS.
GOTTA SAY, NOT WHAT I WAS EXPECTING.
ALWAYS THOUGHT WHEN SUPER VILLAINS ABDUCT YOU THEY TAKE YOU TO AN ABANDONED WAREHOUSE IN THE BAD PART OF TOWN.
WHAT CAN I TELL YOU? THE BLACK CAT LIKES TO HIDE OUT IN STYLE.
ME? I COULD CARE LESS. SEE ALL I CARE ABOUT, JAFFREY...
...IS WHY YOUR COMPANY'S BUILDING TRAPS. JUST TO CATCH *ME.*
TRUST ME, "ELECTRO," I'D RATHER WORK ON *ANY* OTHER ASSIGNMENT.
BUT MY *STUPID* PARTNER, PARKER, HAS MADE *YOU* OUR TOP PRIORITY.
NEXT TIME, WHY DON'T YOU AND MS. SKANKY LEATHER QUEEN TRY KIDNAPPING *HIM?*
I MEAN *LOOK* AT THIS. WHY ARE WE WASTING OUR TIME AND RESOURCES...
...ON WAYS TO CAPTURE AND CURE *YOU?*
WAIT! DID YOU SAY, *"CURE"?*
YEAH. WHATEVER. TOP ME OFF.
SOME OF THE BOLLINGER THIS TIME.

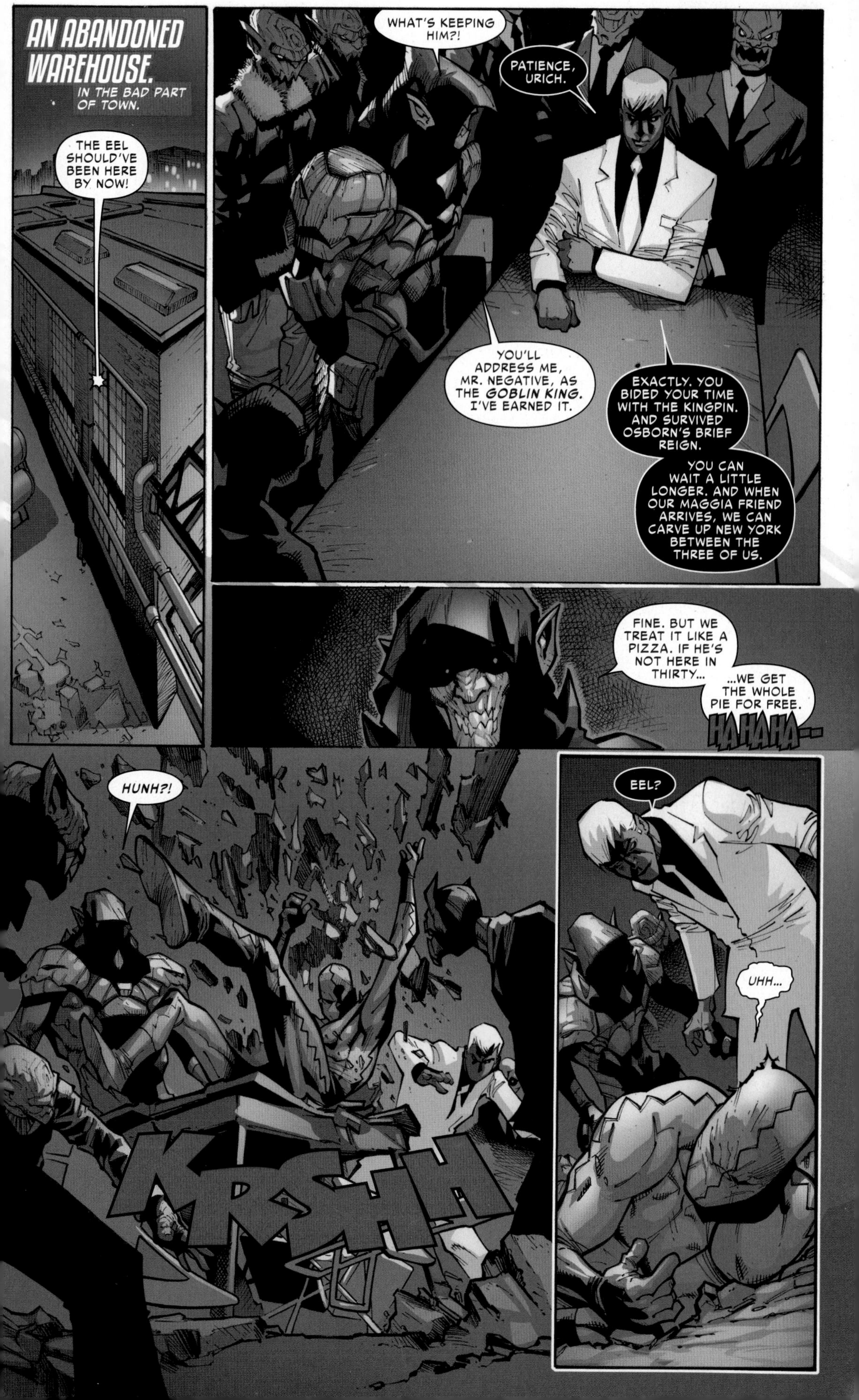

AN ABANDONED WAREHOUSE.
IN THE BAD PART OF TOWN.
THE EEL SHOULD'VE BEEN HERE BY NOW!
WHAT'S KEEPING HIM?!
PATIENCE, URICH.
YOU'LL ADDRESS ME, MR. NEGATIVE, AS THE GOBLIN KING. I'VE EARNED IT.
EXACTLY. YOU BIDED YOUR TIME WITH THE KINGPIN. AND SURVIVED OSBORN'S BRIEF REIGN.
YOU CAN WAIT A LITTLE LONGER. AND WHEN OUR MAGGIA FRIEND ARRIVES, WE CAN CARVE UP NEW YORK BETWEEN THE THREE OF US.
FINE. BUT WE TREAT IT LIKE A PIZZA. IF HE'S NOT HERE IN THIRTY...
...WE GET THE WHOLE PIE FOR FREE.
HAHAHA--
HUNH?!
KRSHH
EEL?
UHH...

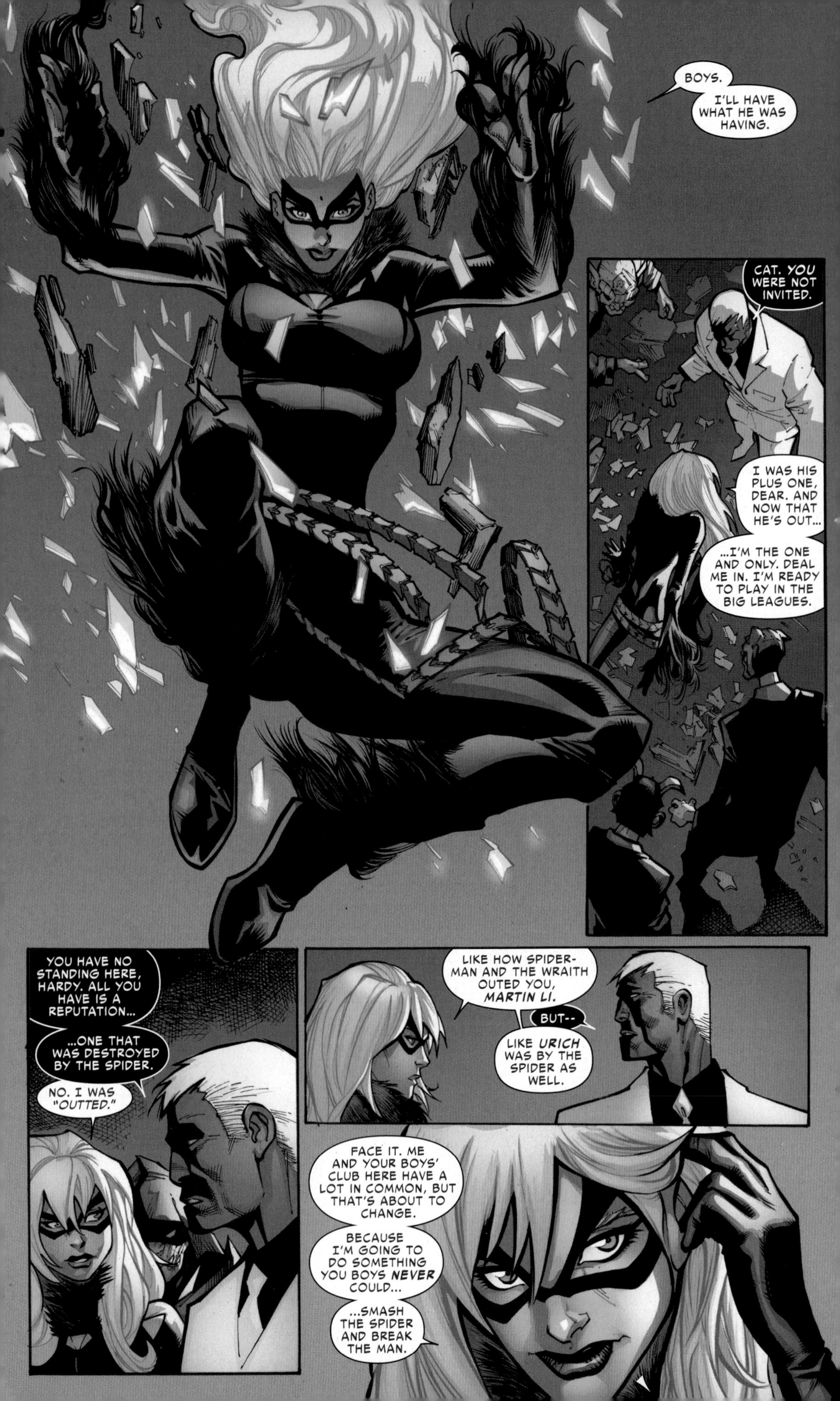
BOYS.
I'LL HAVE WHAT HE WAS HAVING.
CAT. *YOU* WERE NOT INVITED.
I WAS HIS PLUS ONE, DEAR. AND NOW THAT HE'S OUT...
...I'M THE ONE AND ONLY. DEAL ME IN. I'M READY TO PLAY IN THE BIG LEAGUES.
YOU HAVE NO STANDING HERE, HARDY. ALL YOU HAVE IS A REPUTATION...
...ONE THAT WAS DESTROYED BY THE SPIDER.
NO. I WAS "OUTTED."
LIKE HOW SPIDER-MAN AND THE WRAITH OUTED YOU, *MARTIN LI.*
BUT--
LIKE *URICH* WAS BY THE SPIDER AS WELL.
FACE IT. ME AND YOUR BOYS' CLUB HERE HAVE A LOT IN COMMON, BUT THAT'S ABOUT TO CHANGE.
BECAUSE I'M GOING TO DO SOMETHING YOU BOYS *NEVER* COULD...
...SMASH THE SPIDER AND BREAK THE MAN.

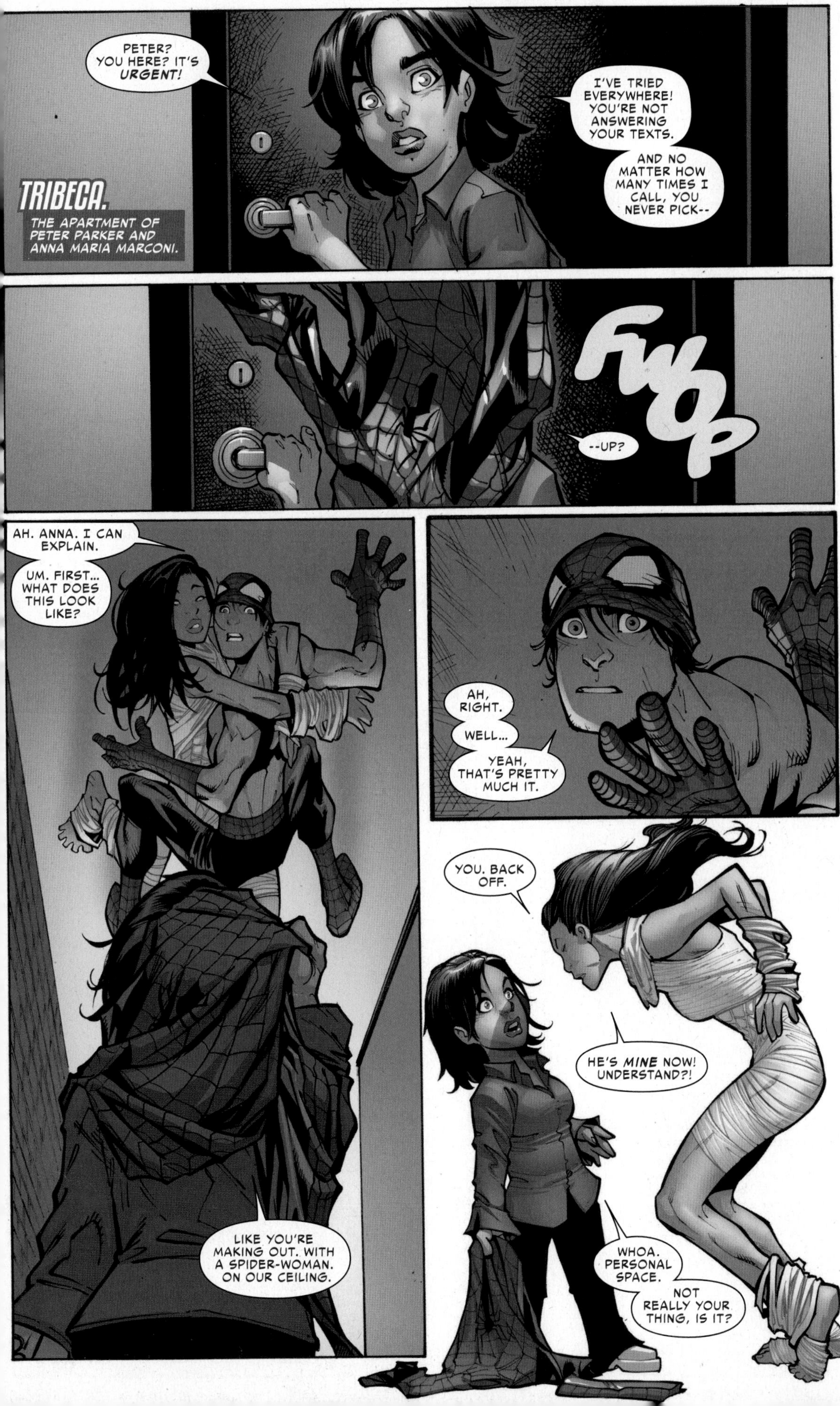
TRIBECA.
THE APARTMENT OF PETER PARKER AND ANNA MARIA MARCONI.
PETER? YOU HERE? IT'S URGENT!
I'VE TRIED EVERYWHERE! YOU'RE NOT ANSWERING YOUR TEXTS.
AND NO MATTER HOW MANY TIMES I CALL, YOU NEVER PICK--
FWOOP
--UP?
AH. ANNA. I CAN EXPLAIN.
UM. FIRST... WHAT DOES THIS LOOK LIKE?
LIKE YOU'RE MAKING OUT. WITH A SPIDER-WOMAN. ON OUR CEILING.
AH, RIGHT.
WELL...
YEAH, THAT'S PRETTY MUCH IT.
YOU. BACK OFF.
HE'S MINE NOW! UNDERSTAND?!
WHOA. PERSONAL SPACE.
NOT REALLY YOUR THING, IS IT?

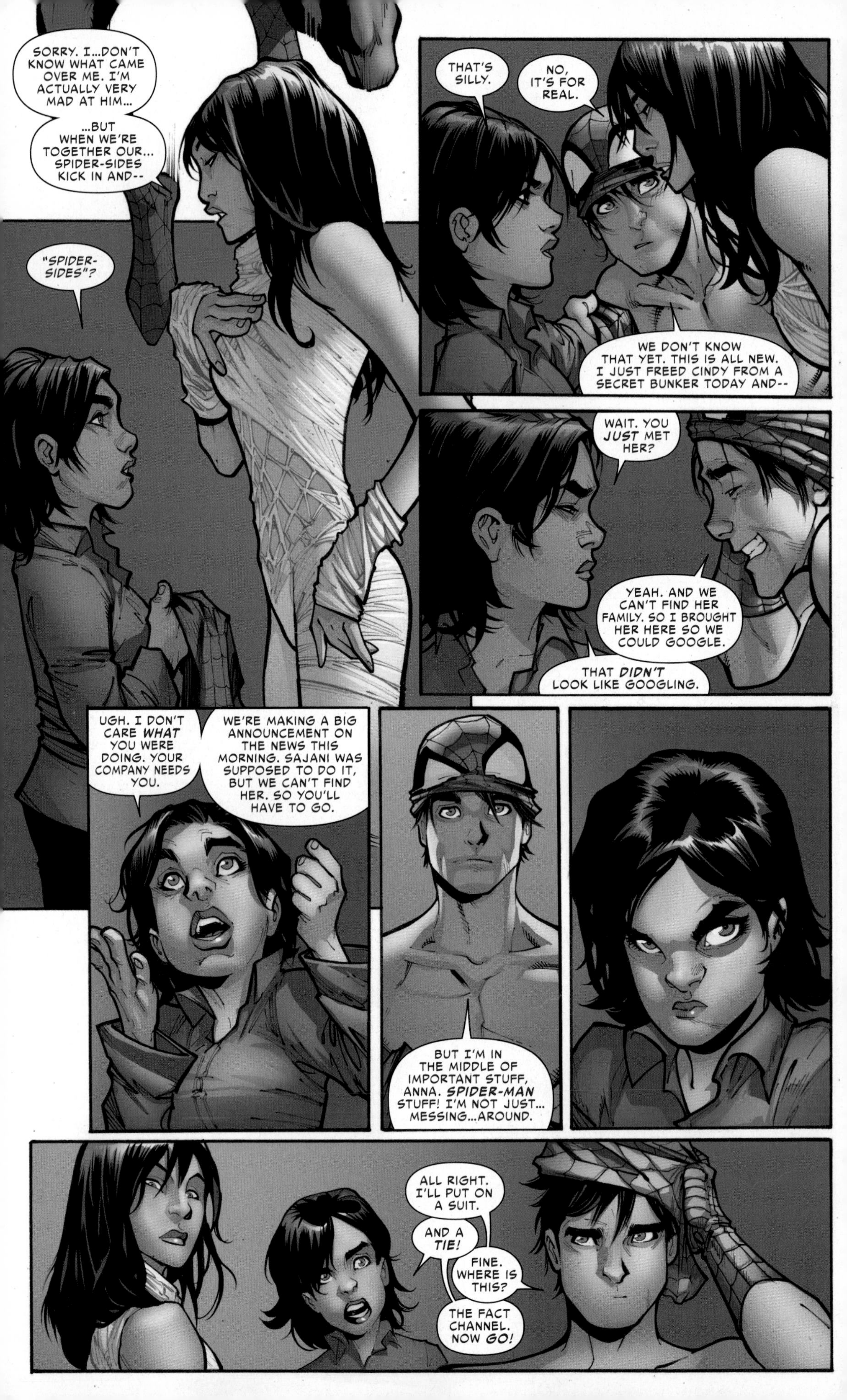
SORRY. I...DON'T KNOW WHAT CAME OVER ME. I'M ACTUALLY VERY MAD AT HIM...
...BUT WHEN WE'RE TOGETHER OUR... SPIDER-SIDES KICK IN AND--
"SPIDER-SIDES"?
THAT'S SILLY.
NO, IT'S FOR REAL.
WE DON'T KNOW THAT YET. THIS IS ALL NEW. I JUST FREED CINDY FROM A SECRET BUNKER TODAY AND--
WAIT. YOU JUST MET HER?
YEAH. AND WE CAN'T FIND HER FAMILY. SO I BROUGHT HER HERE SO WE COULD GOOGLE.
THAT DIDN'T LOOK LIKE GOOGLING.
UGH. I DON'T CARE WHAT YOU WERE DOING. YOUR COMPANY NEEDS YOU.
WE'RE MAKING A BIG ANNOUNCEMENT ON THE NEWS THIS MORNING. SAJANI WAS SUPPOSED TO DO IT, BUT WE CAN'T FIND HER. SO YOU'LL HAVE TO GO.
BUT I'M IN THE MIDDLE OF IMPORTANT STUFF, ANNA. SPIDER-MAN STUFF! I'M NOT JUST... MESSING...AROUND.
ALL RIGHT. I'LL PUT ON A SUIT.
AND A TIE!
FINE. WHERE IS THIS?
THE FACT CHANNEL. NOW GO!

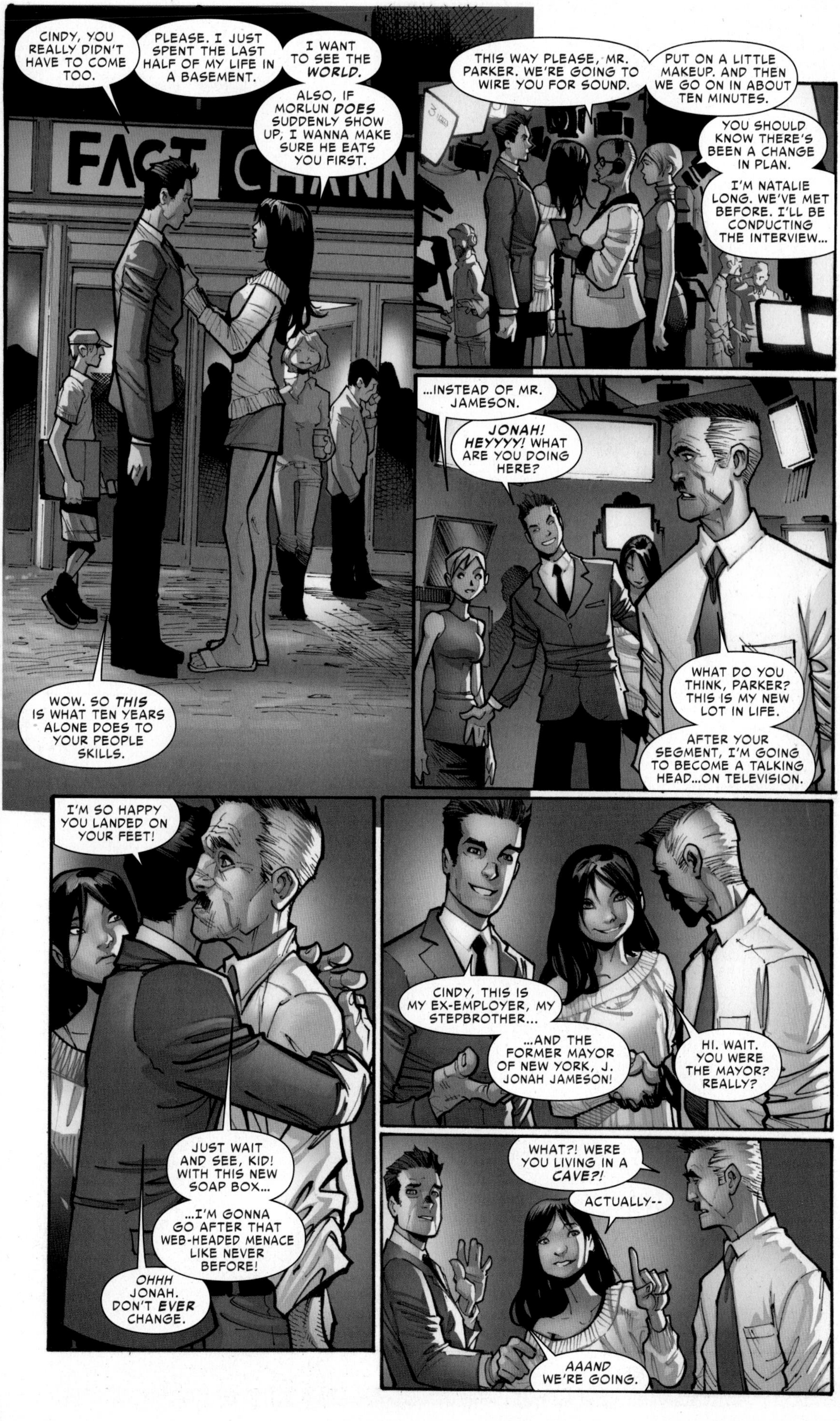

CINDY, YOU REALLY DIDN'T HAVE TO COME TOO.
PLEASE. I JUST SPENT THE LAST HALF OF MY LIFE IN A BASEMENT.
I WANT TO SEE THE *WORLD.*
ALSO, IF MORLUN *DOES* SUDDENLY SHOW UP, I WANNA MAKE SURE HE EATS YOU FIRST.
FACT CHANN
WOW. SO *THIS* IS WHAT TEN YEARS ALONE DOES TO YOUR PEOPLE SKILLS.
THIS WAY PLEASE, MR. PARKER. WE'RE GOING TO WIRE YOU FOR SOUND.
PUT ON A LITTLE MAKEUP. AND THEN WE GO ON IN ABOUT TEN MINUTES.
YOU SHOULD KNOW THERE'S BEEN A CHANGE IN PLAN.
I'M NATALIE LONG. WE'VE MET BEFORE. I'LL BE CONDUCTING THE INTERVIEW...
...INSTEAD OF MR. JAMESON.
JONAH! HEYYYY! WHAT ARE YOU DOING HERE?
WHAT DO YOU THINK, PARKER? THIS IS MY NEW LOT IN LIFE.
AFTER YOUR SEGMENT, I'M GOING TO BECOME A TALKING HEAD...ON TELEVISION.
I'M SO HAPPY YOU LANDED ON YOUR FEET!
JUST WAIT AND SEE, KID! WITH THIS NEW SOAP BOX...
...I'M GONNA GO AFTER THAT WEB-HEADED MENACE LIKE NEVER BEFORE!
OHHH JONAH. DON'T *EVER* CHANGE.
CINDY, THIS IS MY EX-EMPLOYER, MY STEPBROTHER...
...AND THE FORMER MAYOR OF NEW YORK, J. JONAH JAMESON!
HI. WAIT. YOU WERE THE MAYOR? REALLY?
WHAT?! WERE YOU LIVING IN A *CAVE?!*
ACTUALLY--
AAAND WE'RE GOING.

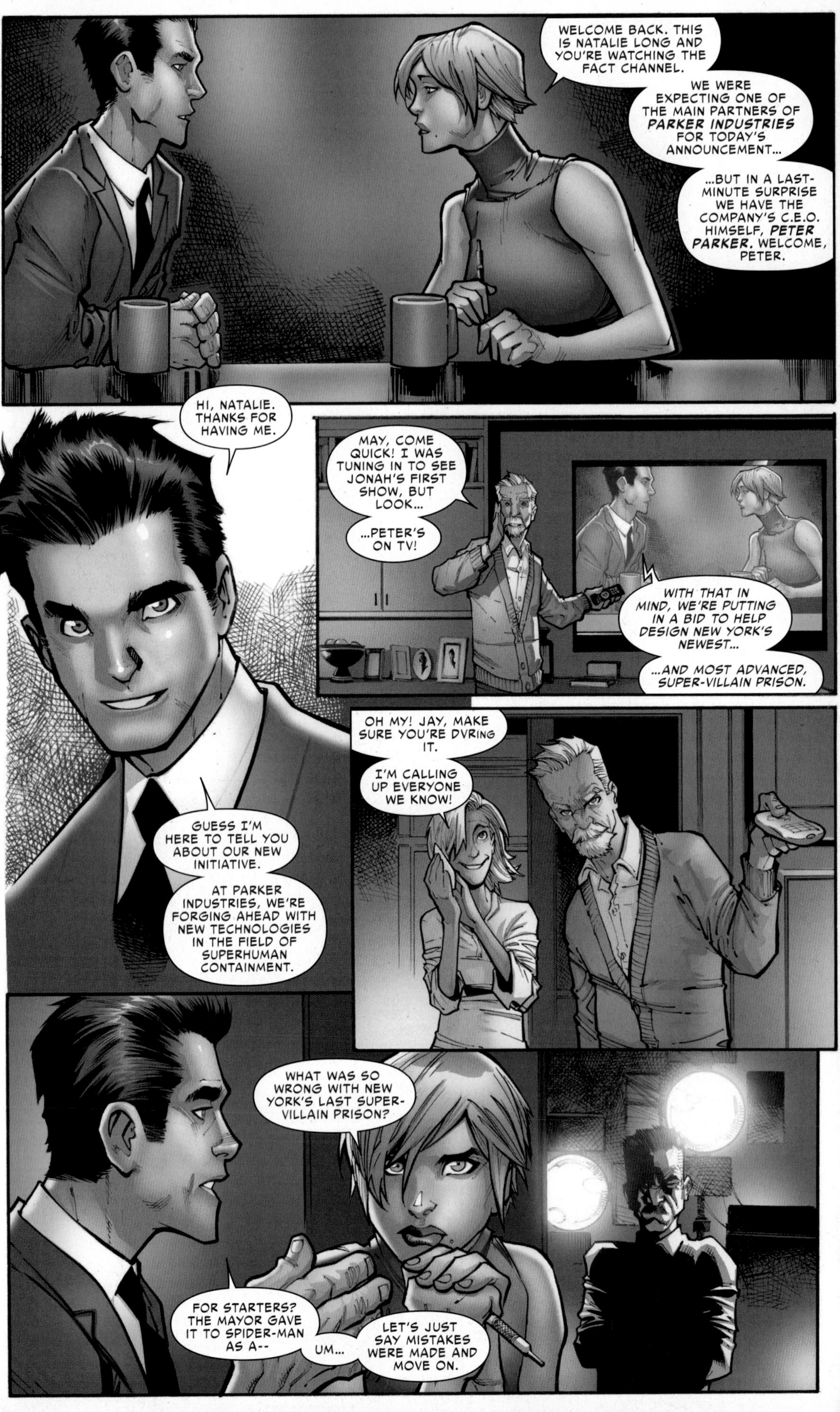
WELCOME BACK. THIS IS NATALIE LONG AND YOU'RE WATCHING THE FACT CHANNEL.
WE WERE EXPECTING ONE OF THE MAIN PARTNERS OF PARKER INDUSTRIES FOR TODAY'S ANNOUNCEMENT...
...BUT IN A LAST-MINUTE SURPRISE WE HAVE THE COMPANY'S C.E.O. HIMSELF, PETER PARKER. WELCOME, PETER.
HI, NATALIE. THANKS FOR HAVING ME.
GUESS I'M HERE TO TELL YOU ABOUT OUR NEW INITIATIVE.
AT PARKER INDUSTRIES, WE'RE FORGING AHEAD WITH NEW TECHNOLOGIES IN THE FIELD OF SUPERHUMAN CONTAINMENT.
MAY, COME QUICK! I WAS TUNING IN TO SEE JONAH'S FIRST SHOW, BUT LOOK...
...PETER'S ON TV!
WITH THAT IN MIND, WE'RE PUTTING IN A BID TO HELP DESIGN NEW YORK'S NEWEST...
...AND MOST ADVANCED, SUPER-VILLAIN PRISON.
OH MY! JAY, MAKE SURE YOU'RE DVRING IT.
I'M CALLING UP EVERYONE WE KNOW!
WHAT WAS SO WRONG WITH NEW YORK'S LAST SUPER-VILLAIN PRISON?
FOR STARTERS? THE MAYOR GAVE IT TO SPIDER-MAN AS A--
UM...
LET'S JUST SAY MISTAKES WERE MADE AND MOVE ON.

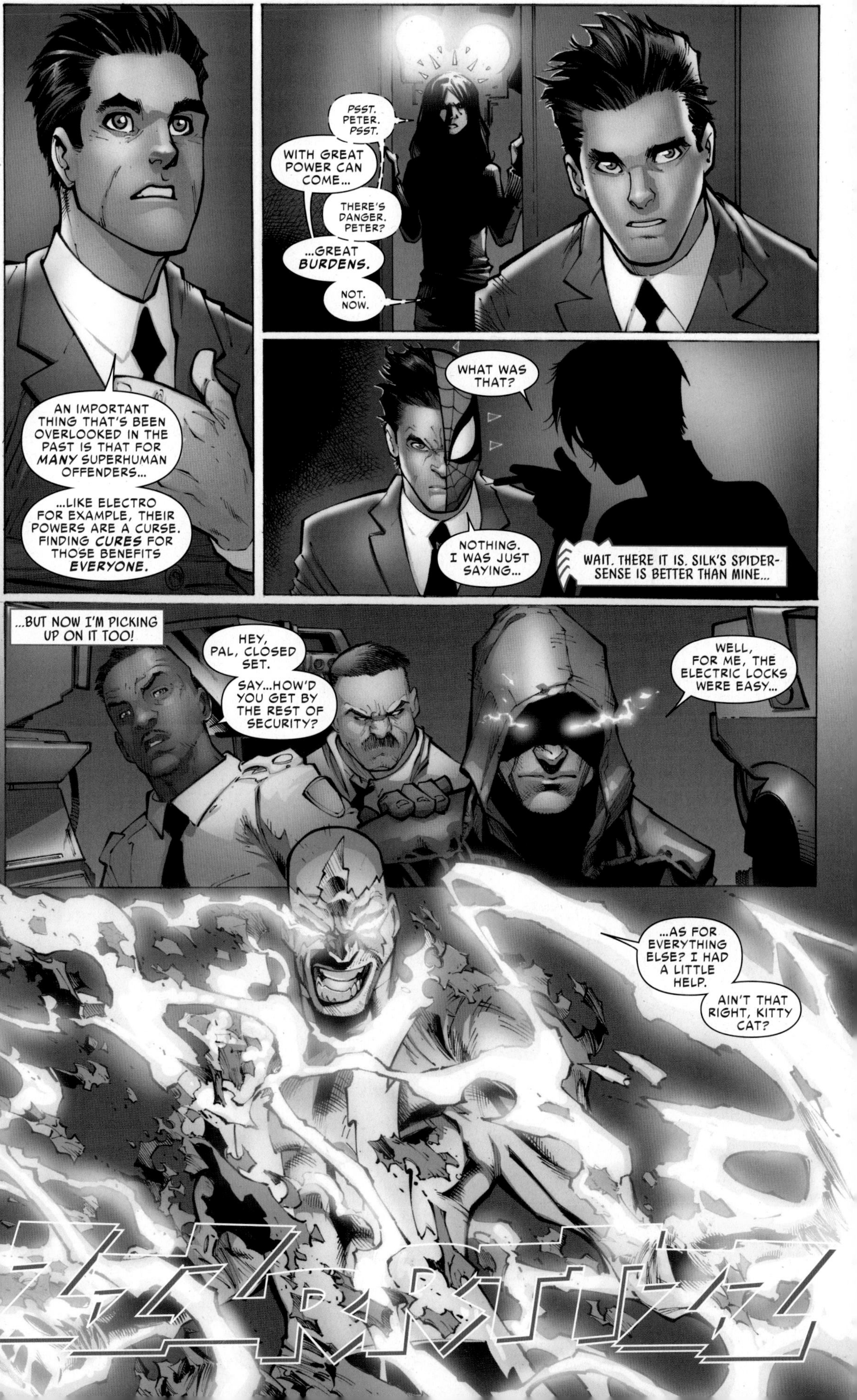
PSST. PETER. PSST.
WITH GREAT POWER CAN COME...
THERE'S DANGER. PETER?
...GREAT BURDENS.
NOT. NOW.
AN IMPORTANT THING THAT'S BEEN OVERLOOKED IN THE PAST IS THAT FOR MANY SUPERHUMAN OFFENDERS...
...LIKE ELECTRO FOR EXAMPLE, THEIR POWERS ARE A CURSE. FINDING CURES FOR THOSE BENEFITS EVERYONE.
WHAT WAS THAT?
NOTHING. I WAS JUST SAYING...
WAIT. THERE IT IS. SILK'S SPIDER-SENSE IS BETTER THAN MINE...
...BUT NOW I'M PICKING UP ON IT TOO!
HEY, PAL, CLOSED SET.
SAY...HOW'D YOU GET BY THE REST OF SECURITY?
WELL, FOR ME, THE ELECTRIC LOCKS WERE EASY...
...AS FOR EVERYTHING ELSE? I HAD A LITTLE HELP.
AIN'T THAT RIGHT, KITTY CAT?

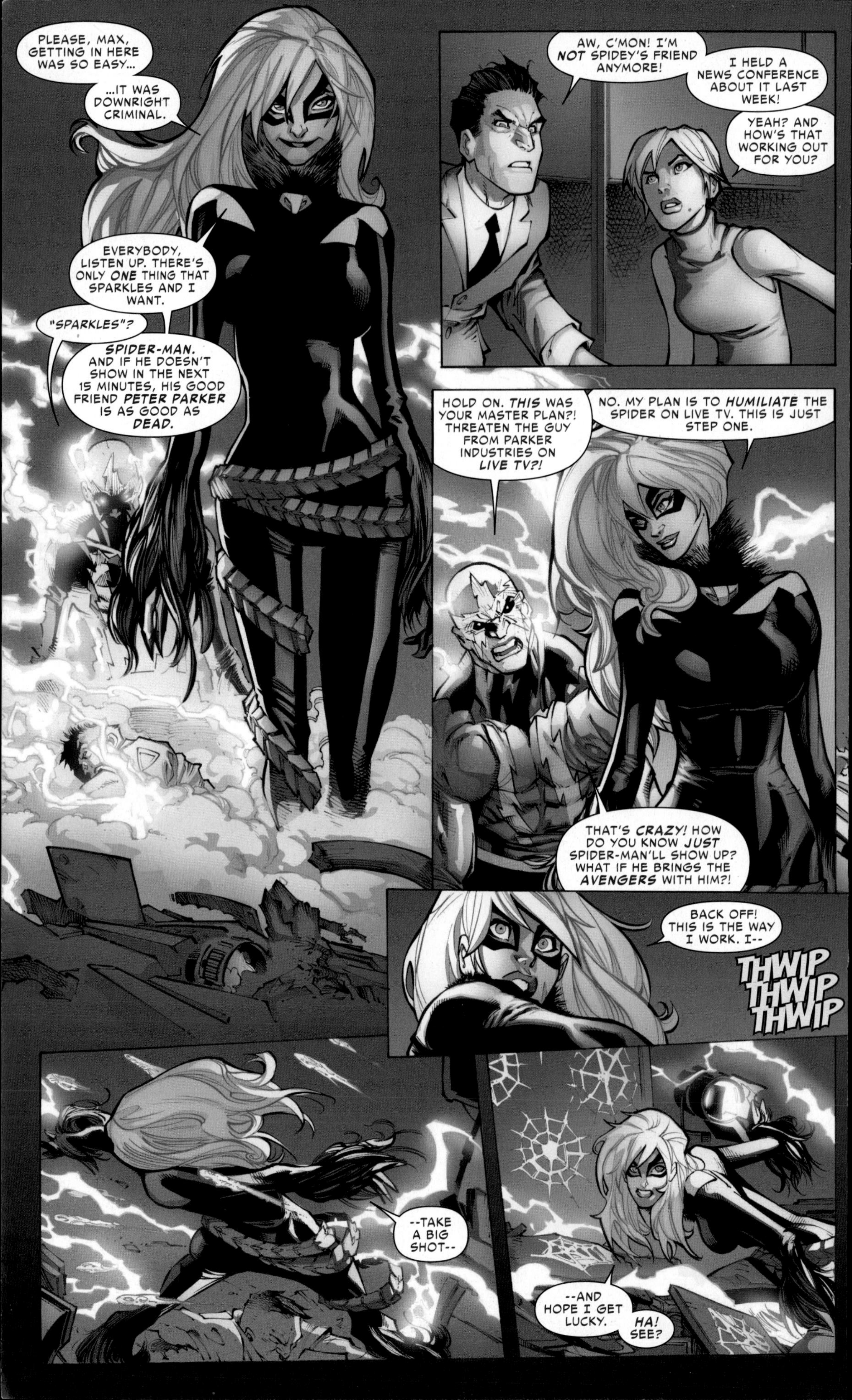
PLEASE, MAX, GETTING IN HERE WAS SO EASY...
...IT WAS DOWNRIGHT CRIMINAL.
EVERYBODY, LISTEN UP. THERE'S ONLY ONE THING THAT SPARKLES AND I WANT.
"SPARKLES"?
SPIDER-MAN. AND IF HE DOESN'T SHOW IN THE NEXT 15 MINUTES, HIS GOOD FRIEND PETER PARKER IS AS GOOD AS DEAD.
AW, C'MON! I'M NOT SPIDEY'S FRIEND ANYMORE!
I HELD A NEWS CONFERENCE ABOUT IT LAST WEEK!
YEAH? AND HOW'S THAT WORKING OUT FOR YOU?
HOLD ON. THIS WAS YOUR MASTER PLAN?! THREATEN THE GUY FROM PARKER INDUSTRIES ON LIVE TV?!
NO. MY PLAN IS TO HUMILIATE THE SPIDER ON LIVE TV. THIS IS JUST STEP ONE.
THAT'S CRAZY! HOW DO YOU KNOW JUST SPIDER-MAN'LL SHOW UP? WHAT IF HE BRINGS THE AVENGERS WITH HIM?!
BACK OFF! THIS IS THE WAY I WORK. I--
THWIP THWIP THWIP
--TAKE A BIG SHOT--
--AND HOPE I GET LUCKY.
HA! SEE?

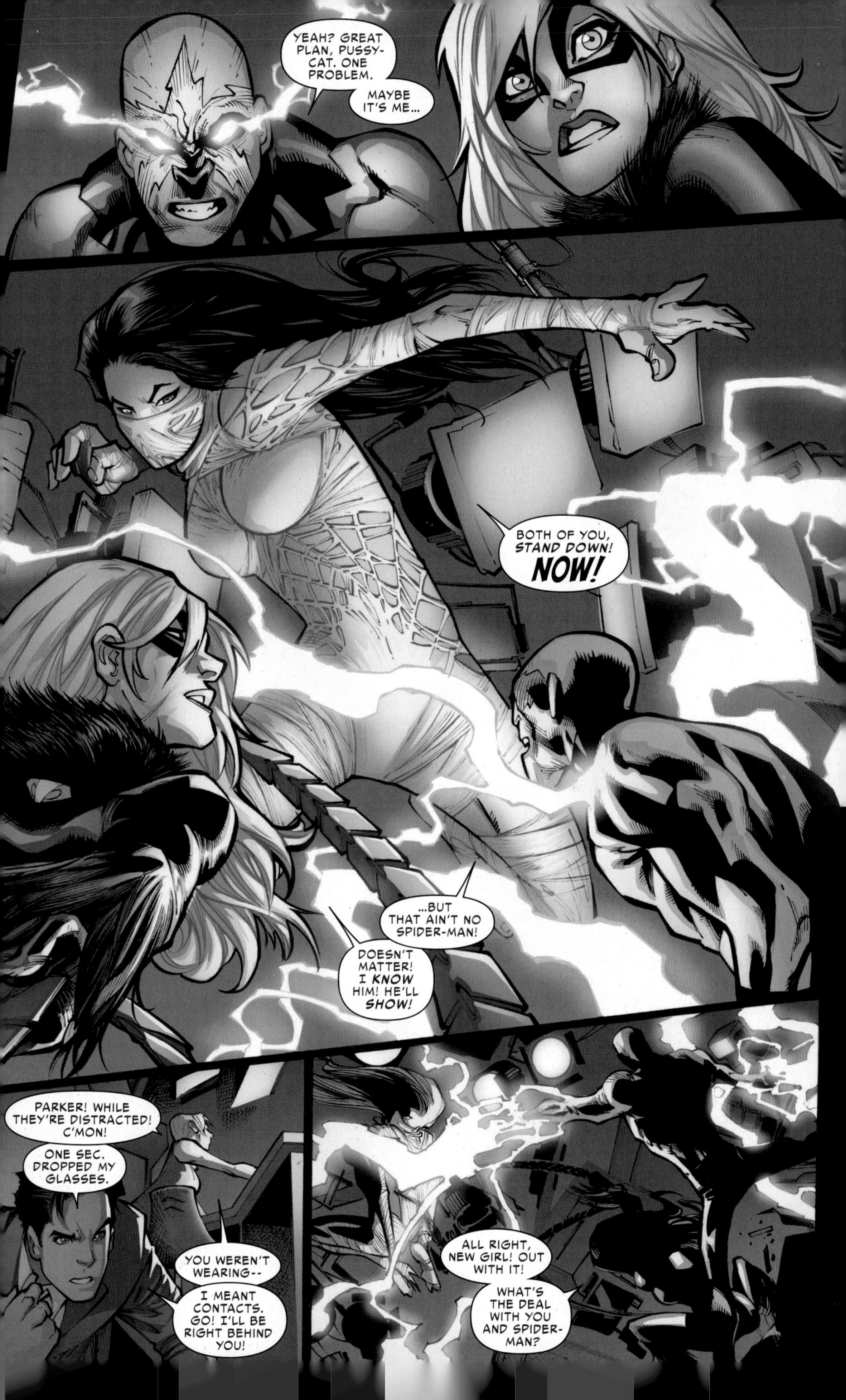
YEAH? GREAT PLAN, PUSSY-CAT. ONE PROBLEM.
MAYBE IT'S ME...
BOTH OF YOU, STAND DOWN! NOW!
...BUT THAT AIN'T NO SPIDER-MAN!
DOESN'T MATTER! I KNOW HIM! HE'LL SHOW!
PARKER! WHILE THEY'RE DISTRACTED! C'MON!
ONE SEC. DROPPED MY GLASSES.
YOU WEREN'T WEARING--
I MEANT CONTACTS. GO! I'LL BE RIGHT BEHIND YOU!
ALL RIGHT, NEW GIRL! OUT WITH IT!
WHAT'S THE DEAL WITH YOU AND SPIDER-MAN?

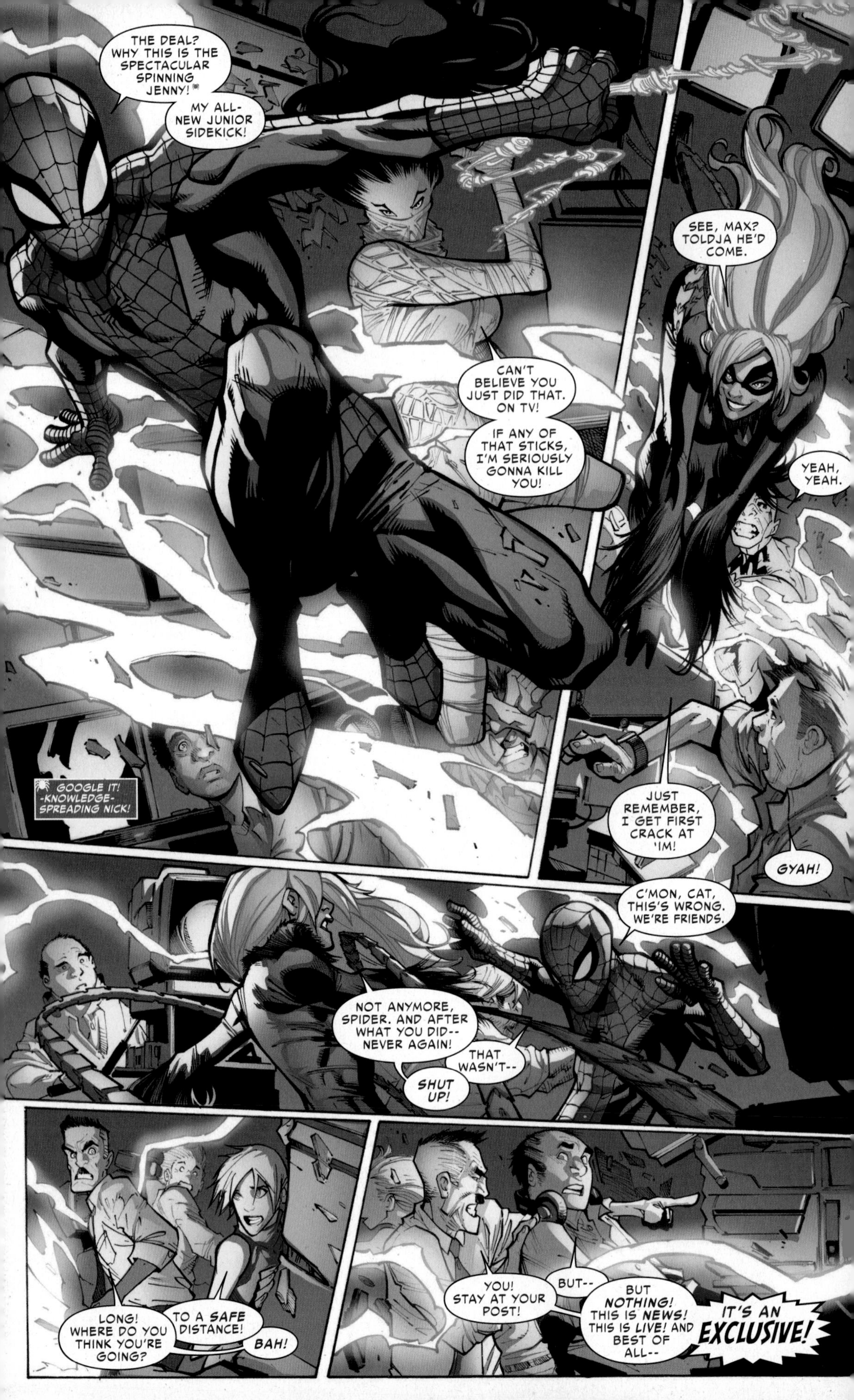
THE DEAL? WHY THIS IS THE SPECTACULAR SPINNING JENNY!
MY ALL-NEW JUNIOR SIDEKICK!
CAN'T BELIEVE YOU JUST DID THAT. ON TV!
IF ANY OF THAT STICKS, I'M SERIOUSLY GONNA KILL YOU!
GOOGLE IT! -KNOWLEDGE-SPREADING NICK!
SEE, MAX? TOLDJA HE'D COME.
YEAH, YEAH.
JUST REMEMBER, I GET FIRST CRACK AT 'IM!
GYAH!
C'MON, CAT, THIS'S WRONG. WE'RE FRIENDS.
NOT ANYMORE, SPIDER. AND AFTER WHAT YOU DID-- NEVER AGAIN!
THAT WASN'T--
SHUT UP!
LONG! WHERE DO YOU THINK YOU'RE GOING?
TO A SAFE DISTANCE!
BAH!
YOU! STAY AT YOUR POST!
BUT--
BUT NOTHING! THIS IS NEWS! THIS IS LIVE! AND BEST OF ALL--
IT'S AN EXCLUSIVE!

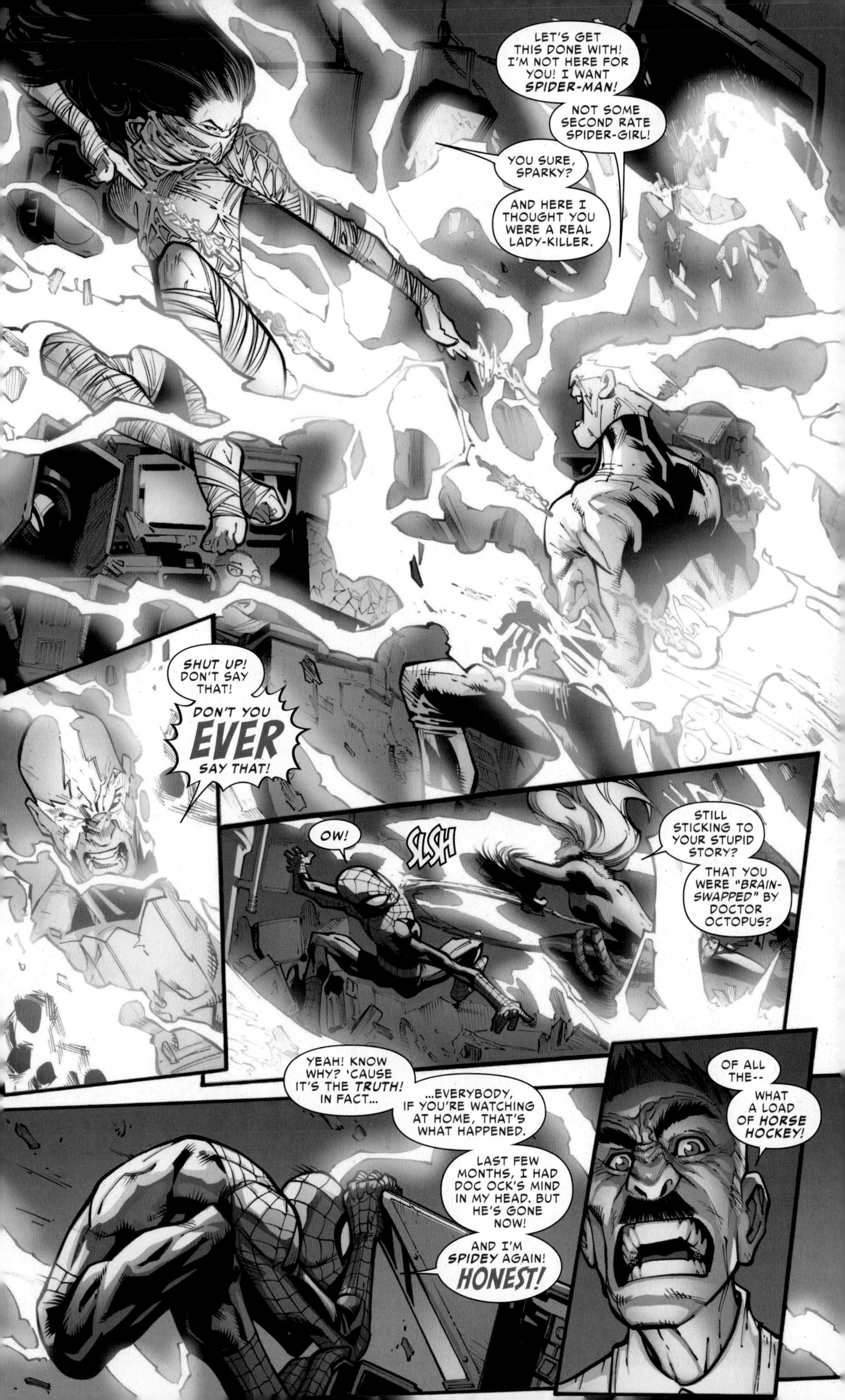
LET'S GET THIS DONE WITH! I'M NOT HERE FOR YOU! I WANT SPIDER-MAN!
NOT SOME SECOND RATE SPIDER-GIRL!
YOU SURE, SPARKY?
AND HERE I THOUGHT YOU WERE A REAL LADY-KILLER.
SHUT UP! DON'T SAY THAT!
DON'T YOU EVER SAY THAT!
OW!
SLSH
STILL STICKING TO YOUR STUPID STORY?
THAT YOU WERE "BRAIN-SWAPPED" BY DOCTOR OCTOPUS?
YEAH! KNOW WHY? 'CAUSE IT'S THE TRUTH! IN FACT...
...EVERYBODY, IF YOU'RE WATCHING AT HOME, THAT'S WHAT HAPPENED.
LAST FEW MONTHS, I HAD DOC OCK'S MIND IN MY HEAD. BUT HE'S GONE NOW!
AND I'M SPIDEY AGAIN! HONEST!
OF ALL THE--
WHAT A LOAD OF HORSE HOCKEY!

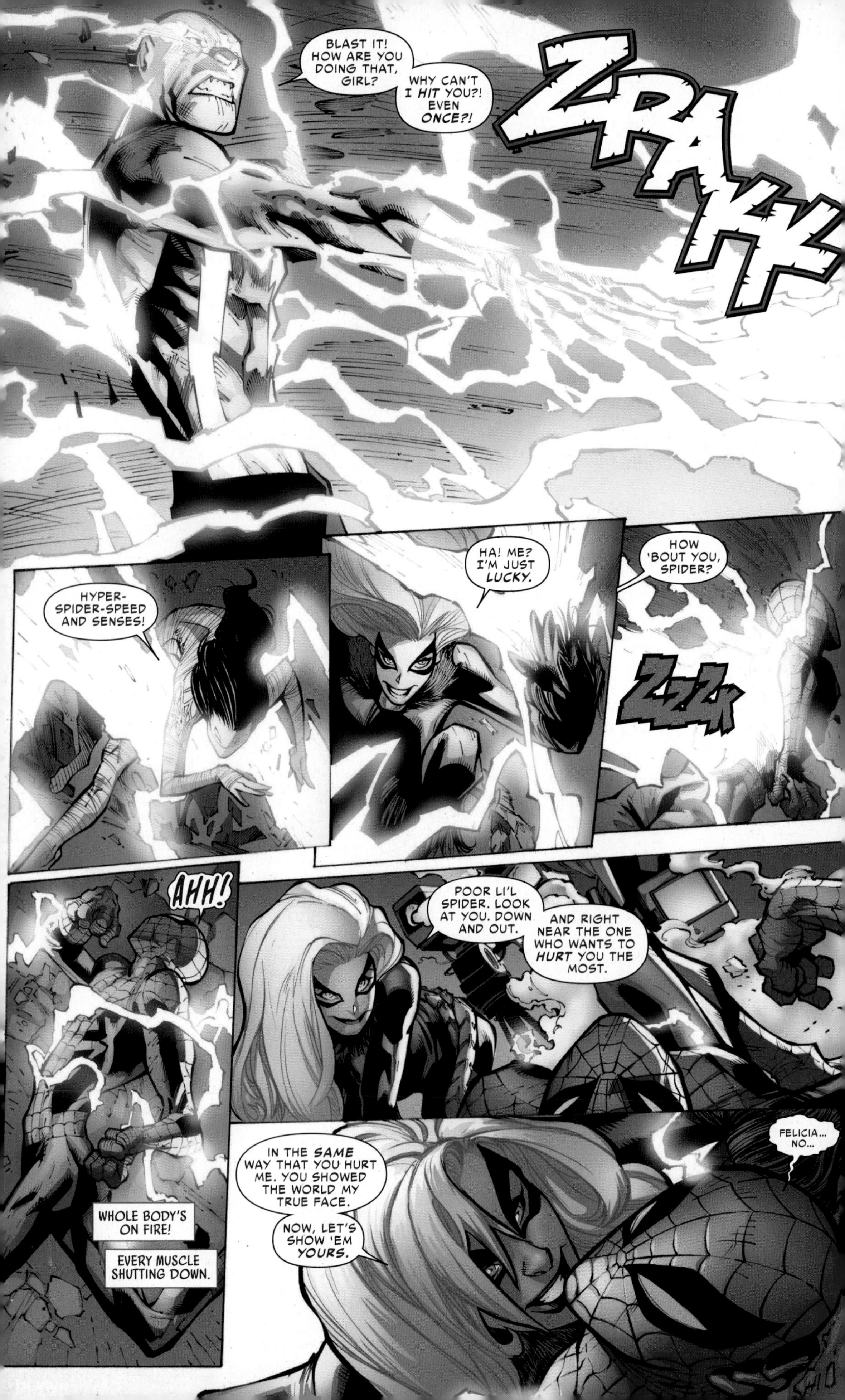
BLAST IT! HOW ARE YOU DOING THAT, GIRL?
WHY CAN'T I HIT YOU?! EVEN ONCE?!
ZRAKK
HYPER-SPIDER-SPEED AND SENSES!
HA! ME? I'M JUST LUCKY.
HOW 'BOUT YOU, SPIDER?
ZZZK
AHH!
POOR LI'L SPIDER. LOOK AT YOU. DOWN AND OUT.
AND RIGHT NEAR THE ONE WHO WANTS TO HURT YOU THE MOST.
IN THE SAME WAY THAT YOU HURT ME. YOU SHOWED THE WORLD MY TRUE FACE.
NOW, LET'S SHOW 'EM YOURS.
FELICIA... NO...
WHOLE BODY'S ON FIRE!
EVERY MUSCLE SHUTTING DOWN.

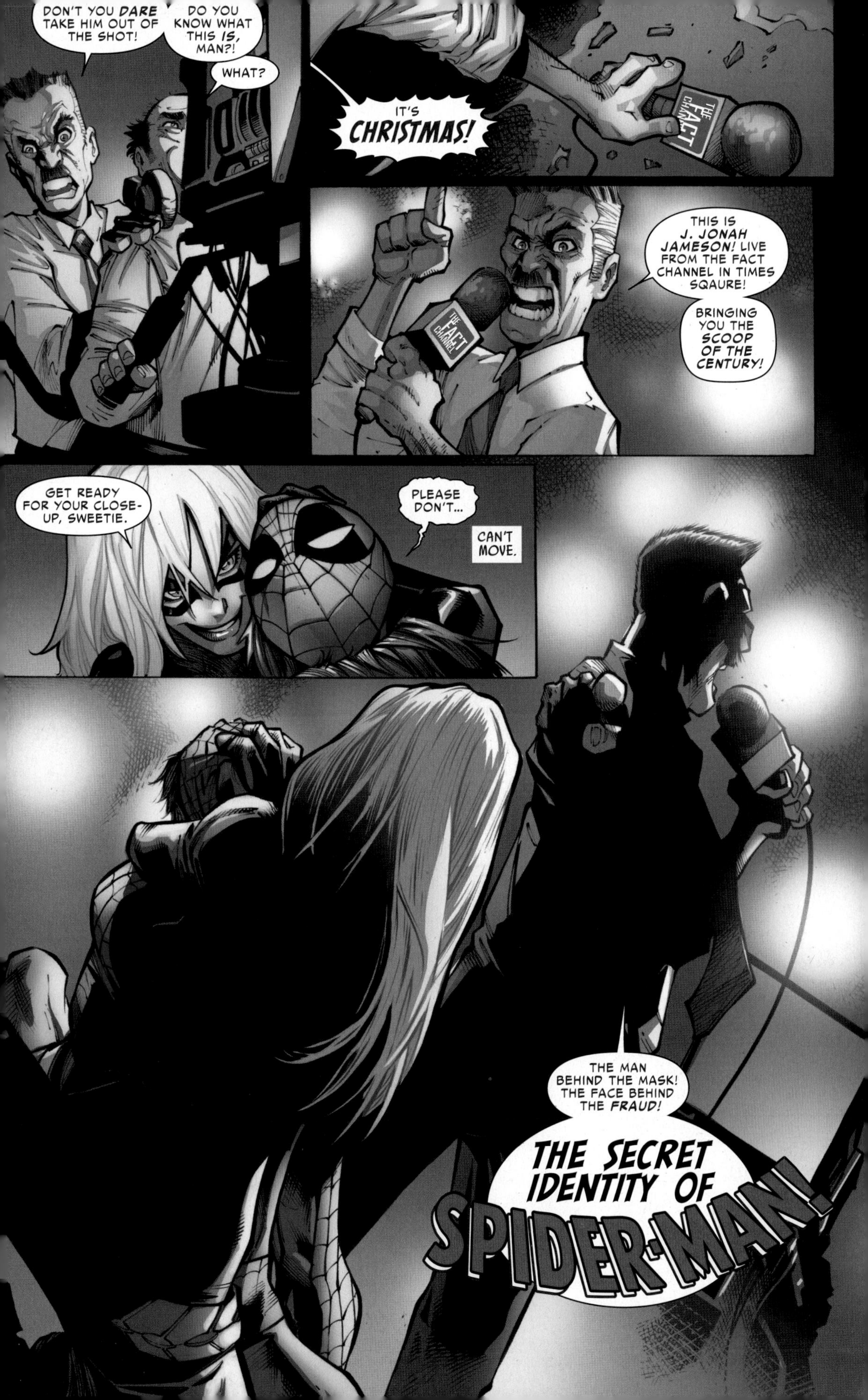
DON'T YOU DARE TAKE HIM OUT OF THE SHOT!
DO YOU KNOW WHAT THIS IS, MAN?!
WHAT?
IT'S CHRISTMAS!
THE FACT CHANNEL
THIS IS J. JONAH JAMESON! LIVE FROM THE FACT CHANNEL IN TIMES SQAURE!
BRINGING YOU THE SCOOP OF THE CENTURY!
GET READY FOR YOUR CLOSE-UP, SWEETIE.
PLEASE DON'T...
CAN'T MOVE.
THE MAN BEHIND THE MASK! THE FACE BEHIND THE FRAUD!
THE SECRET IDENTITY OF SPIDER-MAN!

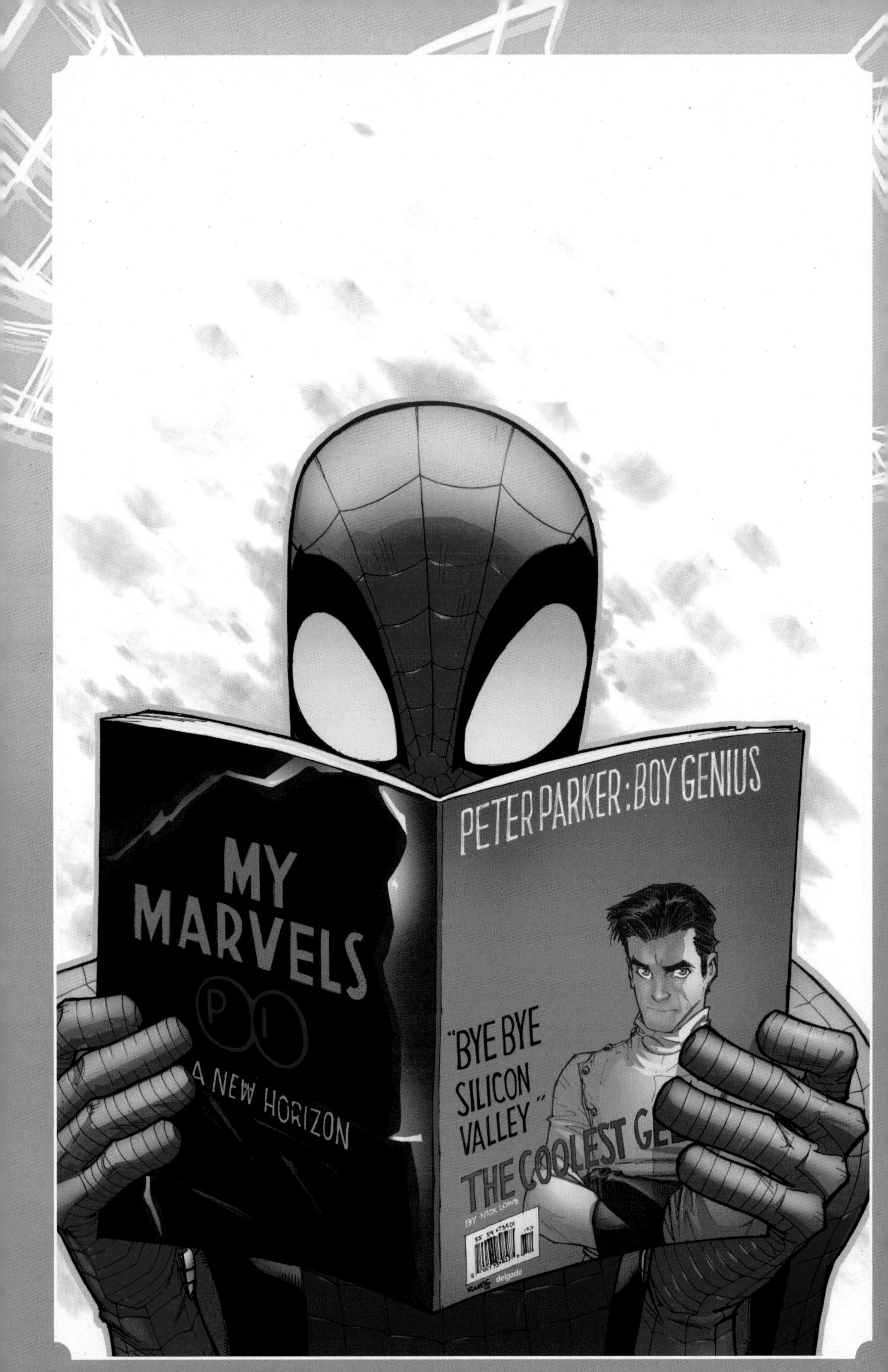
MY MARVELS
PI
A NEW HORIZON
PETER PARKER : BOY GENIUS
"BYE BYE SILICON VALLEY"
THE COOLEST
BY NICK LOWE
delgado

AMAZING SPIDER-MAN (2014) #6

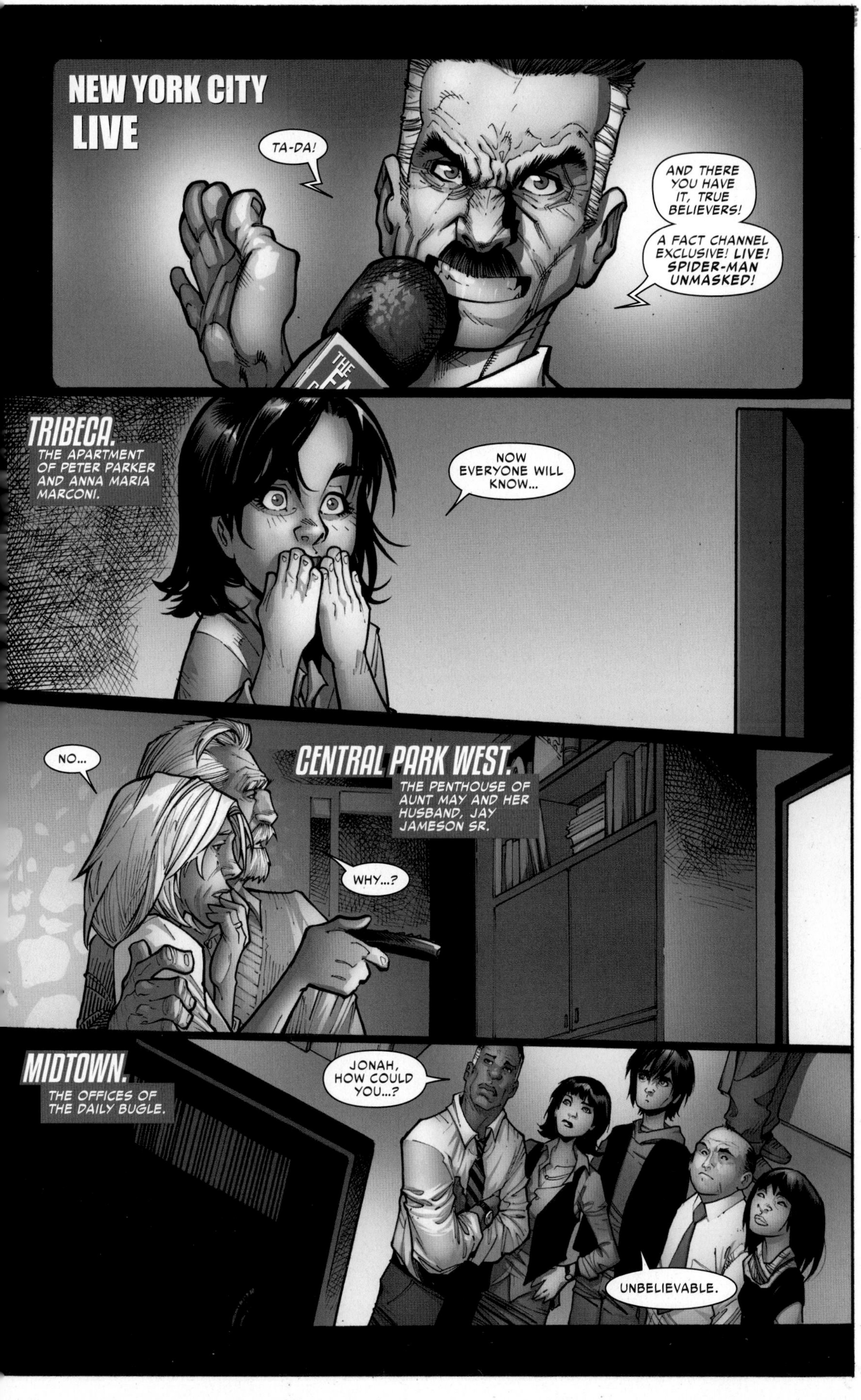
NEW YORK CITY
LIVE
TA-DA!
AND THERE YOU HAVE IT, TRUE BELIEVERS!
A FACT CHANNEL EXCLUSIVE! LIVE! SPIDER-MAN UNMASKED!
TRIBECA.
THE APARTMENT OF PETER PARKER AND ANNA MARIA MARCONI.
NOW EVERYONE WILL KNOW...
NO...
CENTRAL PARK WEST.
THE PENTHOUSE OF AUNT MAY AND HER HUSBAND, JAY JAMESON SR.
WHY...?
MIDTOWN.
THE OFFICES OF THE DAILY BUGLE.
JONAH, HOW COULD YOU...?
UNBELIEVABLE.

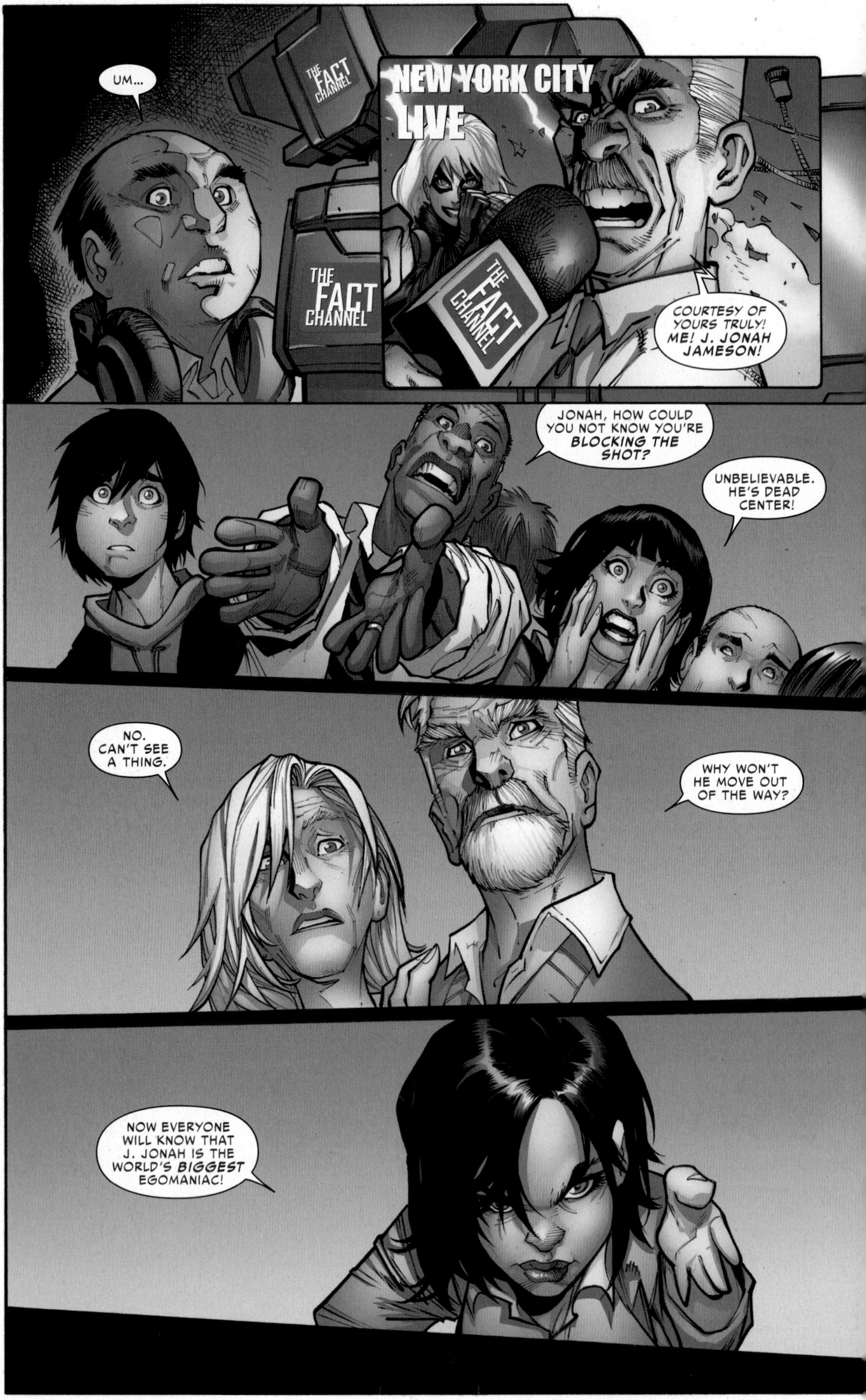

UM...
THE FACT CHANNEL
NEW YORK CITY LIVE
THE FACT CHANNEL
THE FACT CHANNEL
COURTESY OF YOURS TRULY! ME! J. JONAH JAMESON!
JONAH, HOW COULD YOU NOT KNOW YOU'RE BLOCKING THE SHOT?
UNBELIEVABLE. HE'S DEAD CENTER!
NO. CAN'T SEE A THING.
WHY WON'T HE MOVE OUT OF THE WAY?
NOW EVERYONE WILL KNOW THAT J. JONAH IS THE WORLD'S BIGGEST EGOMANIAC!

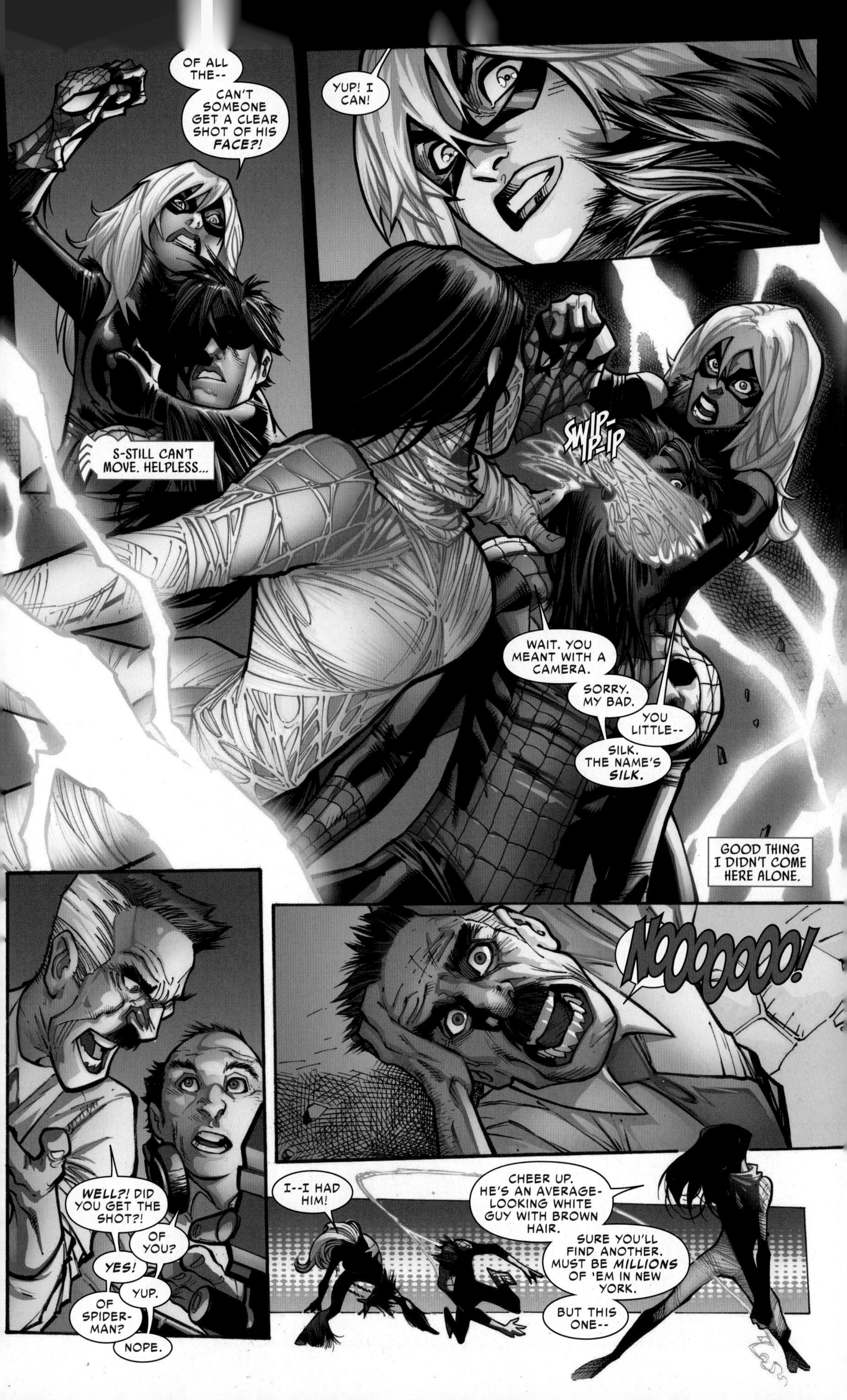
OF ALL THE--
CAN'T SOMEONE GET A CLEAR SHOT OF HIS FACE?!
YUP! I CAN!
S-STILL CAN'T MOVE. HELPLESS...
SWIP-IP-IP
WAIT. YOU MEANT WITH A CAMERA.
SORRY. MY BAD.
YOU LITTLE--
SILK. THE NAME'S SILK.
GOOD THING I DIDN'T COME HERE ALONE.
WELL?! DID YOU GET THE SHOT?!
OF YOU?
YES!
YUP.
OF SPIDER-MAN?
NOPE.
NOOOOOOO!
I--I HAD HIM!
CHEER UP. HE'S AN AVERAGE-LOOKING WHITE GUY WITH BROWN HAIR.
SURE YOU'LL FIND ANOTHER. MUST BE MILLIONS OF 'EM IN NEW YORK.
BUT THIS ONE--

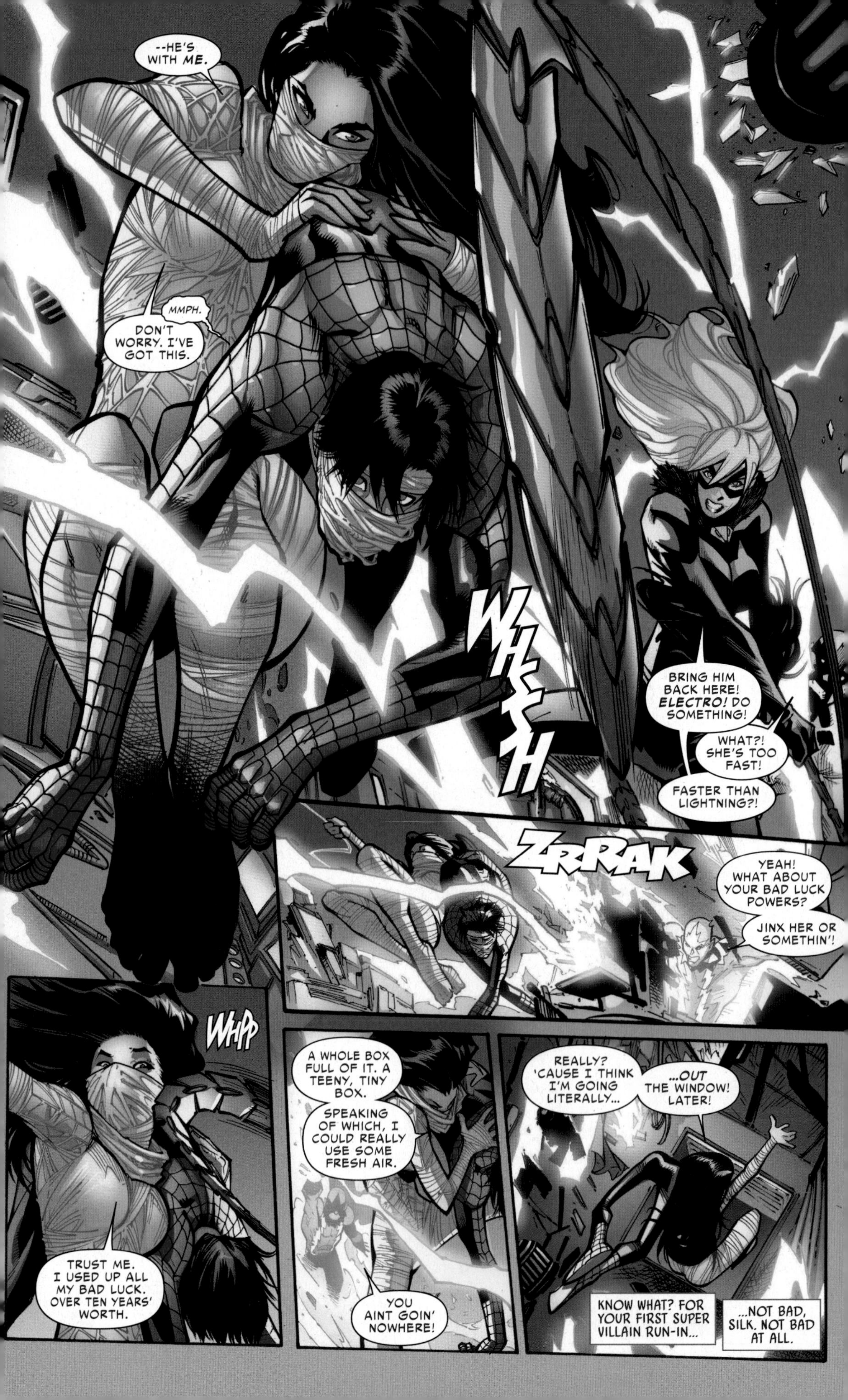
--HE'S WITH ME.
MMPH.
DON'T WORRY. I'VE GOT THIS.
WHSSH
BRING HIM BACK HERE! ELECTRO! DO SOMETHING!
WHAT?! SHE'S TOO FAST!
FASTER THAN LIGHTNING?!
ZRRAK
YEAH! WHAT ABOUT YOUR BAD LUCK POWERS?
JINX HER OR SOMETHIN'!
WHPP
TRUST ME. I USED UP ALL MY BAD LUCK. OVER TEN YEARS' WORTH.
A WHOLE BOX FULL OF IT. A TEENY, TINY BOX.
SPEAKING OF WHICH, I COULD REALLY USE SOME FRESH AIR.
YOU AINT GOIN' NOWHERE!
REALLY? 'CAUSE I THINK I'M GOING LITERALLY...
...OUT THE WINDOW! LATER!
KNOW WHAT? FOR YOUR FIRST SUPER VILLAIN RUN-IN...
...NOT BAD, SILK. NOT BAD AT ALL.

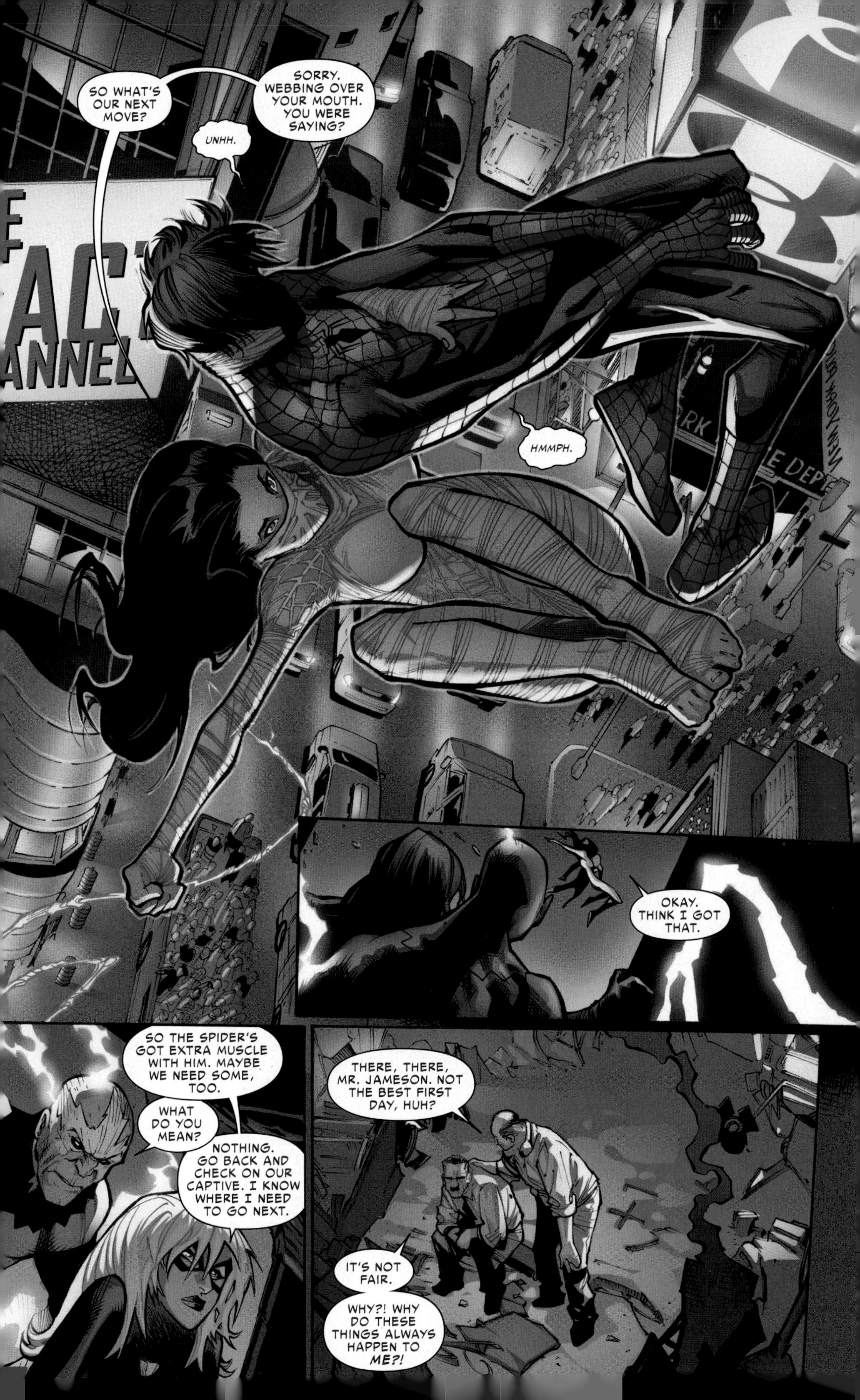
SO WHAT'S OUR NEXT MOVE?
UNHH.
SORRY. WEBBING OVER YOUR MOUTH. YOU WERE SAYING?
HMMPH.
OKAY. THINK I GOT THAT.
SO THE SPIDER'S GOT EXTRA MUSCLE WITH HIM. MAYBE WE NEED SOME, TOO.
WHAT DO YOU MEAN?
NOTHING. GO BACK AND CHECK ON OUR CAPTIVE. I KNOW WHERE I NEED TO GO NEXT.
THERE, THERE, MR. JAMESON. NOT THE BEST FIRST DAY, HUH?
IT'S NOT FAIR.
WHY?! WHY DO THESE THINGS ALWAYS HAPPEN TO *ME?!*

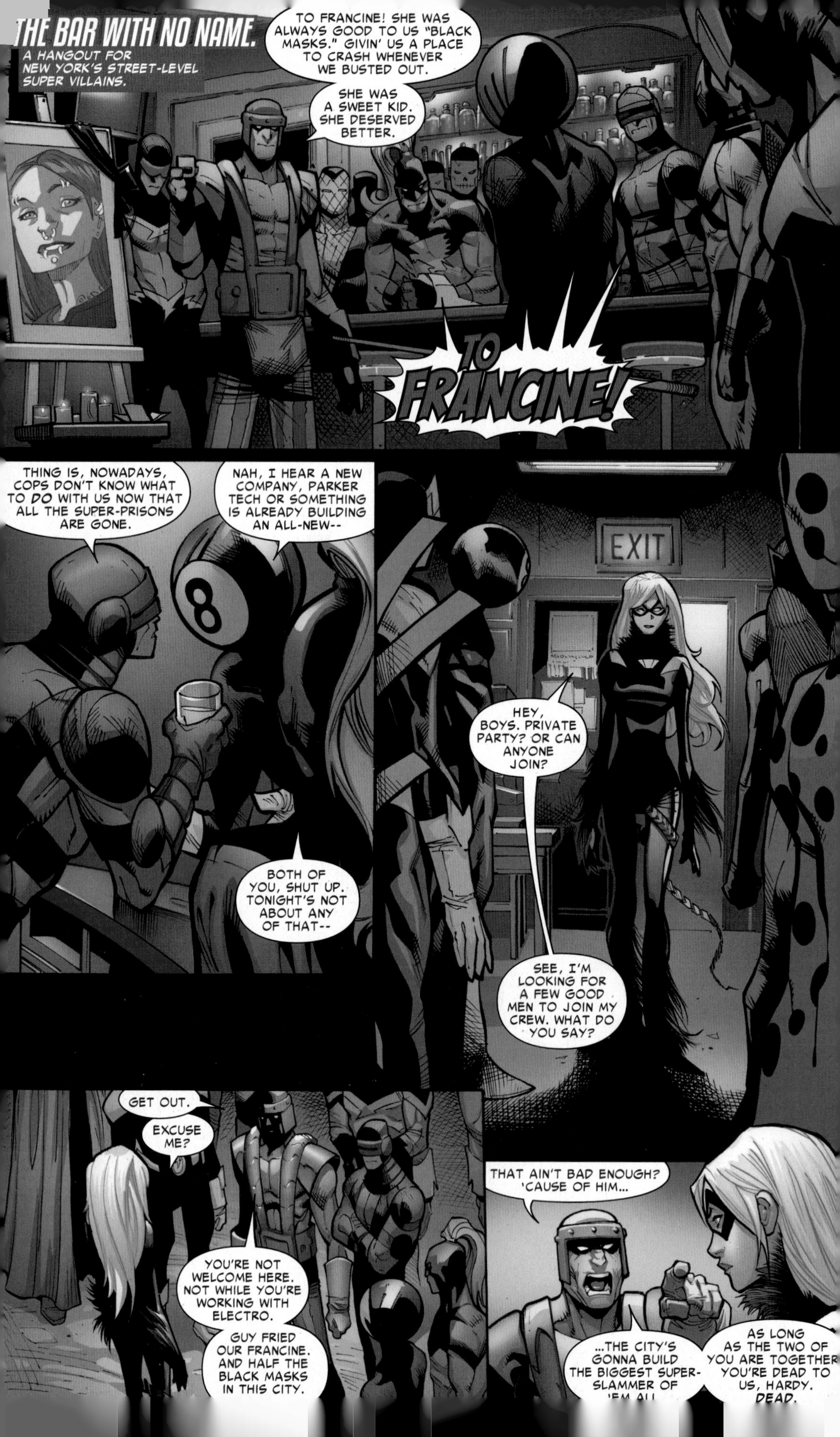
THE BAR WITH NO NAME.
A HANGOUT FOR NEW YORK'S STREET-LEVEL SUPER VILLAINS.
TO FRANCINE! SHE WAS ALWAYS GOOD TO US "BLACK MASKS." GIVIN' US A PLACE TO CRASH WHENEVER WE BUSTED OUT.
SHE WAS A SWEET KID. SHE DESERVED BETTER.
TO FRANCINE!
THING IS, NOWADAYS, COPS DON'T KNOW WHAT TO DO WITH US NOW THAT ALL THE SUPER-PRISONS ARE GONE.
NAH, I HEAR A NEW COMPANY, PARKER TECH OR SOMETHING IS ALREADY BUILDING AN ALL-NEW--
BOTH OF YOU, SHUT UP. TONIGHT'S NOT ABOUT ANY OF THAT--
EXIT
HEY, BOYS. PRIVATE PARTY? OR CAN ANYONE JOIN?
SEE, I'M LOOKING FOR A FEW GOOD MEN TO JOIN MY CREW. WHAT DO YOU SAY?
GET OUT.
EXCUSE ME?
YOU'RE NOT WELCOME HERE. NOT WHILE YOU'RE WORKING WITH ELECTRO.
GUY FRIED OUR FRANCINE. AND HALF THE BLACK MASKS IN THIS CITY.
THAT AIN'T BAD ENOUGH? 'CAUSE OF HIM...
...THE CITY'S GONNA BUILD THE BIGGEST SUPER-SLAMMER OF
AS LONG AS THE TWO OF YOU ARE TOGETHER YOU'RE DEAD TO US, HARDY. DEAD.

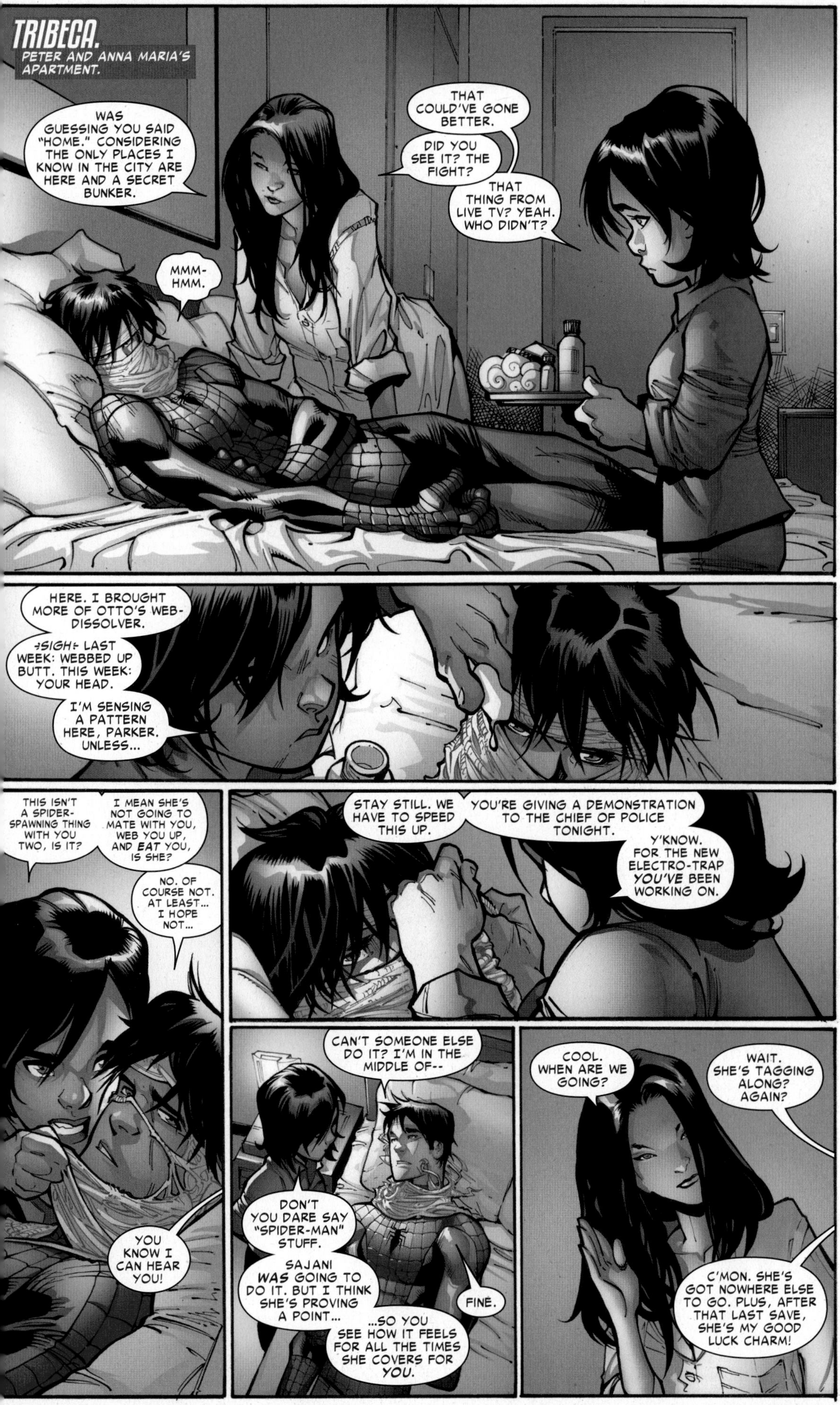
TRIBECA.
PETER AND ANNA MARIA'S APARTMENT.
WAS GUESSING YOU SAID "HOME." CONSIDERING THE ONLY PLACES I KNOW IN THE CITY ARE HERE AND A SECRET BUNKER.
MMM-HMM.
THAT COULD'VE GONE BETTER.
DID YOU SEE IT? THE FIGHT?
THAT THING FROM LIVE TV? YEAH. WHO DIDN'T?
HERE. I BROUGHT MORE OF OTTO'S WEB-DISSOLVER.
=SIGH= LAST WEEK: WEBBED UP BUTT. THIS WEEK: YOUR HEAD.
I'M SENSING A PATTERN HERE, PARKER. UNLESS...
THIS ISN'T A SPIDER-SPAWNING THING WITH YOU TWO, IS IT?
I MEAN SHE'S NOT GOING TO MATE WITH YOU, WEB YOU UP, AND EAT YOU, IS SHE?
NO. OF COURSE NOT. AT LEAST... I HOPE NOT...
YOU KNOW I CAN HEAR YOU!
STAY STILL. WE HAVE TO SPEED THIS UP.
YOU'RE GIVING A DEMONSTRATION TO THE CHIEF OF POLICE TONIGHT.
Y'KNOW. FOR THE NEW ELECTRO-TRAP YOU'VE BEEN WORKING ON.
CAN'T SOMEONE ELSE DO IT? I'M IN THE MIDDLE OF--
DON'T YOU DARE SAY "SPIDER-MAN" STUFF.
SAJANI WAS GOING TO DO IT. BUT I THINK SHE'S PROVING A POINT...
...SO YOU SEE HOW IT FEELS FOR ALL THE TIMES SHE COVERS FOR YOU.
FINE.
COOL. WHEN ARE WE GOING?
WAIT. SHE'S TAGGING ALONG? AGAIN?
C'MON. SHE'S GOT NOWHERE ELSE TO GO. PLUS, AFTER THAT LAST SAVE, SHE'S MY GOOD LUCK CHARM!

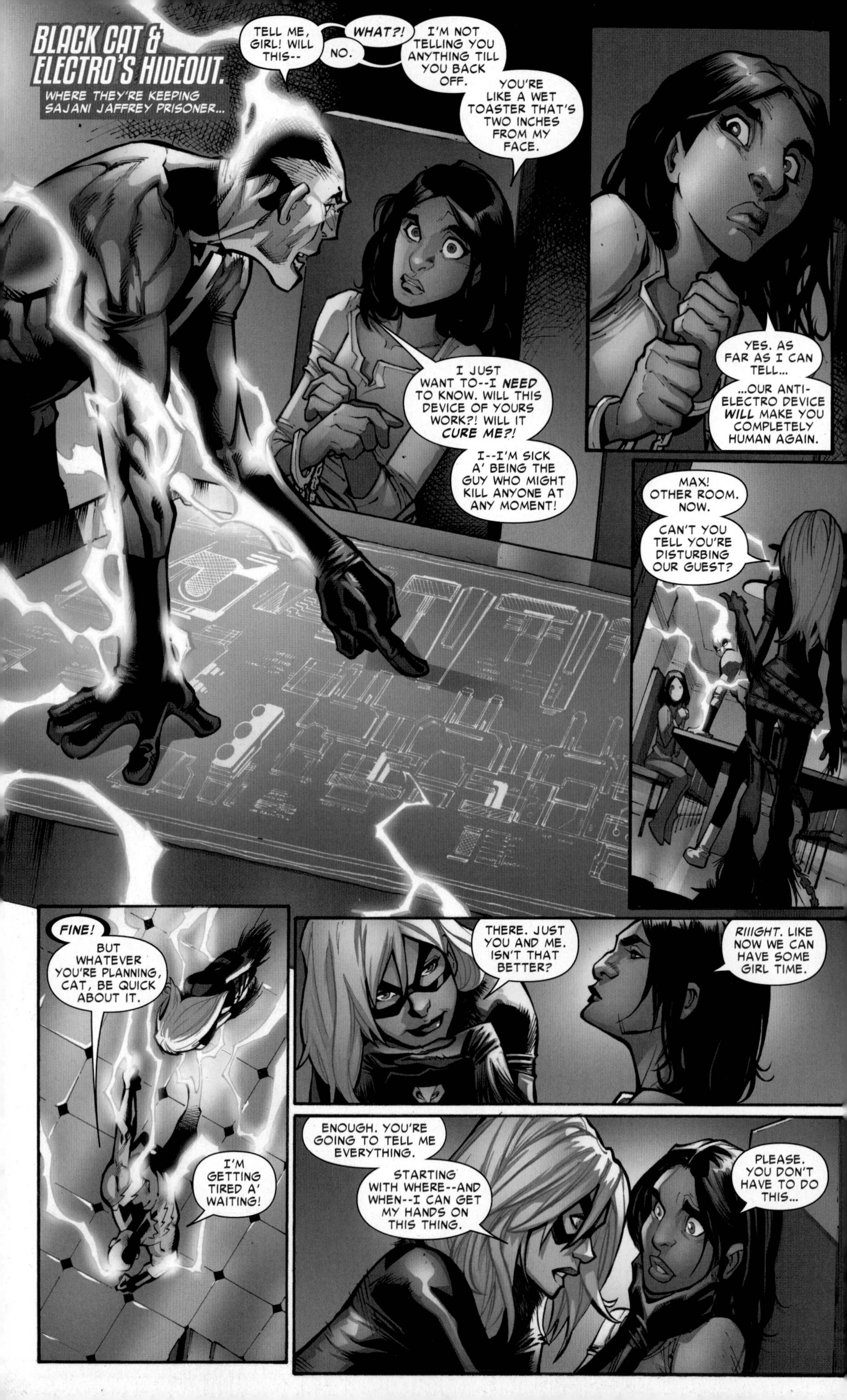
BLACK CAT & ELECTRO'S HIDEOUT.
WHERE THEY'RE KEEPING SAJANI JAFFREY PRISONER...
TELL ME, GIRL! WILL THIS--
NO.
WHAT?!
I'M NOT TELLING YOU ANYTHING TILL YOU BACK OFF.
YOU'RE LIKE A WET TOASTER THAT'S TWO INCHES FROM MY FACE.
I JUST WANT TO--I NEED TO KNOW. WILL THIS DEVICE OF YOURS WORK?! WILL IT CURE ME?!
I--I'M SICK A' BEING THE GUY WHO MIGHT KILL ANYONE AT ANY MOMENT!
YES. AS FAR AS I CAN TELL...
...OUR ANTI-ELECTRO DEVICE WILL MAKE YOU COMPLETELY HUMAN AGAIN.
MAX! OTHER ROOM. NOW.
CAN'T YOU TELL YOU'RE DISTURBING OUR GUEST?
FINE! BUT WHATEVER YOU'RE PLANNING, CAT, BE QUICK ABOUT IT.
I'M GETTING TIRED A' WAITING!
THERE. JUST YOU AND ME. ISN'T THAT BETTER?
RIIIGHT. LIKE NOW WE CAN HAVE SOME GIRL TIME.
ENOUGH. YOU'RE GOING TO TELL ME EVERYTHING.
STARTING WITH WHERE--AND WHEN--I CAN GET MY HANDS ON THIS THING.
PLEASE. YOU DON'T HAVE TO DO THIS...

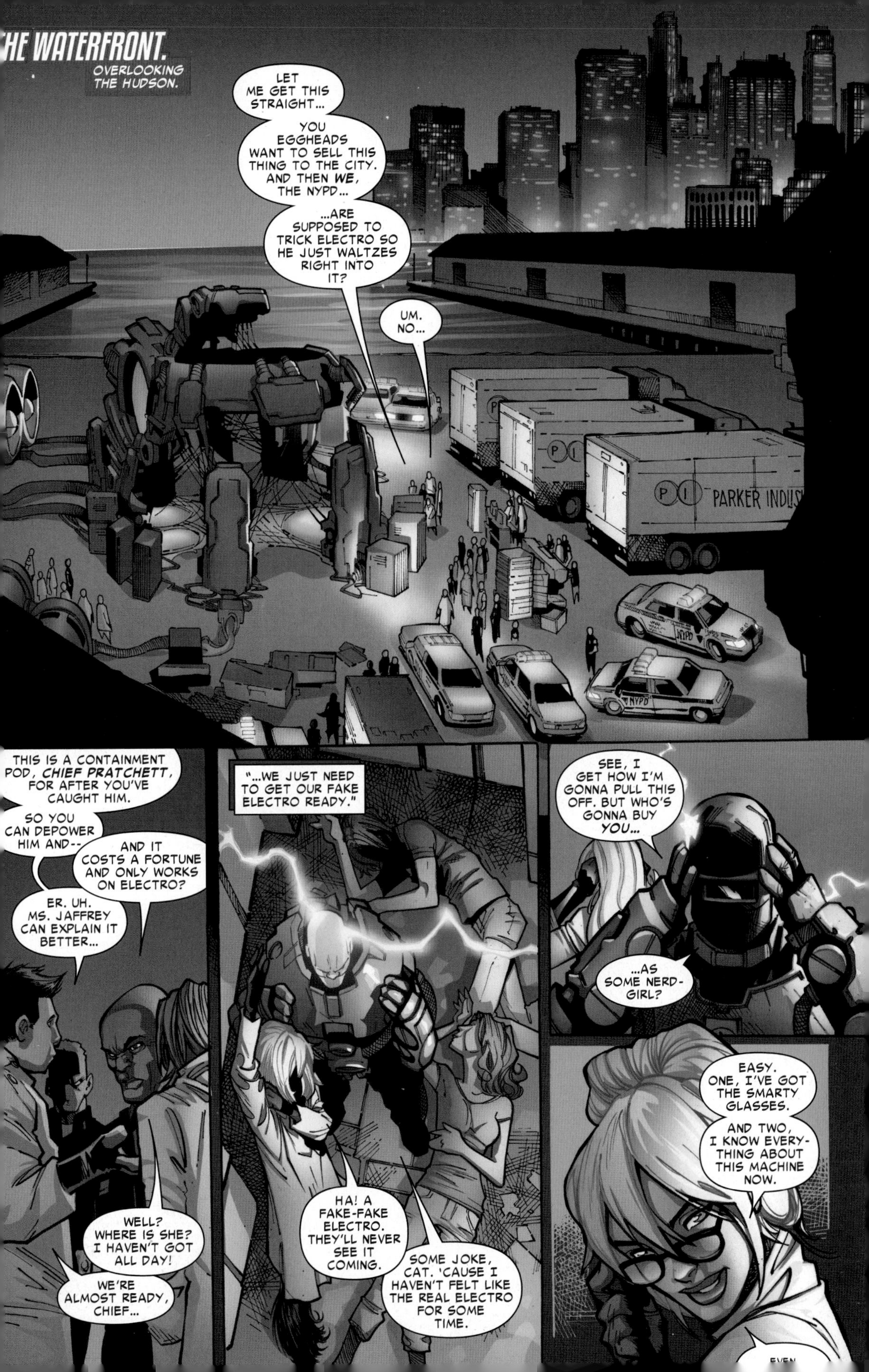
THE WATERFRONT.
OVERLOOKING THE HUDSON.
LET ME GET THIS STRAIGHT...
YOU EGGHEADS WANT TO SELL THIS THING TO THE CITY. AND THEN WE, THE NYPD...
...ARE SUPPOSED TO TRICK ELECTRO SO HE JUST WALTZES RIGHT INTO IT?
UM. NO...
PARKER INDUS
NYPD
THIS IS A CONTAINMENT POD, CHIEF PRATCHETT, FOR AFTER YOU'VE CAUGHT HIM.
SO YOU CAN DEPOWER HIM AND--
AND IT COSTS A FORTUNE AND ONLY WORKS ON ELECTRO?
ER. UH. MS. JAFFREY CAN EXPLAIN IT BETTER...
WELL? WHERE IS SHE? I HAVEN'T GOT ALL DAY!
WE'RE ALMOST READY, CHIEF...
"...WE JUST NEED TO GET OUR FAKE ELECTRO READY."
HA! A FAKE-FAKE ELECTRO. THEY'LL NEVER SEE IT COMING.
SOME JOKE, CAT. 'CAUSE I HAVEN'T FELT LIKE THE REAL ELECTRO FOR SOME TIME.
SEE, I GET HOW I'M GONNA PULL THIS OFF. BUT WHO'S GONNA BUY YOU...
...AS SOME NERD-GIRL?
EASY. ONE, I'VE GOT THE SMARTY GLASSES.
AND TWO, I KNOW EVERY-THING ABOUT THIS MACHINE NOW.

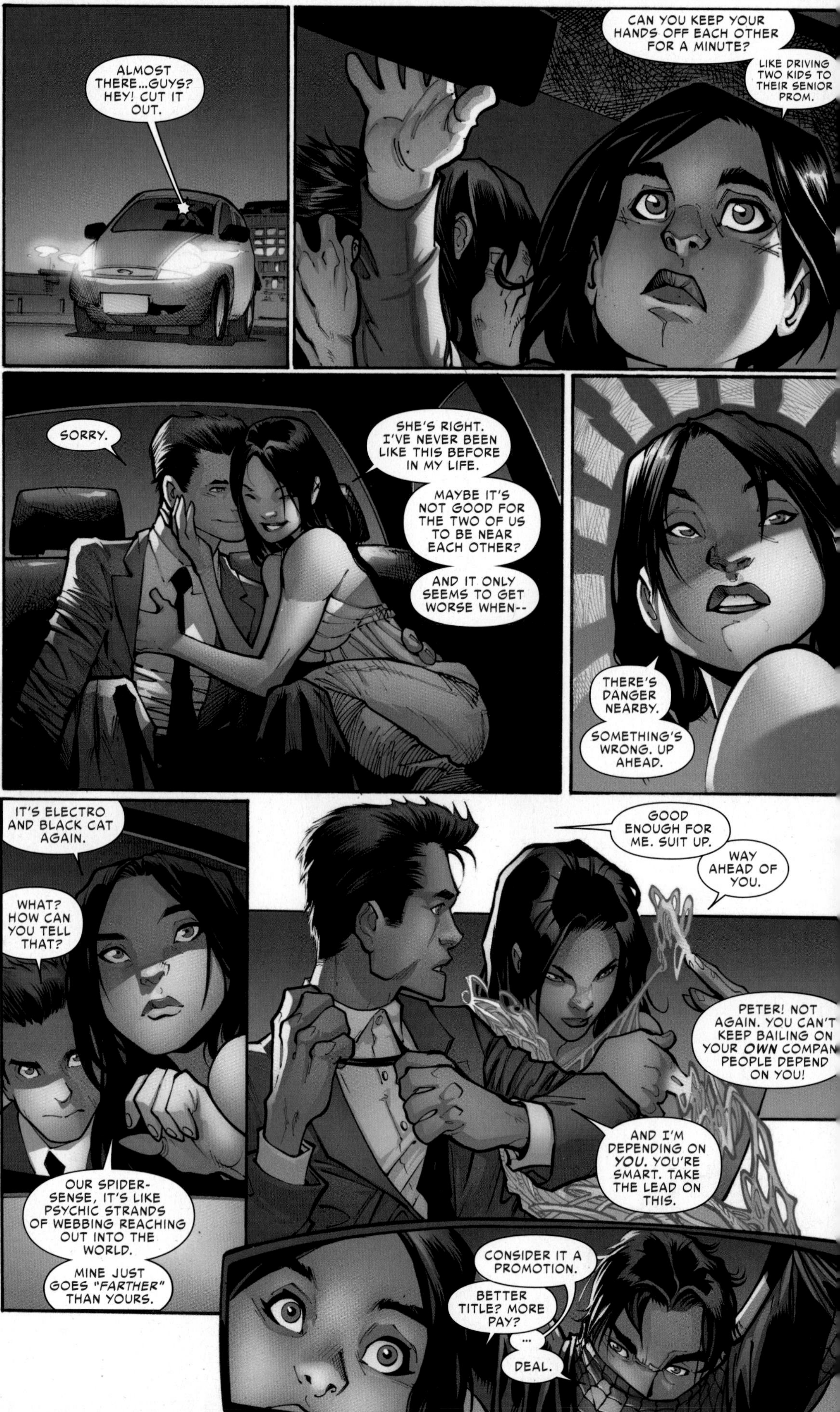

ALMOST THERE...GUYS? HEY! CUT IT OUT.
CAN YOU KEEP YOUR HANDS OFF EACH OTHER FOR A MINUTE?
LIKE DRIVING TWO KIDS TO THEIR SENIOR PROM.
SORRY.
SHE'S RIGHT. I'VE NEVER BEEN LIKE THIS BEFORE IN MY LIFE.
MAYBE IT'S NOT GOOD FOR THE TWO OF US TO BE NEAR EACH OTHER?
AND IT ONLY SEEMS TO GET WORSE WHEN--
THERE'S DANGER NEARBY.
SOMETHING'S WRONG. UP AHEAD.
IT'S ELECTRO AND BLACK CAT AGAIN.
WHAT? HOW CAN YOU TELL THAT?
OUR SPIDER-SENSE, IT'S LIKE PSYCHIC STRANDS OF WEBBING REACHING OUT INTO THE WORLD.
MINE JUST GOES "FARTHER" THAN YOURS.
GOOD ENOUGH FOR ME. SUIT UP.
WAY AHEAD OF YOU.
PETER! NOT AGAIN. YOU CAN'T KEEP BAILING ON YOUR OWN COMPAN PEOPLE DEPEND ON YOU!
AND I'M DEPENDING ON YOU. YOU'RE SMART. TAKE THE LEAD ON THIS.
CONSIDER IT A PROMOTION.
BETTER TITLE? MORE PAY?
...
DEAL.

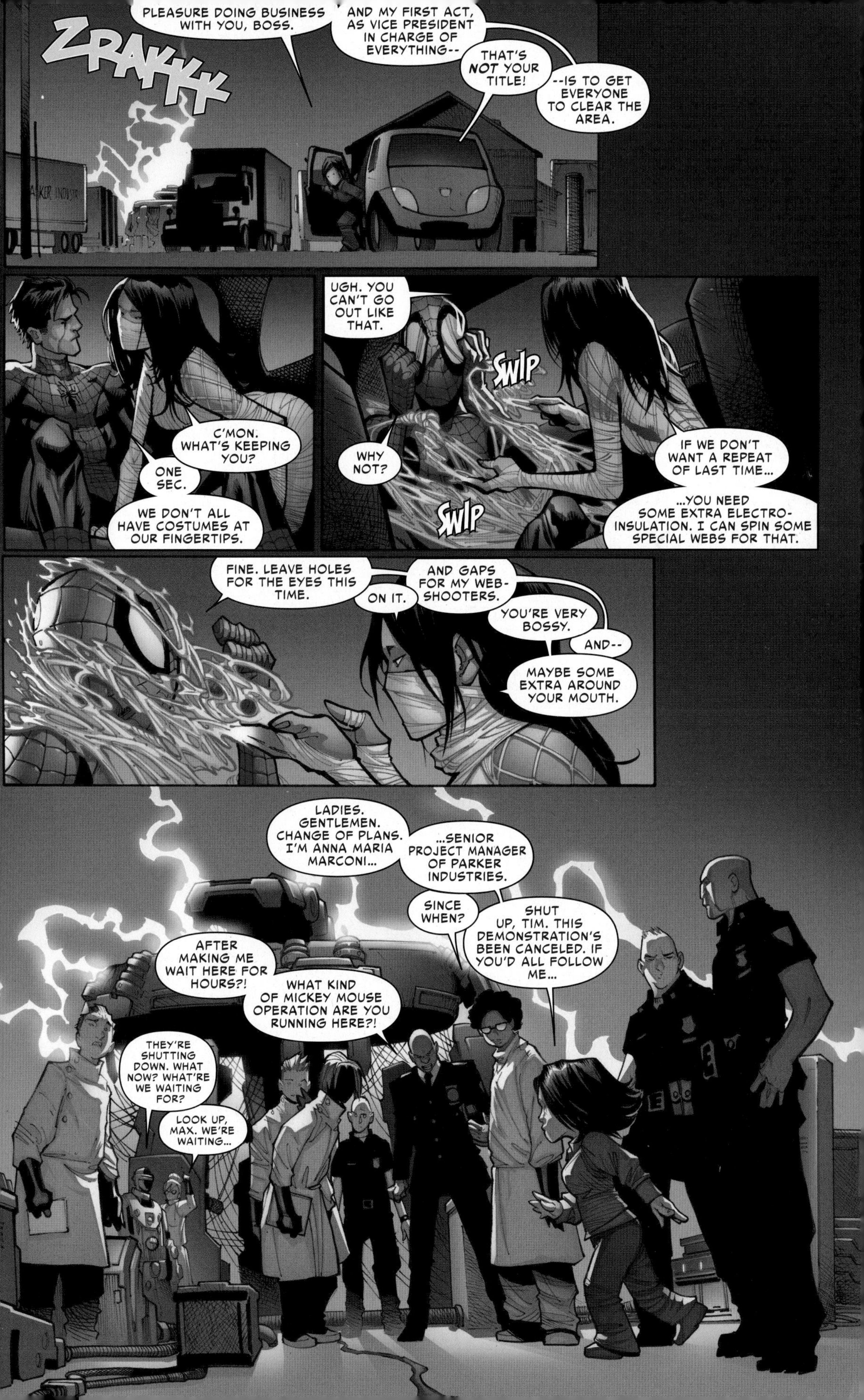
ZRAKKK
PLEASURE DOING BUSINESS WITH YOU, BOSS.
AND MY FIRST ACT, AS VICE PRESIDENT IN CHARGE OF EVERYTHING--
THAT'S NOT YOUR TITLE!
--IS TO GET EVERYONE TO CLEAR THE AREA.
C'MON. WHAT'S KEEPING YOU?
ONE SEC.
WE DON'T ALL HAVE COSTUMES AT OUR FINGERTIPS.
UGH. YOU CAN'T GO OUT LIKE THAT.
SWIP
WHY NOT?
IF WE DON'T WANT A REPEAT OF LAST TIME...
...YOU NEED SOME EXTRA ELECTRO-INSULATION. I CAN SPIN SOME SPECIAL WEBS FOR THAT.
SWIP
FINE. LEAVE HOLES FOR THE EYES THIS TIME.
ON IT.
AND GAPS FOR MY WEB-SHOOTERS.
YOU'RE VERY BOSSY.
AND--
MAYBE SOME EXTRA AROUND YOUR MOUTH.
LADIES. GENTLEMEN. CHANGE OF PLANS. I'M ANNA MARIA MARCONI...
...SENIOR PROJECT MANAGER OF PARKER INDUSTRIES.
SINCE WHEN?
SHUT UP, TIM. THIS DEMONSTRATION'S BEEN CANCELED. IF YOU'D ALL FOLLOW ME...
AFTER MAKING ME WAIT HERE FOR HOURS?!
WHAT KIND OF MICKEY MOUSE OPERATION ARE YOU RUNNING HERE?!
THEY'RE SHUTTING DOWN. WHAT NOW? WHAT'RE WE WAITING FOR?
LOOK UP, MAX. WE'RE WAITING...

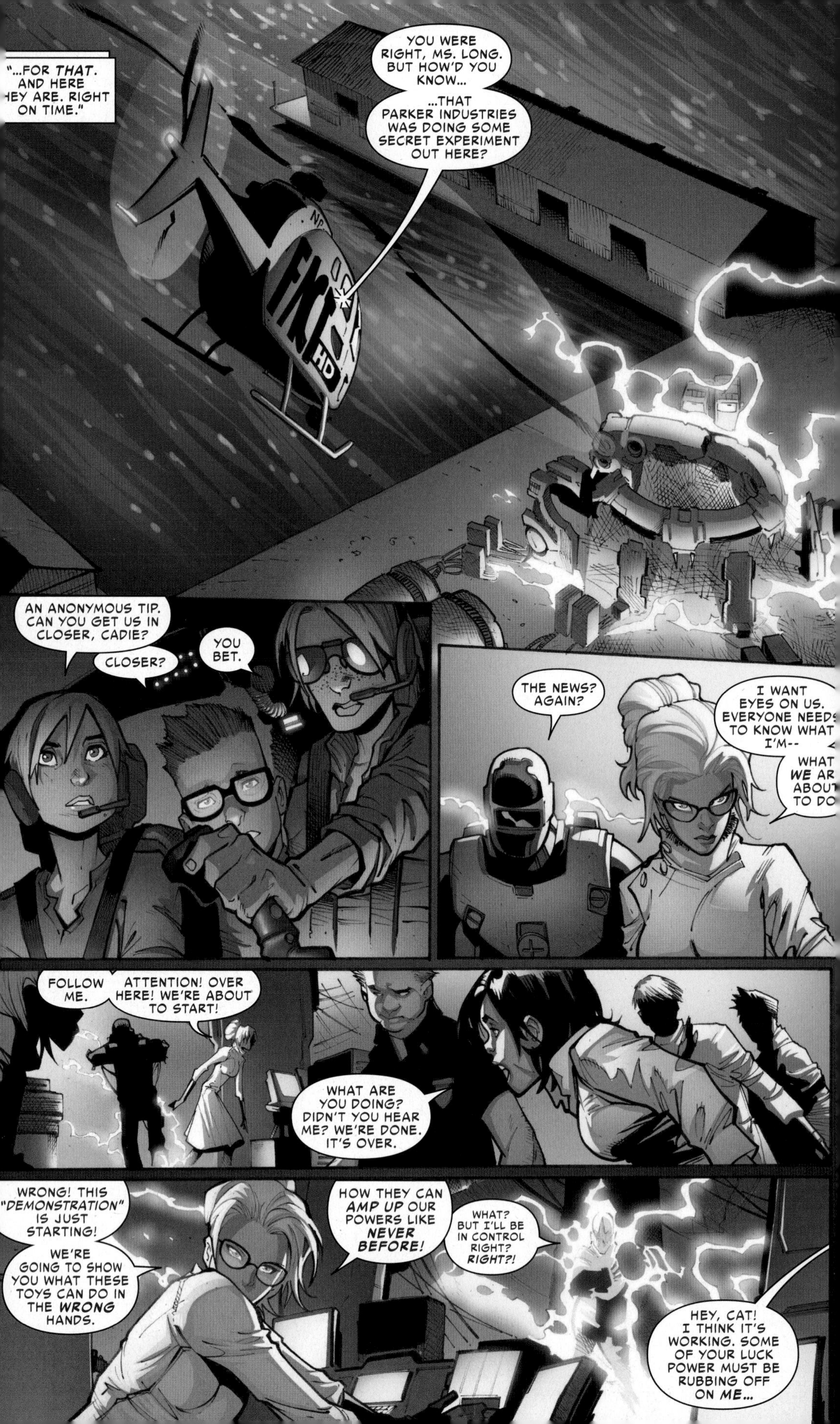
"...FOR *THAT*. AND HERE HEY ARE. RIGHT ON TIME."
YOU WERE RIGHT, MS. LONG. BUT HOW'D YOU KNOW...
...THAT PARKER INDUSTRIES WAS DOING SOME SECRET EXPERIMENT OUT HERE?
AN ANONYMOUS TIP. CAN YOU GET US IN CLOSER, CADIE?
CLOSER?
YOU BET.
THE NEWS? AGAIN?
I WANT EYES ON US. EVERYONE NEEDS TO KNOW WHAT I'M--
WHAT *WE* AR ABOUT TO DO
FOLLOW ME.
ATTENTION! OVER HERE! WE'RE ABOUT TO START!
WHAT ARE YOU DOING? DIDN'T YOU HEAR ME? WE'RE DONE. IT'S OVER.
WRONG! THIS "*DEMONSTRATION*" IS JUST STARTING!
WE'RE GOING TO SHOW YOU WHAT THESE TOYS CAN DO IN THE *WRONG* HANDS.
HOW THEY CAN *AMP UP* OUR POWERS LIKE *NEVER BEFORE!*
WHAT? BUT I'LL BE IN CONTROL RIGHT? *RIGHT?!*
HEY, CAT! I THINK IT'S WORKING. SOME OF YOUR LUCK POWER MUST BE RUBBING OFF ON *ME*...

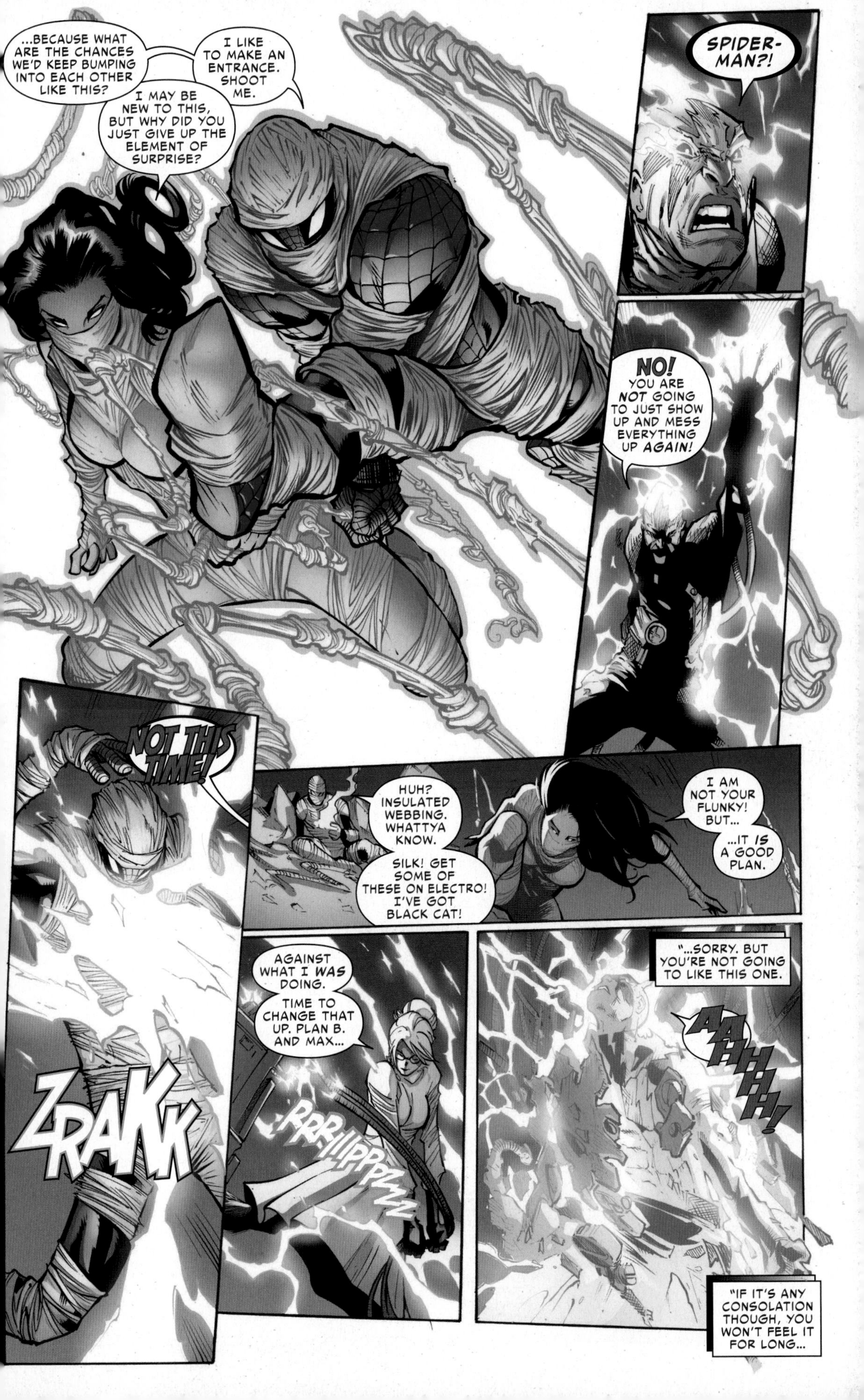

...BECAUSE WHAT ARE THE CHANCES WE'D KEEP BUMPING INTO EACH OTHER LIKE THIS?
I LIKE TO MAKE AN ENTRANCE. SHOOT ME.
I MAY BE NEW TO THIS, BUT WHY DID YOU JUST GIVE UP THE ELEMENT OF SURPRISE?
SPIDER-MAN?!
NO! YOU ARE NOT GOING TO JUST SHOW UP AND MESS EVERYTHING UP AGAIN!
NOT THIS TIME!
ZRAKK
HUH? INSULATED WEBBING. WHATTYA KNOW.
SILK! GET SOME OF THESE ON ELECTRO! I'VE GOT BLACK CAT!
I AM NOT YOUR FLUNKY! BUT...
...IT IS A GOOD PLAN.
AGAINST WHAT I WAS DOING.
TIME TO CHANGE THAT UP. PLAN B. AND MAX...
RRRIIIPPPZZZ
"...SORRY. BUT YOU'RE NOT GOING TO LIKE THIS ONE.
AAHHHH!
"IF IT'S ANY CONSOLATION THOUGH, YOU WON'T FEEL IT FOR LONG...

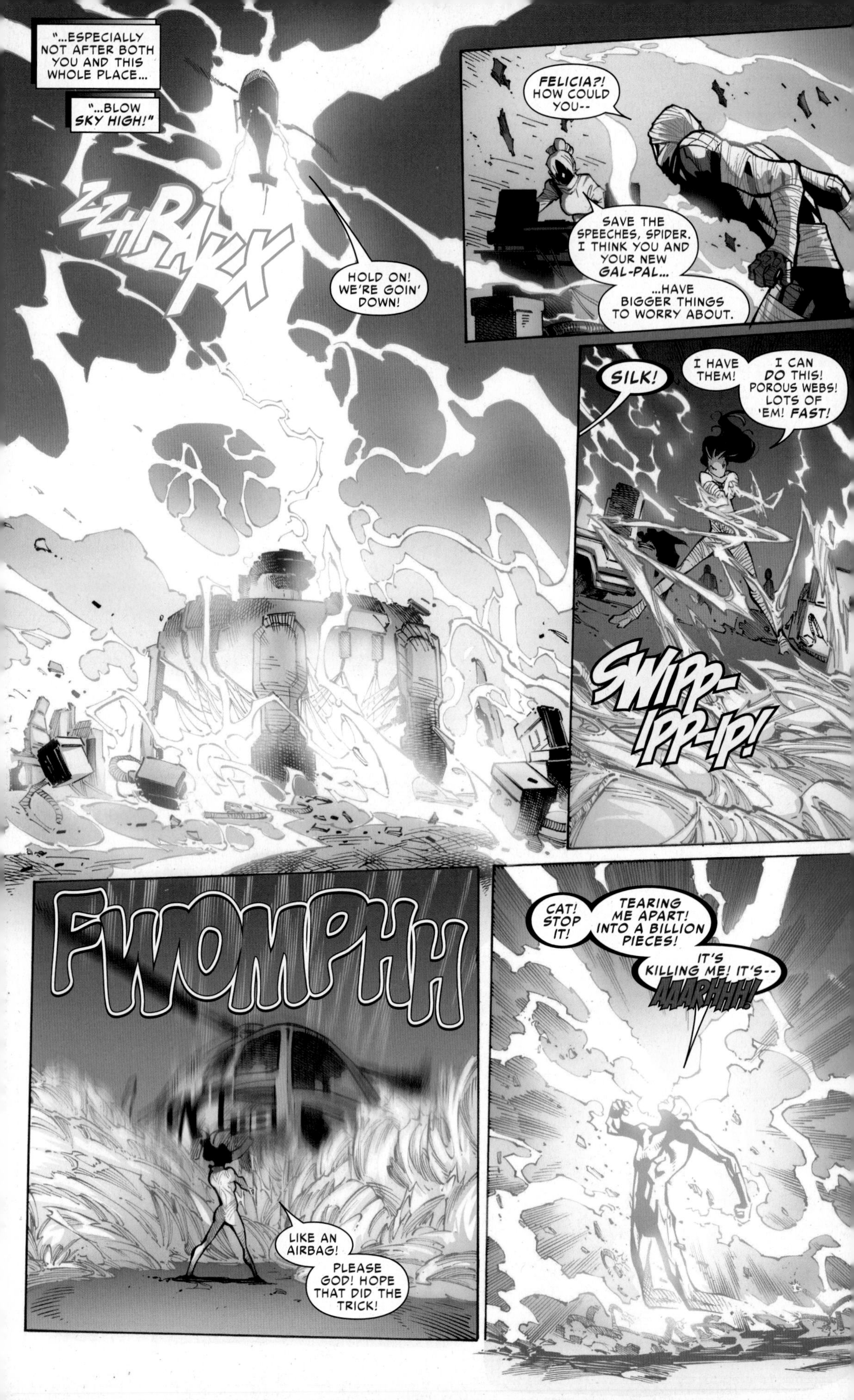
"...ESPECIALLY NOT AFTER BOTH YOU AND THIS WHOLE PLACE...
"...BLOW SKY HIGH!"
ZZHRAKX
HOLD ON! WE'RE GOIN' DOWN!
FELICIA?! HOW COULD YOU--
SAVE THE SPEECHES, SPIDER. I THINK YOU AND YOUR NEW GAL-PAL...
...HAVE BIGGER THINGS TO WORRY ABOUT.
SILK!
I HAVE THEM!
I CAN DO THIS! POROUS WEBS! LOTS OF 'EM! FAST!
SWIPP-IPP-IP!
FWOMPHH
LIKE AN AIRBAG!
PLEASE GOD! HOPE THAT DID THE TRICK!
CAT! STOP IT!
TEARING ME APART! INTO A BILLION PIECES!
IT'S KILLING ME! IT'S-- AAARHHH!

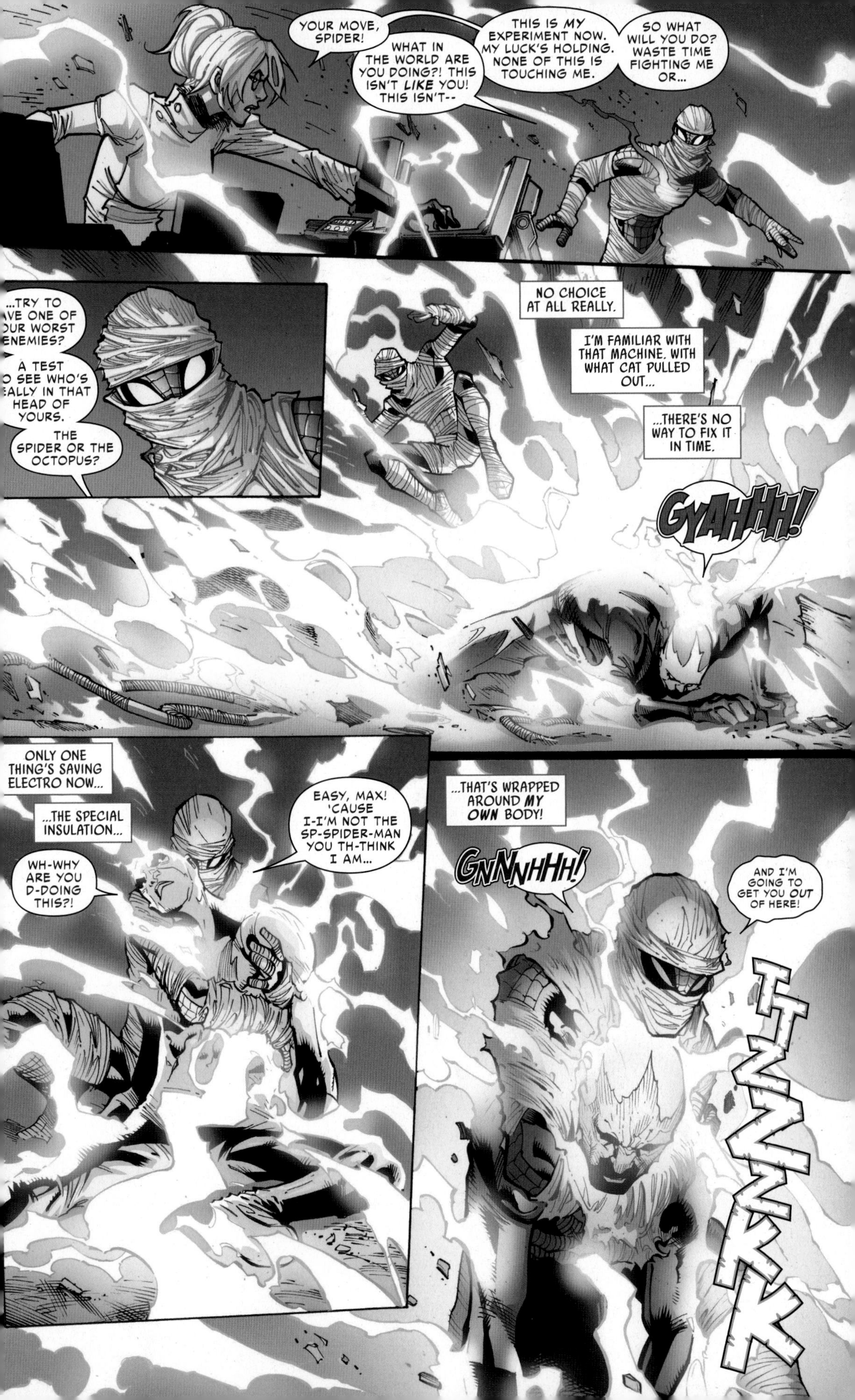
YOUR MOVE, SPIDER!
WHAT IN THE WORLD ARE YOU DOING?! THIS ISN'T LIKE YOU! THIS ISN'T--
THIS IS MY EXPERIMENT NOW. MY LUCK'S HOLDING. NONE OF THIS IS TOUCHING ME.
SO WHAT WILL YOU DO? WASTE TIME FIGHTING ME OR...
...TRY TO AVE ONE OF OUR WORST ENEMIES?
A TEST O SEE WHO'S EALLY IN THAT HEAD OF YOURS.
THE SPIDER OR THE OCTOPUS?
NO CHOICE AT ALL REALLY.
I'M FAMILIAR WITH THAT MACHINE. WITH WHAT CAT PULLED OUT...
...THERE'S NO WAY TO FIX IT IN TIME.
GYAHHH!
ONLY ONE THING'S SAVING ELECTRO NOW...
...THE SPECIAL INSULATION...
WH-WHY ARE YOU D-DOING THIS?!
EASY, MAX! 'CAUSE I-I'M NOT THE SP-SPIDER-MAN YOU TH-THINK I AM...
...THAT'S WRAPPED AROUND MY OWN BODY!
GNNNHHH!
AND I'M GOING TO GET YOU OUT OF HERE!
TTHNNKKK

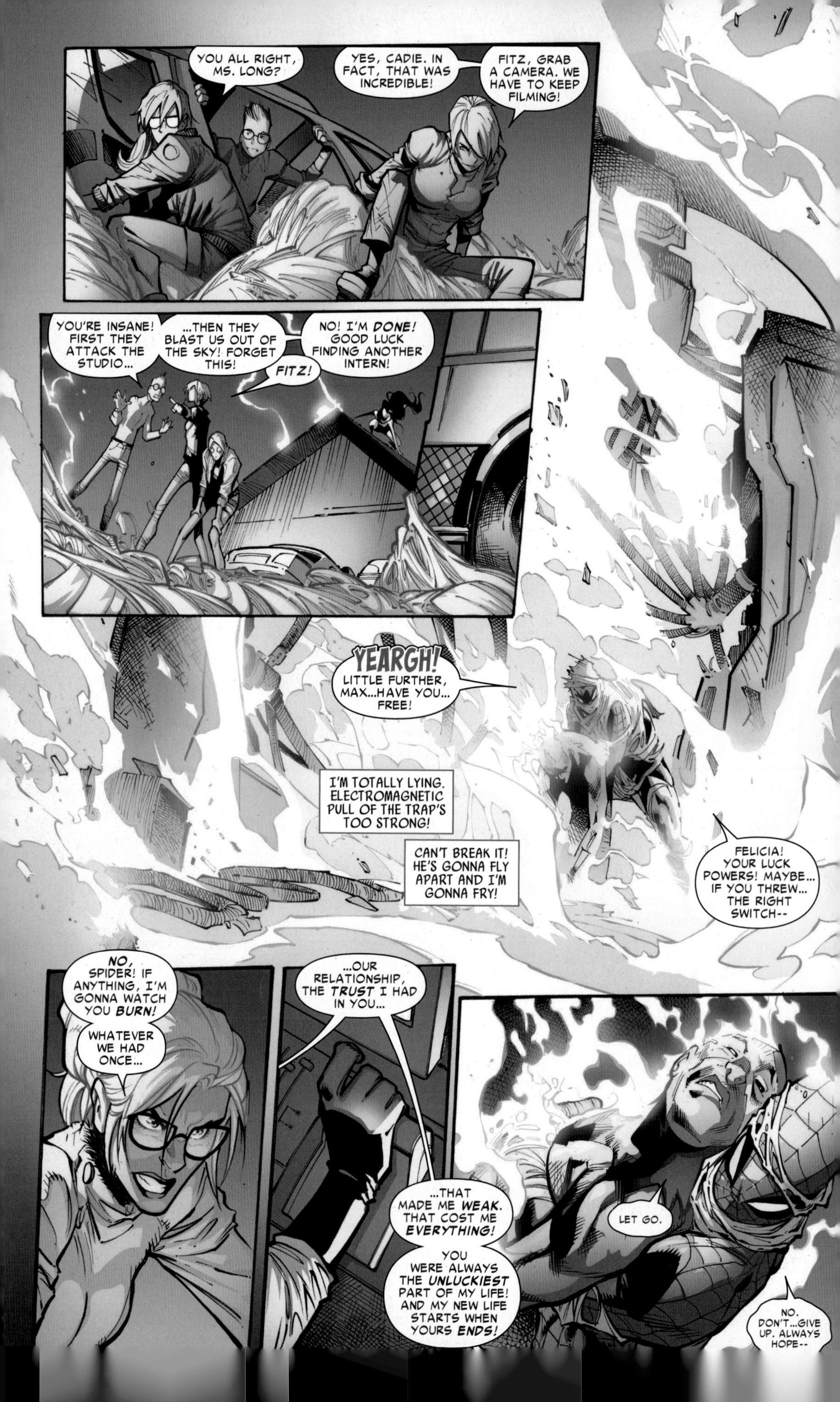

YOU ALL RIGHT, MS. LONG?
YES, CADIE. IN FACT, THAT WAS INCREDIBLE!
FITZ, GRAB A CAMERA. WE HAVE TO KEEP FILMING!
YOU'RE INSANE! FIRST THEY ATTACK THE STUDIO...
...THEN THEY BLAST US OUT OF THE SKY! FORGET THIS!
NO! I'M DONE! GOOD LUCK FINDING ANOTHER INTERN!
FITZ!
YEARGH!
LITTLE FURTHER, MAX...HAVE YOU... FREE!
I'M TOTALLY LYING. ELECTROMAGNETIC PULL OF THE TRAP'S TOO STRONG!
CAN'T BREAK IT! HE'S GONNA FLY APART AND I'M GONNA FRY!
FELICIA! YOUR LUCK POWERS! MAYBE... IF YOU THREW... THE RIGHT SWITCH--
NO, SPIDER! IF ANYTHING, I'M GONNA WATCH YOU BURN!
WHATEVER WE HAD ONCE...
...OUR RELATIONSHIP, THE TRUST I HAD IN YOU...
...THAT MADE ME WEAK. THAT COST ME EVERYTHING!
YOU WERE ALWAYS THE UNLUCKIEST PART OF MY LIFE! AND MY NEW LIFE STARTS WHEN YOURS ENDS!
LET GO.
NO. DON'T...GIVE UP. ALWAYS HOPE--

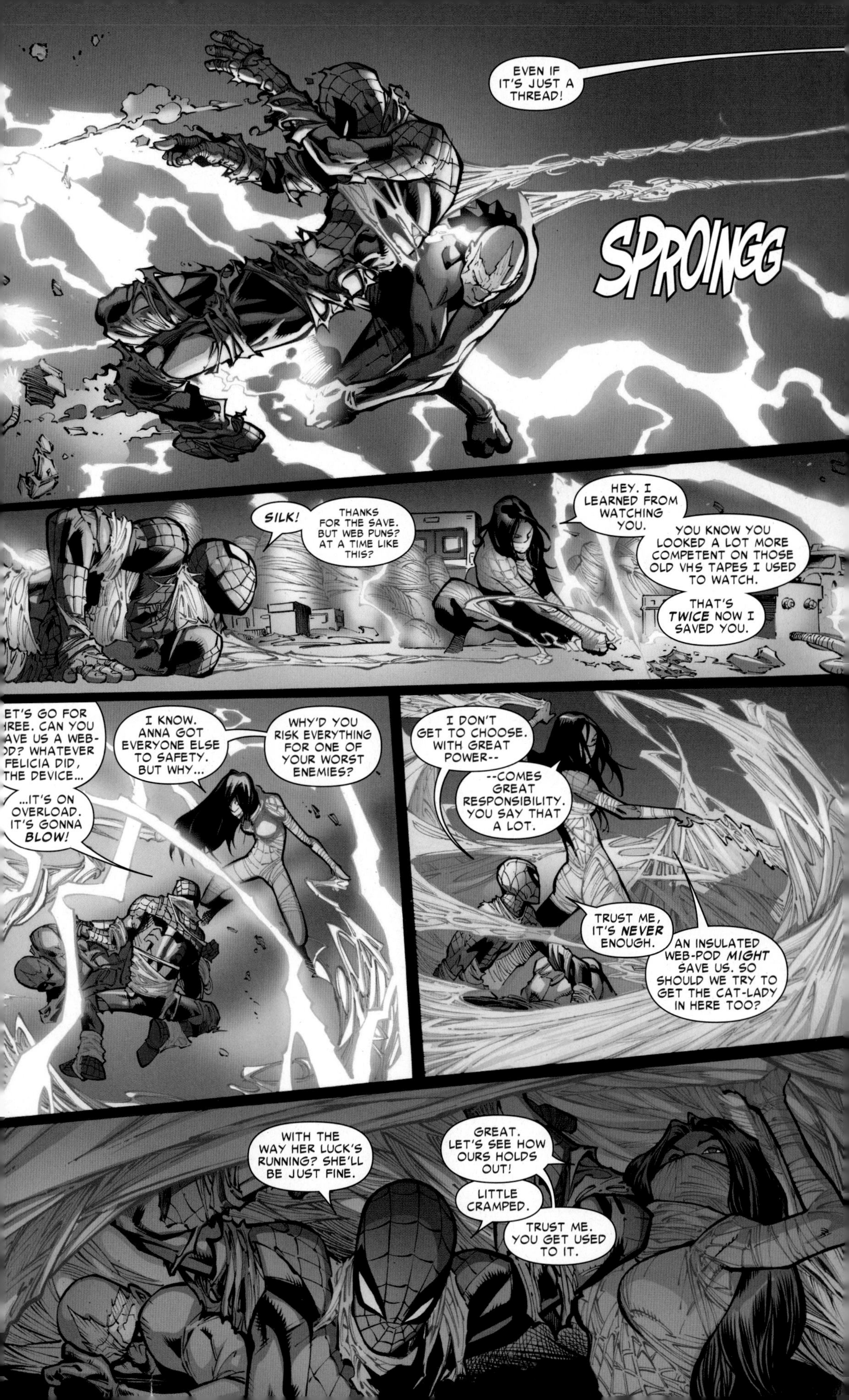

EVEN IF IT'S JUST A THREAD!
SPROINGG
SILK!
THANKS FOR THE SAVE. BUT WEB PUNS? AT A TIME LIKE THIS?
HEY. I LEARNED FROM WATCHING YOU.
YOU KNOW YOU LOOKED A LOT MORE COMPETENT ON THOSE OLD VHS TAPES I USED TO WATCH.
THAT'S TWICE NOW I SAVED YOU.
ET'S GO FOR HREE. CAN YOU AVE US A WEB-OD? WHATEVER FELICIA DID, THE DEVICE...
...IT'S ON OVERLOAD. IT'S GONNA BLOW!
I KNOW. ANNA GOT EVERYONE ELSE TO SAFETY. BUT WHY...
WHY'D YOU RISK EVERYTHING FOR ONE OF YOUR WORST ENEMIES?
I DON'T GET TO CHOOSE. WITH GREAT POWER--
--COMES GREAT RESPONSIBILITY. YOU SAY THAT A LOT.
TRUST ME, IT'S NEVER ENOUGH.
AN INSULATED WEB-POD MIGHT SAVE US. SO SHOULD WE TRY TO GET THE CAT-LADY IN HERE TOO?
WITH THE WAY HER LUCK'S RUNNING? SHE'LL BE JUST FINE.
GREAT. LET'S SEE HOW OURS HOLDS OUT!
LITTLE CRAMPED.
TRUST ME. YOU GET USED TO IT.

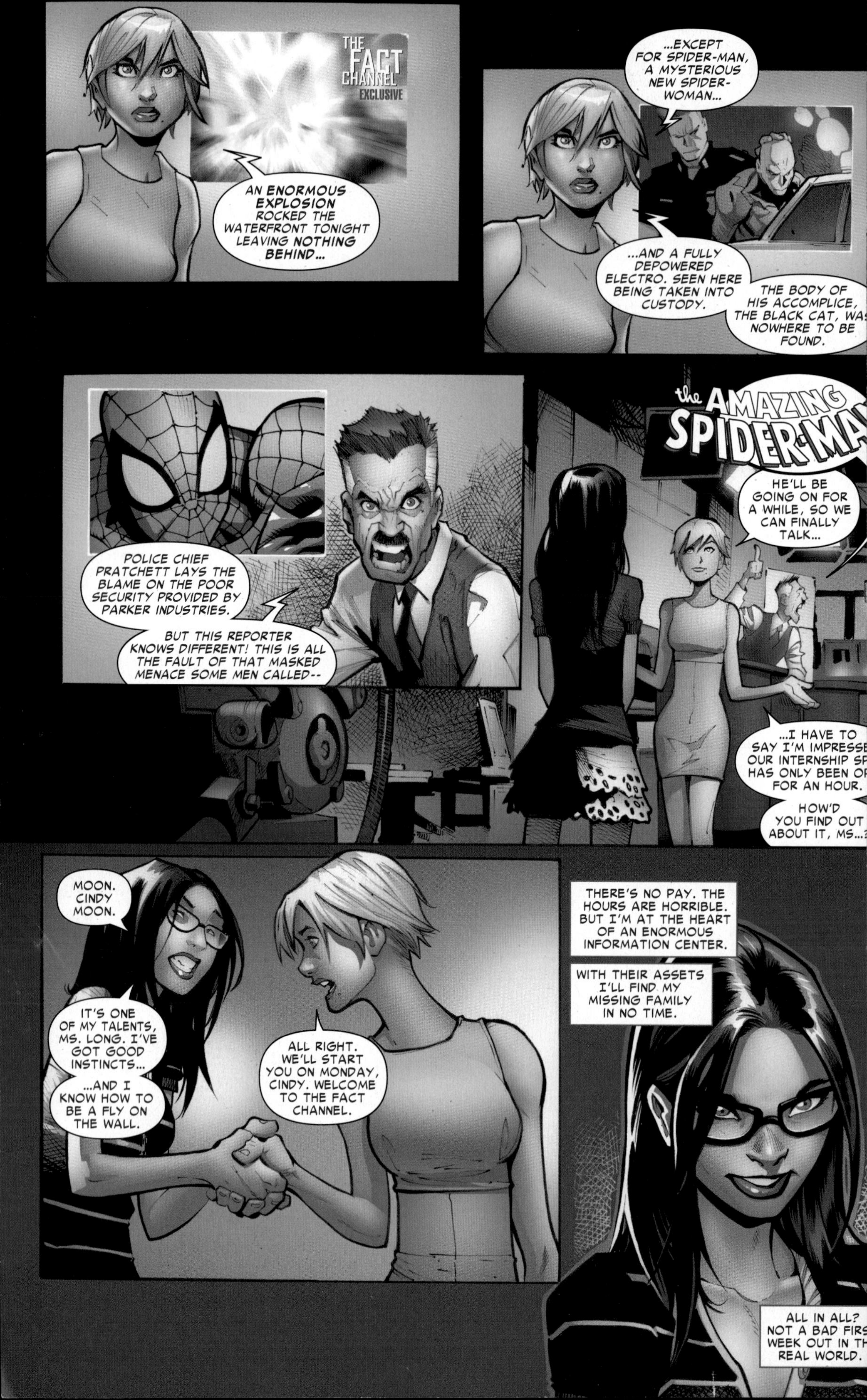
THE FACT CHANNEL EXCLUSIVE
AN ENORMOUS EXPLOSION ROCKED THE WATERFRONT TONIGHT LEAVING NOTHING BEHIND...
...EXCEPT FOR SPIDER-MAN, A MYSTERIOUS NEW SPIDER-WOMAN...
...AND A FULLY DEPOWERED ELECTRO. SEEN HERE BEING TAKEN INTO CUSTODY.
THE BODY OF HIS ACCOMPLICE, THE BLACK CAT, WAS NOWHERE TO BE FOUND.
POLICE CHIEF PRATCHETT LAYS THE BLAME ON THE POOR SECURITY PROVIDED BY PARKER INDUSTRIES.
BUT THIS REPORTER KNOWS DIFFERENT! THIS IS ALL THE FAULT OF THAT MASKED MENACE SOME MEN CALLED--
the AMAZING SPIDER-MAN
HE'LL BE GOING ON FOR A WHILE, SO WE CAN FINALLY TALK...
...I HAVE TO SAY I'M IMPRESSED. OUR INTERNSHIP SP HAS ONLY BEEN OP FOR AN HOUR.
HOW'D YOU FIND OUT ABOUT IT, MS...?
MOON. CINDY MOON.
IT'S ONE OF MY TALENTS, MS. LONG. I'VE GOT GOOD INSTINCTS...
...AND I KNOW HOW TO BE A FLY ON THE WALL.
ALL RIGHT. WE'LL START YOU ON MONDAY, CINDY. WELCOME TO THE FACT CHANNEL.
THERE'S NO PAY. THE HOURS ARE HORRIBLE. BUT I'M AT THE HEART OF AN ENORMOUS INFORMATION CENTER.
WITH THEIR ASSETS I'LL FIND MY MISSING FAMILY IN NO TIME.
ALL IN ALL? NOT A BAD FIRS WEEK OUT IN TH REAL WORLD.

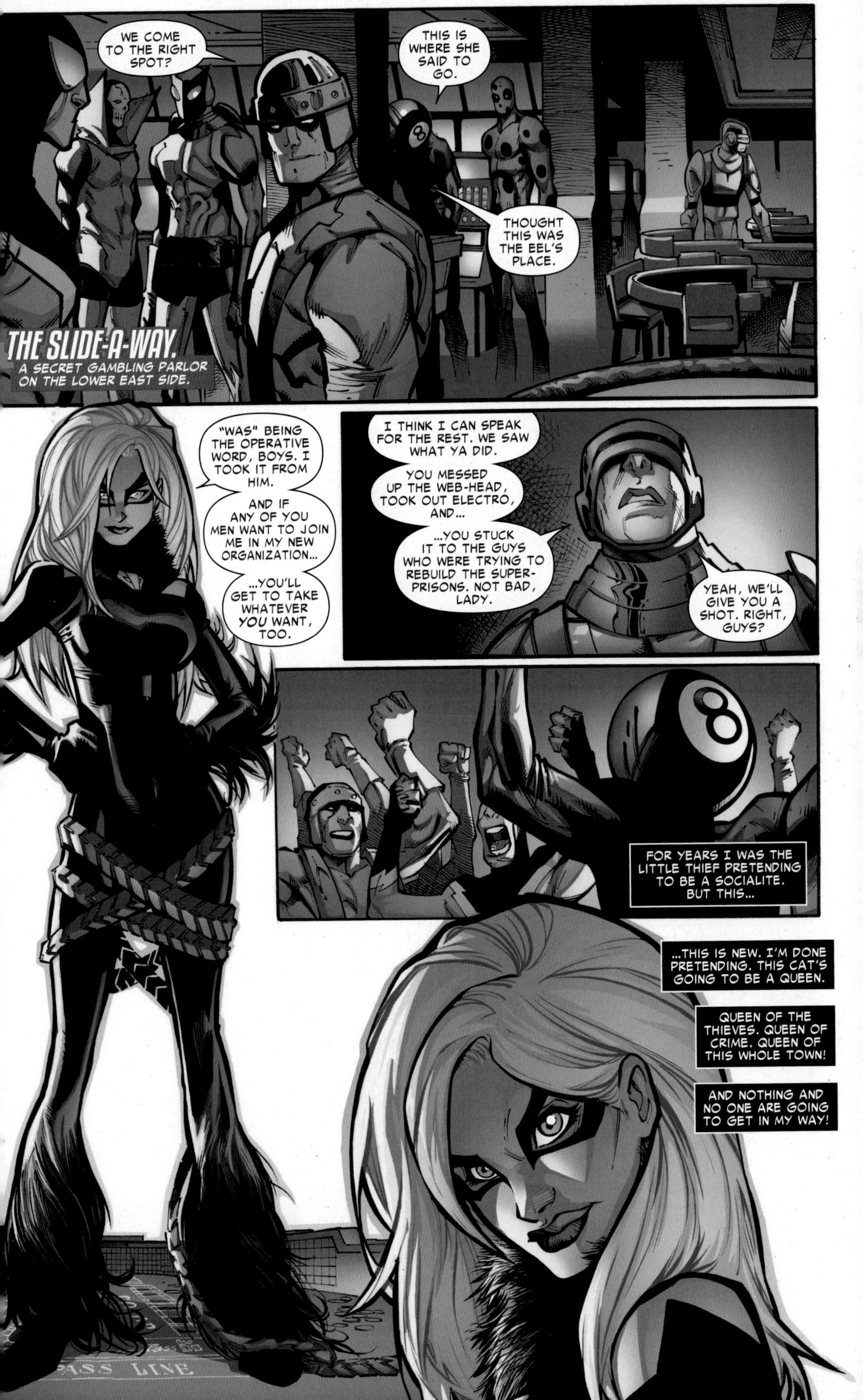
WE COME TO THE RIGHT SPOT?
THIS IS WHERE SHE SAID TO GO.
THOUGHT THIS WAS THE EEL'S PLACE.
THE SLIDE-A-WAY.
A SECRET GAMBLING PARLOR ON THE LOWER EAST SIDE.
"WAS" BEING THE OPERATIVE WORD, BOYS. I TOOK IT FROM HIM.
AND IF ANY OF YOU MEN WANT TO JOIN ME IN MY NEW ORGANIZATION...
...YOU'LL GET TO TAKE WHATEVER YOU WANT, TOO.
I THINK I CAN SPEAK FOR THE REST. WE SAW WHAT YA DID.
YOU MESSED UP THE WEB-HEAD, TOOK OUT ELECTRO, AND...
...YOU STUCK IT TO THE GUYS WHO WERE TRYING TO REBUILD THE SUPER-PRISONS. NOT BAD, LADY.
YEAH, WE'LL GIVE YOU A SHOT. RIGHT, GUYS?
FOR YEARS I WAS THE LITTLE THIEF PRETENDING TO BE A SOCIALITE. BUT THIS...
...THIS IS NEW. I'M DONE PRETENDING. THIS CAT'S GOING TO BE A QUEEN.
QUEEN OF THE THIEVES. QUEEN OF CRIME. QUEEN OF THIS WHOLE TOWN!
AND NOTHING AND NO ONE ARE GOING TO GET IN MY WAY!
PASS LINE

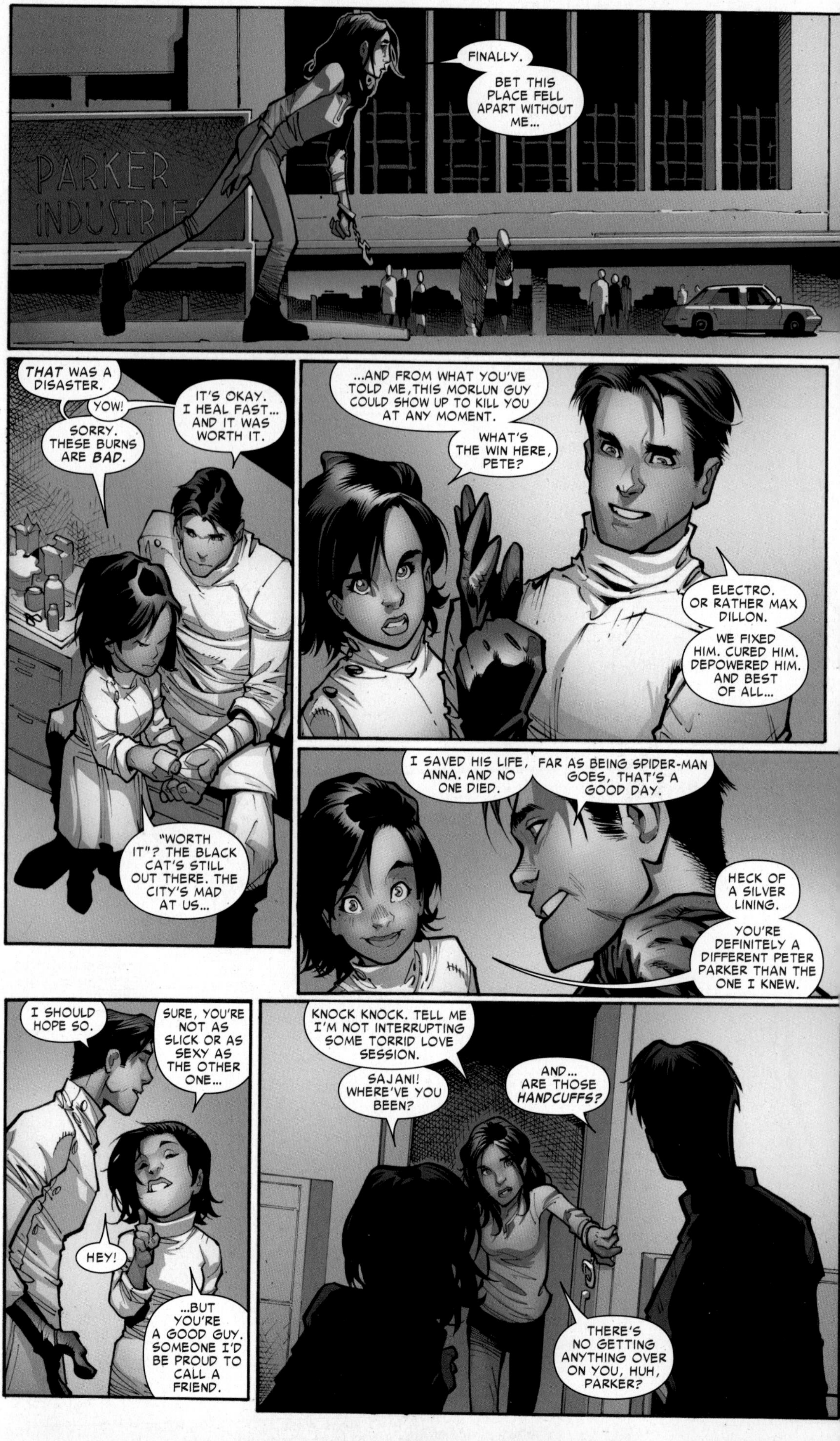
FINALLY.
BET THIS PLACE FELL APART WITHOUT ME...
PARKER INDUSTRIES
THAT WAS A DISASTER.
YOW!
SORRY. THESE BURNS ARE BAD.
IT'S OKAY. I HEAL FAST... AND IT WAS WORTH IT.
"WORTH IT"? THE BLACK CAT'S STILL OUT THERE. THE CITY'S MAD AT US...
...AND FROM WHAT YOU'VE TOLD ME, THIS MORLUN GUY COULD SHOW UP TO KILL YOU AT ANY MOMENT.
WHAT'S THE WIN HERE, PETE?
ELECTRO. OR RATHER MAX DILLON.
WE FIXED HIM. CURED HIM. DEPOWERED HIM. AND BEST OF ALL...
I SAVED HIS LIFE, ANNA. AND NO ONE DIED.
FAR AS BEING SPIDER-MAN GOES, THAT'S A GOOD DAY.
HECK OF A SILVER LINING.
YOU'RE DEFINITELY A DIFFERENT PETER PARKER THAN THE ONE I KNEW.
I SHOULD HOPE SO.
SURE, YOU'RE NOT AS SLICK OR AS SEXY AS THE OTHER ONE...
HEY!
...BUT YOU'RE A GOOD GUY. SOMEONE I'D BE PROUD TO CALL A FRIEND.
KNOCK KNOCK. TELL ME I'M NOT INTERRUPTING SOME TORRID LOVE SESSION.
SAJANI! WHERE'VE YOU BEEN?
AND... ARE THOSE HANDCUFFS?
THERE'S NO GETTING ANYTHING OVER ON YOU, HUH, PARKER?

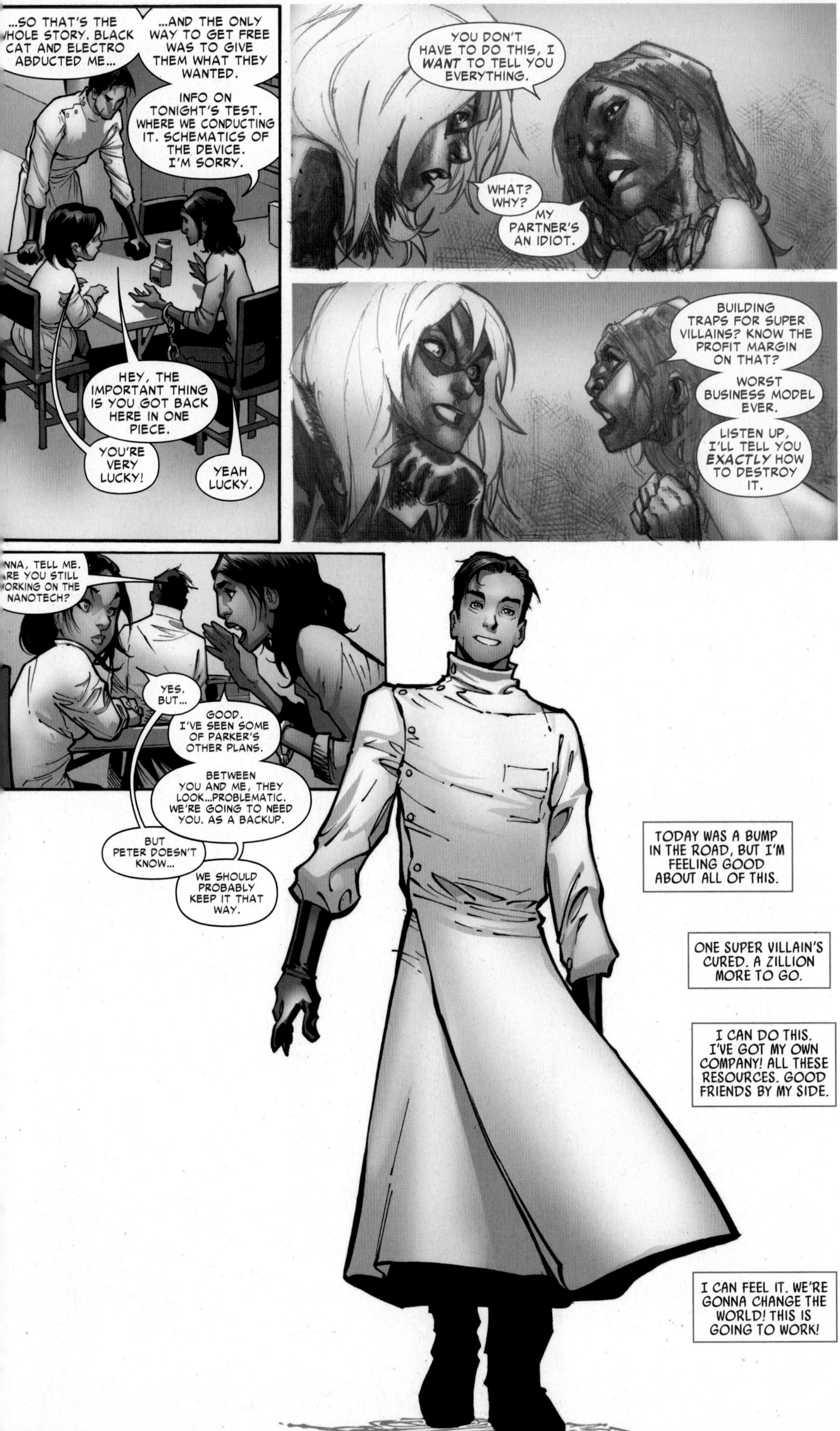
...SO THAT'S THE WHOLE STORY. BLACK CAT AND ELECTRO ABDUCTED ME...
...AND THE ONLY WAY TO GET FREE WAS TO GIVE THEM WHAT THEY WANTED.
INFO ON TONIGHT'S TEST. WHERE WE CONDUCTING IT. SCHEMATICS OF THE DEVICE. I'M SORRY.
HEY, THE IMPORTANT THING IS YOU GOT BACK HERE IN ONE PIECE.
YOU'RE VERY LUCKY!
YEAH LUCKY.
YOU DON'T HAVE TO DO THIS, I WANT TO TELL YOU EVERYTHING.
WHAT? WHY?
MY PARTNER'S AN IDIOT.
BUILDING TRAPS FOR SUPER VILLAINS? KNOW THE PROFIT MARGIN ON THAT?
WORST BUSINESS MODEL EVER.
LISTEN UP, I'LL TELL YOU EXACTLY HOW TO DESTROY IT.
NNA, TELL ME. ARE YOU STILL WORKING ON THE NANOTECH?
YES. BUT...
GOOD. I'VE SEEN SOME OF PARKER'S OTHER PLANS.
BETWEEN YOU AND ME, THEY LOOK...PROBLEMATIC. WE'RE GOING TO NEED YOU. AS A BACKUP.
BUT PETER DOESN'T KNOW...
WE SHOULD PROBABLY KEEP IT THAT WAY.
TODAY WAS A BUMP IN THE ROAD, BUT I'M FEELING GOOD ABOUT ALL OF THIS.
ONE SUPER VILLAIN'S CURED. A ZILLION MORE TO GO.
I CAN DO THIS. I'VE GOT MY OWN COMPANY! ALL THESE RESOURCES. GOOD FRIENDS BY MY SIDE.
I CAN FEEL IT. WE'RE GONNA CHANGE THE WORLD! THIS IS GOING TO WORK!

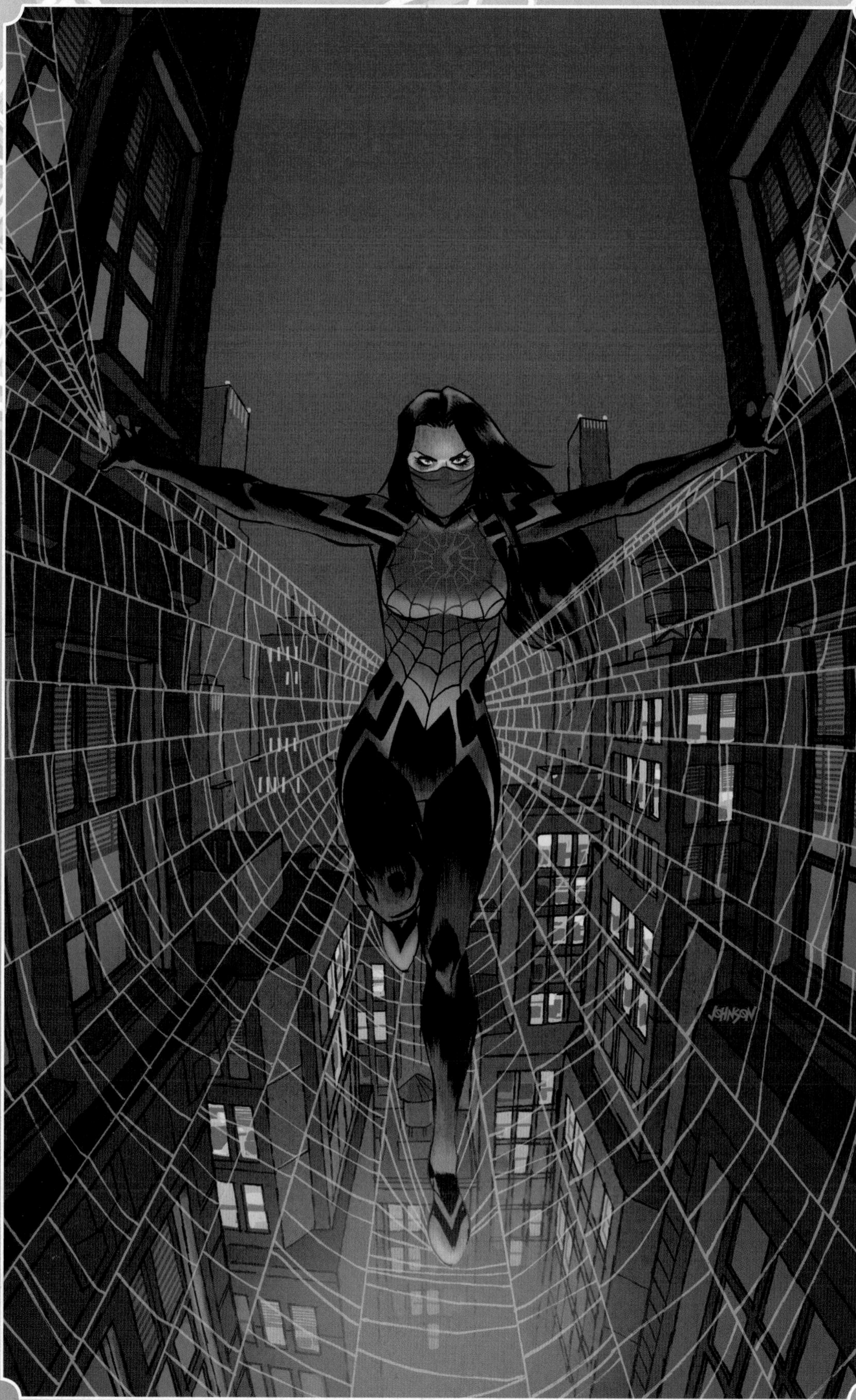
JOHNSON

SILK (2015A) #1

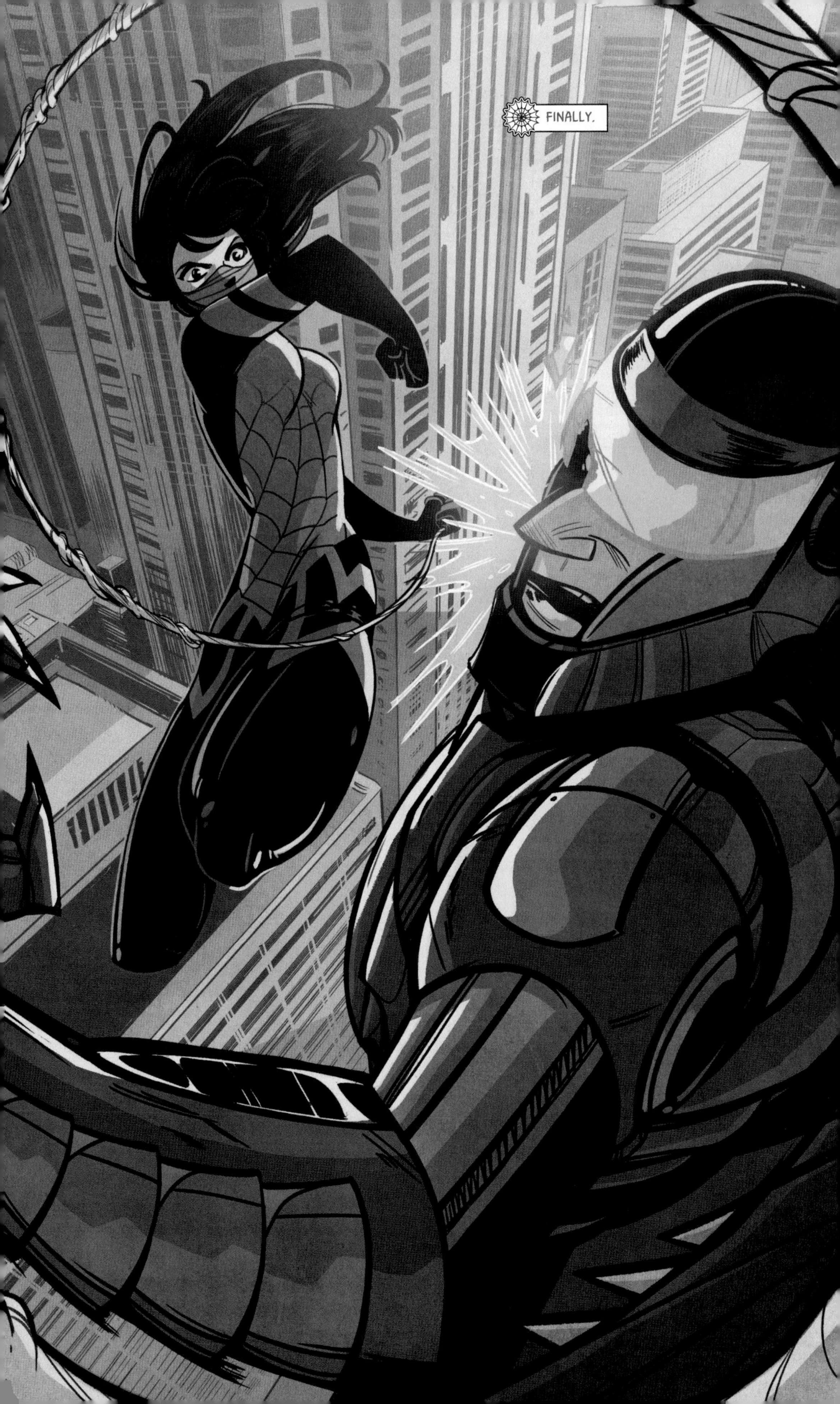
FINALLY.

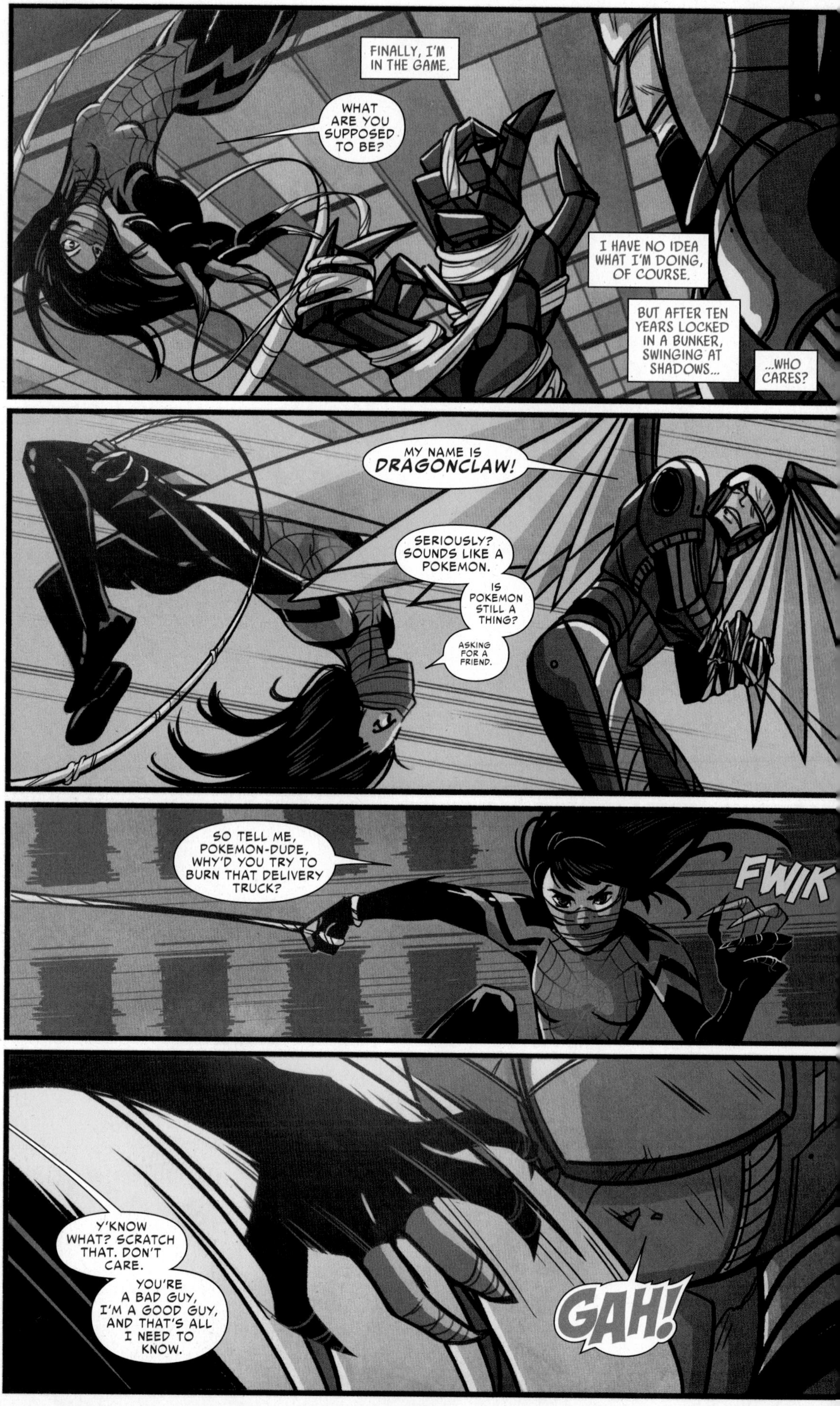
FINALLY, I'M IN THE GAME.
WHAT ARE YOU SUPPOSED TO BE?
I HAVE NO IDEA WHAT I'M DOING, OF COURSE.
BUT AFTER TEN YEARS LOCKED IN A BUNKER, SWINGING AT SHADOWS...
...WHO CARES?
MY NAME IS DRAGONCLAW!
SERIOUSLY? SOUNDS LIKE A POKEMON.
IS POKEMON STILL A THING?
ASKING FOR A FRIEND.
SO TELL ME, POKEMON-DUDE, WHY'D YOU TRY TO BURN THAT DELIVERY TRUCK?
FWIK
Y'KNOW WHAT? SCRATCH THAT. DON'T CARE.
YOU'RE A BAD GUY, I'M A GOOD GUY, AND THAT'S ALL I NEED TO KNOW.
GAH!

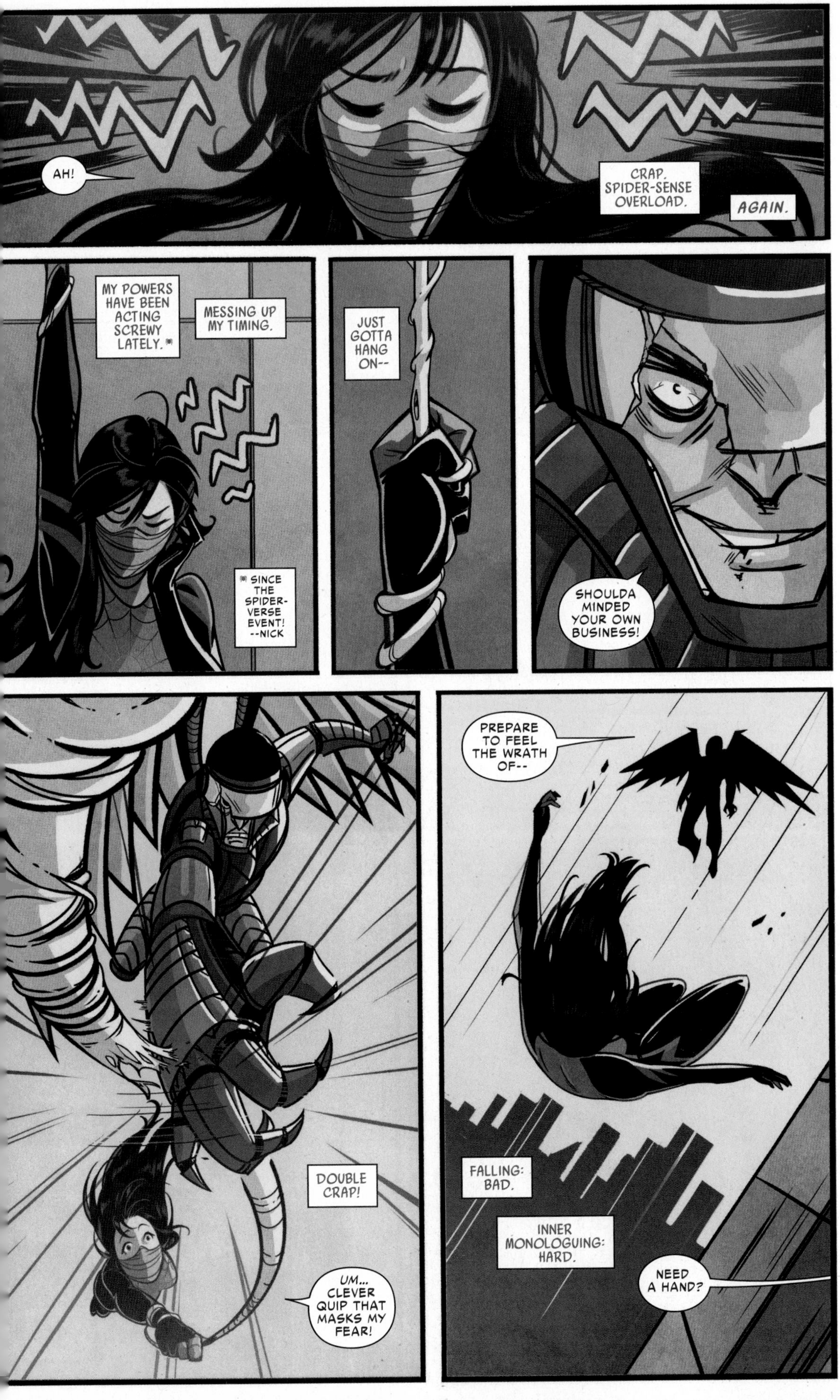
AH!
CRAP. SPIDER-SENSE OVERLOAD.
AGAIN.
MY POWERS HAVE BEEN ACTING SCREWY LATELY.*
MESSING UP MY TIMING.
*SINCE THE SPIDER-VERSE EVENT! --NICK
JUST GOTTA HANG ON--
SHOULDA MINDED YOUR OWN BUSINESS!
DOUBLE CRAP!
UM... CLEVER QUIP THAT MASKS MY FEAR!
PREPARE TO FEEL THE WRATH OF--
FALLING: BAD.
INNER MONOLOGUING: HARD.
NEED A HAND?

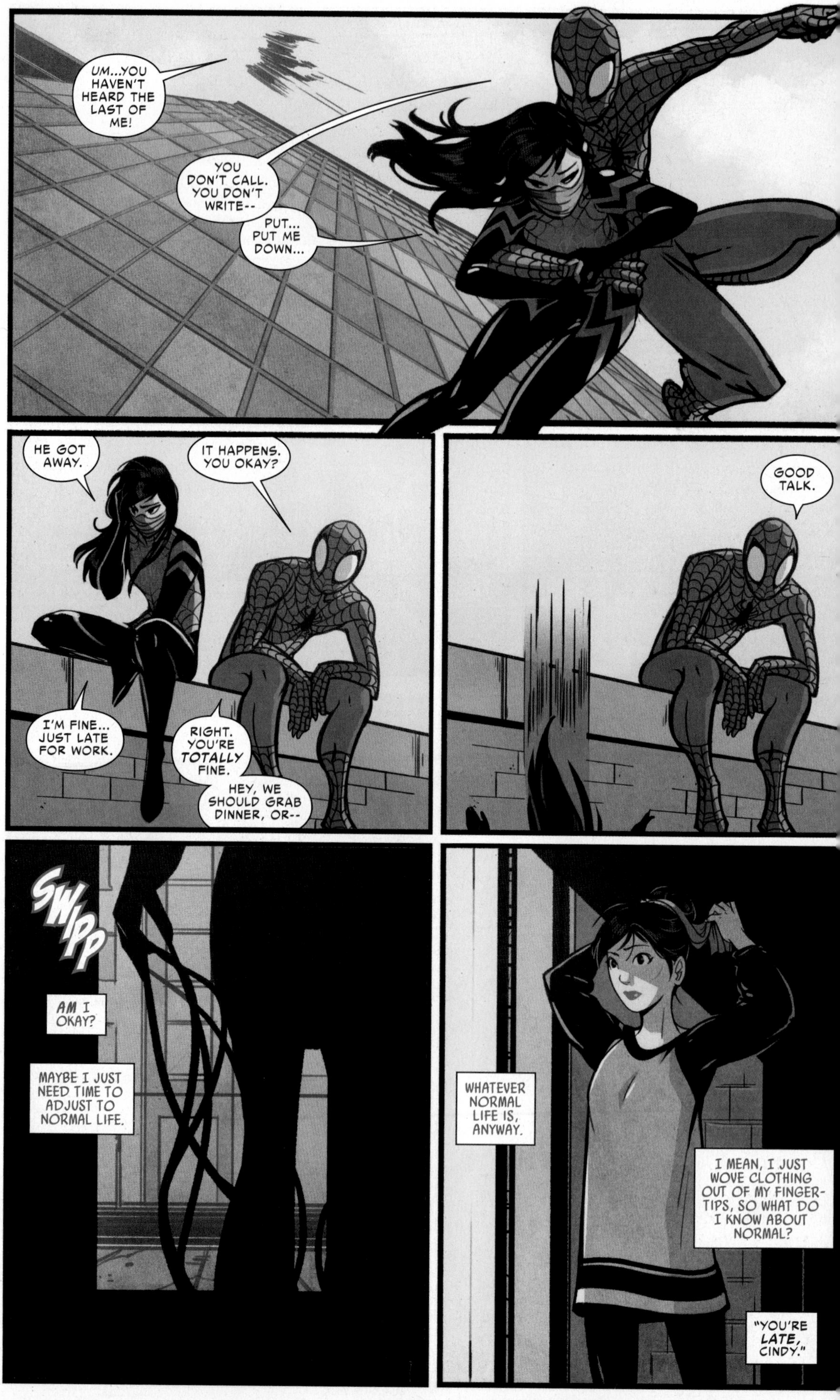
UM...YOU HAVEN'T HEARD THE LAST OF ME!
YOU DON'T CALL. YOU DON'T WRITE--
PUT... PUT ME DOWN...
HE GOT AWAY.
IT HAPPENS. YOU OKAY?
I'M FINE... JUST LATE FOR WORK.
RIGHT. YOU'RE TOTALLY FINE.
HEY, WE SHOULD GRAB DINNER, OR--
GOOD TALK.
SWIPP
AM I OKAY?
MAYBE I JUST NEED TIME TO ADJUST TO NORMAL LIFE.
WHATEVER NORMAL LIFE IS, ANYWAY.
I MEAN, I JUST WOVE CLOTHING OUT OF MY FINGER-TIPS, SO WHAT DO I KNOW ABOUT NORMAL?
"YOU'RE LATE, CINDY."

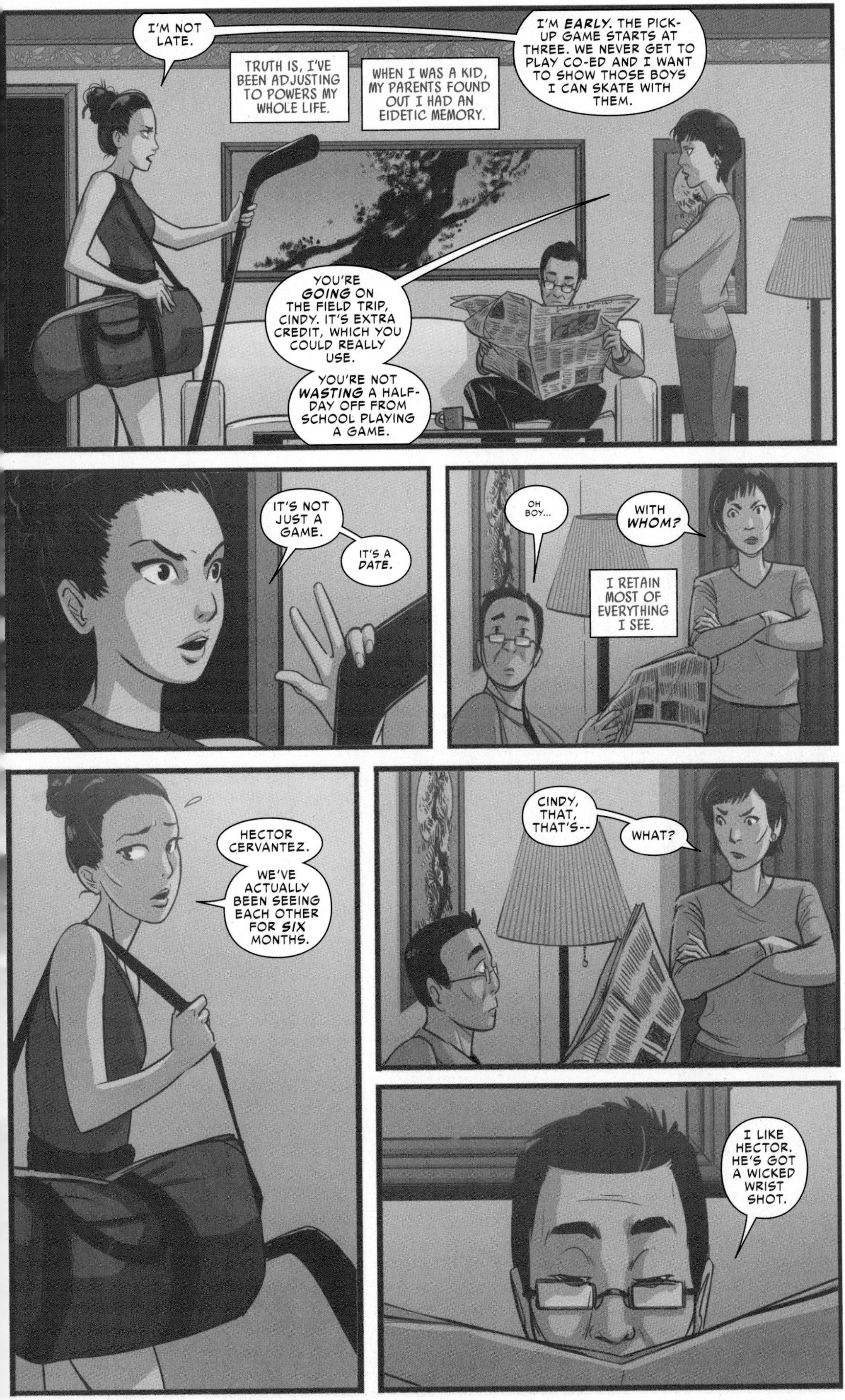

I'M NOT LATE.
TRUTH IS, I'VE BEEN ADJUSTING TO POWERS MY WHOLE LIFE.
WHEN I WAS A KID, MY PARENTS FOUND OUT I HAD AN EIDETIC MEMORY.
I'M EARLY. THE PICK-UP GAME STARTS AT THREE. WE NEVER GET TO PLAY CO-ED AND I WANT TO SHOW THOSE BOYS I CAN SKATE WITH THEM.
YOU'RE GOING ON THE FIELD TRIP, CINDY. IT'S EXTRA CREDIT, WHICH YOU COULD REALLY USE.
YOU'RE NOT WASTING A HALF-DAY OFF FROM SCHOOL PLAYING A GAME.
IT'S NOT JUST A GAME.
IT'S A DATE.
OH BOY...
WITH WHOM?
I RETAIN MOST OF EVERYTHING I SEE.
HECTOR CERVANTEZ.
WE'VE ACTUALLY BEEN SEEING EACH OTHER FOR SIX MONTHS.
CINDY, THAT, THAT'S--
WHAT?
I LIKE HECTOR. HE'S GOT A WICKED WRIST SHOT.

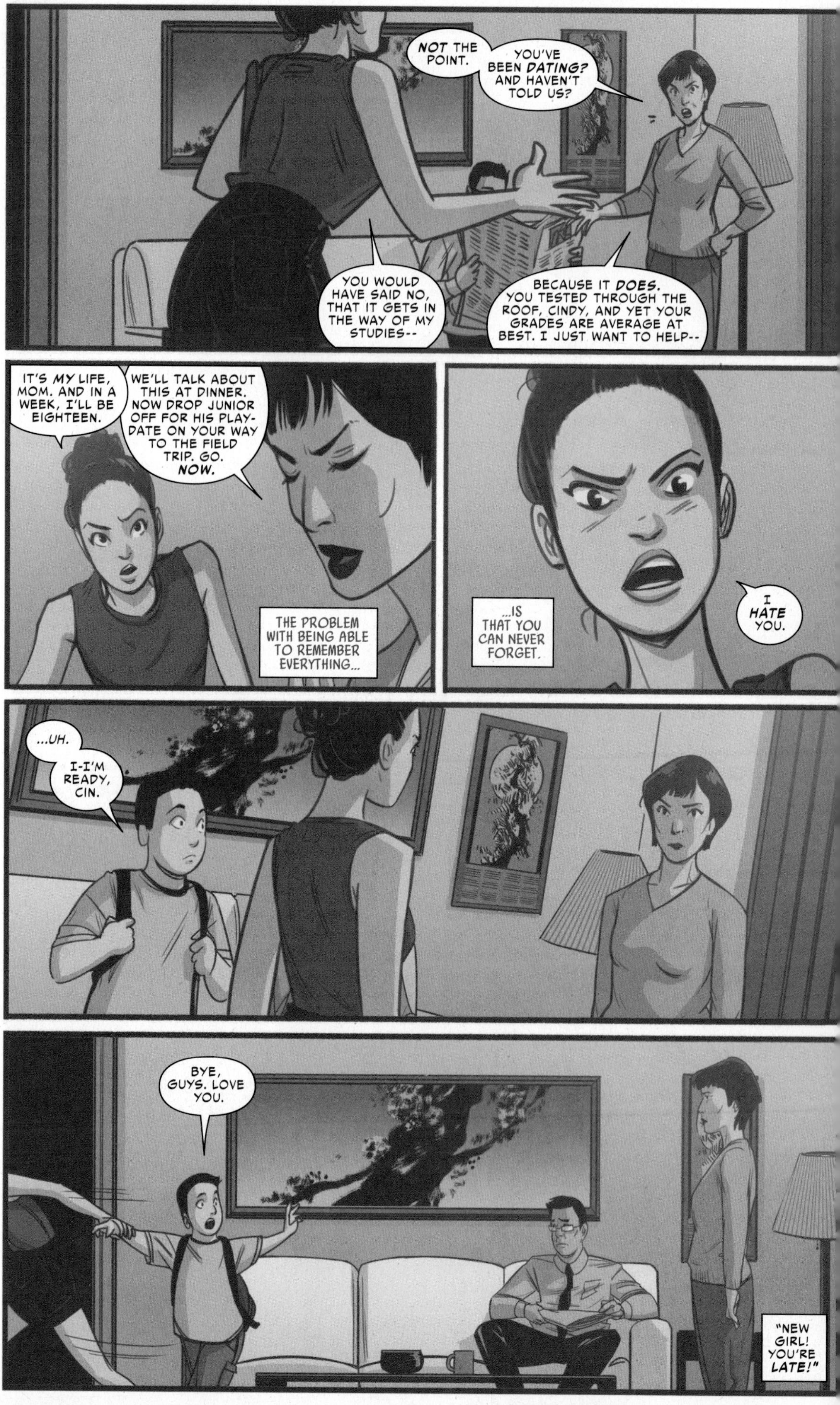
NOT THE POINT.
YOU'VE BEEN DATING? AND HAVEN'T TOLD US?
YOU WOULD HAVE SAID NO, THAT IT GETS IN THE WAY OF MY STUDIES--
BECAUSE IT DOES. YOU TESTED THROUGH THE ROOF, CINDY, AND YET YOUR GRADES ARE AVERAGE AT BEST. I JUST WANT TO HELP--
IT'S MY LIFE, MOM. AND IN A WEEK, I'LL BE EIGHTEEN.
WE'LL TALK ABOUT THIS AT DINNER. NOW DROP JUNIOR OFF FOR HIS PLAY-DATE ON YOUR WAY TO THE FIELD TRIP. GO. NOW.
THE PROBLEM WITH BEING ABLE TO REMEMBER EVERYTHING...
...IS THAT YOU CAN NEVER FORGET.
I HATE YOU.
...UH.
I-I'M READY, CIN.
BYE, GUYS. LOVE YOU.
"NEW GIRL! YOU'RE LATE!"

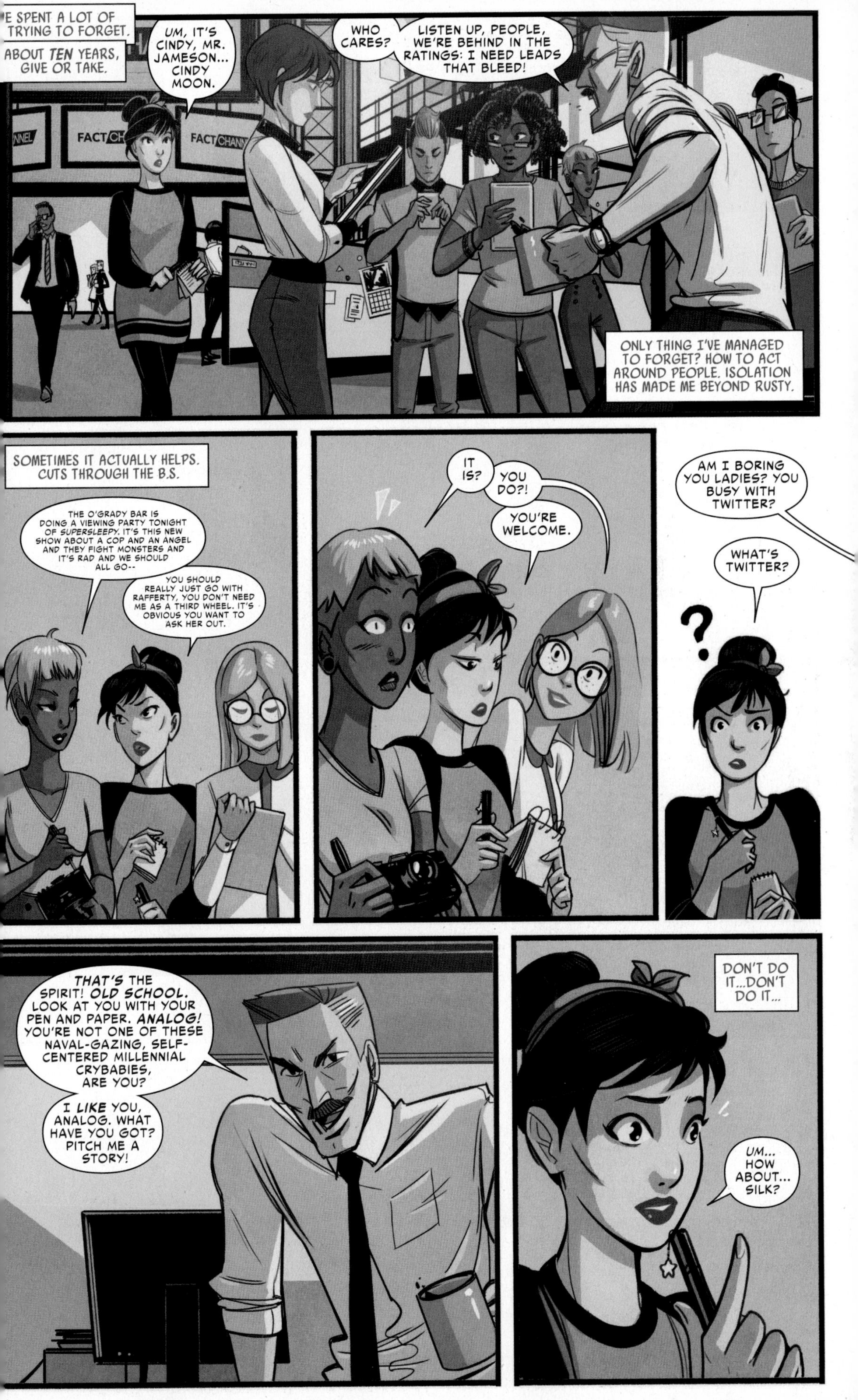
E SPENT A LOT OF TRYING TO FORGET.
ABOUT TEN YEARS, GIVE OR TAKE.
UM, IT'S CINDY, MR. JAMESON... CINDY MOON.
WHO CARES?
LISTEN UP, PEOPLE, WE'RE BEHIND IN THE RATINGS: I NEED LEADS THAT BLEED!
FACT CH
FACT CHANN
ONLY THING I'VE MANAGED TO FORGET? HOW TO ACT AROUND PEOPLE. ISOLATION HAS MADE ME BEYOND RUSTY.
SOMETIMES IT ACTUALLY HELPS. CUTS THROUGH THE B.S.
THE O'GRADY BAR IS DOING A VIEWING PARTY TONIGHT OF SUPERSLEEPY. IT'S THIS NEW SHOW ABOUT A COP AND AN ANGEL AND THEY FIGHT MONSTERS AND IT'S RAD AND WE SHOULD ALL GO--
YOU SHOULD REALLY JUST GO WITH RAFFERTY, YOU DON'T NEED ME AS A THIRD WHEEL. IT'S OBVIOUS YOU WANT TO ASK HER OUT.
IT IS?
YOU DO?!
YOU'RE WELCOME.
AM I BORING YOU LADIES? YOU BUSY WITH TWITTER?
WHAT'S TWITTER?
?
THAT'S THE SPIRIT! OLD SCHOOL. LOOK AT YOU WITH YOUR PEN AND PAPER. ANALOG! YOU'RE NOT ONE OF THESE NAVAL-GAZING, SELF-CENTERED MILLENNIAL CRYBABIES, ARE YOU?
I LIKE YOU, ANALOG. WHAT HAVE YOU GOT? PITCH ME A STORY!
DON'T DO IT...DON'T DO IT...
UM... HOW ABOUT... SILK?

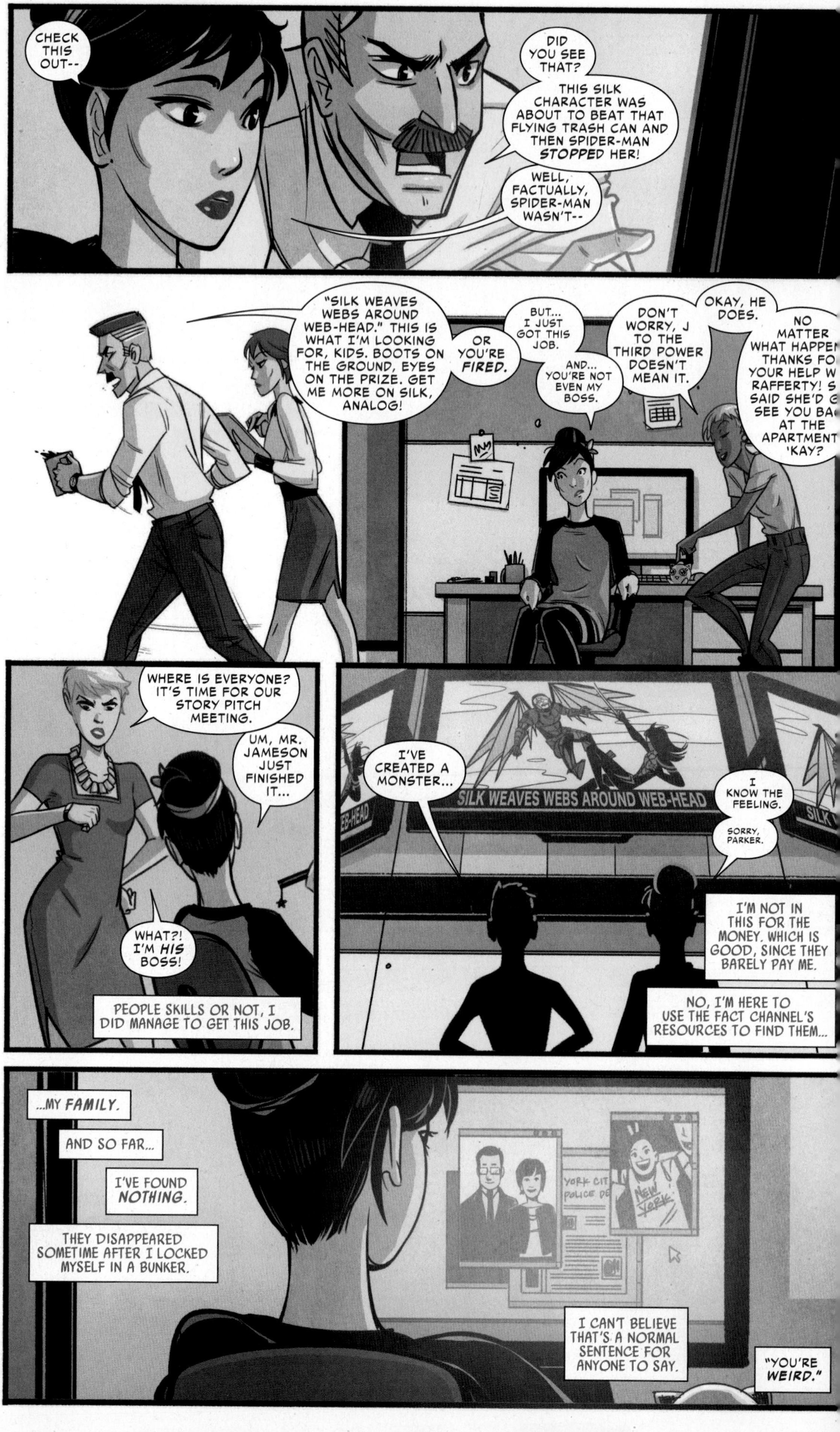

CHECK THIS OUT--
DID YOU SEE THAT?
THIS SILK CHARACTER WAS ABOUT TO BEAT THAT FLYING TRASH CAN AND THEN SPIDER-MAN STOPPED HER!
WELL, FACTUALLY, SPIDER-MAN WASN'T--
"SILK WEAVES WEBS AROUND WEB-HEAD." THIS IS WHAT I'M LOOKING FOR, KIDS. BOOTS ON THE GROUND, EYES ON THE PRIZE. GET ME MORE ON SILK, ANALOG!
OR YOU'RE FIRED.
BUT... I JUST GOT THIS JOB.
AND... YOU'RE NOT EVEN MY BOSS.
DON'T WORRY, J TO THE THIRD POWER DOESN'T MEAN IT.
OKAY, HE DOES.
WHERE IS EVERYONE? IT'S TIME FOR OUR STORY PITCH MEETING.
UM, MR. JAMESON JUST FINISHED IT...
WHAT?! I'M HIS BOSS!
PEOPLE SKILLS OR NOT, I DID MANAGE TO GET THIS JOB.
I'VE CREATED A MONSTER...
SILK WEAVES WEBS AROUND WEB-HEAD
I KNOW THE FEELING.
SORRY, PARKER.
I'M NOT IN THIS FOR THE MONEY. WHICH IS GOOD, SINCE THEY BARELY PAY ME.
NO, I'M HERE TO USE THE FACT CHANNEL'S RESOURCES TO FIND THEM...
...MY FAMILY.
AND SO FAR...
I'VE FOUND NOTHING.
THEY DISAPPEARED SOMETIME AFTER I LOCKED MYSELF IN A BUNKER.
I CAN'T BELIEVE THAT'S A NORMAL SENTENCE FOR ANYONE TO SAY.
"YOU'RE WEIRD."

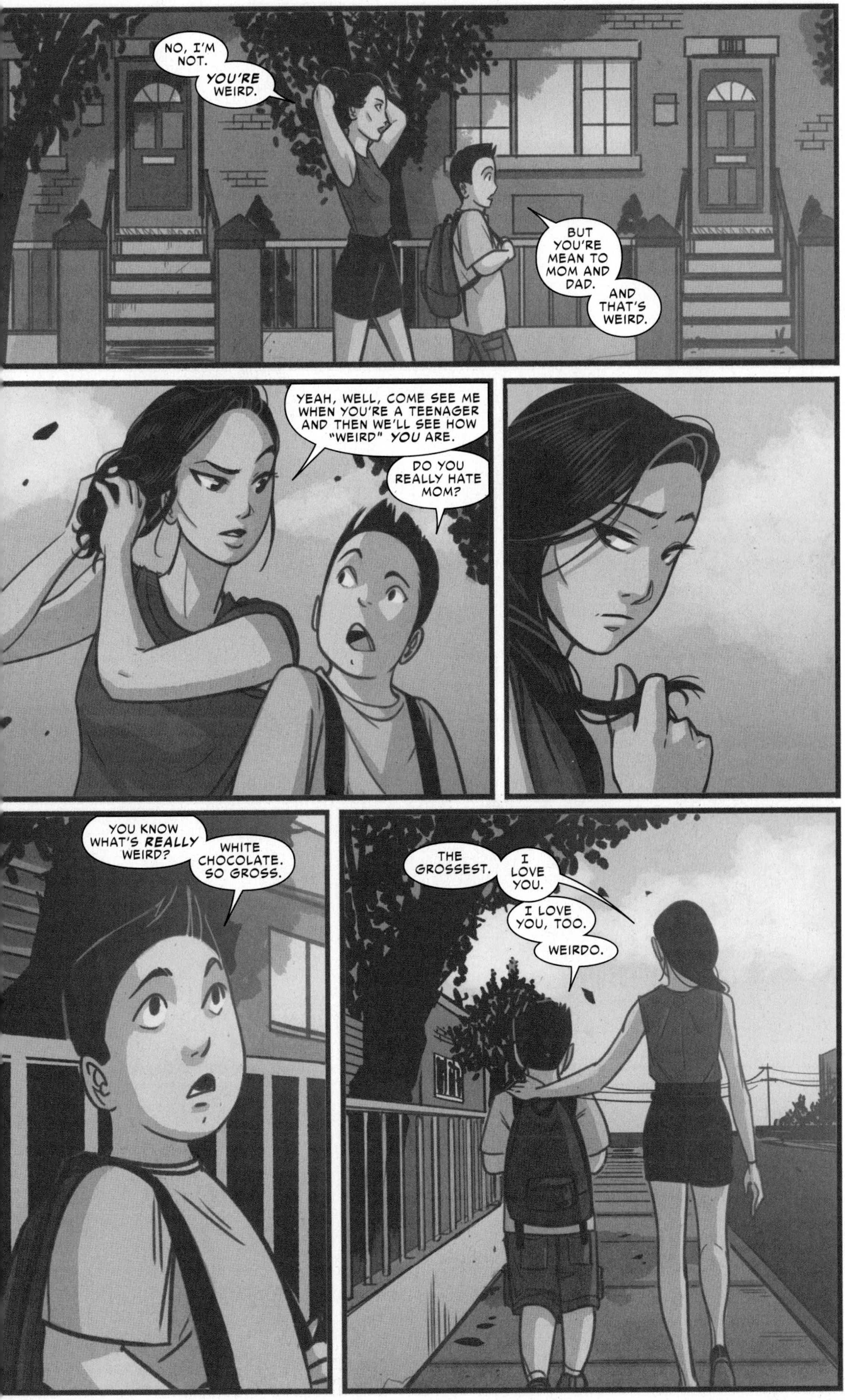
NO, I'M NOT. *YOU'RE* WEIRD.
BUT YOU'RE MEAN TO MOM AND DAD.
AND THAT'S WEIRD.
YEAH, WELL, COME SEE ME WHEN YOU'RE A TEENAGER AND THEN WE'LL SEE HOW "WEIRD" *YOU* ARE.
DO YOU REALLY HATE MOM?
YOU KNOW WHAT'S *REALLY* WEIRD?
WHITE CHOCOLATE. SO GROSS.
THE GROSSEST.
I LOVE YOU.
I LOVE YOU, TOO.
WEIRDO.

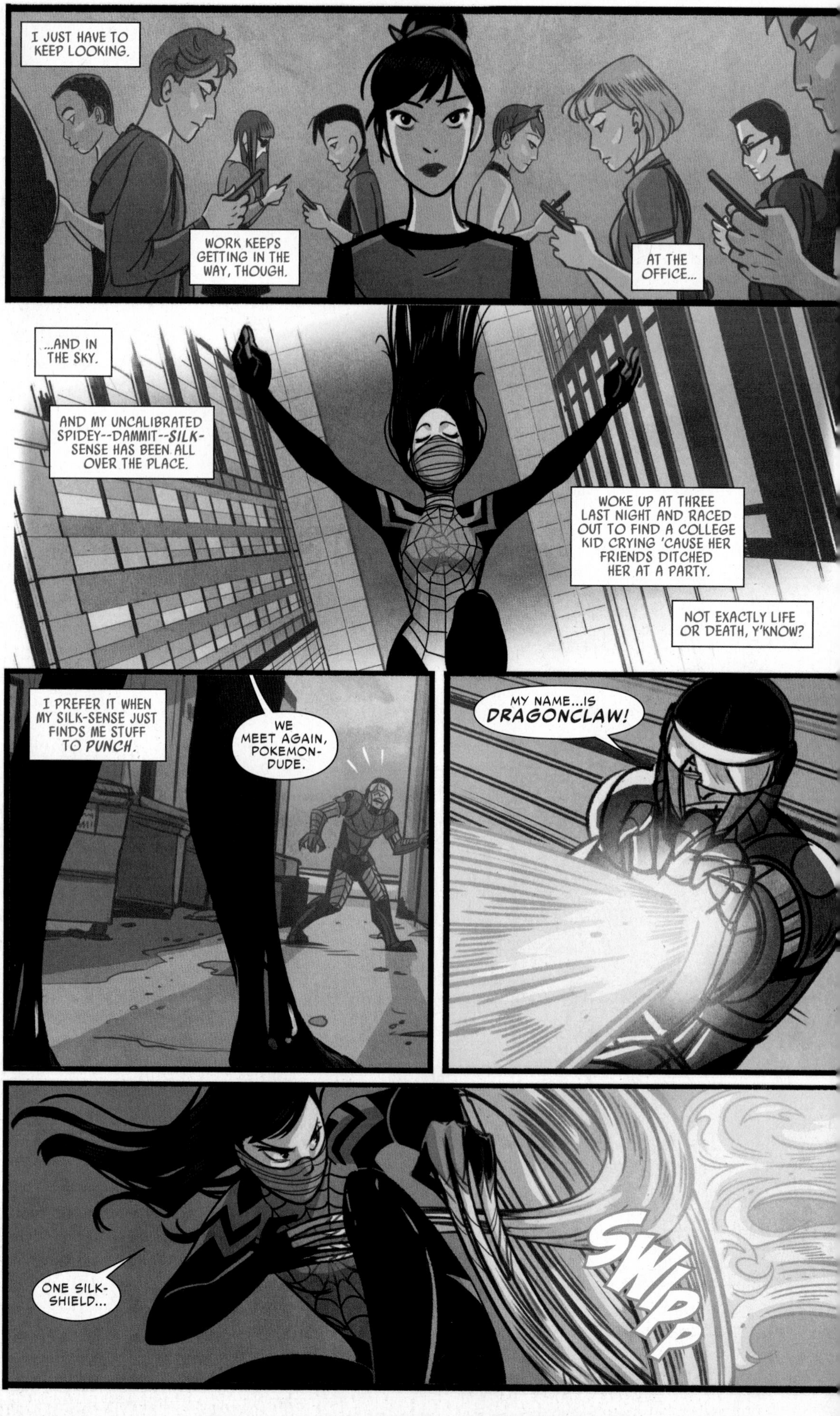
I JUST HAVE TO KEEP LOOKING.
WORK KEEPS GETTING IN THE WAY, THOUGH.
AT THE OFFICE...
...AND IN THE SKY.
AND MY UNCALIBRATED SPIDEY--DAMMIT--SILK-SENSE HAS BEEN ALL OVER THE PLACE.
WOKE UP AT THREE LAST NIGHT AND RACED OUT TO FIND A COLLEGE KID CRYING 'CAUSE HER FRIENDS DITCHED HER AT A PARTY.
NOT EXACTLY LIFE OR DEATH, Y'KNOW?
I PREFER IT WHEN MY SILK-SENSE JUST FINDS ME STUFF TO PUNCH.
WE MEET AGAIN, POKEMON-DUDE.
MY NAME...IS DRAGONCLAW!
ONE SILK-SHIELD...
SWIPP

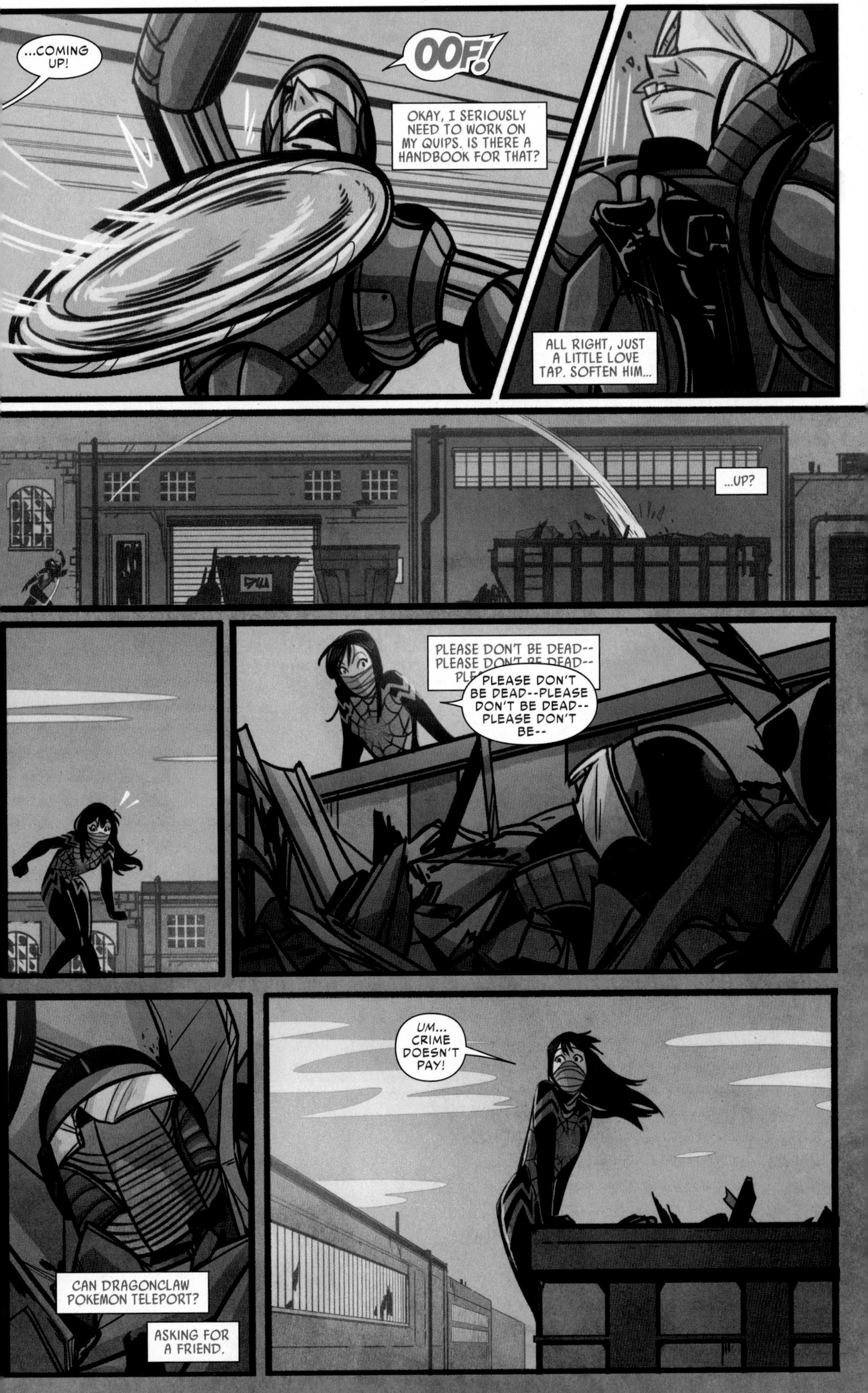
...COMING UP!
OOF!
OKAY, I SERIOUSLY NEED TO WORK ON MY QUIPS. IS THERE A HANDBOOK FOR THAT?
ALL RIGHT, JUST A LITTLE LOVE TAP. SOFTEN HIM...
...UP?
PLEASE DON'T BE DEAD-- PLEASE DON'T BE DEAD--
PLEASE DON'T BE DEAD--PLEASE DON'T BE DEAD-- PLEASE DON'T BE--
CAN DRAGONCLAW POKEMON TELEPORT?
ASKING FOR A FRIEND.
UM... CRIME DOESN'T PAY!

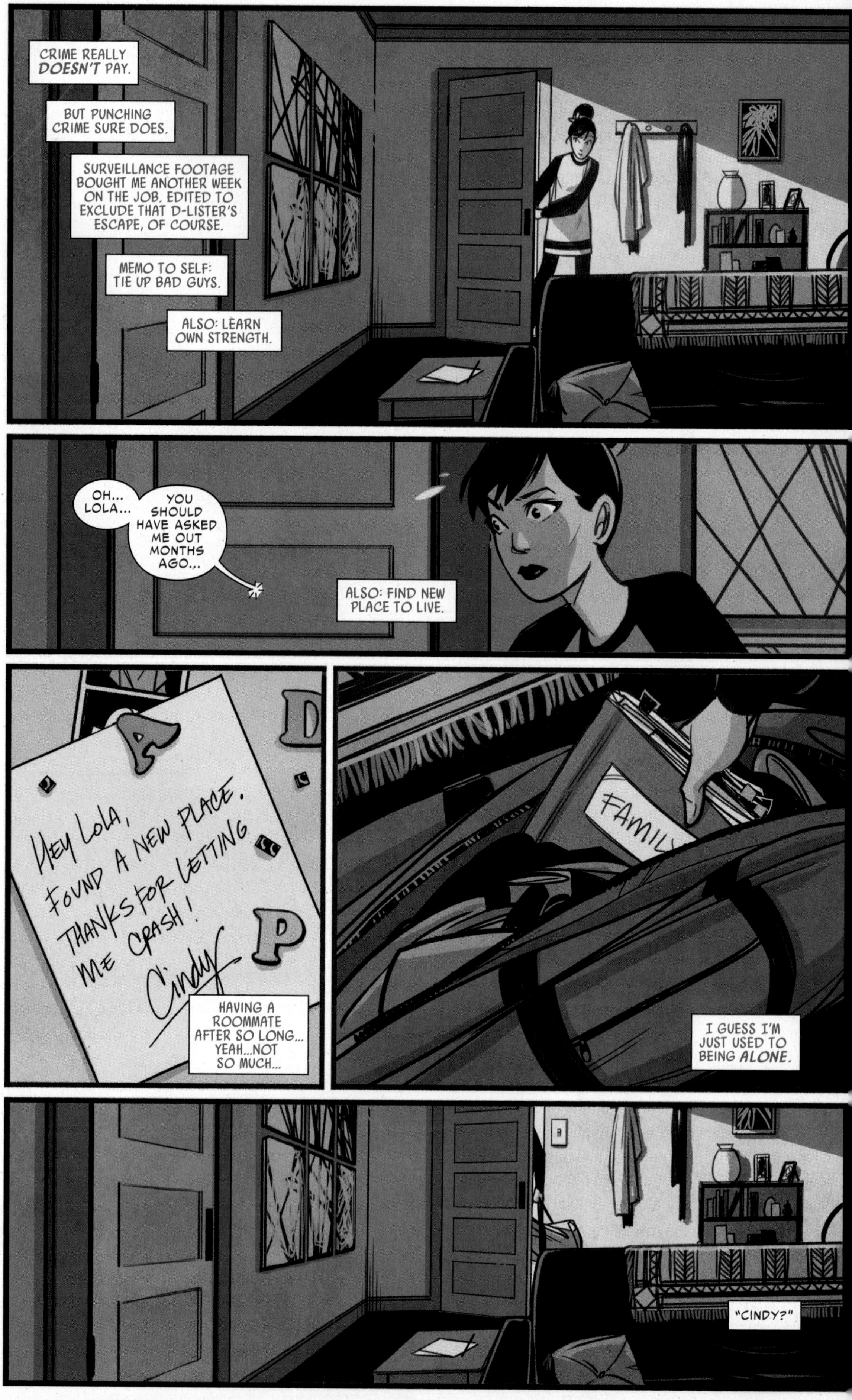

CRIME REALLY DOESN'T PAY.
BUT PUNCHING CRIME SURE DOES.
SURVEILLANCE FOOTAGE BOUGHT ME ANOTHER WEEK ON THE JOB. EDITED TO EXCLUDE THAT D-LISTER'S ESCAPE, OF COURSE.
MEMO TO SELF: TIE UP BAD GUYS.
ALSO: LEARN OWN STRENGTH.
OH... LOLA...
YOU SHOULD HAVE ASKED ME OUT MONTHS AGO...
ALSO: FIND NEW PLACE TO LIVE.
Hey Lola, Found a new place. Thanks for letting me crash! Cindy
HAVING A ROOMMATE AFTER SO LONG... YEAH...NOT SO MUCH...
I GUESS I'M JUST USED TO BEING ALONE.
"CINDY?"

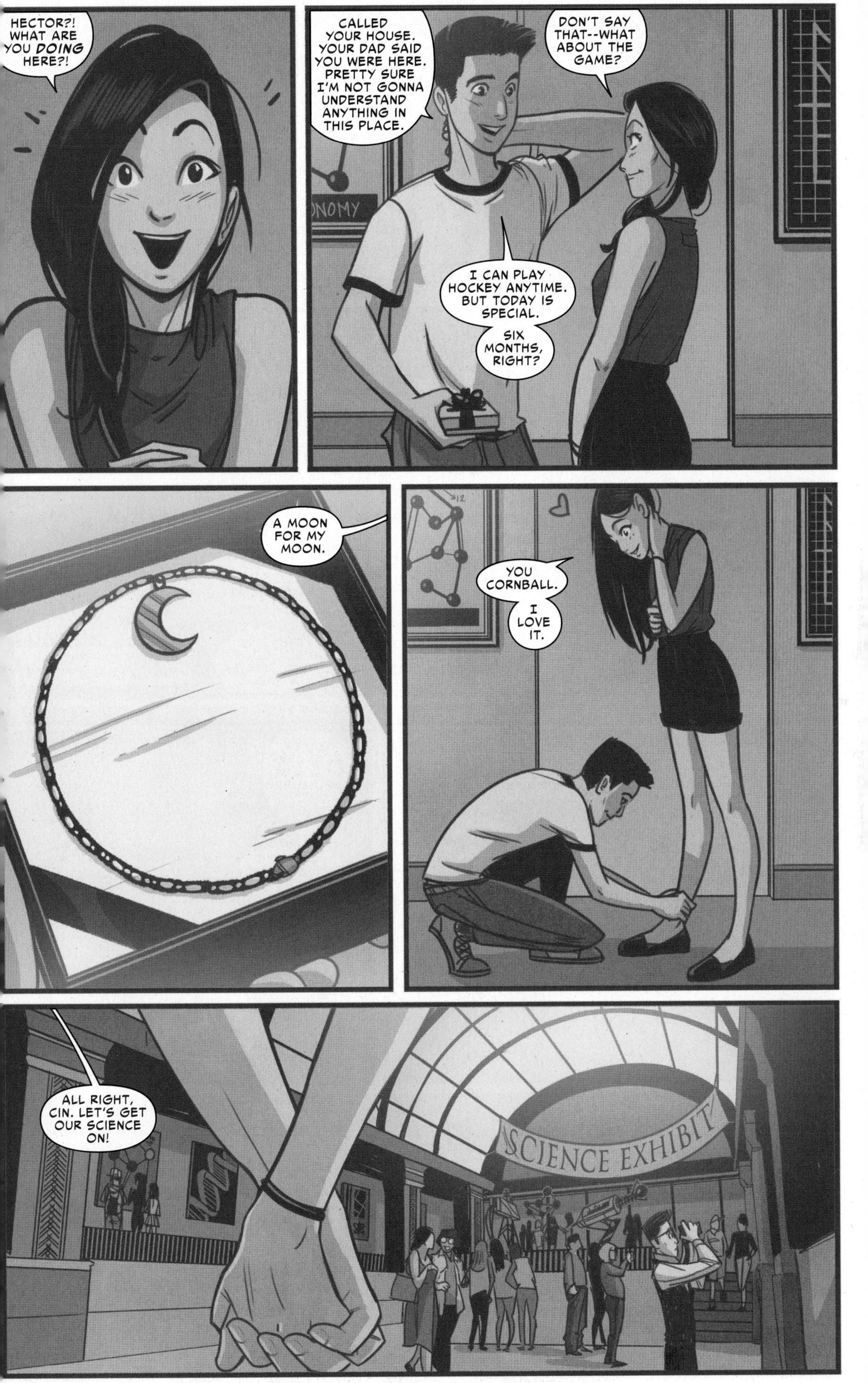
HECTOR?! WHAT ARE YOU *DOING* HERE?!
CALLED YOUR HOUSE. YOUR DAD SAID YOU WERE HERE. PRETTY SURE I'M NOT GONNA UNDERSTAND ANYTHING IN THIS PLACE.
DON'T SAY THAT--WHAT ABOUT THE GAME?
I CAN PLAY HOCKEY ANYTIME. BUT TODAY IS SPECIAL.
SIX MONTHS, RIGHT?
A MOON FOR MY MOON.
YOU CORNBALL.
I LOVE IT.
ALL RIGHT, CIN. LET'S GET OUR SCIENCE ON!
SCIENCE EXHIBIT

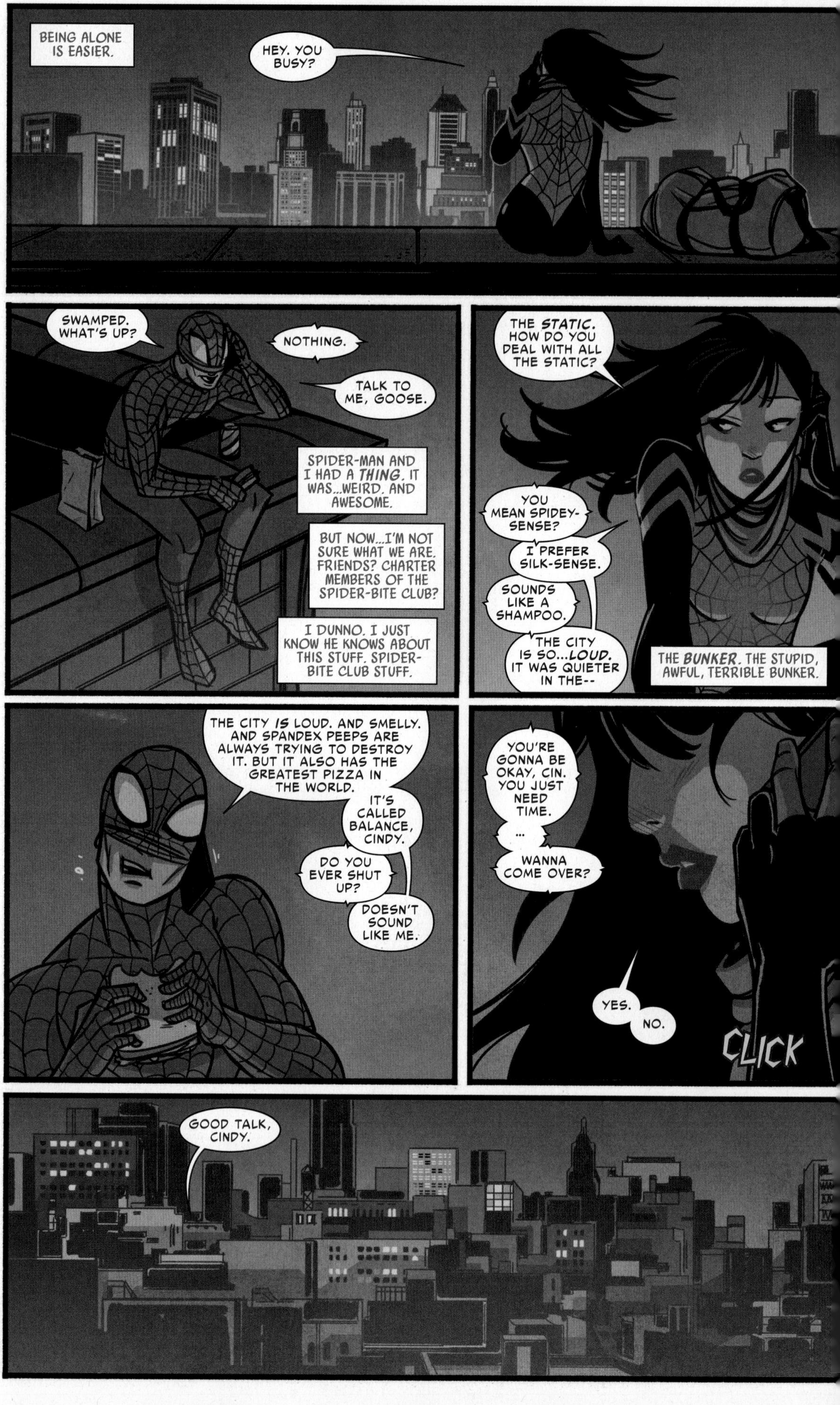
BEING ALONE IS EASIER.
HEY. YOU BUSY?
SWAMPED. WHAT'S UP?
NOTHING.
TALK TO ME, GOOSE.
SPIDER-MAN AND I HAD A *THING*. IT WAS...WEIRD. AND AWESOME.
BUT NOW...I'M NOT SURE WHAT WE ARE. FRIENDS? CHARTER MEMBERS OF THE SPIDER-BITE CLUB?
I DUNNO. I JUST KNOW HE KNOWS ABOUT THIS STUFF. SPIDER-BITE CLUB STUFF.
THE *STATIC*. HOW DO YOU DEAL WITH ALL THE STATIC?
YOU MEAN SPIDEY-SENSE?
I PREFER SILK-SENSE.
SOUNDS LIKE A SHAMPOO.
THE CITY IS SO...*LOUD*. IT WAS QUIETER IN THE--
THE *BUNKER*. THE STUPID, AWFUL, TERRIBLE BUNKER.
THE CITY *IS* LOUD. AND SMELLY. AND SPANDEX PEEPS ARE ALWAYS TRYING TO DESTROY IT. BUT IT ALSO HAS THE GREATEST PIZZA IN THE WORLD.
IT'S CALLED BALANCE, CINDY.
DO YOU EVER SHUT UP?
DOESN'T SOUND LIKE ME.
YOU'RE GONNA BE OKAY, CIN. YOU JUST NEED TIME.
...
WANNA COME OVER?
YES.
NO.
CLICK
GOOD TALK, CINDY.

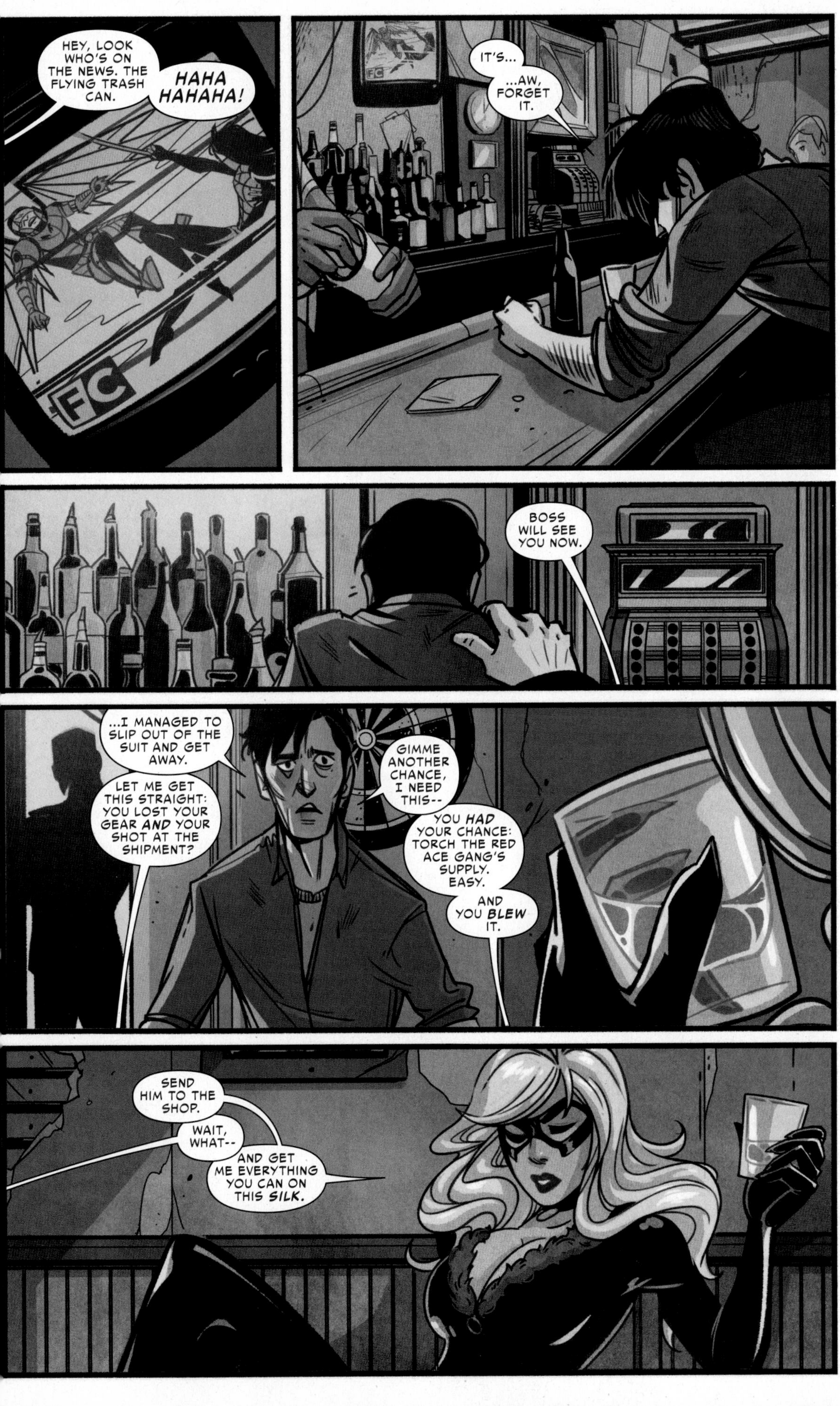
HEY, LOOK WHO'S ON THE NEWS. THE FLYING TRASH CAN.
HAHA HAHAHA!
FC
IT'S...
...AW, FORGET IT.
BOSS WILL SEE YOU NOW.
...I MANAGED TO SLIP OUT OF THE SUIT AND GET AWAY.
LET ME GET THIS STRAIGHT: YOU LOST YOUR GEAR AND YOUR SHOT AT THE SHIPMENT?
GIMME ANOTHER CHANCE, I NEED THIS--
YOU HAD YOUR CHANCE: TORCH THE RED ACE GANG'S SUPPLY. EASY.
AND YOU BLEW IT.
SEND HIM TO THE SHOP.
WAIT, WHAT--
AND GET ME EVERYTHING YOU CAN ON THIS SILK.

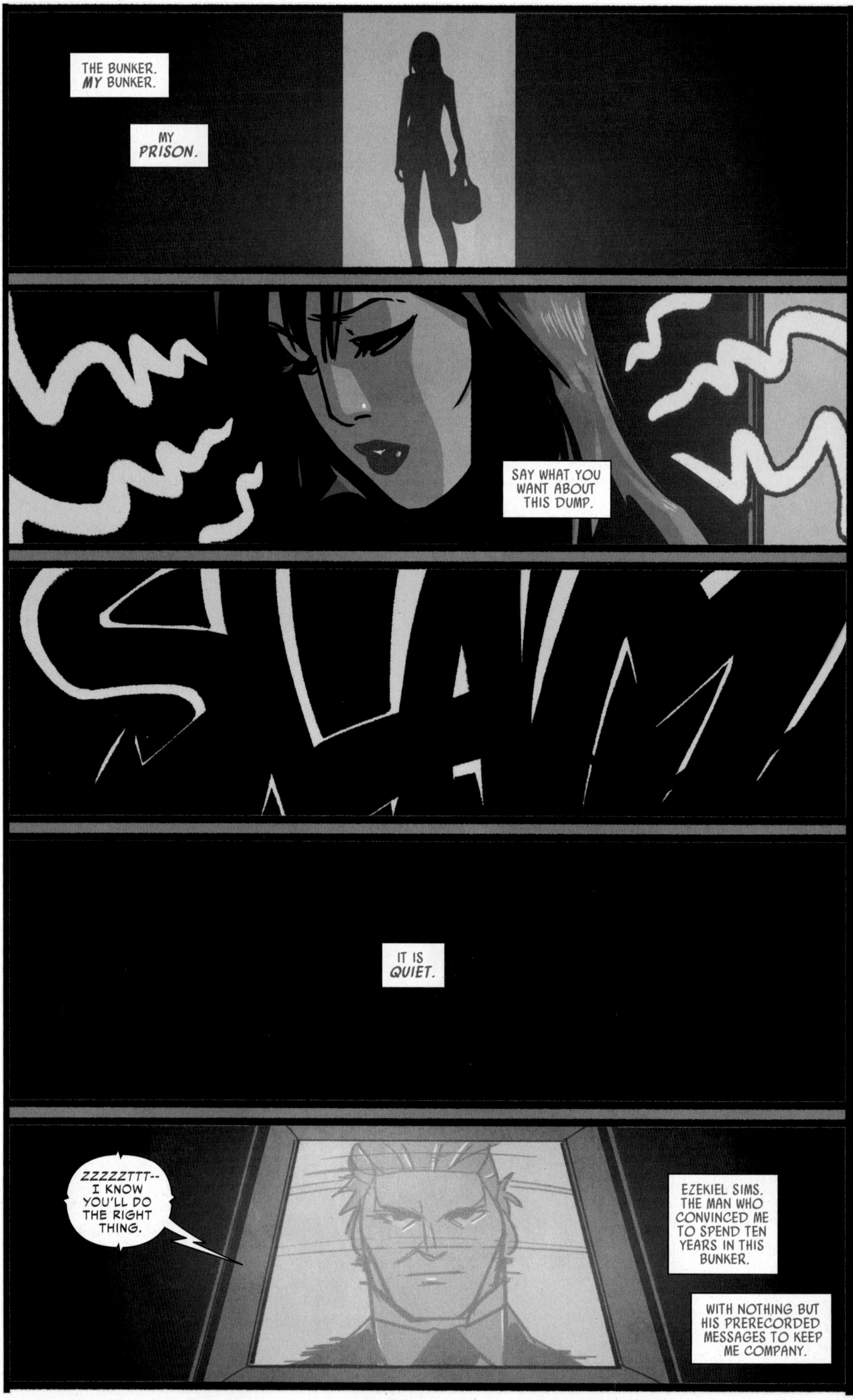
THE BUNKER. MY BUNKER.
MY PRISON.
SAY WHAT YOU WANT ABOUT THIS DUMP.
IT IS QUIET.
ZZZZZTTT-- I KNOW YOU'LL DO THE RIGHT THING.
EZEKIEL SIMS. THE MAN WHO CONVINCED ME TO SPEND TEN YEARS IN THIS BUNKER.
WITH NOTHING BUT HIS PRERECORDED MESSAGES TO KEEP ME COMPANY.

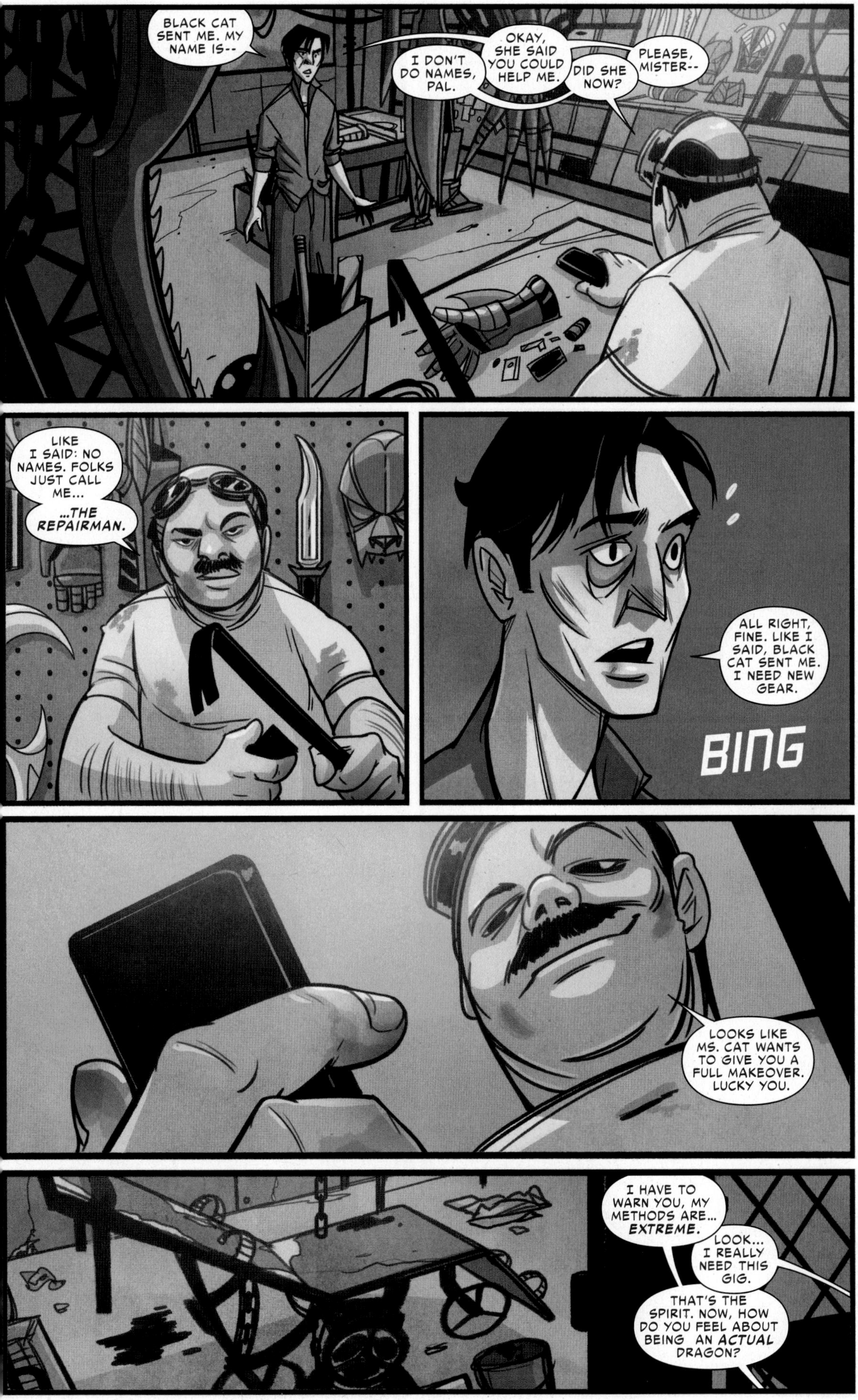
BLACK CAT SENT ME. MY NAME IS--
I DON'T DO NAMES, PAL.
OKAY, SHE SAID YOU COULD HELP ME.
DID SHE NOW?
PLEASE, MISTER--
LIKE I SAID: NO NAMES. FOLKS JUST CALL ME...
...THE REPAIRMAN.
ALL RIGHT, FINE. LIKE I SAID, BLACK CAT SENT ME. I NEED NEW GEAR.
BING
LOOKS LIKE MS. CAT WANTS TO GIVE YOU A FULL MAKEOVER. LUCKY YOU.
I HAVE TO WARN YOU, MY METHODS ARE... EXTREME.
LOOK... I REALLY NEED THIS GIG.
THAT'S THE SPIRIT. NOW, HOW DO YOU FEEL ABOUT BEING AN ACTUAL DRAGON?

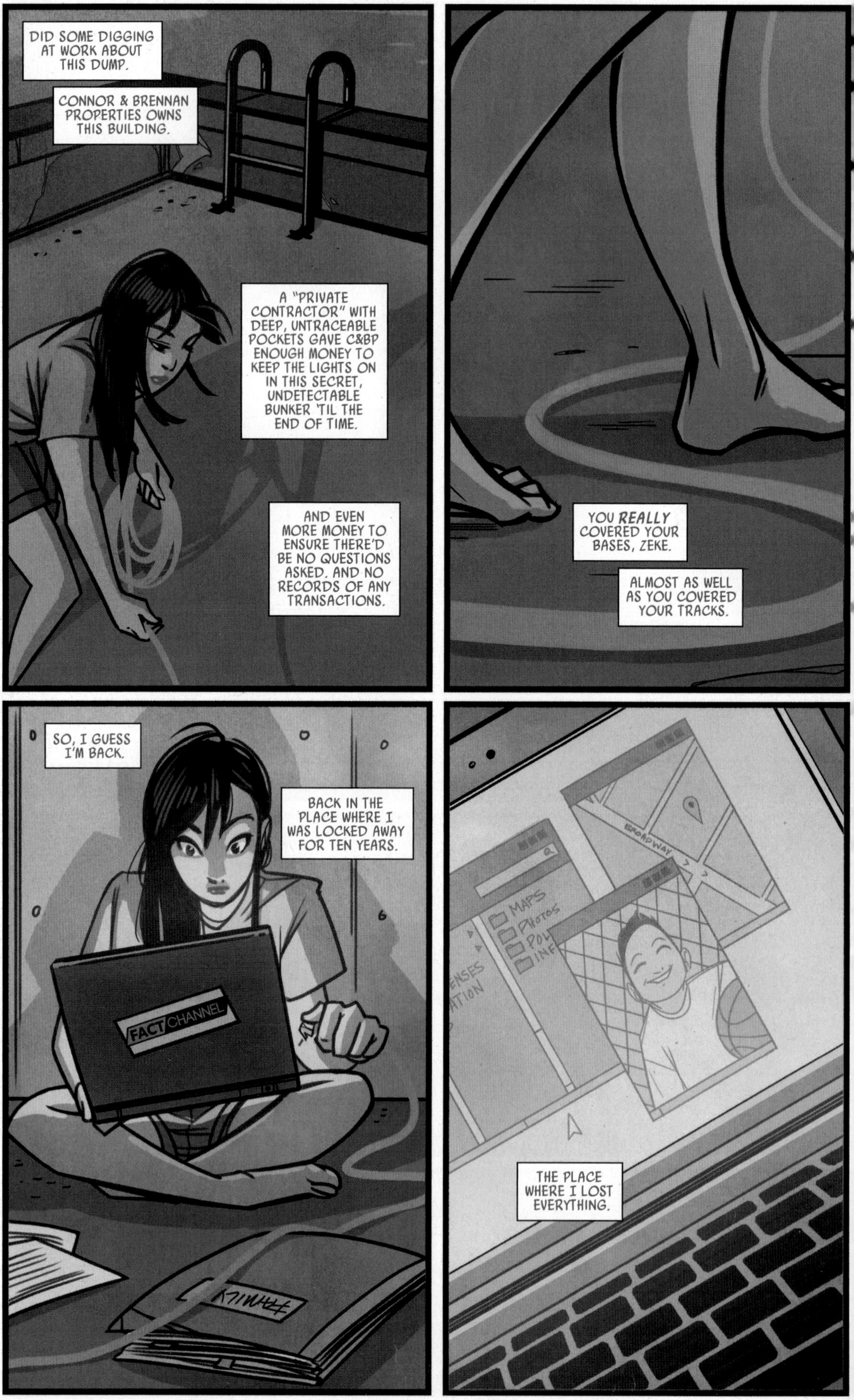
DID SOME DIGGING AT WORK ABOUT THIS DUMP.
CONNOR & BRENNAN PROPERTIES OWNS THIS BUILDING.
A "PRIVATE CONTRACTOR" WITH DEEP, UNTRACEABLE POCKETS GAVE C&BP ENOUGH MONEY TO KEEP THE LIGHTS ON IN THIS SECRET, UNDETECTABLE BUNKER 'TIL THE END OF TIME.
AND EVEN MORE MONEY TO ENSURE THERE'D BE NO QUESTIONS ASKED. AND NO RECORDS OF ANY TRANSACTIONS.
YOU **REALLY** COVERED YOUR BASES, ZEKE.
ALMOST AS WELL AS YOU COVERED YOUR TRACKS.
SO, I GUESS I'M BACK.
BACK IN THE PLACE WHERE I WAS LOCKED AWAY FOR TEN YEARS.
FACT CHANNEL
BROADWAY
MAPS
Photos
THE PLACE WHERE I LOST EVERYTHING.

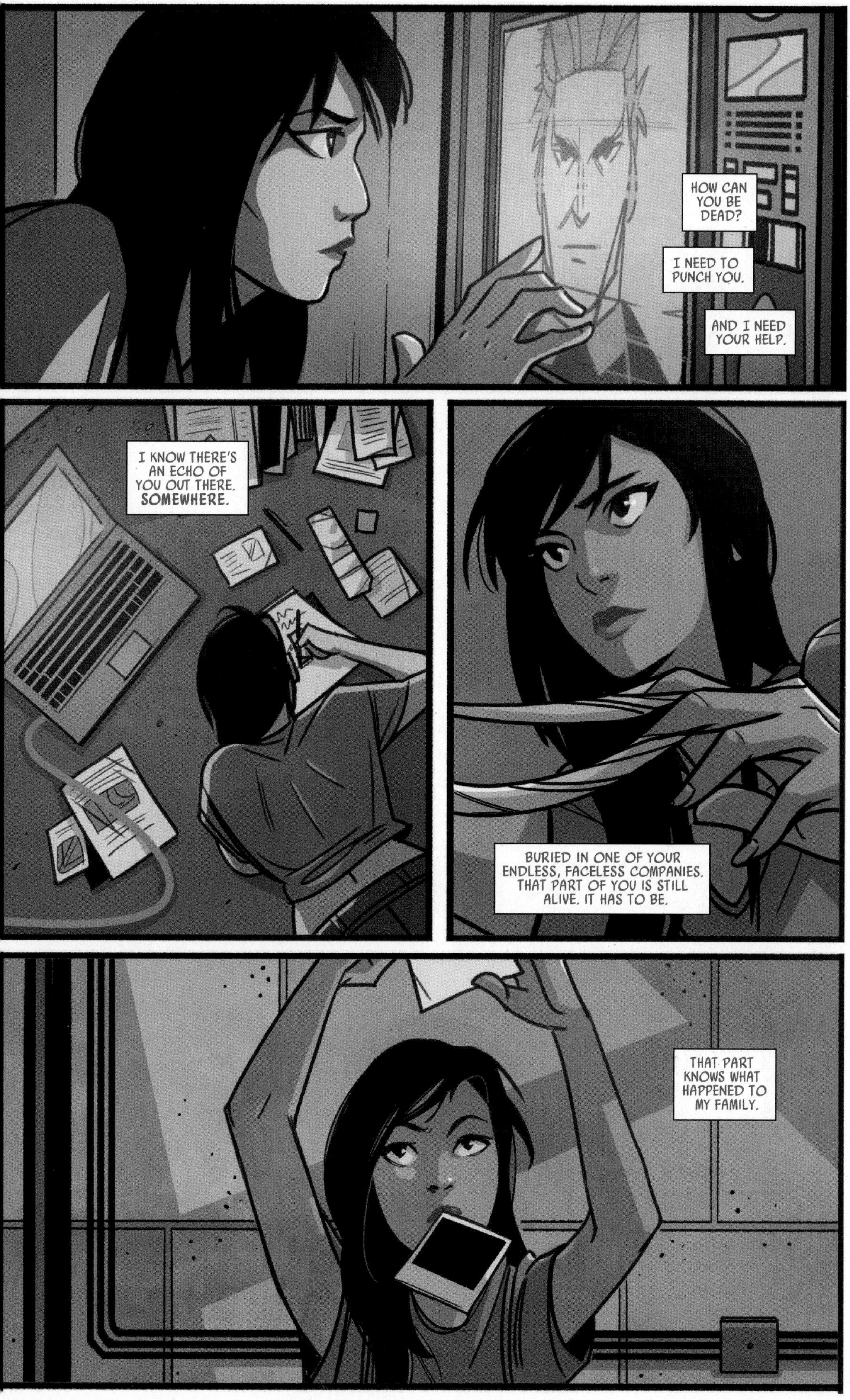
HOW CAN YOU BE DEAD?
I NEED TO PUNCH YOU.
AND I NEED YOUR HELP.
I KNOW THERE'S AN ECHO OF YOU OUT THERE. SOMEWHERE.
BURIED IN ONE OF YOUR ENDLESS, FACELESS COMPANIES. THAT PART OF YOU IS STILL ALIVE. IT HAS TO BE.
THAT PART KNOWS WHAT HAPPENED TO MY FAMILY.

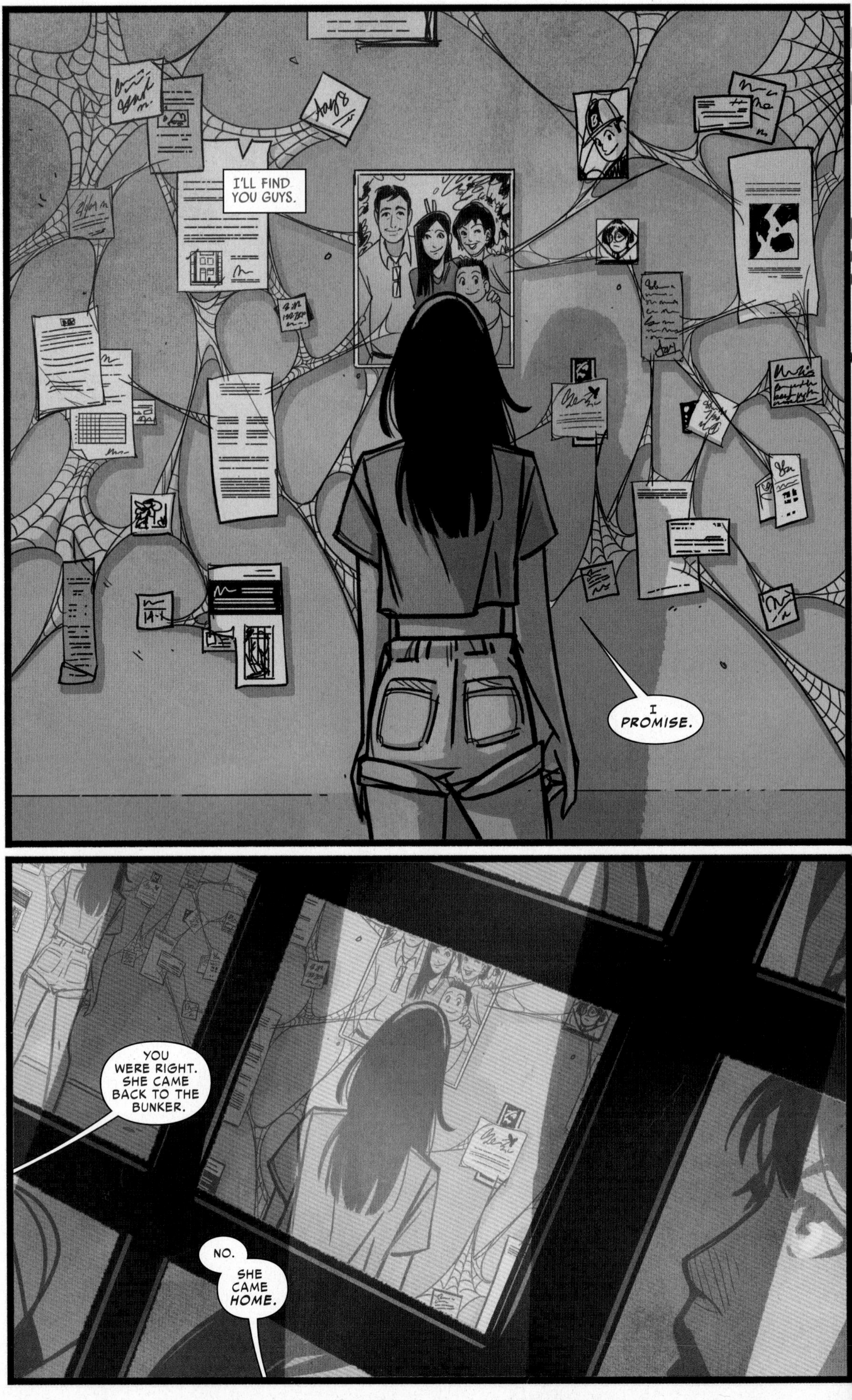
I'LL FIND YOU GUYS.
I PROMISE.
YOU WERE RIGHT. SHE CAME BACK TO THE BUNKER.
NO.
SHE CAME *HOME.*

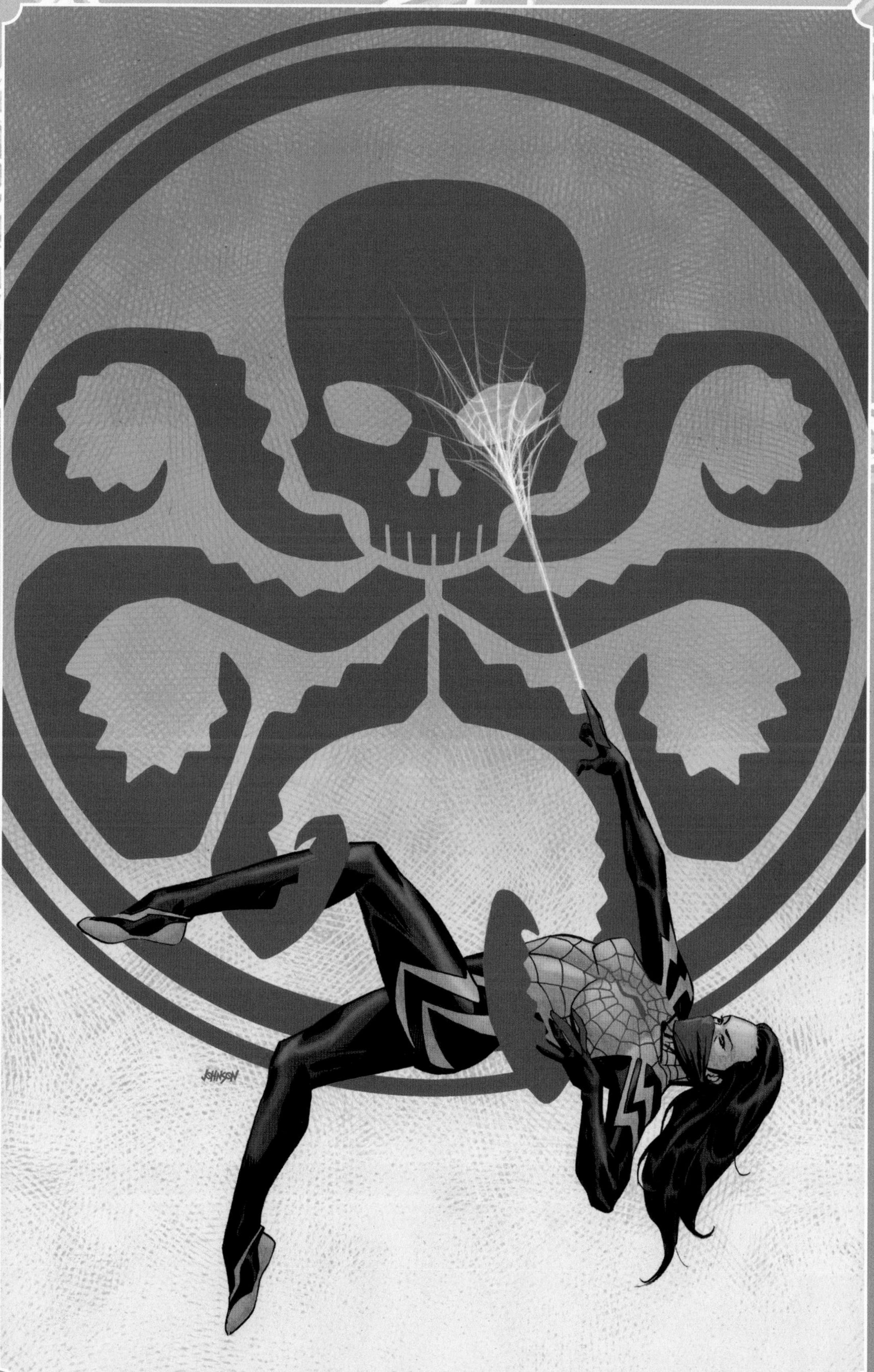
JOHNSON

SILK (2015A) #2

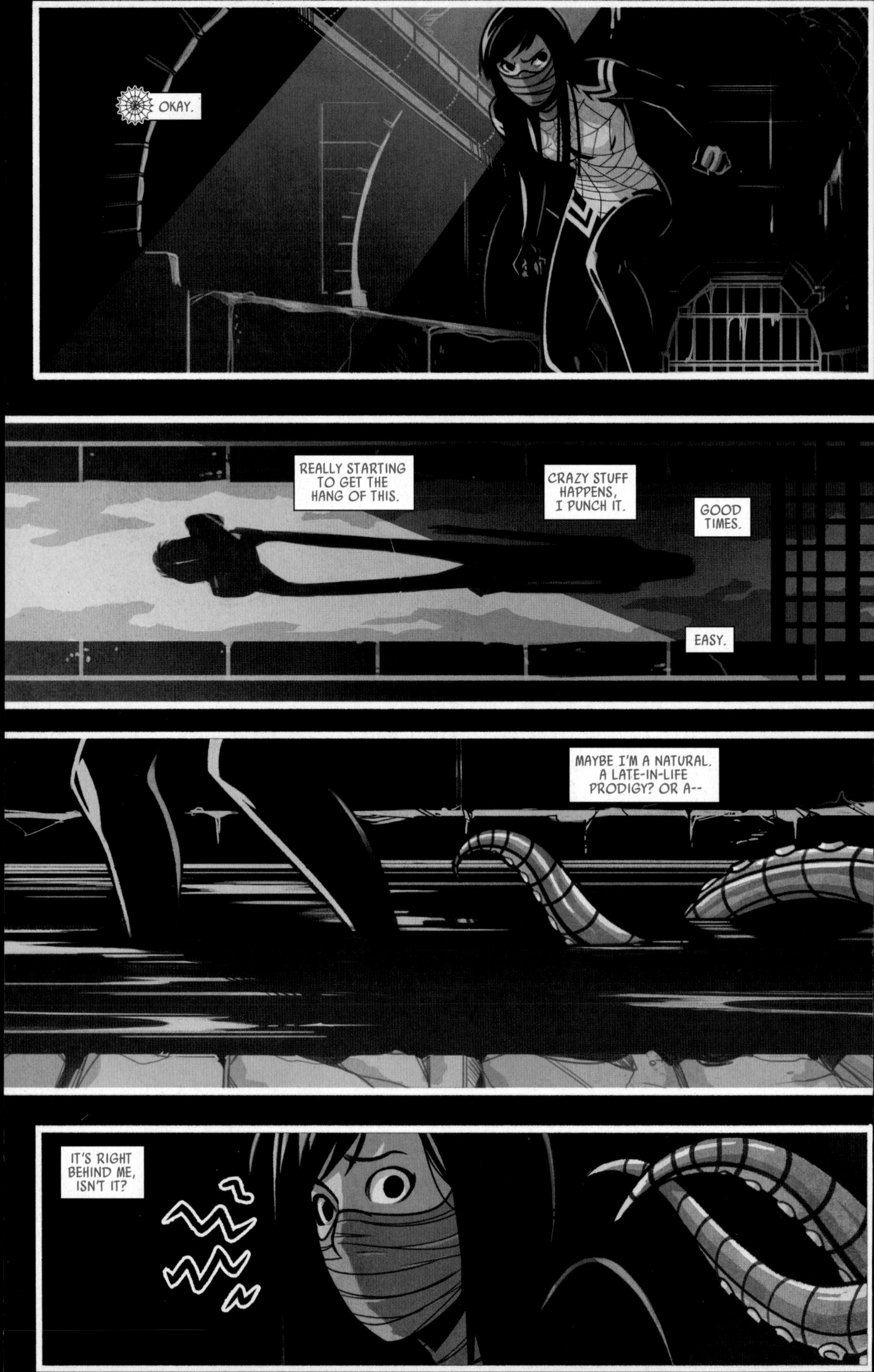
OKAY.
REALLY STARTING TO GET THE HANG OF THIS.
CRAZY STUFF HAPPENS, I PUNCH IT.
GOOD TIMES.
EASY.
MAYBE I'M A NATURAL. A LATE-IN-LIFE PRODIGY? OR A--
IT'S RIGHT BEHIND ME, ISN'T IT?

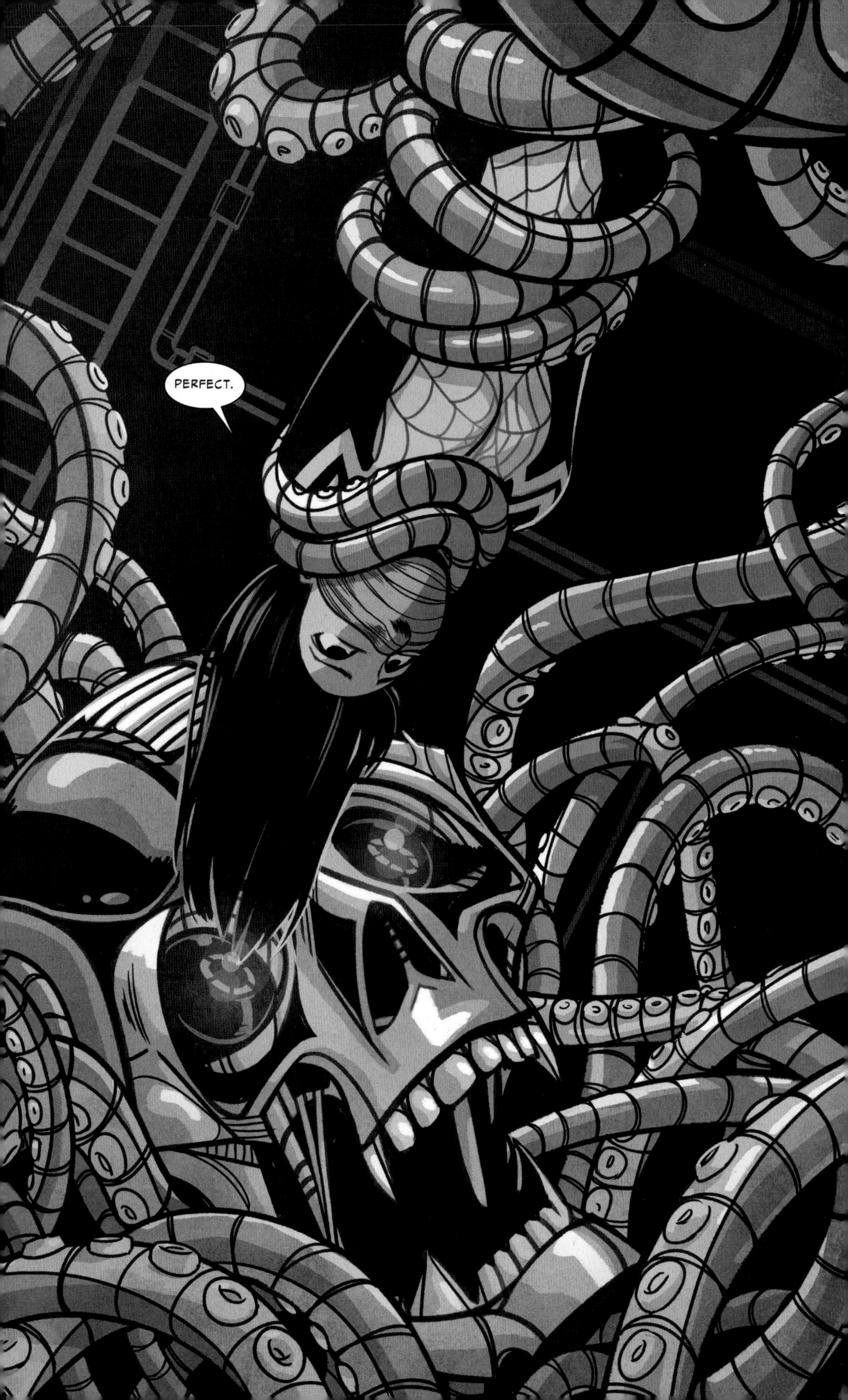
PERFECT.

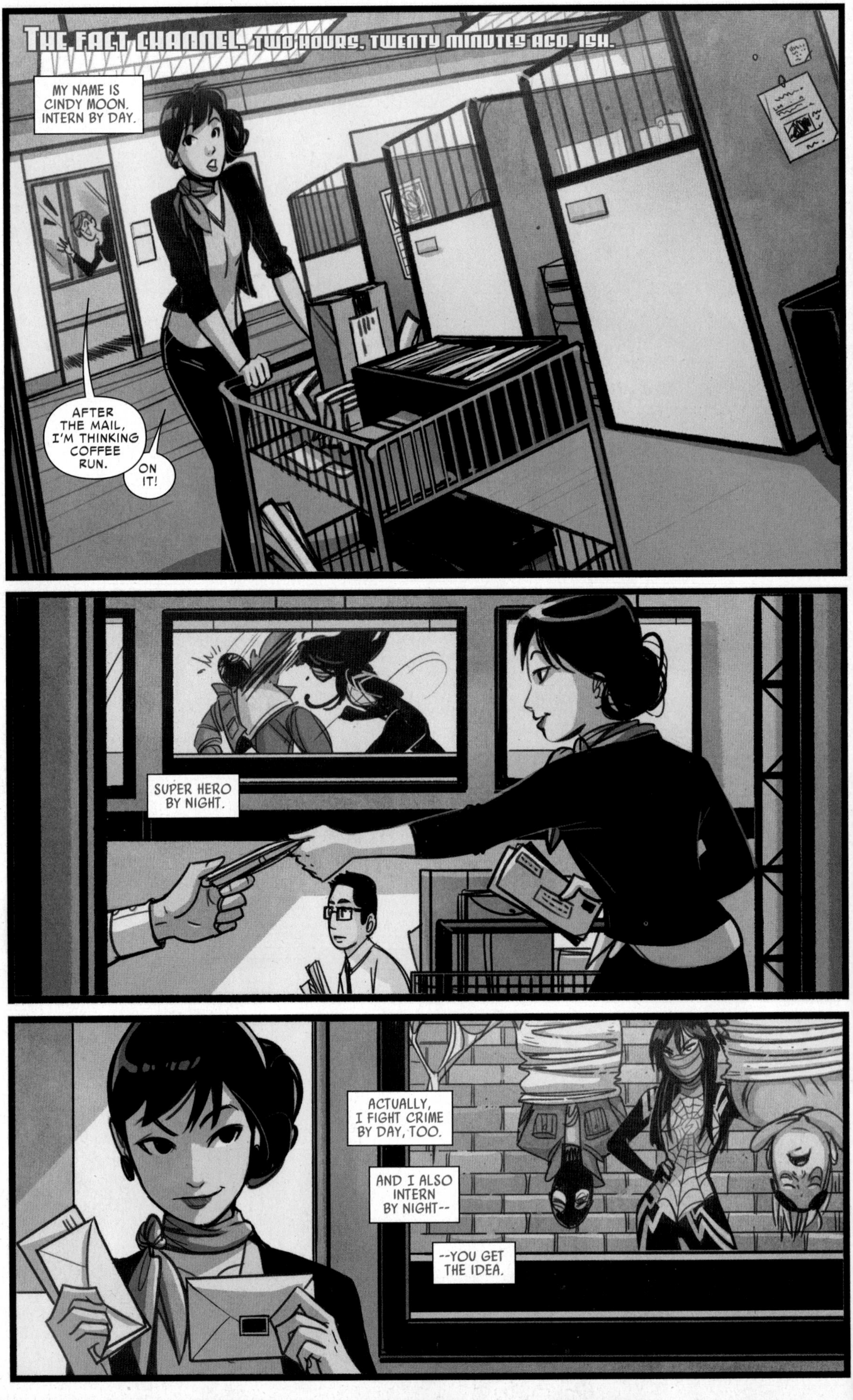
THE FACT CHANNEL. TWO HOURS, TWENTY MINUTES AGO. ISH.
MY NAME IS CINDY MOON. INTERN BY DAY.
AFTER THE MAIL, I'M THINKING COFFEE RUN.
ON IT!
SUPER HERO BY NIGHT.
ACTUALLY, I FIGHT CRIME BY DAY, TOO.
AND I ALSO INTERN BY NIGHT--
--YOU GET THE IDEA.

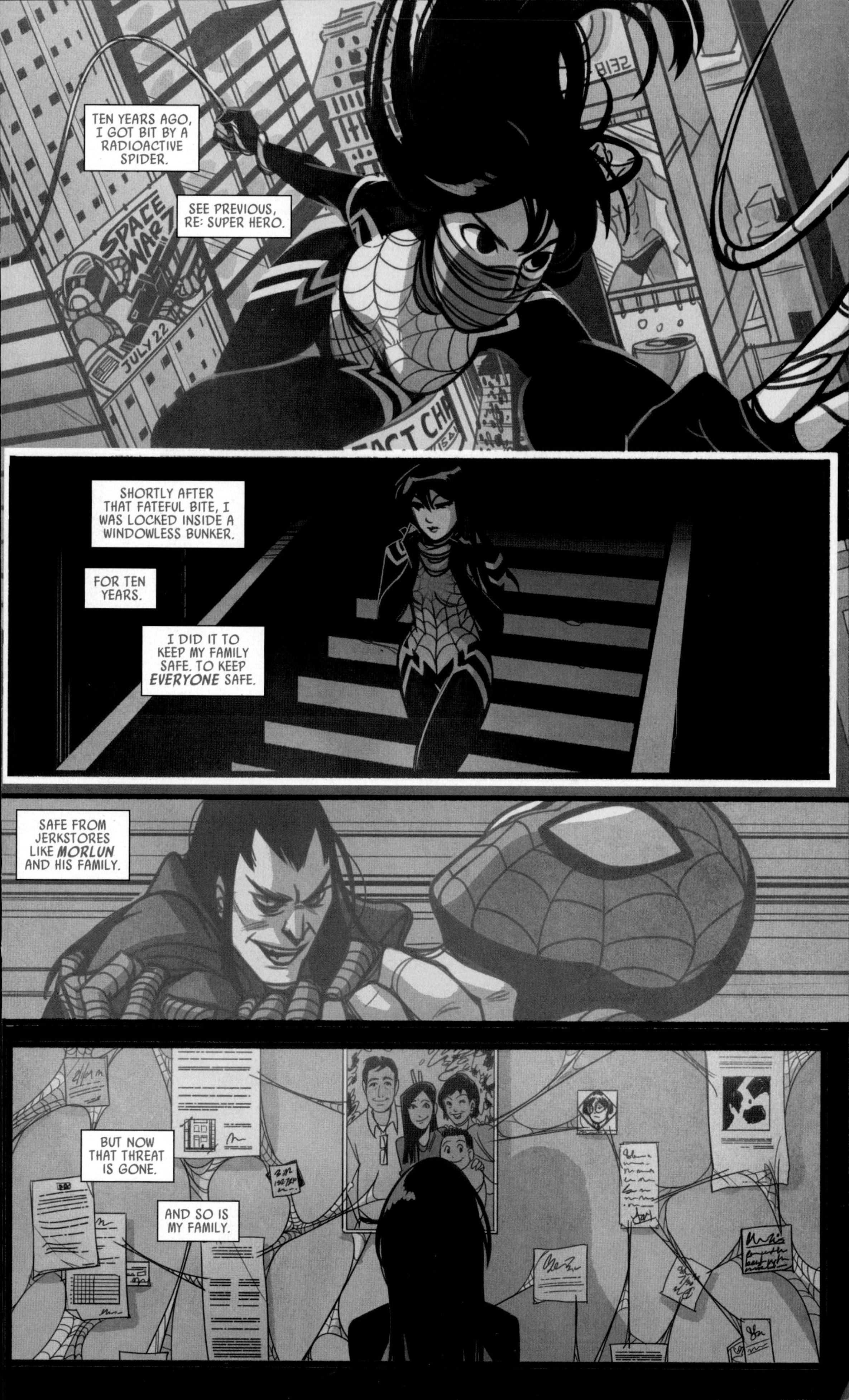
TEN YEARS AGO, I GOT BIT BY A RADIOACTIVE SPIDER.
SEE PREVIOUS, RE: SUPER HERO.
SPACE WAR 7
JULY 22
SHORTLY AFTER THAT FATEFUL BITE, I WAS LOCKED INSIDE A WINDOWLESS BUNKER.
FOR TEN YEARS.
I DID IT TO KEEP MY FAMILY SAFE. TO KEEP *EVERYONE* SAFE.
SAFE FROM JERKSTORES LIKE *MORLUN* AND HIS FAMILY.
BUT NOW THAT THREAT IS GONE.
AND SO IS MY FAMILY.

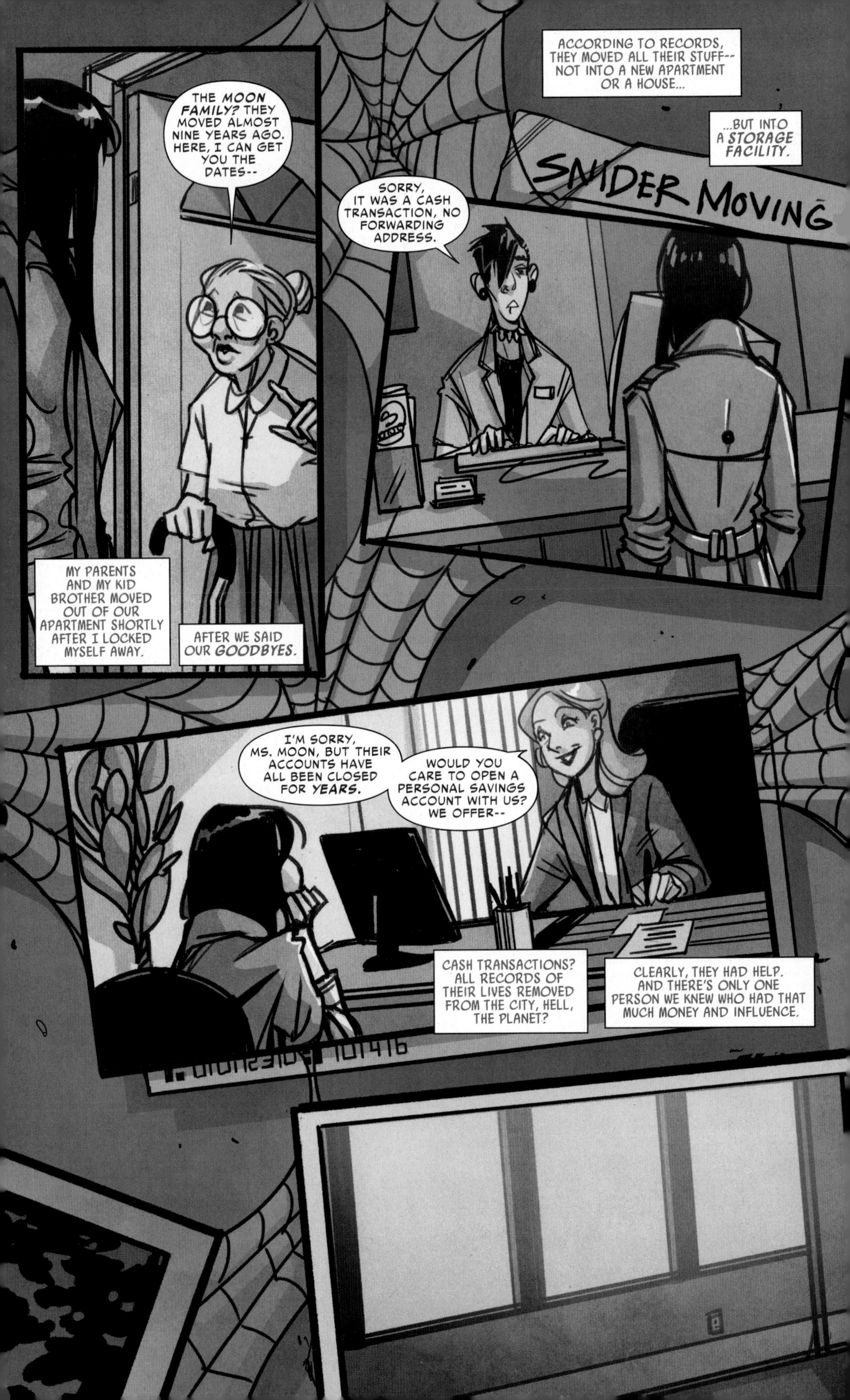
THE MOON FAMILY? THEY MOVED ALMOST NINE YEARS AGO. HERE, I CAN GET YOU THE DATES--
MY PARENTS AND MY KID BROTHER MOVED OUT OF OUR APARTMENT SHORTLY AFTER I LOCKED MYSELF AWAY.
AFTER WE SAID OUR GOODBYES.
ACCORDING TO RECORDS, THEY MOVED ALL THEIR STUFF-- NOT INTO A NEW APARTMENT OR A HOUSE...
...BUT INTO A STORAGE FACILITY.
SNIDER MOVING
SORRY, IT WAS A CASH TRANSACTION, NO FORWARDING ADDRESS.
I'M SORRY, MS. MOON, BUT THEIR ACCOUNTS HAVE ALL BEEN CLOSED FOR YEARS.
WOULD YOU CARE TO OPEN A PERSONAL SAVINGS ACCOUNT WITH US? WE OFFER--
CASH TRANSACTIONS? ALL RECORDS OF THEIR LIVES REMOVED FROM THE CITY, HELL, THE PLANET?
CLEARLY, THEY HAD HELP. AND THERE'S ONLY ONE PERSON WE KNEW WHO HAD THAT MUCH MONEY AND INFLUENCE.

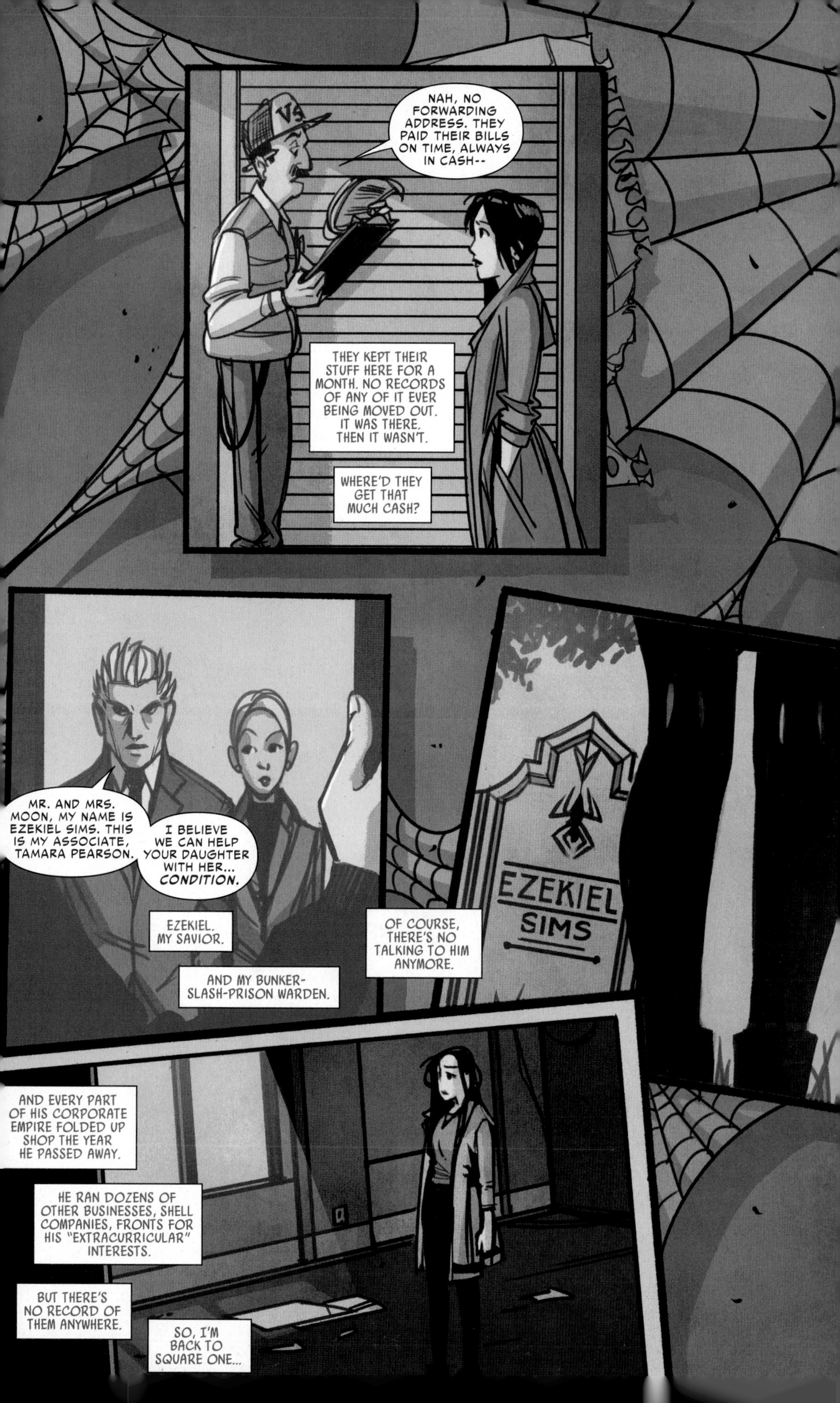

NAH, NO FORWARDING ADDRESS. THEY PAID THEIR BILLS ON TIME, ALWAYS IN CASH--
THEY KEPT THEIR STUFF HERE FOR A MONTH. NO RECORDS OF ANY OF IT EVER BEING MOVED OUT. IT WAS THERE. THEN IT WASN'T.
WHERE'D THEY GET THAT MUCH CASH?
MR. AND MRS. MOON, MY NAME IS EZEKIEL SIMS. THIS IS MY ASSOCIATE, TAMARA PEARSON.
I BELIEVE WE CAN HELP YOUR DAUGHTER WITH HER... CONDITION.
EZEKIEL. MY SAVIOR.
AND MY BUNKER-SLASH-PRISON WARDEN.
EZEKIEL SIMS
OF COURSE, THERE'S NO TALKING TO HIM ANYMORE.
AND EVERY PART OF HIS CORPORATE EMPIRE FOLDED UP SHOP THE YEAR HE PASSED AWAY.
HE RAN DOZENS OF OTHER BUSINESSES, SHELL COMPANIES, FRONTS FOR HIS "EXTRACURRICULAR" INTERESTS.
BUT THERE'S NO RECORD OF THEM ANYWHERE.
SO, I'M BACK TO SQUARE ONE...

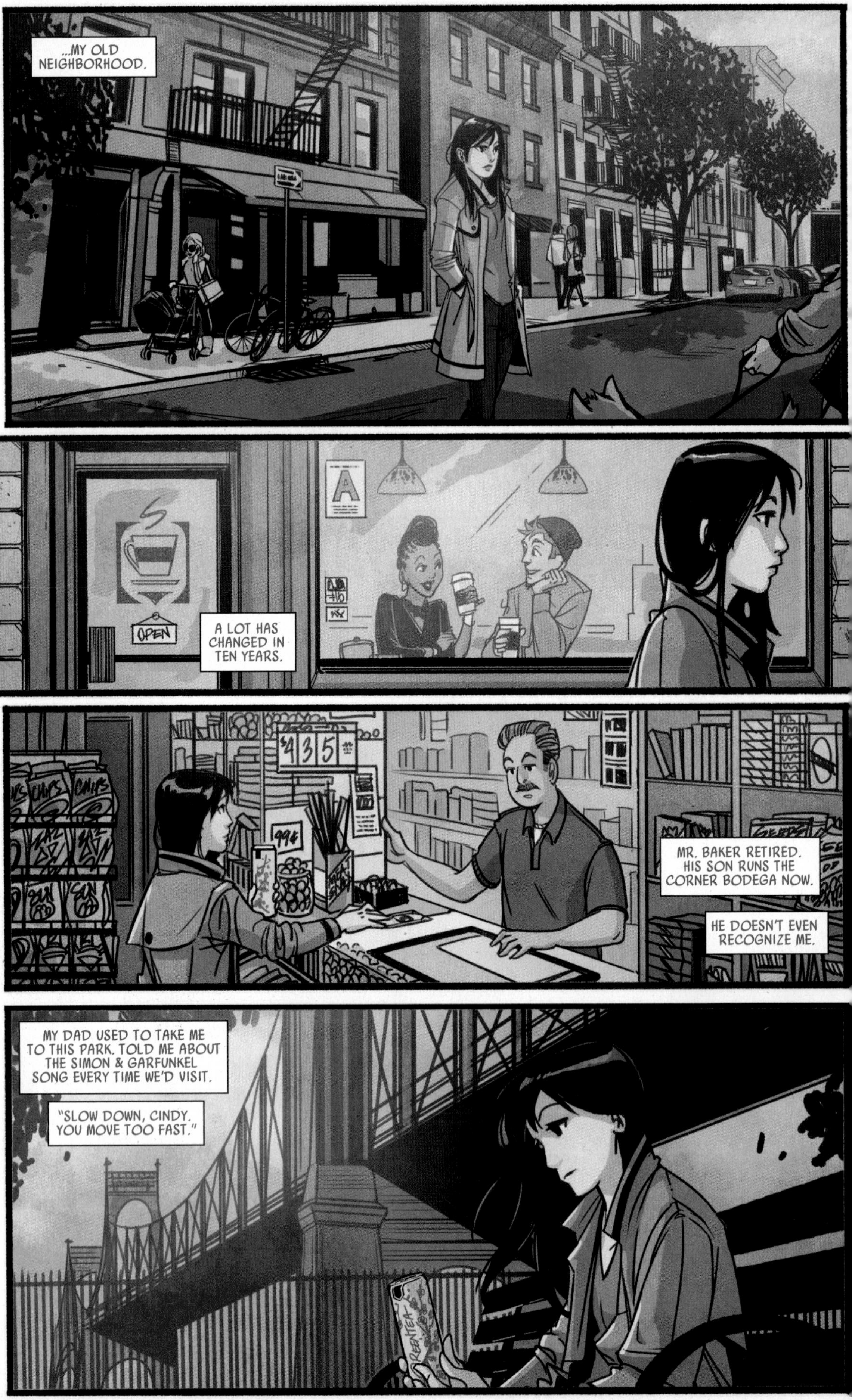

...MY OLD NEIGHBORHOOD.
OPEN
A LOT HAS CHANGED IN TEN YEARS.
$4 3 5
99¢
MR. BAKER RETIRED. HIS SON RUNS THE CORNER BODEGA NOW.
HE DOESN'T EVEN RECOGNIZE ME.
MY DAD USED TO TAKE ME TO THIS PARK. TOLD ME ABOUT THE SIMON & GARFUNKEL SONG EVERY TIME WE'D VISIT.
"SLOW DOWN, CINDY. YOU MOVE TOO FAST."
GREEN TEA

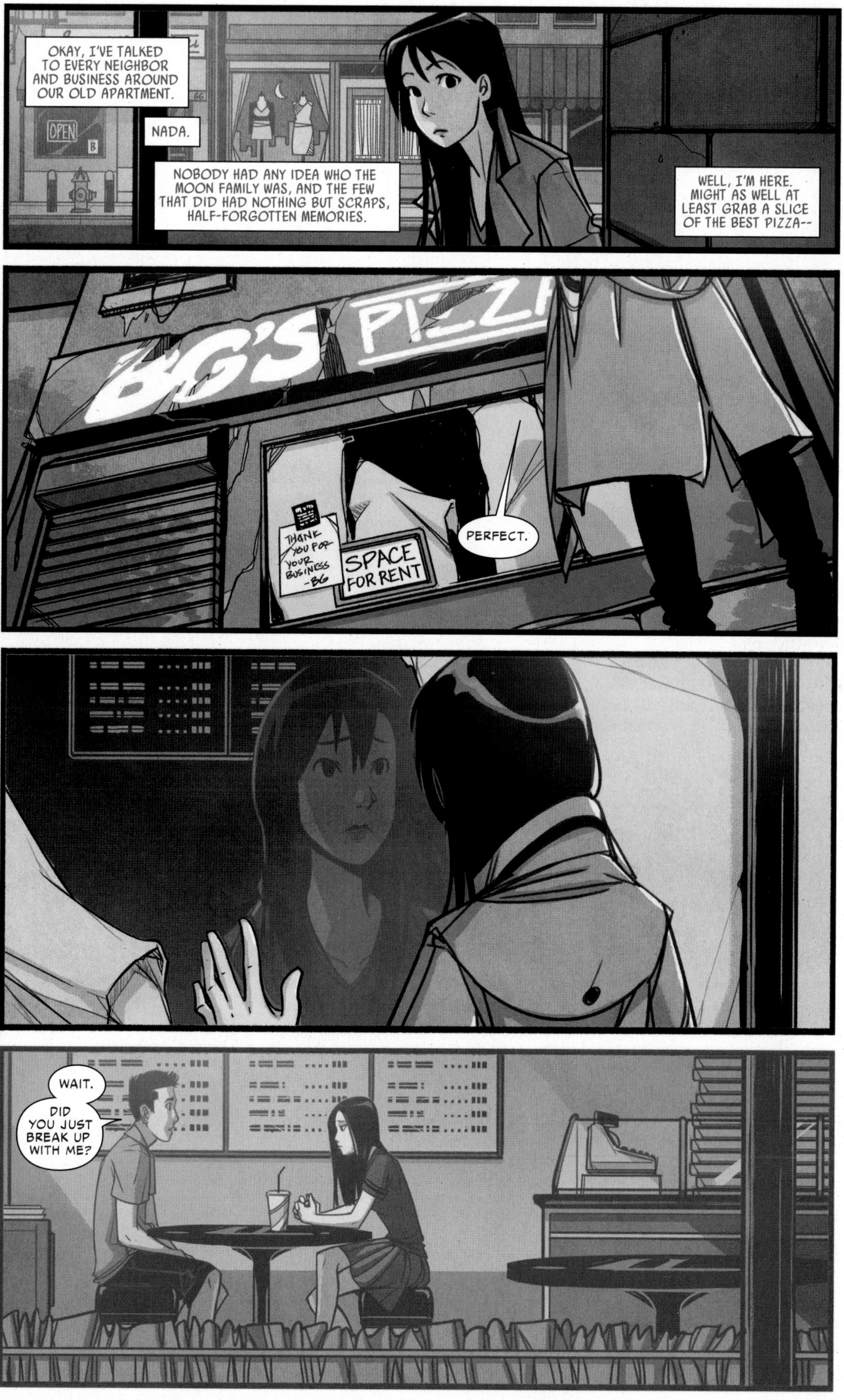

OKAY, I'VE TALKED TO EVERY NEIGHBOR AND BUSINESS AROUND OUR OLD APARTMENT.
NADA.
NOBODY HAD ANY IDEA WHO THE MOON FAMILY WAS, AND THE FEW THAT DID HAD NOTHING BUT SCRAPS, HALF-FORGOTTEN MEMORIES.
WELL, I'M HERE. MIGHT AS WELL AT LEAST GRAB A SLICE OF THE BEST PIZZA--
OPEN
BG'S PIZZ
THANK YOU FOR YOUR BUSINESS -BG
SPACE FOR RENT
PERFECT.
WAIT.
DID YOU JUST BREAK UP WITH ME?

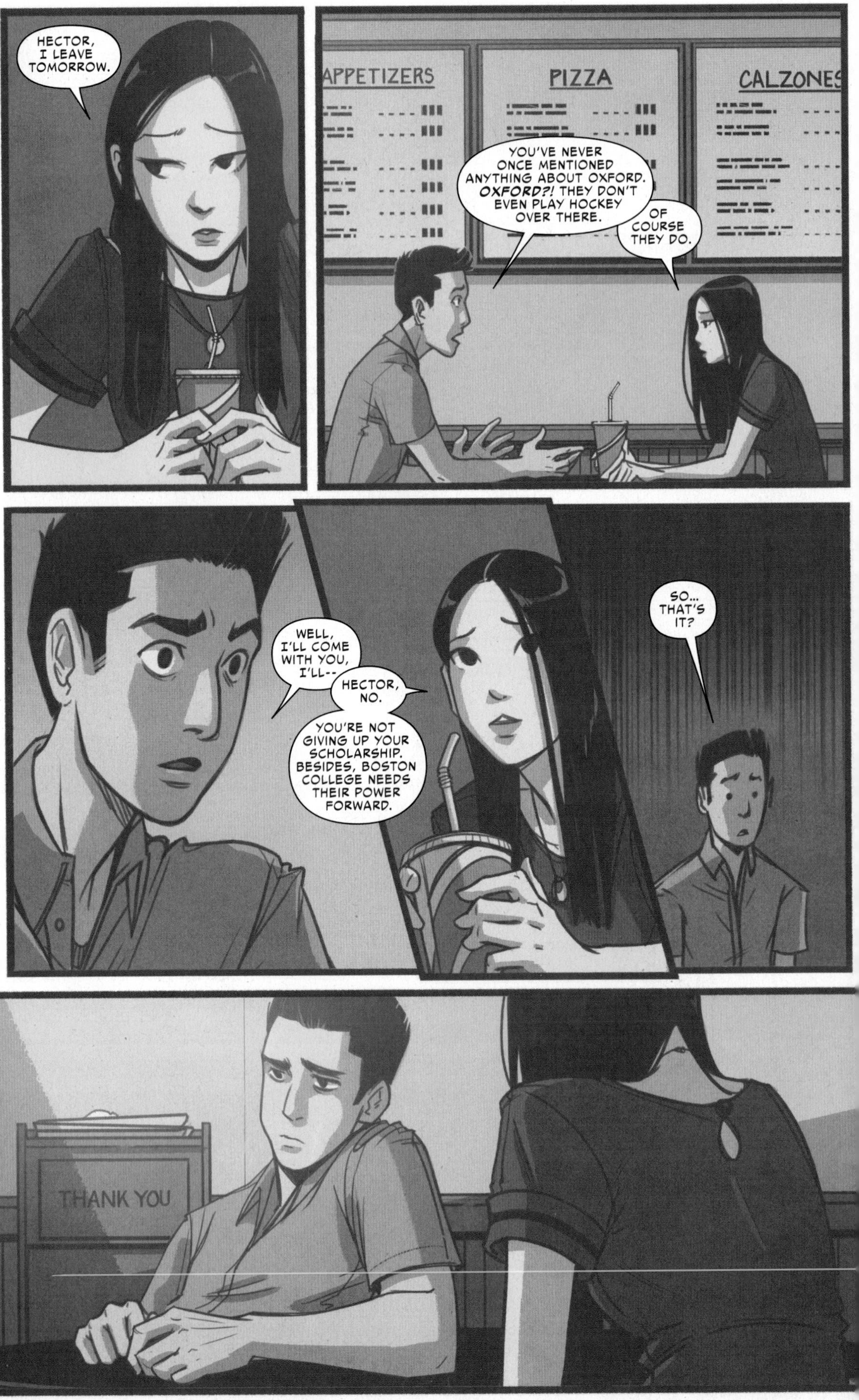
HECTOR, I LEAVE TOMORROW.
APPETIZERS
PIZZA
CALZONES
YOU'VE NEVER ONCE MENTIONED ANYTHING ABOUT OXFORD. *OXFORD?!* THEY DON'T EVEN PLAY HOCKEY OVER THERE.
OF COURSE THEY DO.
WELL, I'LL COME WITH YOU, I'LL--
HECTOR, NO.
YOU'RE NOT GIVING UP YOUR SCHOLARSHIP. BESIDES, BOSTON COLLEGE NEEDS THEIR POWER FORWARD.
SO... THAT'S IT?
THANK YOU

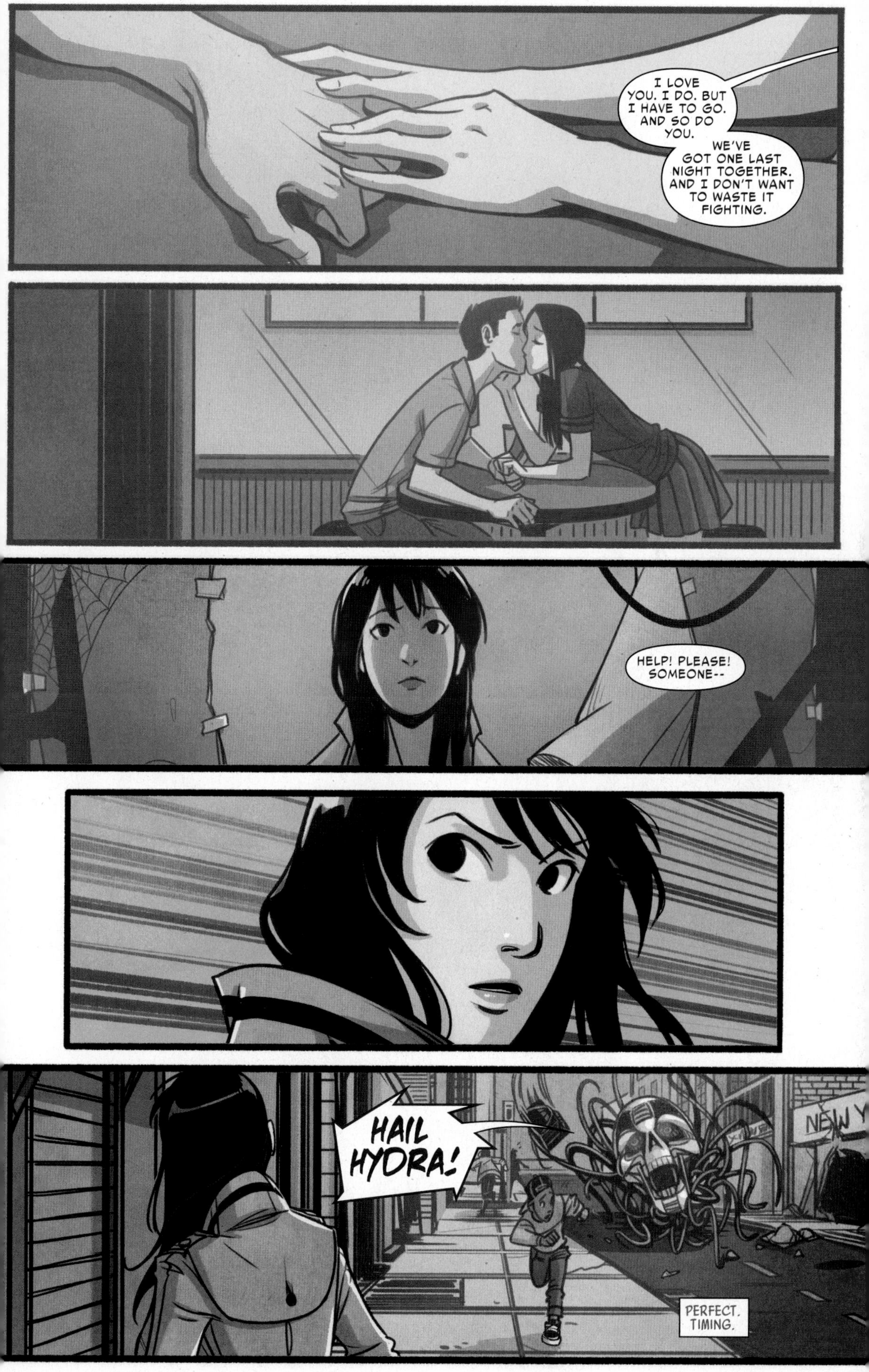

I LOVE YOU. I DO. BUT I HAVE TO GO. AND SO DO YOU.
WE'VE GOT ONE LAST NIGHT TOGETHER. AND I DON'T WANT TO WASTE IT FIGHTING.
HELP! PLEASE! SOMEONE--
HAIL HYDRA!
PERFECT. TIMING.

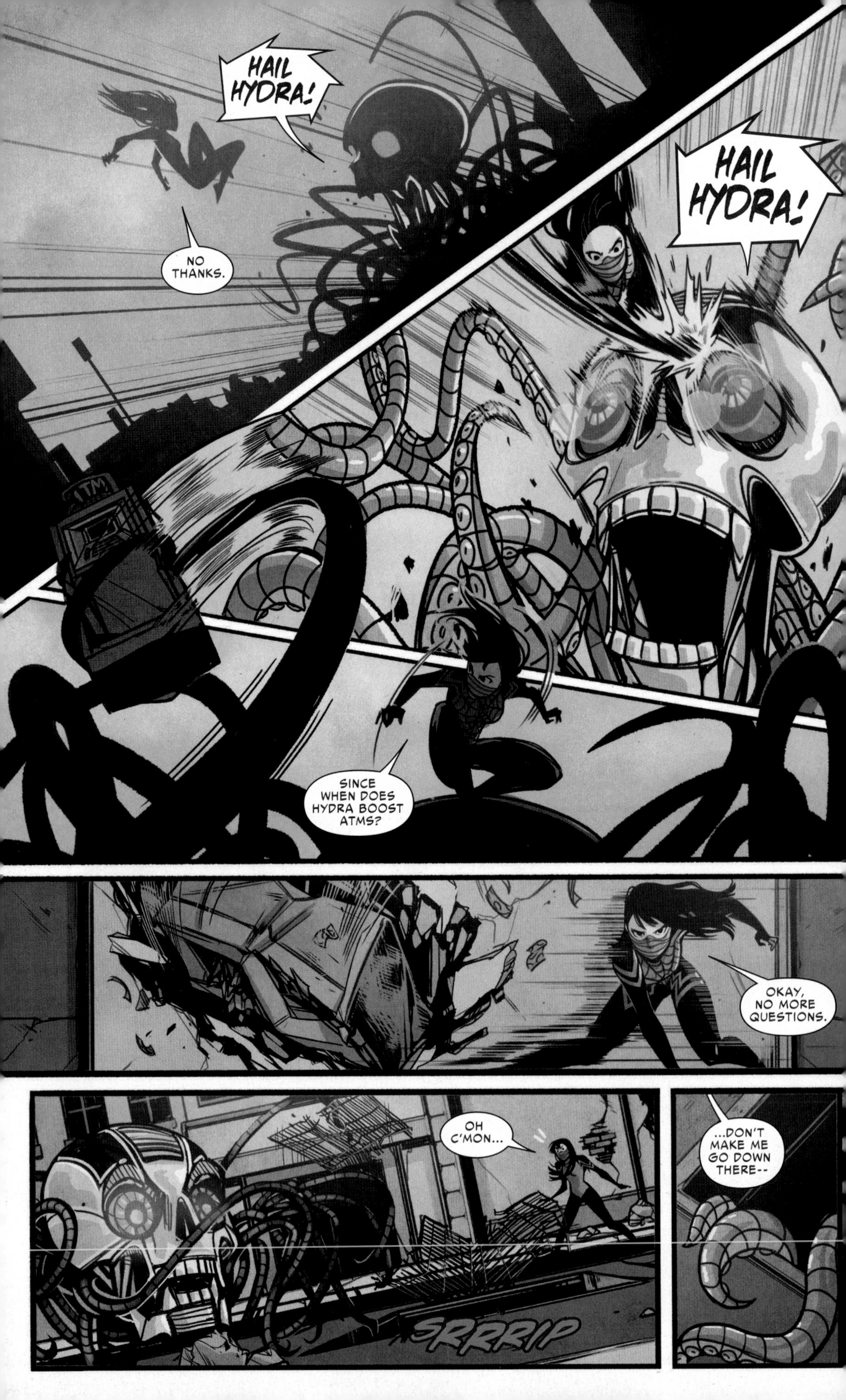
HAIL HYDRA!
NO THANKS.
HAIL HYDRA!
SINCE WHEN DOES HYDRA BOOST ATMS?
ATM
OKAY, NO MORE QUESTIONS.
OH C'MON...
...DON'T MAKE ME GO DOWN THERE--
SRRRIP

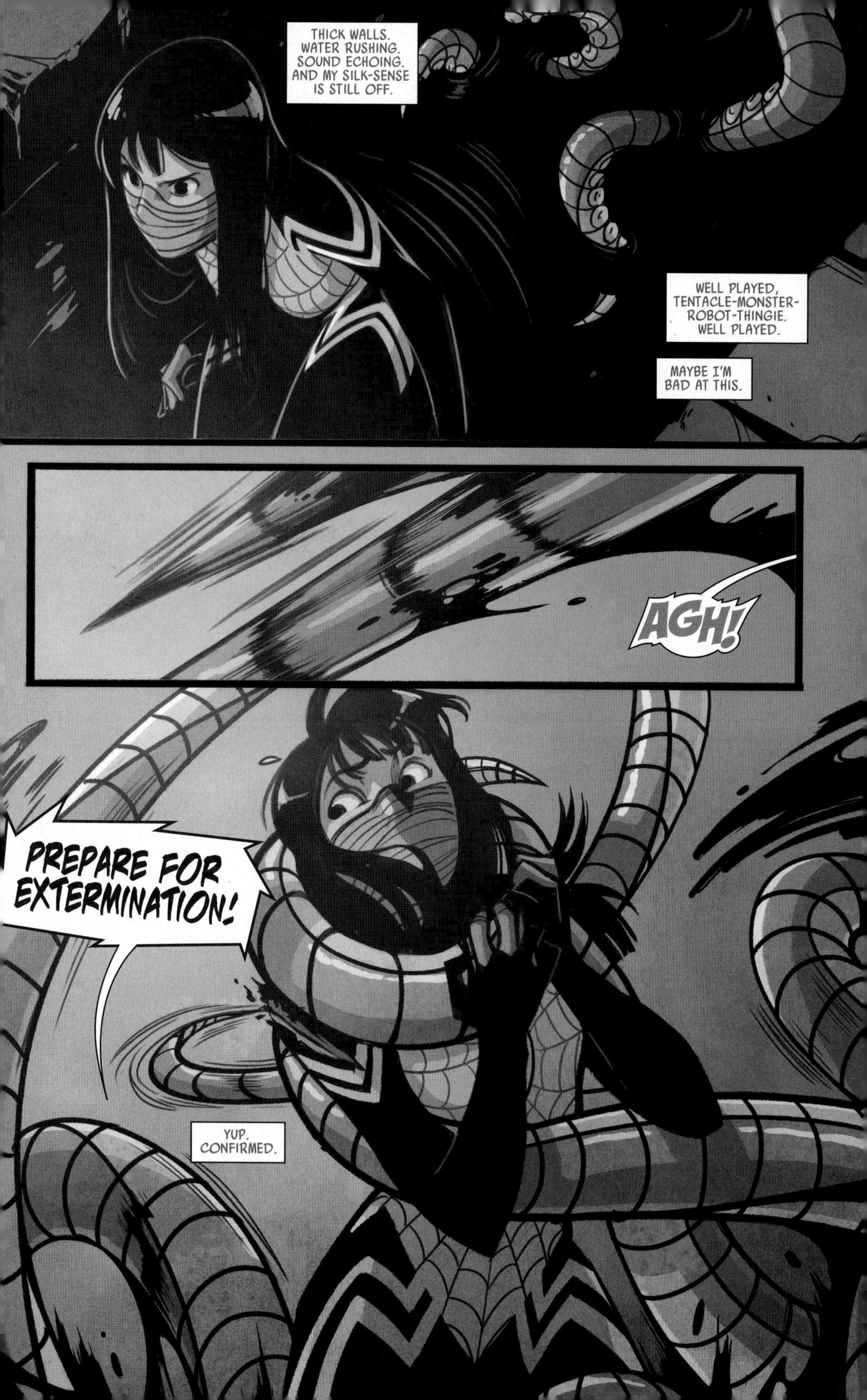
THICK WALLS. WATER RUSHING. SOUND ECHOING. AND MY SILK-SENSE IS STILL OFF.
WELL PLAYED, TENTACLE-MONSTER-ROBOT-THINGIE. WELL PLAYED.
MAYBE I'M BAD AT THIS.
AGH!
PREPARE FOR EXTERMINATION!
YUP. CONFIRMED.

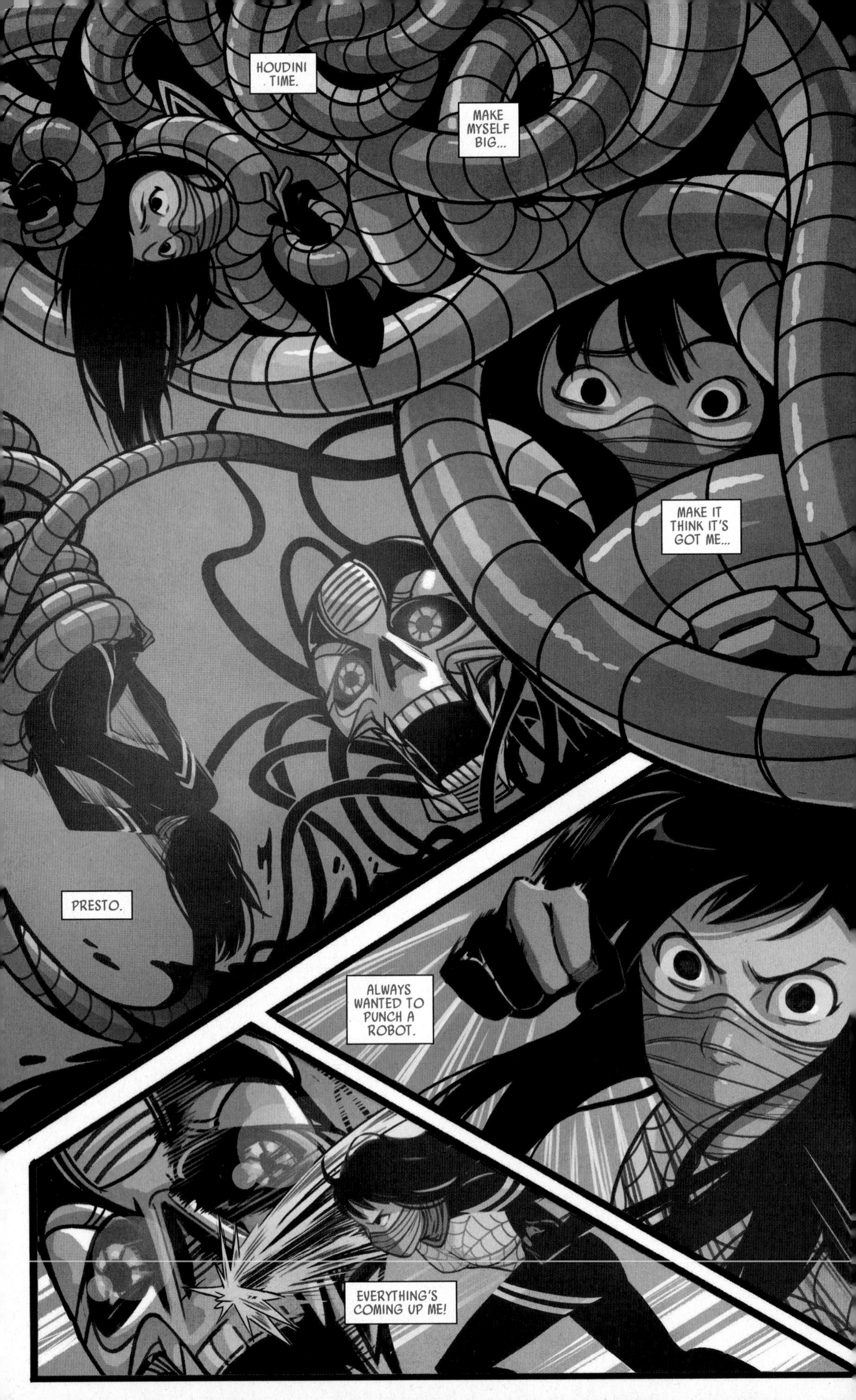
HOUDINI TIME.
MAKE MYSELF BIG...
MAKE IT THINK IT'S GOT ME...
PRESTO.
ALWAYS WANTED TO PUNCH A ROBOT.
EVERYTHING'S COMING UP ME!

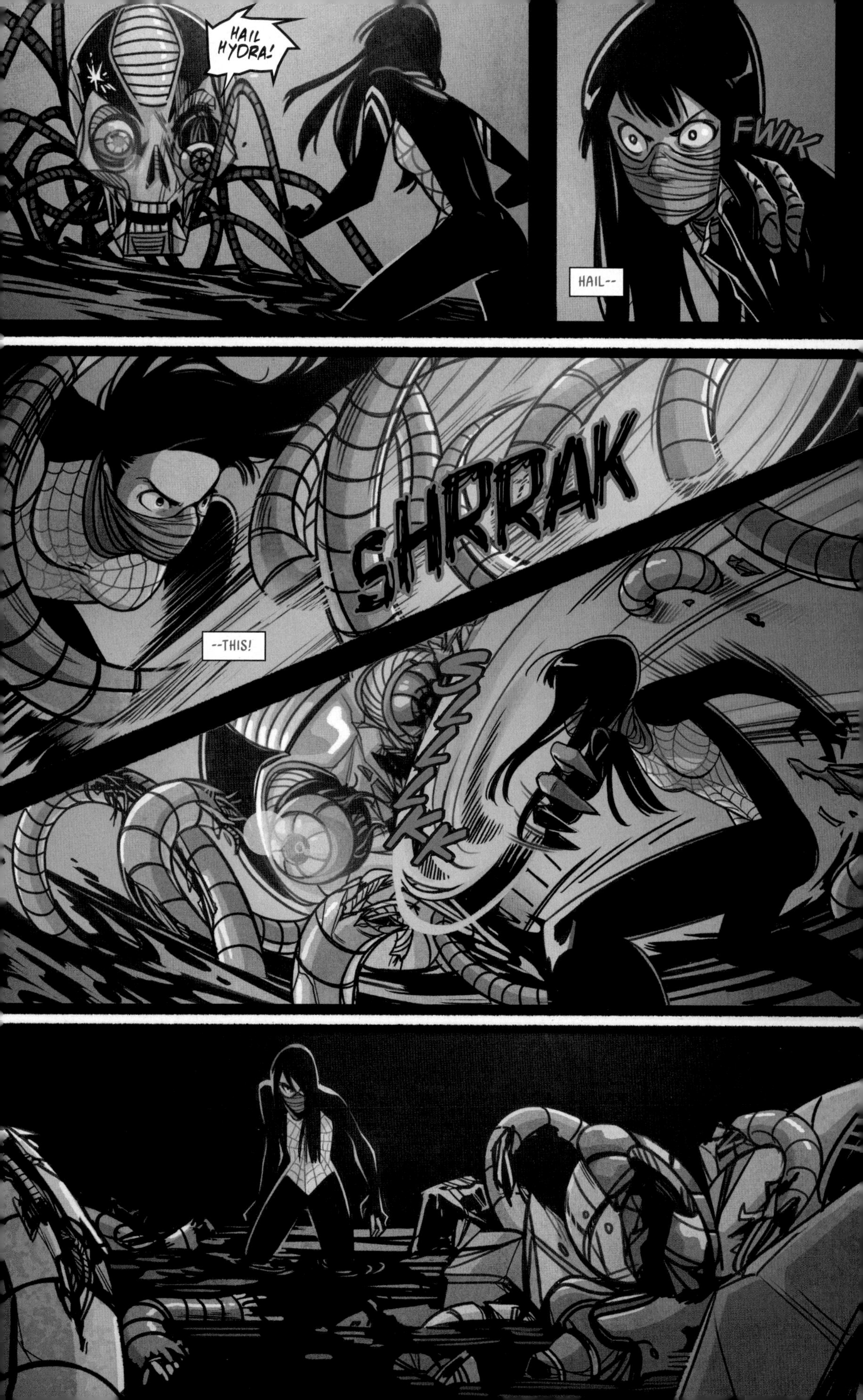
HAIL HYDRA!
FWIK
HAIL--
SHRRAK
--THIS!
SNIKKK

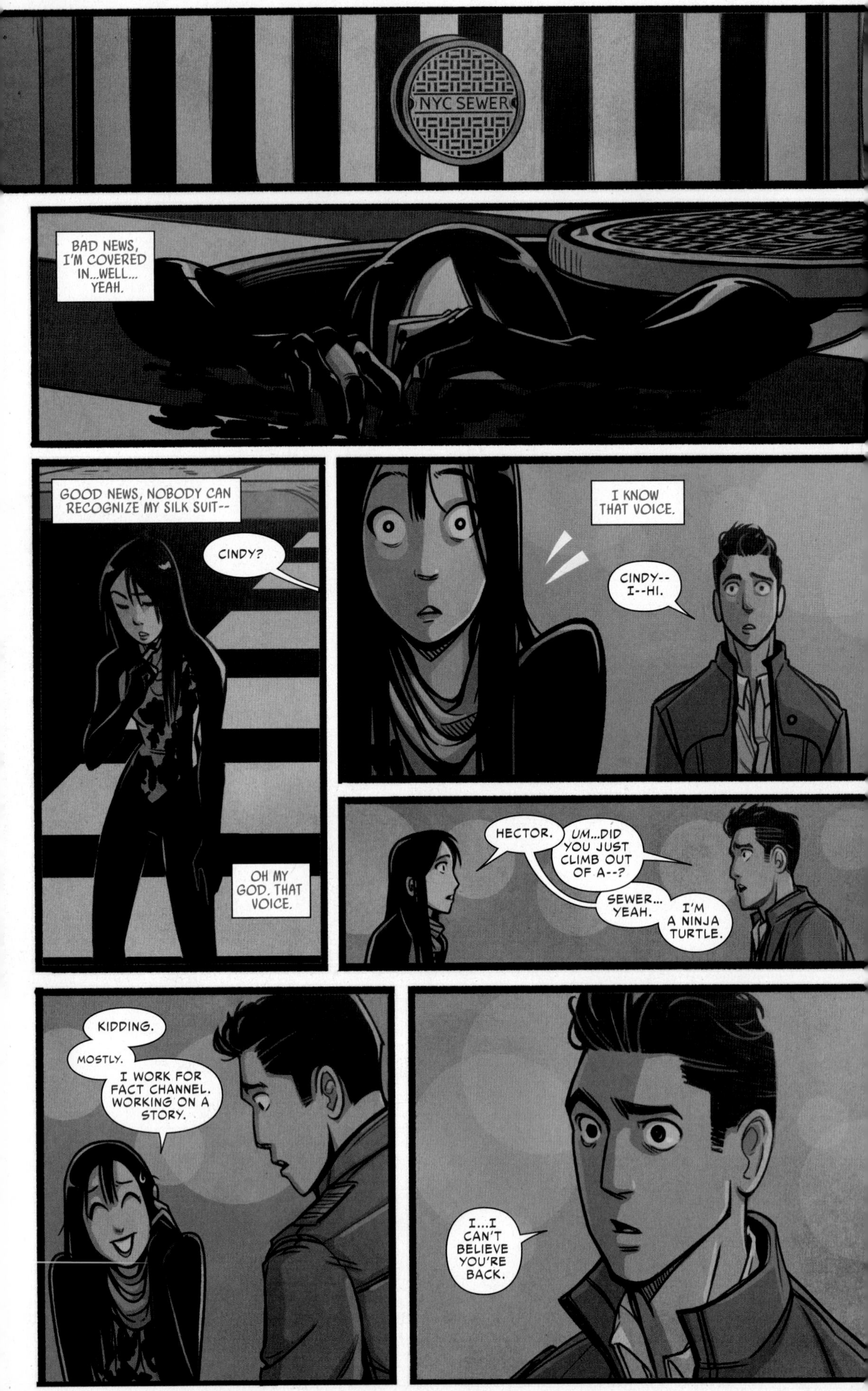
NYC SEWER
BAD NEWS, I'M COVERED IN...WELL... YEAH.
GOOD NEWS, NOBODY CAN RECOGNIZE MY SILK SUIT--
CINDY?
OH MY GOD. THAT VOICE.
I KNOW THAT VOICE.
CINDY-- I--HI.
HECTOR.
UM...DID YOU JUST CLIMB OUT OF A--?
SEWER... YEAH.
I'M A NINJA TURTLE.
KIDDING.
MOSTLY.
I WORK FOR FACT CHANNEL. WORKING ON A STORY.
I...I CAN'T BELIEVE YOU'RE BACK.

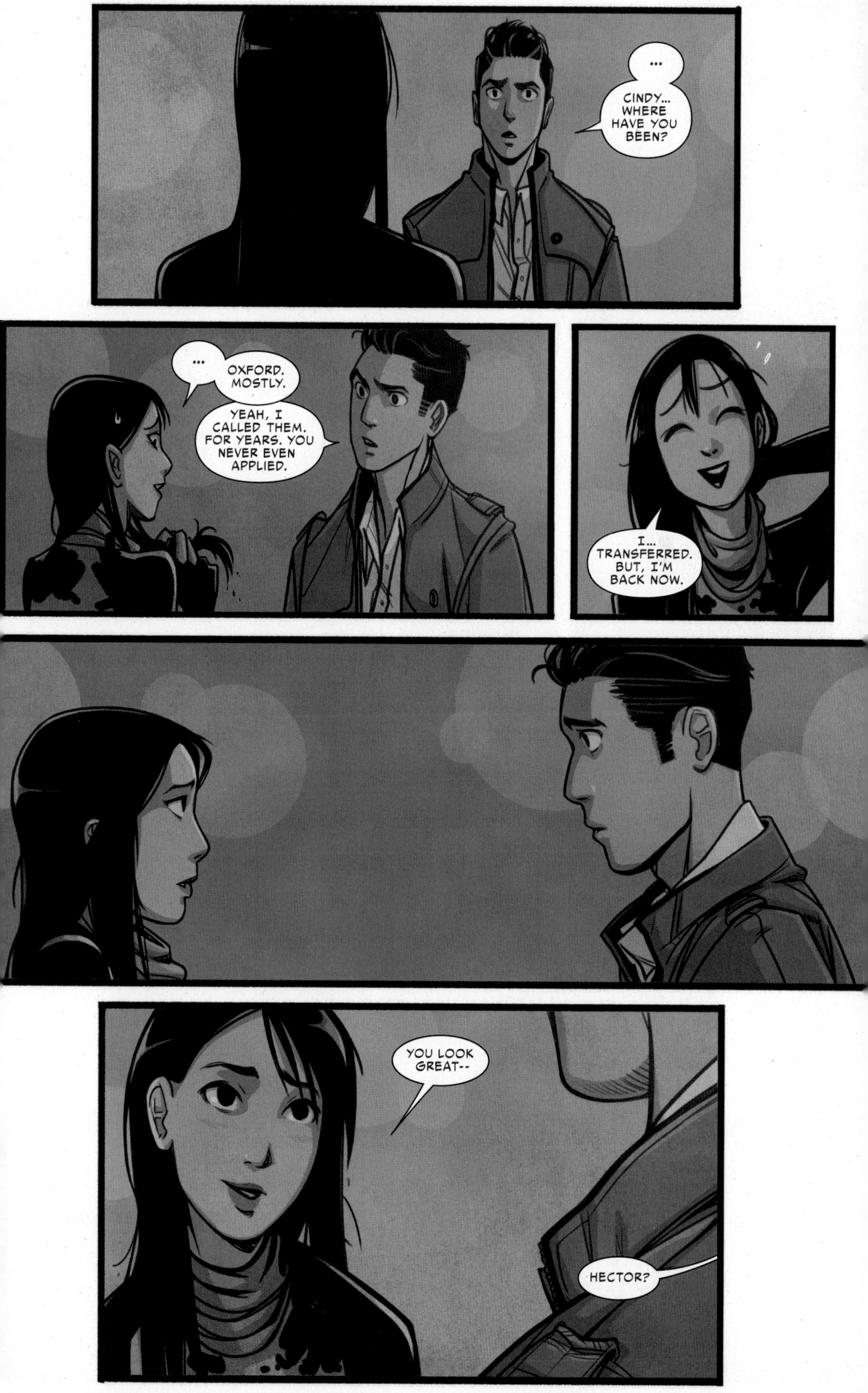
...
CINDY... WHERE HAVE YOU BEEN?
...
OXFORD. MOSTLY.
YEAH, I CALLED THEM. FOR YEARS. YOU NEVER EVEN APPLIED.
I... TRANSFERRED. BUT, I'M BACK NOW.
YOU LOOK GREAT--
HECTOR?

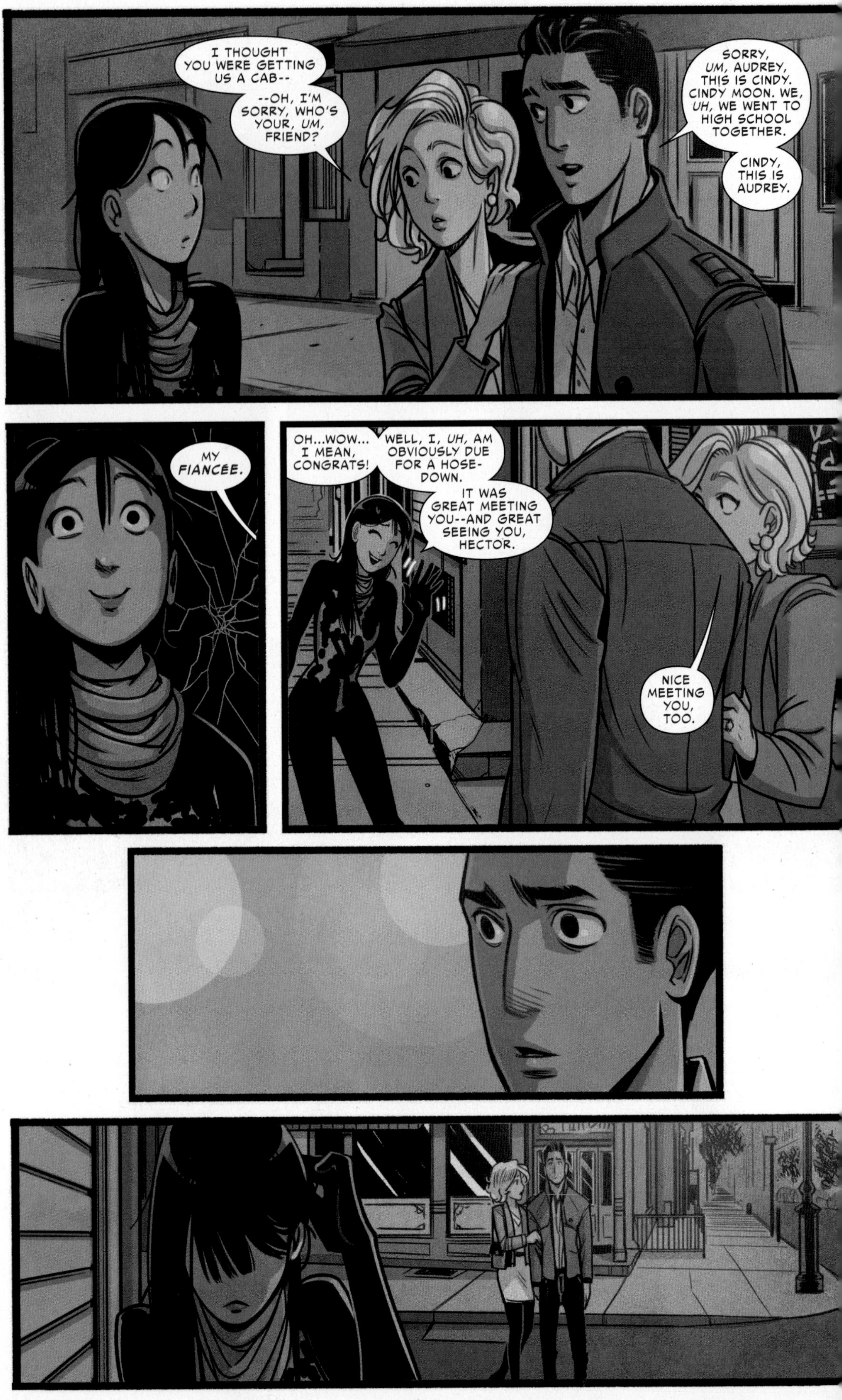
I THOUGHT YOU WERE GETTING US A CAB--
--OH, I'M SORRY, WHO'S YOUR, UM, FRIEND?
SORRY, UM, AUDREY, THIS IS CINDY. CINDY MOON. WE, UH, WE WENT TO HIGH SCHOOL TOGETHER.
CINDY, THIS IS AUDREY.
MY FIANCÉE.
OH...WOW... I MEAN, CONGRATS!
WELL, I, UH, AM OBVIOUSLY DUE FOR A HOSE-DOWN.
IT WAS GREAT MEETING YOU--AND GREAT SEEING YOU, HECTOR.
NICE MEETING YOU, TOO.

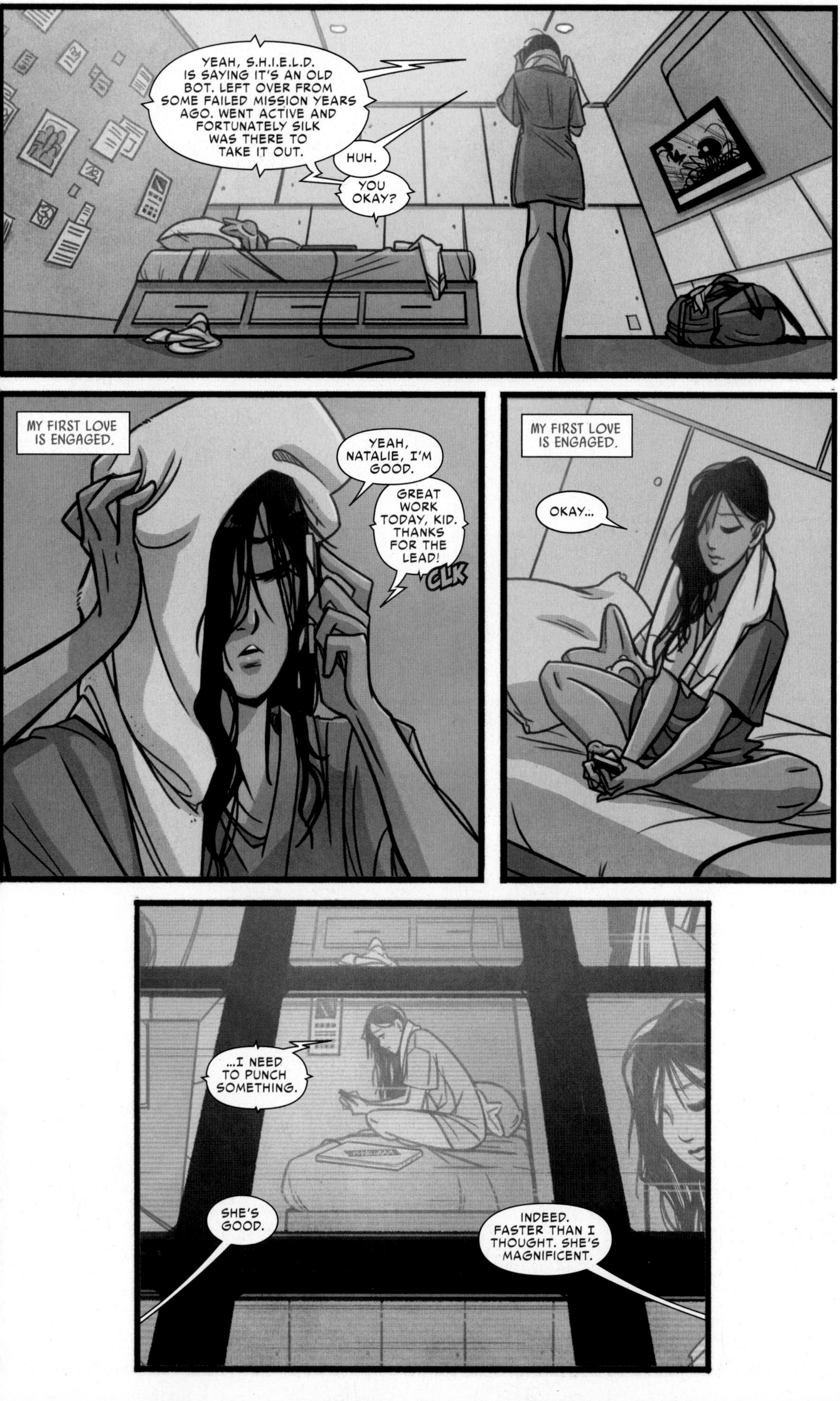
YEAH, S.H.I.E.L.D. IS SAYING IT'S AN OLD BOT. LEFT OVER FROM SOME FAILED MISSION YEARS AGO. WENT ACTIVE AND FORTUNATELY SILK WAS THERE TO TAKE IT OUT.
HUH.
YOU OKAY?
MY FIRST LOVE IS ENGAGED.
YEAH, NATALIE, I'M GOOD.
GREAT WORK TODAY, KID. THANKS FOR THE LEAD!
CLK
MY FIRST LOVE IS ENGAGED.
OKAY...
...I NEED TO PUNCH SOMETHING.
SHE'S GOOD.
INDEED. FASTER THAN I THOUGHT. SHE'S MAGNIFICENT.

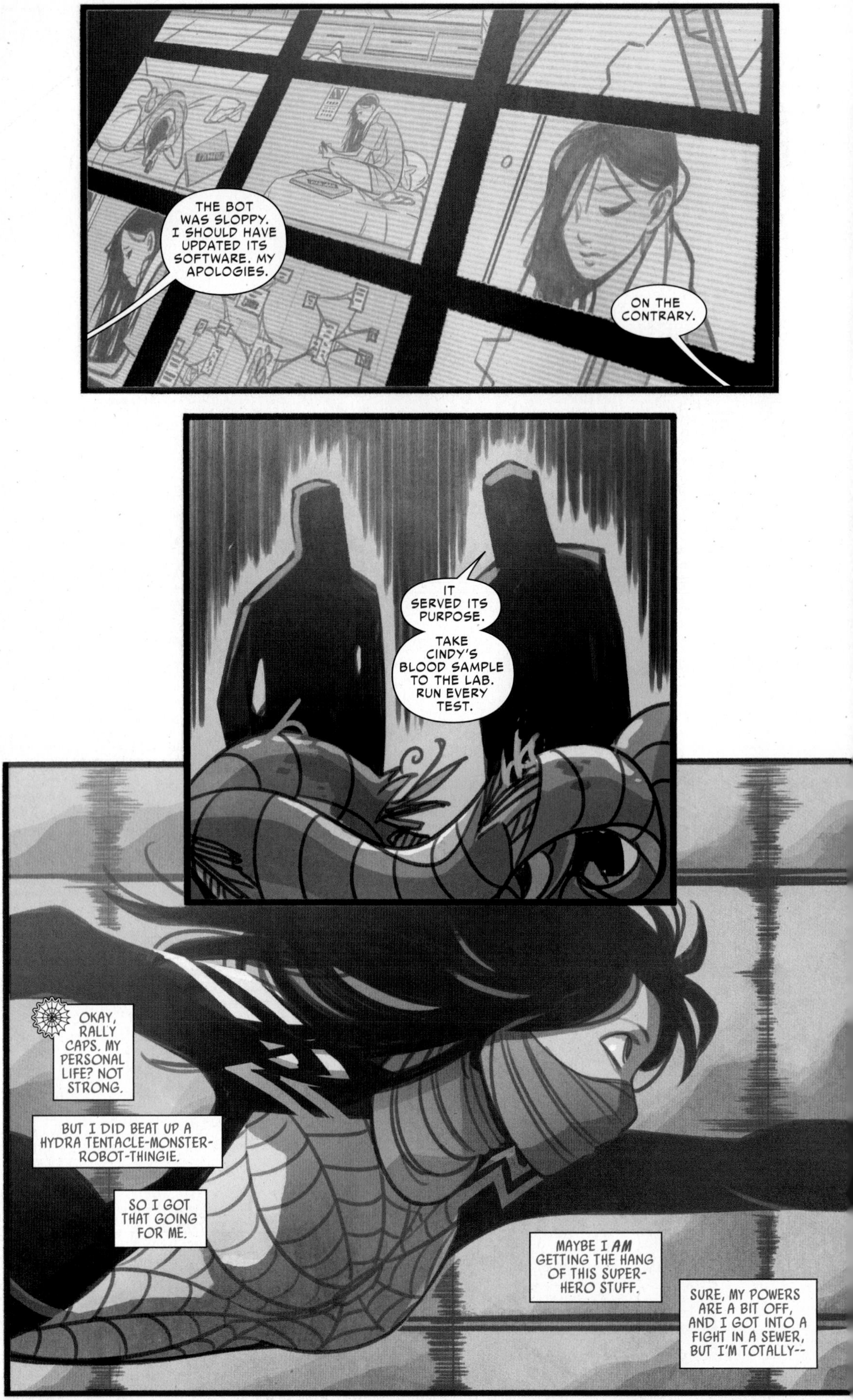
THE BOT WAS SLOPPY. I SHOULD HAVE UPDATED ITS SOFTWARE. MY APOLOGIES.
ON THE CONTRARY.
IT SERVED ITS PURPOSE.
TAKE CINDY'S BLOOD SAMPLE TO THE LAB. RUN EVERY TEST.
OKAY, RALLY CAPS. MY PERSONAL LIFE? NOT STRONG.
BUT I DID BEAT UP A HYDRA TENTACLE-MONSTER-ROBOT-THINGIE.
SO I GOT THAT GOING FOR ME.
MAYBE I AM GETTING THE HANG OF THIS SUPER-HERO STUFF.
SURE, MY POWERS ARE A BIT OFF, AND I GOT INTO A FIGHT IN A SEWER, BUT I'M TOTALLY--

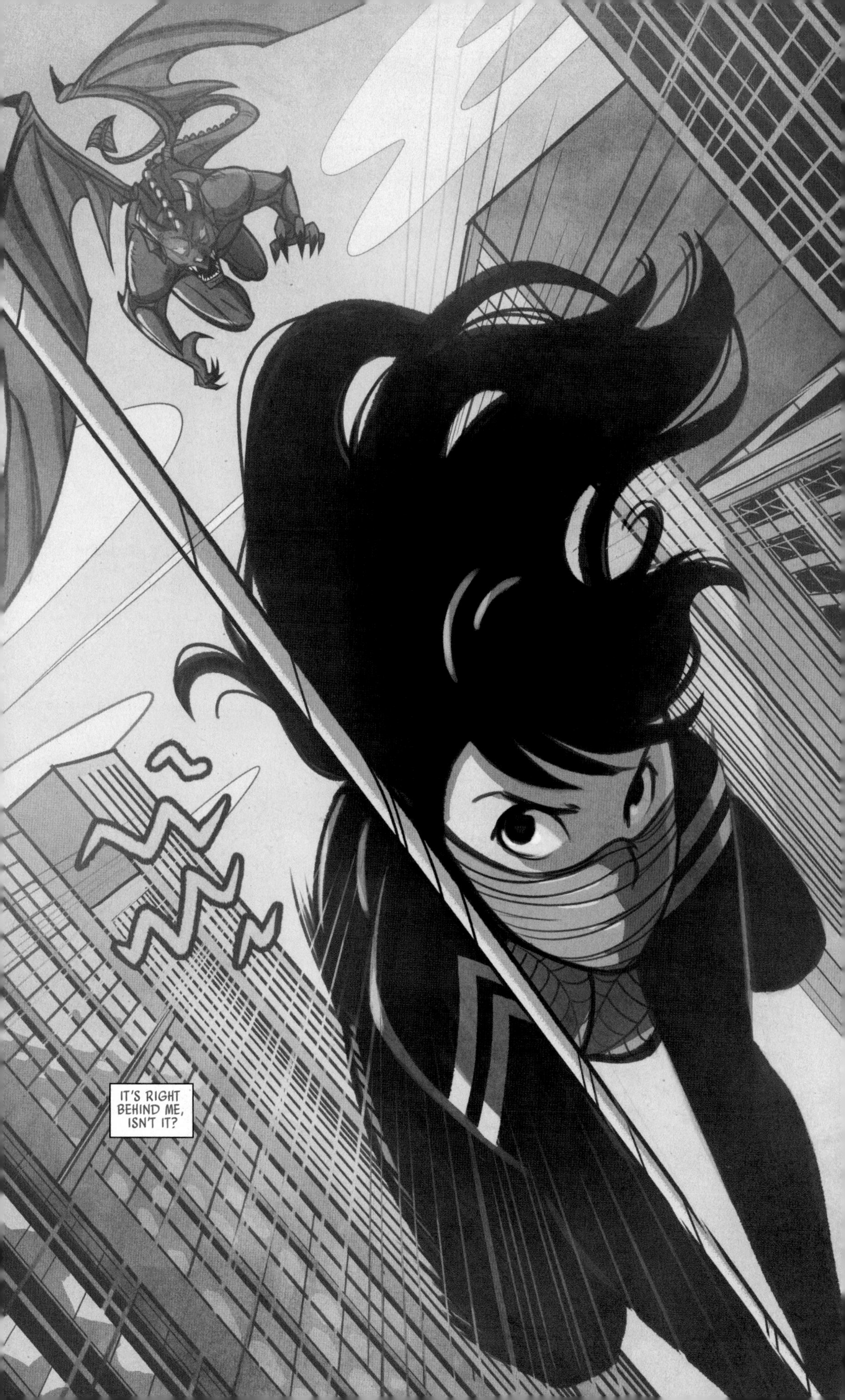
IT'S RIGHT
BEHIND ME,
ISN'T IT?

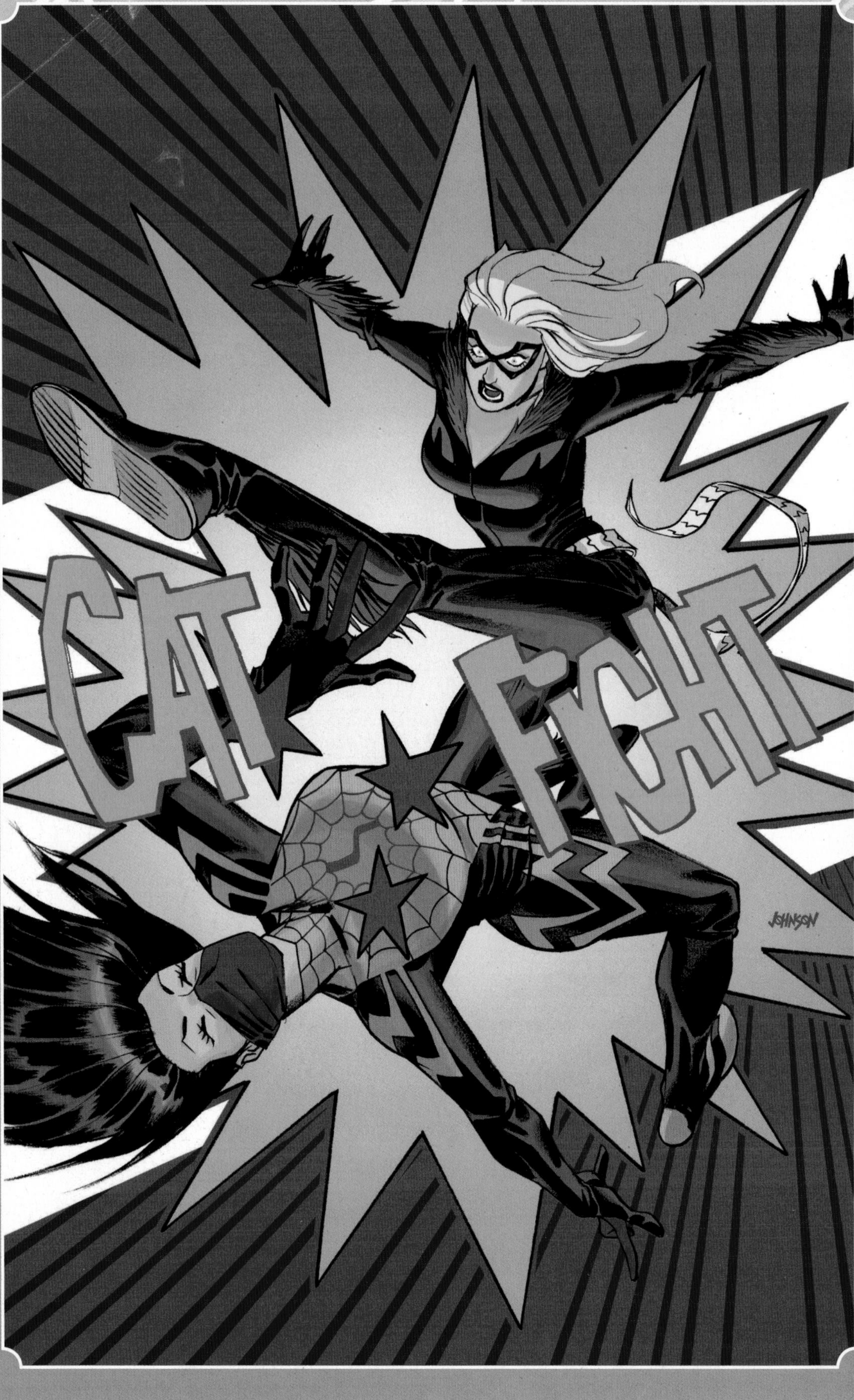
CAT FIGHT
JOHNSON

SILK (2015A) #3

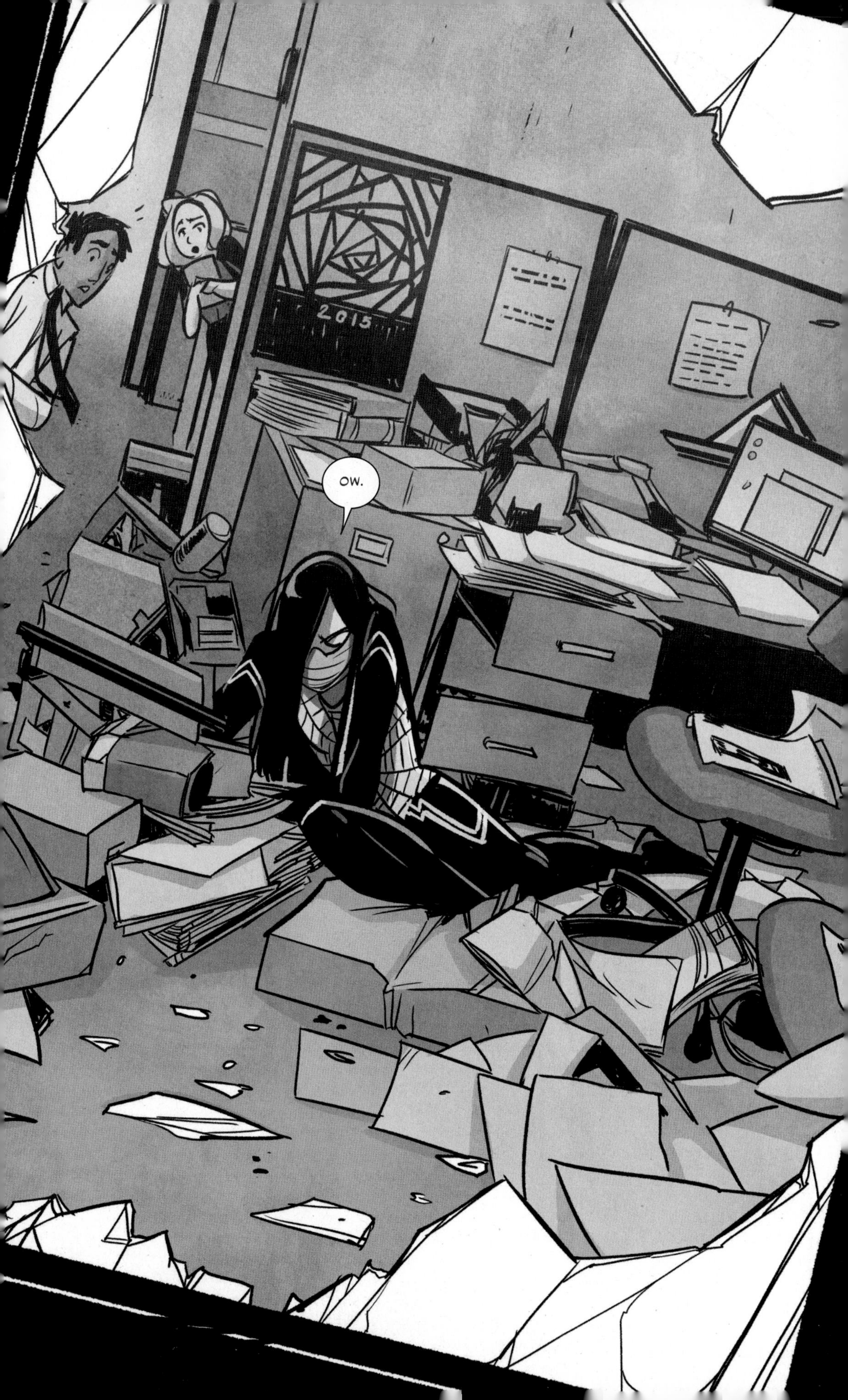

2015
OW.

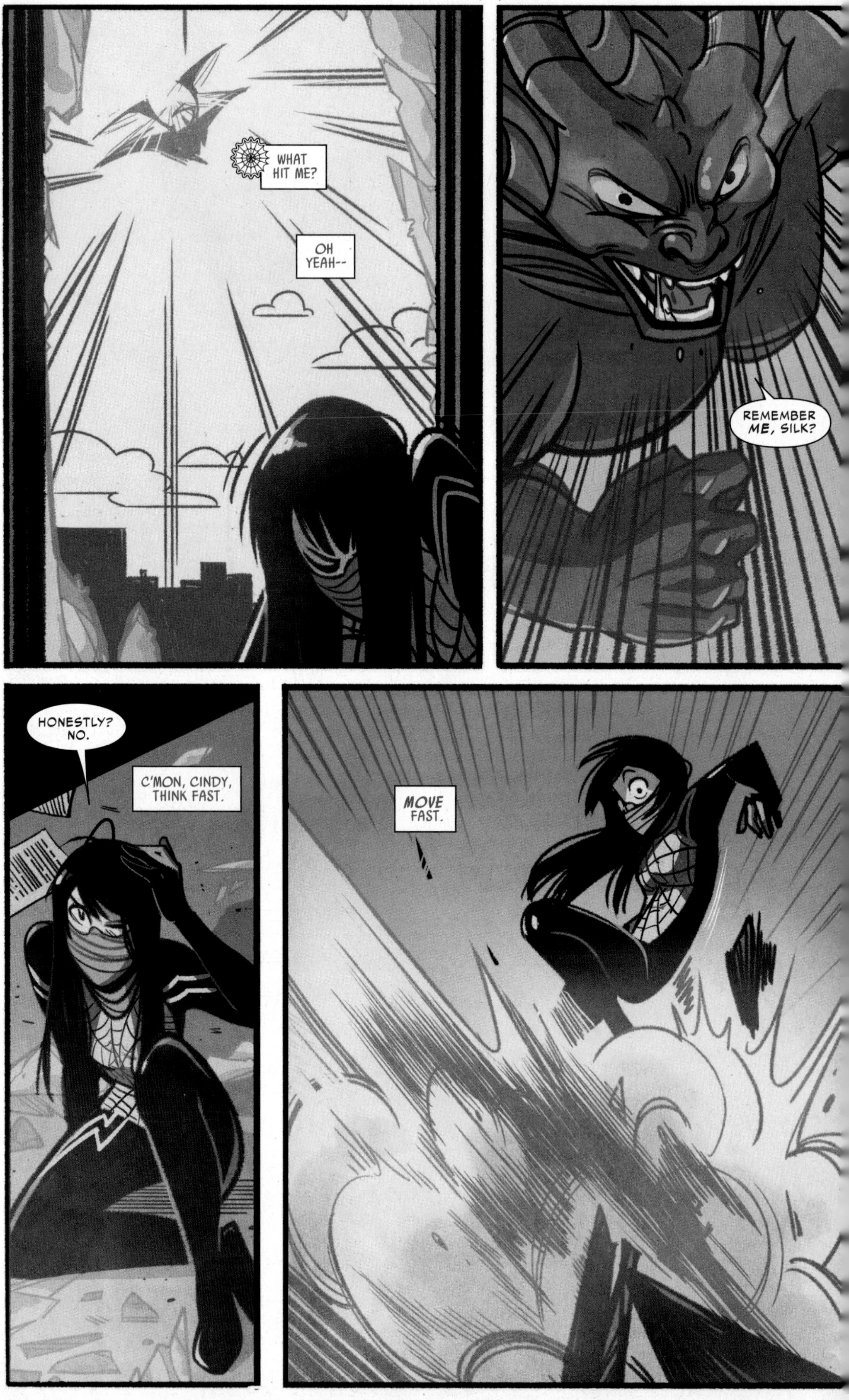
WHAT HIT ME?
OH YEAH--
REMEMBER ME, SILK?
HONESTLY? NO.
C'MON, CINDY, THINK FAST.
MOVE FAST.

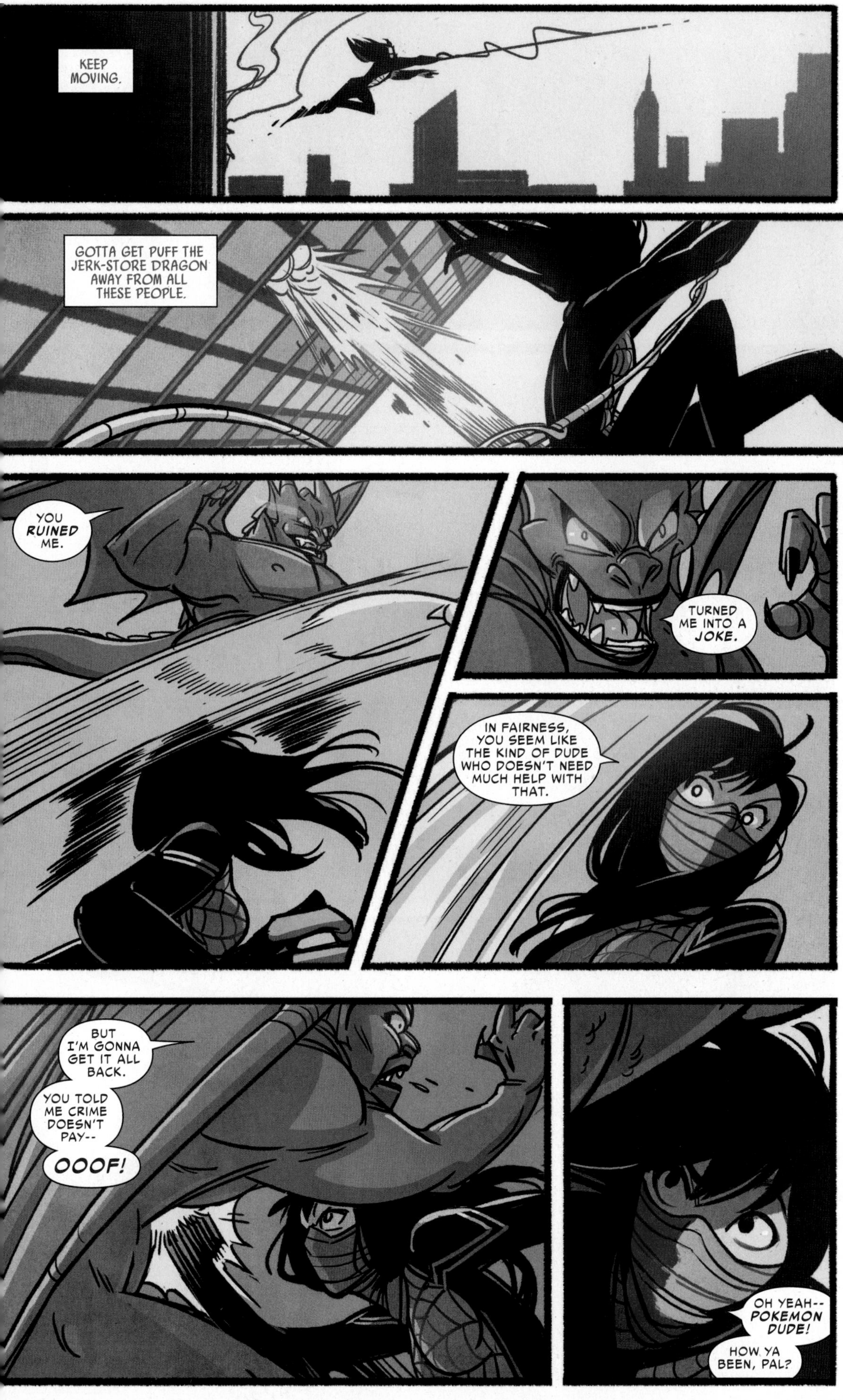
KEEP MOVING.
GOTTA GET PUFF THE JERK-STORE DRAGON AWAY FROM ALL THESE PEOPLE.
YOU RUINED ME.
TURNED ME INTO A JOKE.
IN FAIRNESS, YOU SEEM LIKE THE KIND OF DUDE WHO DOESN'T NEED MUCH HELP WITH THAT.
BUT I'M GONNA GET IT ALL BACK.
YOU TOLD ME CRIME DOESN'T PAY--
OOOF!
OH YEAH-- POKEMON DUDE!
HOW YA BEEN, PAL?

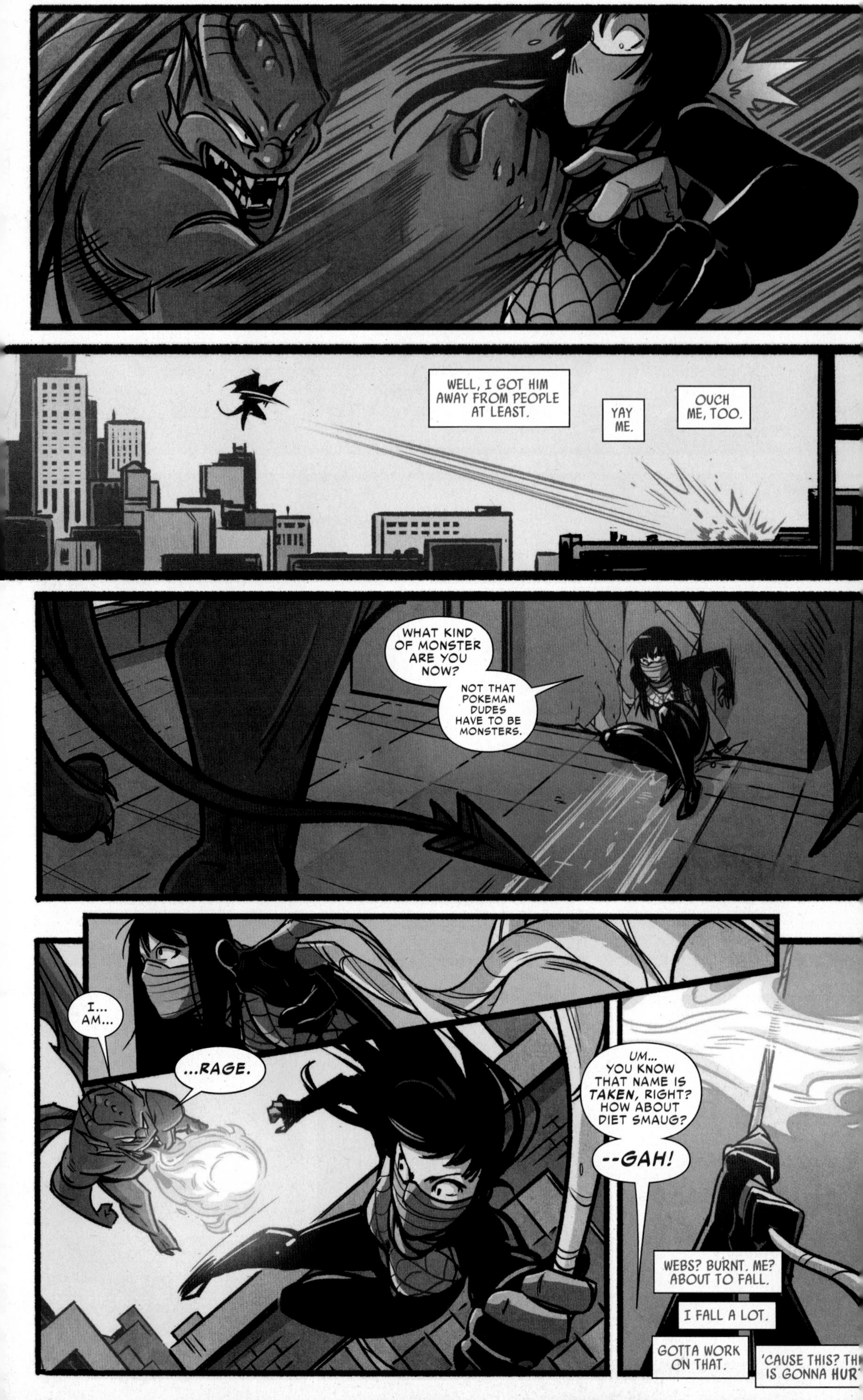

WELL, I GOT HIM AWAY FROM PEOPLE AT LEAST.
YAY ME.
OUCH ME, TOO.
WHAT KIND OF MONSTER ARE YOU NOW?
NOT THAT POKEMAN DUDES HAVE TO BE MONSTERS.
I... AM...
...RAGE.
UM... YOU KNOW THAT NAME IS *TAKEN*, RIGHT? HOW ABOUT DIET SMAUG?
--GAH!
WEBS? BURNT. ME? ABOUT TO FALL.
I FALL A LOT.
GOTTA WORK ON THAT.
'CAUSE THIS? TH IS GONNA **HUR**

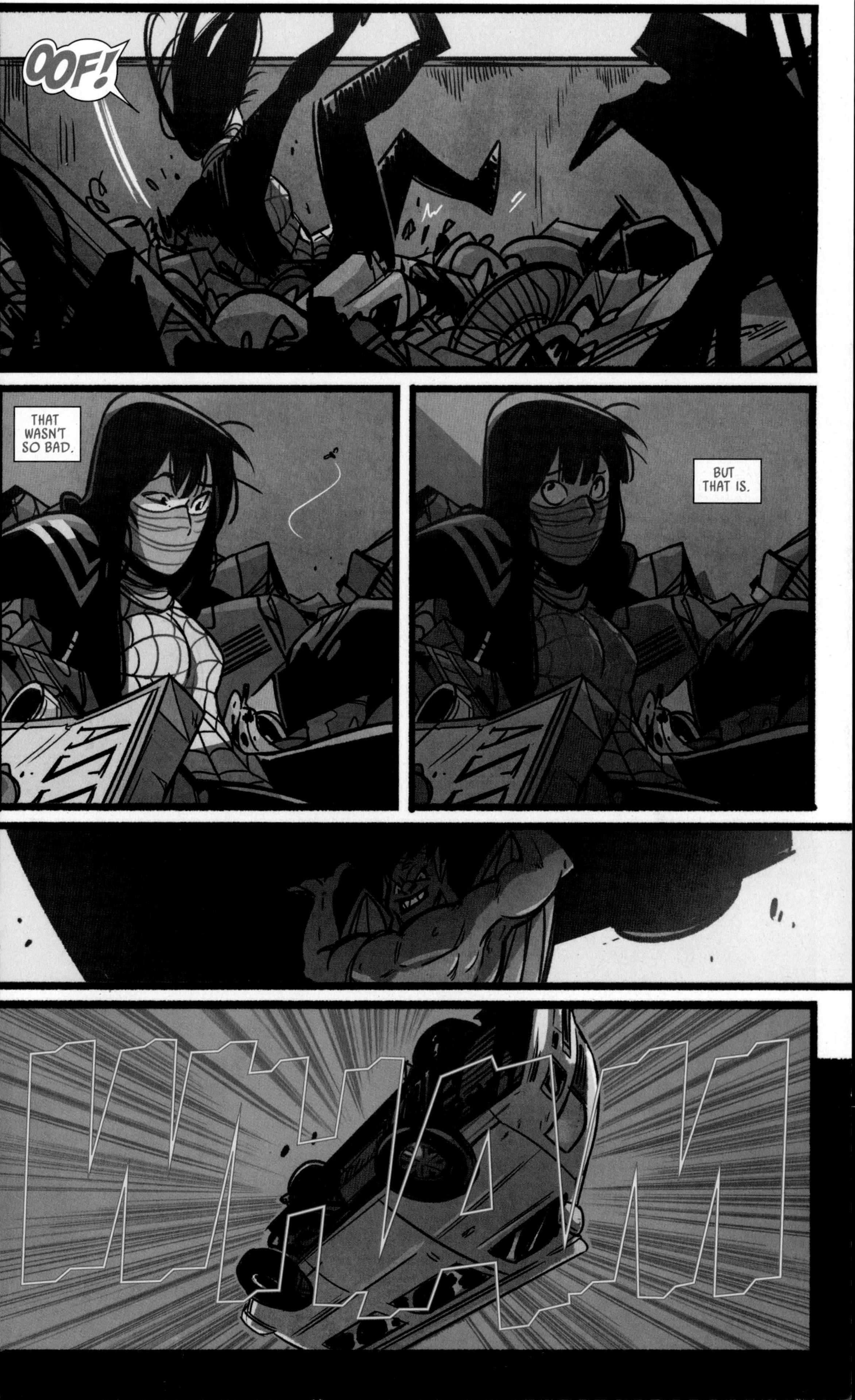
OOF!
THAT WASN'T SO BAD.
BUT THAT IS.
WHAM

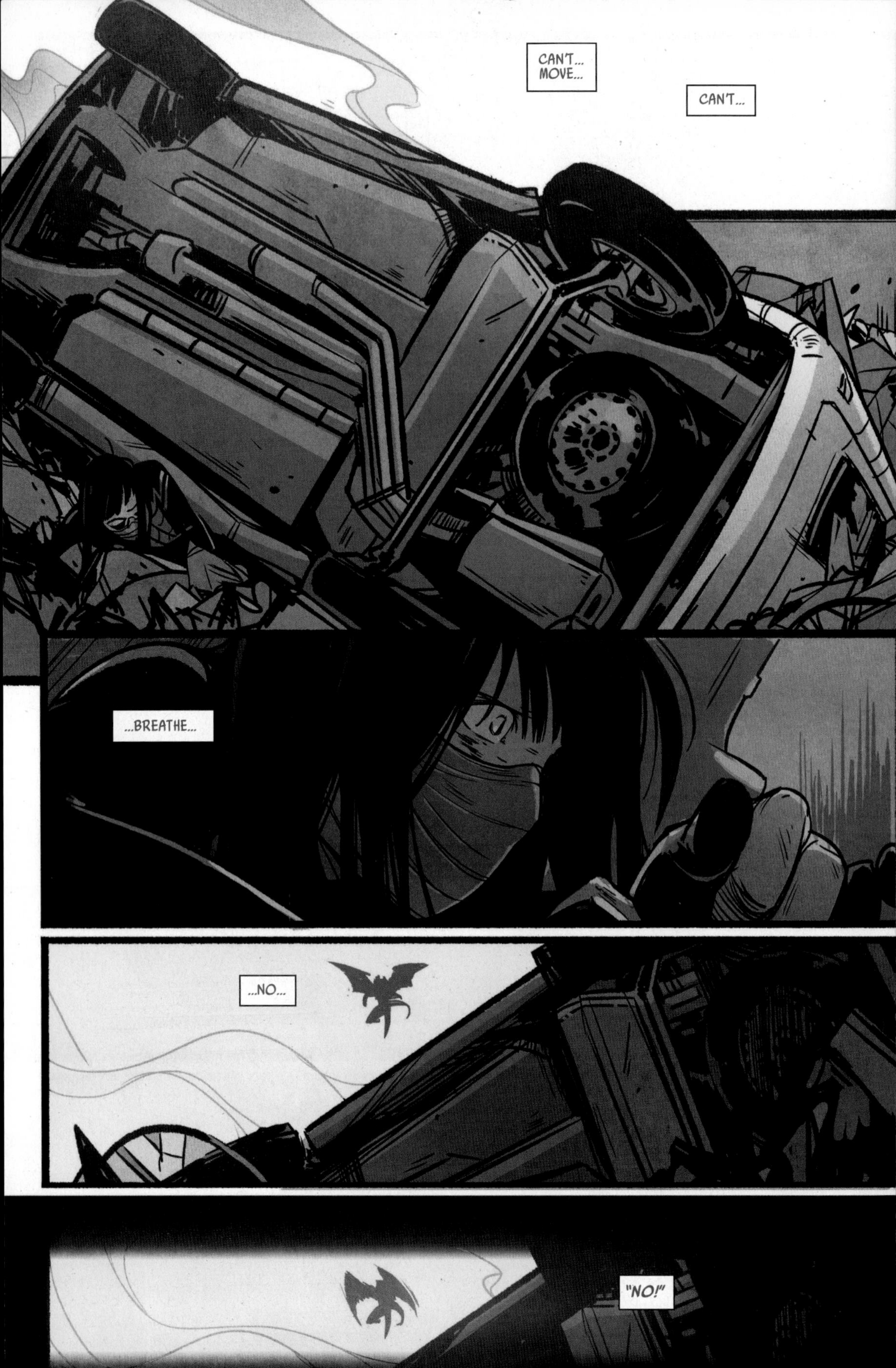
CAN'T... MOVE...
CAN'T...
...BREATHE...
...NO...
"NO!"

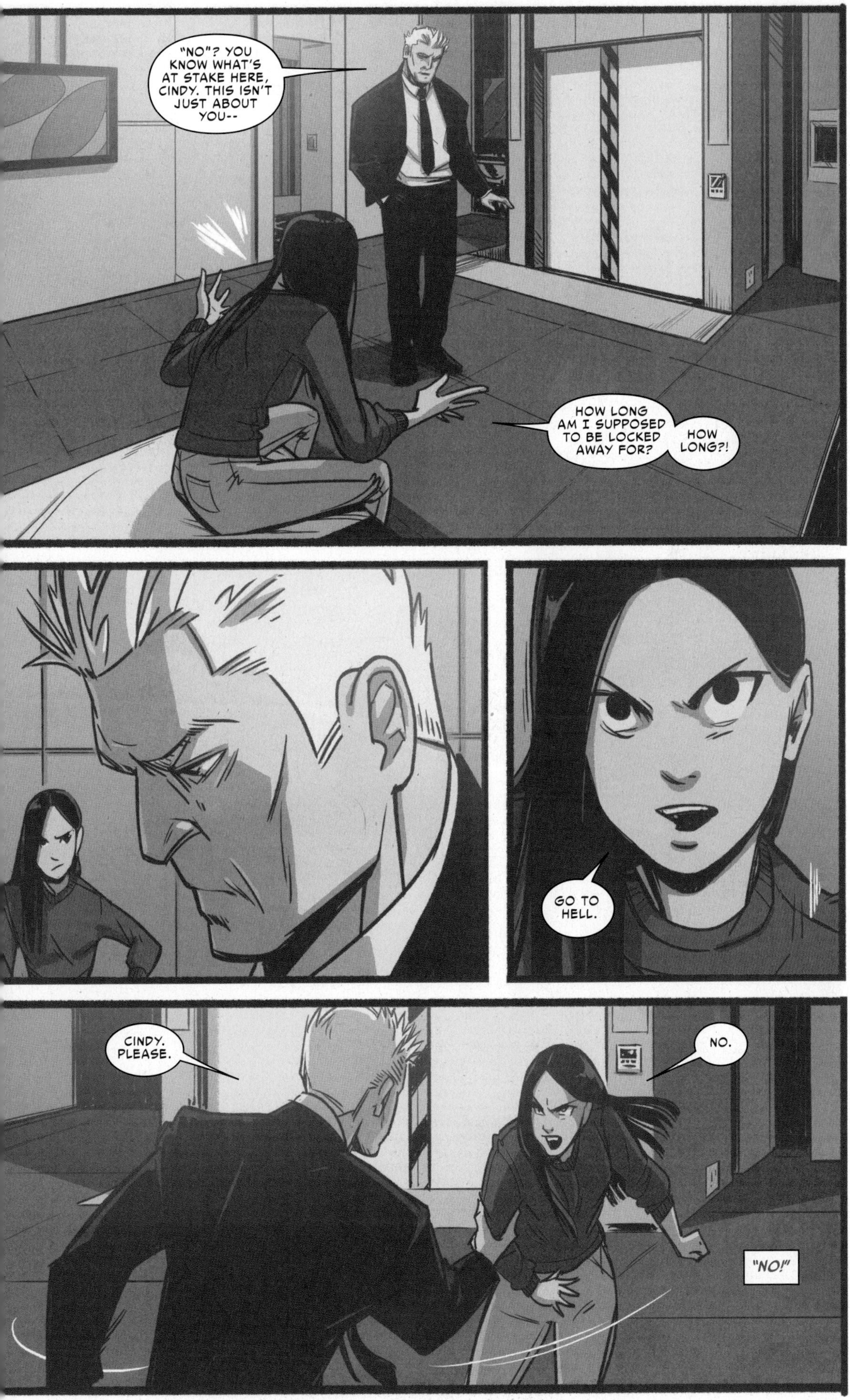
"NO"? YOU KNOW WHAT'S AT STAKE HERE, CINDY. THIS ISN'T JUST ABOUT YOU--
HOW LONG AM I SUPPOSED TO BE LOCKED AWAY FOR?
HOW LONG?!
GO TO HELL.
CINDY. PLEASE.
NO.
"NO!"

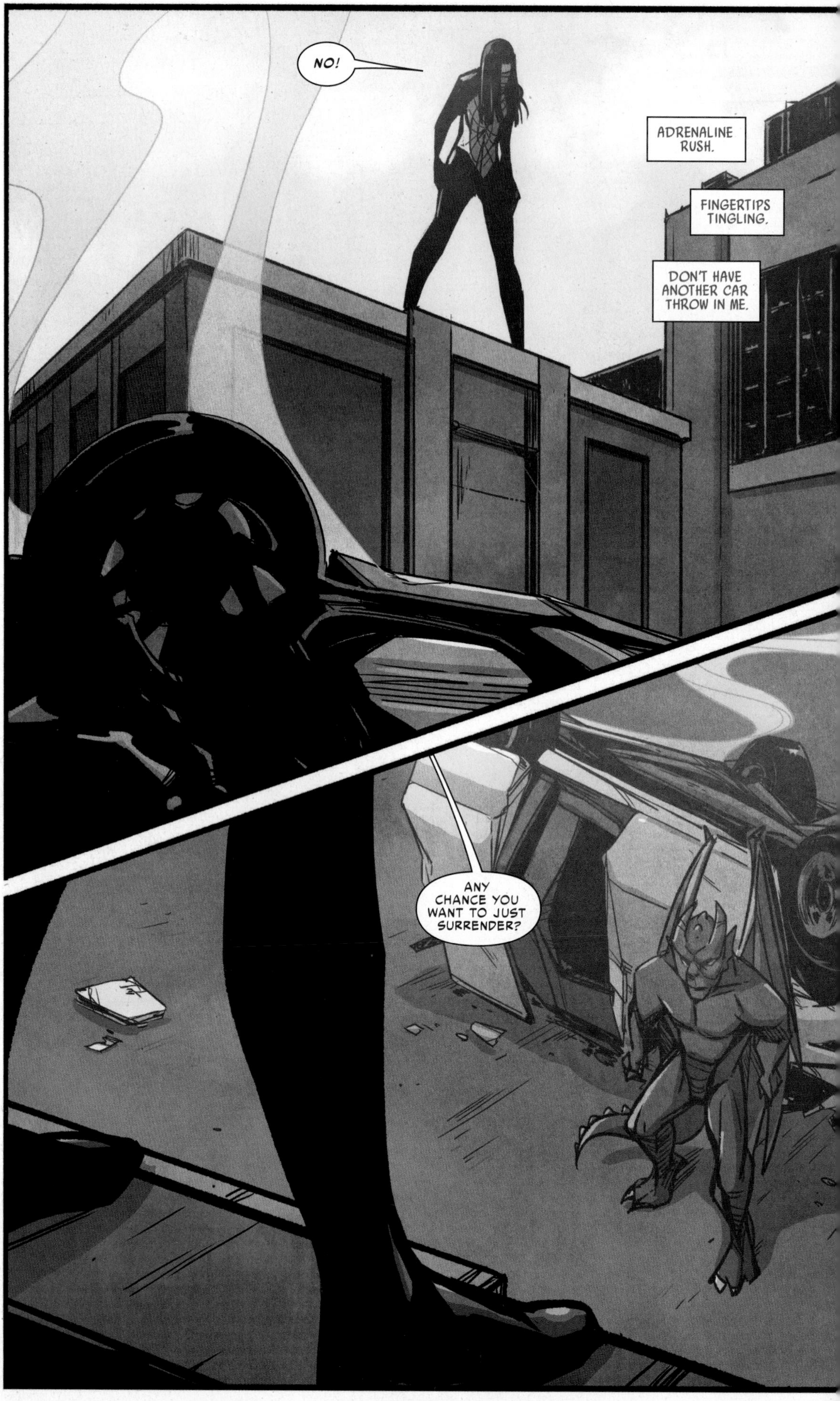
NO!
ADRENALINE RUSH.
FINGERTIPS TINGLING.
DON'T HAVE ANOTHER CAR THROW IN ME.
ANY CHANCE YOU WANT TO JUST SURRENDER?

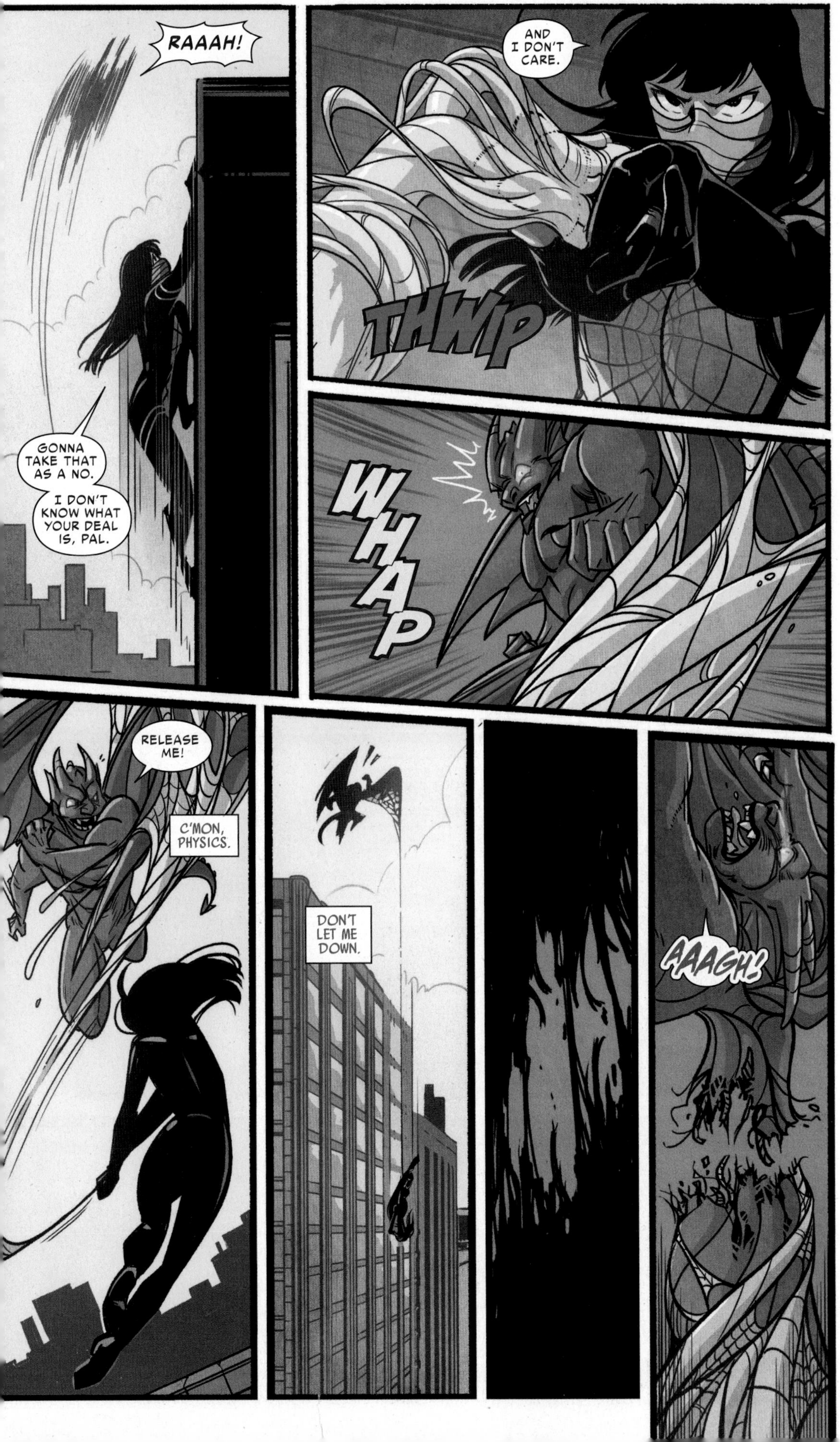
RAAAH!
GONNA TAKE THAT AS A NO.
I DON'T KNOW WHAT YOUR DEAL IS, PAL.
AND I DON'T CARE.
THWIP
WHAP
RELEASE ME!
C'MON, PHYSICS.
DON'T LET ME DOWN.
AAAGH!

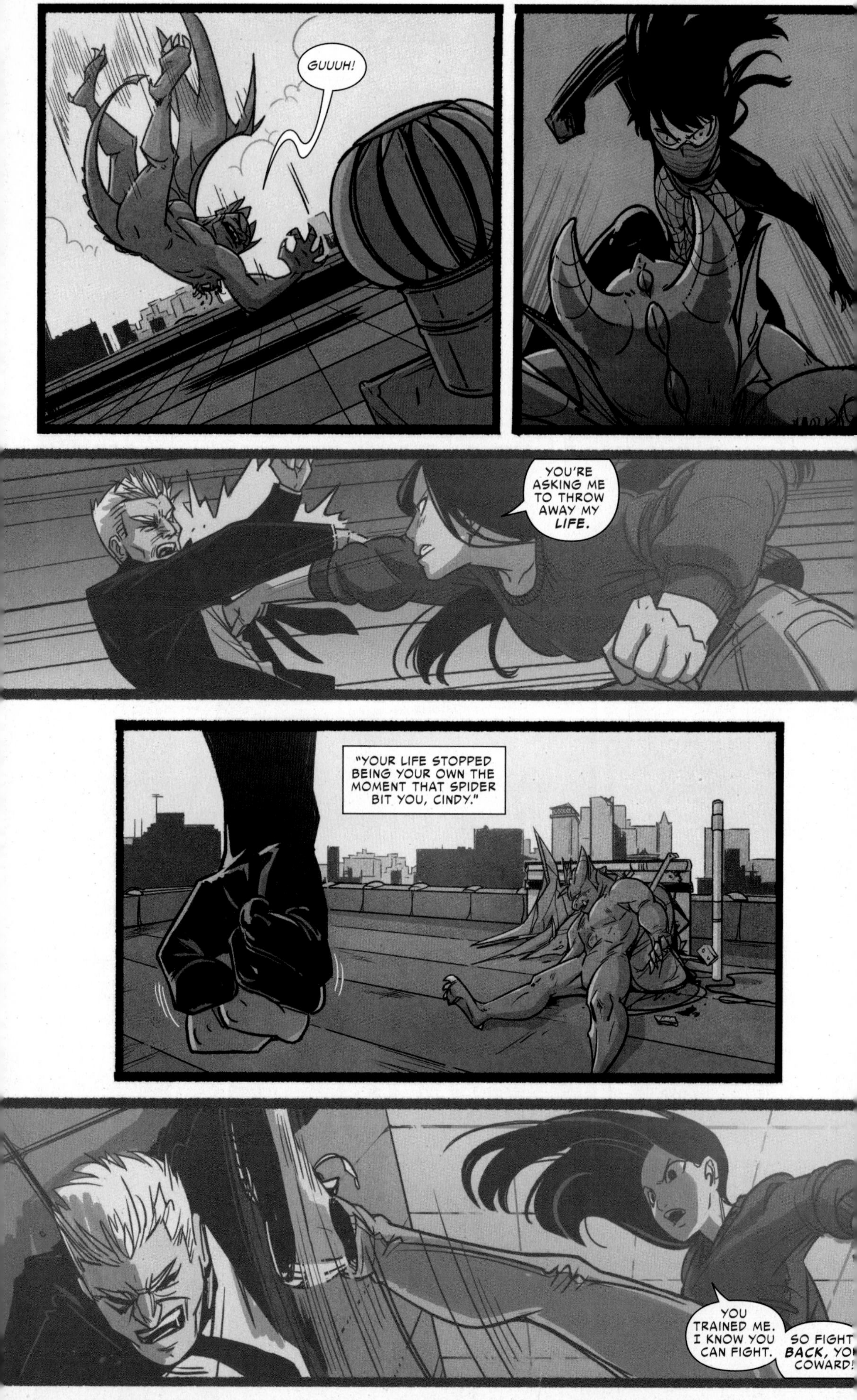
GUUUH!
YOU'RE ASKING ME TO THROW AWAY MY LIFE.
"YOUR LIFE STOPPED BEING YOUR OWN THE MOMENT THAT SPIDER BIT YOU, CINDY."
YOU TRAINED ME. I KNOW YOU CAN FIGHT.
SO FIGHT BACK, YO COWARD!

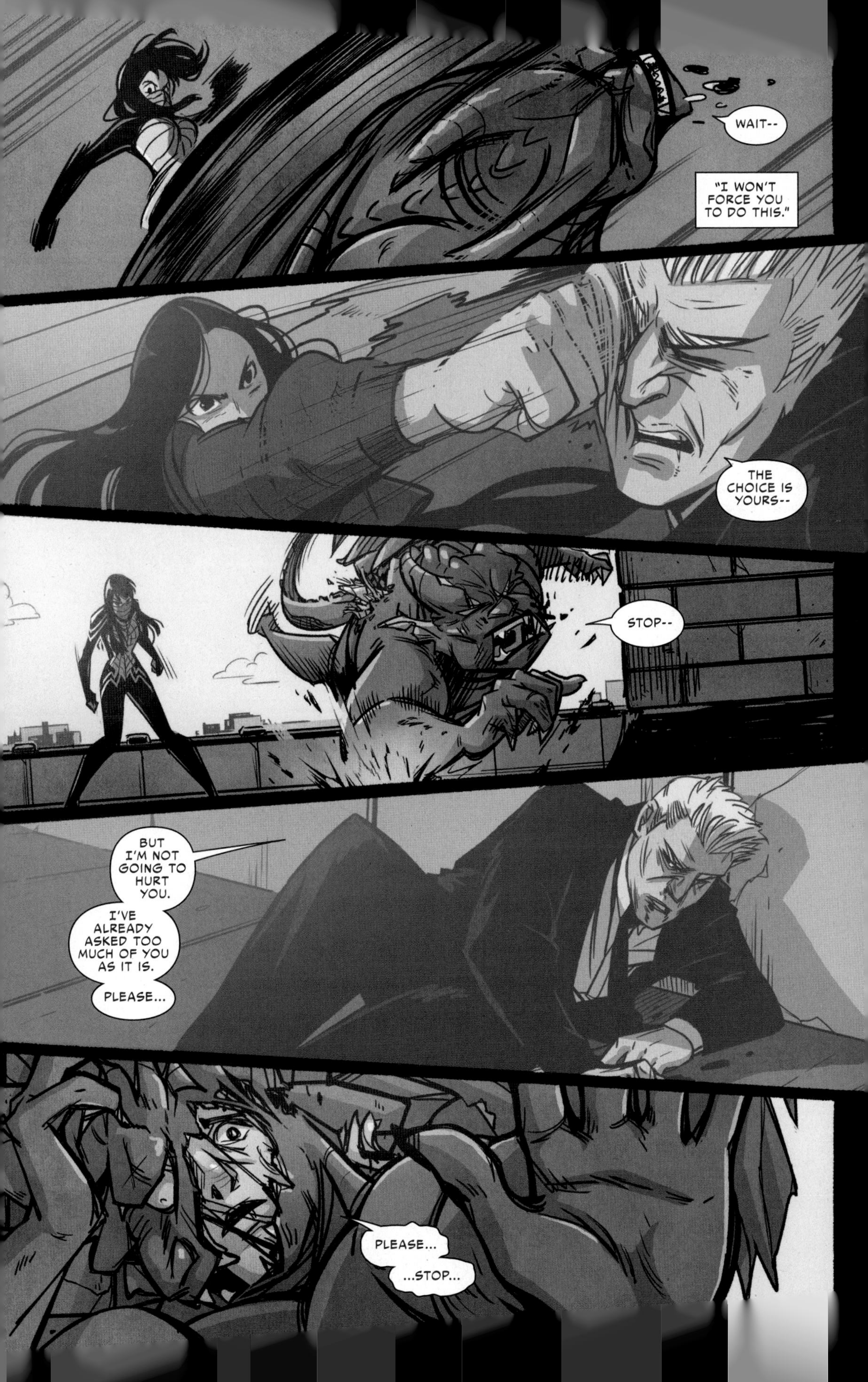
WAIT--
"I WON'T FORCE YOU TO DO THIS."
THE CHOICE IS YOURS--
STOP--
BUT I'M NOT GOING TO HURT YOU.
I'VE ALREADY ASKED TOO MUCH OF YOU AS IT IS.
PLEASE...
PLEASE...
...STOP...

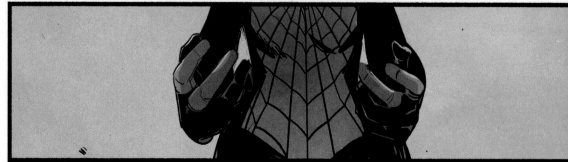

OKAY. ENOUGH WITH THE PUNCHING AND KICKING.

WHAT'S YOUR NAME? YOUR *REAL* NAME.

HARRIS. HARRIS PORTER.

ALL RIGHT, HARRIS. I LOST MY TEMPER. MY BAD. BUT YOU THREW A VAN AT ME. SO, IT HAPPENS.

WHAT'S WITH THE WHOLE BAD-GUY THING?

I...I GOT A KID.

MY WIFE LEFT US A FEW YEARS AGO. MY LITTLE GIRL IS ALL I GOT.

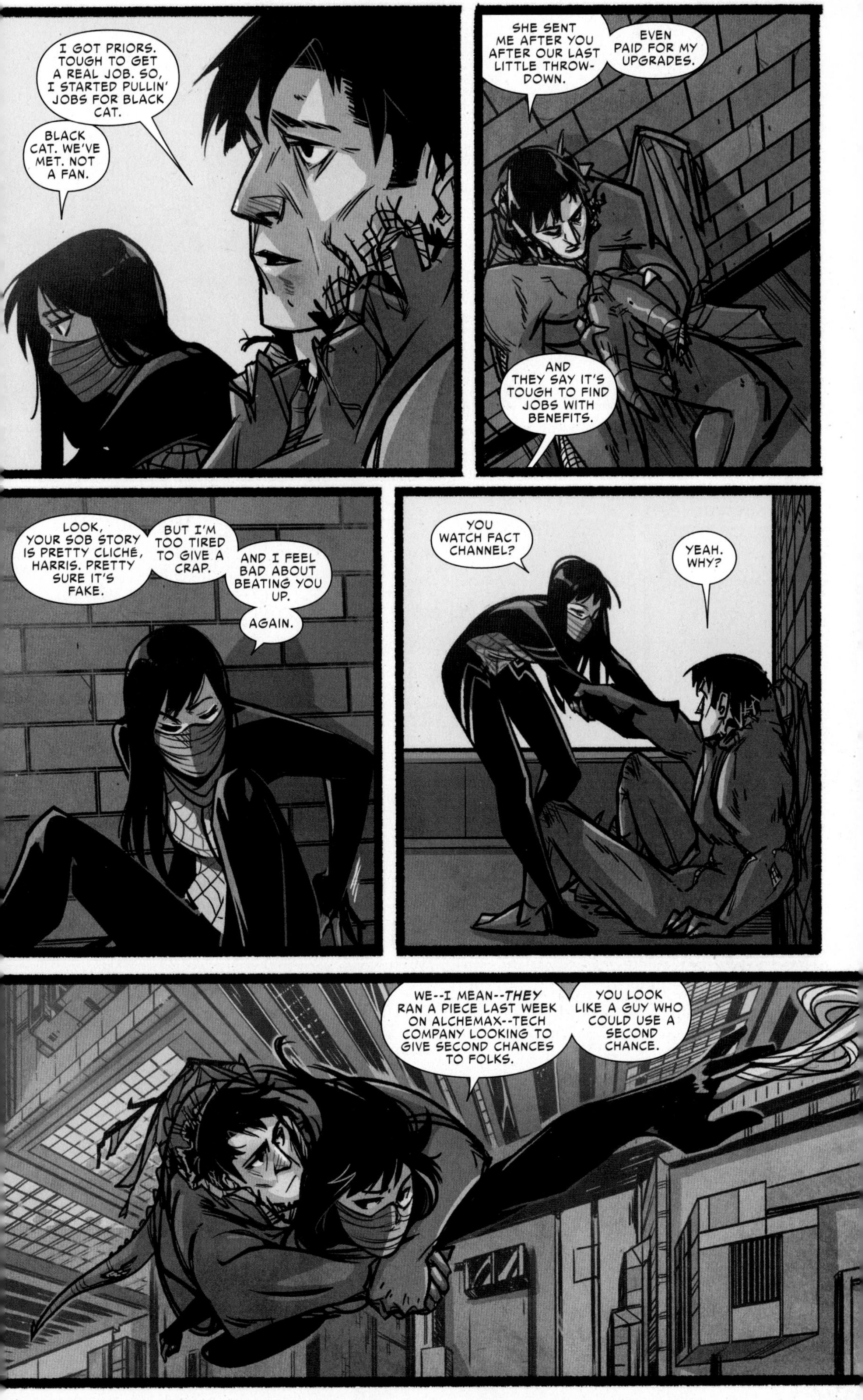
I GOT PRIORS. TOUGH TO GET A REAL JOB. SO, I STARTED PULLIN' JOBS FOR BLACK CAT.
BLACK CAT. WE'VE MET. NOT A FAN.
SHE SENT ME AFTER YOU AFTER OUR LAST LITTLE THROW-DOWN.
EVEN PAID FOR MY UPGRADES.
AND THEY SAY IT'S TOUGH TO FIND JOBS WITH BENEFITS.
LOOK, YOUR SOB STORY IS PRETTY CLICHÉ, HARRIS. PRETTY SURE IT'S FAKE.
BUT I'M TOO TIRED TO GIVE A CRAP.
AND I FEEL BAD ABOUT BEATING YOU UP.
AGAIN.
YOU WATCH FACT CHANNEL?
YEAH. WHY?
WE--I MEAN--*THEY* RAN A PIECE LAST WEEK ON ALCHEMAX--TECH COMPANY LOOKING TO GIVE SECOND CHANCES TO FOLKS.
YOU LOOK LIKE A GUY WHO COULD USE A SECOND CHANCE.

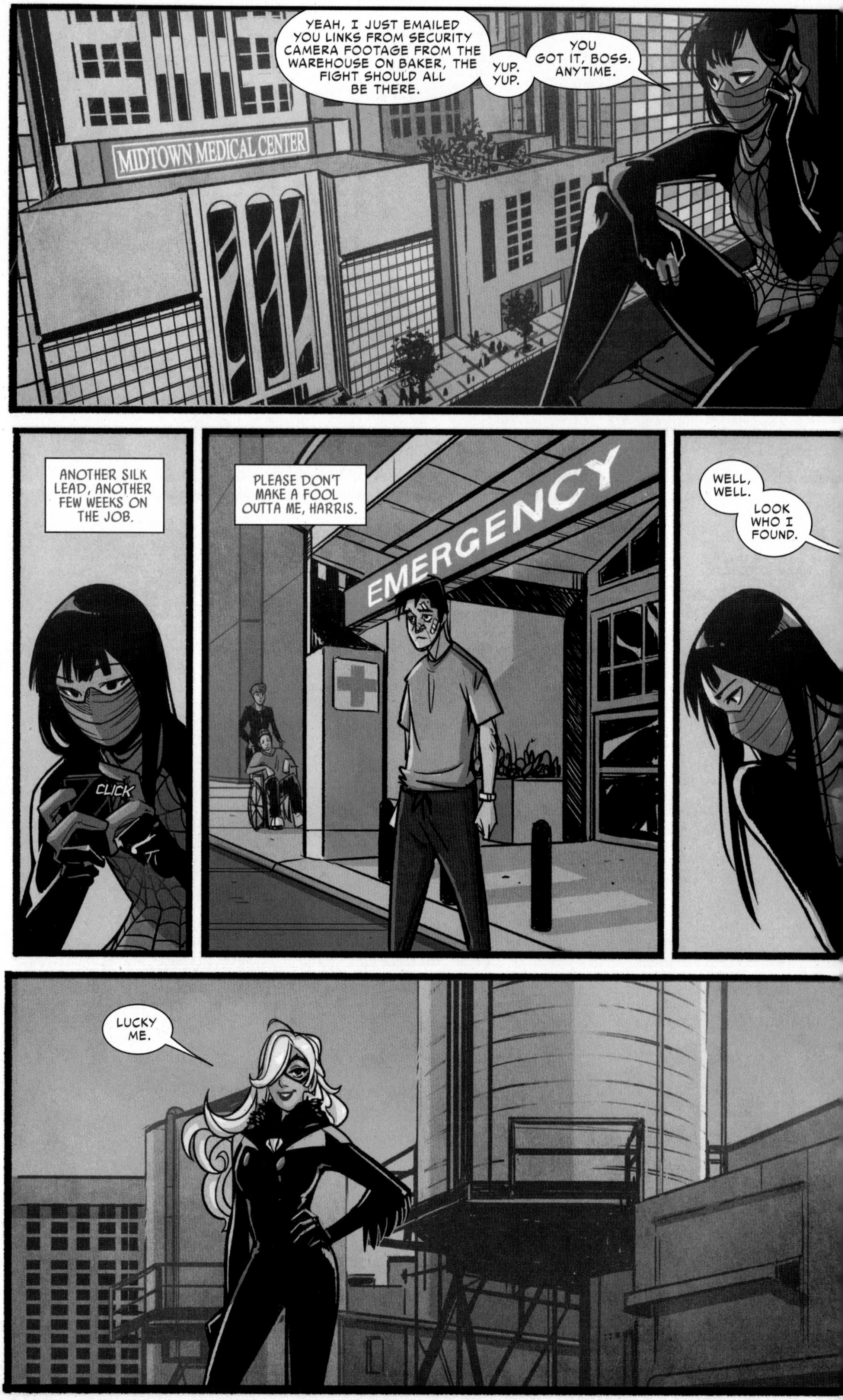

YEAH, I JUST EMAILED YOU LINKS FROM SECURITY CAMERA FOOTAGE FROM THE WAREHOUSE ON BAKER, THE FIGHT SHOULD ALL BE THERE.
YUP. YUP.
YOU GOT IT, BOSS. ANYTIME.
MIDTOWN MEDICAL CENTER
ANOTHER SILK LEAD, ANOTHER FEW WEEKS ON THE JOB.
CLICK
PLEASE DON'T MAKE A FOOL OUTTA ME, HARRIS.
EMERGENCY
WELL, WELL.
LOOK WHO I FOUND.
LUCKY ME.

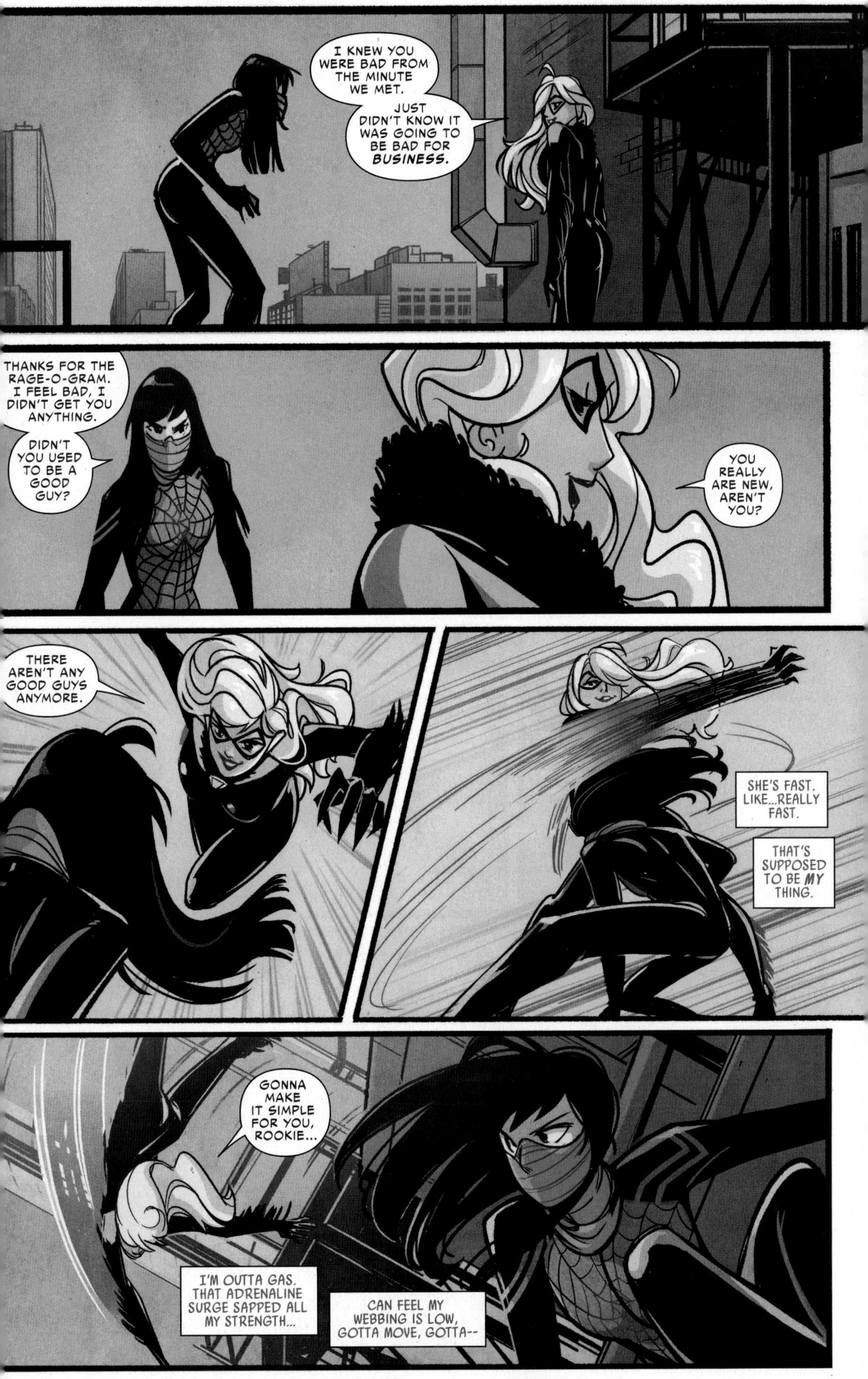

I KNEW YOU WERE BAD FROM THE MINUTE WE MET.
JUST DIDN'T KNOW IT WAS GOING TO BE BAD FOR BUSINESS.
THANKS FOR THE RAGE-O-GRAM. I FEEL BAD, I DIDN'T GET YOU ANYTHING.
DIDN'T YOU USED TO BE A GOOD GUY?
YOU REALLY ARE NEW, AREN'T YOU?
THERE AREN'T ANY GOOD GUYS ANYMORE.
SHE'S FAST. LIKE...REALLY FAST.
THAT'S SUPPOSED TO BE MY THING.
GONNA MAKE IT SIMPLE FOR YOU, ROOKIE...
I'M OUTTA GAS. THAT ADRENALINE SURGE SAPPED ALL MY STRENGTH...
CAN FEEL MY WEBBING IS LOW, GOTTA MOVE, GOTTA--

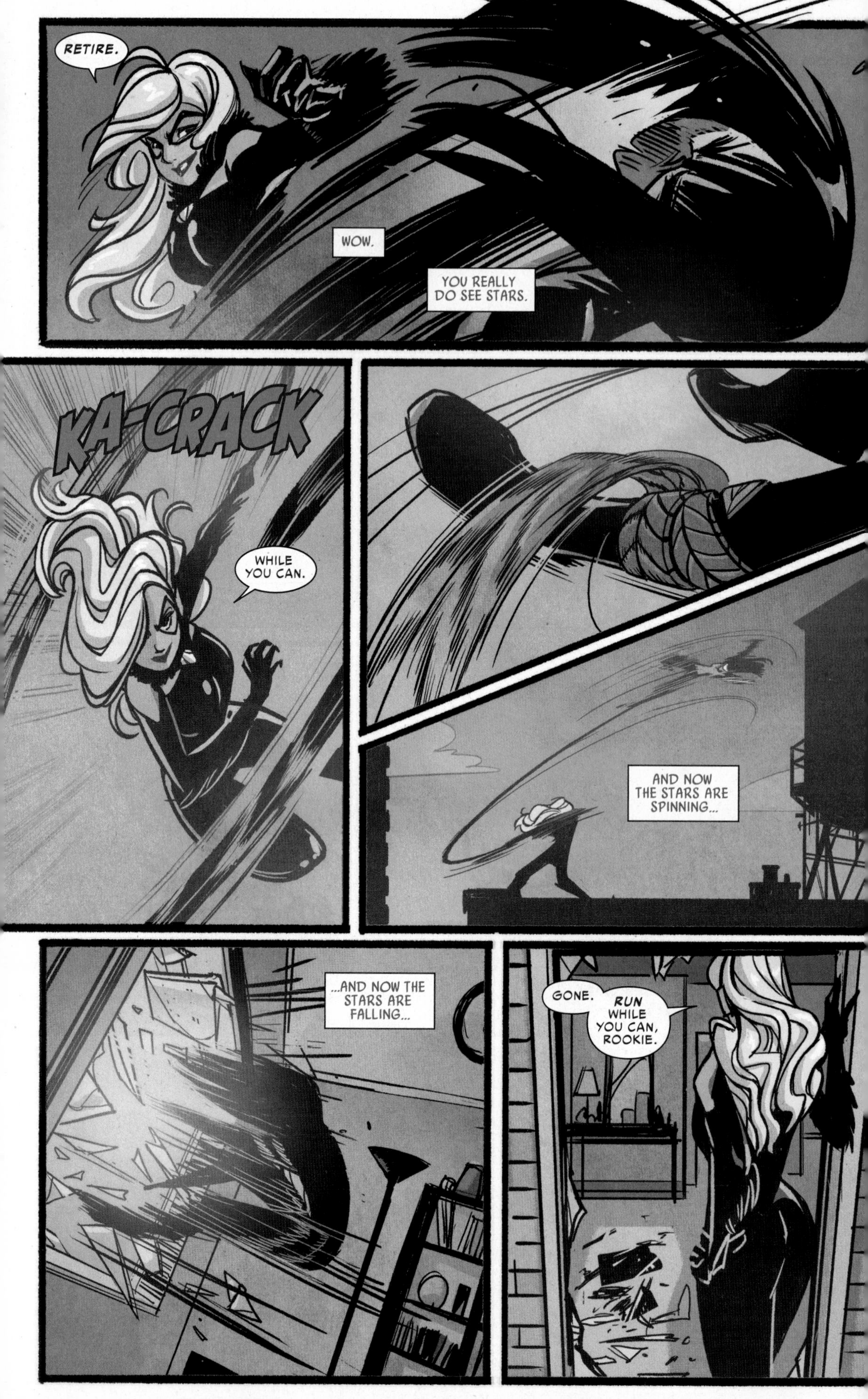
RETIRE.
WOW.
YOU REALLY DO SEE STARS.
KA-CRACK
WHILE YOU CAN.
AND NOW THE STARS ARE SPINNING...
...AND NOW THE STARS ARE FALLING...
GONE.
RUN WHILE YOU CAN, ROOKIE.

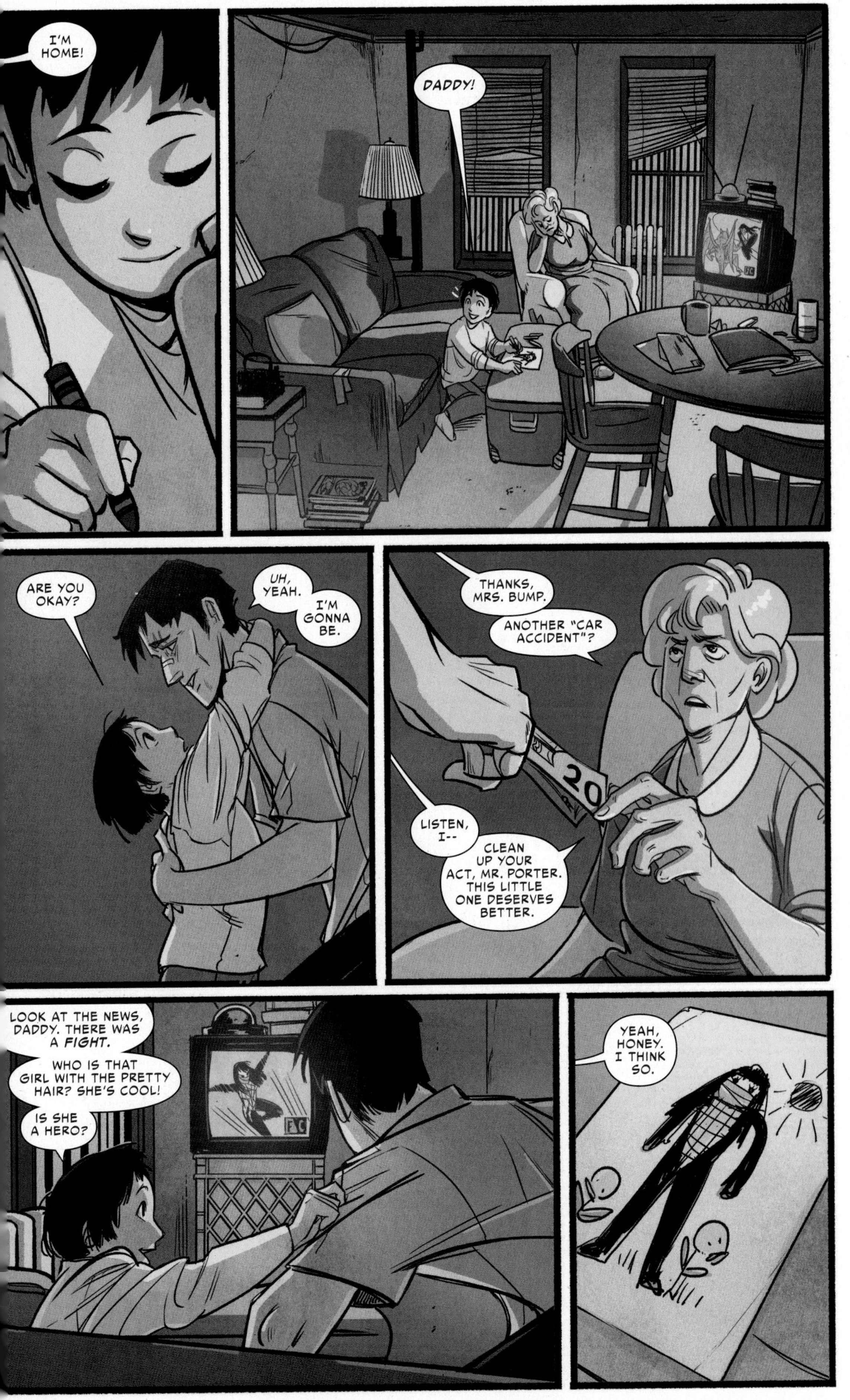

I'M HOME!
DADDY!
ARE YOU OKAY?
UH, YEAH.
I'M GONNA BE.
THANKS, MRS. BUMP.
ANOTHER "CAR ACCIDENT"?
LISTEN, I--
CLEAN UP YOUR ACT, MR. PORTER. THIS LITTLE ONE DESERVES BETTER.
LOOK AT THE NEWS, DADDY. THERE WAS A *FIGHT*.
WHO IS THAT GIRL WITH THE PRETTY HAIR? SHE'S COOL!
IS SHE A HERO?
YEAH, HONEY. I THINK SO.

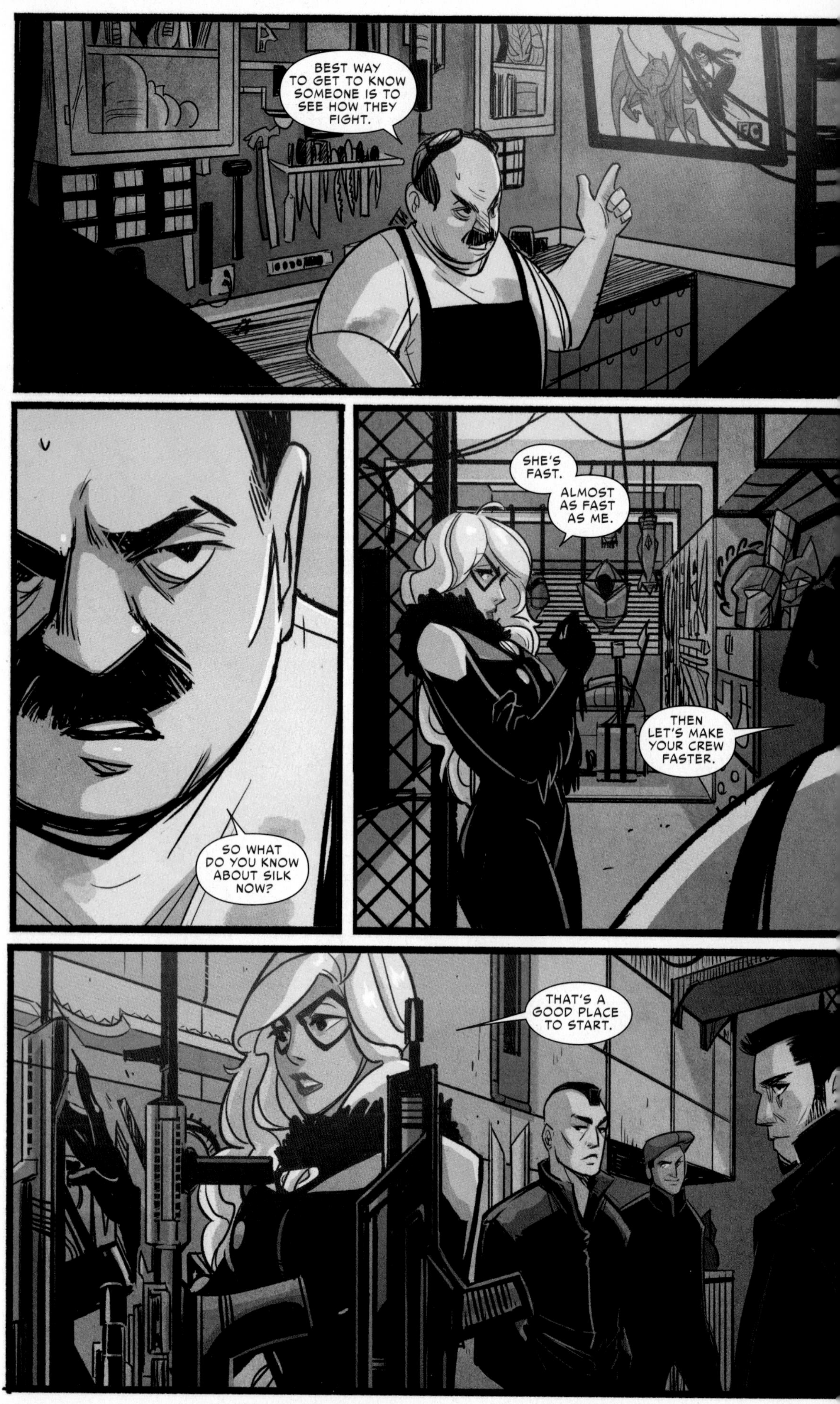
BEST WAY TO GET TO KNOW SOMEONE IS TO SEE HOW THEY FIGHT.
SO WHAT DO YOU KNOW ABOUT SILK NOW?
SHE'S FAST.
ALMOST AS FAST AS ME.
THEN LET'S MAKE YOUR CREW FASTER.
THAT'S A GOOD PLACE TO START.

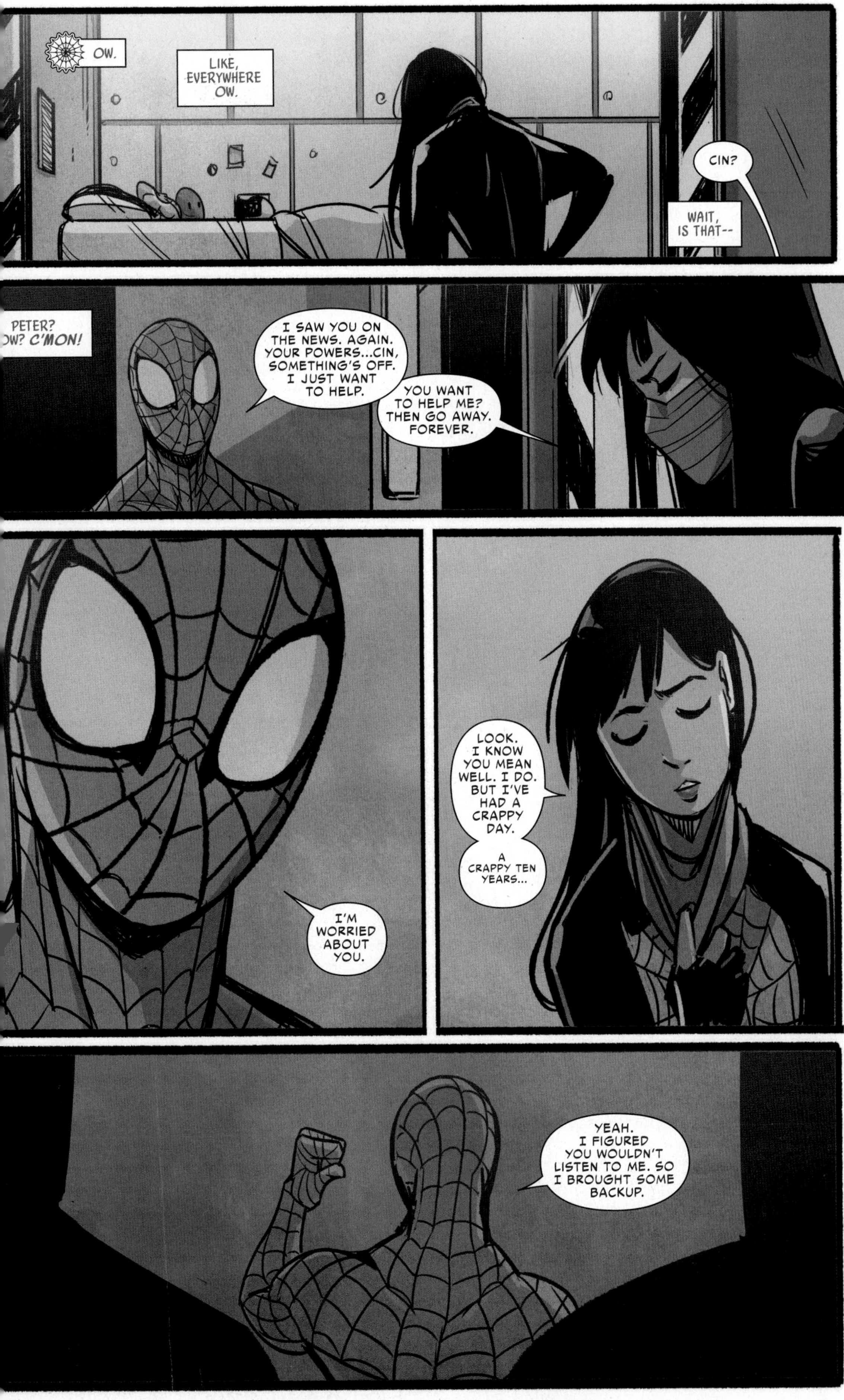

OW.
LIKE, EVERYWHERE OW.
CIN?
WAIT, IS THAT--
PETER?
OW? C'MON!
I SAW YOU ON THE NEWS. AGAIN. YOUR POWERS...CIN, SOMETHING'S OFF. I JUST WANT TO HELP.
YOU WANT TO HELP ME? THEN GO AWAY. FOREVER.
I'M WORRIED ABOUT YOU.
LOOK. I KNOW YOU MEAN WELL. I DO. BUT I'VE HAD A CRAPPY DAY.
A CRAPPY TEN YEARS...
YEAH. I FIGURED YOU WOULDN'T LISTEN TO ME. SO I BROUGHT SOME BACKUP.

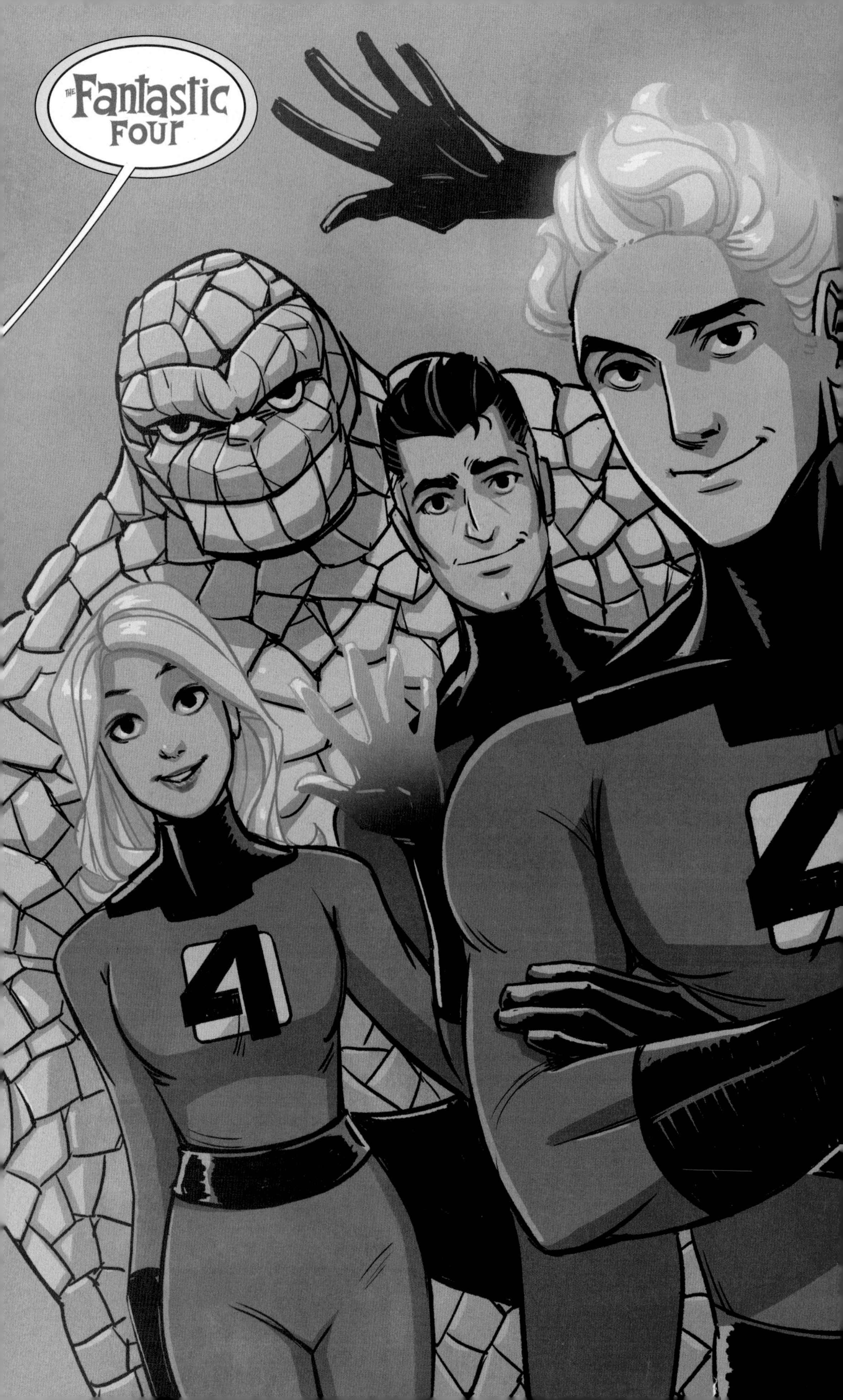
The Fantastic Four

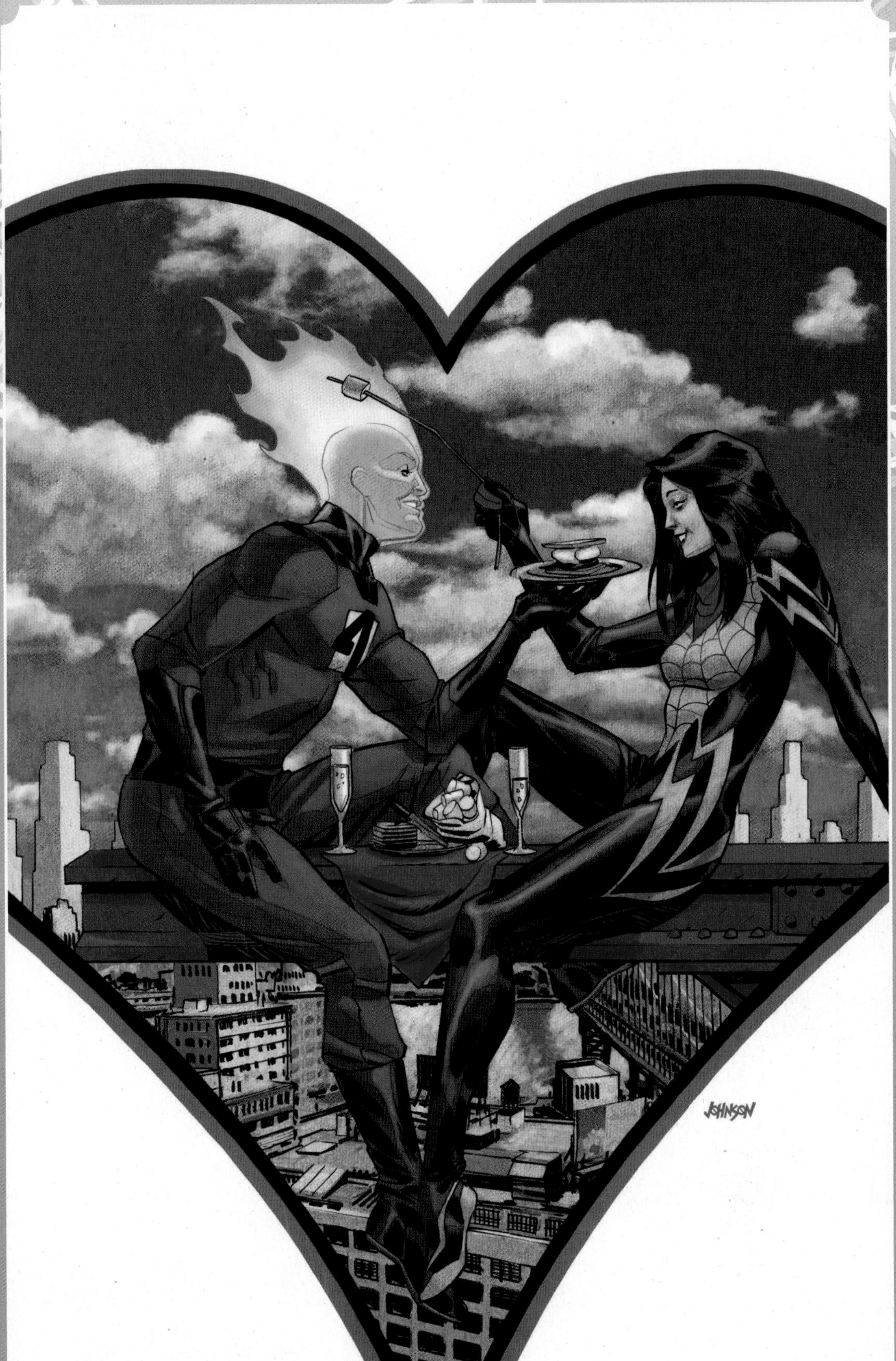
JOHNSON

SILK (2015A) #4

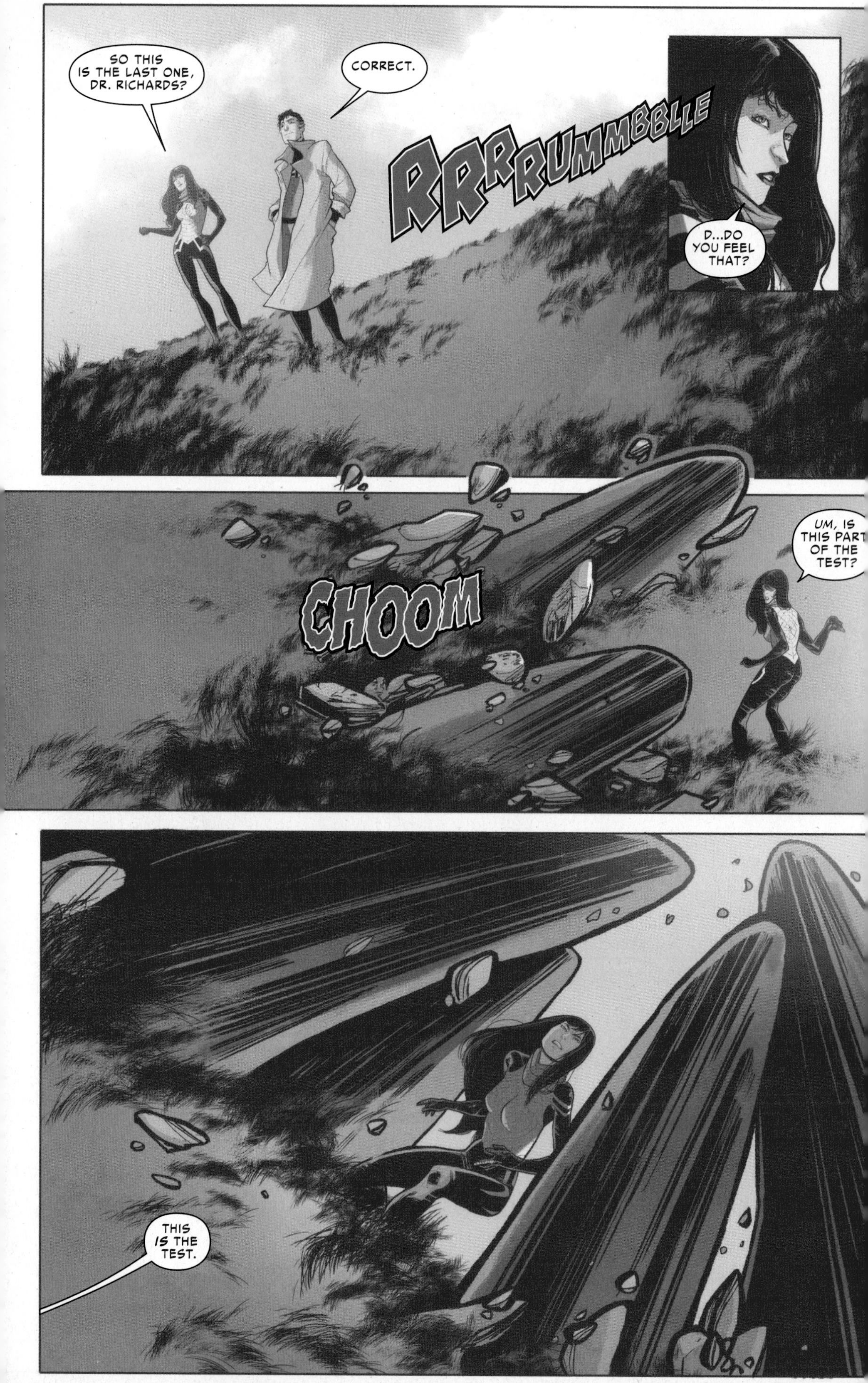
SO THIS IS THE LAST ONE, DR. RICHARDS?
CORRECT.
RRRRUMMBBLLE
D...DO YOU FEEL THAT?
CHOOM
UM, IS THIS PART OF THE TEST?
THIS IS THE TEST.

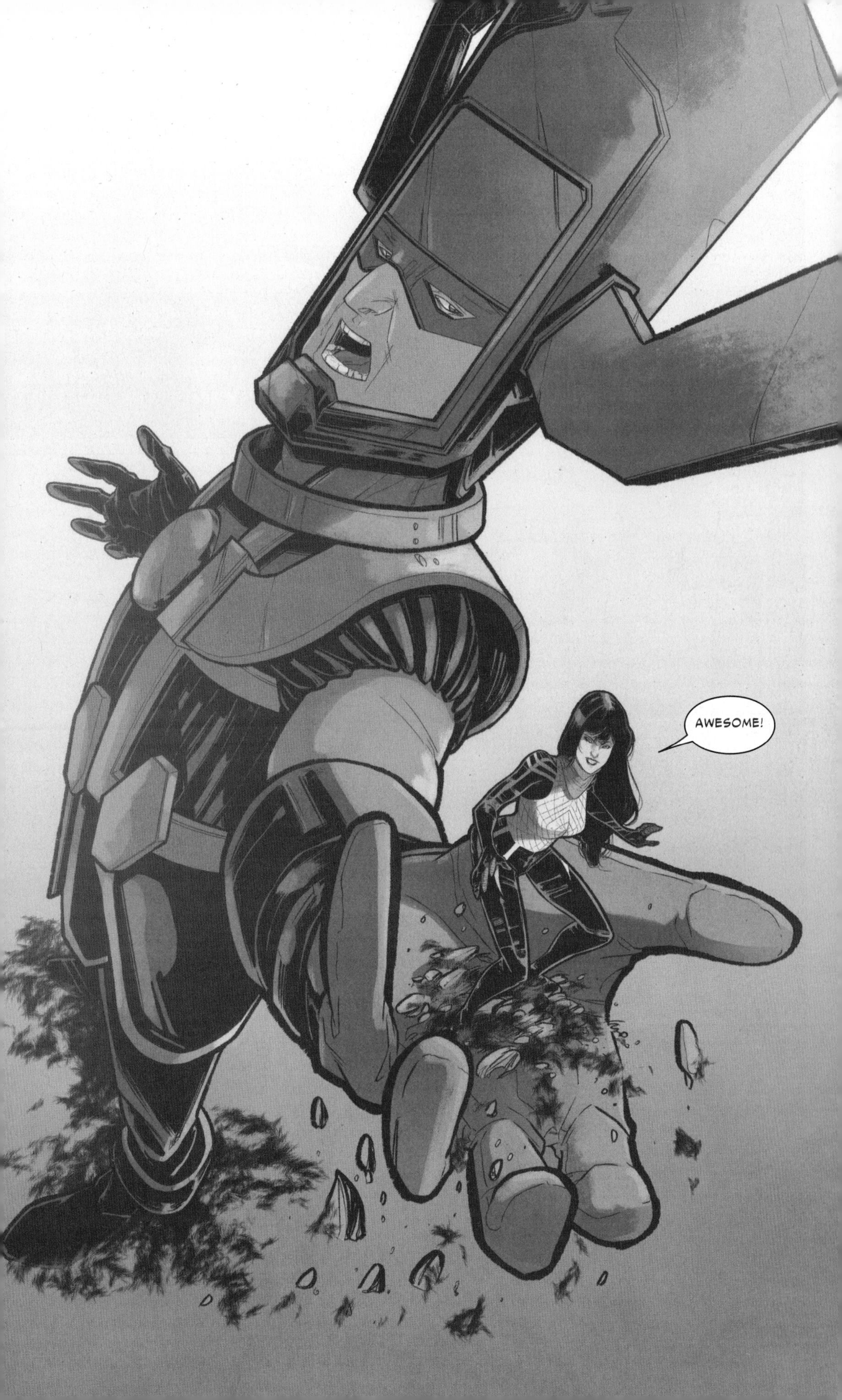
AWESOME!

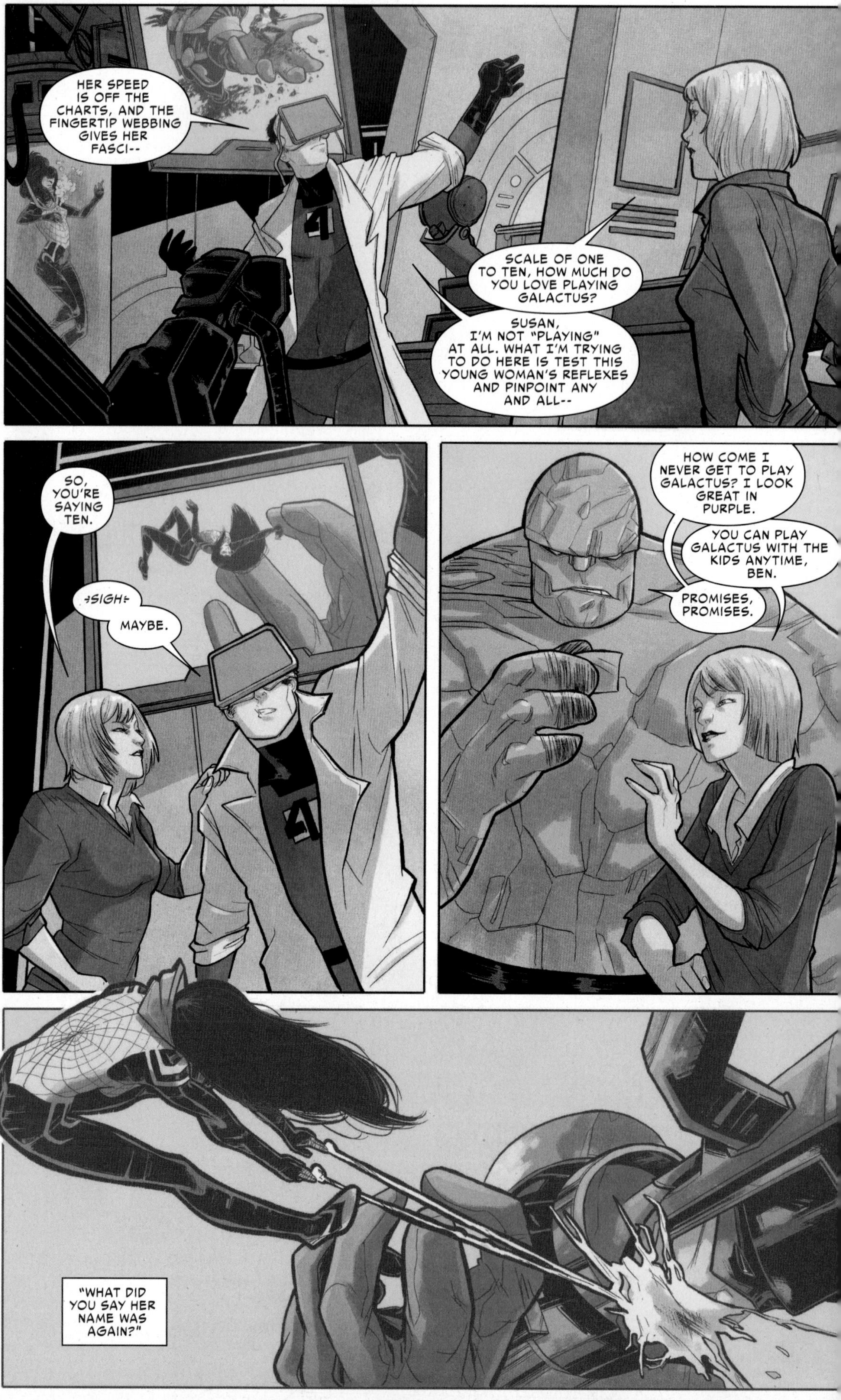
HER SPEED IS OFF THE CHARTS, AND THE FINGERTIP WEBBING GIVES HER FASCI--
SCALE OF ONE TO TEN, HOW MUCH DO YOU LOVE PLAYING GALACTUS?
SUSAN, I'M NOT "PLAYING" AT ALL. WHAT I'M TRYING TO DO HERE IS TEST THIS YOUNG WOMAN'S REFLEXES AND PINPOINT ANY AND ALL--
SO, YOU'RE SAYING TEN.
-SIGH-
MAYBE.
HOW COME I NEVER GET TO PLAY GALACTUS? I LOOK GREAT IN PURPLE.
YOU CAN PLAY GALACTUS WITH THE KIDS ANYTIME, BEN.
PROMISES, PROMISES.
"WHAT DID YOU SAY HER NAME WAS AGAIN?"

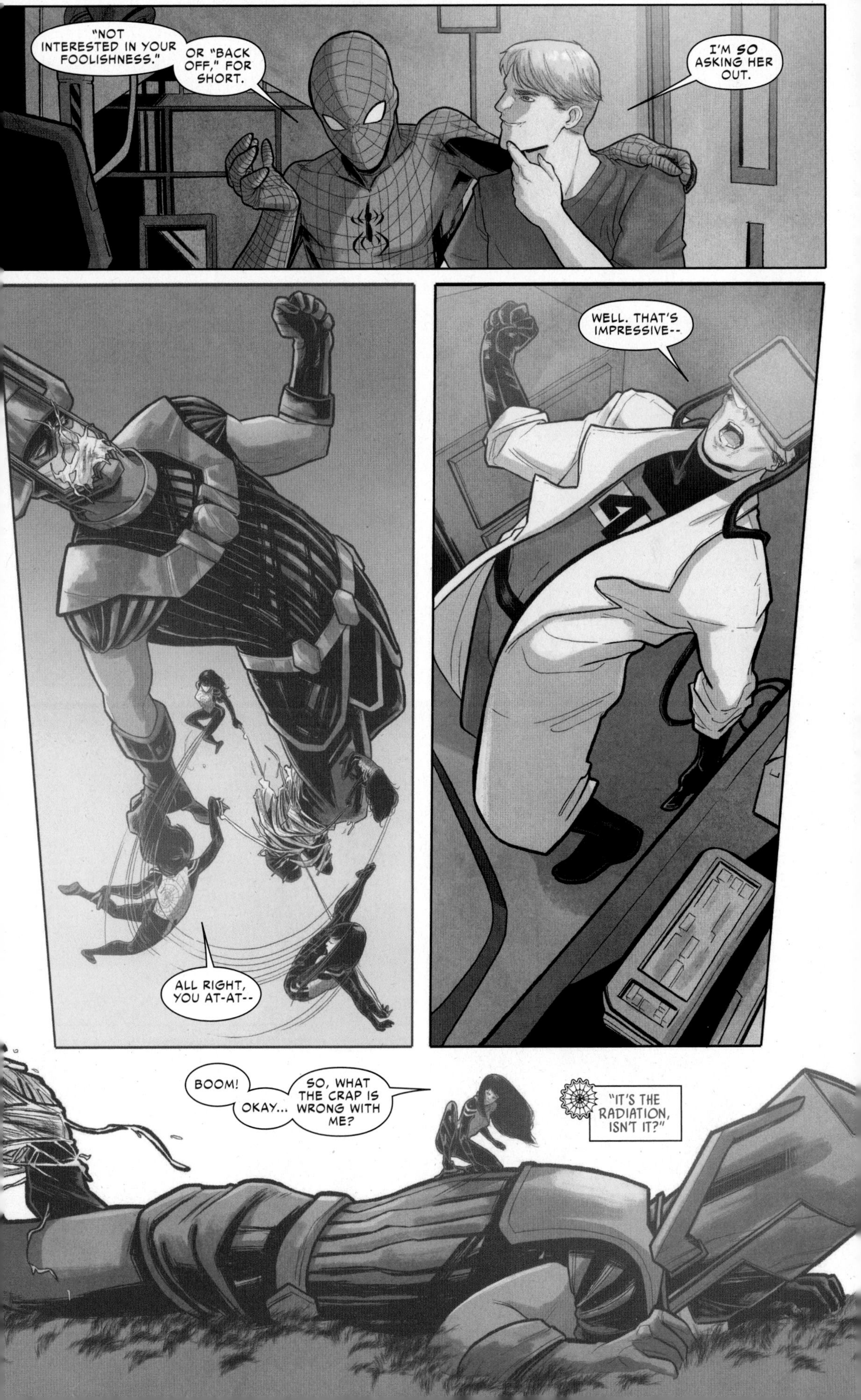
"NOT INTERESTED IN YOUR FOOLISHNESS."
OR "BACK OFF," FOR SHORT.
I'M SO ASKING HER OUT.
ALL RIGHT, YOU AT-AT--
WELL. THAT'S IMPRESSIVE--
BOOM!
OKAY...
SO, WHAT THE CRAP IS WRONG WITH ME?
"IT'S THE RADIATION, ISN'T IT?"

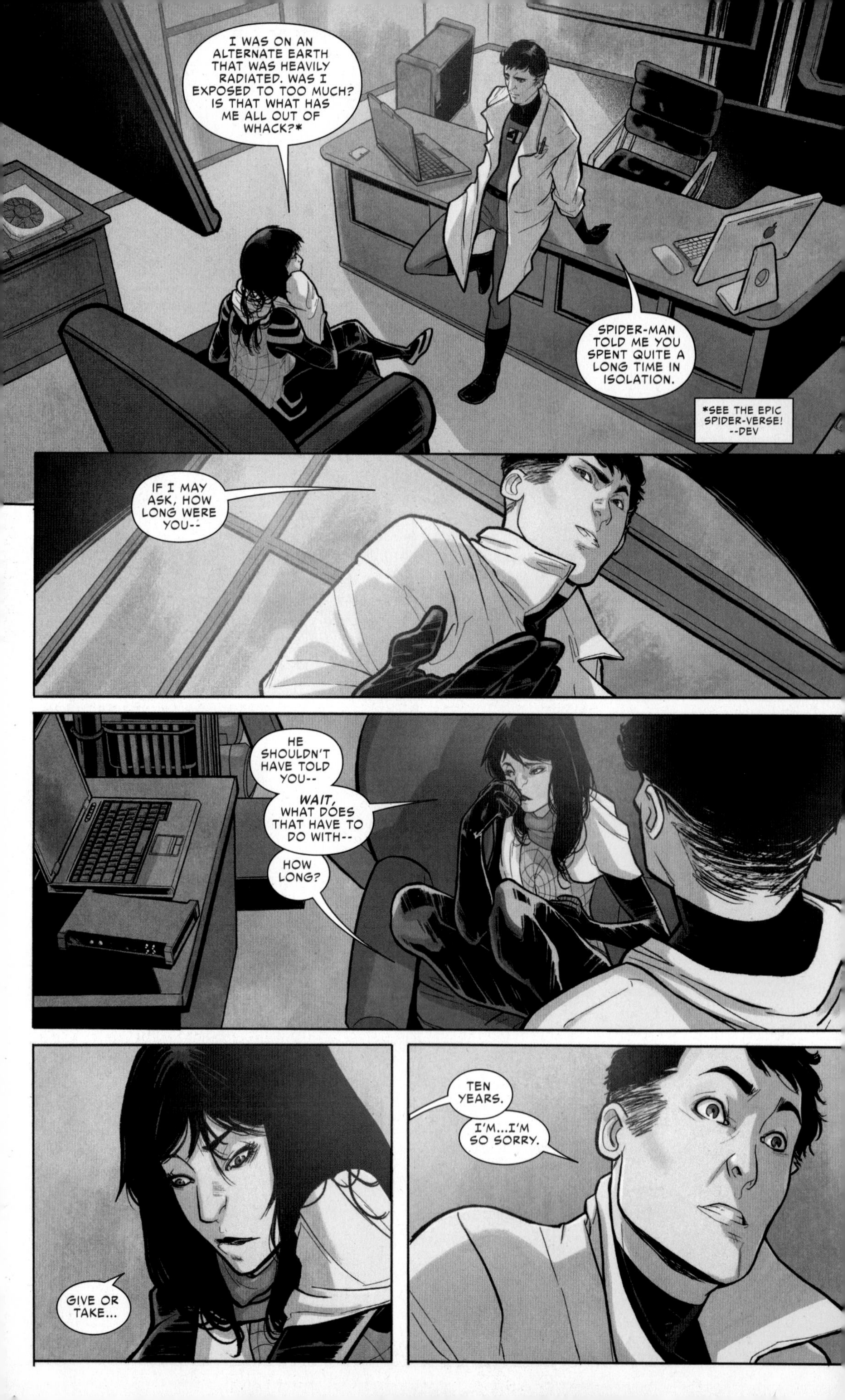
I WAS ON AN ALTERNATE EARTH THAT WAS HEAVILY RADIATED. WAS I EXPOSED TO TOO MUCH? IS THAT WHAT HAS ME ALL OUT OF WHACK?*
SPIDER-MAN TOLD ME YOU SPENT QUITE A LONG TIME IN ISOLATION.
*SEE THE EPIC SPIDER-VERSE! --DEV
IF I MAY ASK, HOW LONG WERE YOU--
HE SHOULDN'T HAVE TOLD YOU--
WAIT, WHAT DOES THAT HAVE TO DO WITH--
HOW LONG?
GIVE OR TAKE...
TEN YEARS.
I'M...I'M SO SORRY.

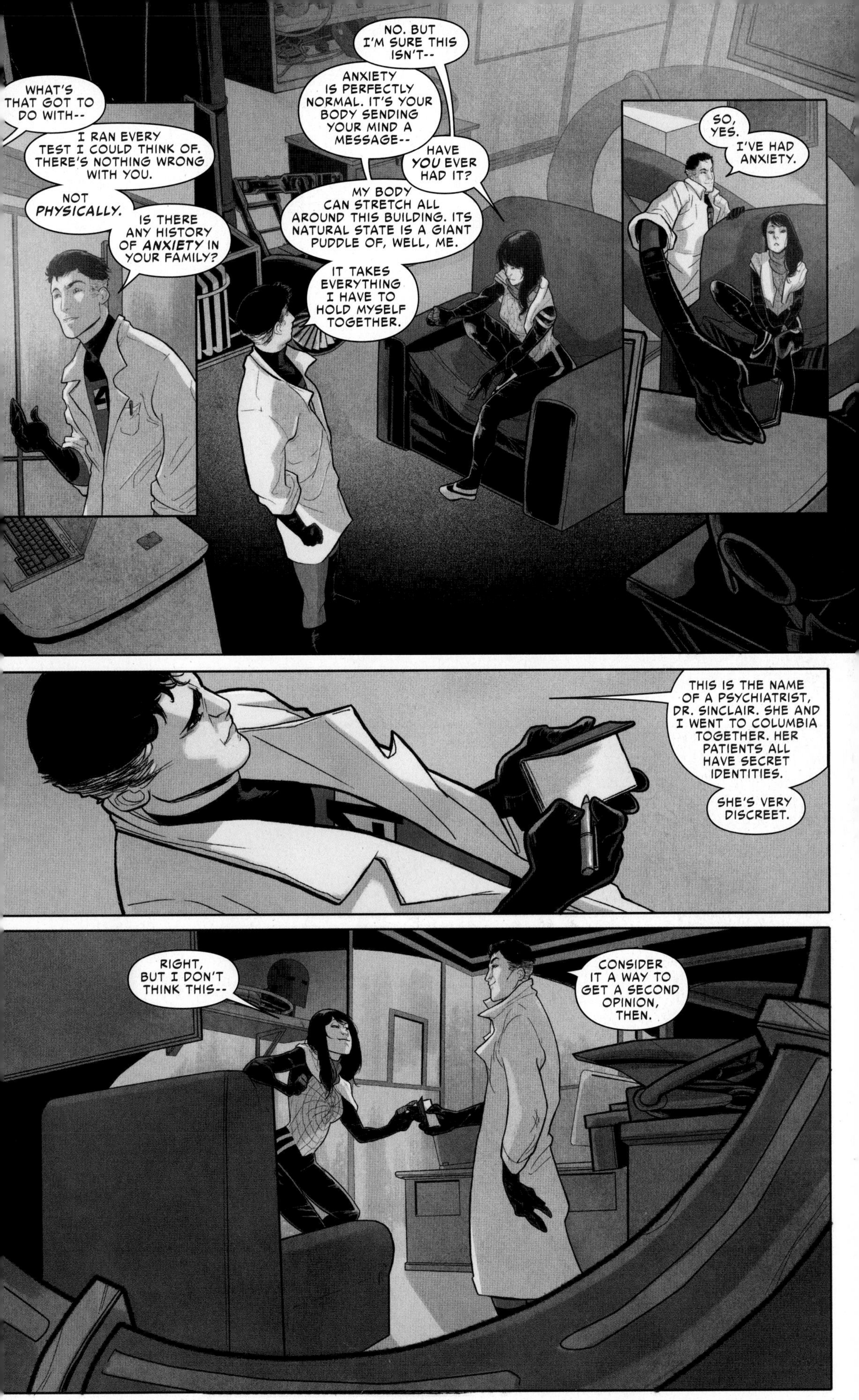
WHAT'S THAT GOT TO DO WITH--
I RAN EVERY TEST I COULD THINK OF. THERE'S NOTHING WRONG WITH YOU.
NOT *PHYSICALLY.*
IS THERE ANY HISTORY OF *ANXIETY* IN YOUR FAMILY?
NO. BUT I'M SURE THIS ISN'T--
ANXIETY IS PERFECTLY NORMAL. IT'S YOUR BODY SENDING YOUR MIND A MESSAGE--
HAVE *YOU* EVER HAD IT?
MY BODY CAN STRETCH ALL AROUND THIS BUILDING. ITS NATURAL STATE IS A GIANT PUDDLE OF, WELL, ME.
IT TAKES EVERYTHING I HAVE TO HOLD MYSELF TOGETHER.
SO, YES. I'VE HAD ANXIETY.
THIS IS THE NAME OF A PSYCHIATRIST, DR. SINCLAIR. SHE AND I WENT TO COLUMBIA TOGETHER. HER PATIENTS ALL HAVE SECRET IDENTITIES.
SHE'S VERY DISCREET.
RIGHT, BUT I DON'T THINK THIS--
CONSIDER IT A WAY TO GET A SECOND OPINION, THEN.

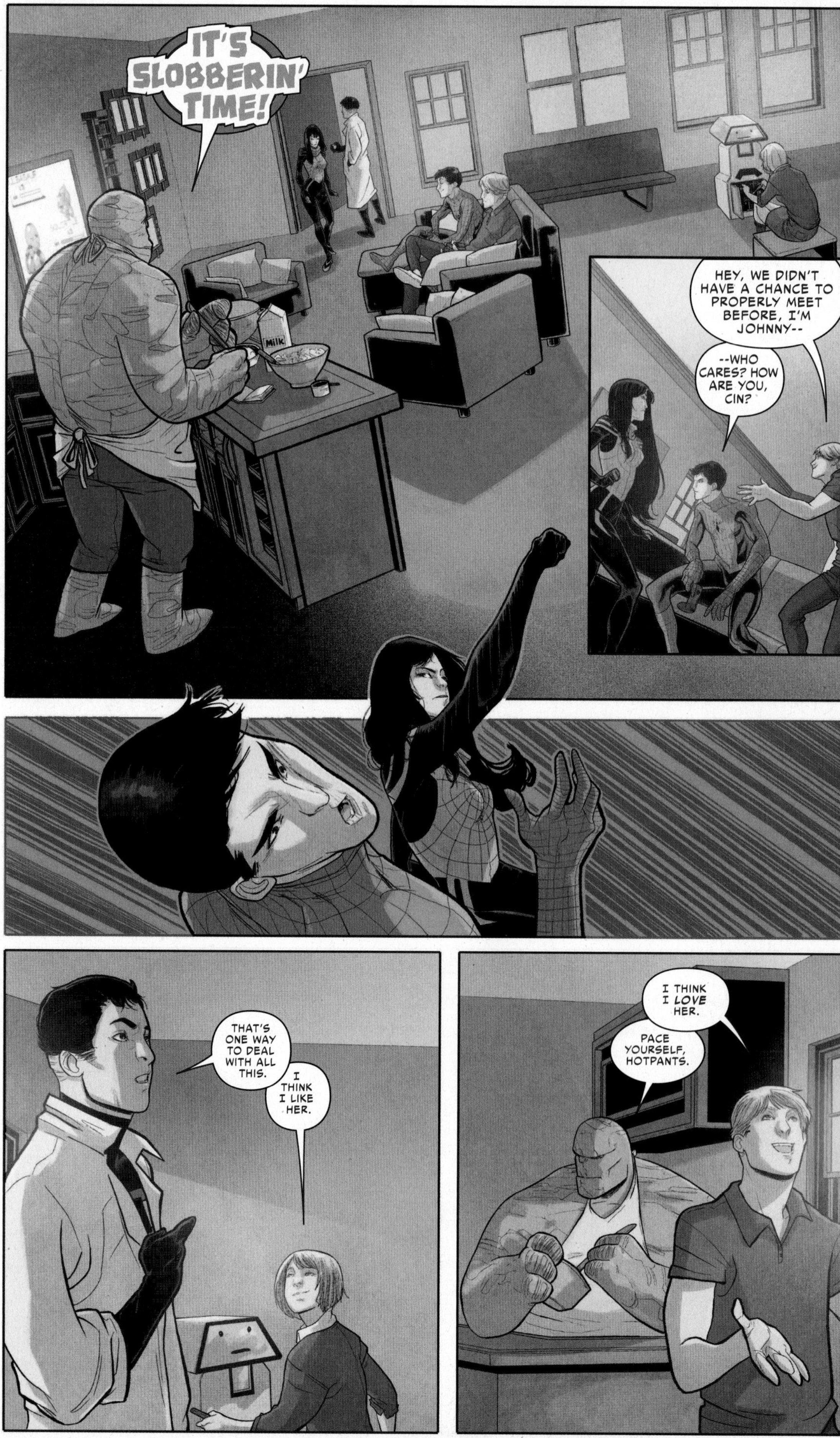
IT'S SLOBBERIN' TIME!
HEY, WE DIDN'T HAVE A CHANCE TO PROPERLY MEET BEFORE, I'M JOHNNY--
--WHO CARES? HOW ARE YOU, CIN?
Milk
THAT'S ONE WAY TO DEAL WITH ALL THIS.
I THINK I LIKE HER.
I THINK I *LOVE* HER.
PACE YOURSELF, HOTPANTS.

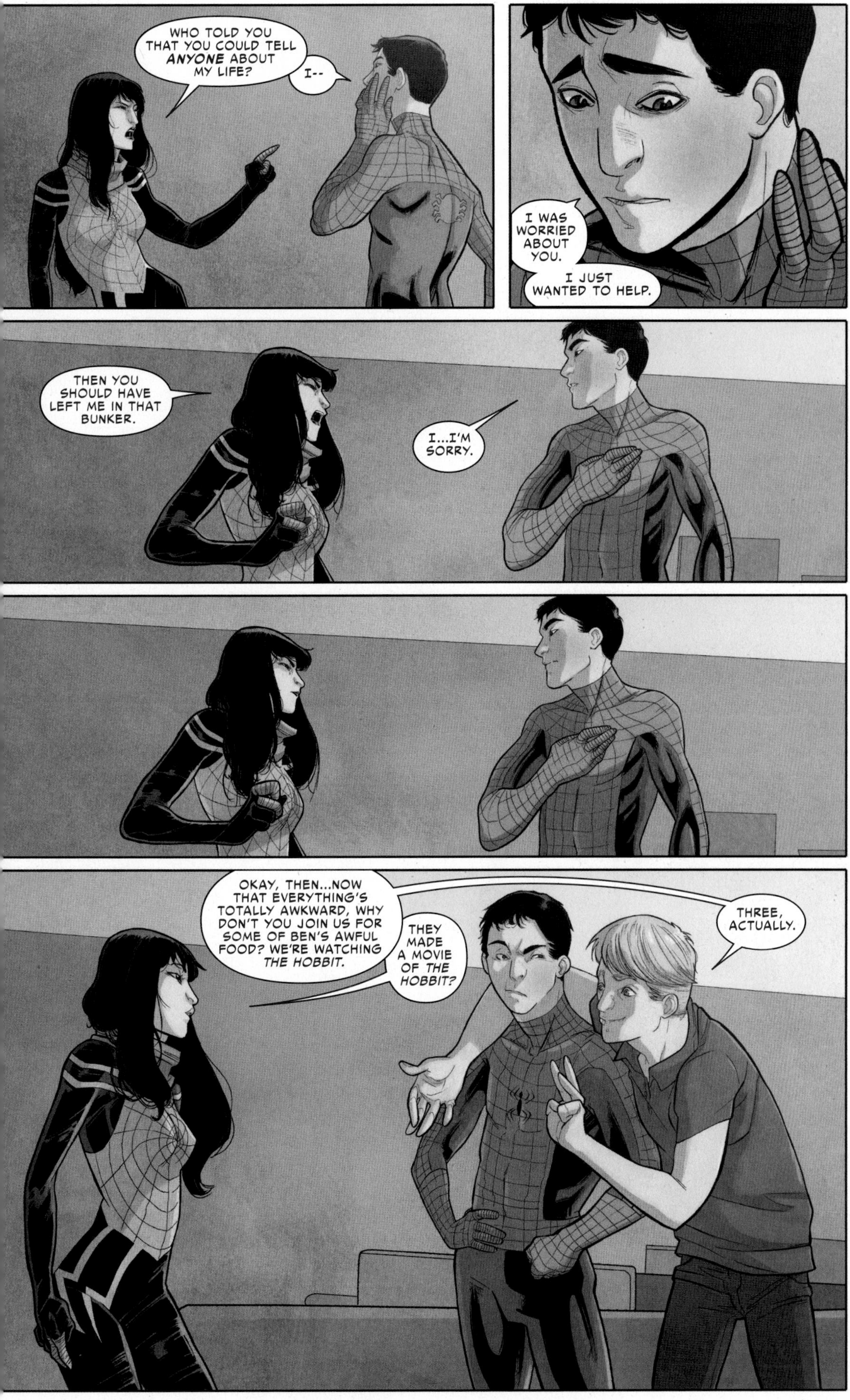
WHO TOLD YOU THAT YOU COULD TELL *ANYONE* ABOUT MY LIFE?
I--
I WAS WORRIED ABOUT YOU.
I JUST WANTED TO HELP.
THEN YOU SHOULD HAVE LEFT ME IN THAT BUNKER.
I...I'M SORRY.
OKAY, THEN...NOW THAT EVERYTHING'S TOTALLY AWKWARD, WHY DON'T YOU JOIN US FOR SOME OF BEN'S AWFUL FOOD? WE'RE WATCHING *THE HOBBIT.*
THEY MADE A MOVIE OF *THE HOBBIT?*
THREE, ACTUALLY.

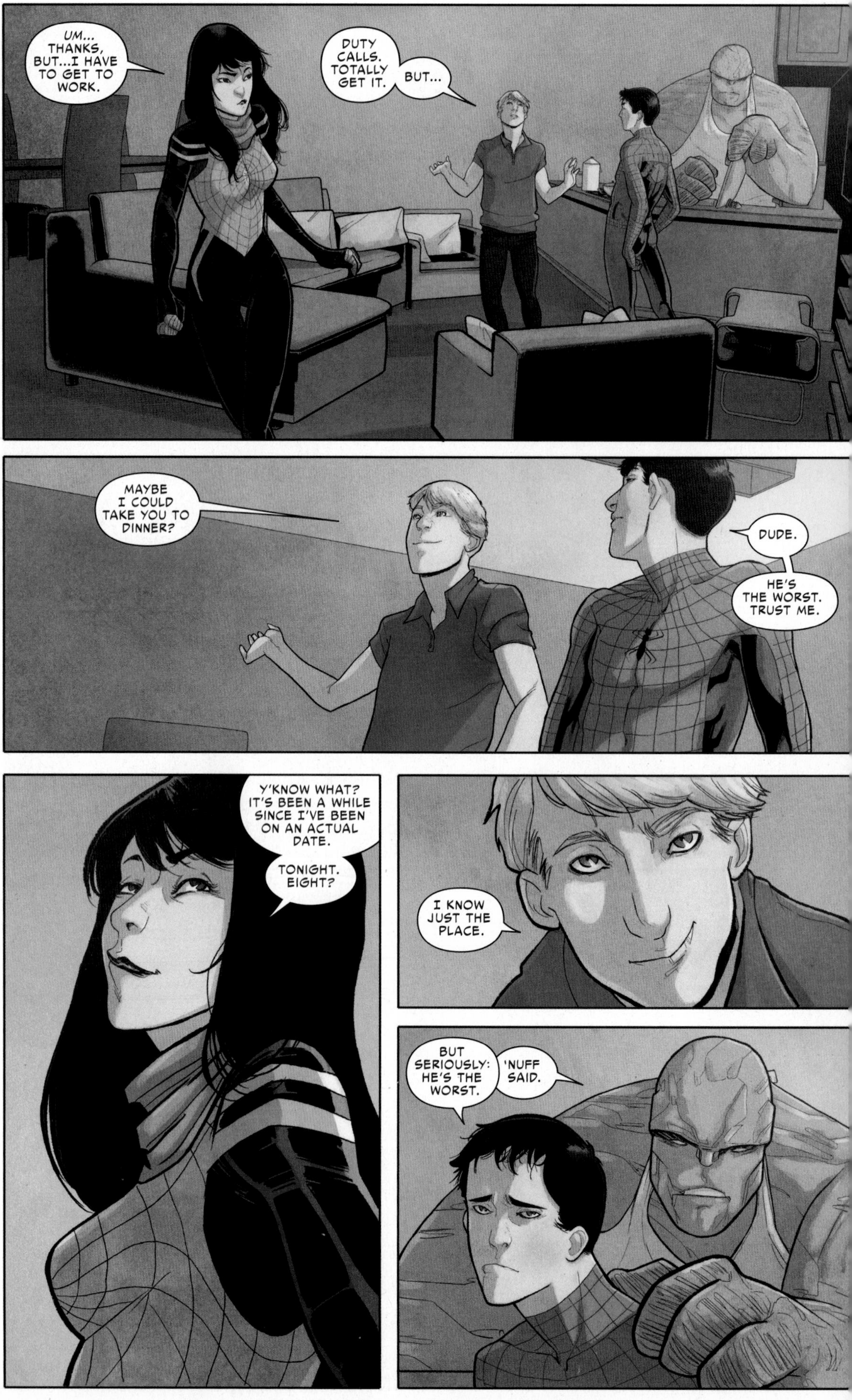

UM... THANKS, BUT...I HAVE TO GET TO WORK.
DUTY CALLS. TOTALLY GET IT.
BUT...
MAYBE I COULD TAKE YOU TO DINNER?
DUDE.
HE'S THE WORST. TRUST ME.
Y'KNOW WHAT? IT'S BEEN A WHILE SINCE I'VE BEEN ON AN ACTUAL DATE.
TONIGHT. EIGHT?
I KNOW JUST THE PLACE.
BUT SERIOUSLY: HE'S THE WORST.
'NUFF SAID.

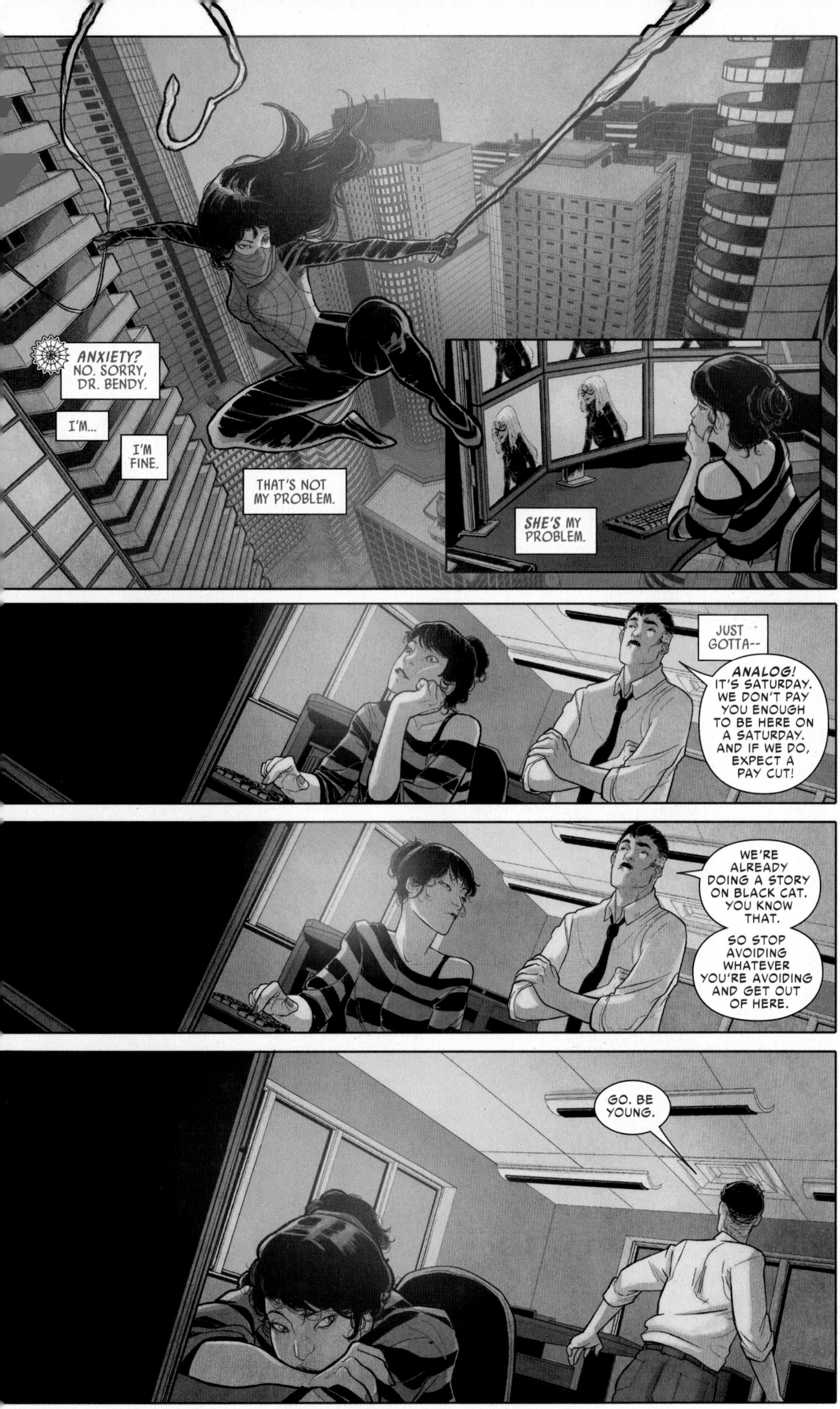
ANXIETY? NO. SORRY, DR. BENDY.
I'M...
I'M FINE.
THAT'S NOT MY PROBLEM.
SHE'S MY PROBLEM.
JUST GOTTA--
ANALOG! IT'S SATURDAY. WE DON'T PAY YOU ENOUGH TO BE HERE ON A SATURDAY. AND IF WE DO, EXPECT A PAY CUT!
WE'RE ALREADY DOING A STORY ON BLACK CAT. YOU KNOW THAT.
SO STOP AVOIDING WHATEVER YOU'RE AVOIDING AND GET OUT OF HERE.
GO. BE YOUNG.

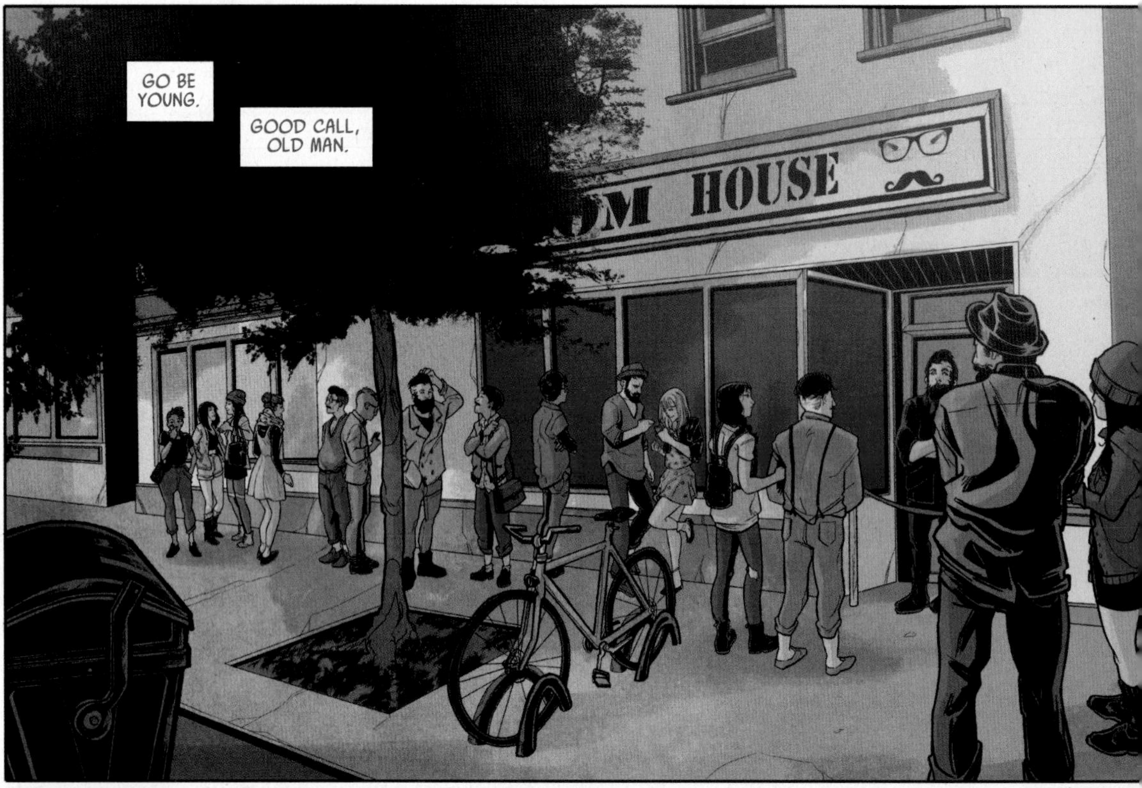
GO BE YOUNG.
GOOD CALL, OLD MAN.
OM HOUSE

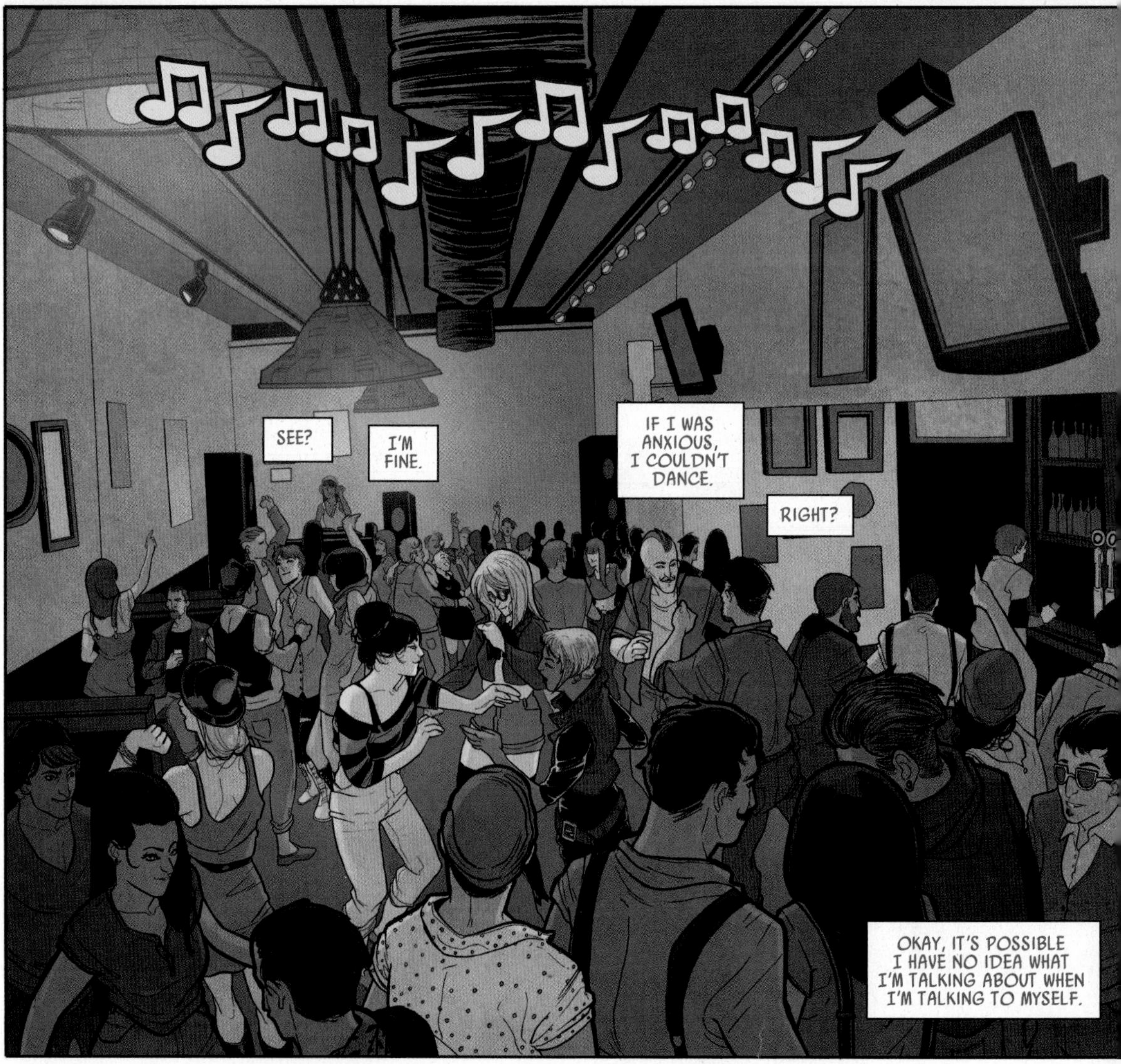
SEE?
I'M FINE.
IF I WAS ANXIOUS, I COULDN'T DANCE.
RIGHT?
OKAY, IT'S POSSIBLE I HAVE NO IDEA WHAT I'M TALKING ABOUT WHEN I'M TALKING TO MYSELF.

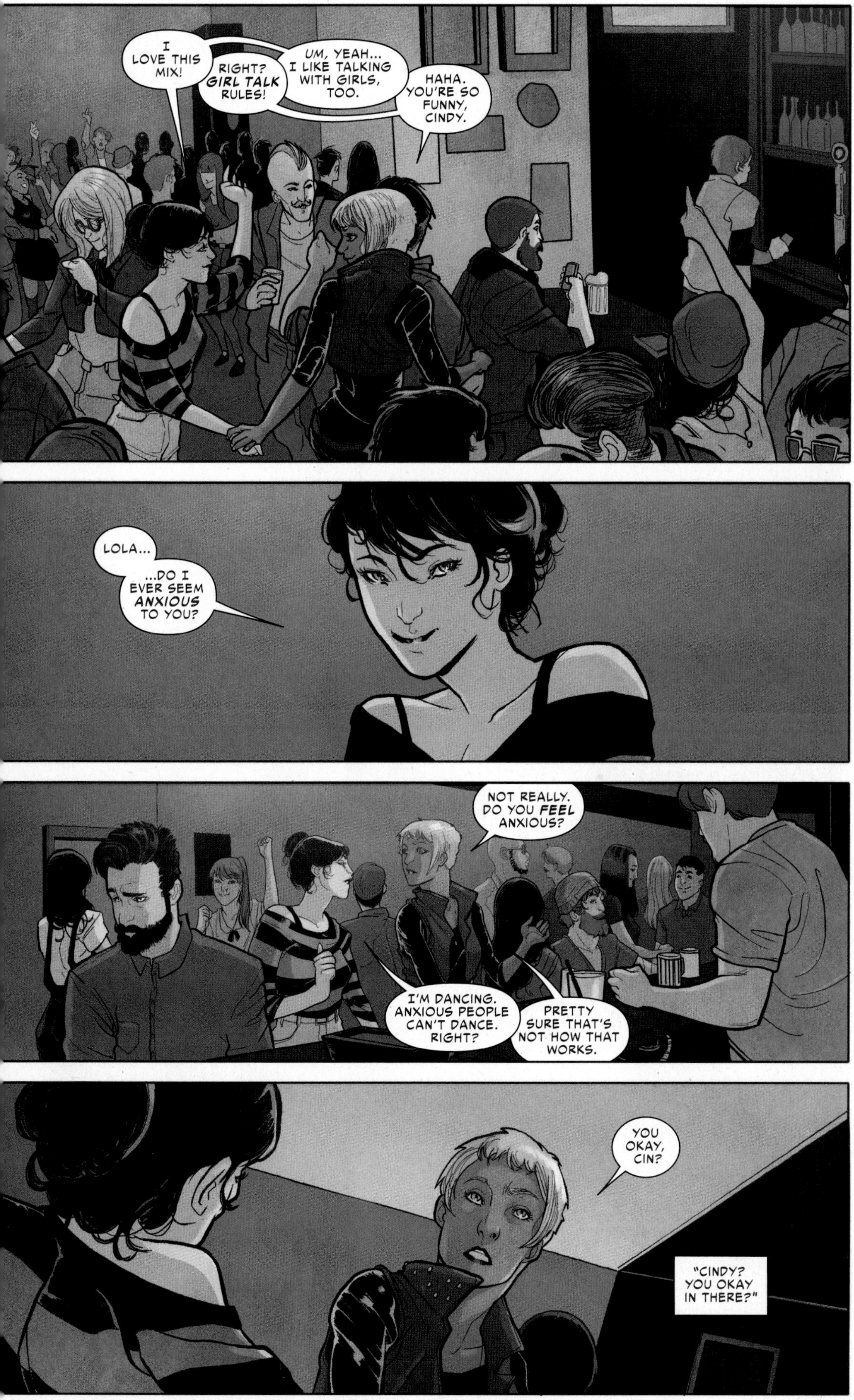
I LOVE THIS MIX!
RIGHT? GIRL TALK RULES!
UM, YEAH... I LIKE TALKING WITH GIRLS, TOO.
HAHA. YOU'RE SO FUNNY, CINDY.
LOLA...
...DO I EVER SEEM ANXIOUS TO YOU?
NOT REALLY. DO YOU FEEL ANXIOUS?
I'M DANCING. ANXIOUS PEOPLE CAN'T DANCE. RIGHT?
PRETTY SURE THAT'S NOT HOW THAT WORKS.
YOU OKAY, CIN?
"CINDY? YOU OKAY IN THERE?"

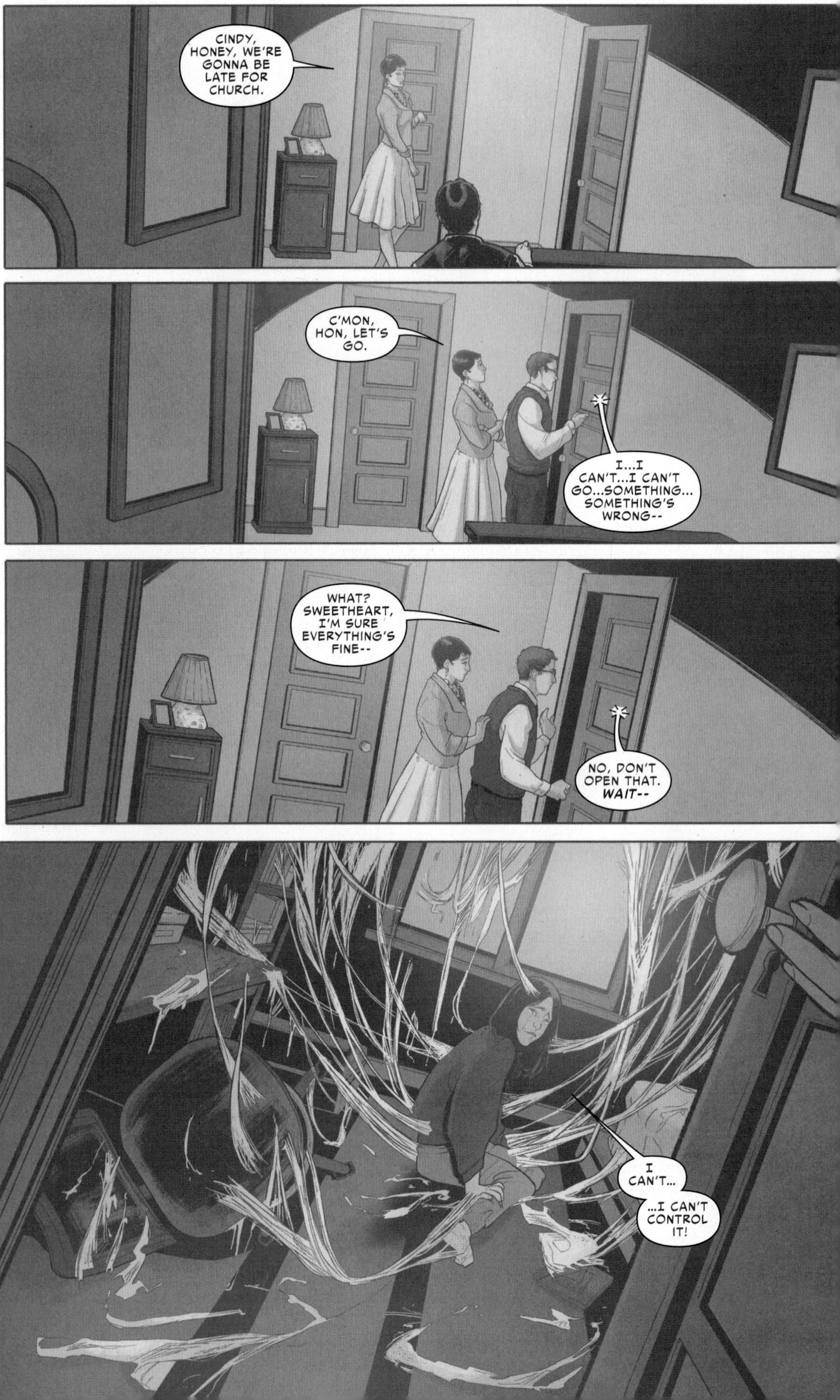
CINDY, HONEY, WE'RE GONNA BE LATE FOR CHURCH.
C'MON, HON, LET'S GO.
I...I CAN'T...I CAN'T GO...SOMETHING... SOMETHING'S WRONG--
WHAT? SWEETHEART, I'M SURE EVERYTHING'S FINE--
NO, DON'T OPEN THAT. *WAIT--*
I CAN'T...
...I CAN'T CONTROL IT!

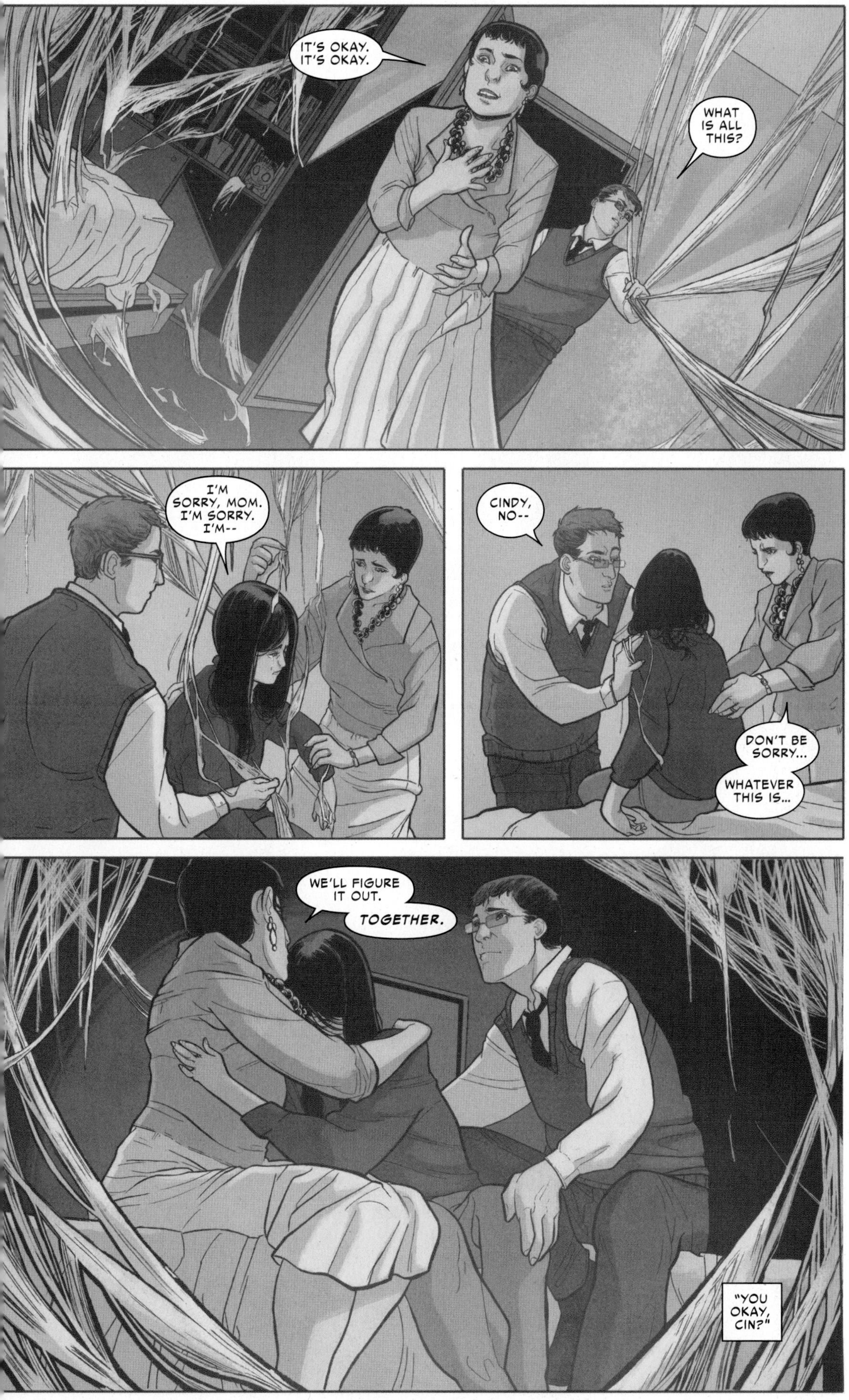
IT'S OKAY. IT'S OKAY.
WHAT IS ALL THIS?
I'M SORRY, MOM. I'M SORRY. I'M--
CINDY, NO--
DON'T BE SORRY...
WHATEVER THIS IS...
WE'LL FIGURE IT OUT.
TOGETHER.
"YOU OKAY, CIN?"

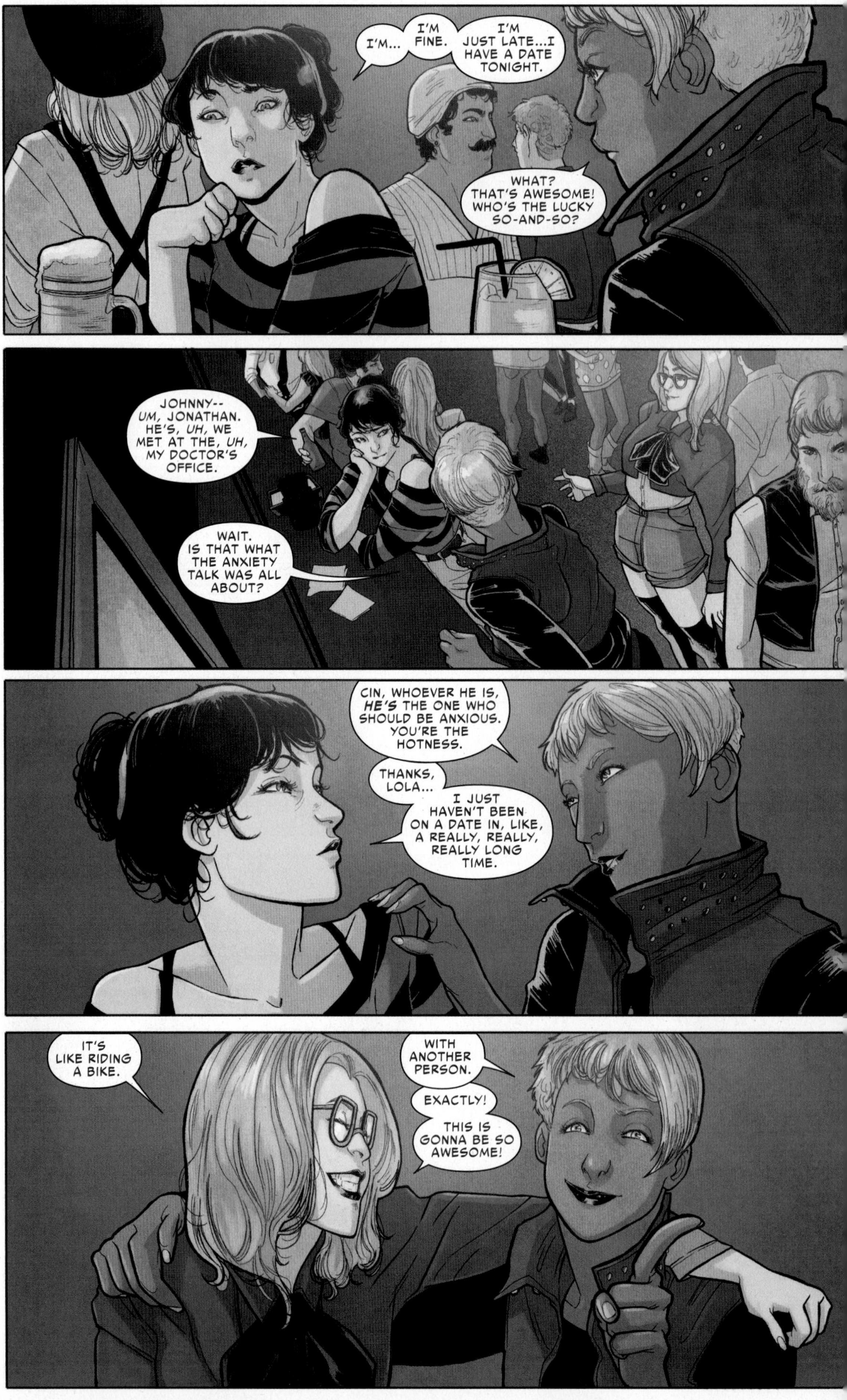
I'M...
I'M FINE.
I'M JUST LATE...I HAVE A DATE TONIGHT.
WHAT? THAT'S AWESOME! WHO'S THE LUCKY SO-AND-SO?
JOHNNY-- *UM*, JONATHAN. HE'S, *UH*, WE MET AT THE, *UH*, MY DOCTOR'S OFFICE.
WAIT. IS THAT WHAT THE ANXIETY TALK WAS ALL ABOUT?
CIN, WHOEVER HE IS, ***HE'S*** THE ONE WHO SHOULD BE ANXIOUS. YOU'RE THE HOTNESS.
THANKS, LOLA...
I JUST HAVEN'T BEEN ON A DATE IN, LIKE, A REALLY, REALLY, REALLY LONG TIME.
IT'S LIKE RIDING A BIKE.
WITH ANOTHER PERSON.
EXACTLY!
THIS IS GONNA BE SO AWESOME!

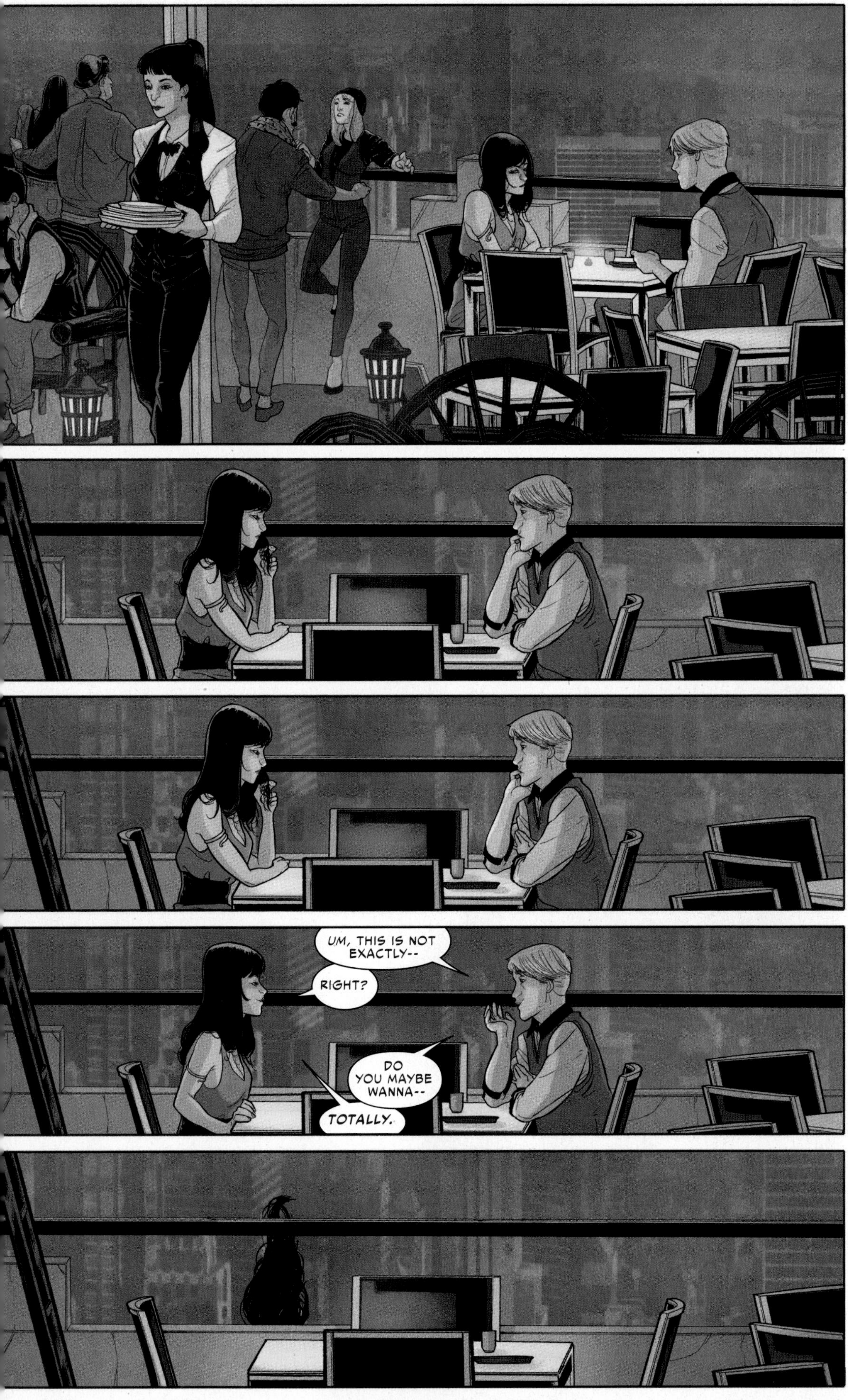
UM, THIS IS NOT EXACTLY--
RIGHT?
DO YOU MAYBE WANNA--
TOTALLY.

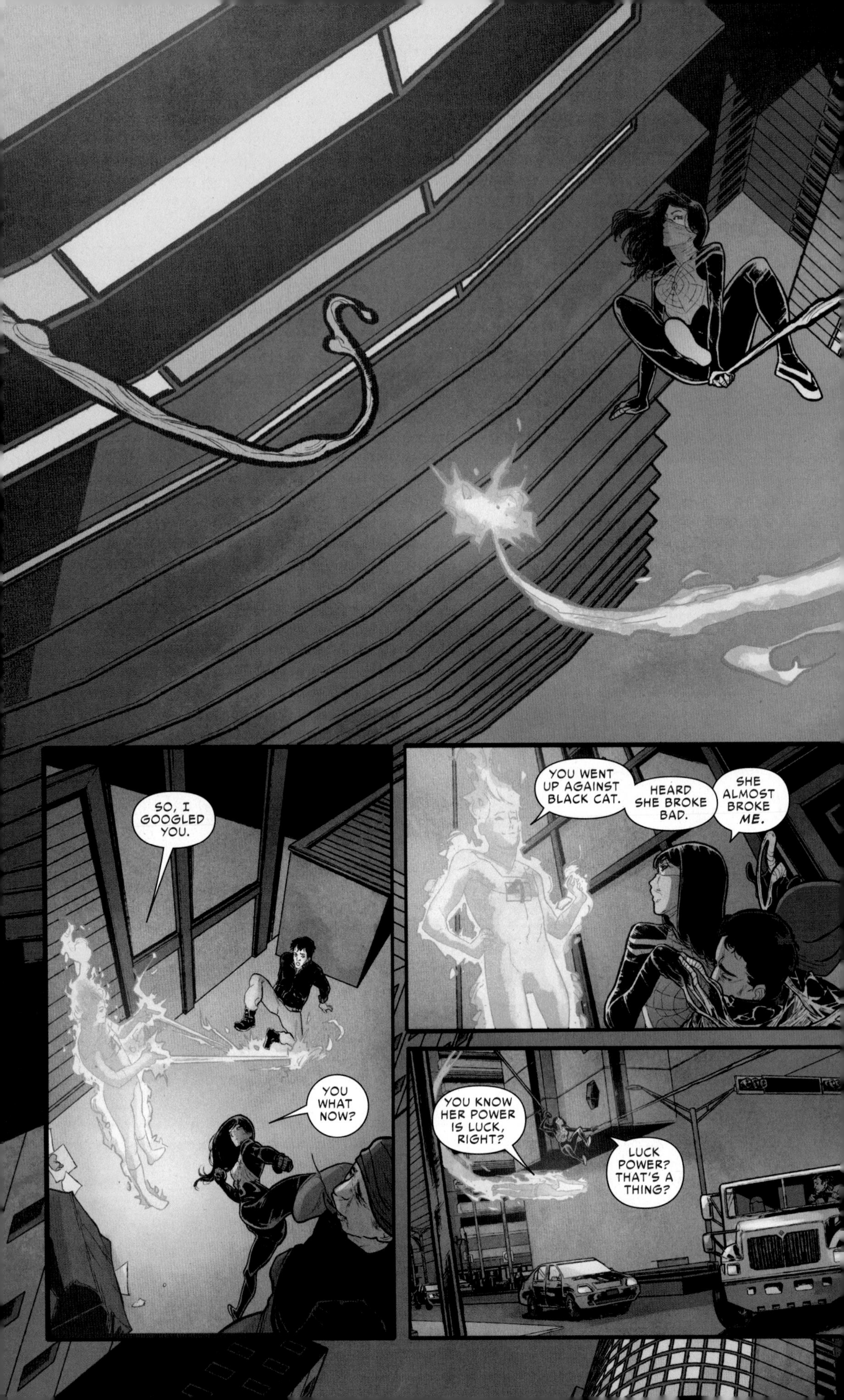
SO, I GOOGLED YOU.
YOU WHAT NOW?
YOU WENT UP AGAINST BLACK CAT.
HEARD SHE BROKE BAD.
SHE ALMOST BROKE ME.
YOU KNOW HER POWER IS LUCK, RIGHT?
LUCK POWER? THAT'S A THING?

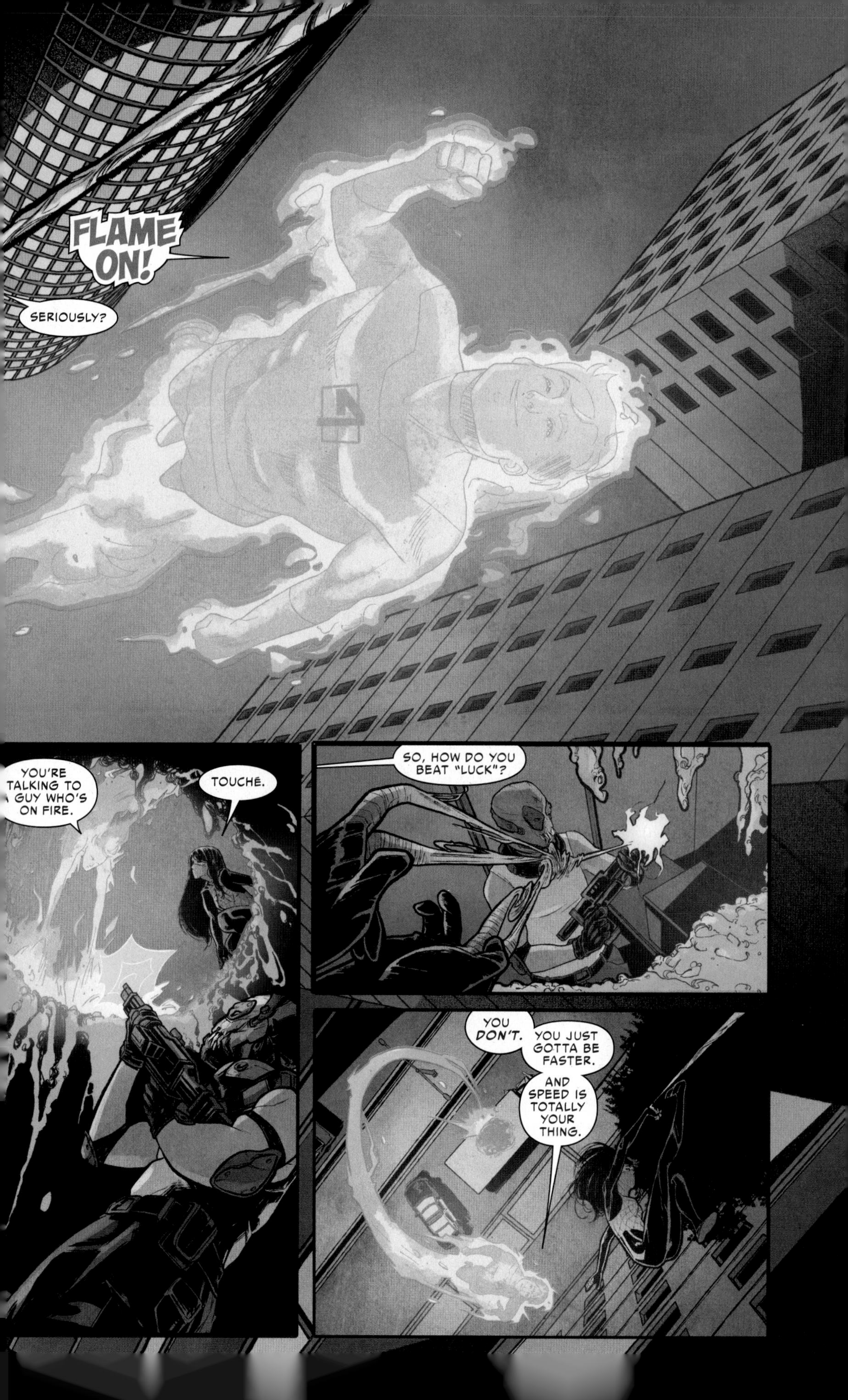
FLAME ON!
SERIOUSLY?
YOU'RE TALKING TO A GUY WHO'S ON FIRE.
TOUCHÉ.
SO, HOW DO YOU BEAT "LUCK"?
YOU *DON'T.*
YOU JUST GOTTA BE FASTER.
AND SPEED IS TOTALLY YOUR THING.

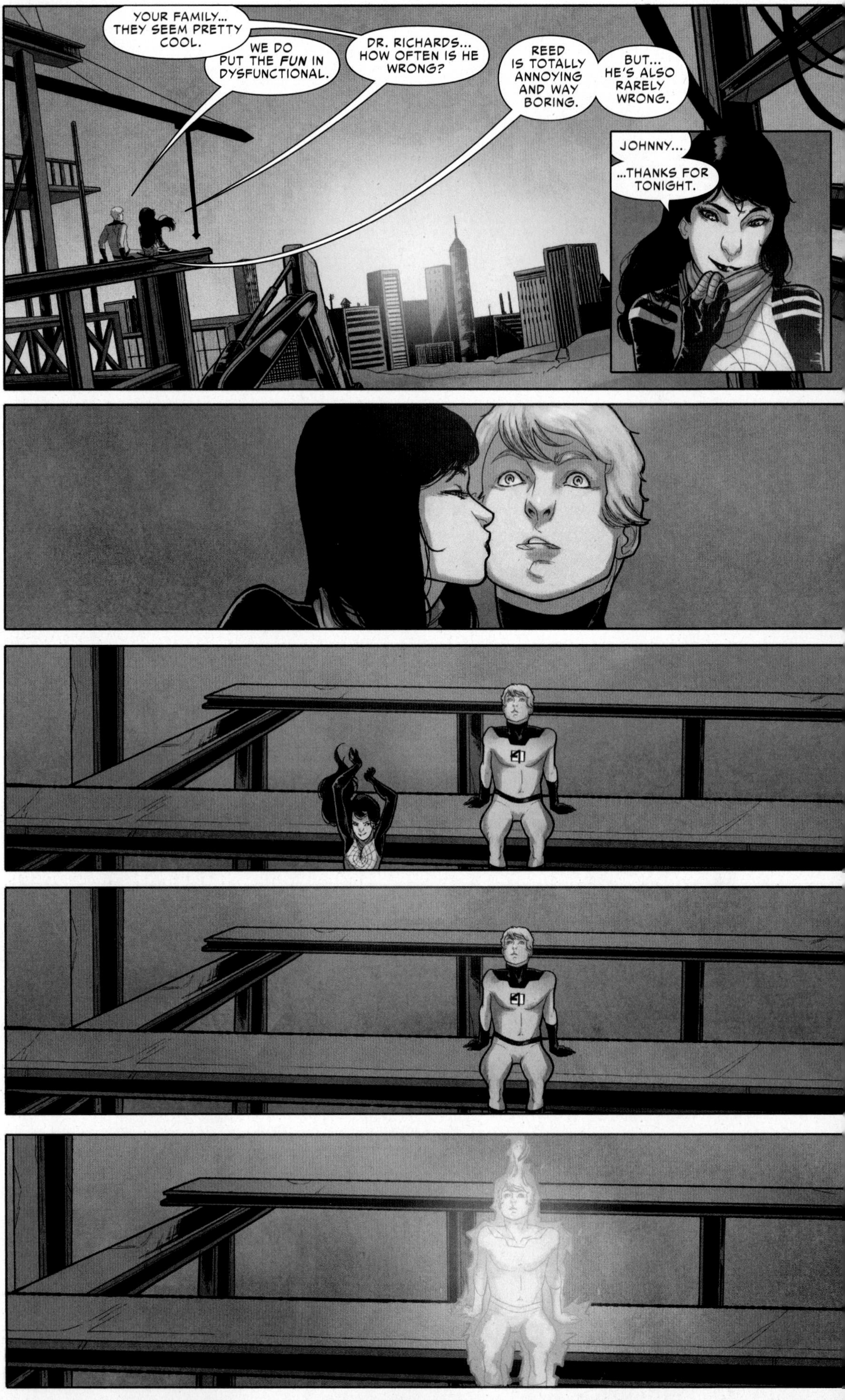
YOUR FAMILY... THEY SEEM PRETTY COOL.
WE DO PUT THE *FUN* IN DYSFUNCTIONAL.
DR. RICHARDS... HOW OFTEN IS HE WRONG?
REED IS TOTALLY ANNOYING AND WAY BORING.
BUT... HE'S ALSO RARELY WRONG.
JOHNNY...
...THANKS FOR TONIGHT.

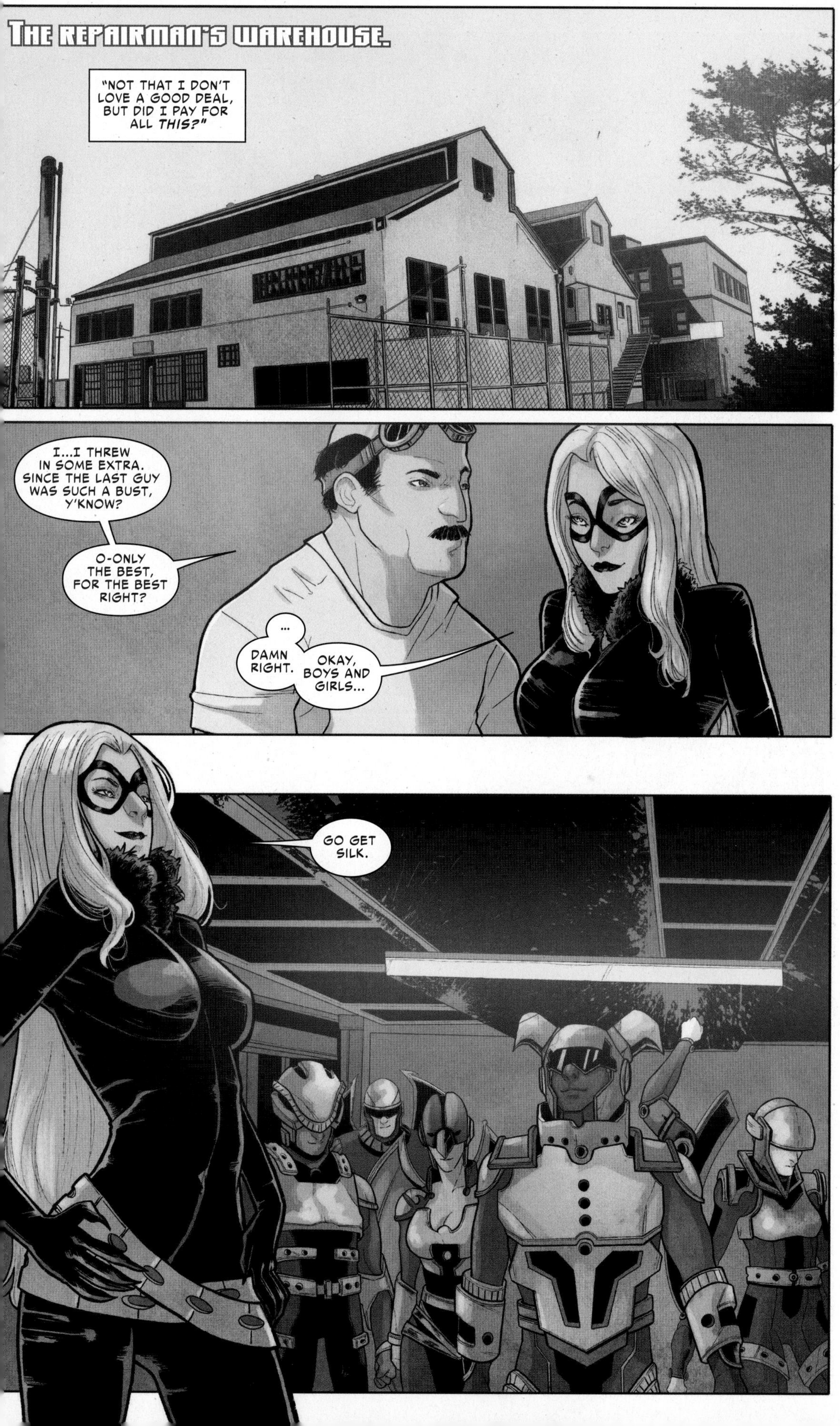
THE REPAIRMAN'S WAREHOUSE.
"NOT THAT I DON'T LOVE A GOOD DEAL, BUT DID I PAY FOR ALL *THIS?*"
I...I THREW IN SOME EXTRA. SINCE THE LAST GUY WAS SUCH A BUST, Y'KNOW?
O-ONLY THE BEST, FOR THE BEST RIGHT?
...
DAMN RIGHT.
OKAY, BOYS AND GIRLS...
GO GET SILK.

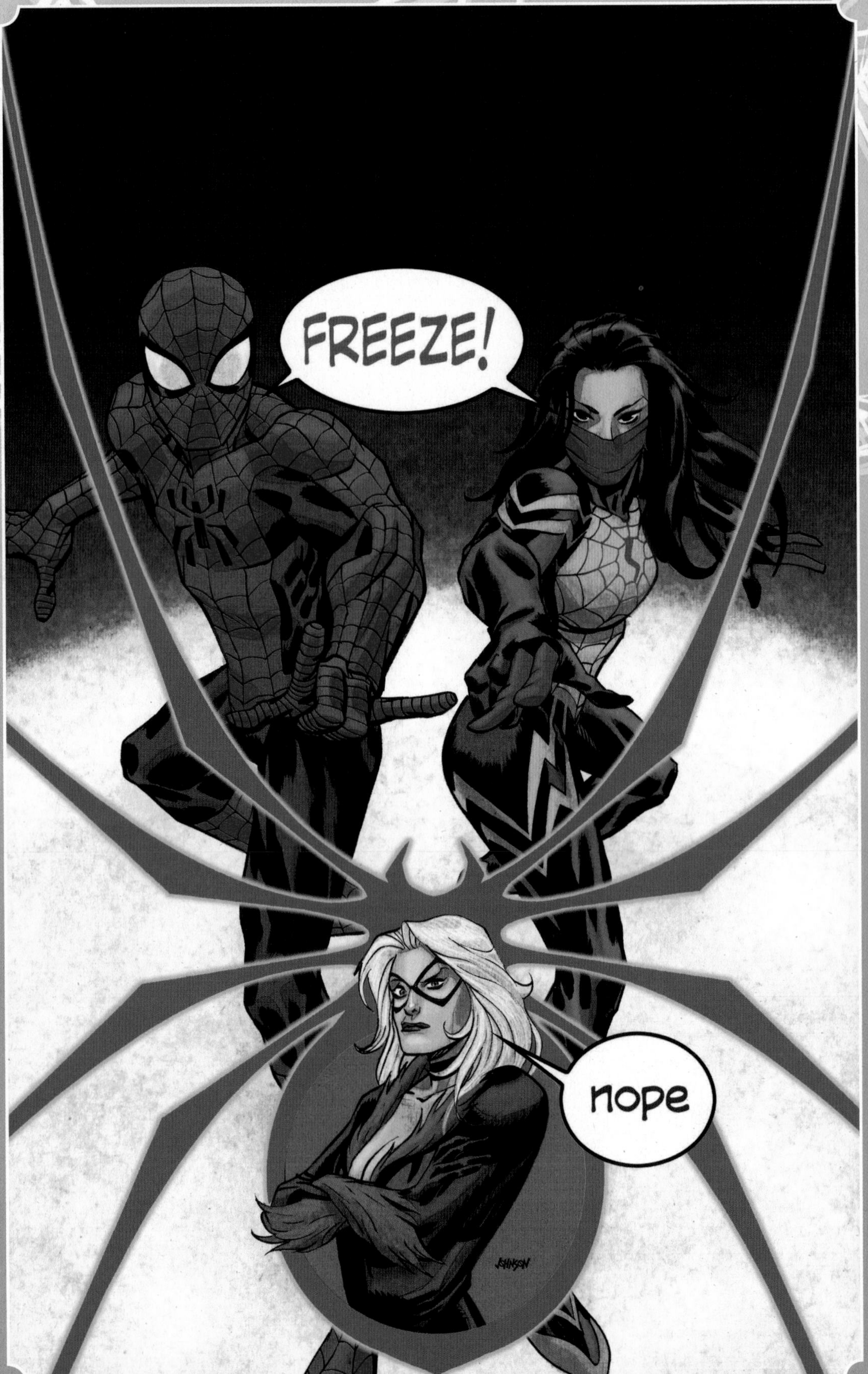
FREEZE!
nope
JOHNSON

SILK (2015A) #5

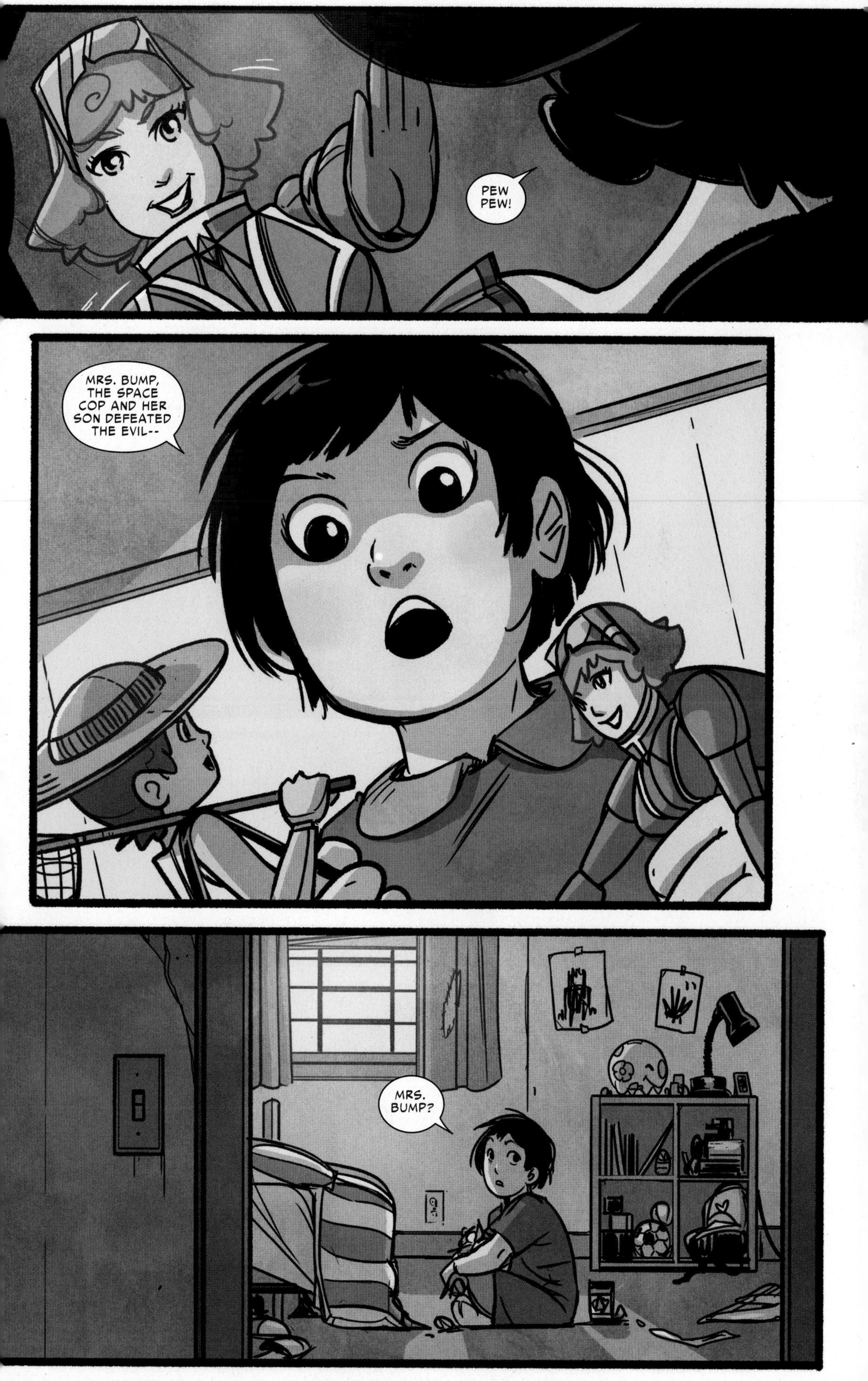
PEW PEW!
MRS. BUMP, THE SPACE COP AND HER SON DEFEATED THE EVIL--
MRS. BUMP?

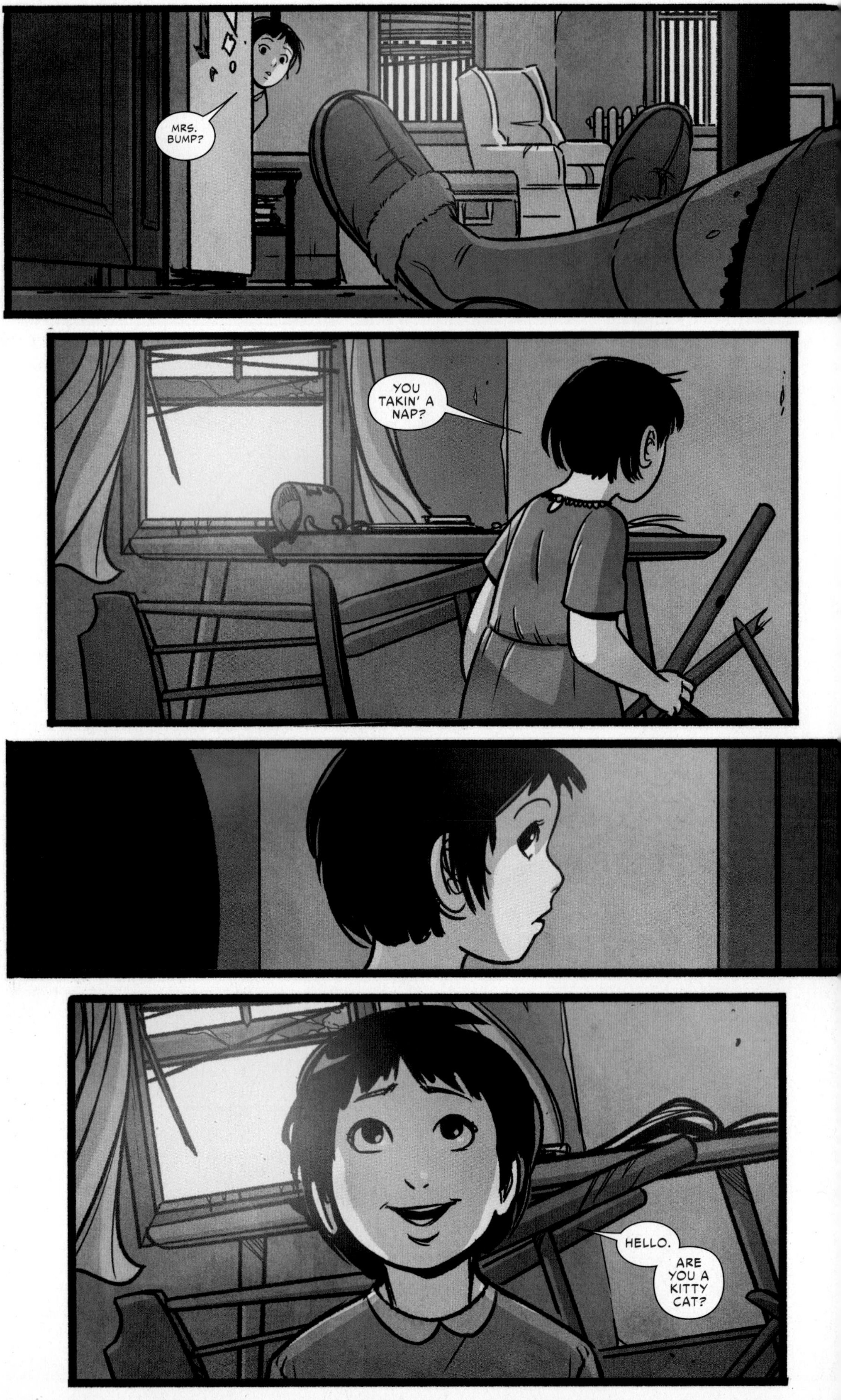
MRS. BUMP?
YOU TAKIN' A NAP?
HELLO.
ARE YOU A KITTY CAT?

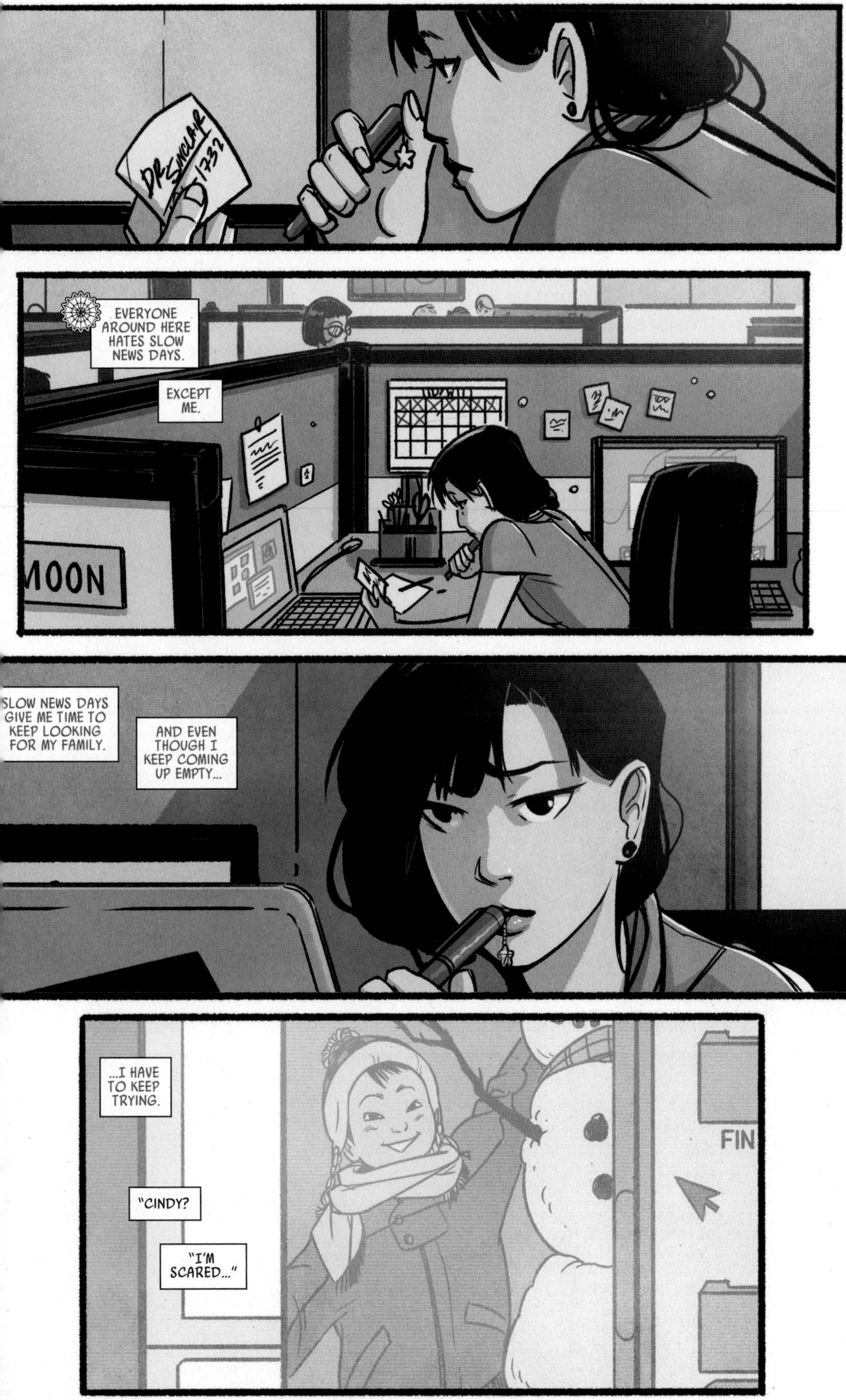
DR. SINCLAIR
EVERYONE AROUND HERE HATES SLOW NEWS DAYS.
EXCEPT ME.
MOON
SLOW NEWS DAYS GIVE ME TIME TO KEEP LOOKING FOR MY FAMILY.
AND EVEN THOUGH I KEEP COMING UP EMPTY...
...I HAVE TO KEEP TRYING.
"CINDY?
"I'M SCARED..."

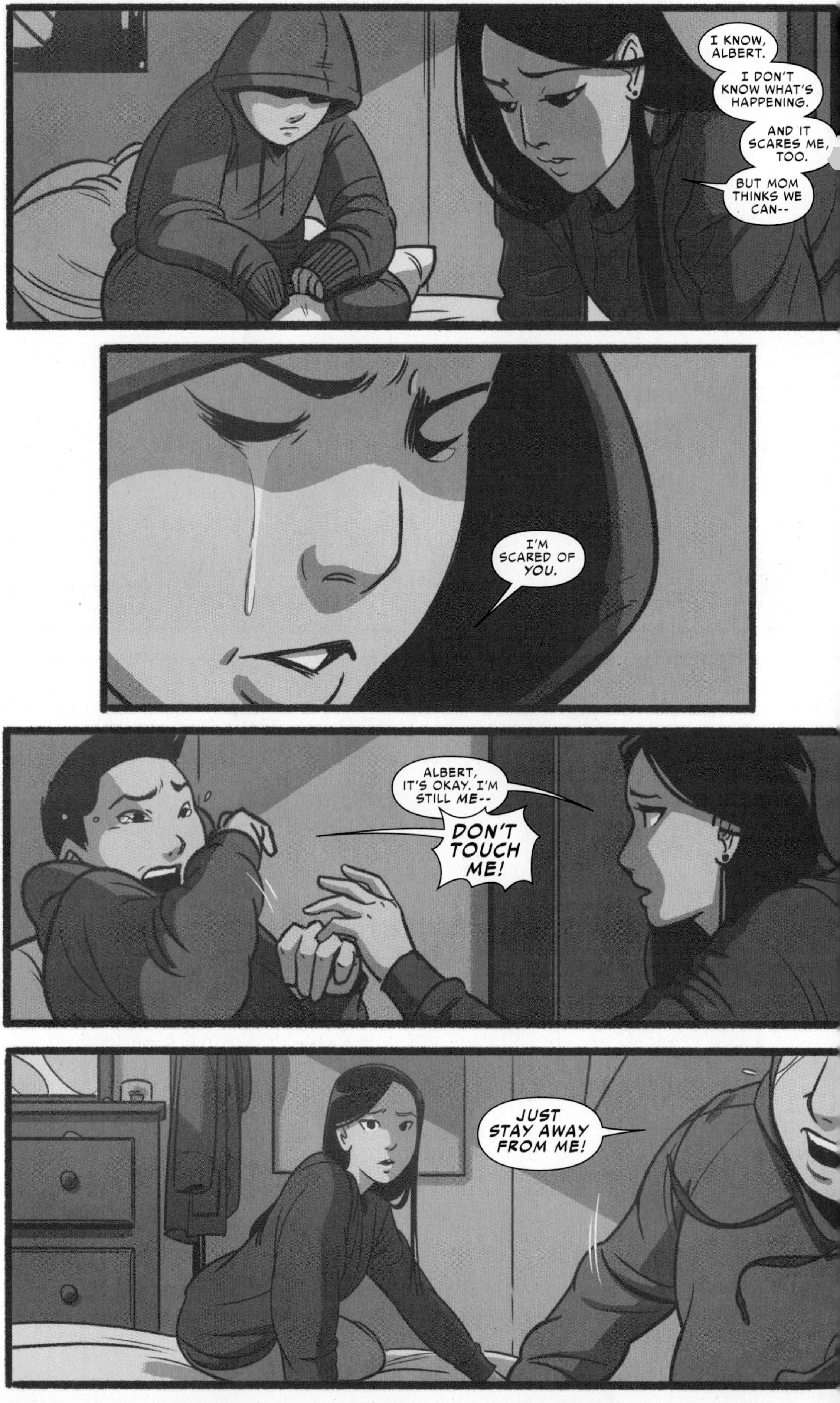
I KNOW, ALBERT.
I DON'T KNOW WHAT'S HAPPENING.
AND IT SCARES ME, TOO.
BUT MOM THINKS WE CAN--
I'M SCARED OF YOU.
ALBERT, IT'S OKAY. I'M STILL ME--
DON'T TOUCH ME!
JUST STAY AWAY FROM ME!

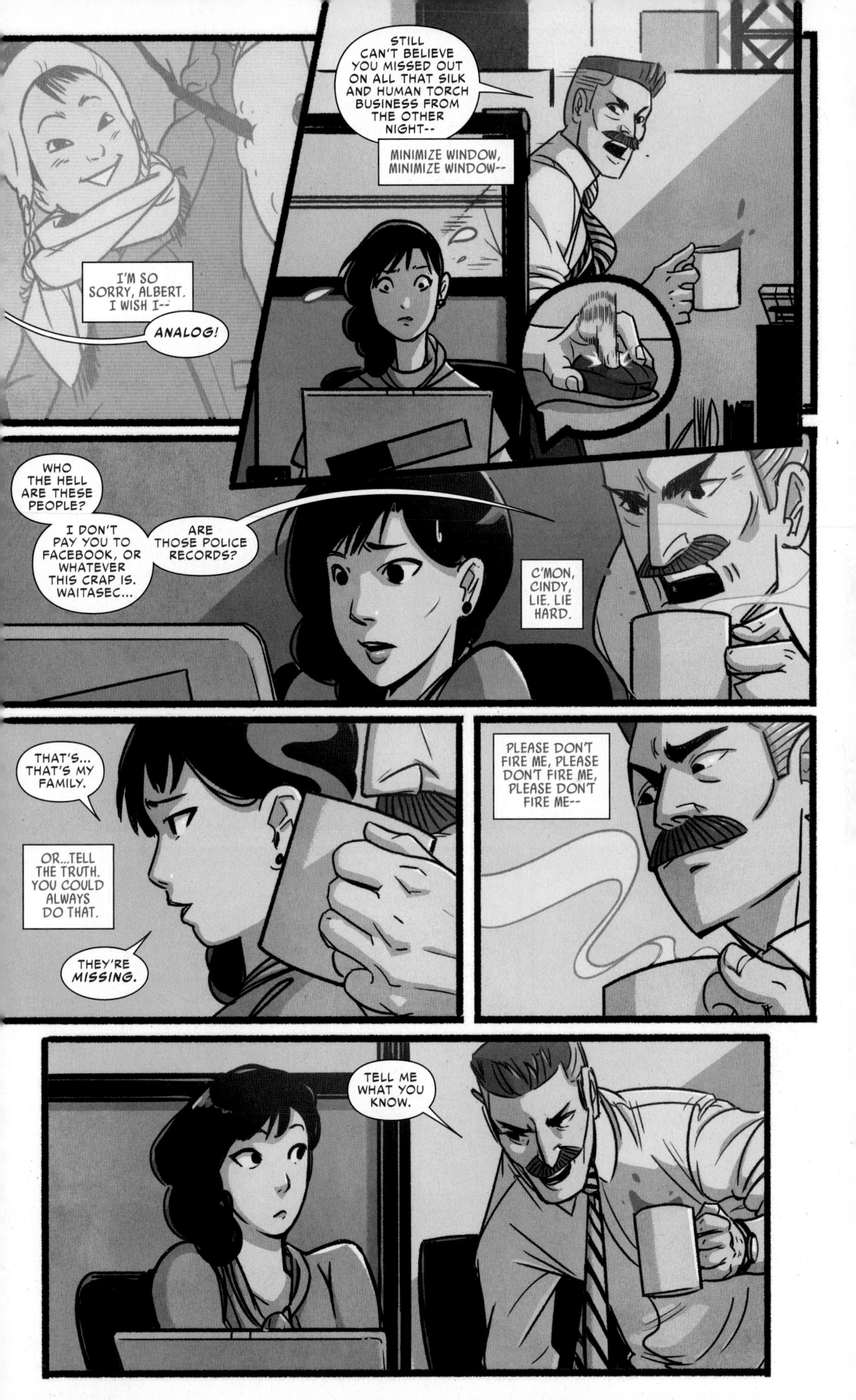
I'M SO SORRY, ALBERT. I WISH I--
ANALOG!
STILL CAN'T BELIEVE YOU MISSED OUT ON ALL THAT SILK AND HUMAN TORCH BUSINESS FROM THE OTHER NIGHT--
MINIMIZE WINDOW, MINIMIZE WINDOW--
WHO THE HELL ARE THESE PEOPLE?
I DON'T PAY YOU TO FACEBOOK, OR WHATEVER THIS CRAP IS. WAITASEC...
ARE THOSE POLICE RECORDS?
C'MON, CINDY, LIE. LIE HARD.
THAT'S... THAT'S MY FAMILY.
OR...TELL THE TRUTH. YOU COULD ALWAYS DO THAT.
THEY'RE MISSING.
PLEASE DON'T FIRE ME, PLEASE DON'T FIRE ME, PLEASE DON'T FIRE ME--
TELL ME WHAT YOU KNOW.

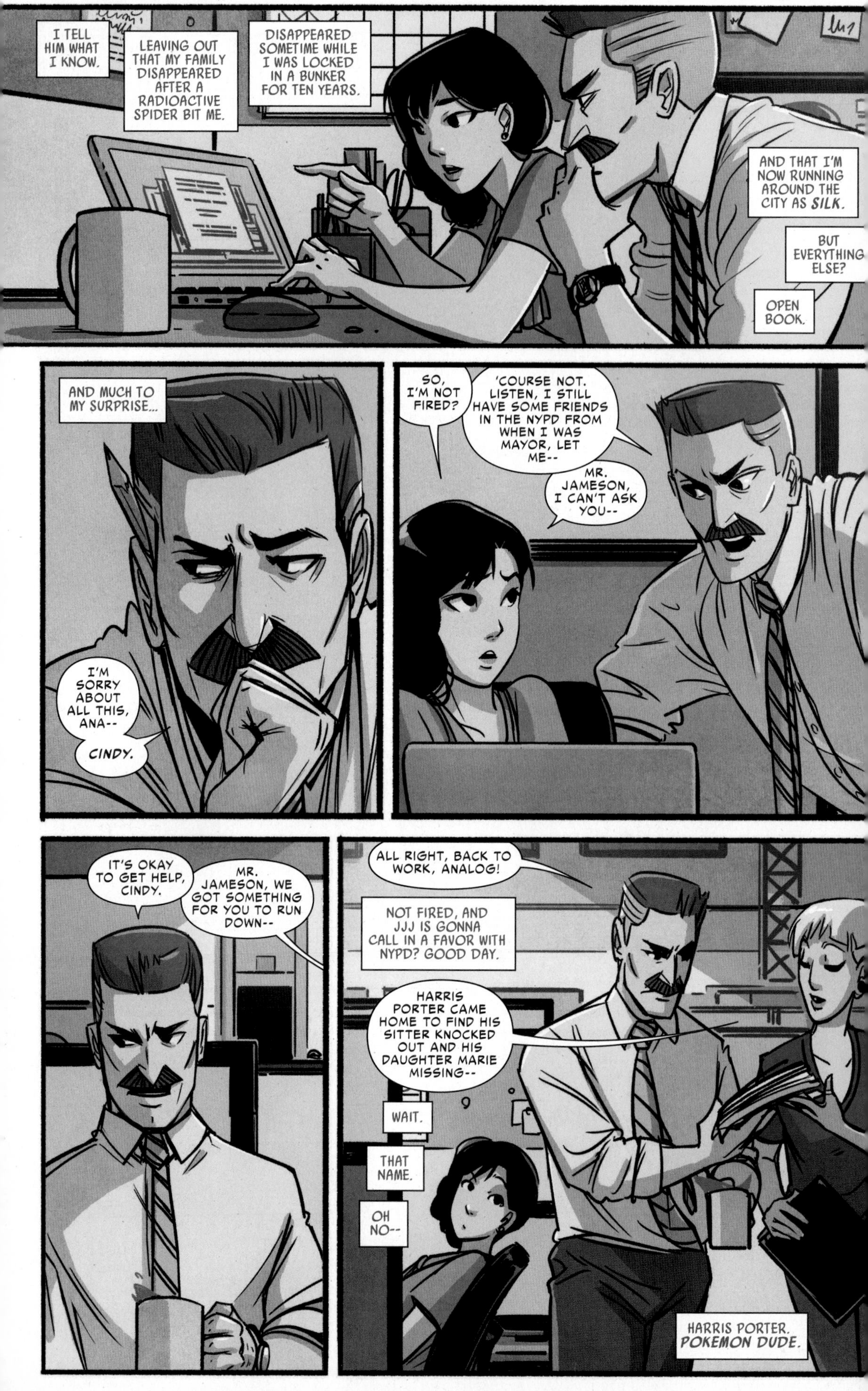
I TELL HIM WHAT I KNOW.
LEAVING OUT THAT MY FAMILY DISAPPEARED AFTER A RADIOACTIVE SPIDER BIT ME.
DISAPPEARED SOMETIME WHILE I WAS LOCKED IN A BUNKER FOR TEN YEARS.
AND THAT I'M NOW RUNNING AROUND THE CITY AS SILK.
BUT EVERYTHING ELSE?
OPEN BOOK.
AND MUCH TO MY SURPRISE...
I'M SORRY ABOUT ALL THIS, ANA--
CINDY.
SO, I'M NOT FIRED?
'COURSE NOT. LISTEN, I STILL HAVE SOME FRIENDS IN THE NYPD FROM WHEN I WAS MAYOR, LET ME--
MR. JAMESON, I CAN'T ASK YOU--
IT'S OKAY TO GET HELP, CINDY.
MR. JAMESON, WE GOT SOMETHING FOR YOU TO RUN DOWN--
ALL RIGHT, BACK TO WORK, ANALOG!
NOT FIRED, AND JJJ IS GONNA CALL IN A FAVOR WITH NYPD? GOOD DAY.
HARRIS PORTER CAME HOME TO FIND HIS SITTER KNOCKED OUT AND HIS DAUGHTER MARIE MISSING--
WAIT.
THAT NAME.
OH NO--
HARRIS PORTER. POKEMON DUDE.

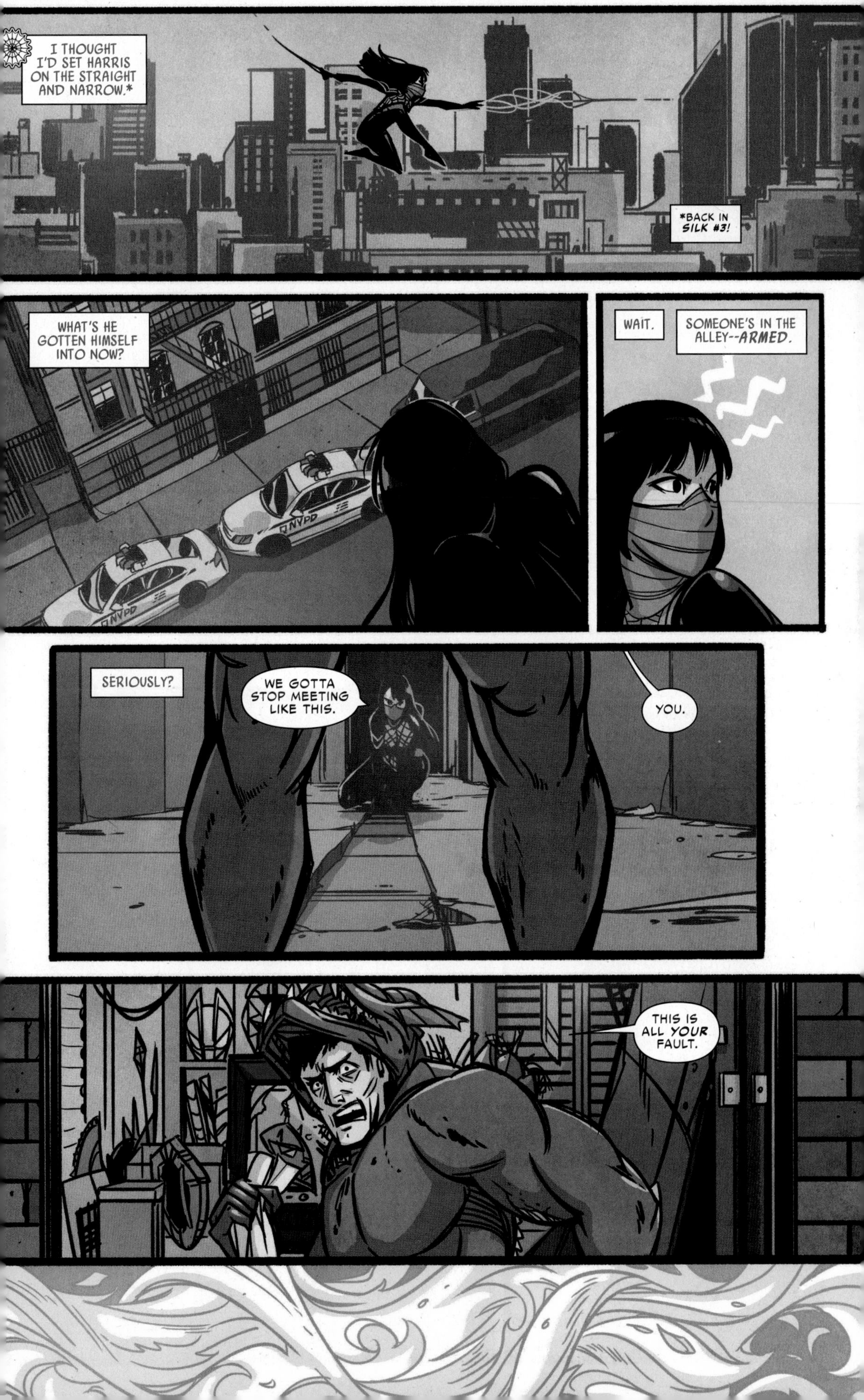
I THOUGHT I'D SET HARRIS ON THE STRAIGHT AND NARROW.*
*BACK IN SILK #3!
WHAT'S HE GOTTEN HIMSELF INTO NOW?
WAIT.
SOMEONE'S IN THE ALLEY--ARMED.
SERIOUSLY?
WE GOTTA STOP MEETING LIKE THIS.
YOU.
THIS IS ALL YOUR FAULT.

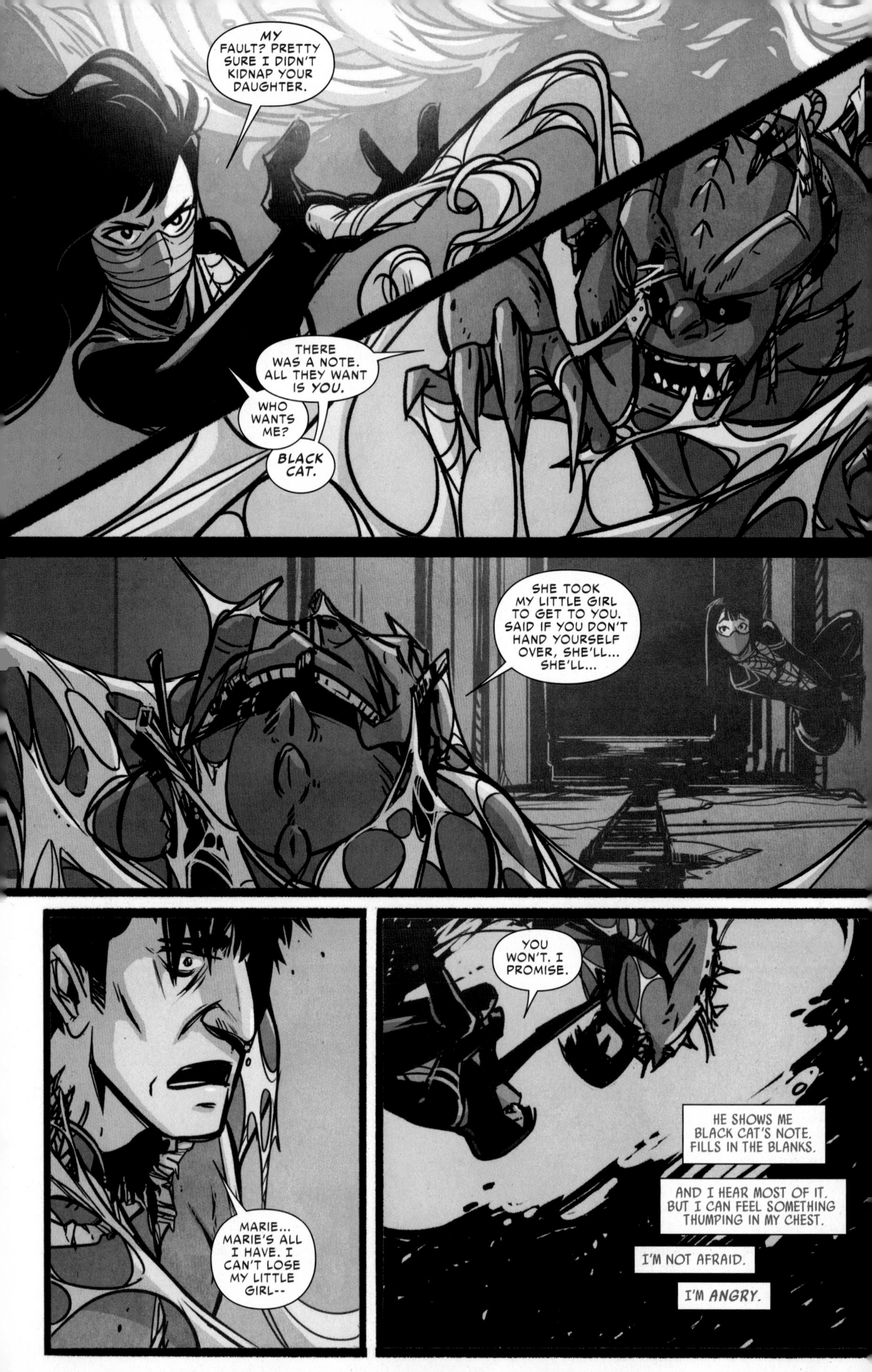
MY FAULT? PRETTY SURE I DIDN'T KIDNAP YOUR DAUGHTER.
THERE WAS A NOTE. ALL THEY WANT IS YOU.
WHO WANTS ME?
BLACK CAT.
SHE TOOK MY LITTLE GIRL TO GET TO YOU. SAID IF YOU DON'T HAND YOURSELF OVER, SHE'LL... SHE'LL...
MARIE... MARIE'S ALL I HAVE. I CAN'T LOSE MY LITTLE GIRL--
YOU WON'T. I PROMISE.
HE SHOWS ME BLACK CAT'S NOTE. FILLS IN THE BLANKS.
AND I HEAR MOST OF IT. BUT I CAN FEEL SOMETHING THUMPING IN MY CHEST.
I'M NOT AFRAID.
I'M ANGRY.

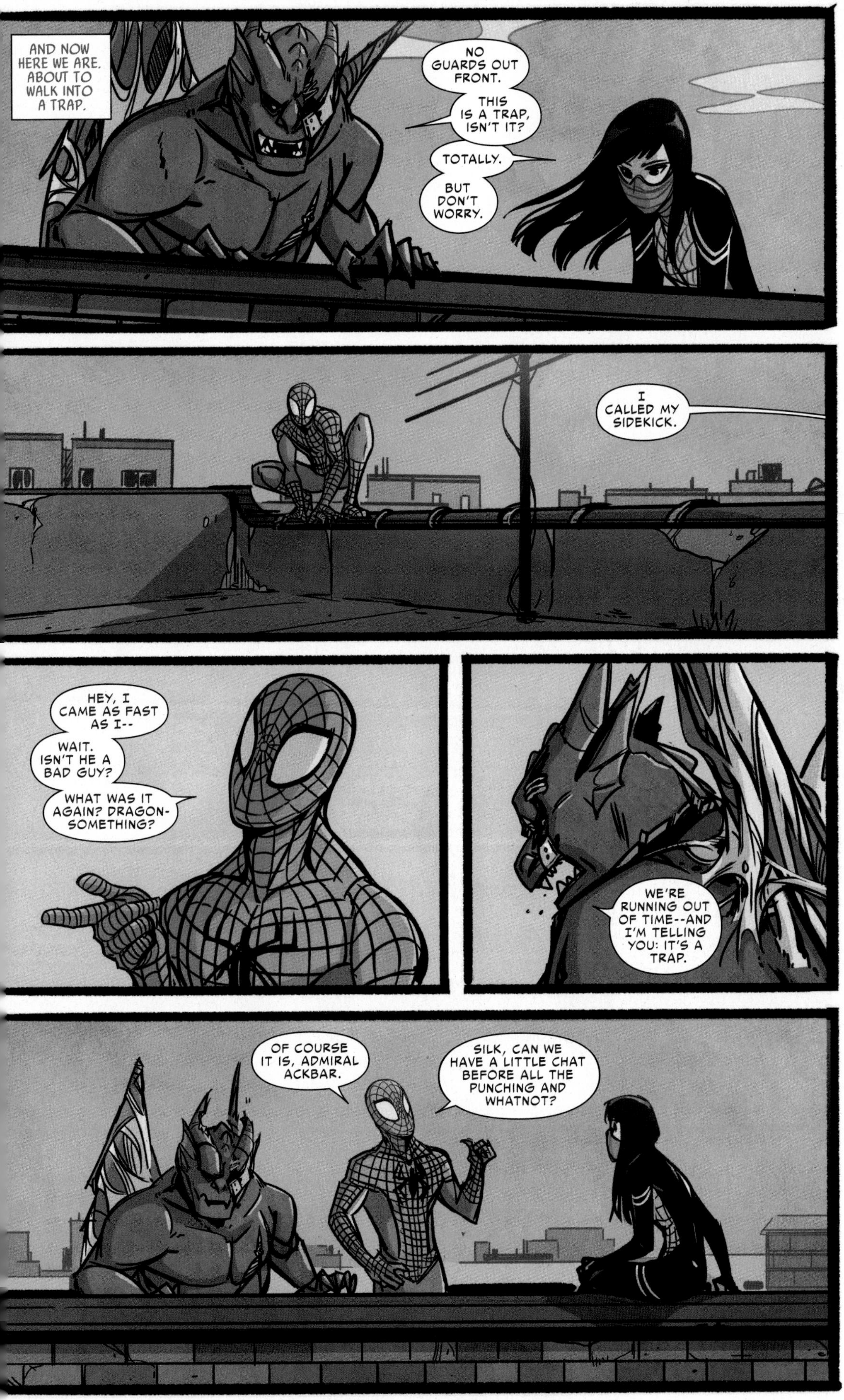

AND NOW HERE WE ARE. ABOUT TO WALK INTO A TRAP.
NO GUARDS OUT FRONT.
THIS IS A TRAP, ISN'T IT?
TOTALLY.
BUT DON'T WORRY.
I CALLED MY SIDEKICK.
HEY, I CAME AS FAST AS I--
WAIT. ISN'T HE A BAD GUY?
WHAT WAS IT AGAIN? DRAGON-SOMETHING?
WE'RE RUNNING OUT OF TIME--AND I'M TELLING YOU: IT'S A TRAP.
OF COURSE IT IS, ADMIRAL ACKBAR.
SILK, CAN WE HAVE A LITTLE CHAT BEFORE ALL THE PUNCHING AND WHATNOT?

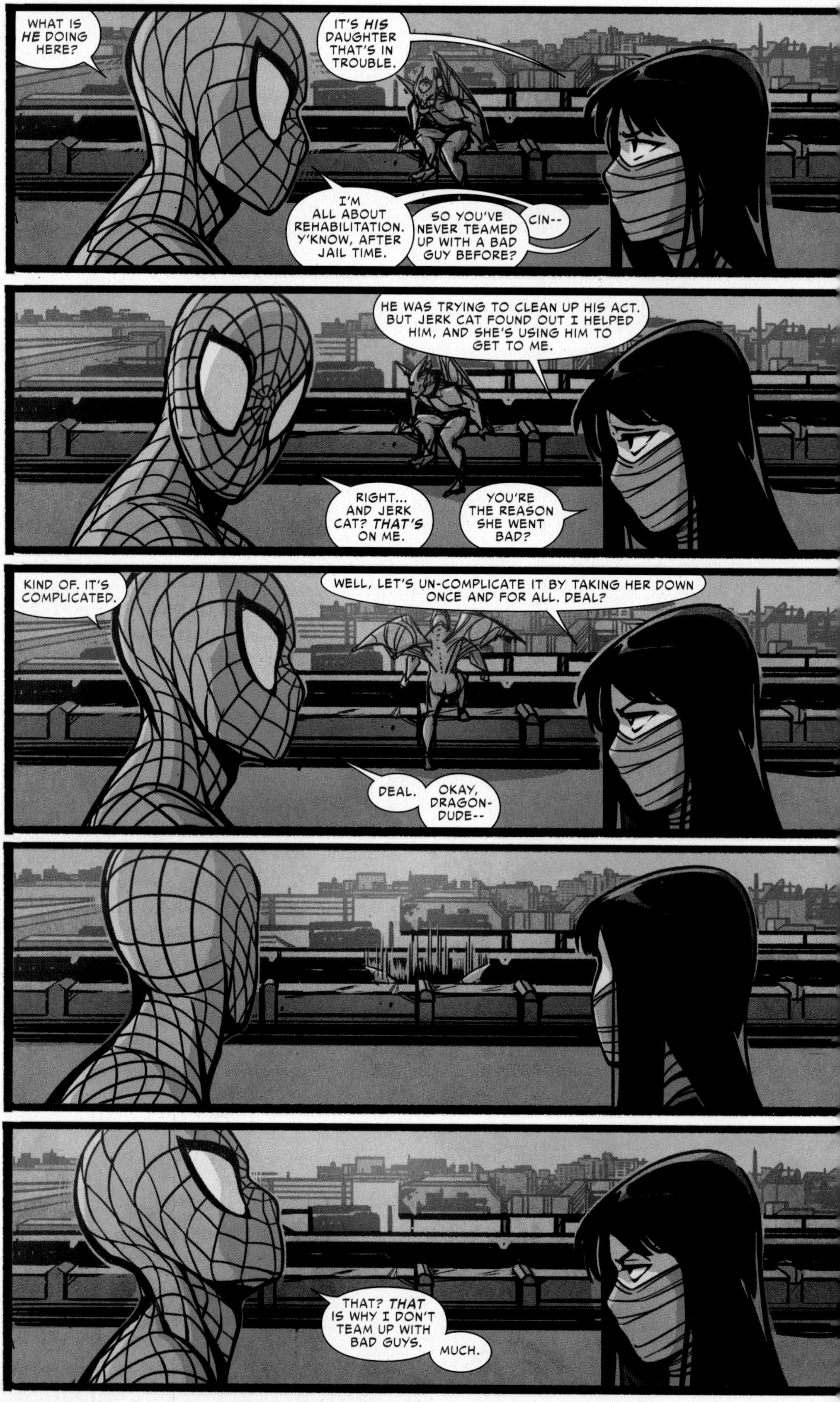
WHAT IS HE DOING HERE?
IT'S HIS DAUGHTER THAT'S IN TROUBLE.
I'M ALL ABOUT REHABILITATION. Y'KNOW, AFTER JAIL TIME.
CIN--
SO YOU'VE NEVER TEAMED UP WITH A BAD GUY BEFORE?
HE WAS TRYING TO CLEAN UP HIS ACT. BUT JERK CAT FOUND OUT I HELPED HIM, AND SHE'S USING HIM TO GET TO ME.
RIGHT... AND JERK CAT? THAT'S ON ME.
YOU'RE THE REASON SHE WENT BAD?
KIND OF. IT'S COMPLICATED.
WELL, LET'S UN-COMPLICATE IT BY TAKING HER DOWN ONCE AND FOR ALL. DEAL?
DEAL.
OKAY, DRAGON-DUDE--
THAT? THAT IS WHY I DON'T TEAM UP WITH BAD GUYS.
MUCH.

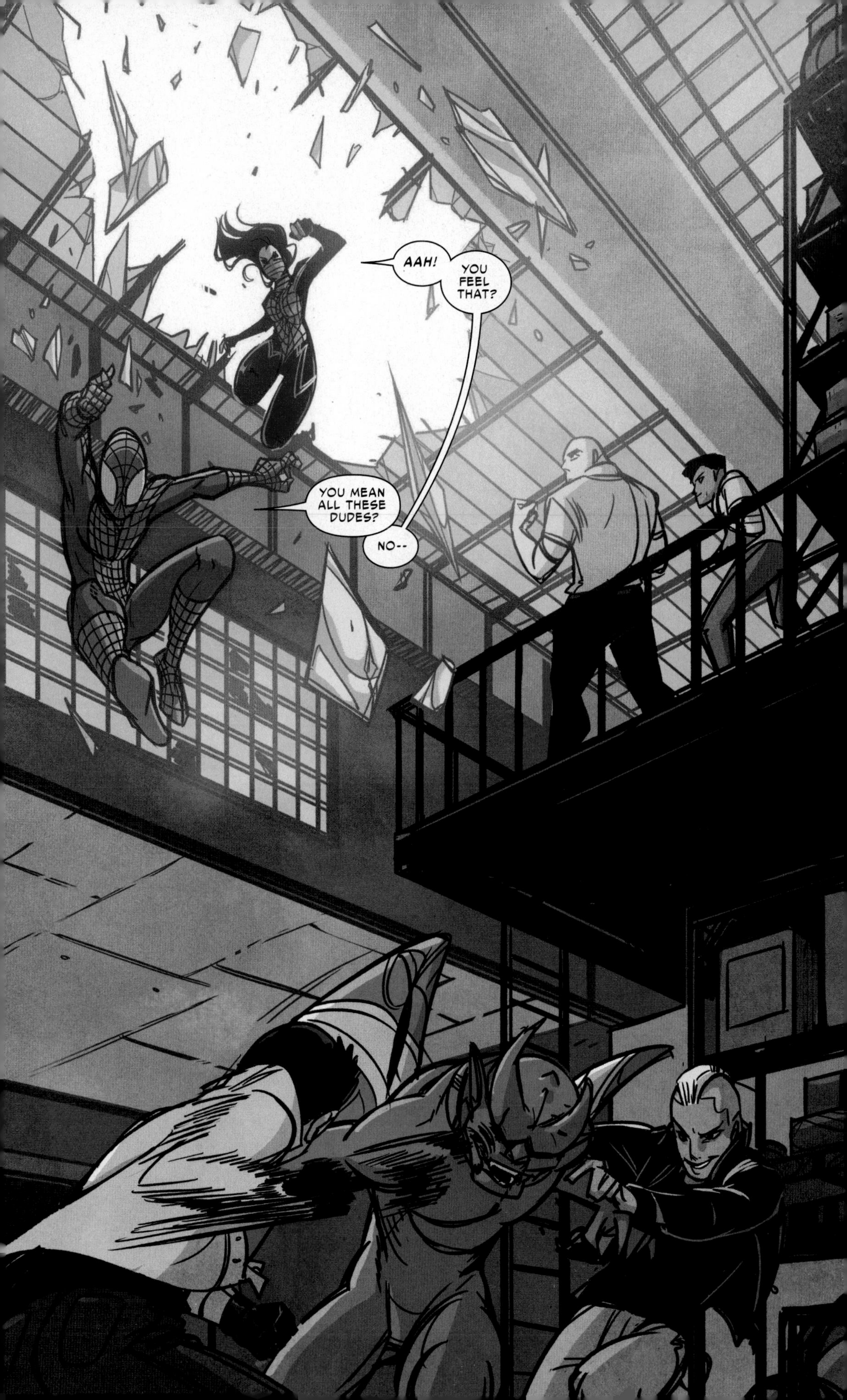
AAH!
YOU FEEL THAT?
YOU MEAN ALL THESE DUDES?
NO--

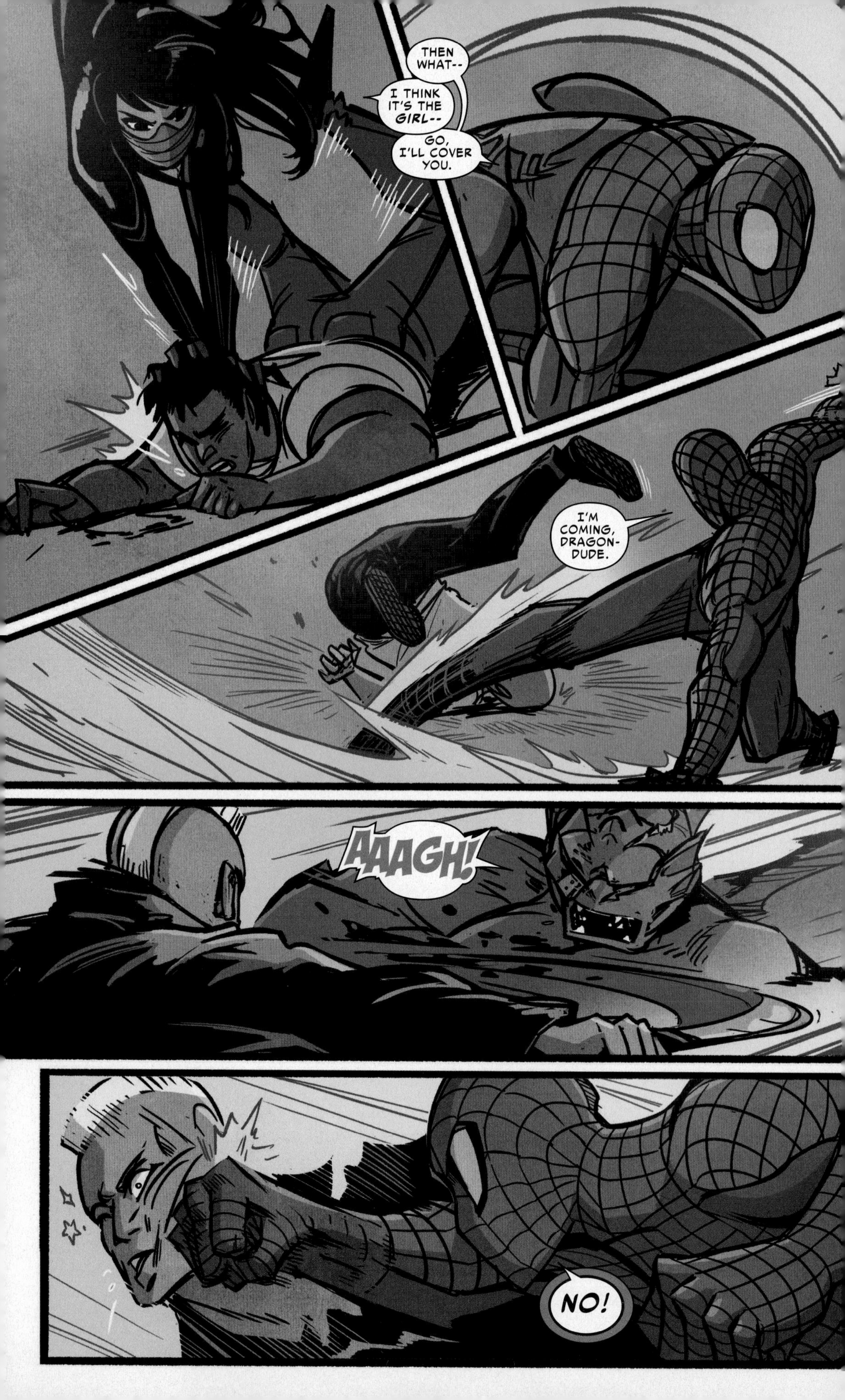
THEN WHAT--
I THINK IT'S THE GIRL--
GO, I'LL COVER YOU.
I'M COMING, DRAGON-DUDE.
AAAGH!
NO!

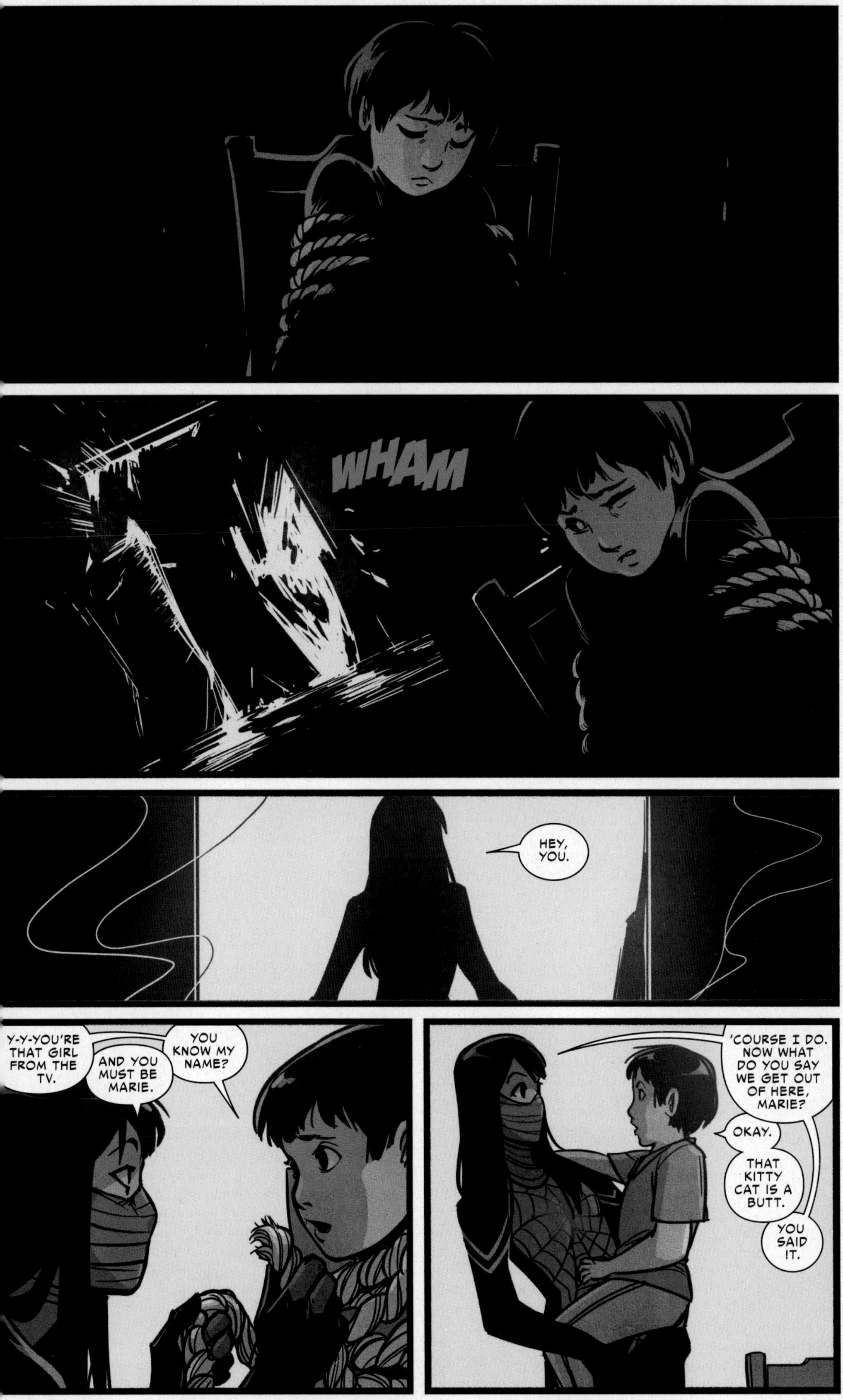
WHAM
HEY, YOU.
Y-Y-YOU'RE THAT GIRL FROM THE TV.
AND YOU MUST BE MARIE.
YOU KNOW MY NAME?
'COURSE I DO. NOW WHAT DO YOU SAY WE GET OUT OF HERE, MARIE?
OKAY.
THAT KITTY CAT IS A BUTT.
YOU SAID IT.

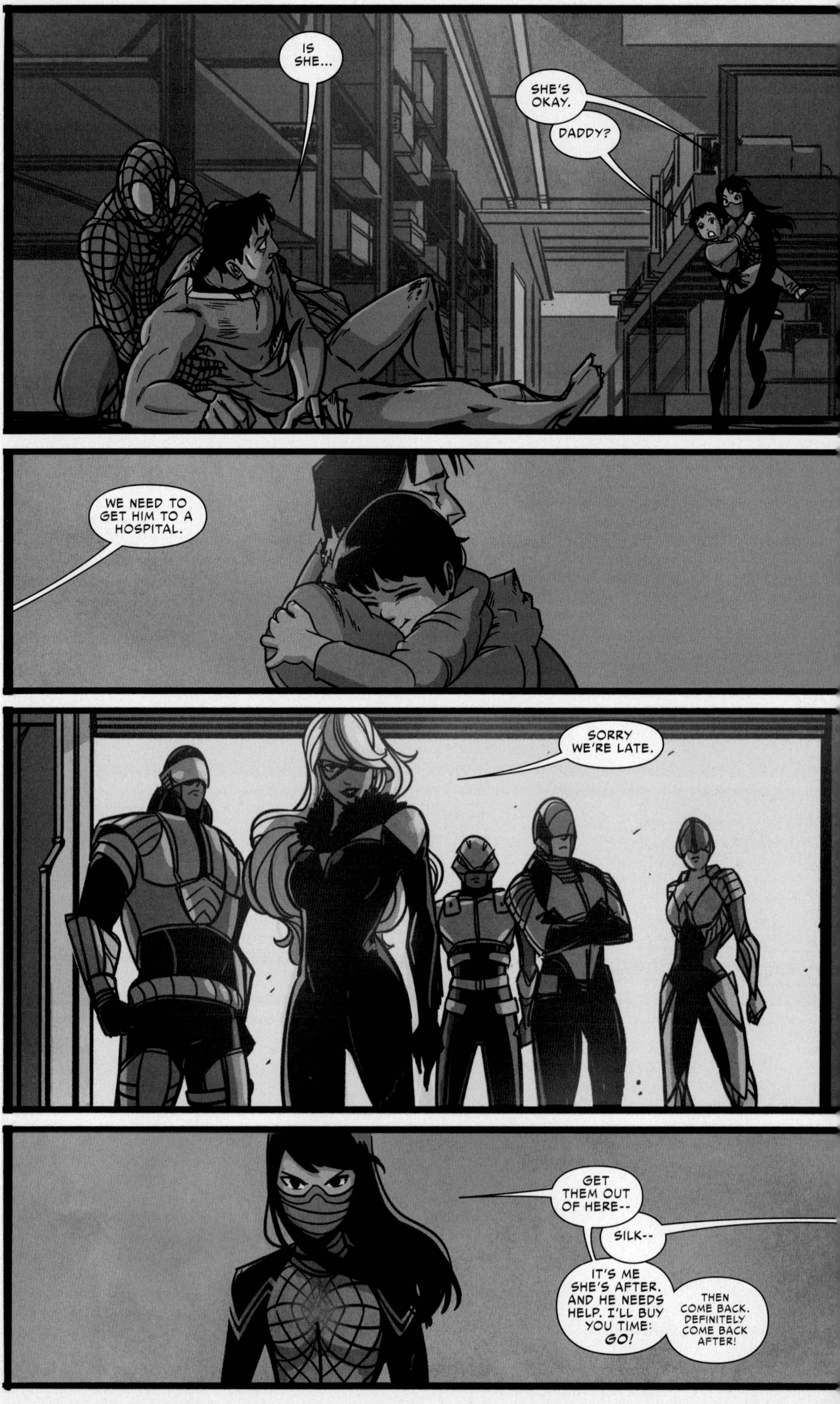
IS SHE...
SHE'S OKAY.
DADDY?
WE NEED TO GET HIM TO A HOSPITAL.
SORRY WE'RE LATE.
GET THEM OUT OF HERE--
SILK--
IT'S ME SHE'S AFTER. AND HE NEEDS HELP. I'LL BUY YOU TIME: GO!
THEN COME BACK. DEFINITELY COME BACK AFTER!

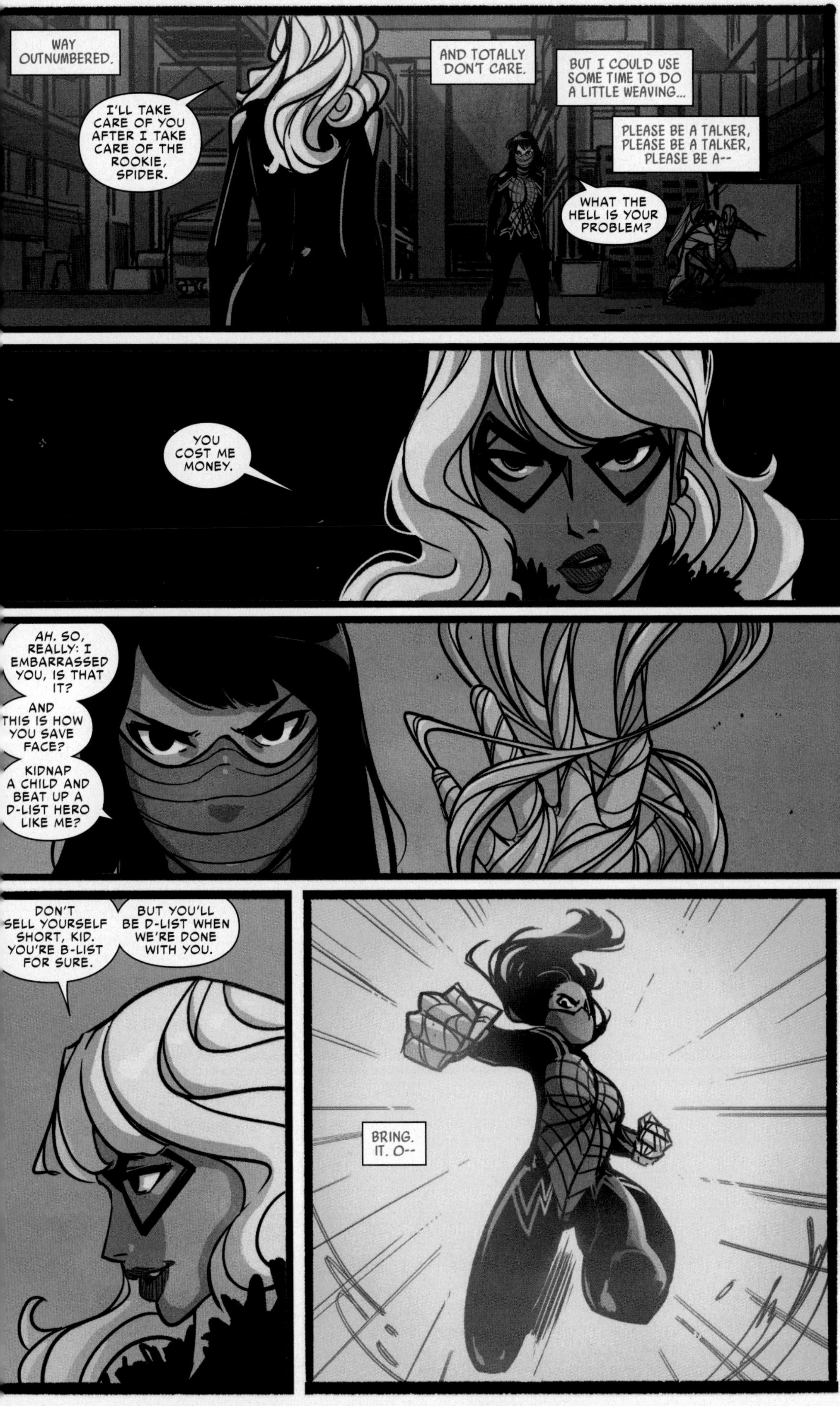
WAY OUTNUMBERED.
I'LL TAKE CARE OF YOU AFTER I TAKE CARE OF THE ROOKIE, SPIDER.
AND TOTALLY DON'T CARE.
BUT I COULD USE SOME TIME TO DO A LITTLE WEAVING...
PLEASE BE A TALKER, PLEASE BE A TALKER, PLEASE BE A--
WHAT THE HELL IS YOUR PROBLEM?
YOU COST ME MONEY.
AH. SO, REALLY: I EMBARRASSED YOU, IS THAT IT?
AND THIS IS HOW YOU SAVE FACE?
KIDNAP A CHILD AND BEAT UP A D-LIST HERO LIKE ME?
DON'T SELL YOURSELF SHORT, KID. YOU'RE B-LIST FOR SURE.
BUT YOU'LL BE D-LIST WHEN WE'RE DONE WITH YOU.
BRING. IT. O--

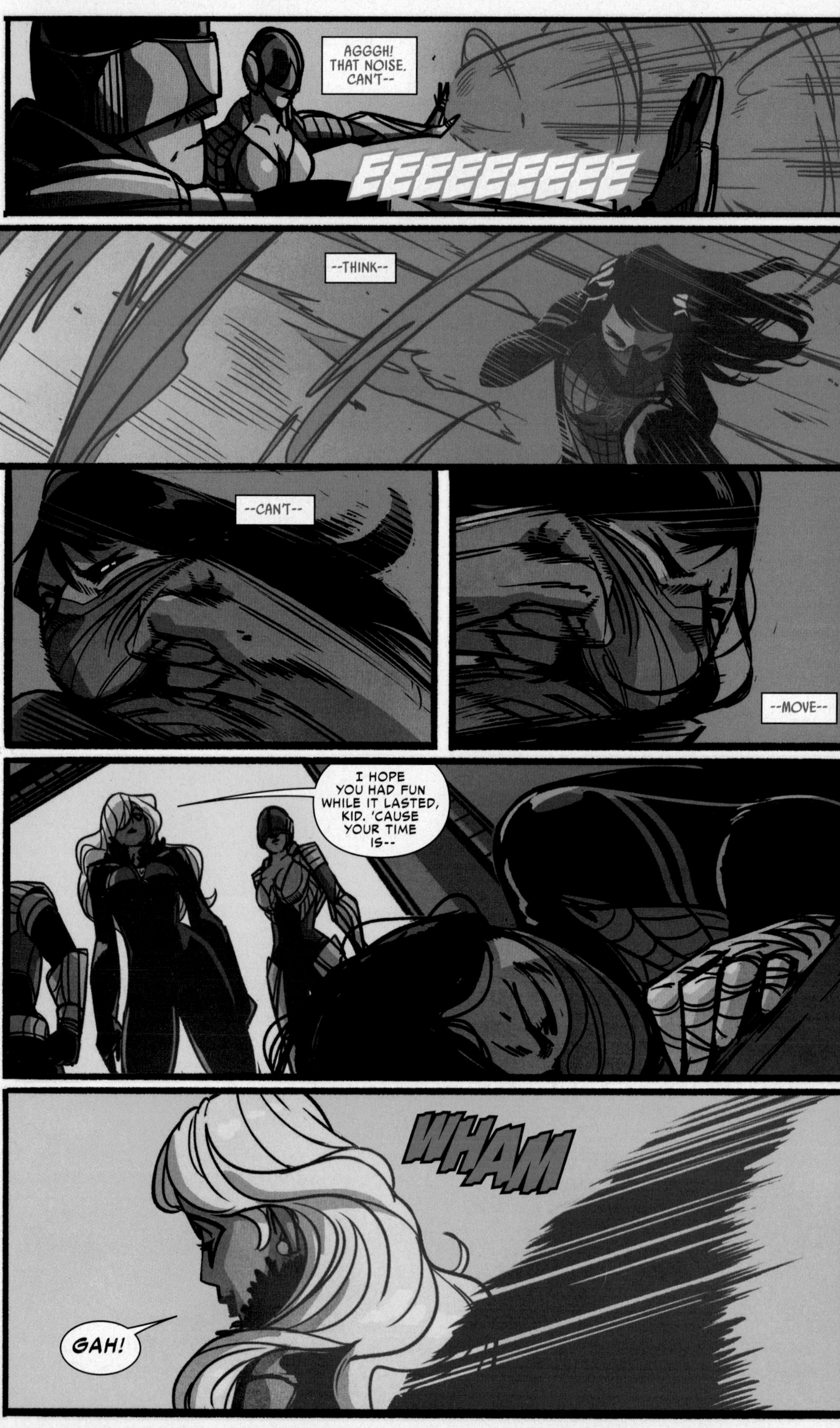
AGGGH! THAT NOISE. CAN'T--
EEEEEEEEEE
--THINK--
--CAN'T--
--MOVE--
I HOPE YOU HAD FUN WHILE IT LASTED, KID. 'CAUSE YOUR TIME IS--
WHAM
GAH!

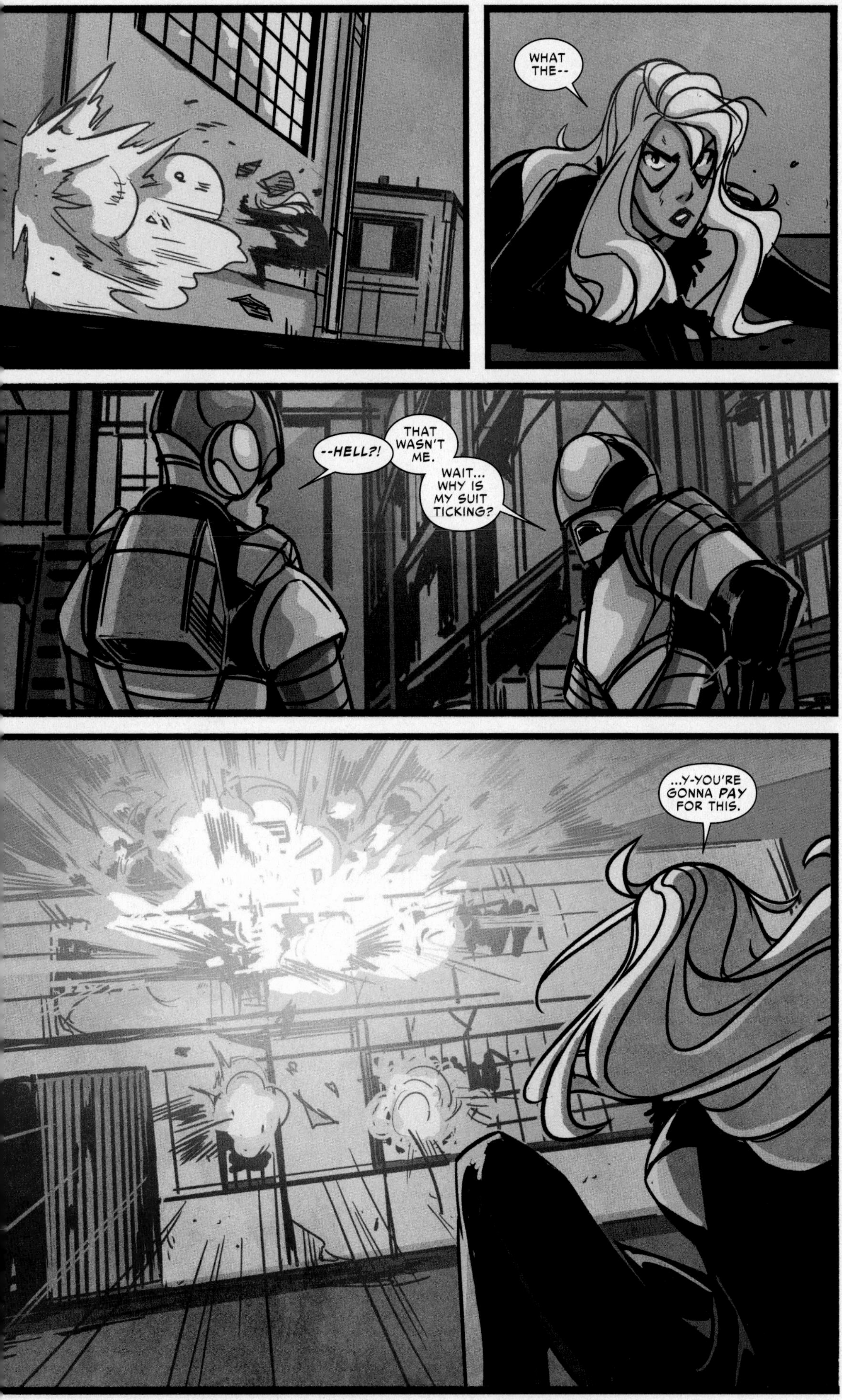
WHAT THE--
--HELL?!
THAT WASN'T ME.
WAIT... WHY IS MY SUIT TICKING?
...Y-YOU'RE GONNA PAY FOR THIS.

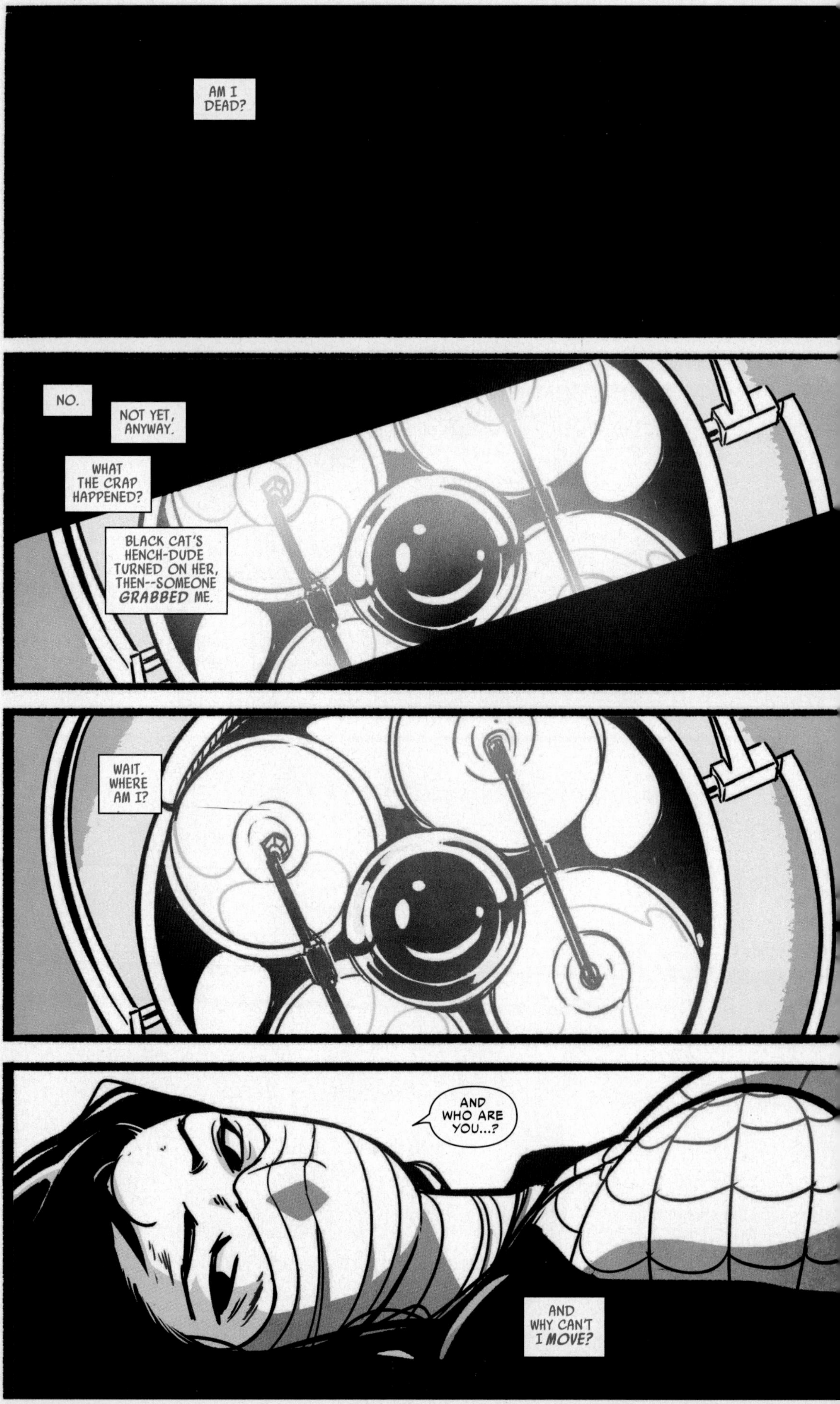
AM I DEAD?
NO.
NOT YET, ANYWAY.
WHAT THE CRAP HAPPENED?
BLACK CAT'S HENCH-DUDE TURNED ON HER, THEN--SOMEONE *GRABBED* ME.
WAIT. WHERE AM I?
AND WHO ARE YOU...?
AND WHY CAN'T I *MOVE?*

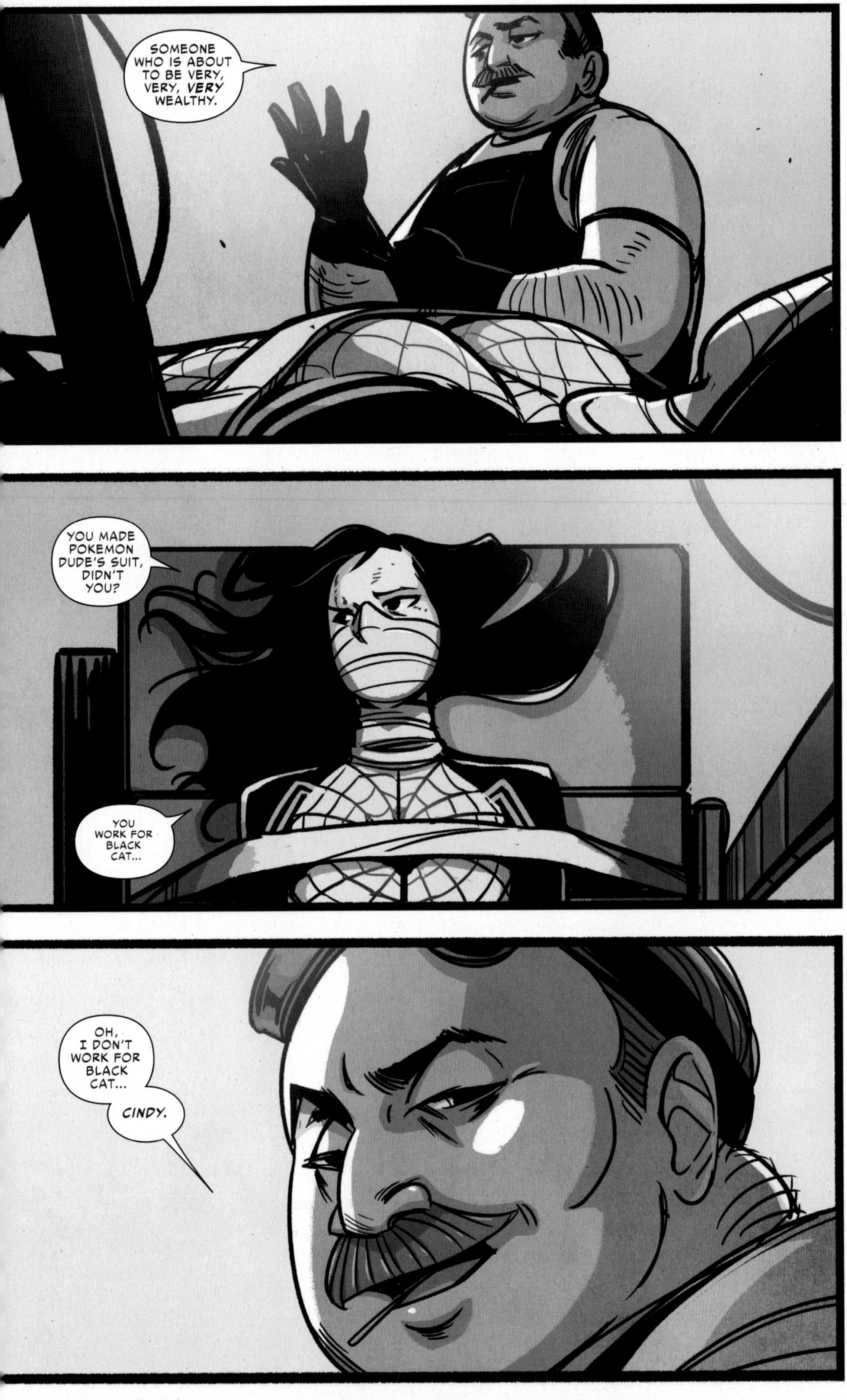
SOMEONE WHO IS ABOUT TO BE VERY, VERY, *VERY* WEALTHY.
YOU MADE POKEMON DUDE'S SUIT, DIDN'T YOU?
YOU WORK FOR BLACK CAT...
OH, I DON'T WORK FOR BLACK CAT...
CINDY.

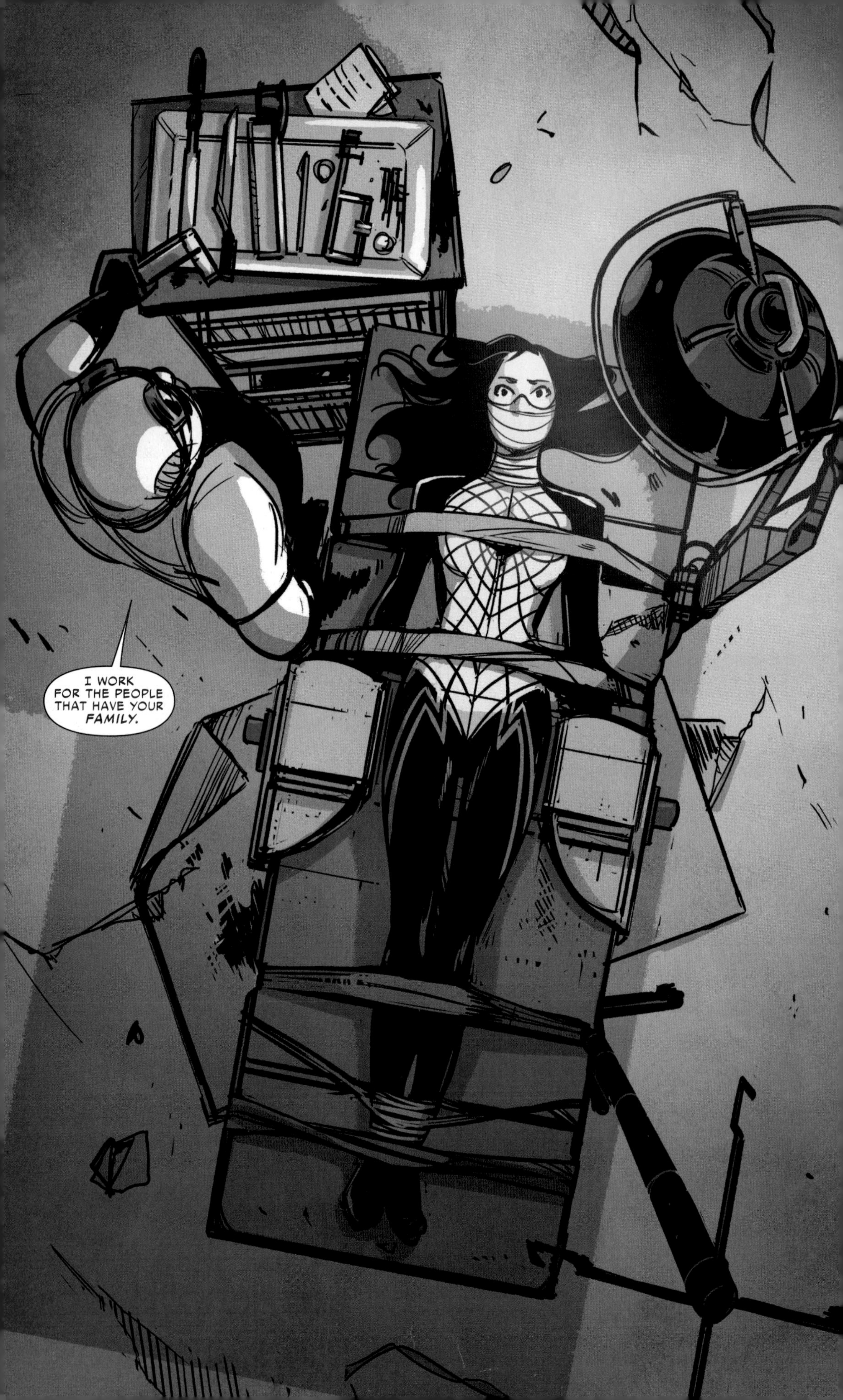
I WORK FOR THE PEOPLE THAT HAVE YOUR *FAMILY.*

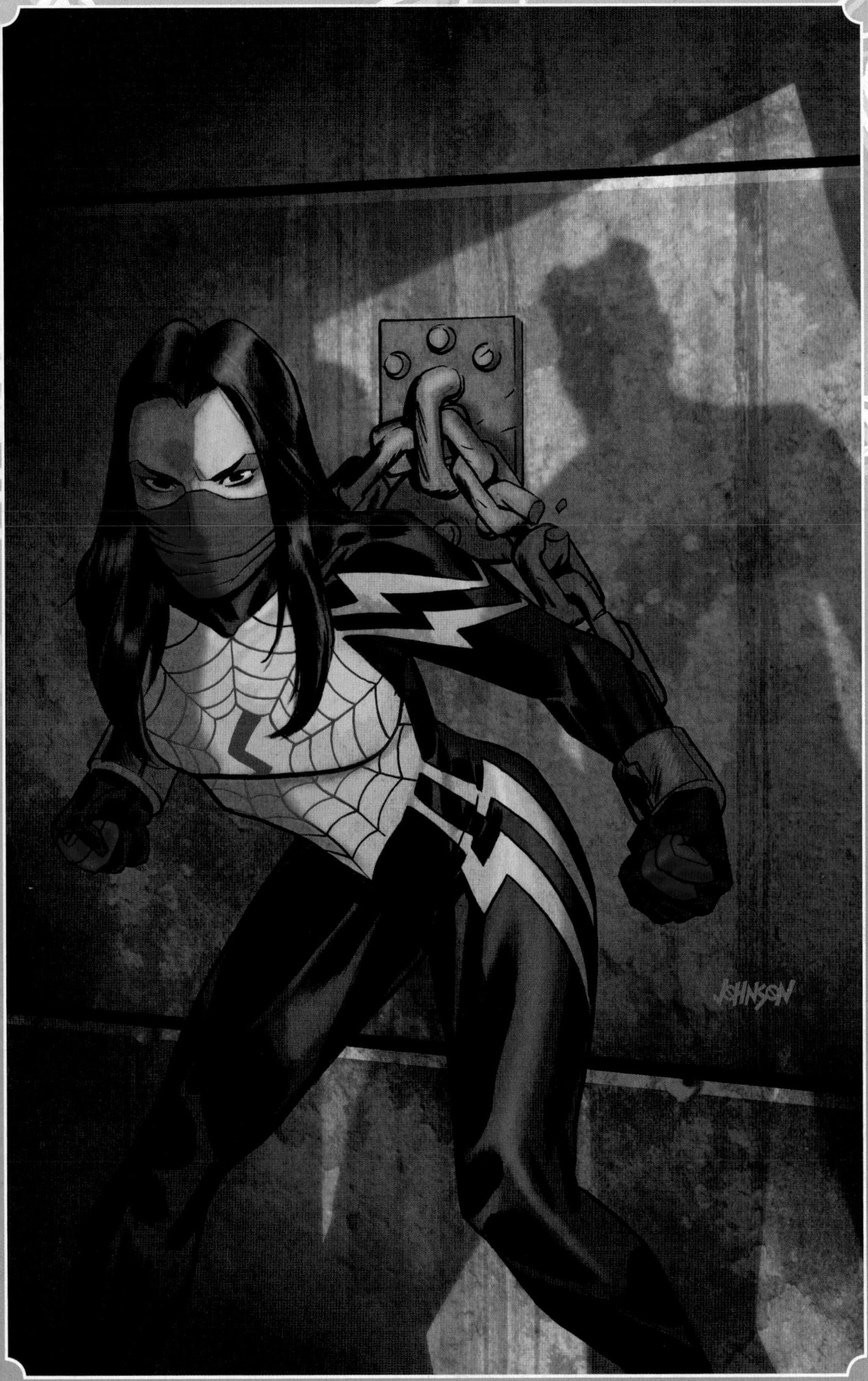
JOHNSON

SILK (2015A) #6

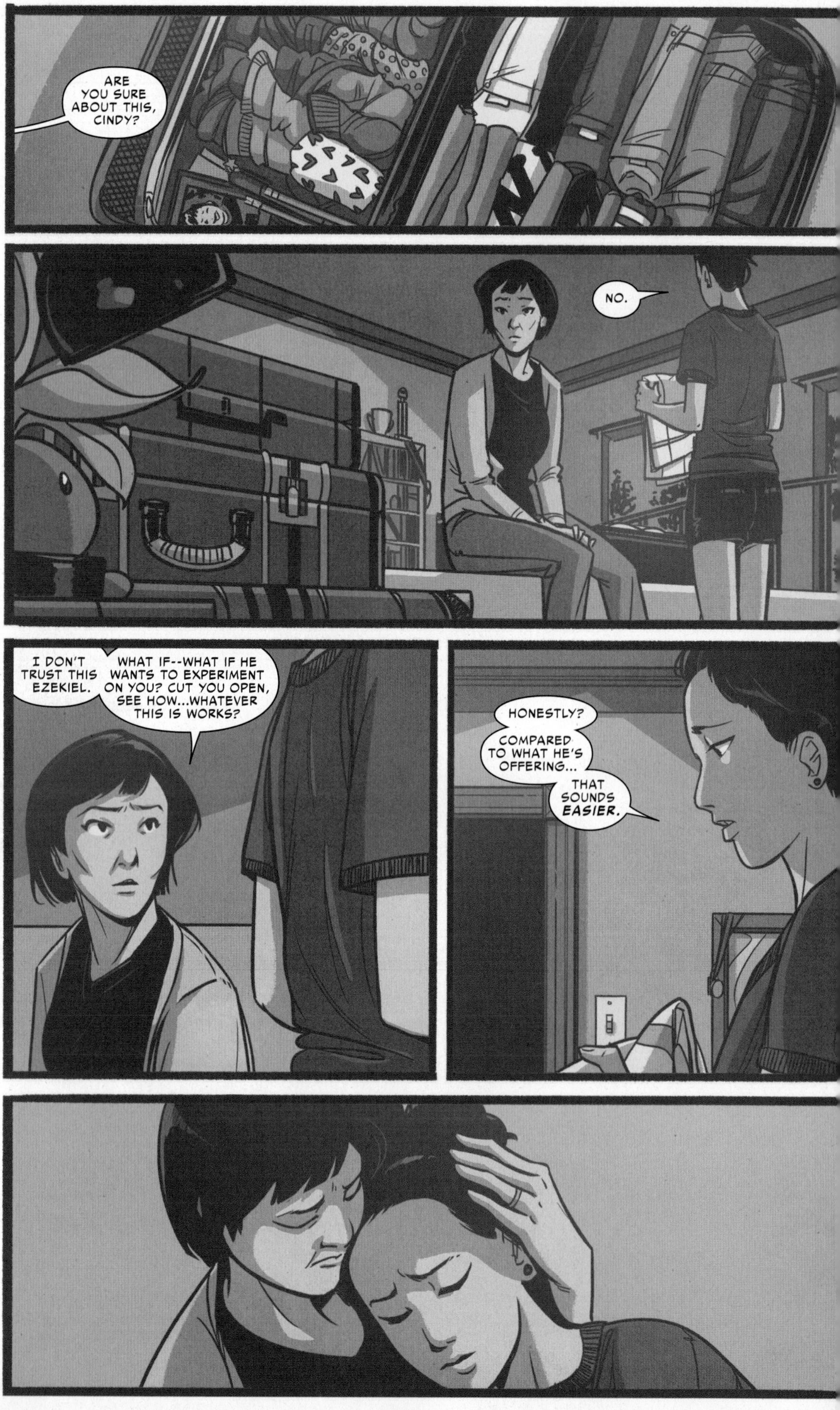
ARE YOU SURE ABOUT THIS, CINDY?
NO.
I DON'T TRUST THIS EZEKIEL.
WHAT IF--WHAT IF HE WANTS TO EXPERIMENT ON YOU? CUT YOU OPEN, SEE HOW...WHATEVER THIS IS WORKS?
HONESTLY?
COMPARED TO WHAT HE'S OFFERING...
THAT SOUNDS *EASIER*.

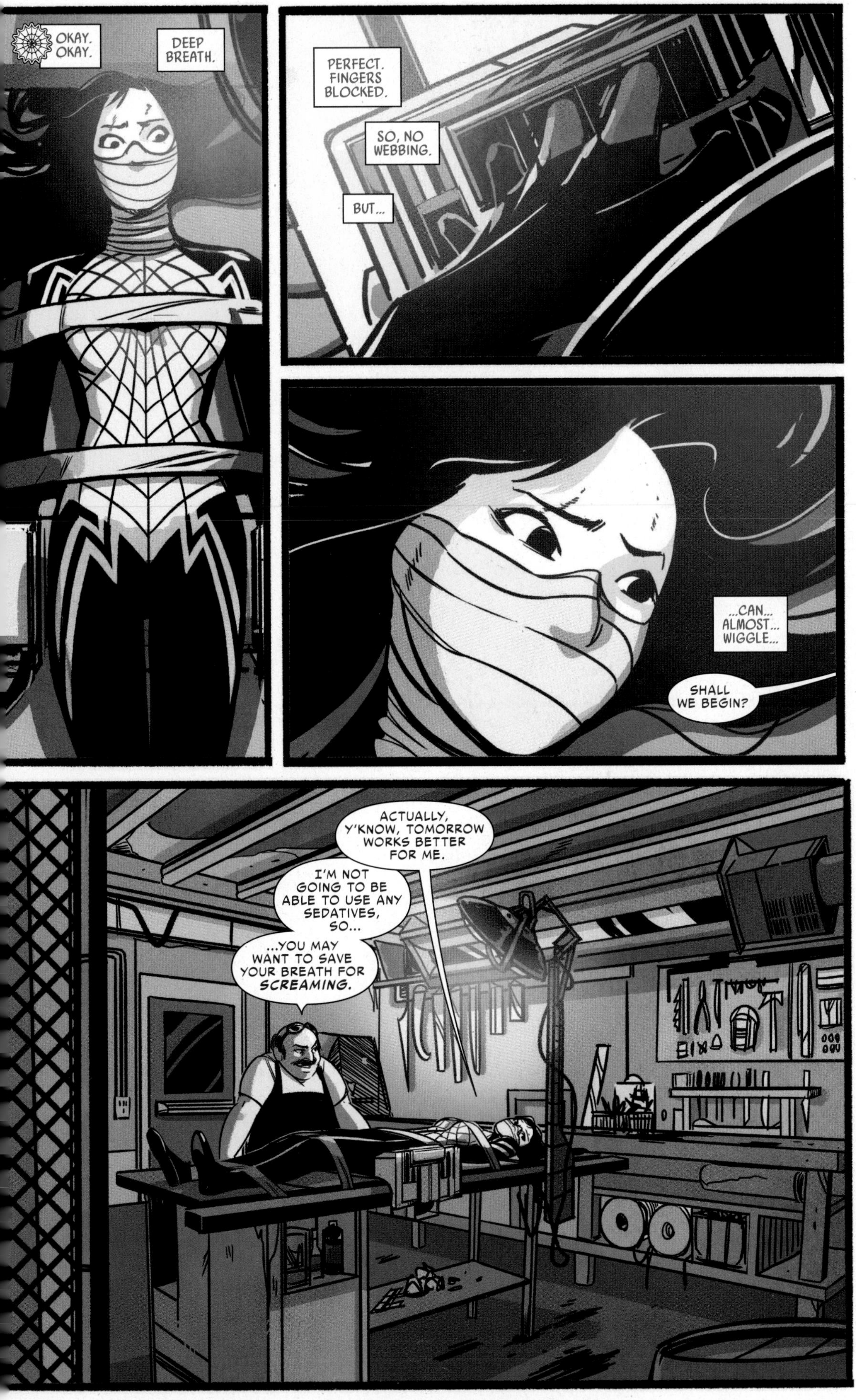
OKAY. OKAY.
DEEP BREATH.
PERFECT. FINGERS BLOCKED.
SO, NO WEBBING.
BUT...
...CAN... ALMOST... WIGGLE...
SHALL WE BEGIN?
ACTUALLY, Y'KNOW, TOMORROW WORKS BETTER FOR ME.
I'M NOT GOING TO BE ABLE TO USE ANY SEDATIVES, SO...
...YOU MAY WANT TO SAVE YOUR BREATH FOR SCREAMING.

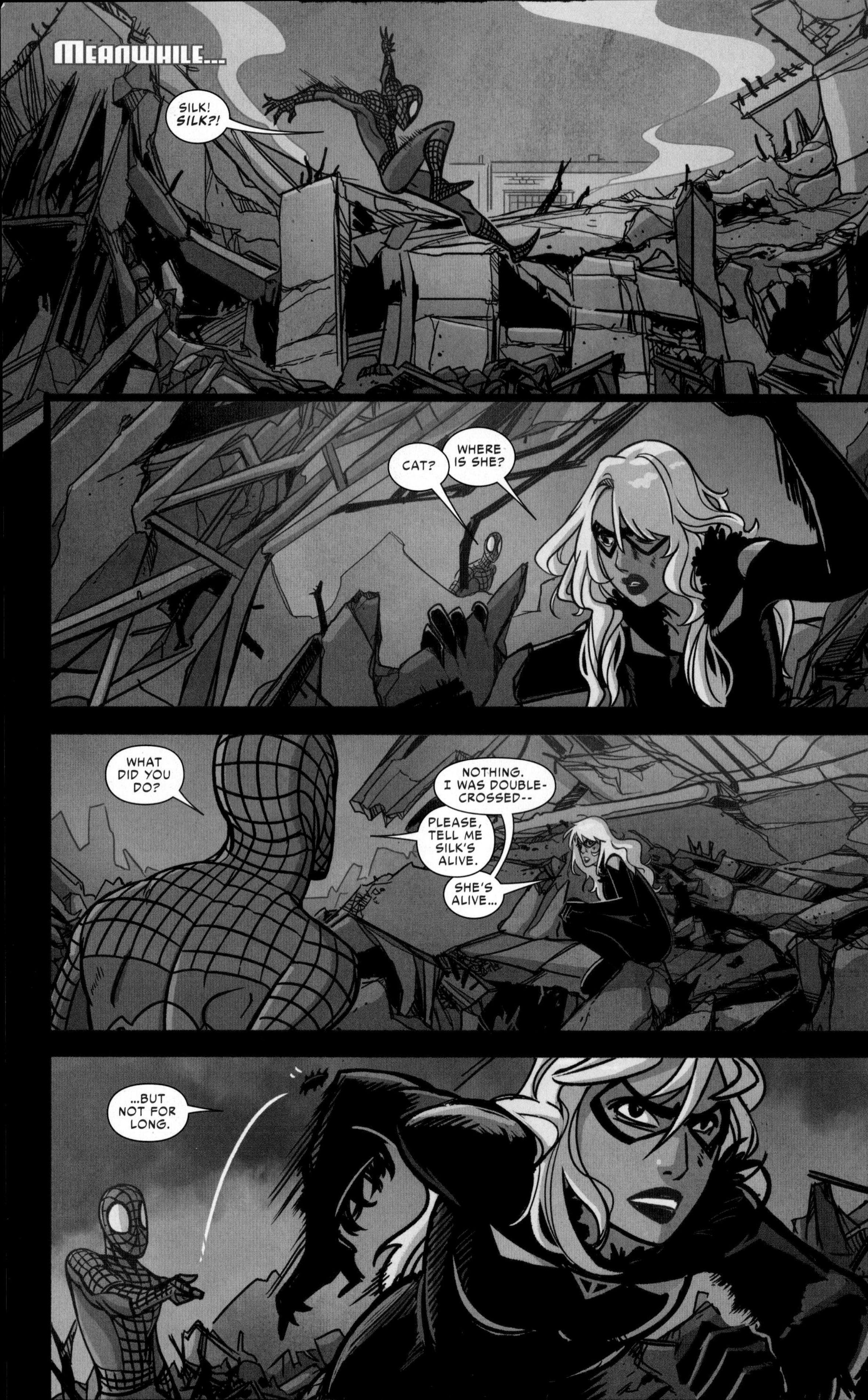
MEANWHILE...
SILK! SILK?!
CAT?
WHERE IS SHE?
WHAT DID YOU DO?
NOTHING. I WAS DOUBLE-CROSSED--
PLEASE, TELL ME SILK'S ALIVE.
SHE'S ALIVE...
...BUT NOT FOR LONG.

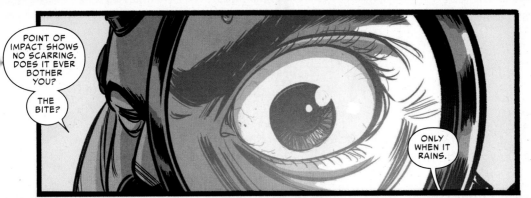

POINT OF IMPACT SHOWS NO SCARRING. DOES IT EVER BOTHER YOU?

THE BITE?

ONLY WHEN IT RAINS.

HOW DOES HE KNOW ABOUT THE BITE?

WHO THE HELL IS THIS GUY?

FOCUS. GET FREE. THEN GET ANSWERS.

KEEP HIM TALKING. DISTRACTED.

AND, Y'KNOW, NOT CUTTING INTO ME.

MY FAMILY.

YOU'VE SEEN THEM?

YOUR PARENTS? NO. BUT THE PEOPLE WHO HAVE THEM... MY GOODNESS, THEY'VE GOT THE DEEPEST POCKETS I'VE EVER SEEN.

BUT THEY PLAYED THEIR HAND...

C'MON...

THEY'VE GONE TO SUCH GREAT LENGTHS. WATCHED YOUR EVERY MOVE IN THAT BUNKER.

SO, I KNEW ANYONE WORTH THAT MUCH TO THEM...

...WOULD BE WORTH A WHOLE LOT MORE ON THE BLACK MARKET.

THEY'VE BEEN WATCHING ME? IN THE BUNKER? HOW?

AND THEY WHO?

WHO THE HELL ARE THEY?

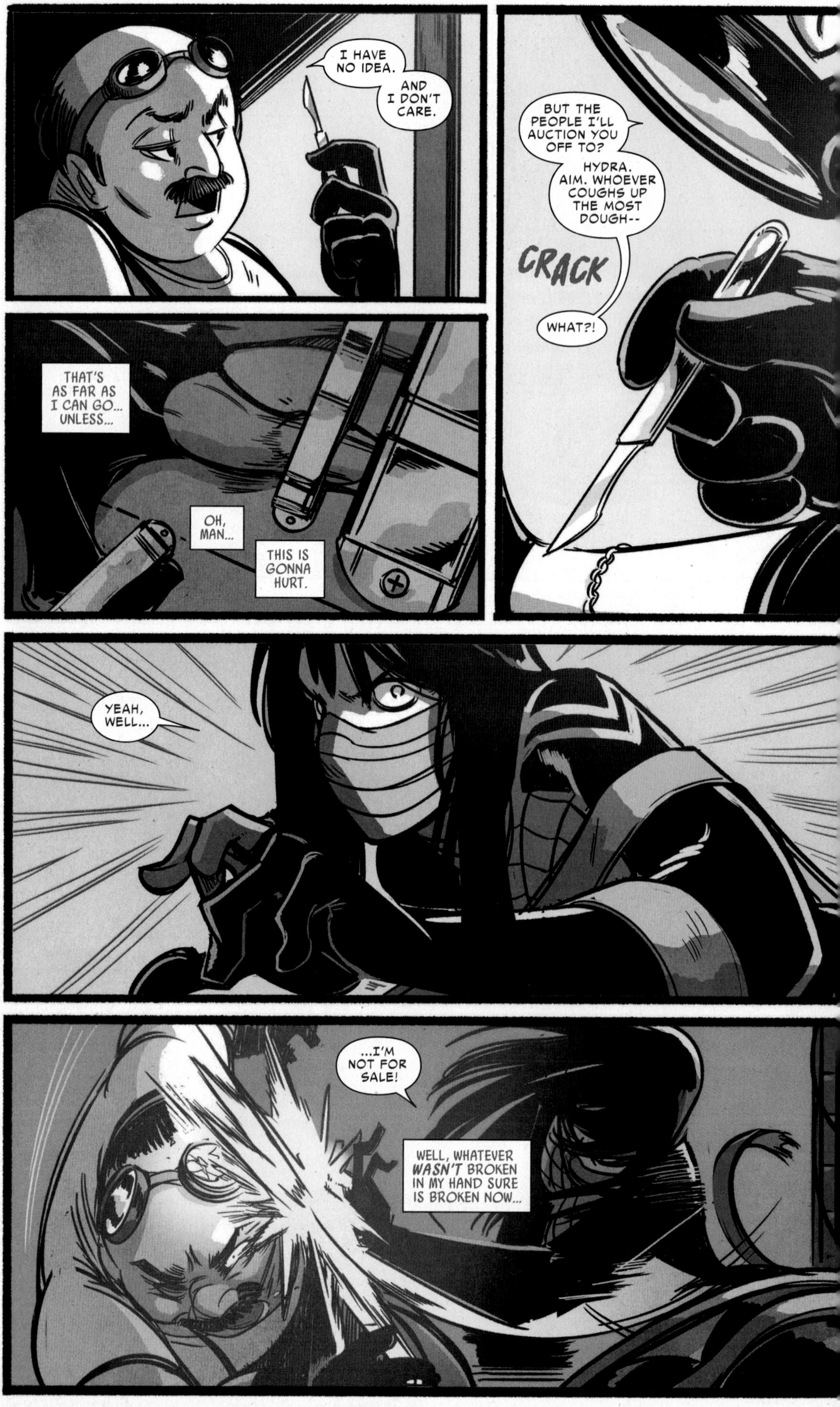
I HAVE NO IDEA.
AND I DON'T CARE.
BUT THE PEOPLE I'LL AUCTION YOU OFF TO?
HYDRA. AIM. WHOEVER COUGHS UP THE MOST DOUGH--
CRACK
WHAT?!
THAT'S AS FAR AS I CAN GO... UNLESS...
OH, MAN...
THIS IS GONNA HURT.
YEAH, WELL...
...I'M NOT FOR SALE!
WELL, WHATEVER *WASN'T* BROKEN IN MY HAND SURE IS BROKEN NOW...

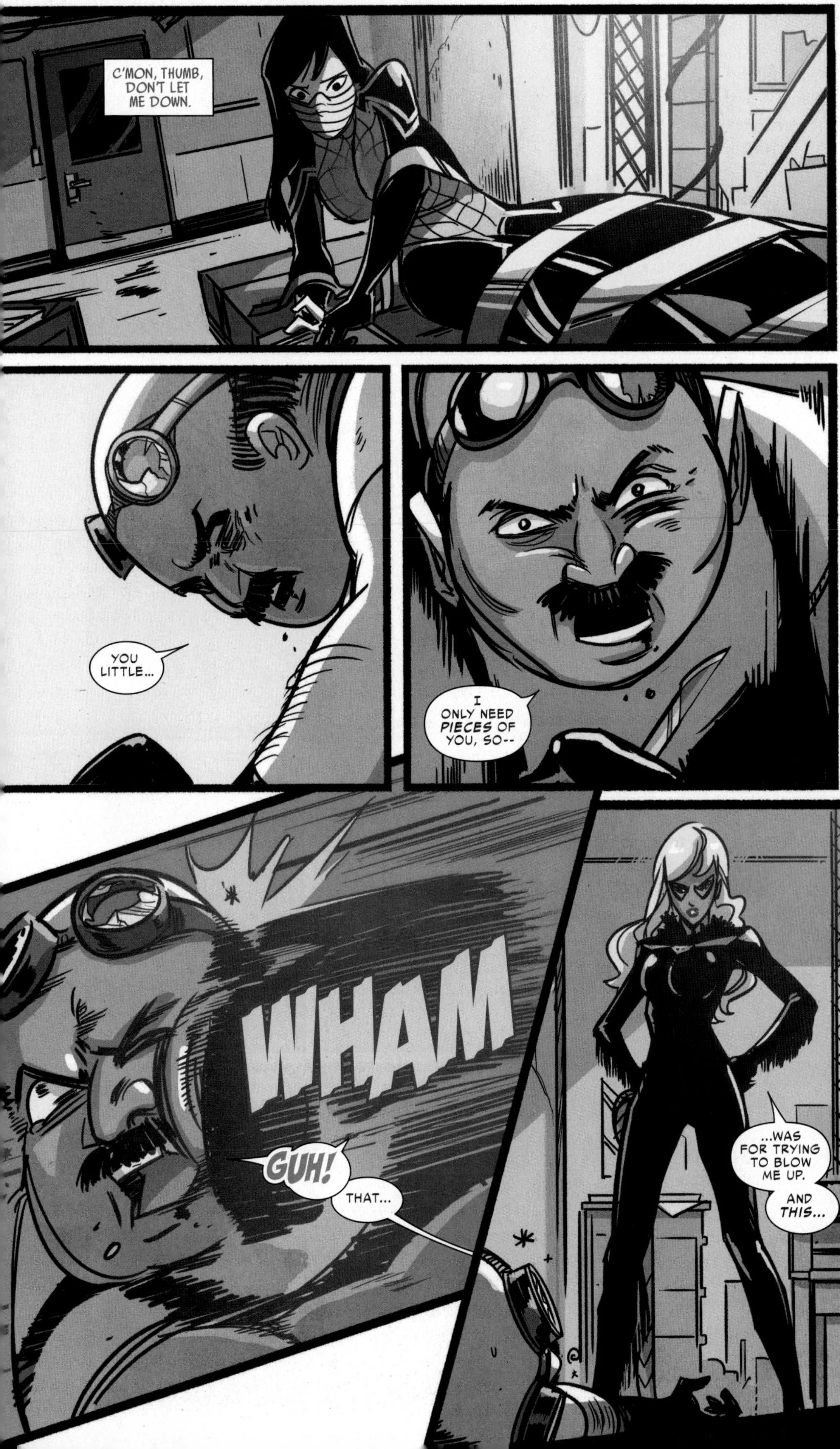
C'MON, THUMB, DON'T LET ME DOWN.
YOU LITTLE...
I ONLY NEED PIECES OF YOU, SO--
WHAM
GUH!
THAT...
...WAS FOR TRYING TO BLOW ME UP.
AND THIS...

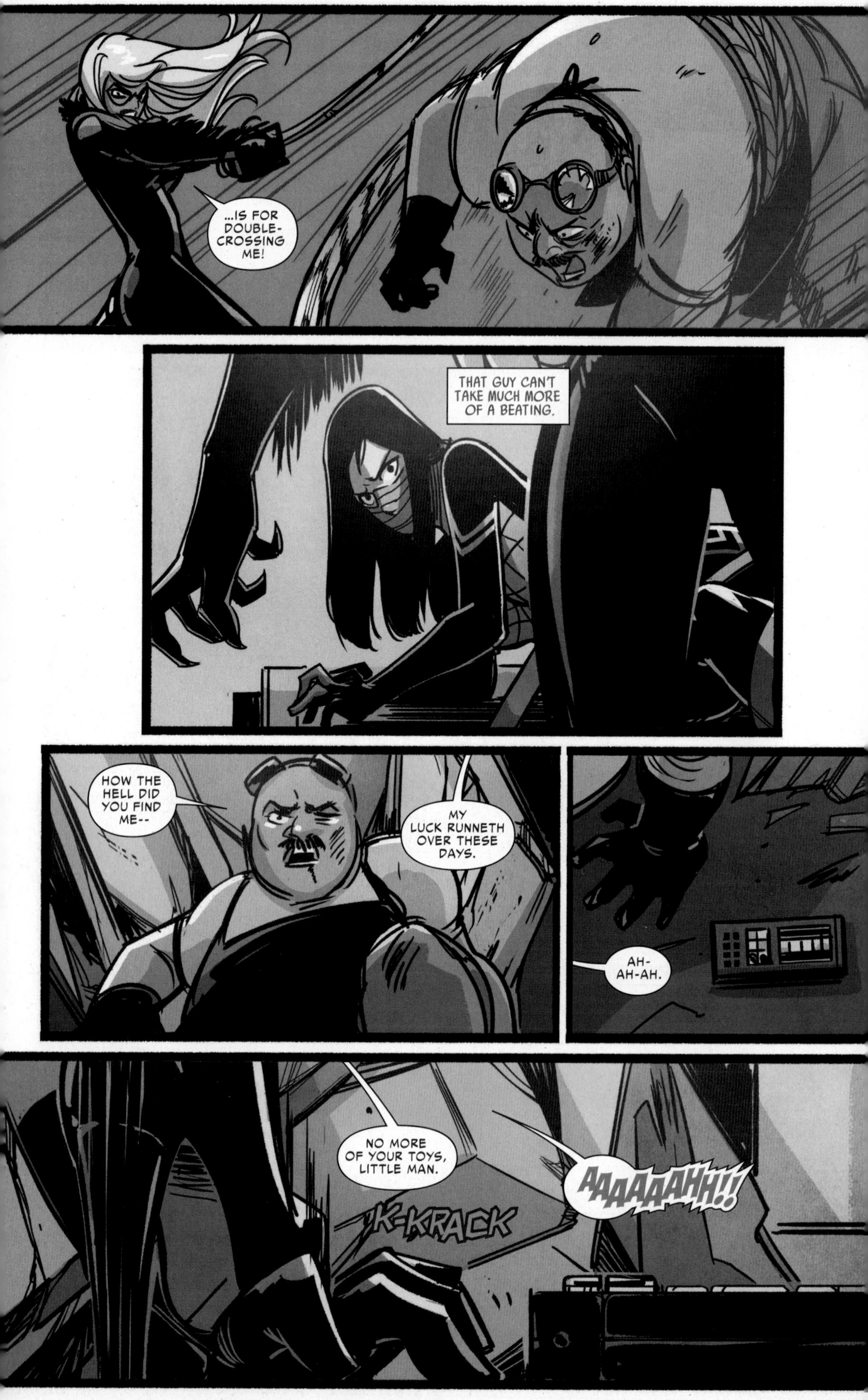
...IS FOR DOUBLE-CROSSING ME!
THAT GUY CAN'T TAKE MUCH MORE OF A BEATING.
HOW THE HELL DID YOU FIND ME--
MY LUCK RUNNETH OVER THESE DAYS.
AH-AH-AH.
NO MORE OF YOUR TOYS, LITTLE MAN.
K-KRACK
AAAAAAHH!!

CRAP.

THE CEILING...

...IT'S GONNA COLLAPSE!

MUST MOVE FASTER. MUST MOVE FASTER!

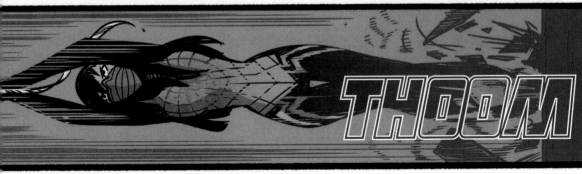

THOOM

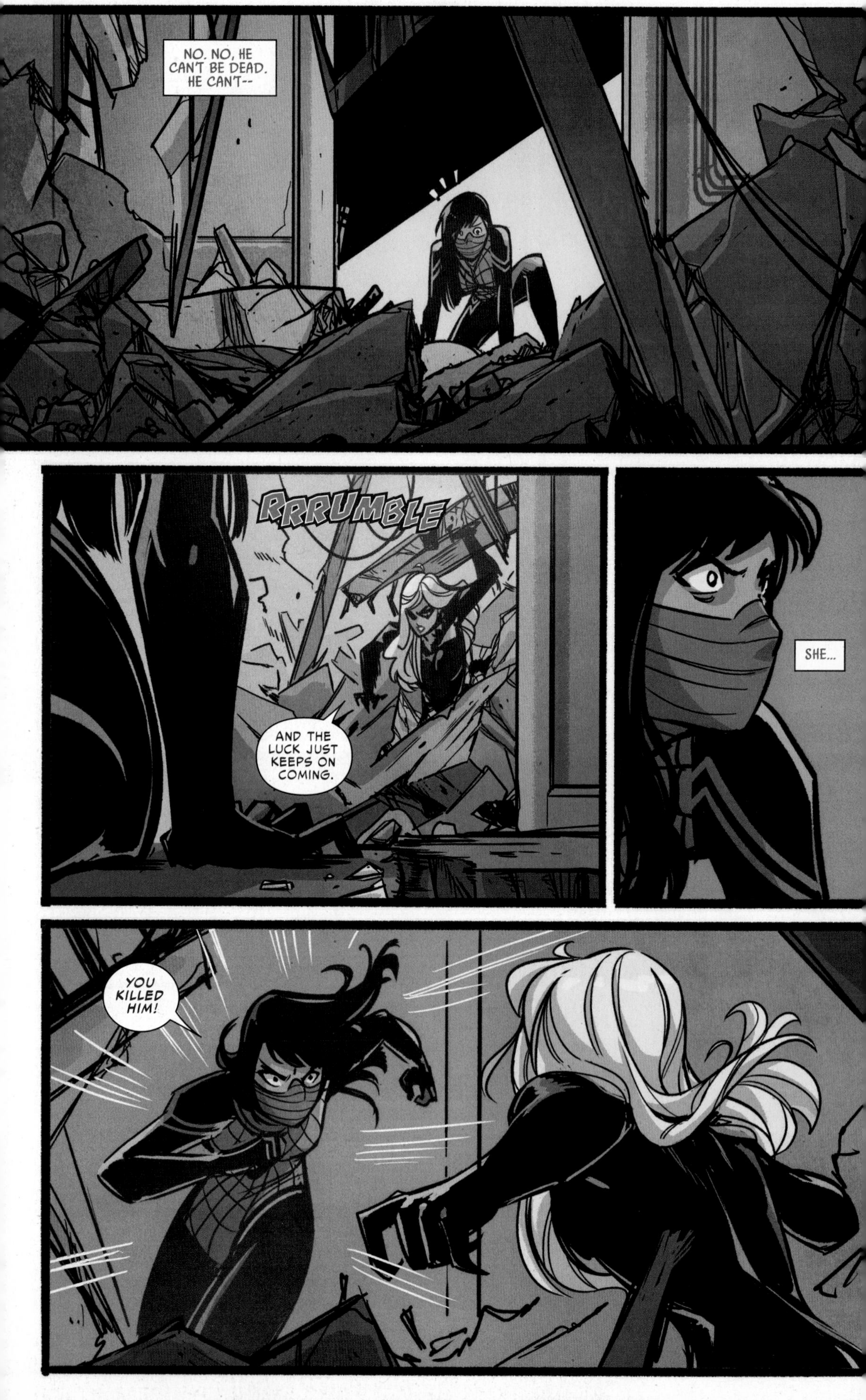
NO. NO, HE CAN'T BE DEAD. HE CAN'T--
!!
RRRUMBLE
AND THE LUCK JUST KEEPS ON COMING.
SHE...
YOU KILLED HIM!

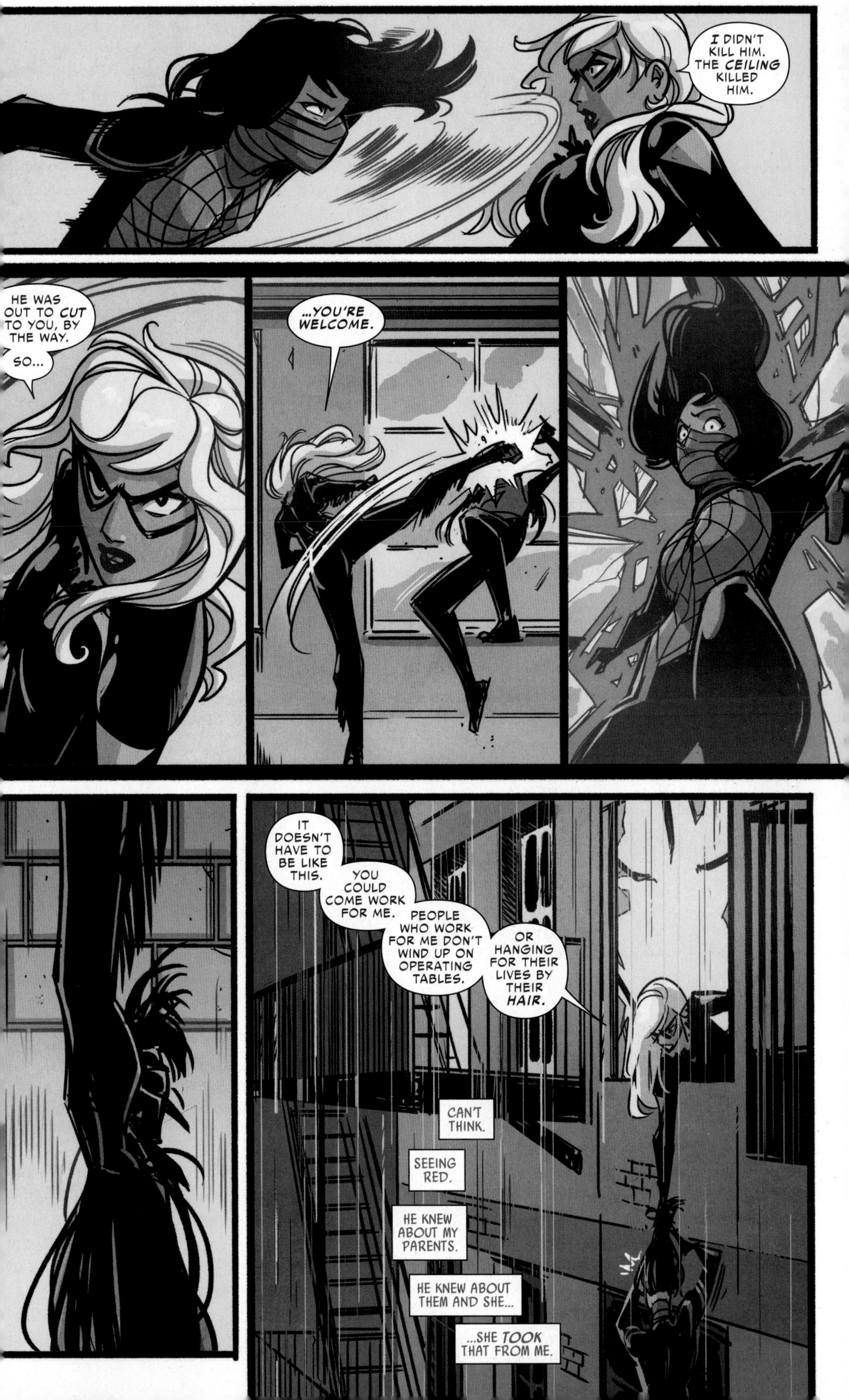
I DIDN'T KILL HIM. THE CEILING KILLED HIM.
HE WAS OUT TO CUT TO YOU, BY THE WAY.
SO...
...YOU'RE WELCOME.
IT DOESN'T HAVE TO BE LIKE THIS.
YOU COULD COME WORK FOR ME.
PEOPLE WHO WORK FOR ME DON'T WIND UP ON OPERATING TABLES.
OR HANGING FOR THEIR LIVES BY THEIR HAIR.
CAN'T THINK.
SEEING RED.
HE KNEW ABOUT MY PARENTS.
HE KNEW ABOUT THEM AND SHE...
...SHE TOOK THAT FROM ME.

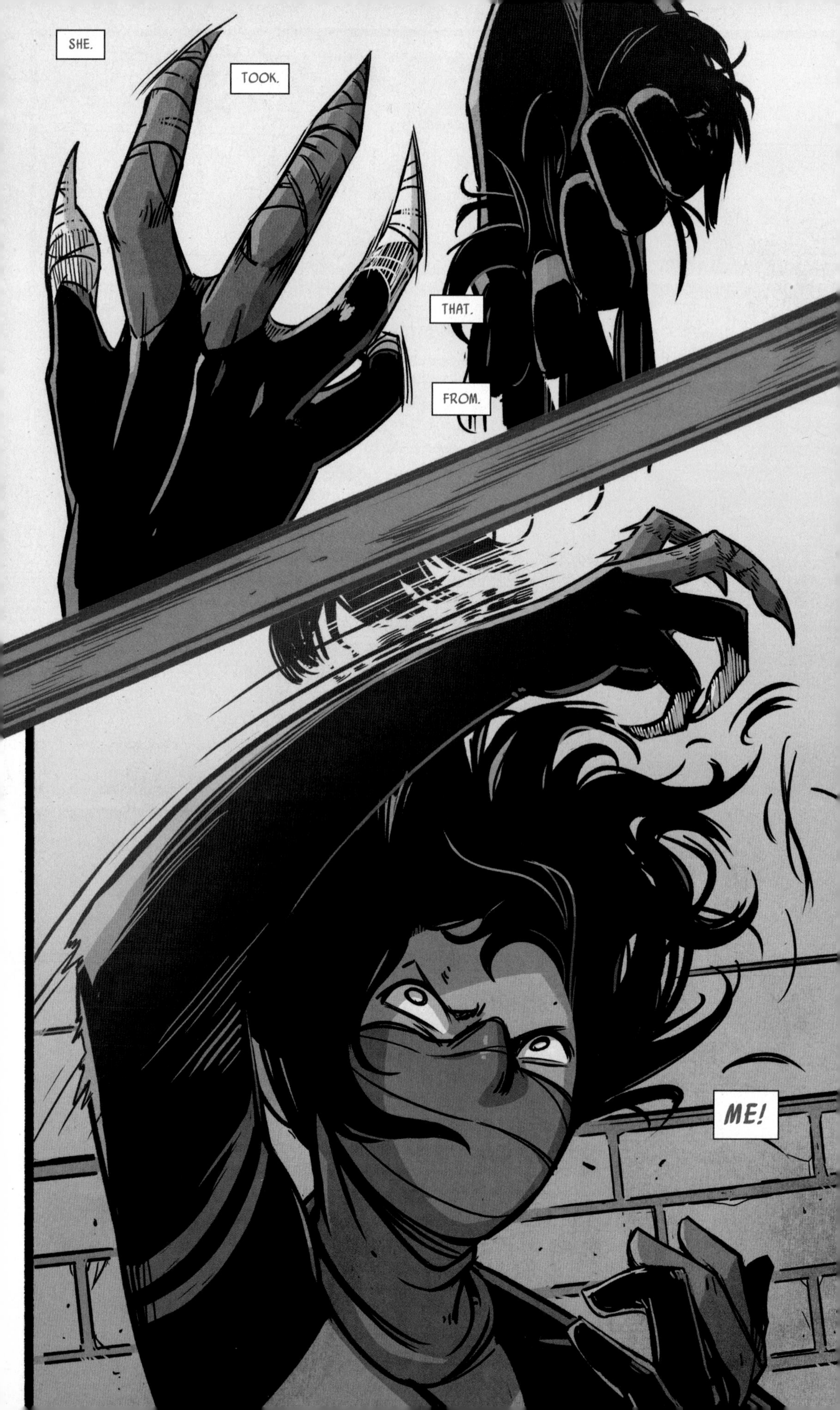
SHE.
TOOK.
THAT.
FROM.
ME!

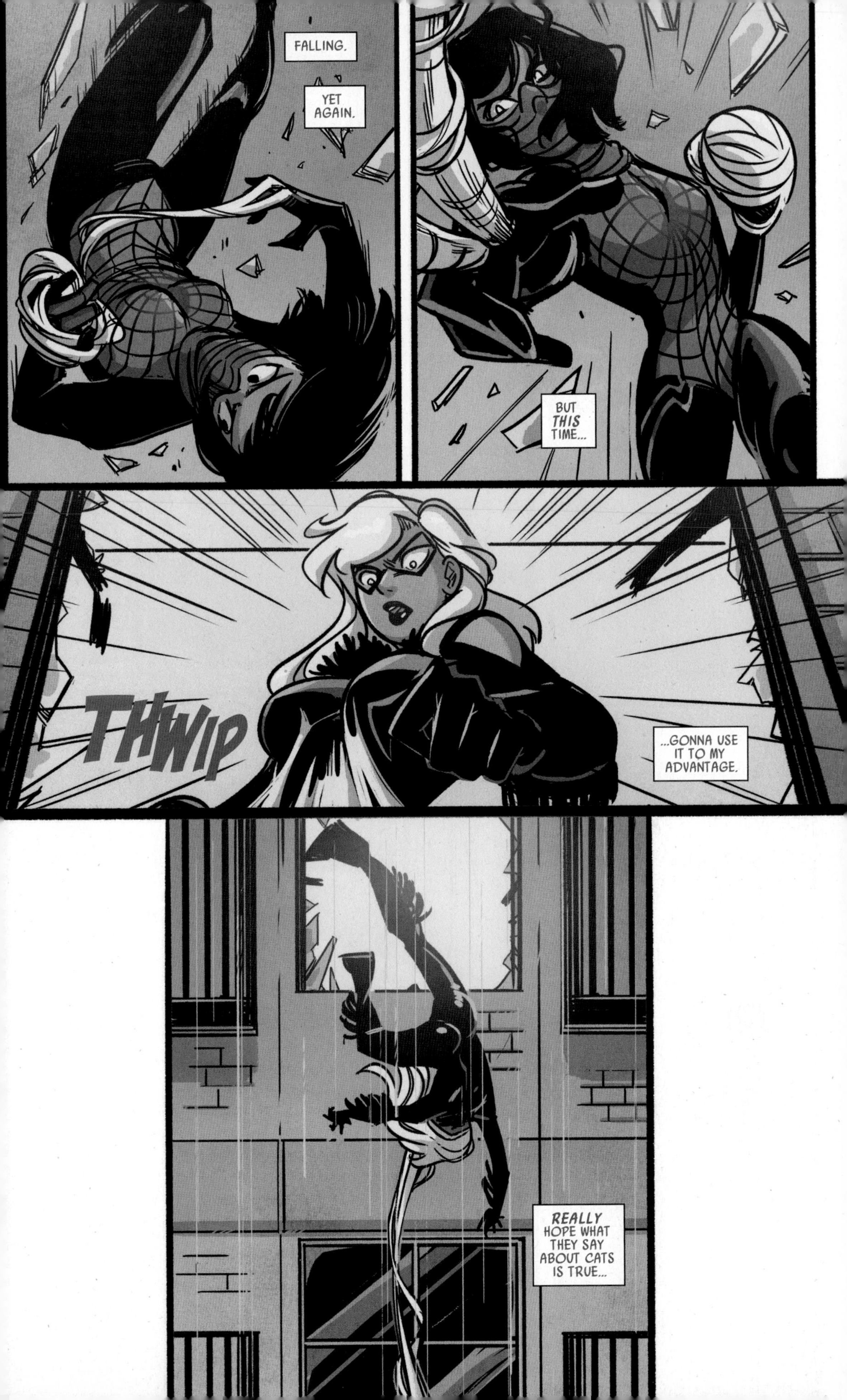
FALLING.
YET AGAIN.
BUT THIS TIME...
THWIP
...GONNA USE IT TO MY ADVANTAGE.
REALLY HOPE WHAT THEY SAY ABOUT CATS IS TRUE...

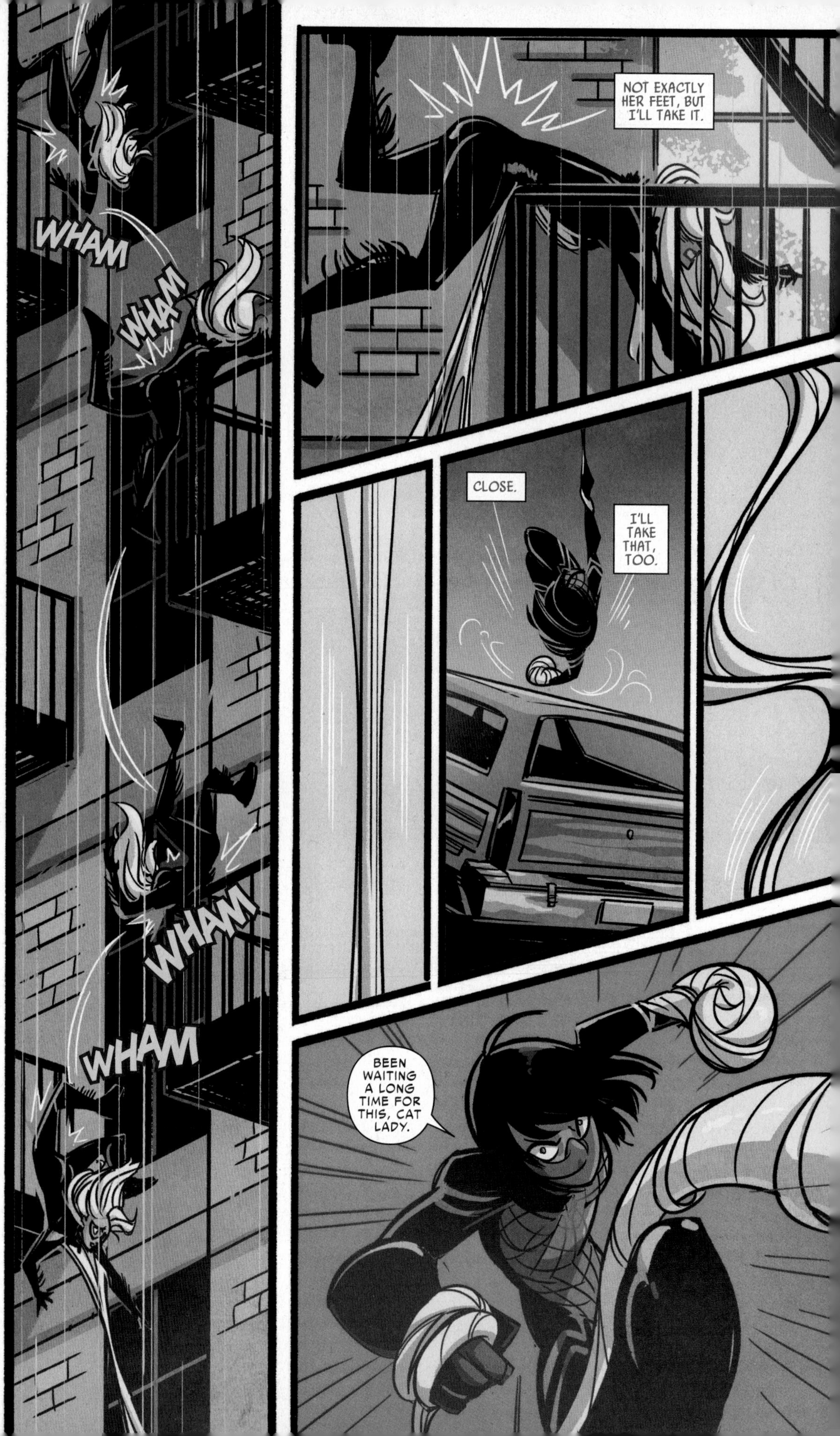
WHAM
WHAM
WHAM
WHAM
NOT EXACTLY HER FEET, BUT I'LL TAKE IT.
CLOSE.
I'LL TAKE THAT, TOO.
BEEN WAITING A LONG TIME FOR THIS, CAT LADY.

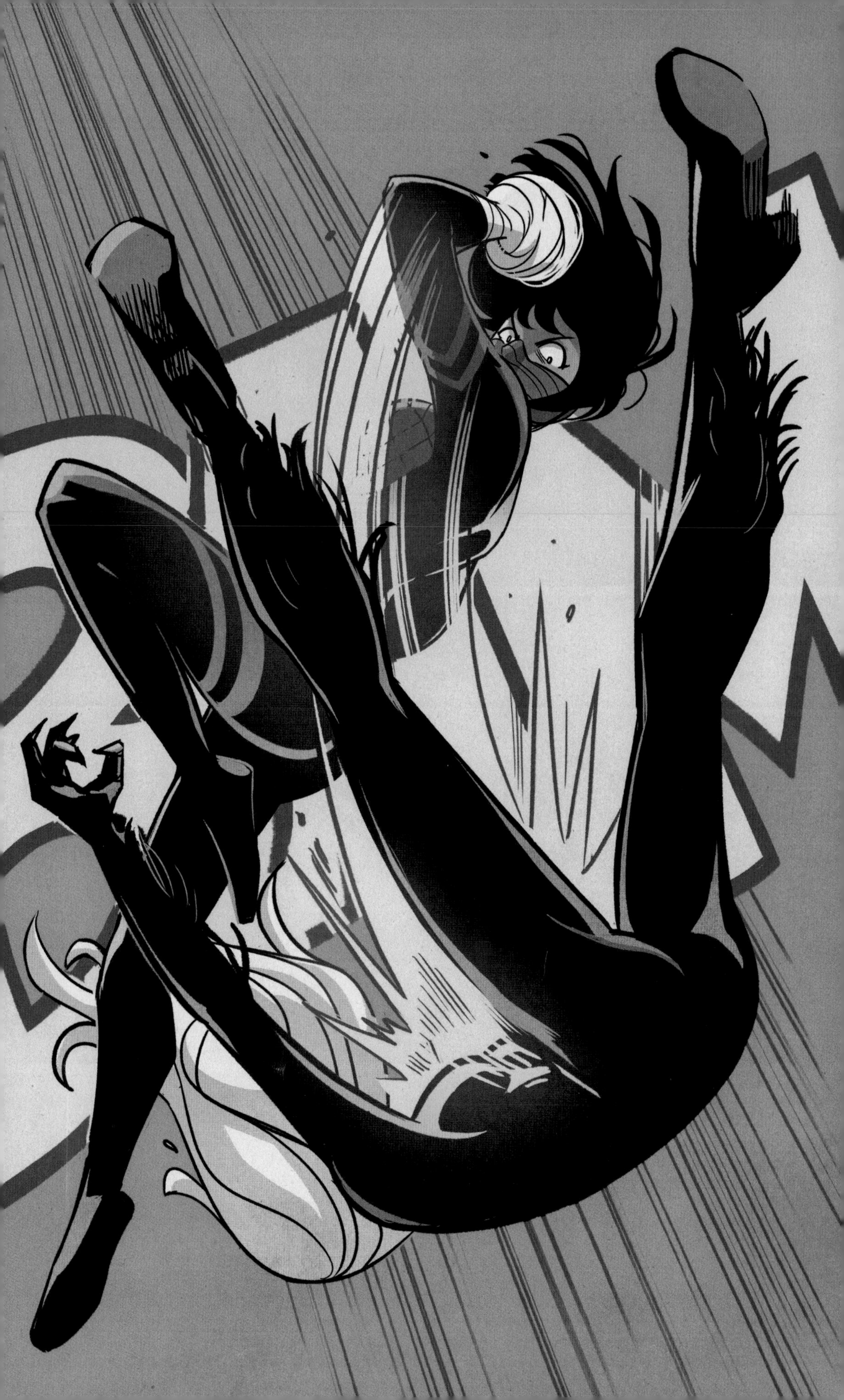

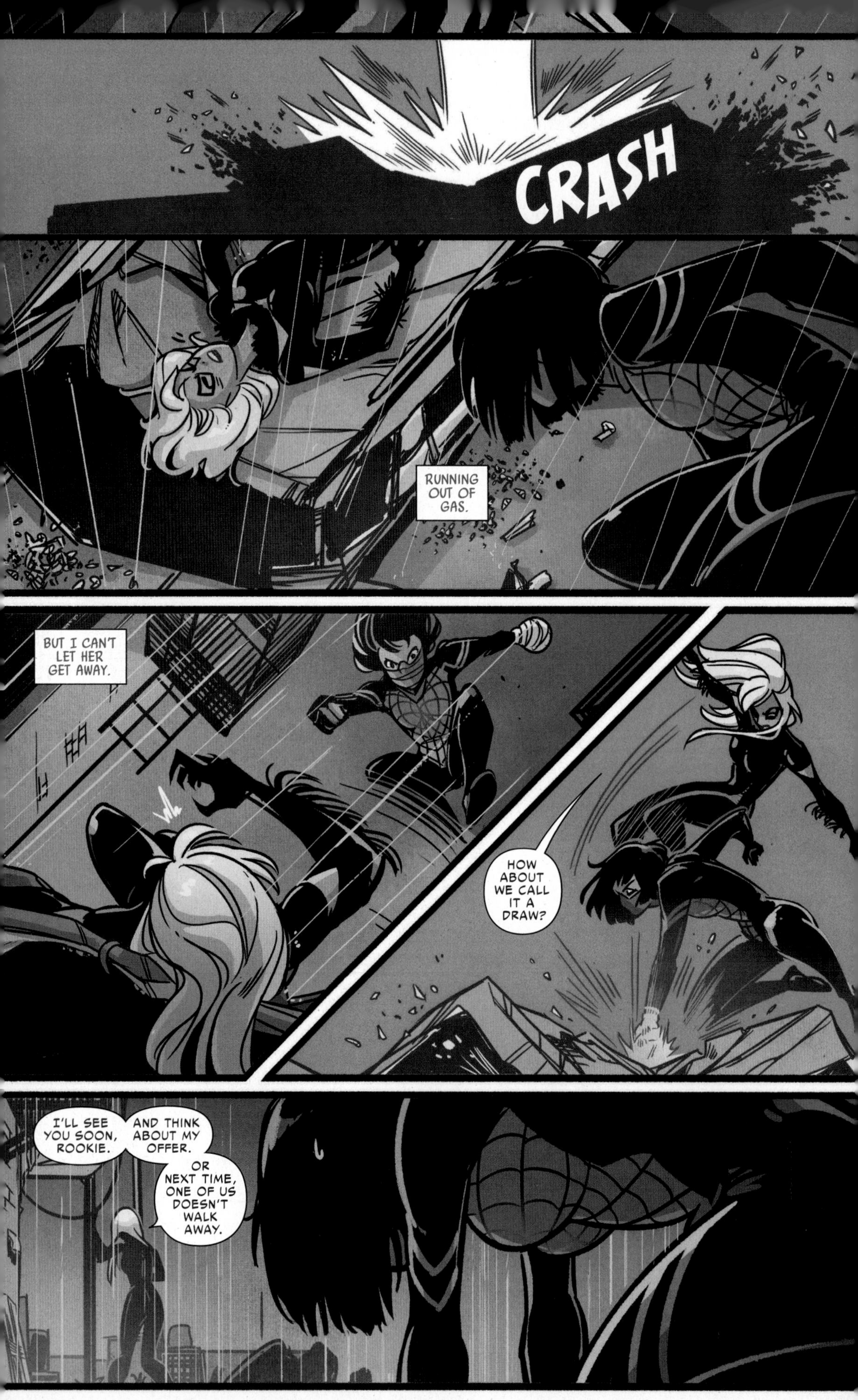
CRASH
RUNNING OUT OF GAS.
BUT I CAN'T LET HER GET AWAY.
HOW ABOUT WE CALL IT A DRAW?
I'LL SEE YOU SOON, ROOKIE.
AND THINK ABOUT MY OFFER.
OR NEXT TIME, ONE OF US DOESN'T WALK AWAY.

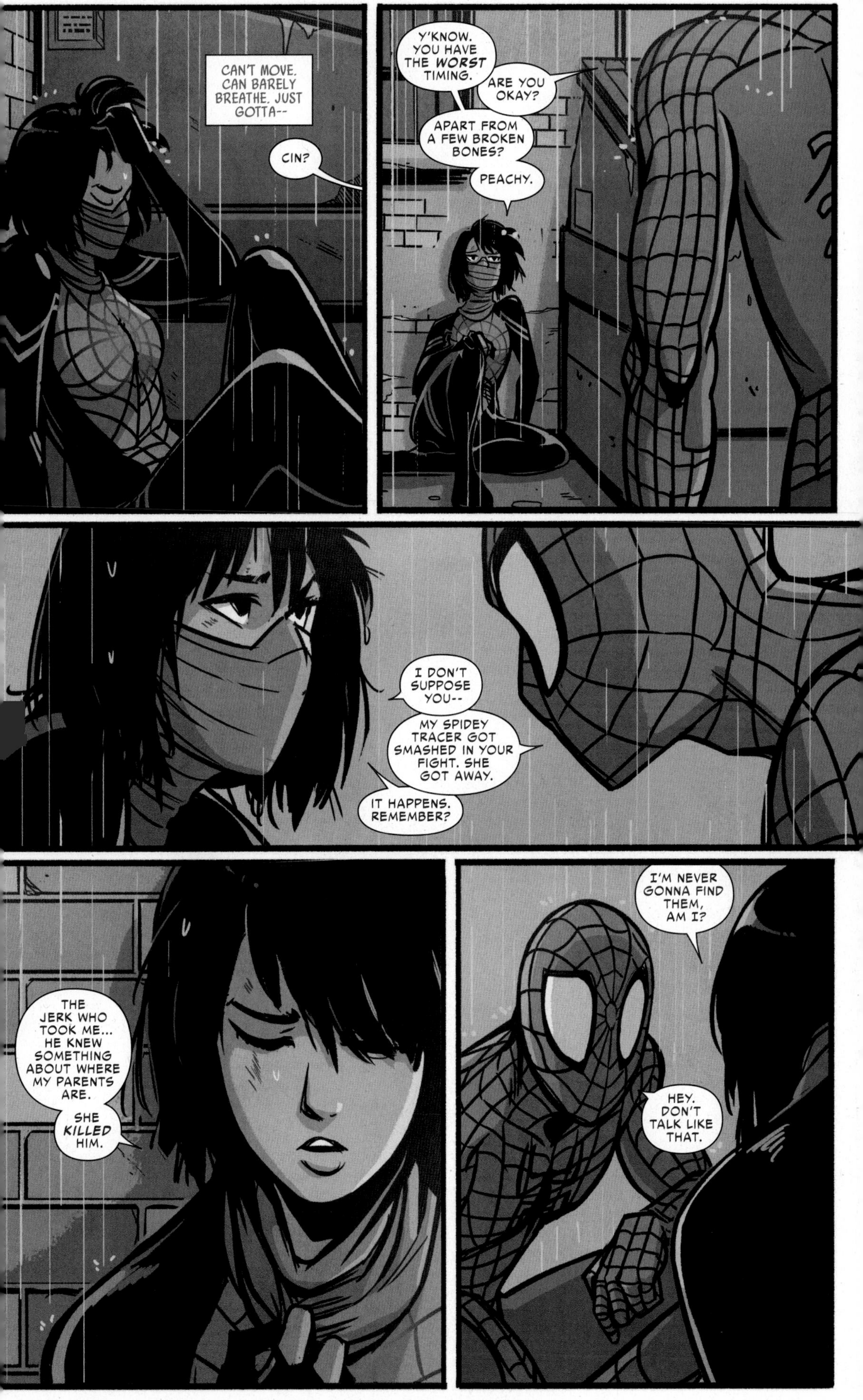

CAN'T MOVE. CAN BARELY BREATHE. JUST GOTTA--
CIN?
ARE YOU OKAY?
Y'KNOW. YOU HAVE THE **WORST** TIMING.
APART FROM A FEW BROKEN BONES?
PEACHY.
I DON'T SUPPOSE YOU--
MY SPIDEY TRACER GOT SMASHED IN YOUR FIGHT. SHE GOT AWAY.
IT HAPPENS. REMEMBER?
THE JERK WHO TOOK ME... HE KNEW SOMETHING ABOUT WHERE MY PARENTS ARE.
SHE ***KILLED*** HIM.
I'M NEVER GONNA FIND THEM, AM I?
HEY. DON'T TALK LIKE THAT.

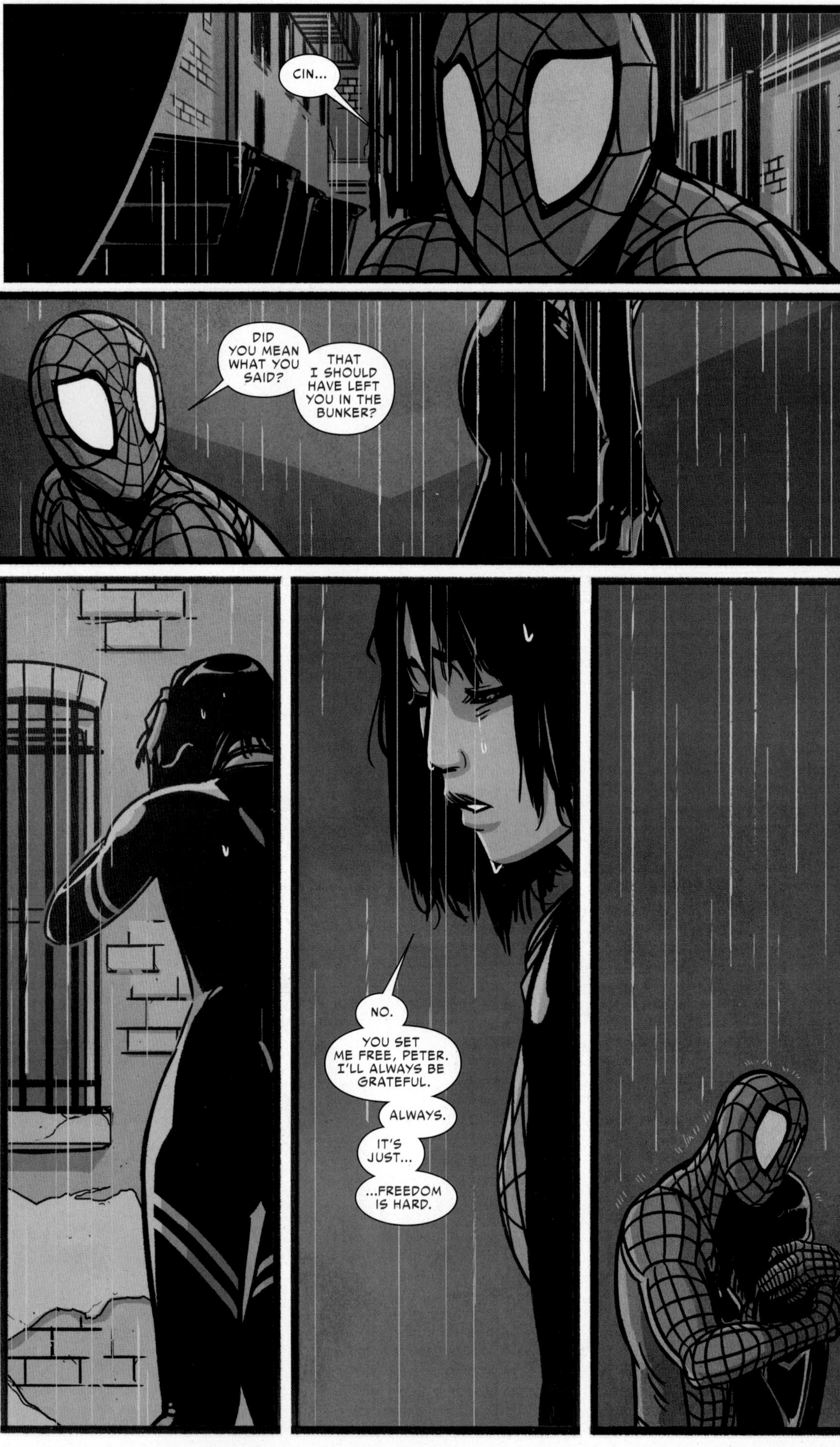
CIN...
DID YOU MEAN WHAT YOU SAID?
THAT I SHOULD HAVE LEFT YOU IN THE BUNKER?
NO.
YOU SET ME FREE, PETER. I'LL ALWAYS BE GRATEFUL.
ALWAYS.
IT'S JUST...
...FREEDOM IS HARD.

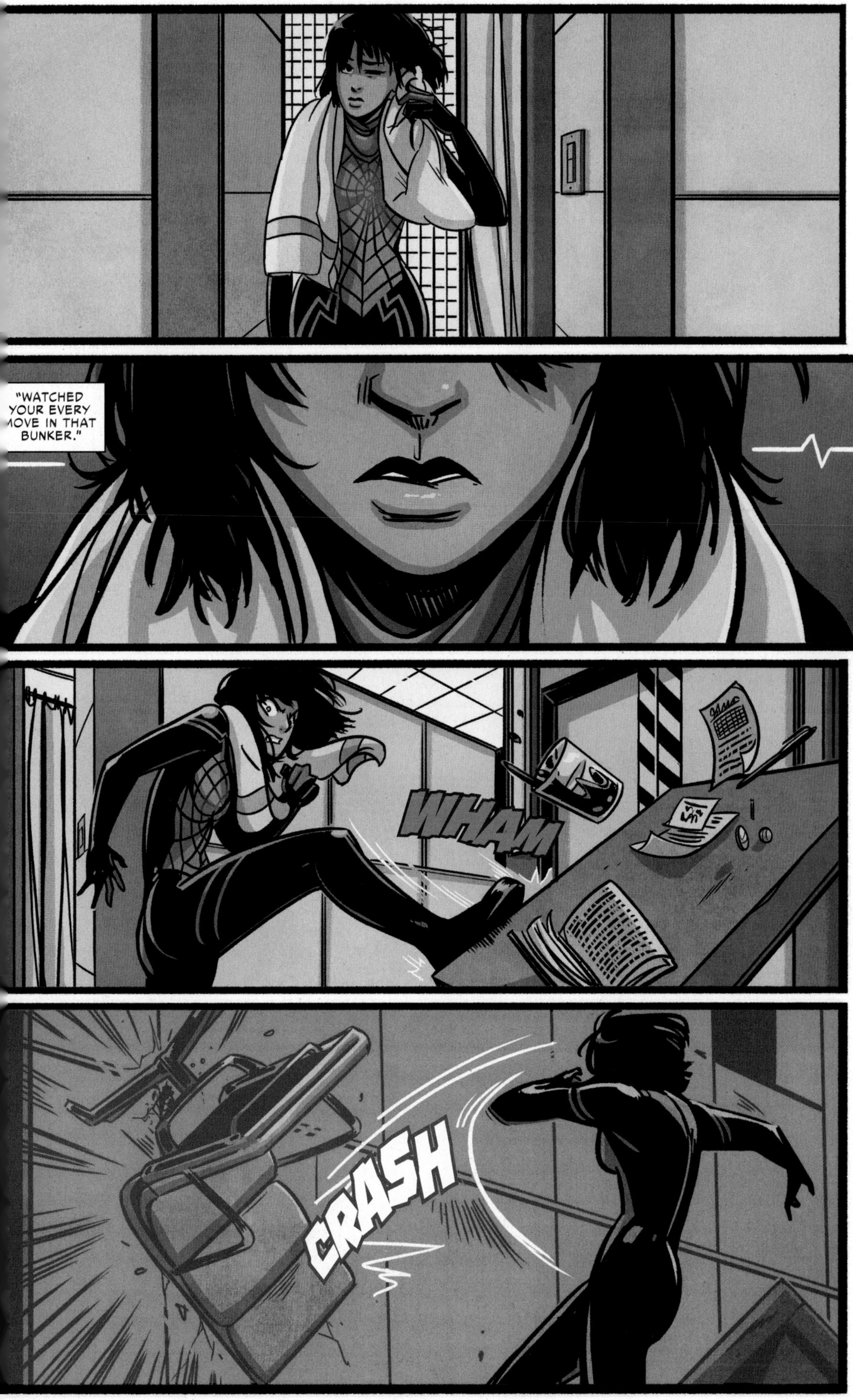

"WATCHED YOUR EVERY MOVE IN THAT BUNKER."
WHAM
CRASH

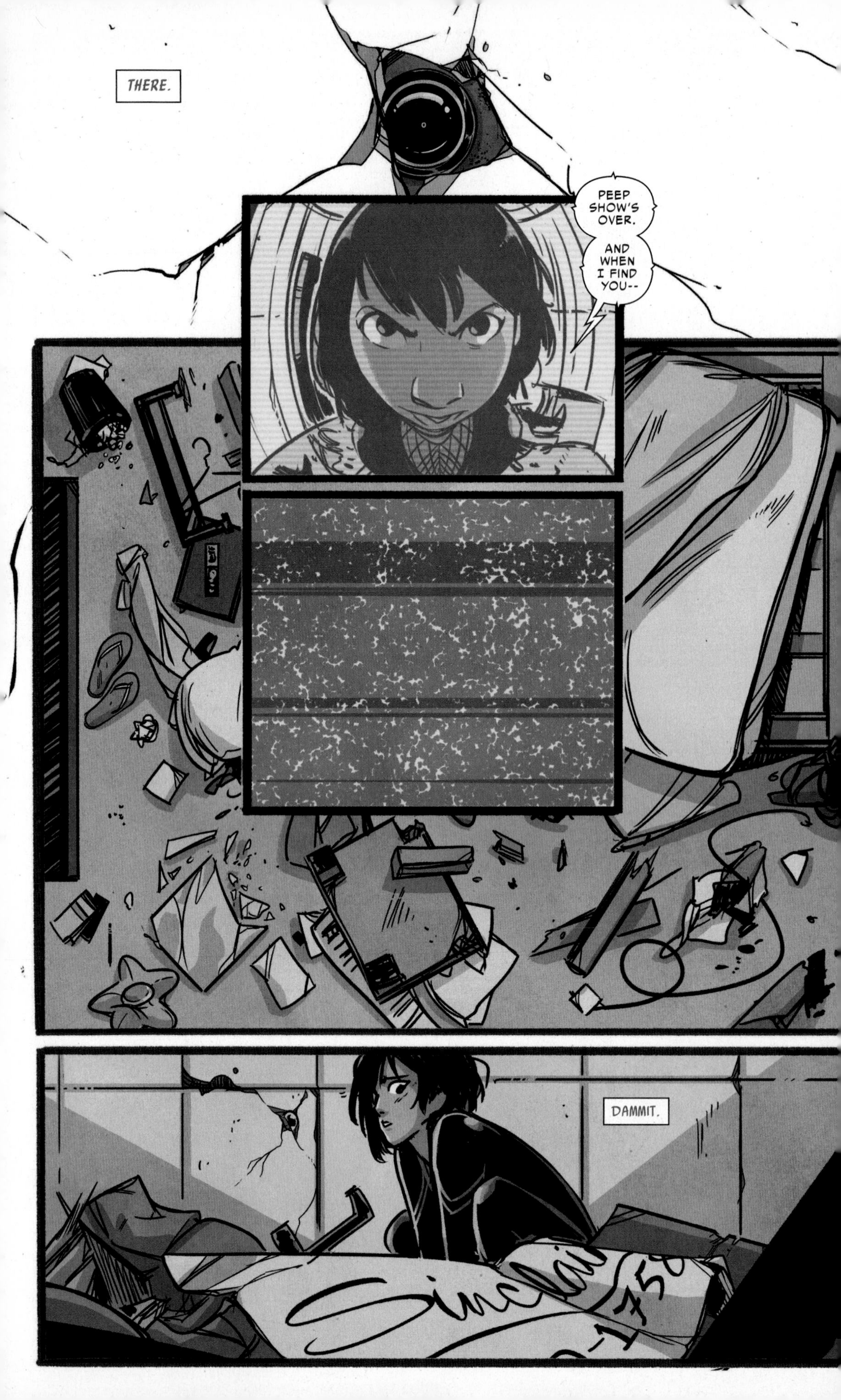
THERE.
PEEP SHOW'S OVER.
AND WHEN I FIND YOU--
DAMMIT.

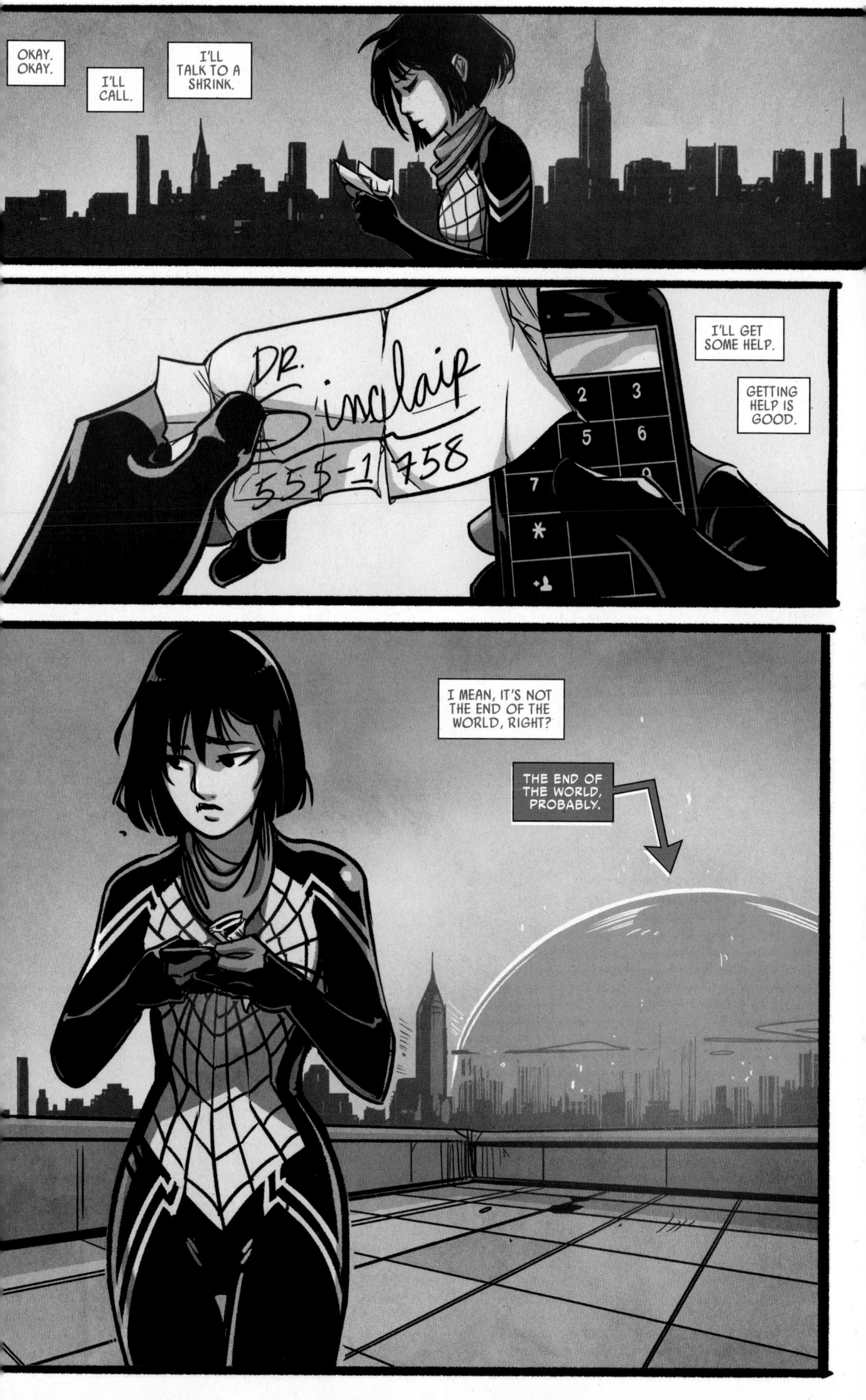
OKAY. OKAY.
I'LL CALL.
I'LL TALK TO A SHRINK.
DR. Sinclair
555-1758
I'LL GET SOME HELP.
GETTING HELP IS GOOD.
I MEAN, IT'S NOT THE END OF THE WORLD, RIGHT?
THE END OF THE WORLD, PROBABLY.

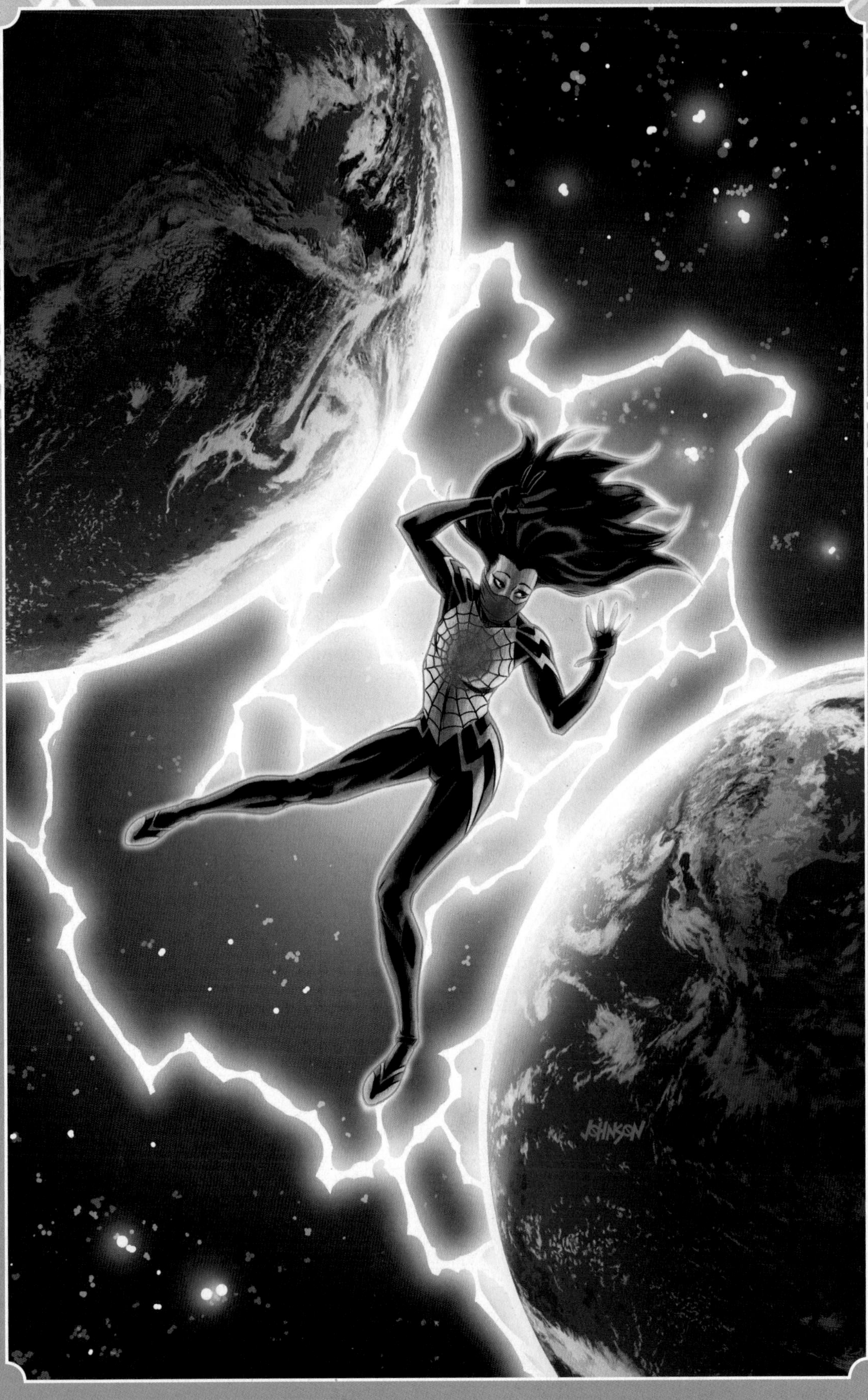
JOHNSON

SILK (2015A) #7

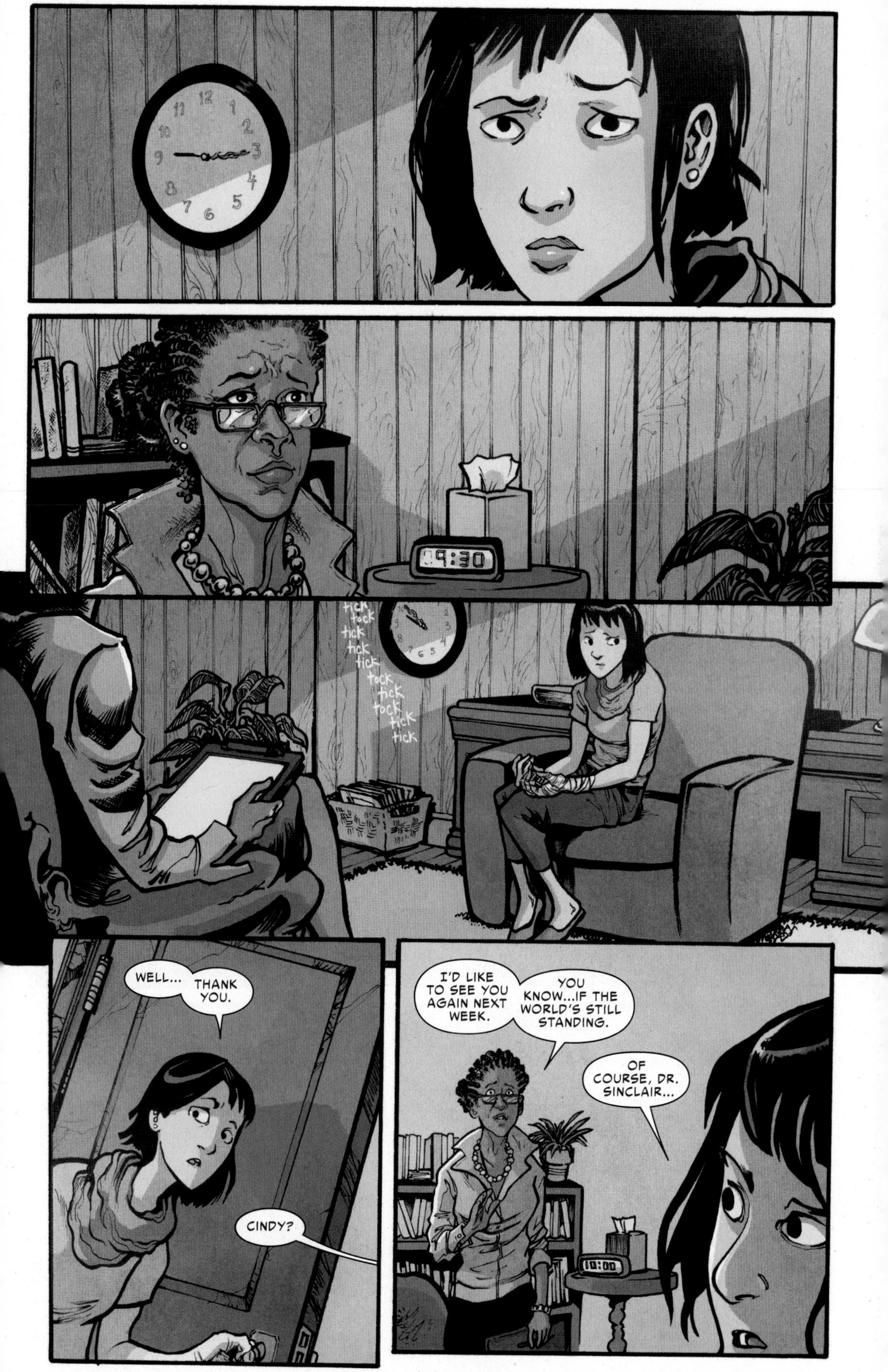
tick
tock
tick
tick
tick
tock
tick
tock
tick
tick
WELL...
THANK YOU.
CINDY?
I'D LIKE TO SEE YOU AGAIN NEXT WEEK.
YOU KNOW...IF THE WORLD'S STILL STANDING.
OF COURSE, DR. SINCLAIR...

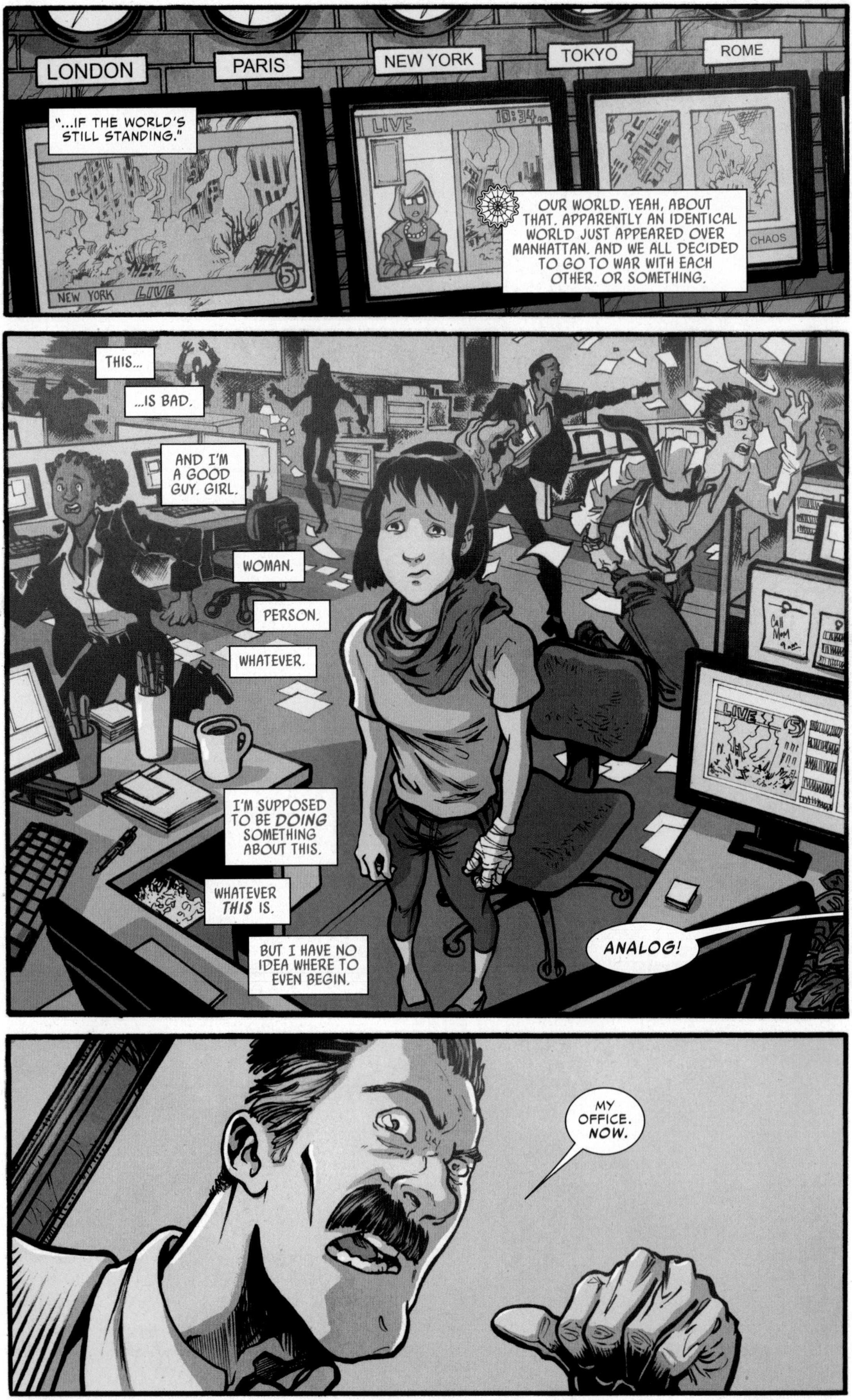

LONDON
PARIS
NEW YORK
TOKYO
ROME
"...IF THE WORLD'S STILL STANDING."
NEW YORK LIVE
LIVE 10:34 AM
CHAOS
OUR WORLD. YEAH, ABOUT THAT. APPARENTLY AN IDENTICAL WORLD JUST APPEARED OVER MANHATTAN. AND WE ALL DECIDED TO GO TO WAR WITH EACH OTHER. OR SOMETHING.
THIS...
...IS BAD.
AND I'M A GOOD GUY. GIRL.
WOMAN.
PERSON.
WHATEVER.
I'M SUPPOSED TO BE DOING SOMETHING ABOUT THIS.
WHATEVER THIS IS.
BUT I HAVE NO IDEA WHERE TO EVEN BEGIN.
ANALOG!
MY OFFICE. NOW.

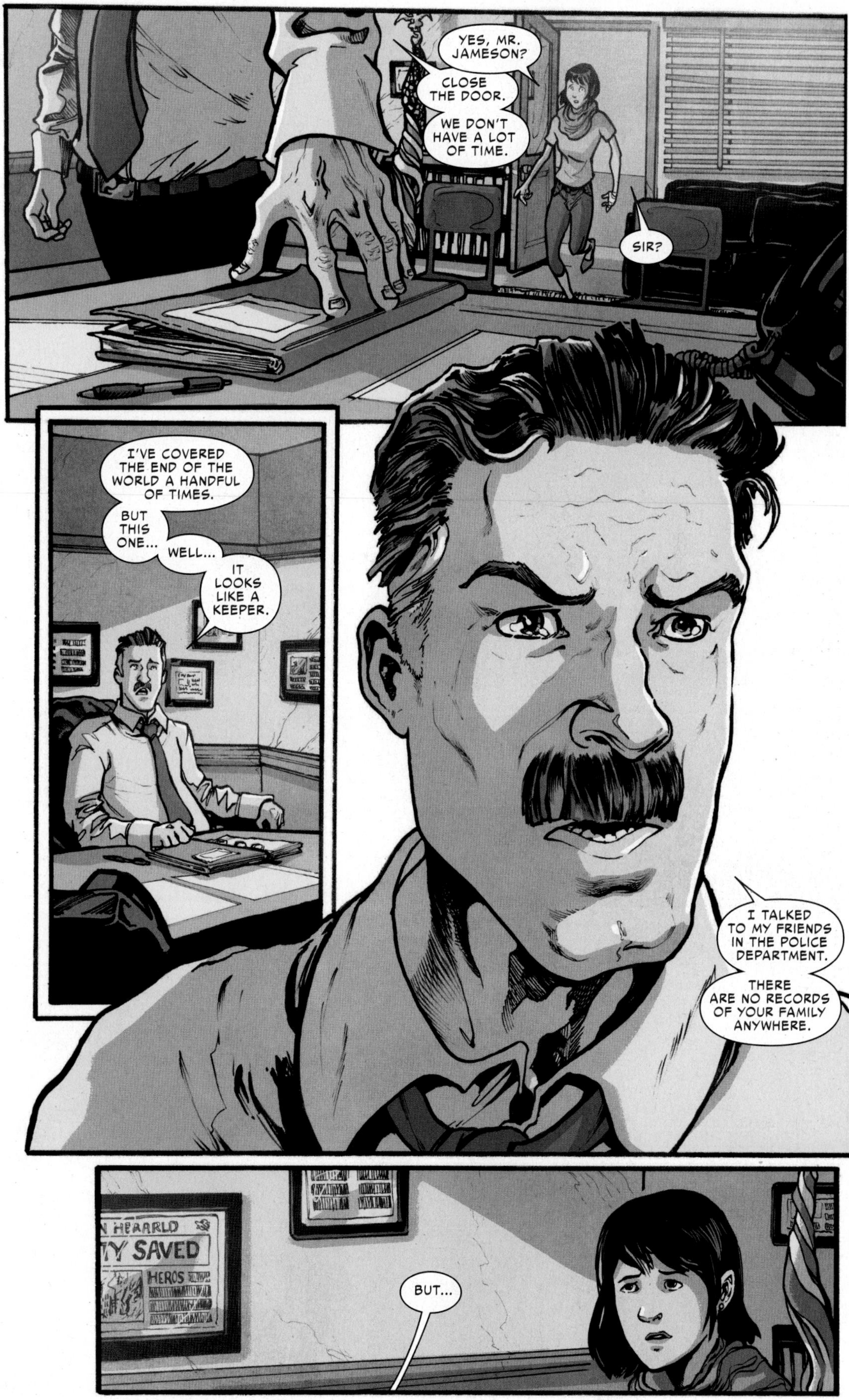

YES, MR. JAMESON?
CLOSE THE DOOR.
WE DON'T HAVE A LOT OF TIME.
SIR?
I'VE COVERED THE END OF THE WORLD A HANDFUL OF TIMES.
BUT THIS ONE...
WELL...
IT LOOKS LIKE A KEEPER.
I TALKED TO MY FRIENDS IN THE POLICE DEPARTMENT.
THERE ARE NO RECORDS OF YOUR FAMILY ANYWHERE.
N HERARLD
TY SAVED
HEROS
BUT...

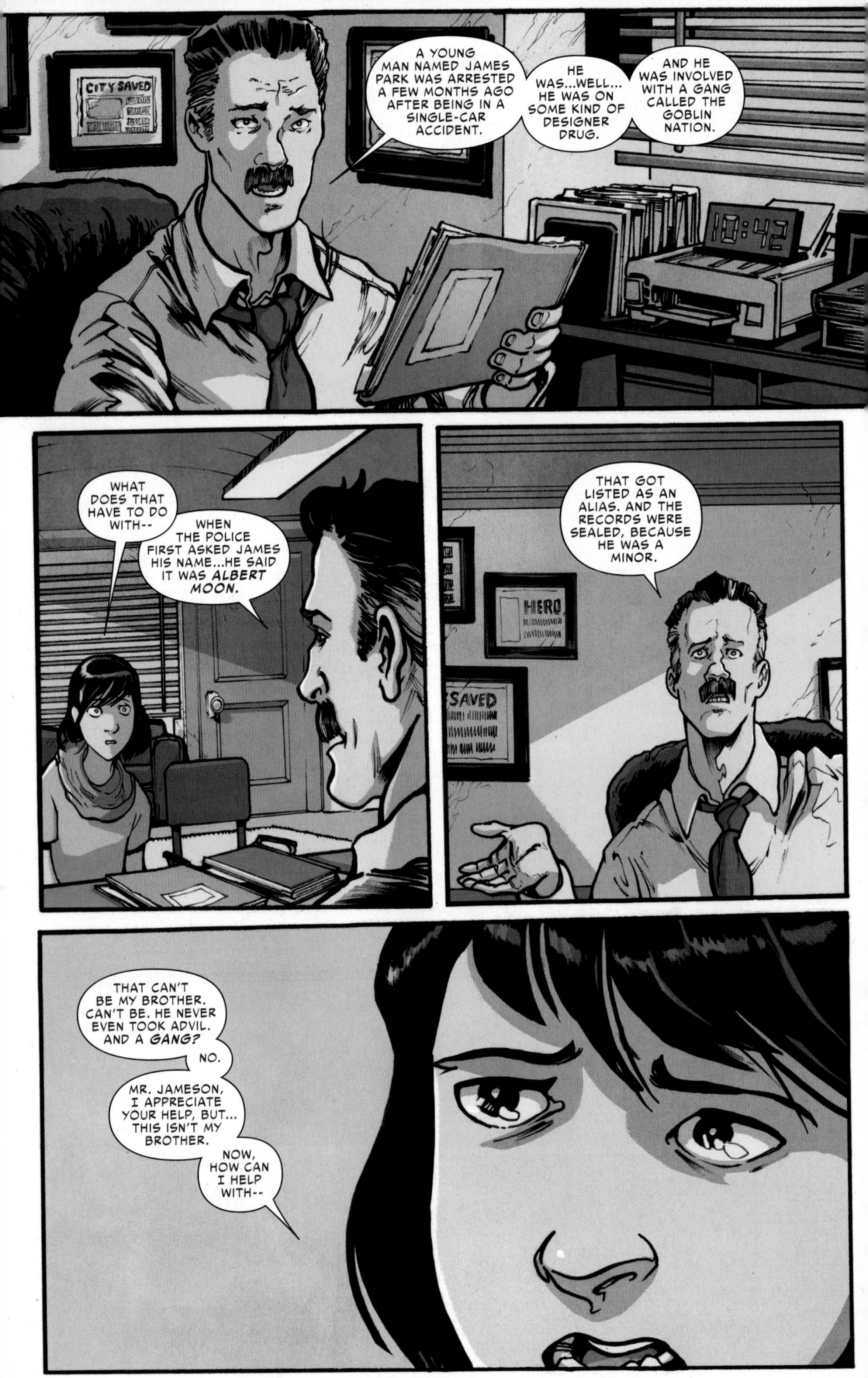
CITY SAVED
A YOUNG MAN NAMED JAMES PARK WAS ARRESTED A FEW MONTHS AGO AFTER BEING IN A SINGLE-CAR ACCIDENT.
HE WAS...WELL... HE WAS ON SOME KIND OF DESIGNER DRUG.
AND HE WAS INVOLVED WITH A GANG CALLED THE GOBLIN NATION.
10:42
WHAT DOES THAT HAVE TO DO WITH--
WHEN THE POLICE FIRST ASKED JAMES HIS NAME...HE SAID IT WAS *ALBERT MOON.*
THAT GOT LISTED AS AN ALIAS. AND THE RECORDS WERE SEALED, BECAUSE HE WAS A MINOR.
HERO
SAVED
THAT CAN'T BE MY BROTHER. CAN'T BE. HE NEVER EVEN TOOK ADVIL. AND A *GANG?*
NO.
MR. JAMESON, I APPRECIATE YOUR HELP, BUT... THIS ISN'T MY BROTHER.
NOW, HOW CAN I HELP WITH--

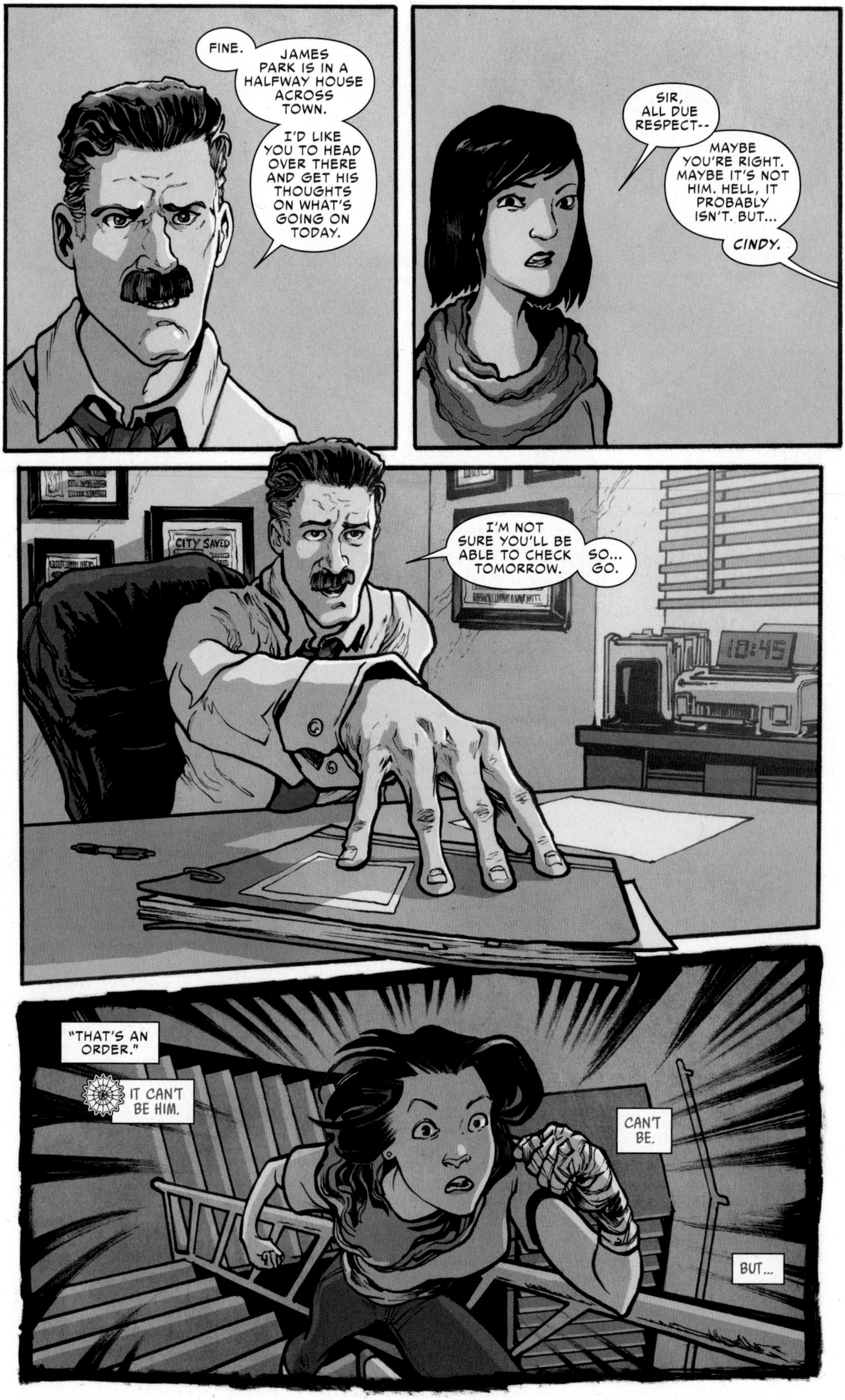
FINE.
JAMES PARK IS IN A HALFWAY HOUSE ACROSS TOWN.
I'D LIKE YOU TO HEAD OVER THERE AND GET HIS THOUGHTS ON WHAT'S GOING ON TODAY.
SIR, ALL DUE RESPECT--
MAYBE YOU'RE RIGHT. MAYBE IT'S NOT HIM. HELL, IT PROBABLY ISN'T. BUT...
CINDY.
CITY SAVED
I'M NOT SURE YOU'LL BE ABLE TO CHECK TOMORROW.
SO... GO.
10:45
"THAT'S AN ORDER."
IT CAN'T BE HIM.
CAN'T BE.
BUT...

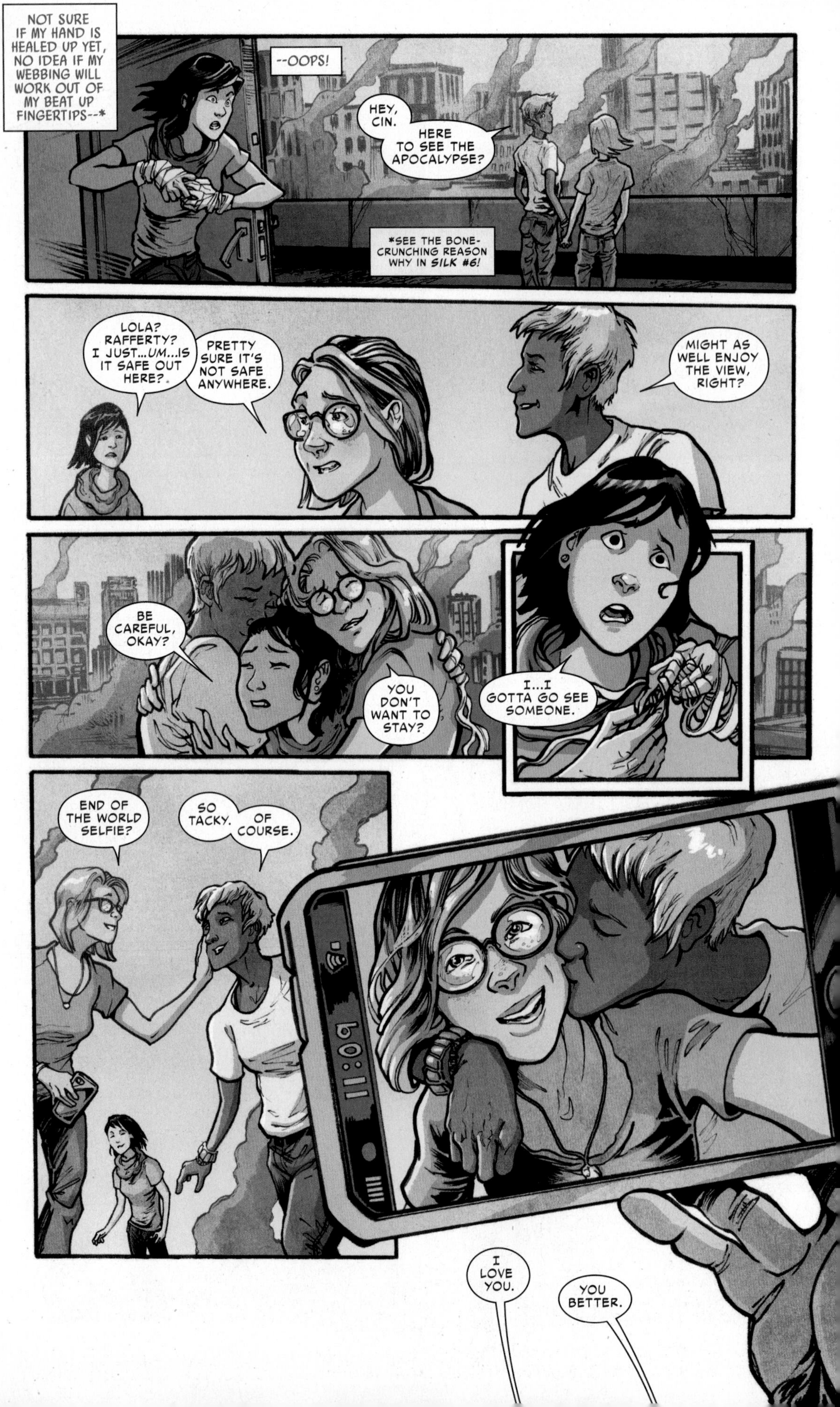

NOT SURE IF MY HAND IS HEALED UP YET, NO IDEA IF MY WEBBING WILL WORK OUT OF MY BEAT UP FINGERTIPS--*
--OOPS!
HEY, CIN.
HERE TO SEE THE APOCALYPSE?
*SEE THE BONE-CRUNCHING REASON WHY IN SILK #6!
LOLA? RAFFERTY? I JUST...UM...IS IT SAFE OUT HERE?
PRETTY SURE IT'S NOT SAFE ANYWHERE.
MIGHT AS WELL ENJOY THE VIEW, RIGHT?
BE CAREFUL, OKAY?
YOU DON'T WANT TO STAY?
I...I GOTTA GO SEE SOMEONE.
END OF THE WORLD SELFIE?
SO TACKY.
OF COURSE.
I LOVE YOU.
YOU BETTER.

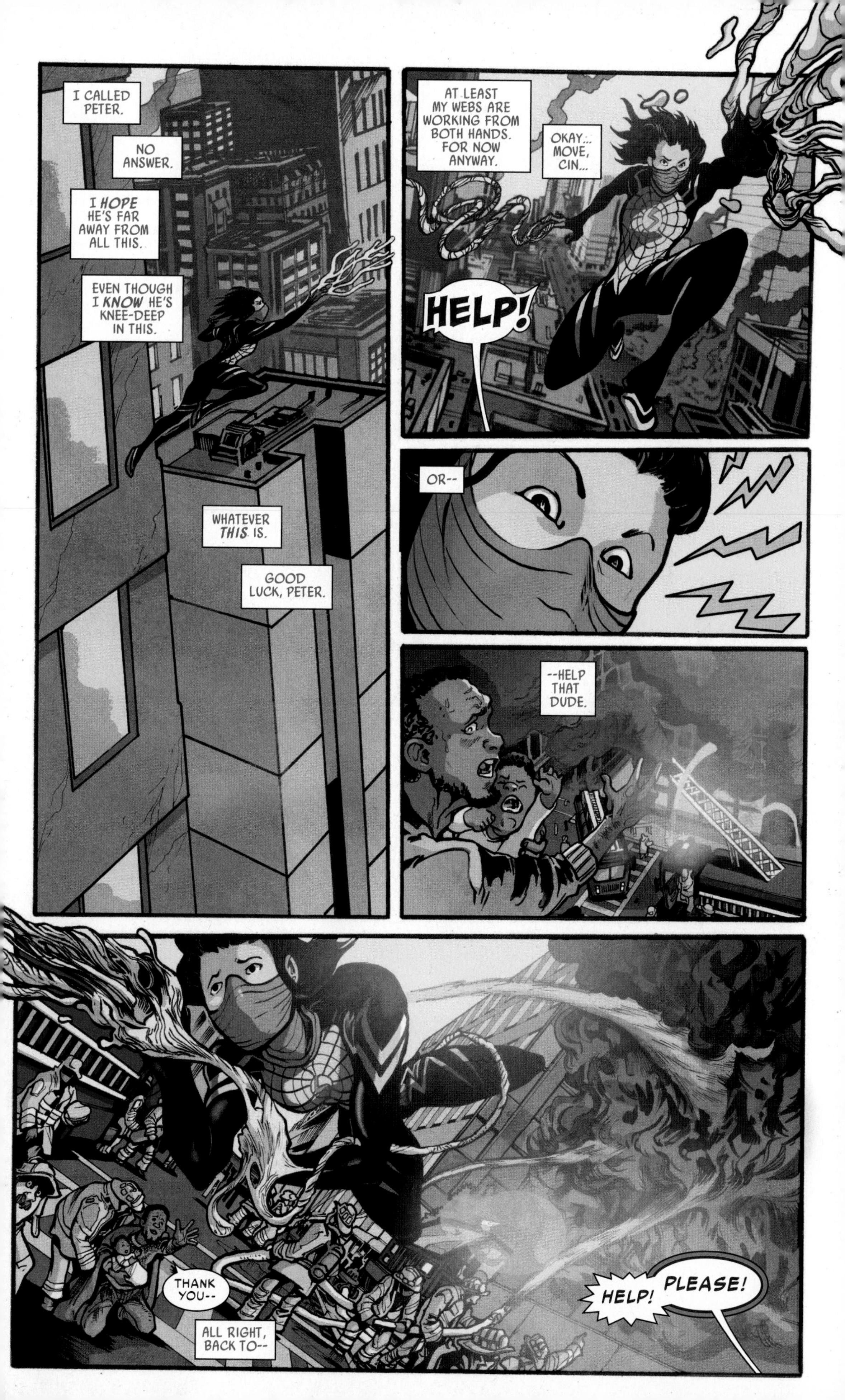
I CALLED PETER.
NO ANSWER.
I HOPE HE'S FAR AWAY FROM ALL THIS.
EVEN THOUGH I KNOW HE'S KNEE-DEEP IN THIS.
WHATEVER THIS IS.
GOOD LUCK, PETER.
AT LEAST MY WEBS ARE WORKING FROM BOTH HANDS. FOR NOW ANYWAY.
OKAY... MOVE, CIN...
HELP!
OR--
--HELP THAT DUDE.
THANK YOU--
ALL RIGHT, BACK TO--
HELP!
PLEASE!

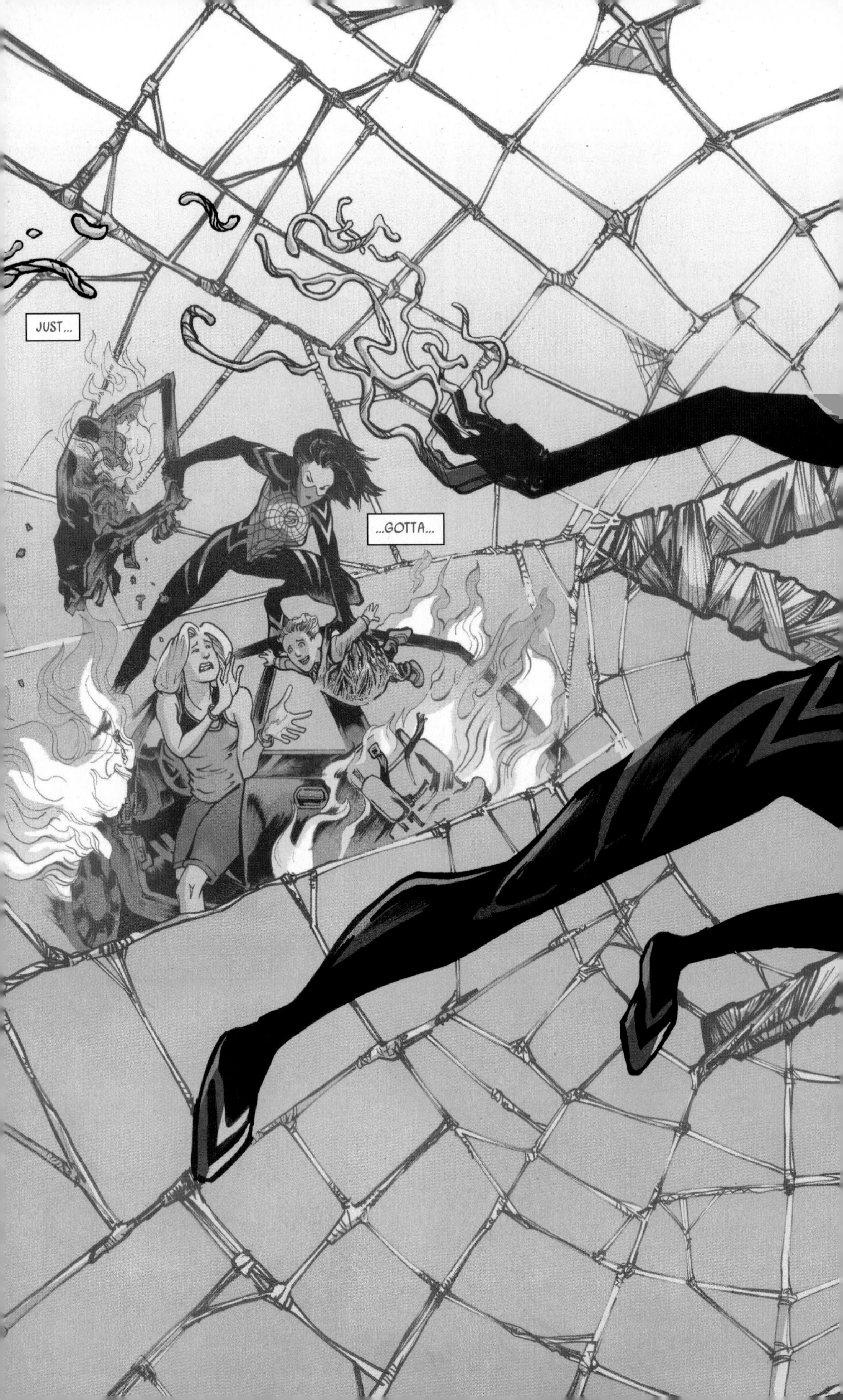
JUST...
...GOTTA...

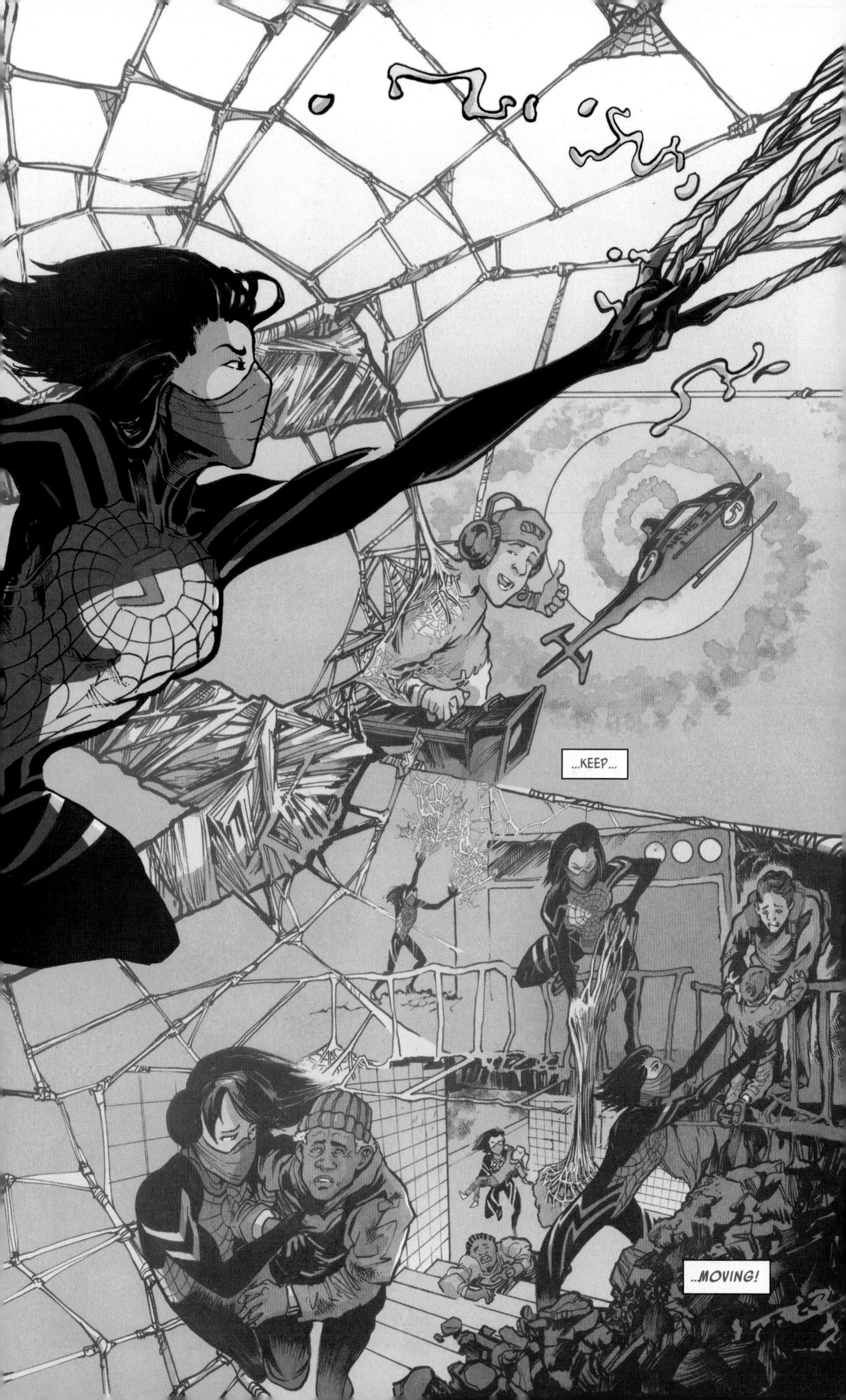

...KEEP...
...MOVING!

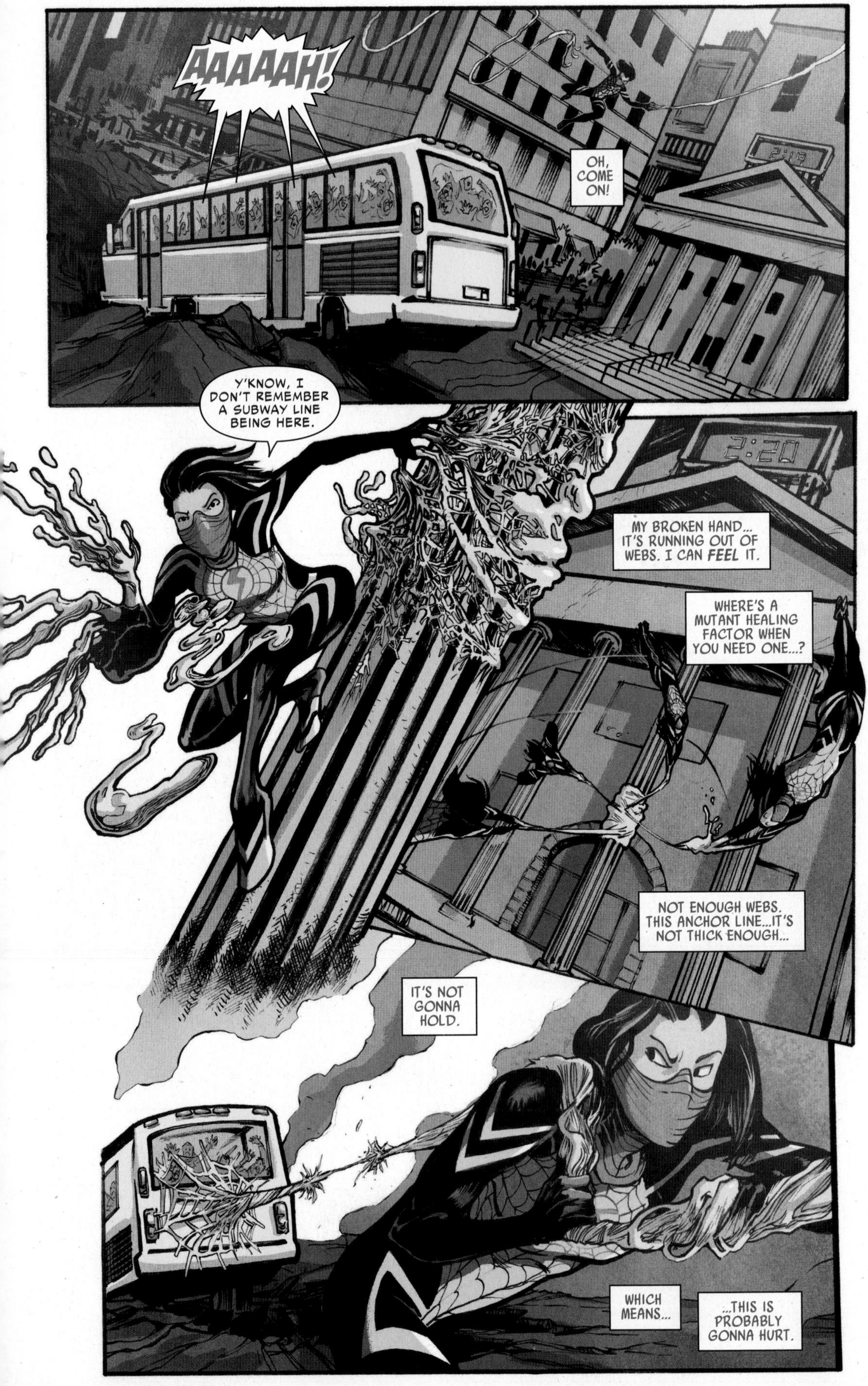
AAAAAH!
OH, COME ON!
Y'KNOW, I DON'T REMEMBER A SUBWAY LINE BEING HERE.
MY BROKEN HAND... IT'S RUNNING OUT OF WEBS. I CAN FEEL IT.
WHERE'S A MUTANT HEALING FACTOR WHEN YOU NEED ONE...?
NOT ENOUGH WEBS. THIS ANCHOR LINE...IT'S NOT THICK ENOUGH...
IT'S NOT GONNA HOLD.
WHICH MEANS...
...THIS IS PROBABLY GONNA HURT.

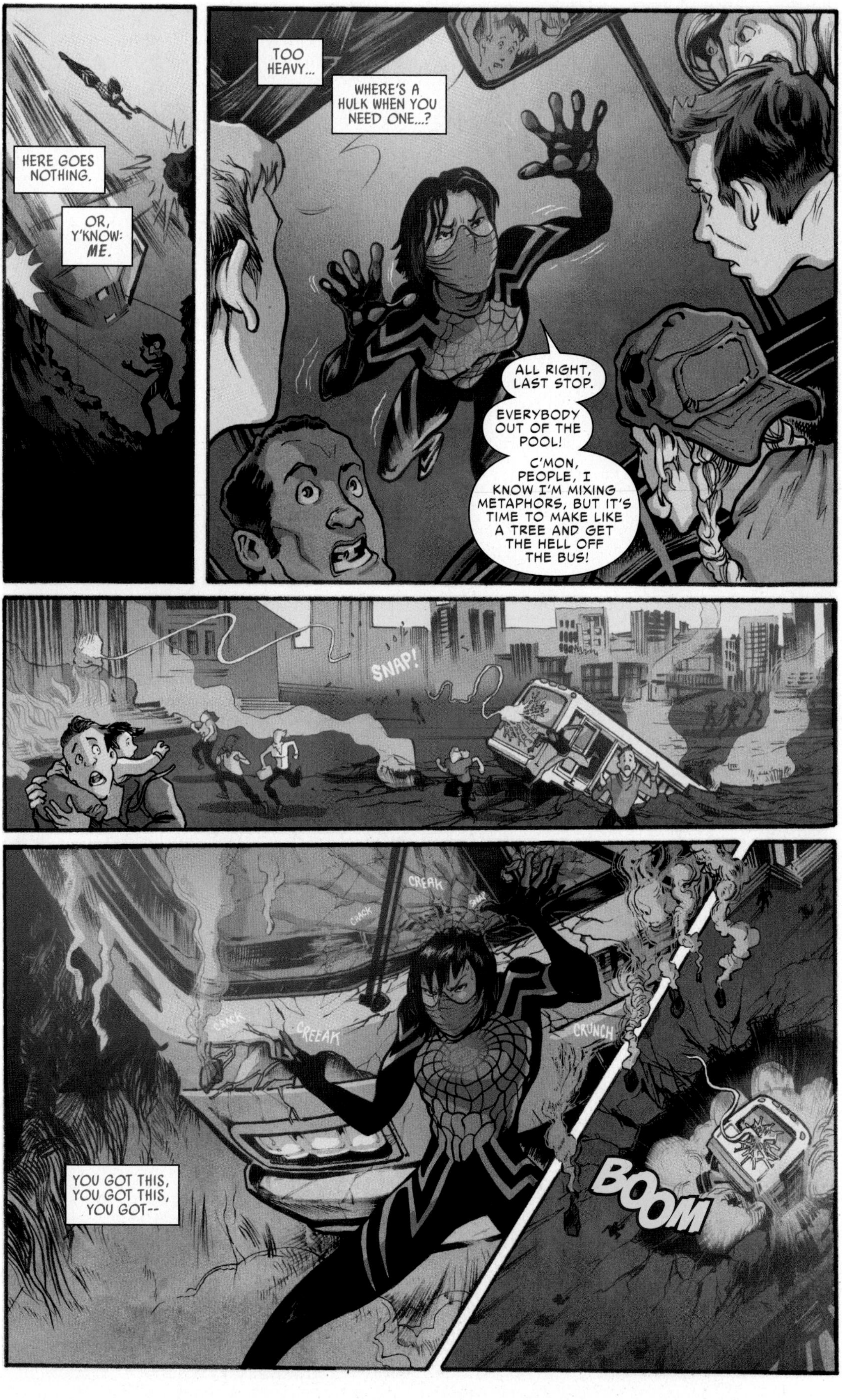

HERE GOES NOTHING.
OR, Y'KNOW: *ME.*
TOO HEAVY...
WHERE'S A HULK WHEN YOU NEED ONE...?
ALL RIGHT, LAST STOP.
EVERYBODY OUT OF THE POOL!
C'MON, PEOPLE, I KNOW I'M MIXING METAPHORS, BUT IT'S TIME TO MAKE LIKE A TREE AND GET THE HELL OFF THE BUS!
SNAP!
CREAK
SNAP
CRACK
CRACK
CREEAK
CRUNCH
YOU GOT THIS, YOU GOT THIS, YOU GOT--
BOOM

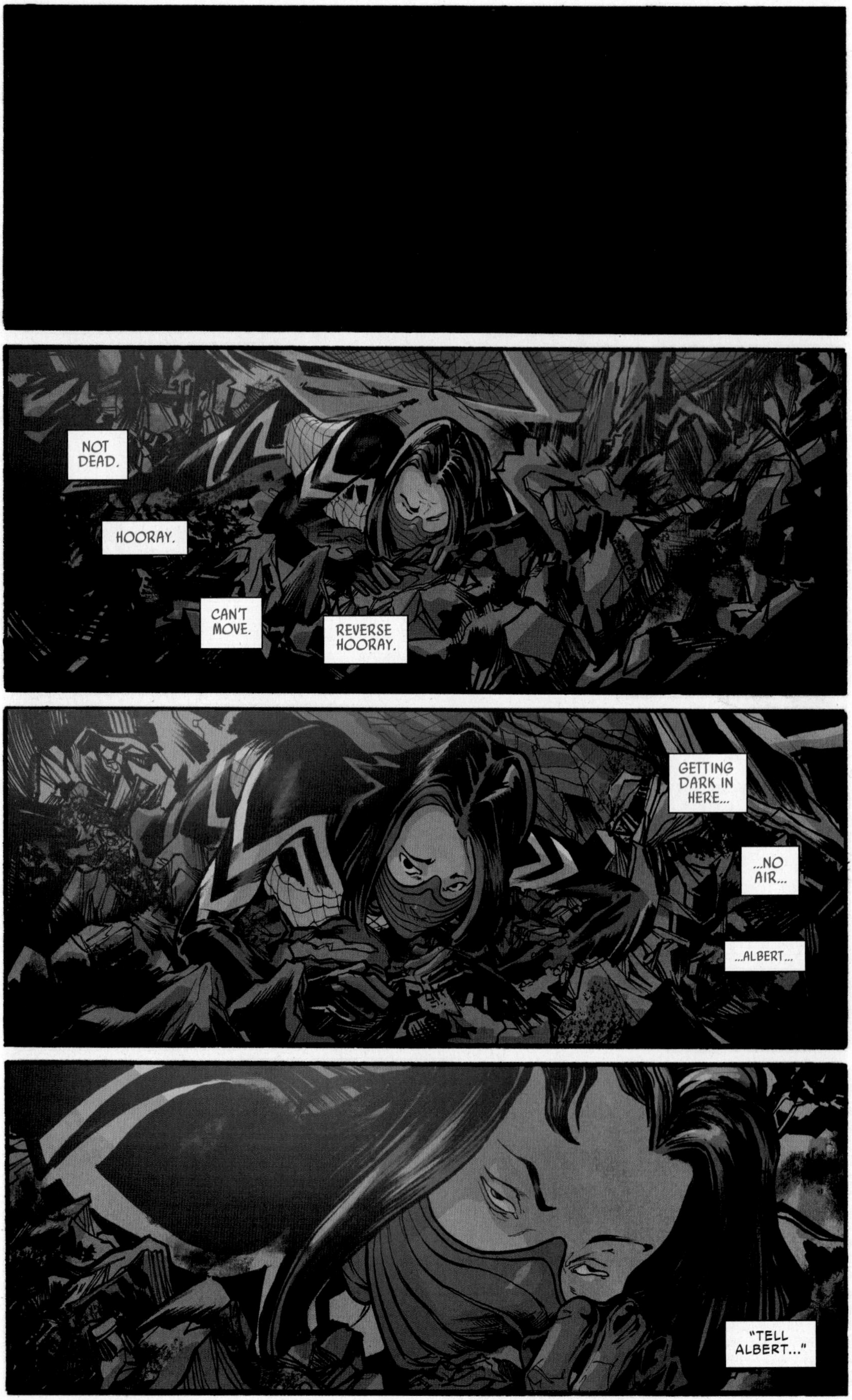
NOT DEAD.
HOORAY.
CAN'T MOVE.
REVERSE HOORAY.
GETTING DARK IN HERE...
...NO AIR...
...ALBERT...
"TELL ALBERT..."

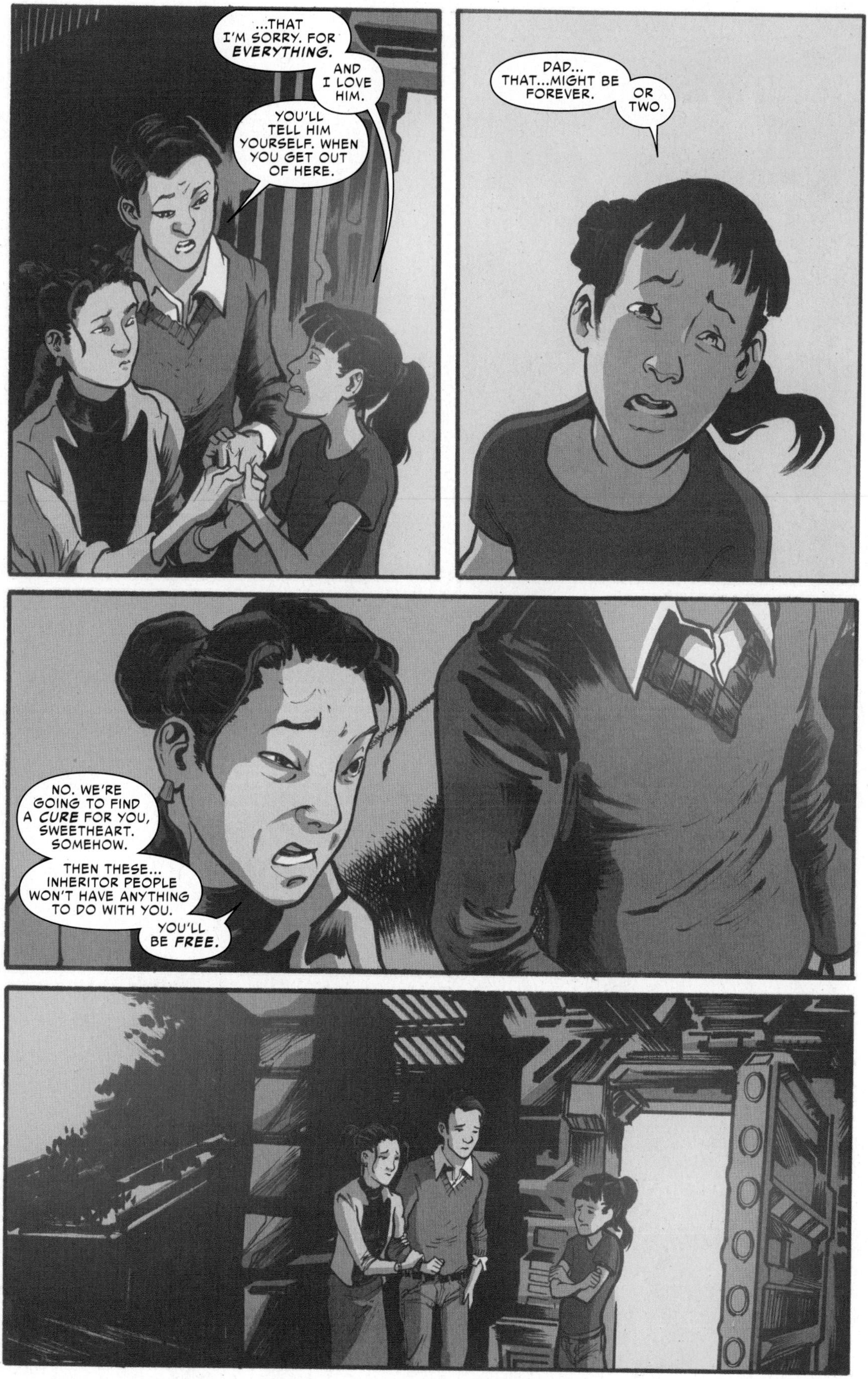
...THAT I'M SORRY. FOR EVERYTHING.
AND I LOVE HIM.
YOU'LL TELL HIM YOURSELF. WHEN YOU GET OUT OF HERE.
DAD... THAT...MIGHT BE FOREVER.
OR TWO.
NO. WE'RE GOING TO FIND A CURE FOR YOU, SWEETHEART. SOMEHOW.
THEN THESE... INHERITOR PEOPLE WON'T HAVE ANYTHING TO DO WITH YOU.
YOU'LL BE FREE.

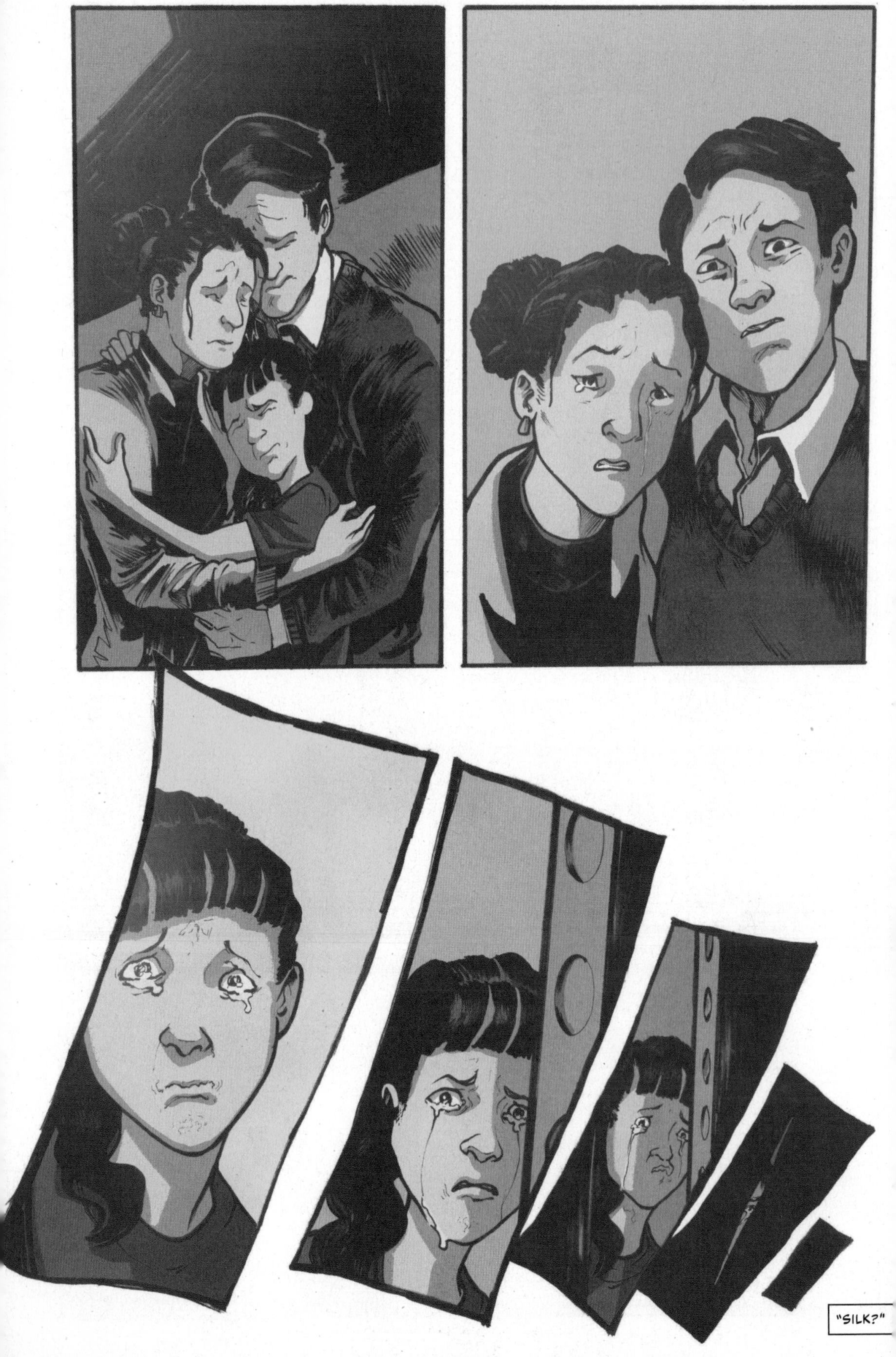
"SILK?"

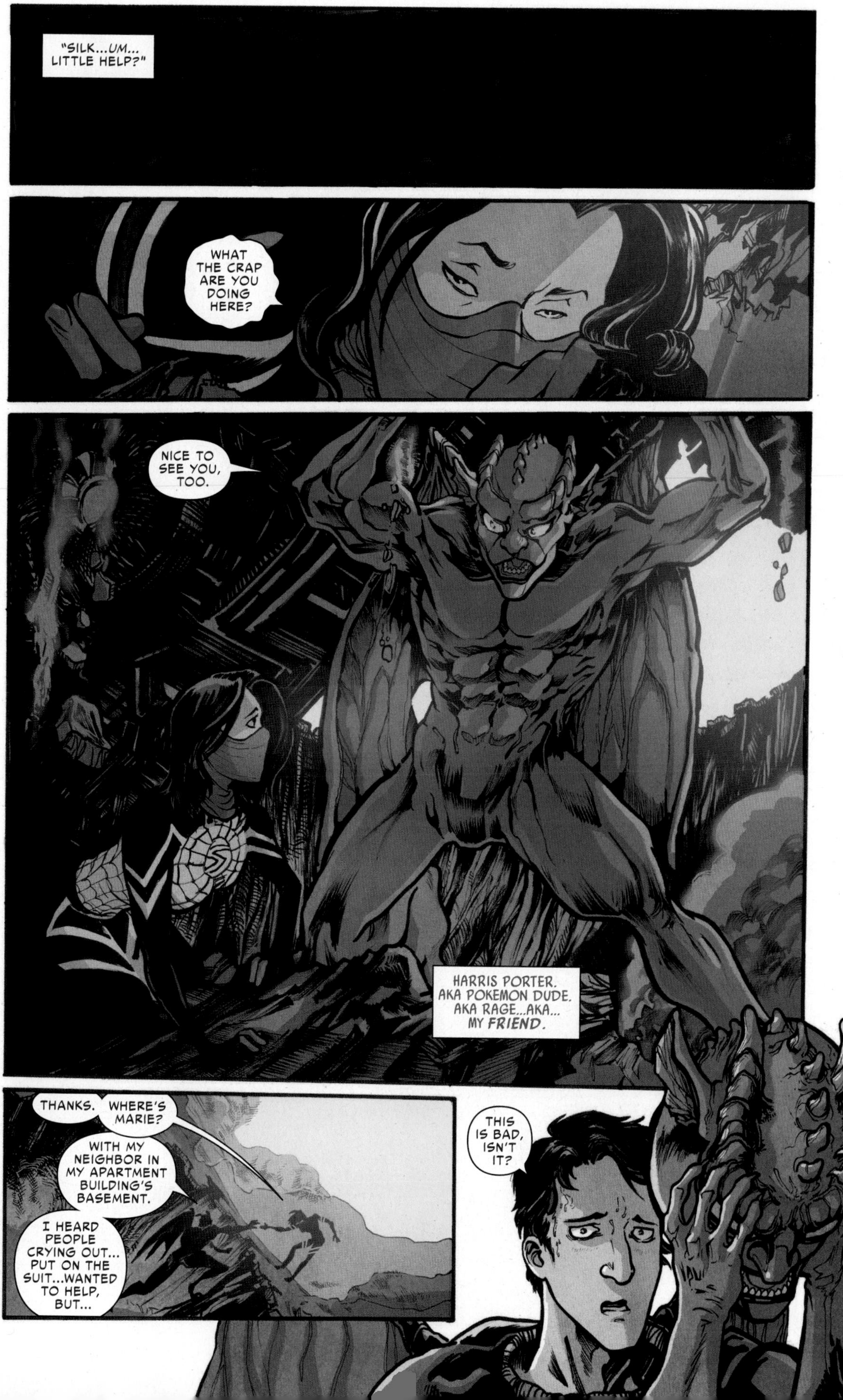
"SILK...UM... LITTLE HELP?"
WHAT THE CRAP ARE YOU DOING HERE?
NICE TO SEE YOU, TOO.
HARRIS PORTER. AKA POKEMON DUDE. AKA RAGE...AKA... MY FRIEND.
THANKS.
WHERE'S MARIE?
WITH MY NEIGHBOR IN MY APARTMENT BUILDING'S BASEMENT.
I HEARD PEOPLE CRYING OUT... PUT ON THE SUIT...WANTED TO HELP, BUT...
THIS IS BAD, ISN'T IT?

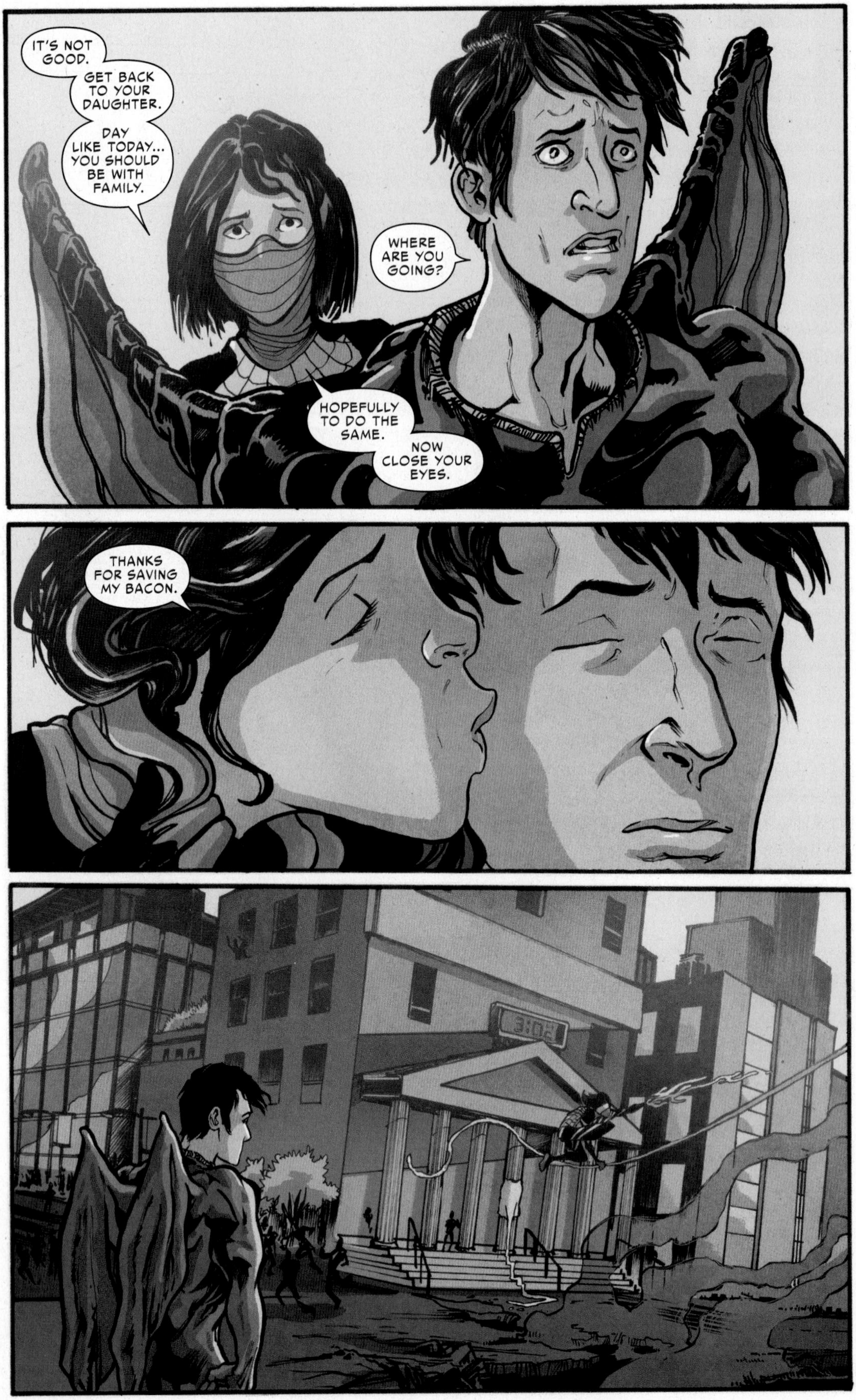
IT'S NOT GOOD.
GET BACK TO YOUR DAUGHTER.
DAY LIKE TODAY... YOU SHOULD BE WITH FAMILY.
WHERE ARE YOU GOING?
HOPEFULLY TO DO THE SAME.
NOW CLOSE YOUR EYES.
THANKS FOR SAVING MY BACON.

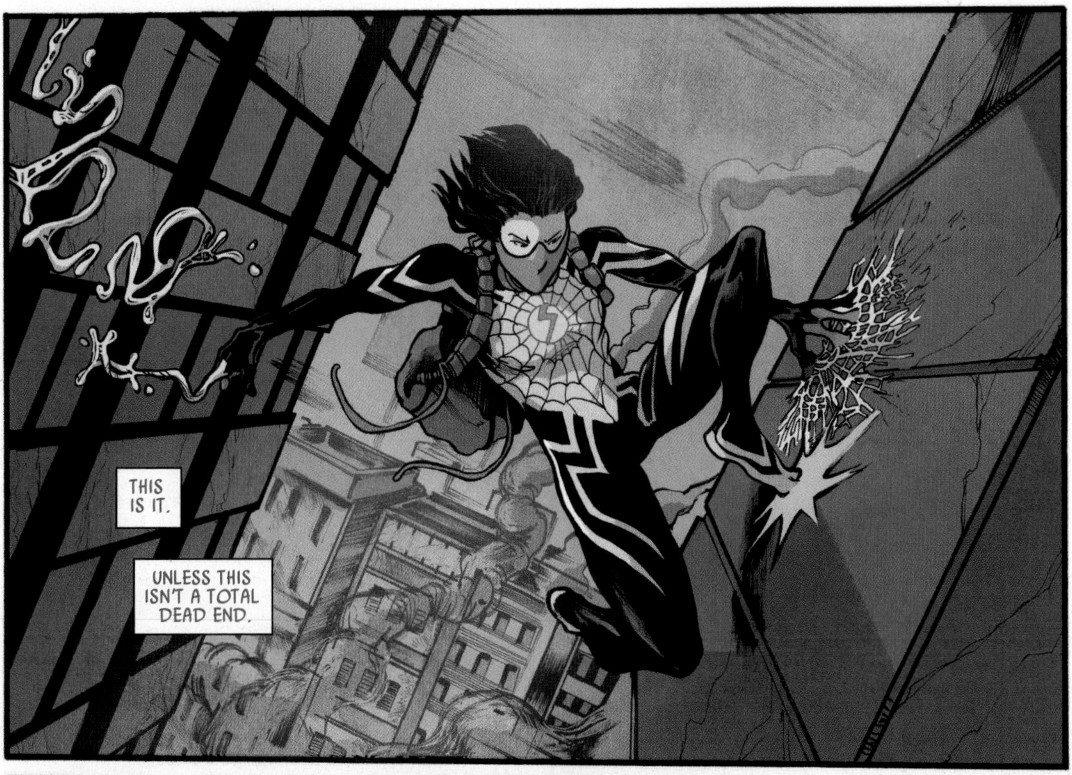
THIS IS IT.
UNLESS THIS ISN'T A TOTAL DEAD END.
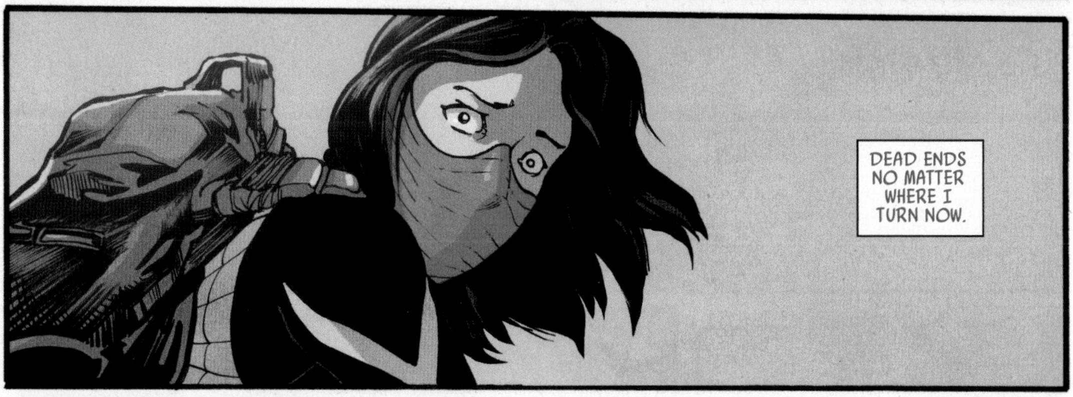
DEAD ENDS NO MATTER WHERE I TURN NOW.
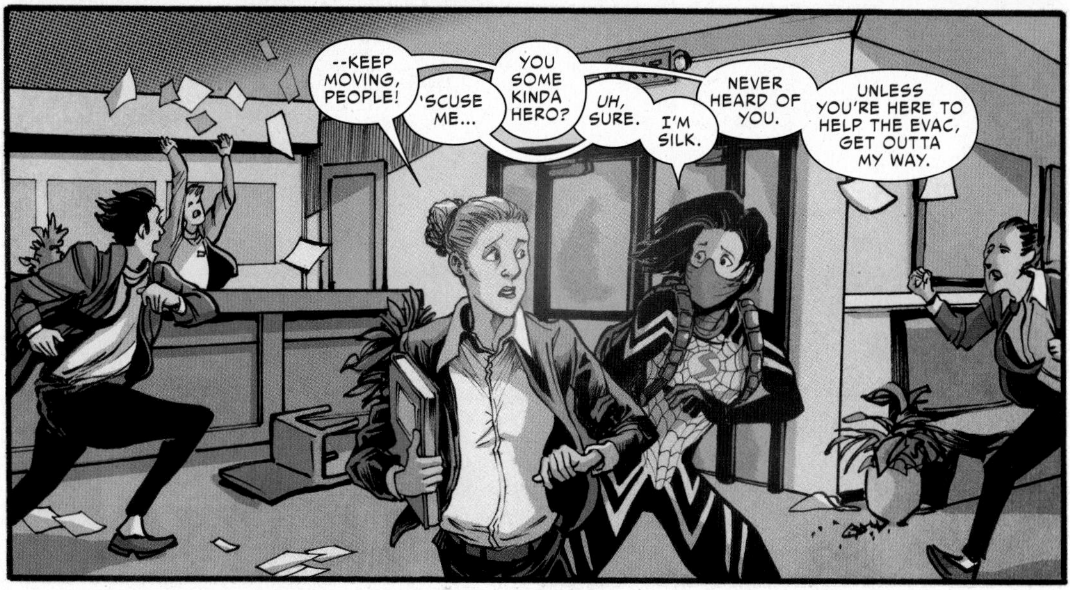
--KEEP MOVING, PEOPLE!
'SCUSE ME...
YOU SOME KINDA HERO?
UH, SURE.
I'M SILK.
NEVER HEARD OF YOU.
UNLESS YOU'RE HERE TO HELP THE EVAC, GET OUTTA MY WAY.

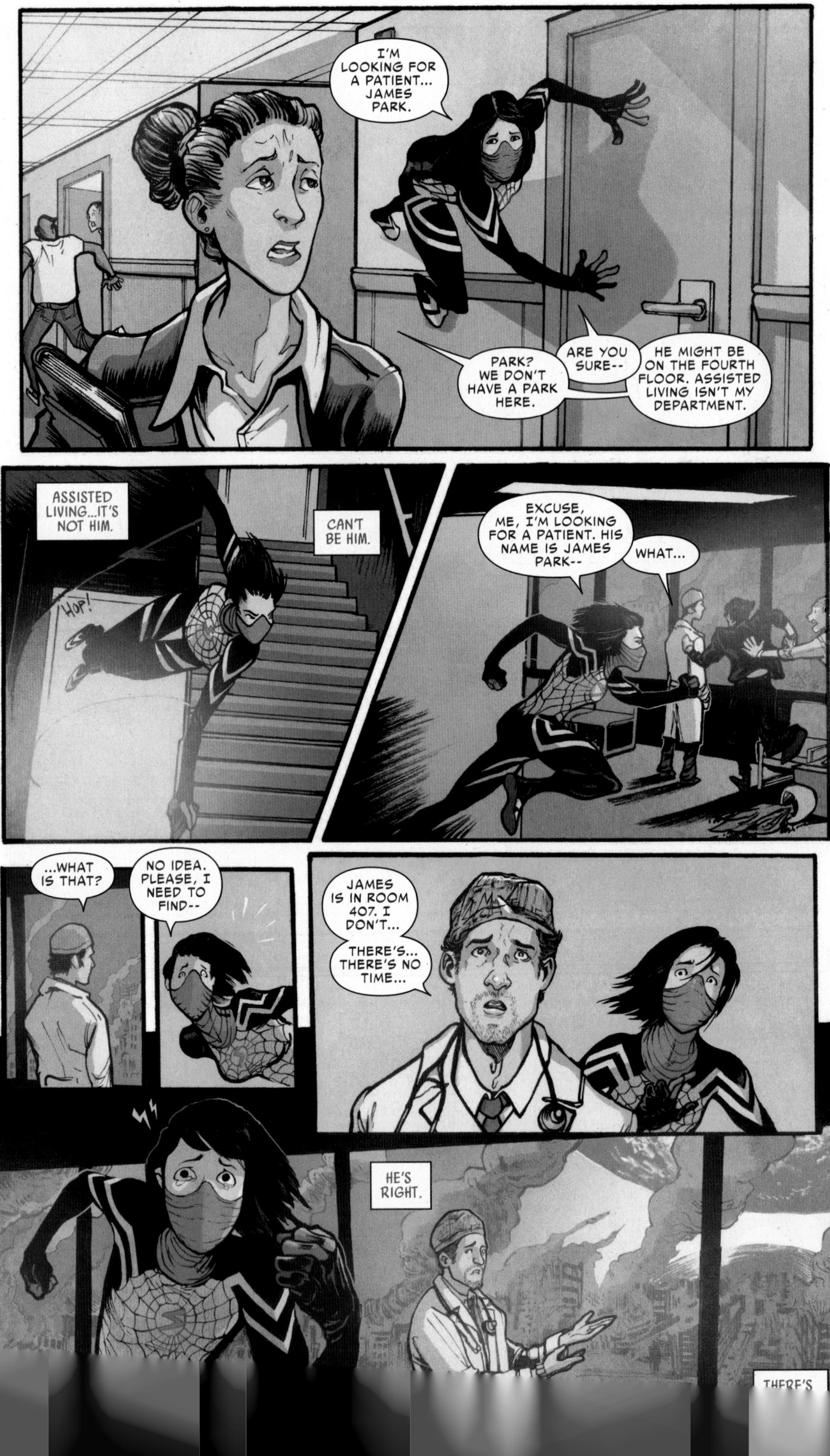
I'M LOOKING FOR A PATIENT... JAMES PARK.
PARK? WE DON'T HAVE A PARK HERE.
ARE YOU SURE--
HE MIGHT BE ON THE FOURTH FLOOR. ASSISTED LIVING ISN'T MY DEPARTMENT.
ASSISTED LIVING...IT'S NOT HIM.
HOP!
CAN'T BE HIM.
EXCUSE, ME, I'M LOOKING FOR A PATIENT. HIS NAME IS JAMES PARK--
WHAT...
...WHAT IS THAT?
NO IDEA. PLEASE, I NEED TO FIND--
JAMES IS IN ROOM 407. I DON'T...
THERE'S... THERE'S NO TIME...
HE'S RIGHT.
THERE'S

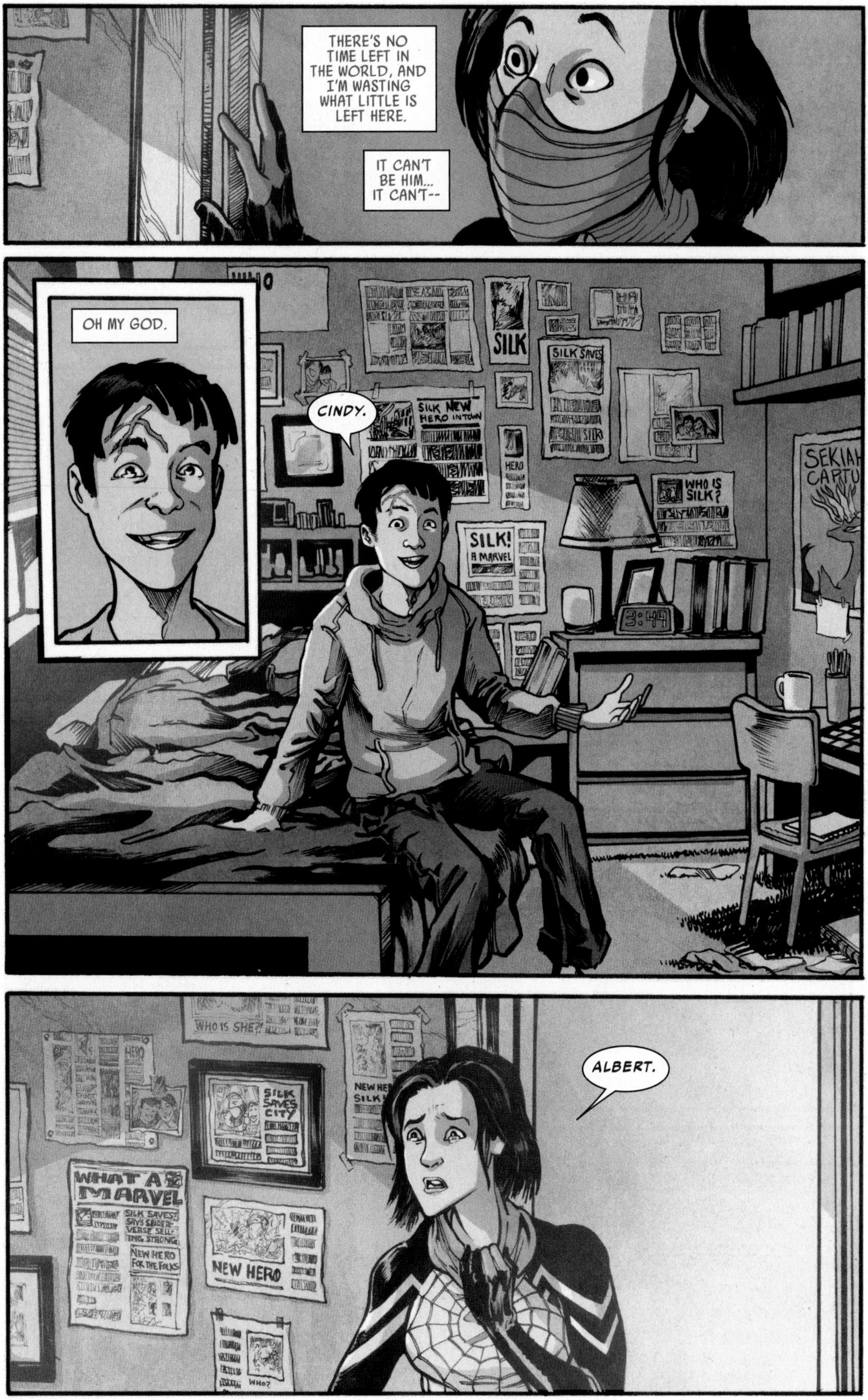
THERE'S NO TIME LEFT IN THE WORLD, AND I'M WASTING WHAT LITTLE IS LEFT HERE.
IT CAN'T BE HIM... IT CAN'T--
OH MY GOD.
CINDY.
ALBERT.

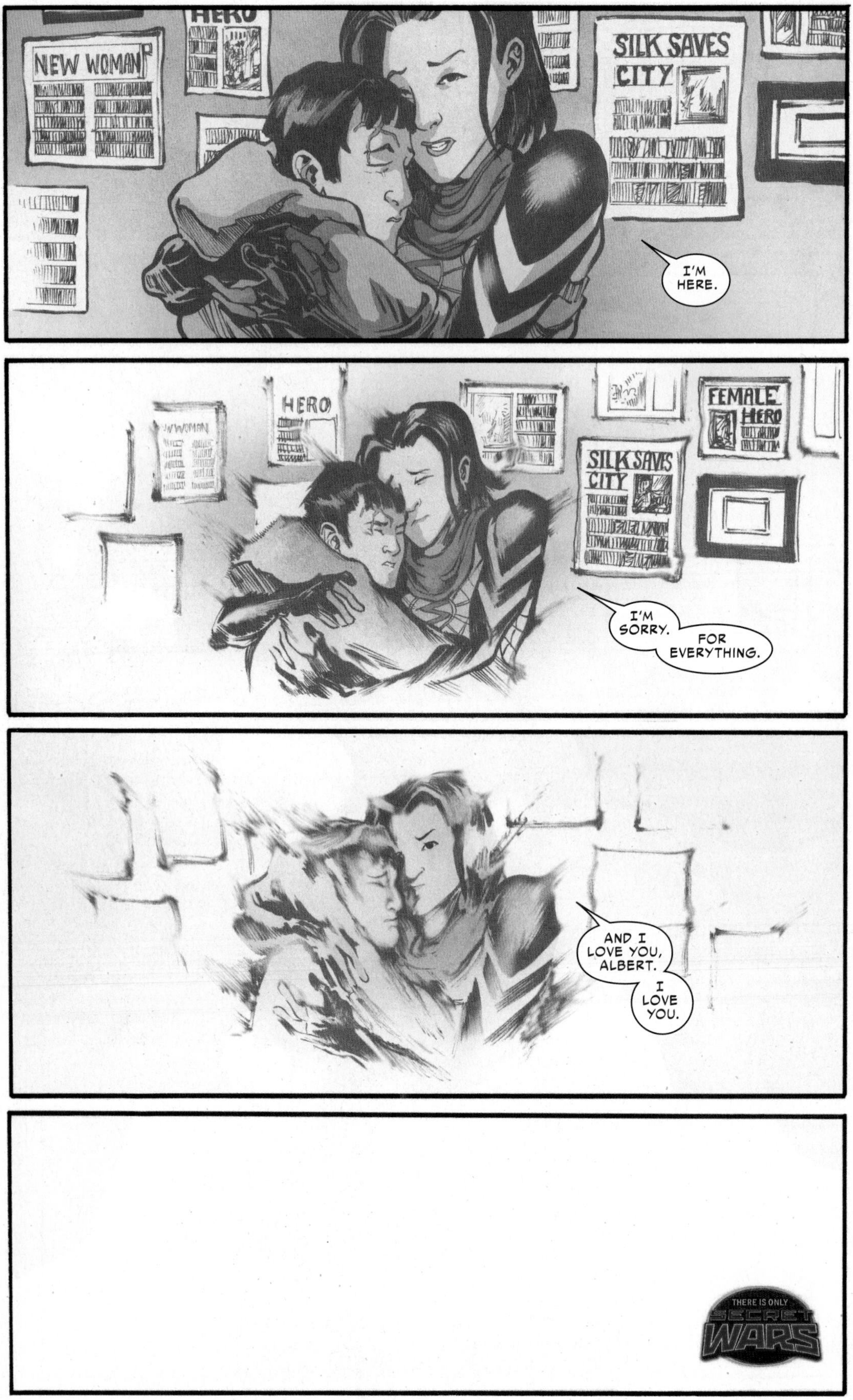
NEW WOMAN
HERO
SILK SAVES CITY
I'M HERE.
HERO
FEMALE HERO
SILK SAVES CITY
I'M SORRY.
FOR EVERYTHING.
AND I LOVE YOU, ALBERT.
I LOVE YOU.
THERE IS ONLY SECRET WARS

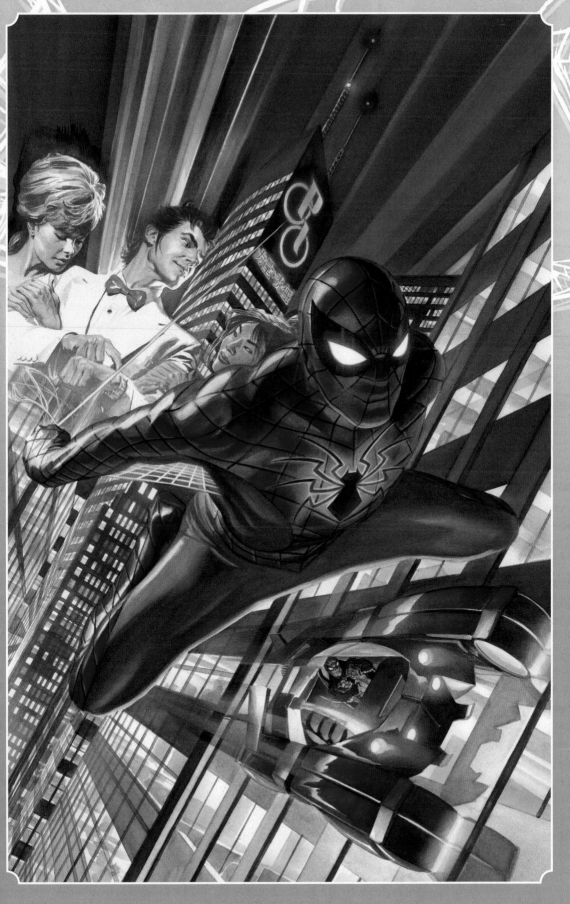

AMASING SPIDER-MAN [2015] #1 — "BREAKING BAD"

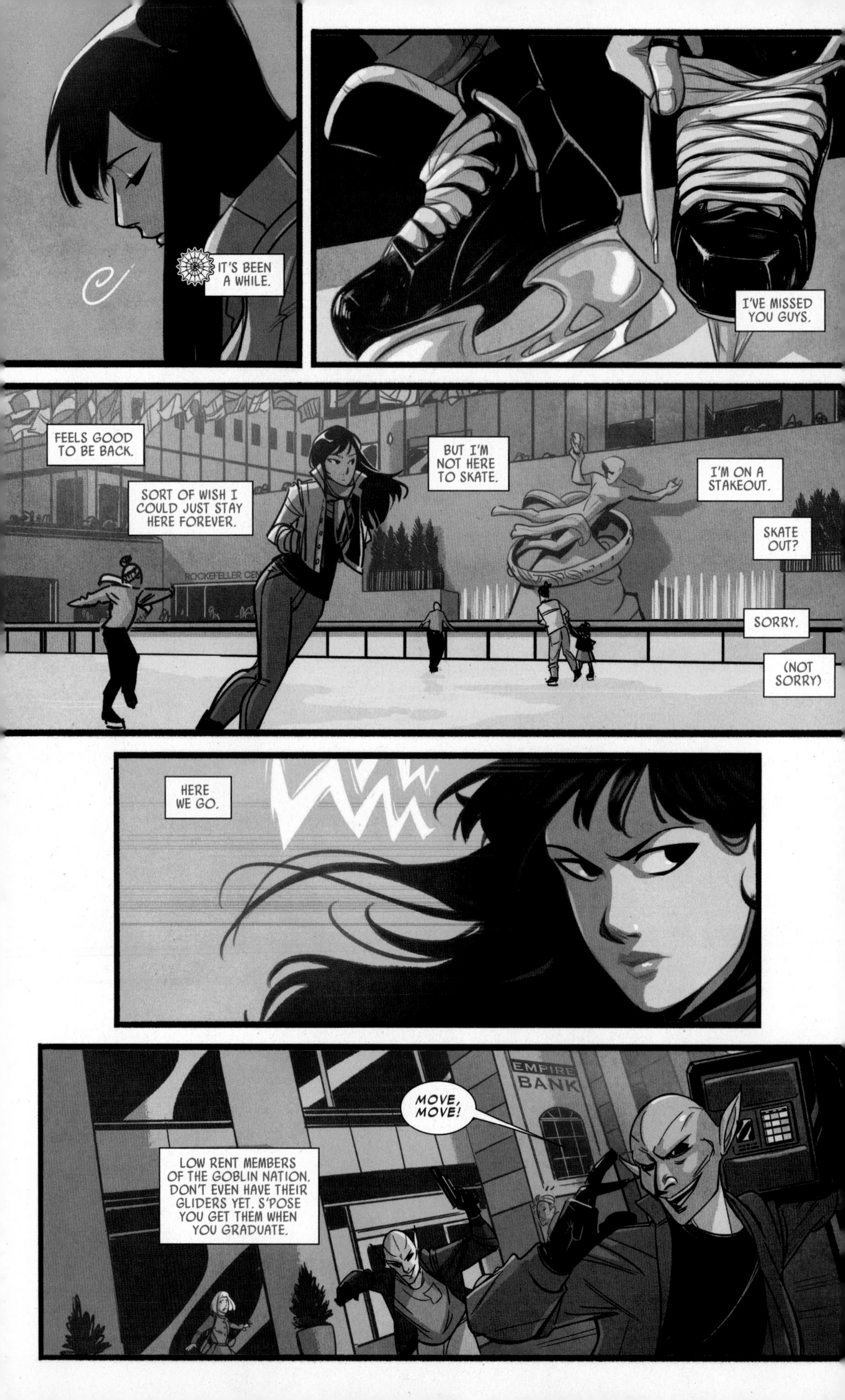
IT'S BEEN A WHILE.
I'VE MISSED YOU GUYS.
FEELS GOOD TO BE BACK.
SORT OF WISH I COULD JUST STAY HERE FOREVER.
ROCKEFELLER CEN
BUT I'M NOT HERE TO SKATE.
I'M ON A STAKEOUT.
SKATE OUT?
SORRY.
(NOT SORRY)
HERE WE GO.
EMPIRE BANK
MOVE, MOVE!
LOW RENT MEMBERS OF THE GOBLIN NATION. DON'T EVEN HAVE THEIR GLIDERS YET. S'POSE YOU GET THEM WHEN YOU GRADUATE.

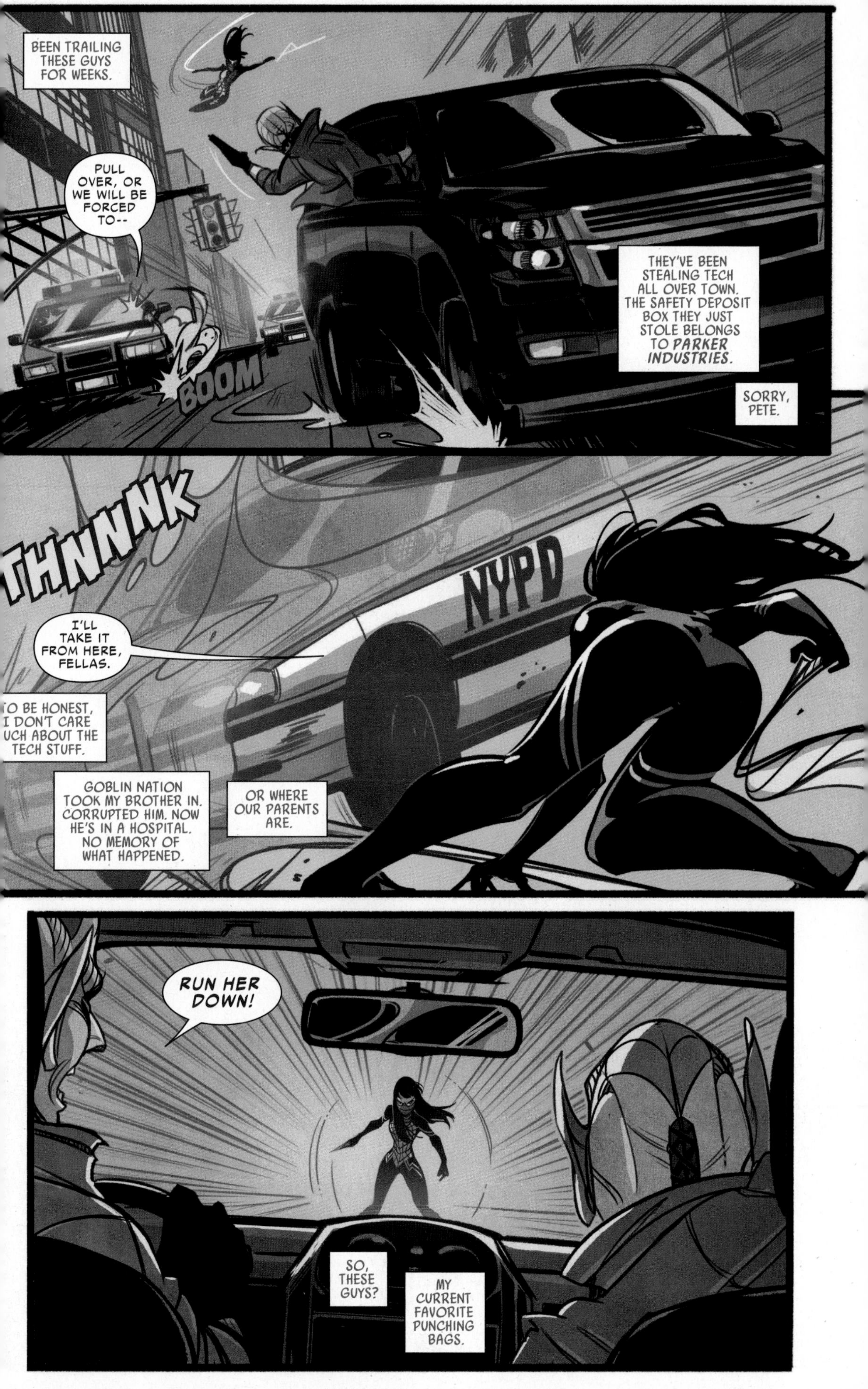
BEEN TRAILING THESE GUYS FOR WEEKS.
PULL OVER, OR WE WILL BE FORCED TO--
BOOM
THEY'VE BEEN STEALING TECH ALL OVER TOWN. THE SAFETY DEPOSIT BOX THEY JUST STOLE BELONGS TO PARKER INDUSTRIES.
SORRY, PETE.
THHNNNK
NYPD
I'LL TAKE IT FROM HERE, FELLAS.
TO BE HONEST, I DON'T CARE UCH ABOUT THE TECH STUFF.
GOBLIN NATION TOOK MY BROTHER IN. CORRUPTED HIM. NOW HE'S IN A HOSPITAL. NO MEMORY OF WHAT HAPPENED.
OR WHERE OUR PARENTS ARE.
RUN HER DOWN!
SO, THESE GUYS?
MY CURRENT FAVORITE PUNCHING BAGS.

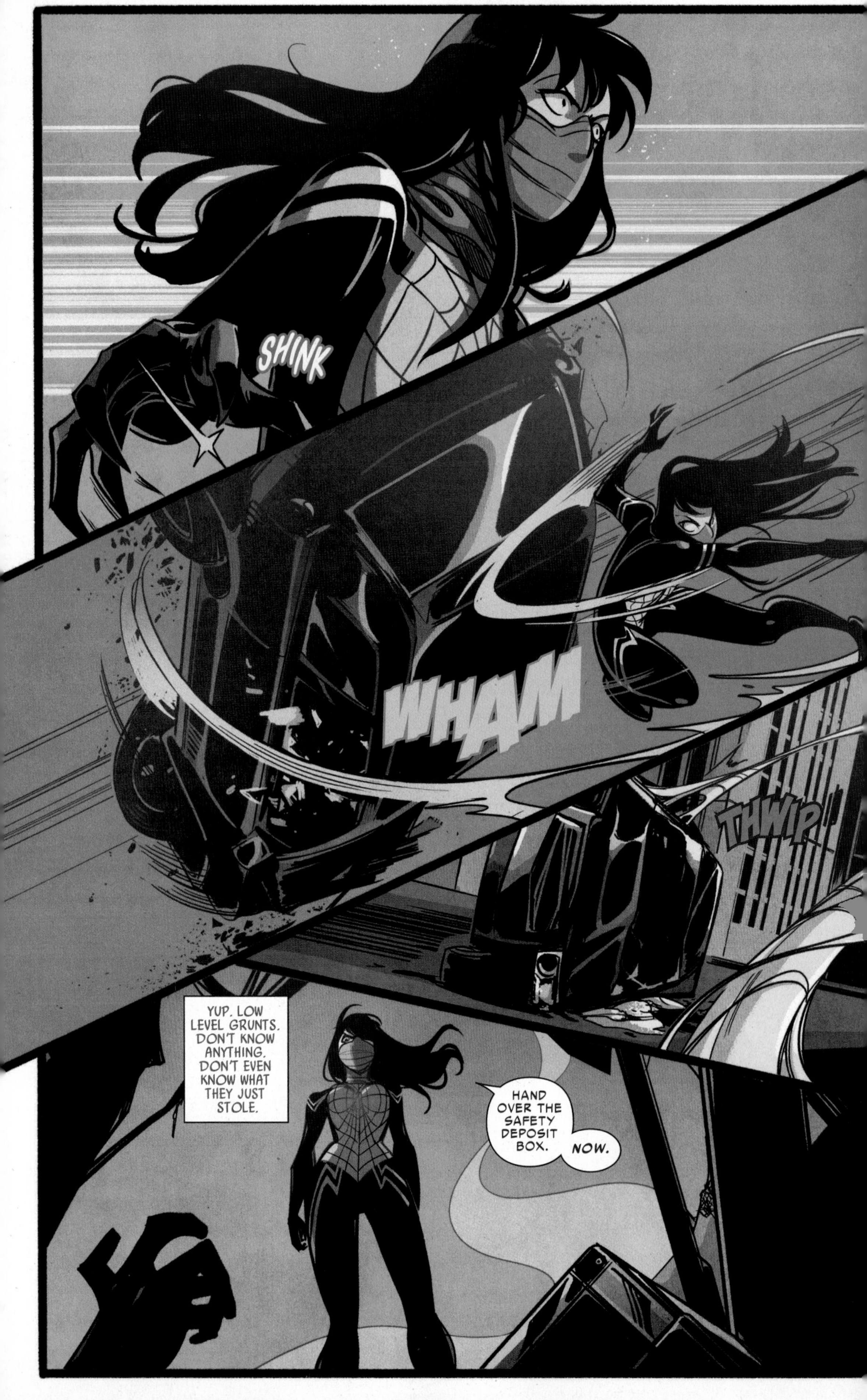
SHINK
WHAM
THWIP
YUP. LOW LEVEL GRUNTS. DON'T KNOW ANYTHING. DON'T EVEN KNOW WHAT THEY JUST STOLE.
HAND OVER THE SAFETY DEPOSIT BOX.
NOW.

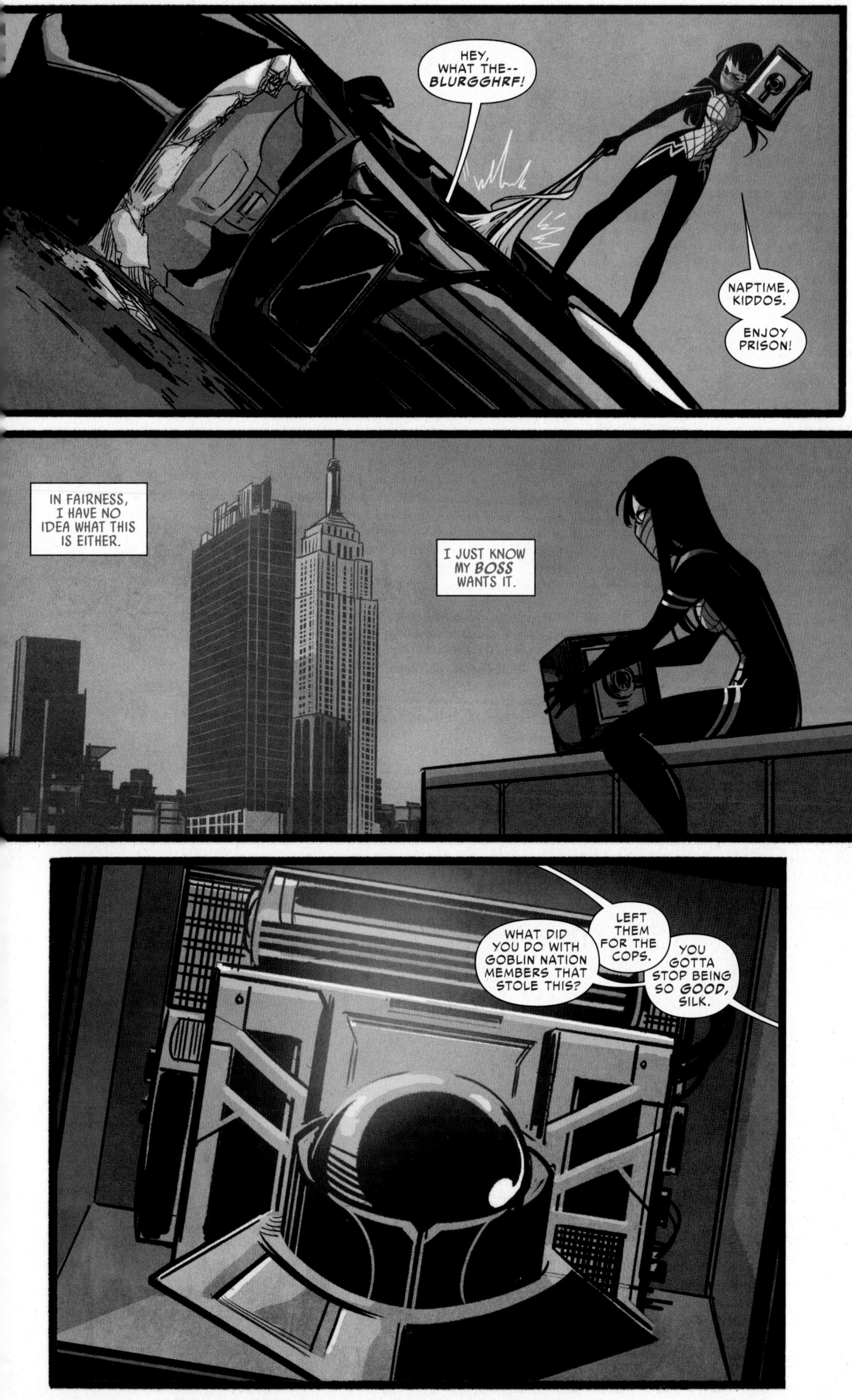
HEY, WHAT THE-- BLURGGHRF!
NAPTIME, KIDDOS.
ENJOY PRISON!
IN FAIRNESS, I HAVE NO IDEA WHAT THIS IS EITHER.
I JUST KNOW MY BOSS WANTS IT.
WHAT DID YOU DO WITH GOBLIN NATION MEMBERS THAT STOLE THIS?
LEFT THEM FOR THE COPS.
YOU GOTTA STOP BEING SO GOOD, SILK.

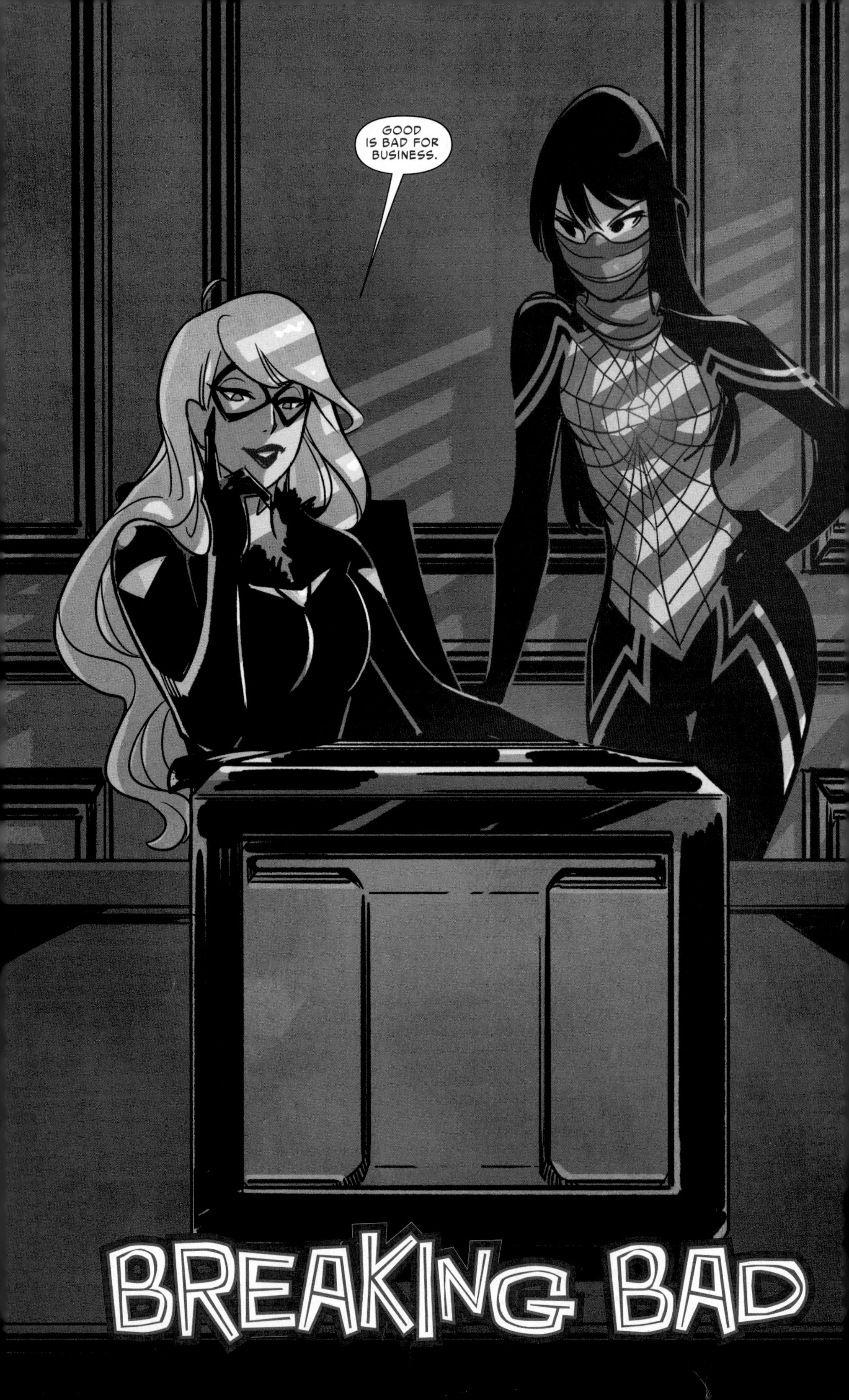
GOOD IS BAD FOR BUSINESS.
BREAKING BAD

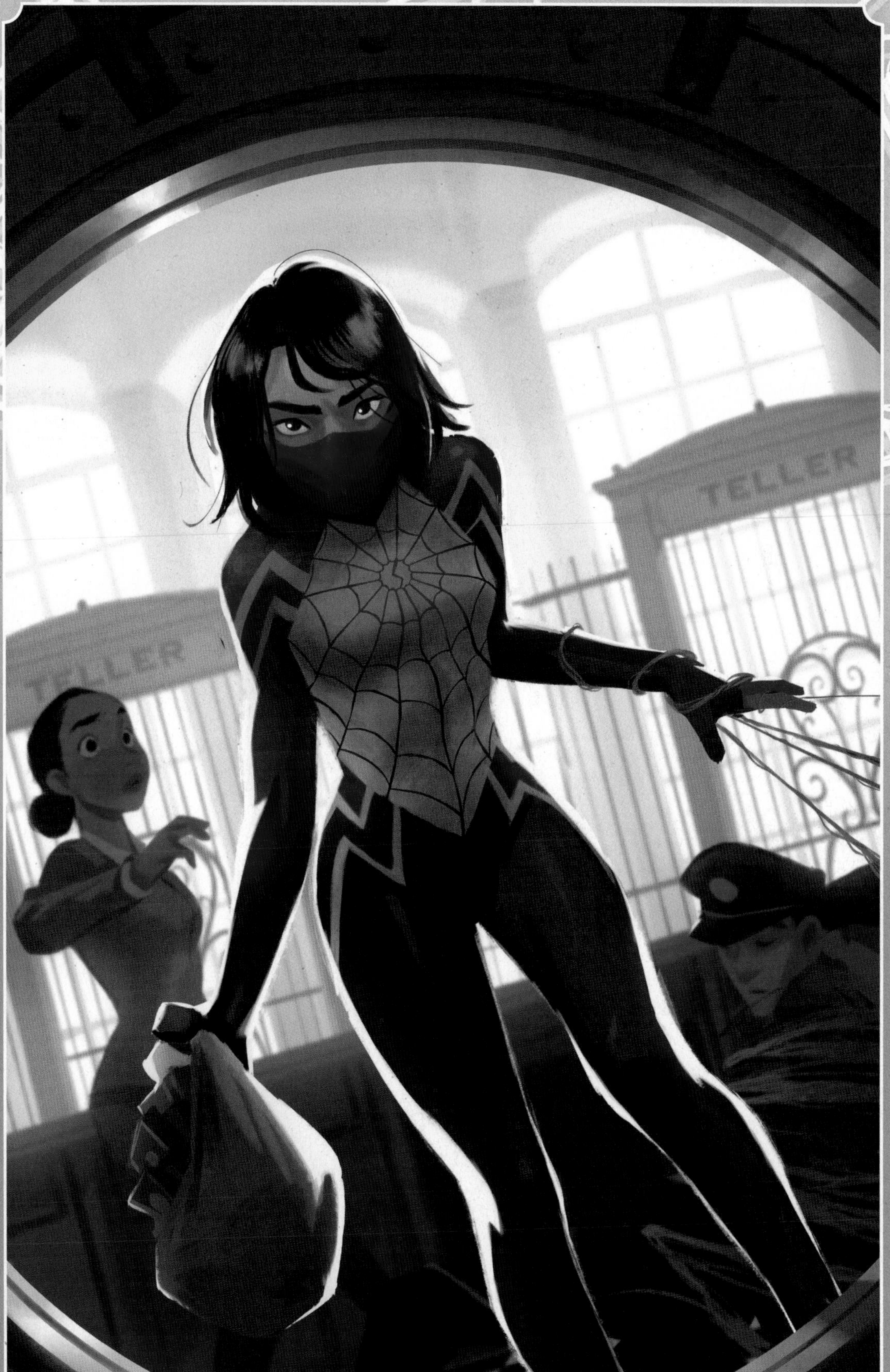
TELLER
TELLER

SILK (2015B) #1

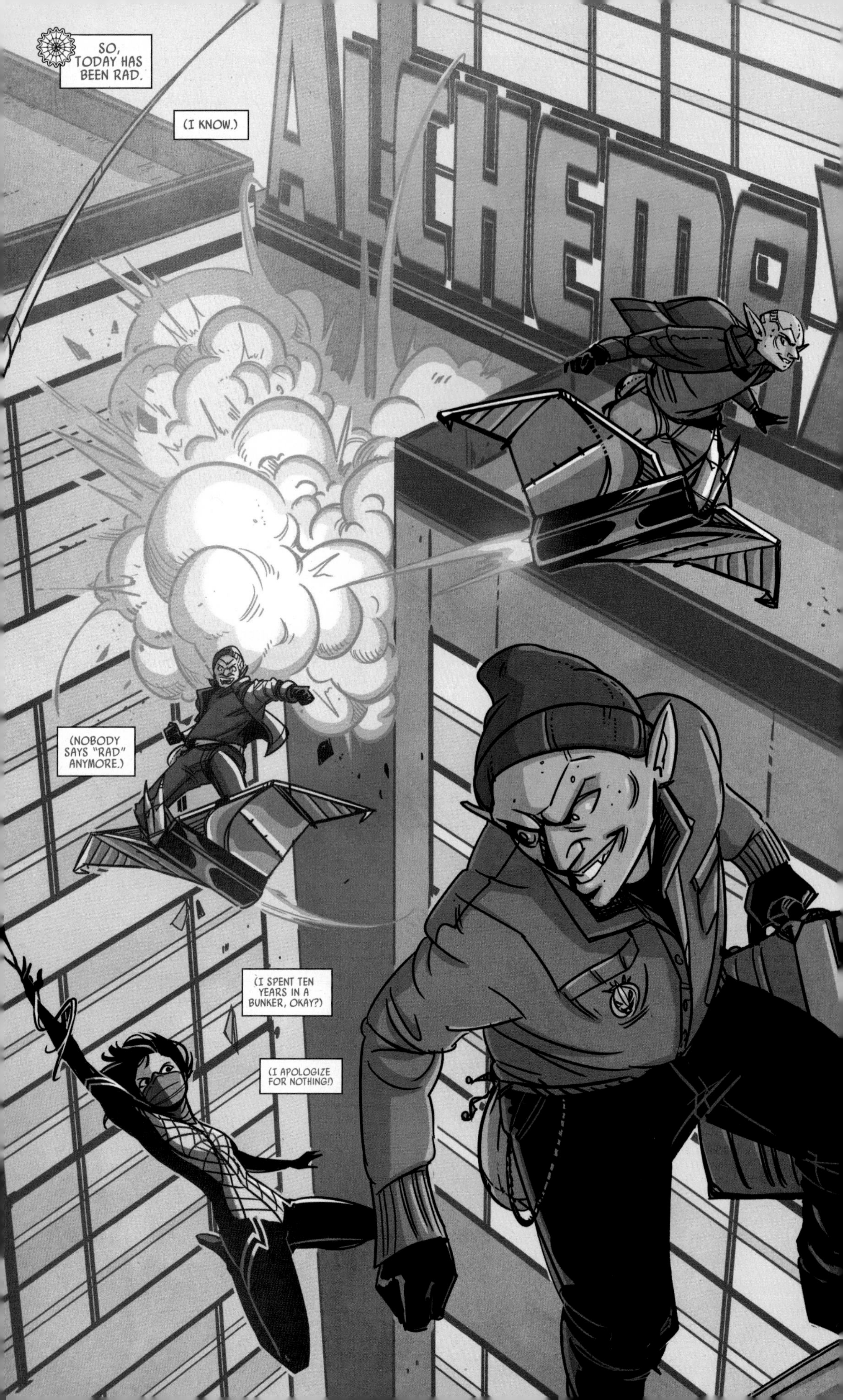
SO, TODAY HAS BEEN RAD.
(I KNOW.)
(NOBODY SAYS "RAD" ANYMORE.)
(I SPENT TEN YEARS IN A BUNKER, OKAY?)
(I APOLOGIZE FOR NOTHING!)

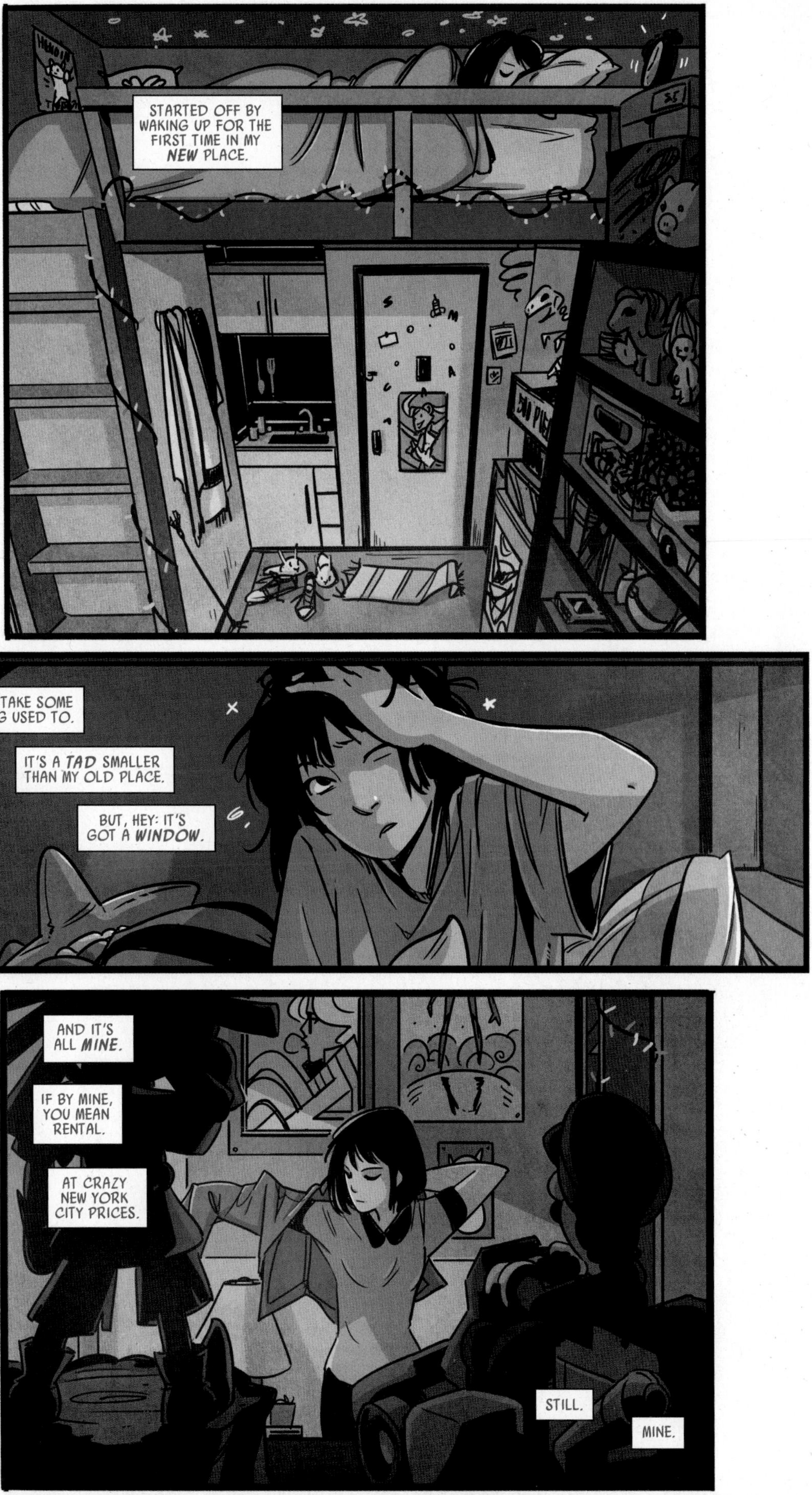
STARTED OFF BY WAKING UP FOR THE FIRST TIME IN MY *NEW* PLACE.
GONNA TAKE SOME GETTING USED TO.
IT'S A *TAD* SMALLER THAN MY OLD PLACE.
BUT, HEY: IT'S GOT A *WINDOW*.
AND IT'S ALL *MINE*.
IF BY MINE, YOU MEAN RENTAL.
AT CRAZY NEW YORK CITY PRICES.
STILL.
MINE.

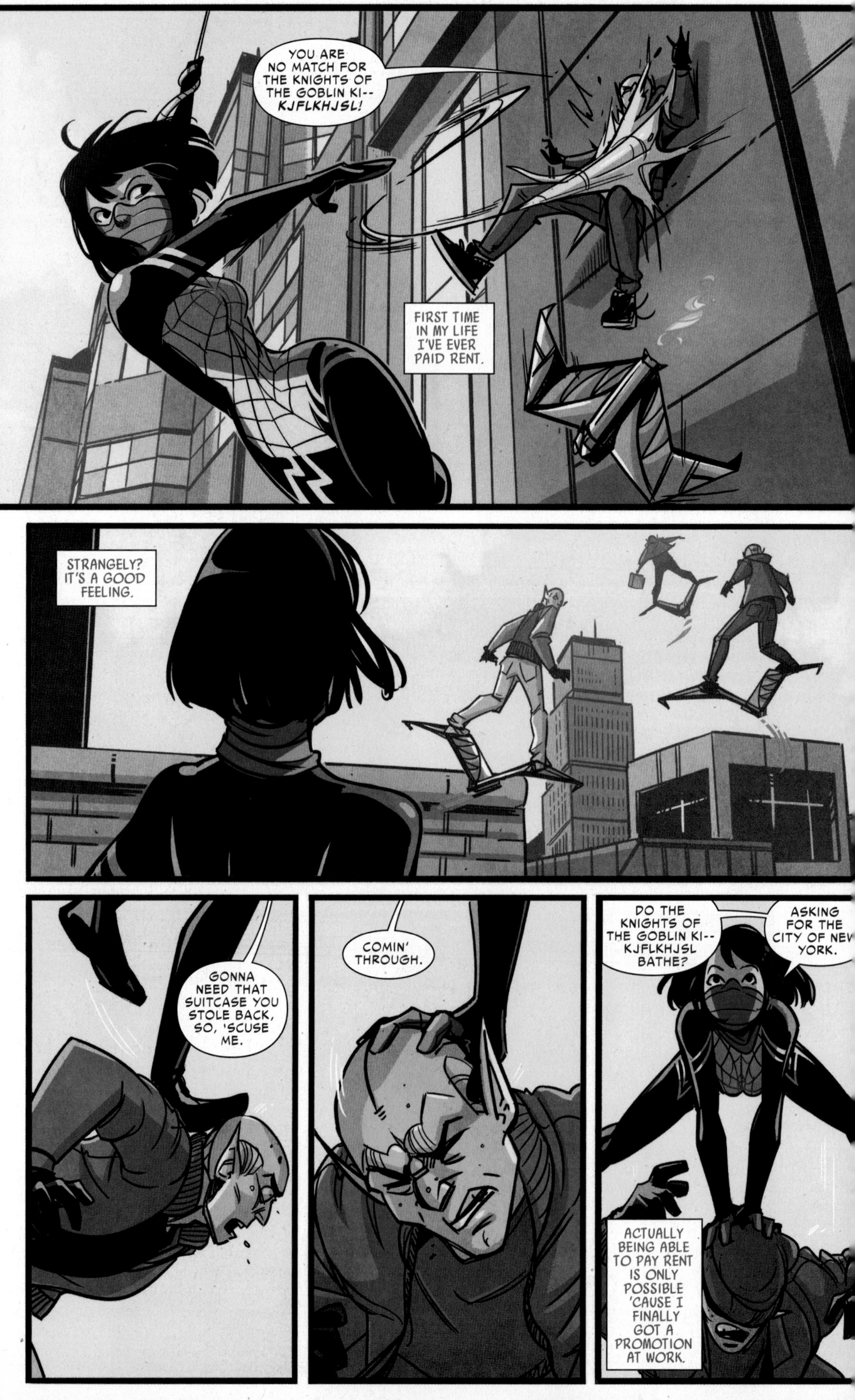

YOU ARE NO MATCH FOR THE KNIGHTS OF THE GOBLIN KI-- KJFLKHJSL!
FIRST TIME IN MY LIFE I'VE EVER PAID RENT.
STRANGELY? IT'S A GOOD FEELING.
GONNA NEED THAT SUITCASE YOU STOLE BACK, SO, 'SCUSE ME.
COMIN' THROUGH.
DO THE KNIGHTS OF THE GOBLIN KI-- KJFLKHJSL BATHE?
ASKING FOR THE CITY OF NEW YORK.
ACTUALLY BEING ABLE TO PAY RENT IS ONLY POSSIBLE 'CAUSE I FINALLY GOT A PROMOTION AT WORK.

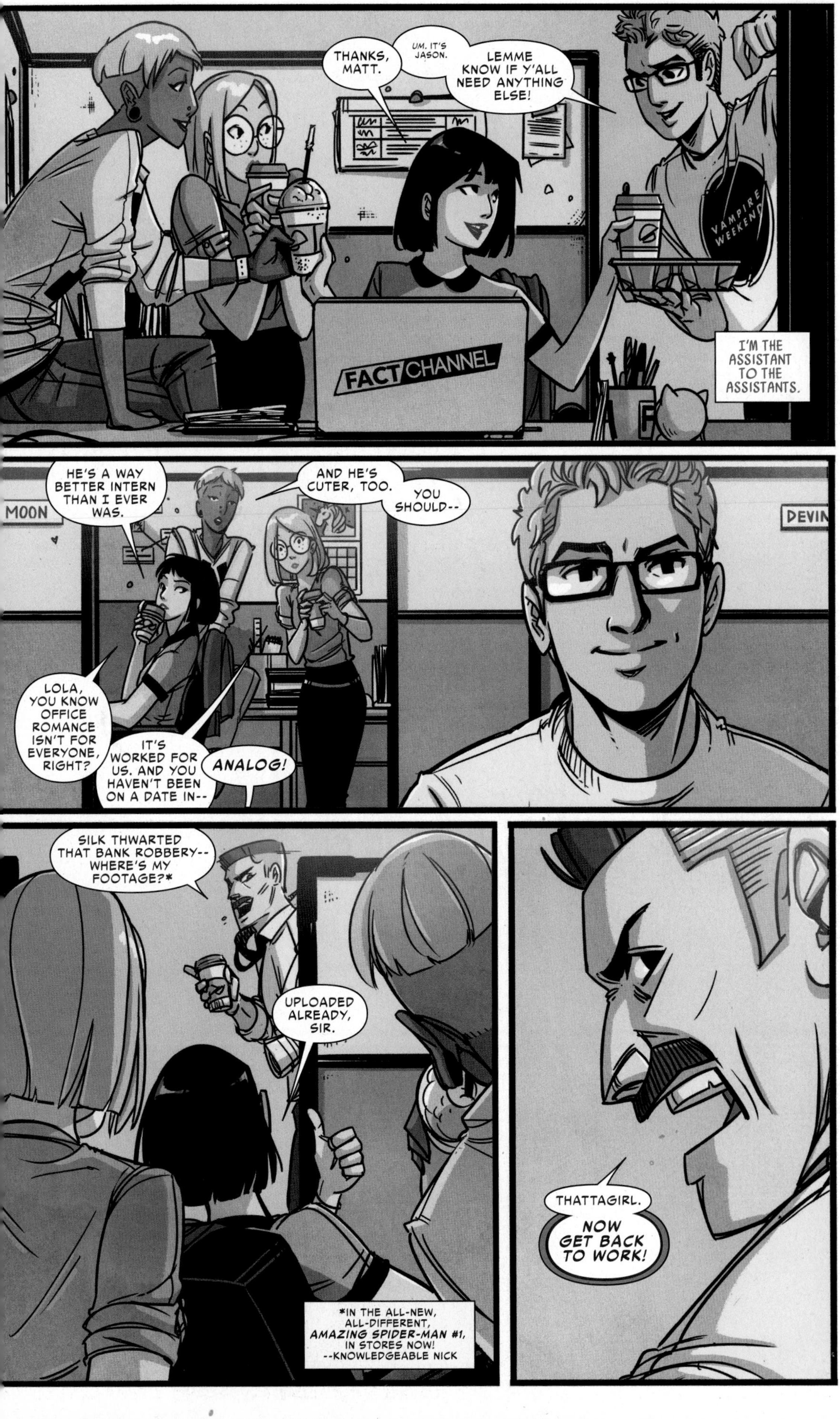
THANKS, MATT.
UM. IT'S JASON.
LEMME KNOW IF Y'ALL NEED ANYTHING ELSE!
VAMPIRE WEEKEND
FACT CHANNEL
I'M THE ASSISTANT TO THE ASSISTANTS.
MOON
DEVIN
HE'S A WAY BETTER INTERN THAN I EVER WAS.
AND HE'S CUTER, TOO.
YOU SHOULD--
LOLA, YOU KNOW OFFICE ROMANCE ISN'T FOR EVERYONE, RIGHT?
IT'S WORKED FOR US. AND YOU HAVEN'T BEEN ON A DATE IN--
ANALOG!
SILK THWARTED THAT BANK ROBBERY--WHERE'S MY FOOTAGE?*
UPLOADED ALREADY, SIR.
*IN THE ALL-NEW, ALL-DIFFERENT, AMAZING SPIDER-MAN #1, IN STORES NOW! --KNOWLEDGEABLE NICK
THATTAGIRL.
NOW GET BACK TO WORK!

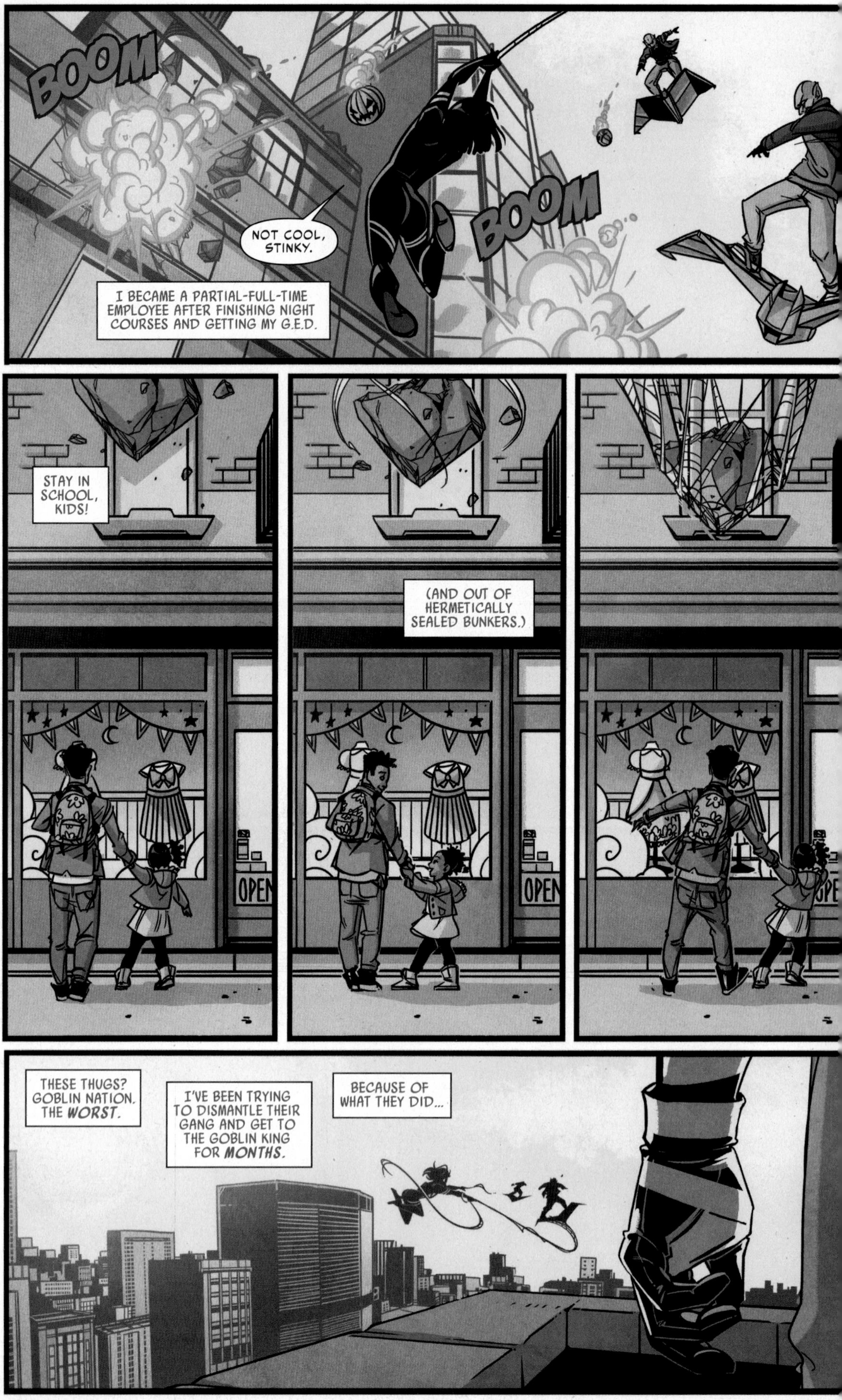
BOOM
NOT COOL, STINKY.
BOOM
I BECAME A PARTIAL-FULL-TIME EMPLOYEE AFTER FINISHING NIGHT COURSES AND GETTING MY G.E.D.
STAY IN SCHOOL, KIDS!
(AND OUT OF HERMETICALLY SEALED BUNKERS.)
OPEN
OPEN
THESE THUGS? GOBLIN NATION. THE *WORST.*
I'VE BEEN TRYING TO DISMANTLE THEIR GANG AND GET TO THE GOBLIN KING FOR *MONTHS.*
BECAUSE OF WHAT THEY DID...

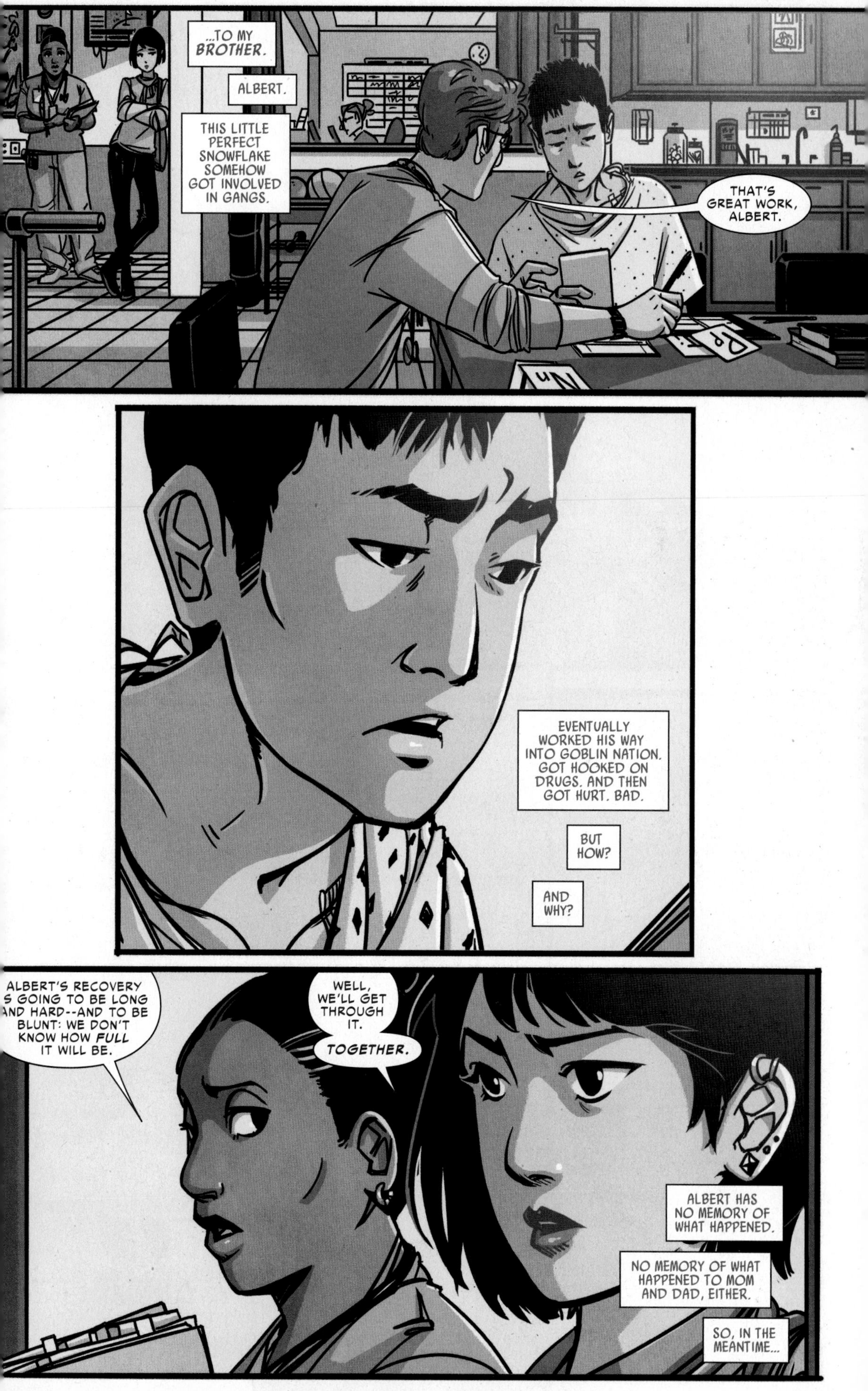
...TO MY BROTHER.
ALBERT.
THIS LITTLE PERFECT SNOWFLAKE SOMEHOW GOT INVOLVED IN GANGS.
THAT'S GREAT WORK, ALBERT.
EVENTUALLY WORKED HIS WAY INTO GOBLIN NATION. GOT HOOKED ON DRUGS. AND THEN GOT HURT. BAD.
BUT HOW?
AND WHY?
ALBERT'S RECOVERY S GOING TO BE LONG ND HARD--AND TO BE BLUNT: WE DON'T KNOW HOW FULL IT WILL BE.
WELL, WE'LL GET THROUGH IT.
TOGETHER.
ALBERT HAS NO MEMORY OF WHAT HAPPENED.
NO MEMORY OF WHAT HAPPENED TO MOM AND DAD, EITHER.
SO, IN THE MEANTIME...

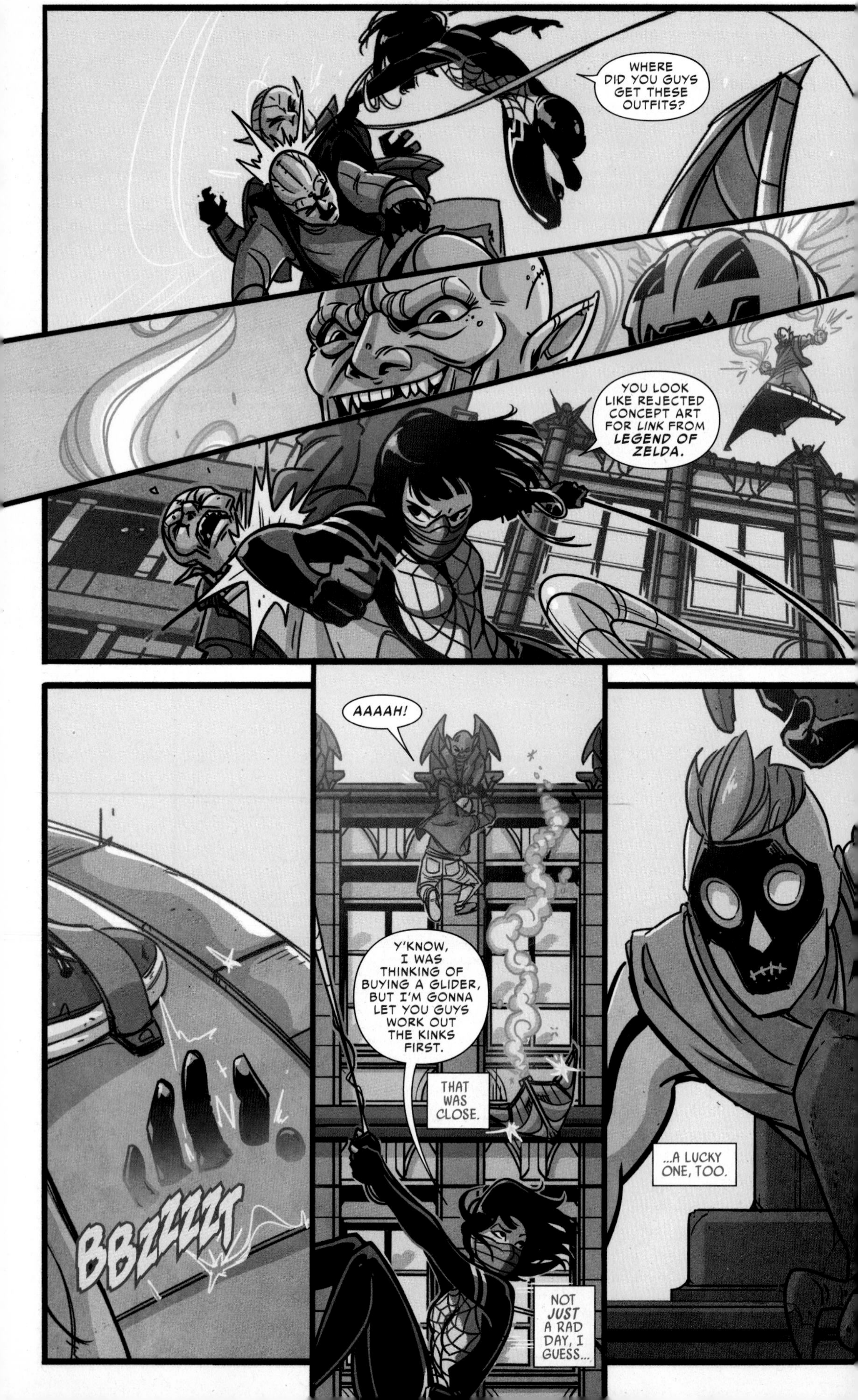
WHERE DID YOU GUYS GET THESE OUTFITS?
YOU LOOK LIKE REJECTED CONCEPT ART FOR LINK FROM *LEGEND OF ZELDA.*
BBZZZZT
AAAAH!
Y'KNOW, I WAS THINKING OF BUYING A GLIDER, BUT I'M GONNA LET YOU GUYS WORK OUT THE KINKS FIRST.
THAT WAS CLOSE.
NOT *JUST* A RAD DAY, I GUESS...
...A LUCKY ONE, TOO.

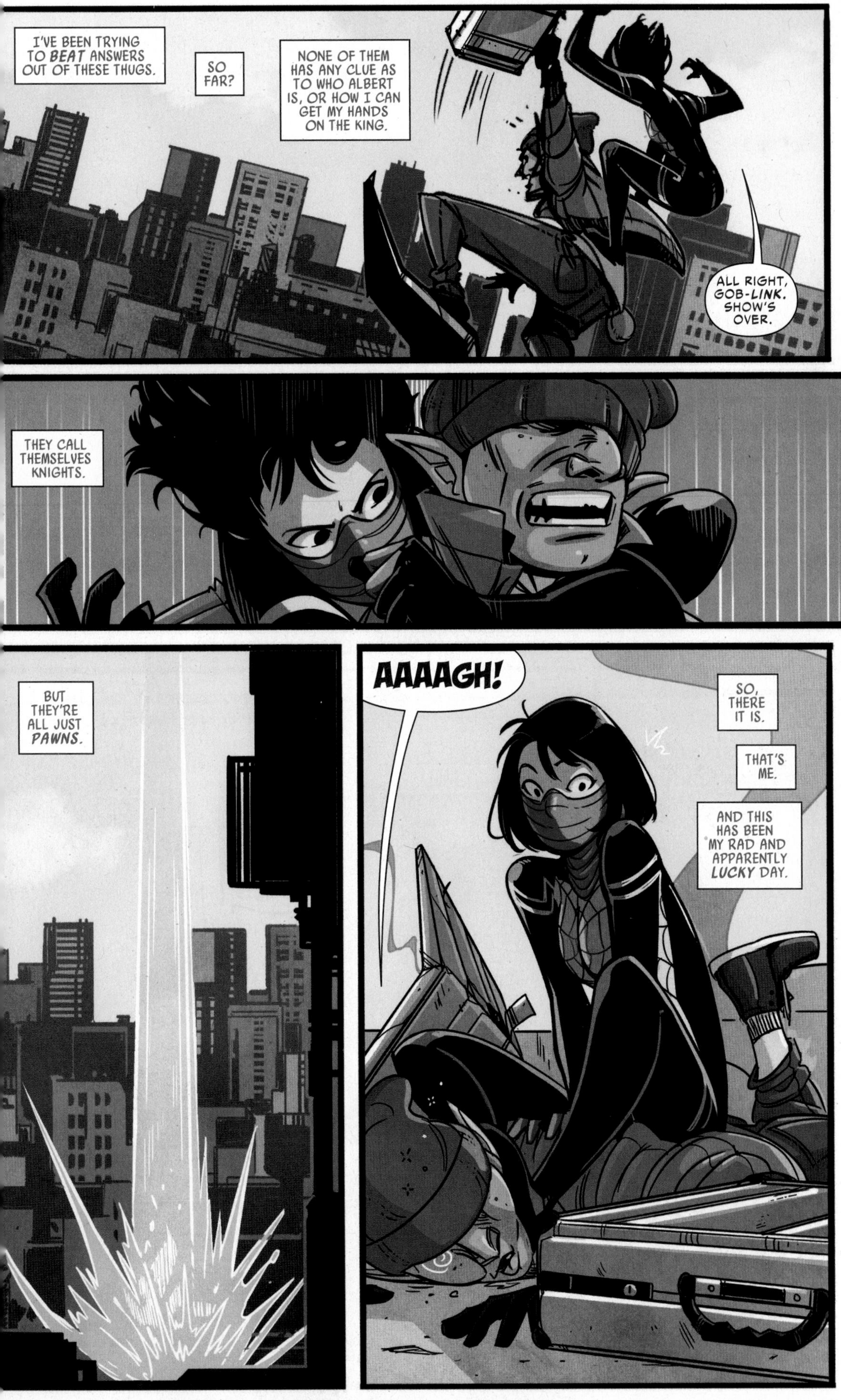
I'VE BEEN TRYING TO BEAT ANSWERS OUT OF THESE THUGS.
SO FAR?
NONE OF THEM HAS ANY CLUE AS TO WHO ALBERT IS, OR HOW I CAN GET MY HANDS ON THE KING.
ALL RIGHT, GOB-LINK. SHOW'S OVER.
THEY CALL THEMSELVES KNIGHTS.
BUT THEY'RE ALL JUST PAWNS.
AAAAGH!
SO, THERE IT IS.
THAT'S ME.
AND THIS HAS BEEN MY RAD AND APPARENTLY LUCKY DAY.

I'M SURE THE COPS WILL FIND YOU.

SOMEDAY.

THANKS FOR DOING THE HEAVY LIFTING.

WE'RE ALL CAUGHT UP.

RIGHT?

HEY... THAT BELONGS TO THE KING.

NO...

IT BELONGS TO ME.

NO...

IT BELONGS TO ALCHEMAX.

OH, YEAH...

...ACTUALLY...

MOCKINGBIRD.

AND ON BEHALF OF S.H.I.E.L.D., I'LL BE TAKING IT BACK THERE, THANKS VERY MUCH.

...THERE IS ONE OTHER THING.

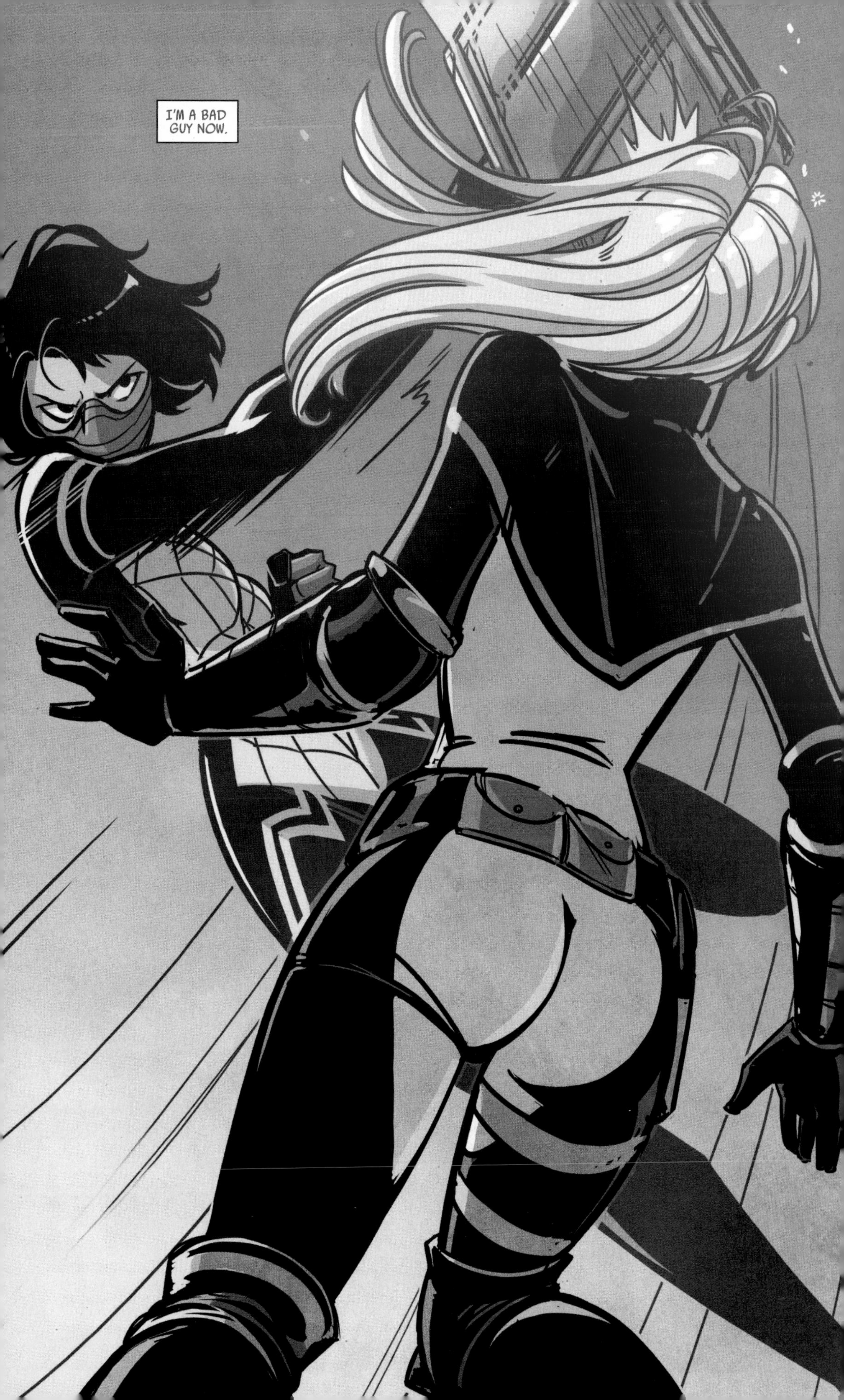
I'M A BAD GUY NOW.

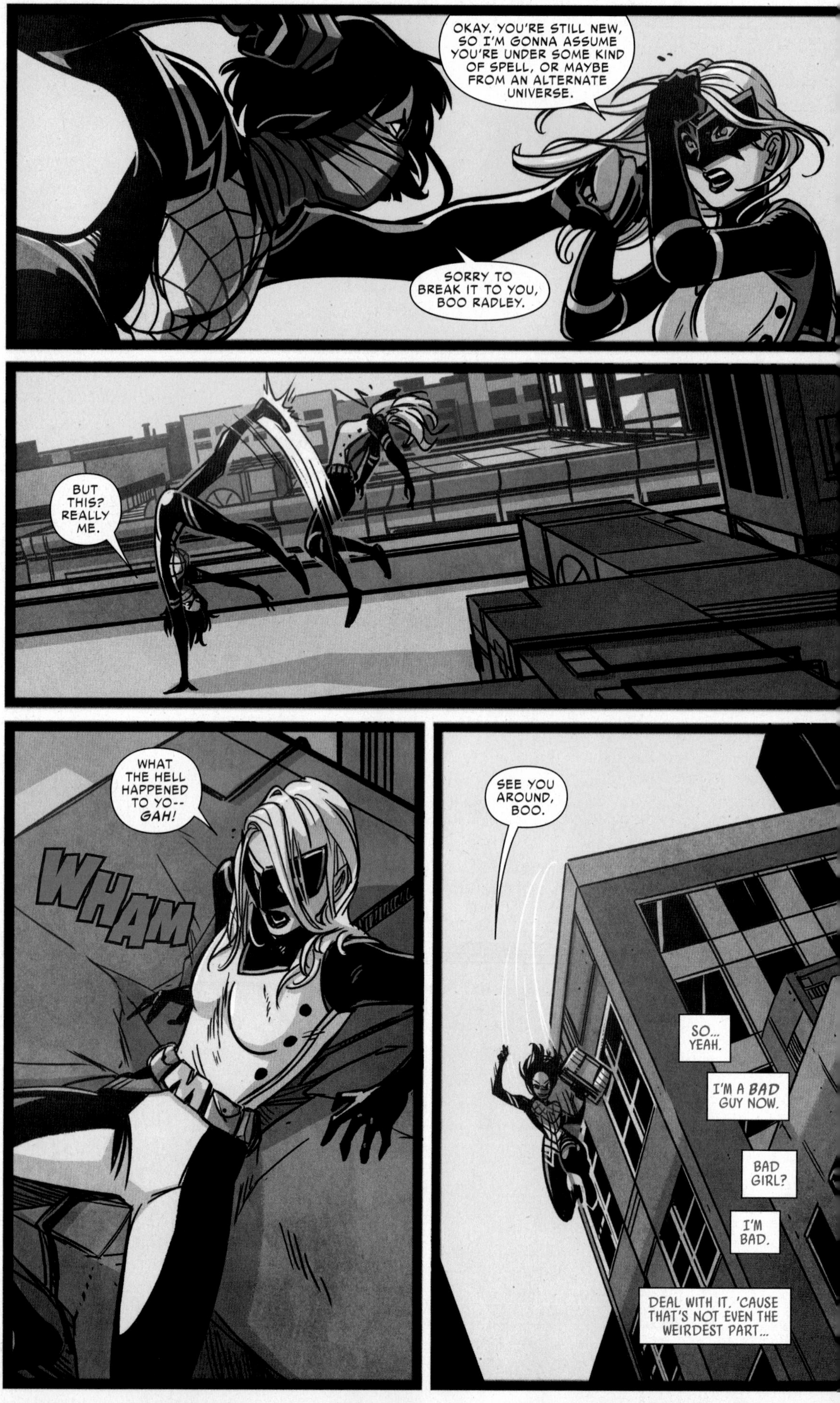
OKAY. YOU'RE STILL NEW, SO I'M GONNA ASSUME YOU'RE UNDER SOME KIND OF SPELL, OR MAYBE FROM AN ALTERNATE UNIVERSE.
SORRY TO BREAK IT TO YOU, BOO RADLEY.
BUT THIS? REALLY ME.
WHAT THE HELL HAPPENED TO YO-- GAH!
WHAM
SEE YOU AROUND, BOO.
SO... YEAH.
I'M A BAD GUY NOW.
BAD GIRL?
I'M BAD.
DEAL WITH IT. 'CAUSE THAT'S NOT EVEN THE WEIRDEST PART...

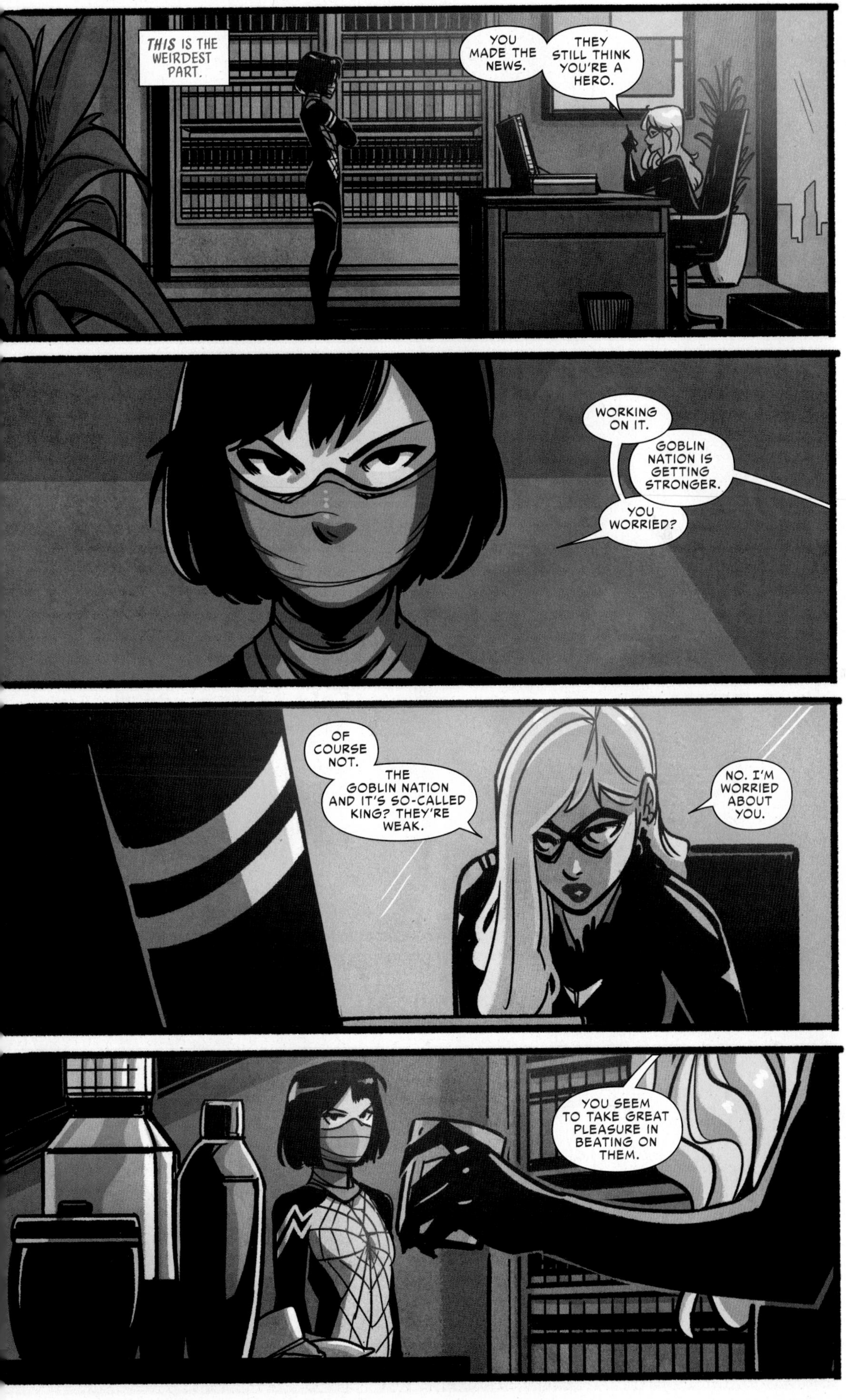
THIS IS THE WEIRDEST PART.
YOU MADE THE NEWS.
THEY STILL THINK YOU'RE A HERO.
WORKING ON IT.
GOBLIN NATION IS GETTING STRONGER.
YOU WORRIED?
OF COURSE NOT.
THE GOBLIN NATION AND IT'S SO-CALLED KING? THEY'RE WEAK.
NO. I'M WORRIED ABOUT YOU.
YOU SEEM TO TAKE GREAT PLEASURE IN BEATING ON THEM.

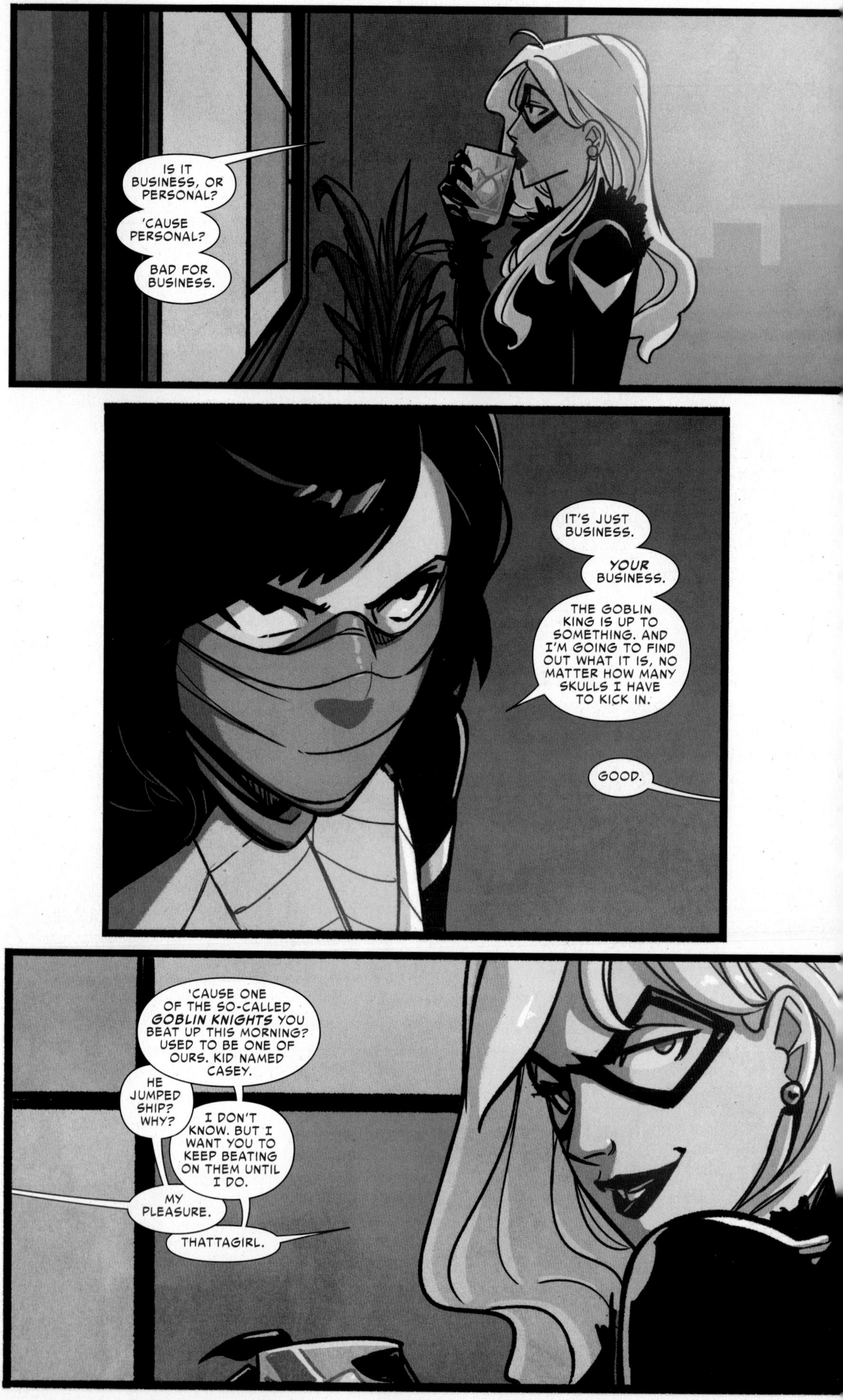
IS IT BUSINESS, OR PERSONAL?
'CAUSE PERSONAL?
BAD FOR BUSINESS.
IT'S JUST BUSINESS.
YOUR BUSINESS.
THE GOBLIN KING IS UP TO SOMETHING. AND I'M GOING TO FIND OUT WHAT IT IS, NO MATTER HOW MANY SKULLS I HAVE TO KICK IN.
GOOD.
'CAUSE ONE OF THE SO-CALLED ***GOBLIN KNIGHTS*** YOU BEAT UP THIS MORNING? USED TO BE ONE OF OURS. KID NAMED CASEY.
HE JUMPED SHIP? WHY?
I DON'T KNOW. BUT I WANT YOU TO KEEP BEATING ON THEM UNTIL I DO.
MY PLEASURE.
THATTAGIRL.

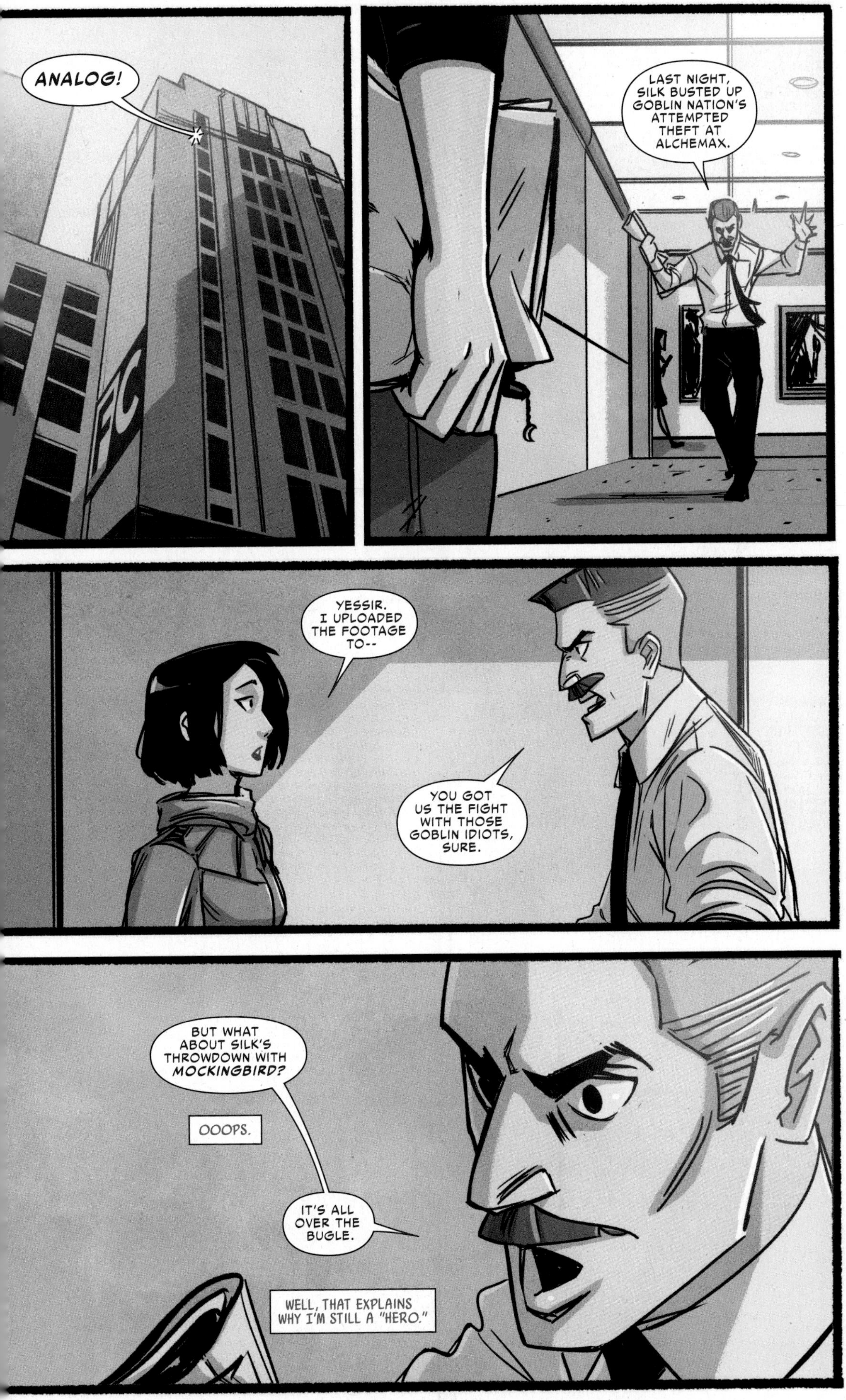
ANALOG!
LAST NIGHT, SILK BUSTED UP GOBLIN NATION'S ATTEMPTED THEFT AT ALCHEMAX.
YESSIR. I UPLOADED THE FOOTAGE TO--
YOU GOT US THE FIGHT WITH THOSE GOBLIN IDIOTS, SURE.
BUT WHAT ABOUT SILK'S THROWDOWN WITH *MOCKINGBIRD?*
OOOPS.
IT'S ALL OVER THE BUGLE.
WELL, THAT EXPLAINS WHY I'M STILL A "HERO."

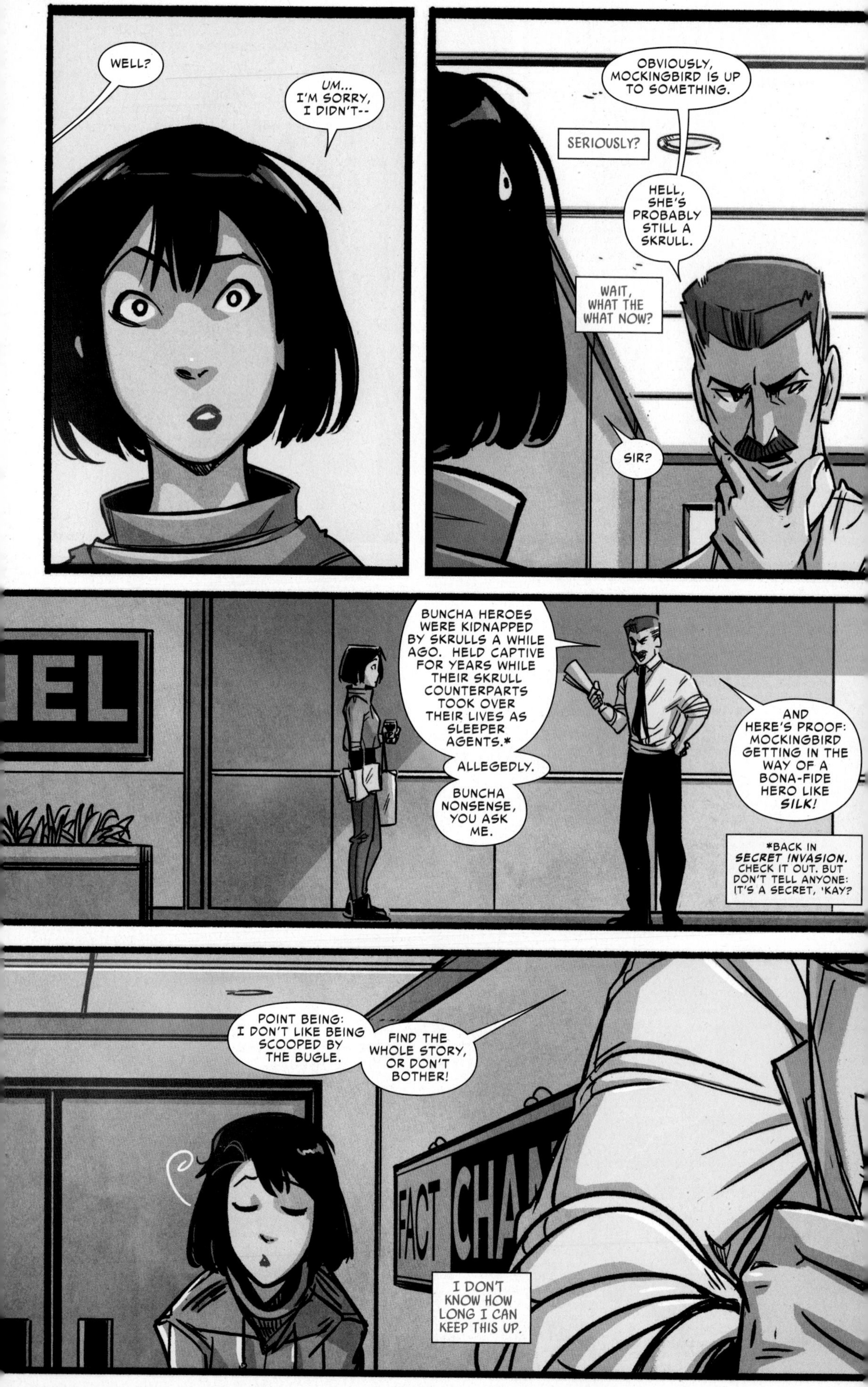
WELL?
UM... I'M SORRY, I DIDN'T--
OBVIOUSLY, MOCKINGBIRD IS UP TO SOMETHING.
SERIOUSLY?
HELL, SHE'S PROBABLY STILL A SKRULL.
WAIT, WHAT THE WHAT NOW?
SIR?
BUNCHA HEROES WERE KIDNAPPED BY SKRULLS A WHILE AGO. HELD CAPTIVE FOR YEARS WHILE THEIR SKRULL COUNTERPARTS TOOK OVER THEIR LIVES AS SLEEPER AGENTS.*
ALLEGEDLY.
BUNCHA NONSENSE, YOU ASK ME.
AND HERE'S PROOF: MOCKINGBIRD GETTING IN THE WAY OF A BONA-FIDE HERO LIKE *SILK!*
*BACK IN ***SECRET INVASION.*** CHECK IT OUT. BUT DON'T TELL ANYONE: IT'S A SECRET, 'KAY?
POINT BEING: I DON'T LIKE BEING SCOOPED BY THE BUGLE.
FIND THE WHOLE STORY, OR DON'T BOTHER!
FACT CHA
I DON'T KNOW HOW LONG I CAN KEEP THIS UP.

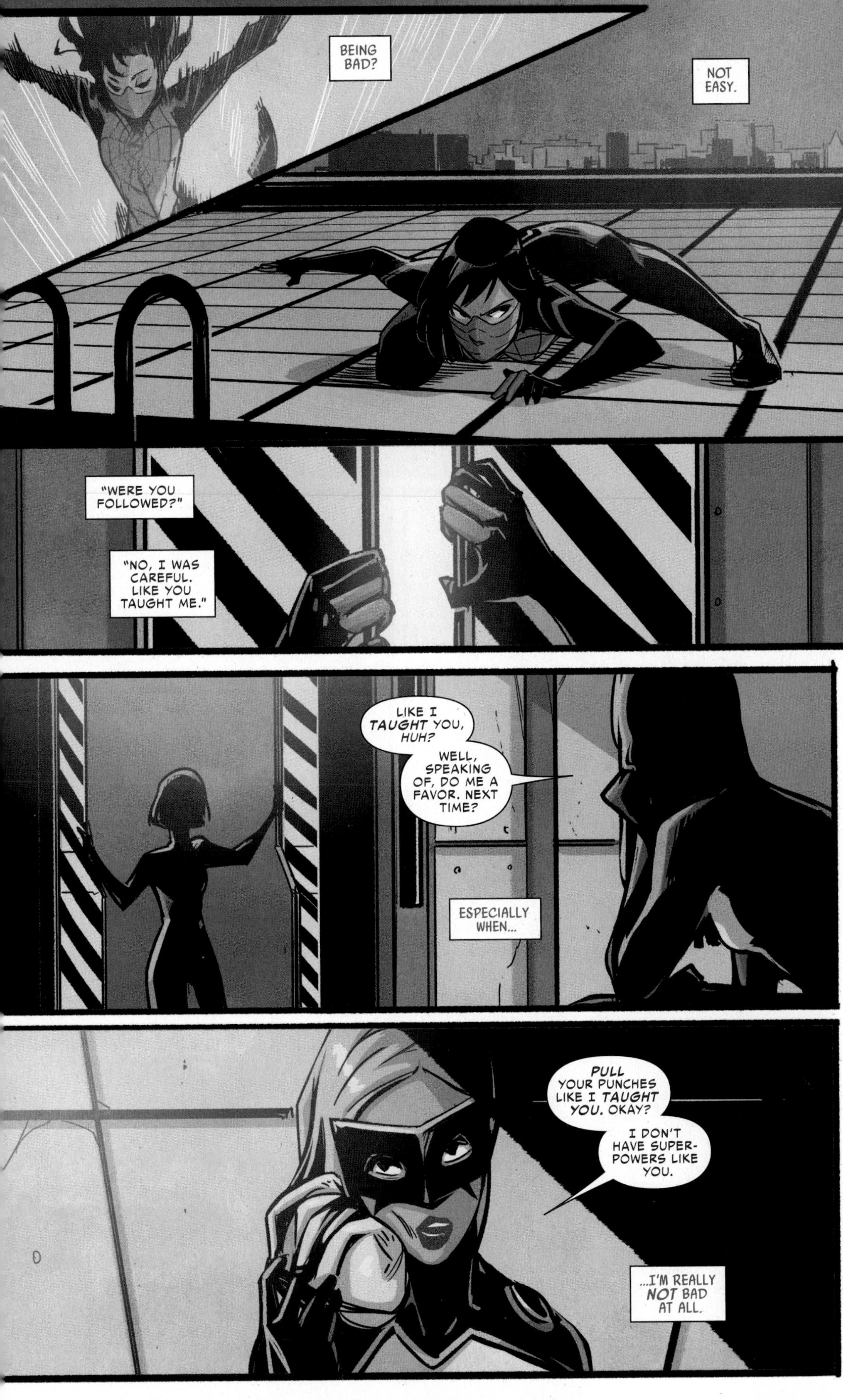
BEING BAD?
NOT EASY.
"WERE YOU FOLLOWED?"
"NO, I WAS CAREFUL. LIKE YOU TAUGHT ME."
LIKE I *TAUGHT* YOU, HUH?
WELL, SPEAKING OF, DO ME A FAVOR. NEXT TIME?
ESPECIALLY WHEN...
PULL YOUR PUNCHES LIKE I *TAUGHT YOU.* OKAY?
I DON'T HAVE SUPER-POWERS LIKE YOU.
...I'M REALLY *NOT* BAD AT ALL.

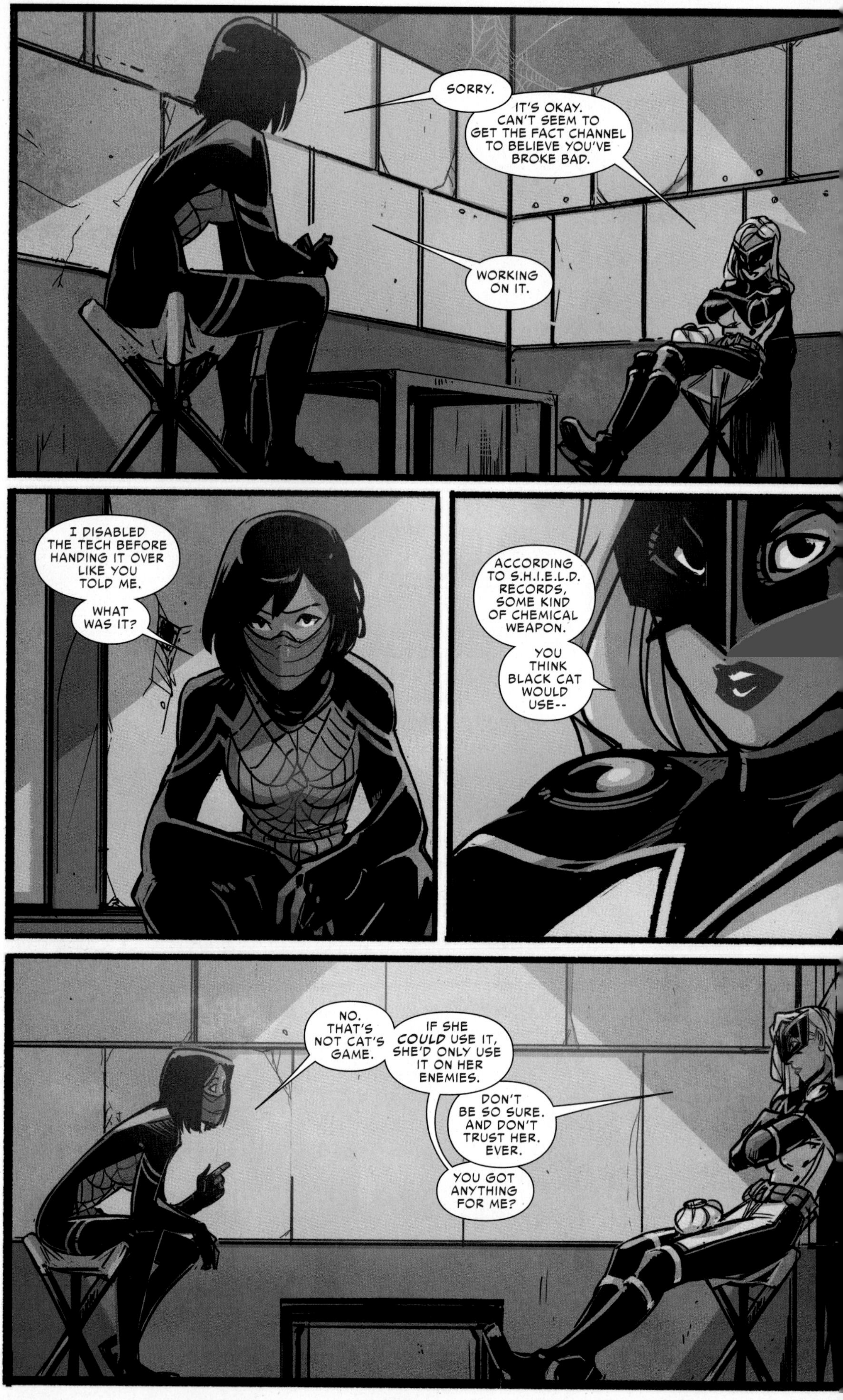

SORRY.
IT'S OKAY. CAN'T SEEM TO GET THE FACT CHANNEL TO BELIEVE YOU'VE BROKE BAD.
WORKING ON IT.
I DISABLED THE TECH BEFORE HANDING IT OVER LIKE YOU TOLD ME.
WHAT WAS IT?
ACCORDING TO S.H.I.E.L.D. RECORDS, SOME KIND OF CHEMICAL WEAPON.
YOU THINK BLACK CAT WOULD USE--
NO. THAT'S NOT CAT'S GAME.
IF SHE *COULD* USE IT, SHE'D ONLY USE IT ON HER ENEMIES.
DON'T BE SO SURE. AND DON'T TRUST HER. EVER.
YOU GOT ANYTHING FOR ME?

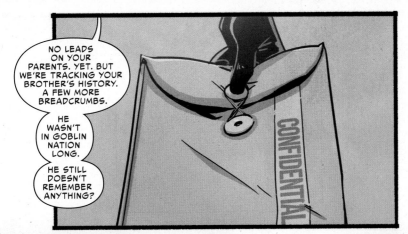

NO LEADS ON YOUR PARENTS. YET. BUT WE'RE TRACKING YOUR BROTHER'S HISTORY. A FEW MORE BREADCRUMBS.

HE WASN'T IN GOBLIN NATION LONG.

HE STILL DOESN'T REMEMBER ANYTHING?

CONFIDENTIAL

NO. BUT HE'S GETTING BETTER. THANK YOU FOR GETTING HIM INTO THAT HOSPITAL. THEY'VE BEEN GREAT.

WE HOLD UP OUR END AT S.H.I.E.L.D.

ALRIGHT, I'M GONNA GO SLEEP THIS BRUISE AWAY. KEEP DIGGING INTO CAT.

HEY, BOO...

YOU WERE HELD CAPTIVE BY SKRULLS?

FOR YEARS. YEAH.

HOW...

HOW DID YOU GET OVER THAT?

I DIDN'T.

BE CAREFUL OUT THERE, KIDDO.

WORKING UNDERCOVER? ONLY PERSON TO WATCH YOUR BACK IS YOU.

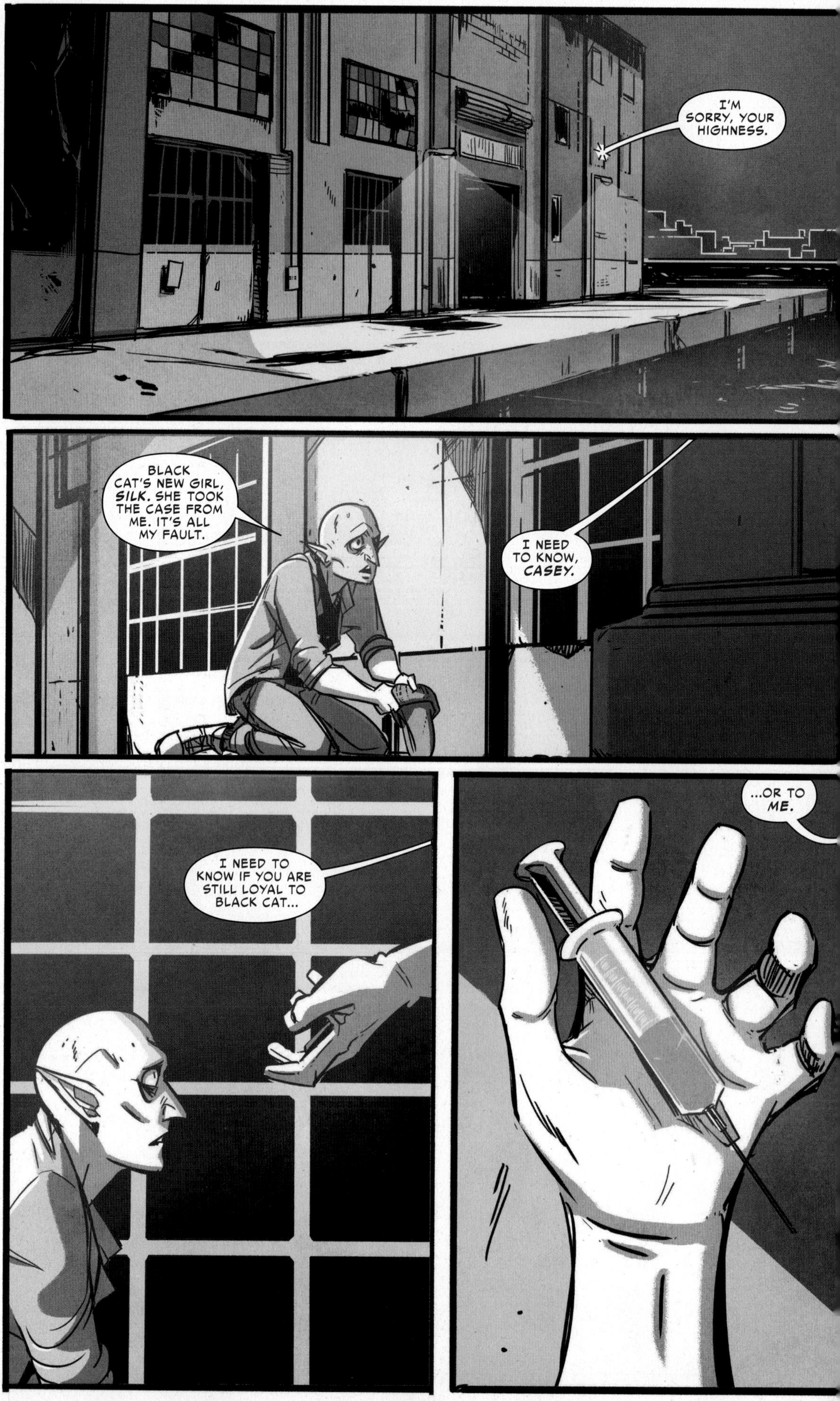
I'M SORRY, YOUR HIGHNESS.
BLACK CAT'S NEW GIRL, SILK. SHE TOOK THE CASE FROM ME. IT'S ALL MY FAULT.
I NEED TO KNOW, CASEY.
I NEED TO KNOW IF YOU ARE STILL LOYAL TO BLACK CAT...
...OR TO ME.

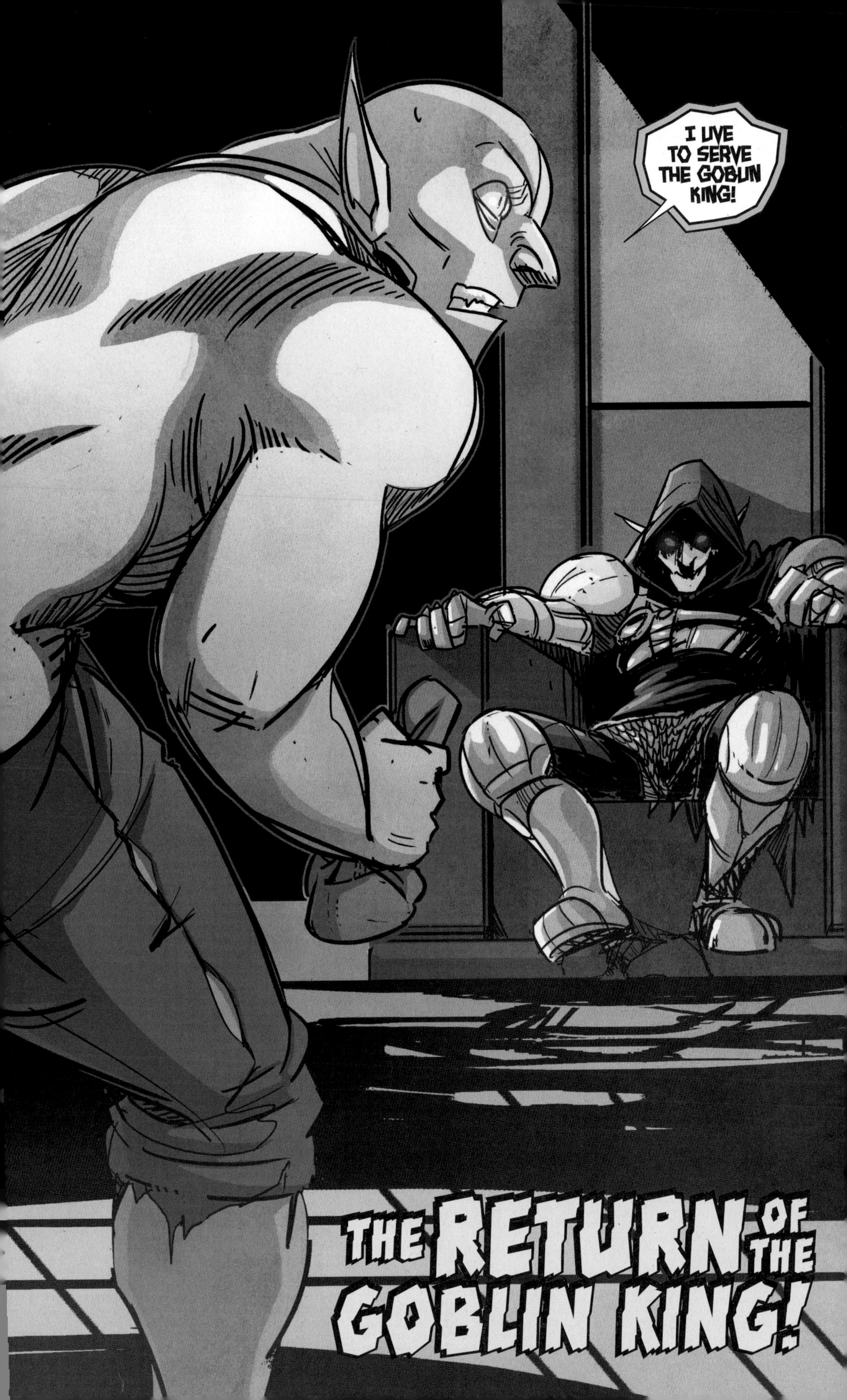
I LIVE TO SERVE THE GOBLIN KING!
THE RETURN OF THE GOBLIN KING!

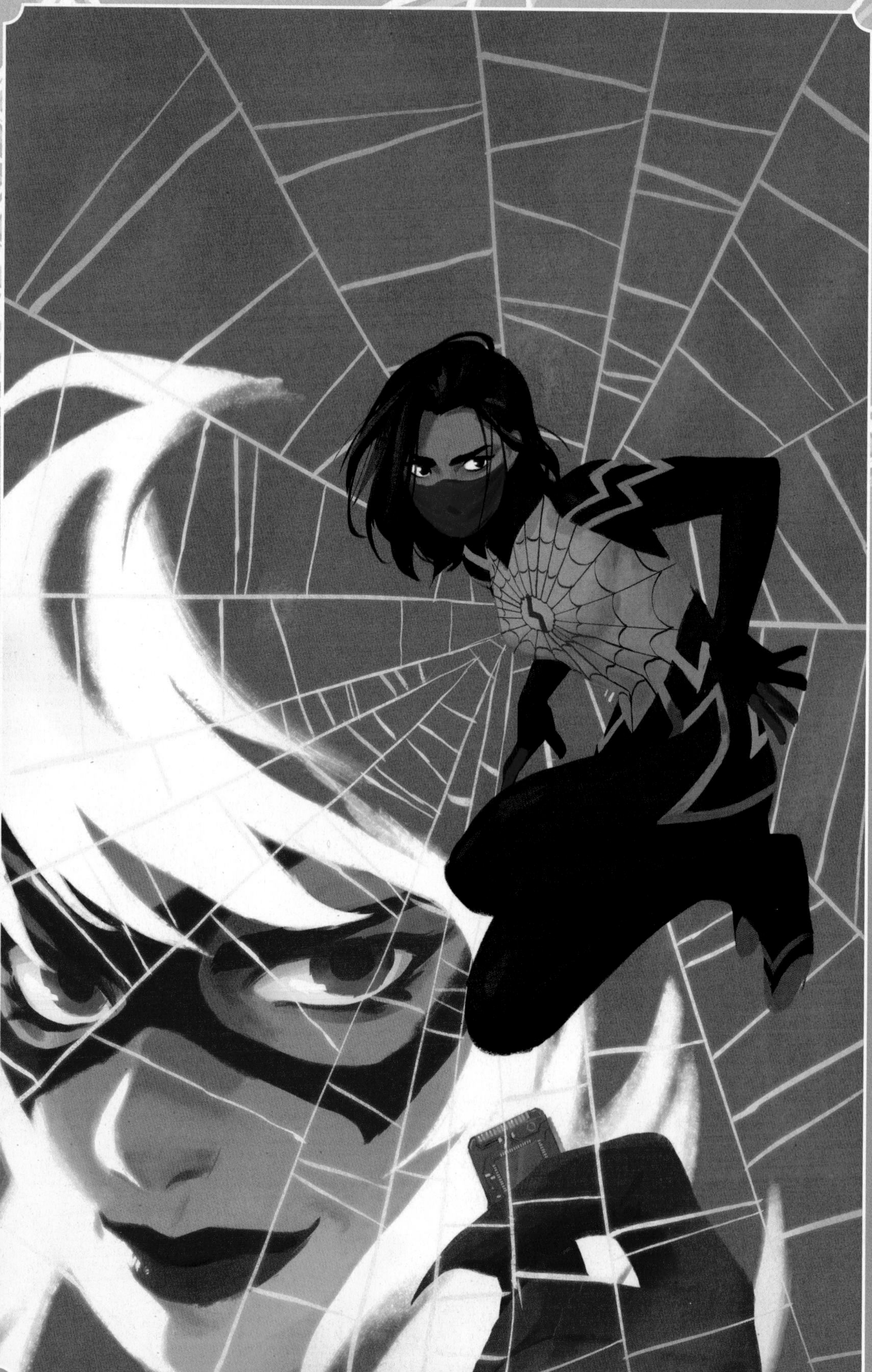

SILK (2015B) #2

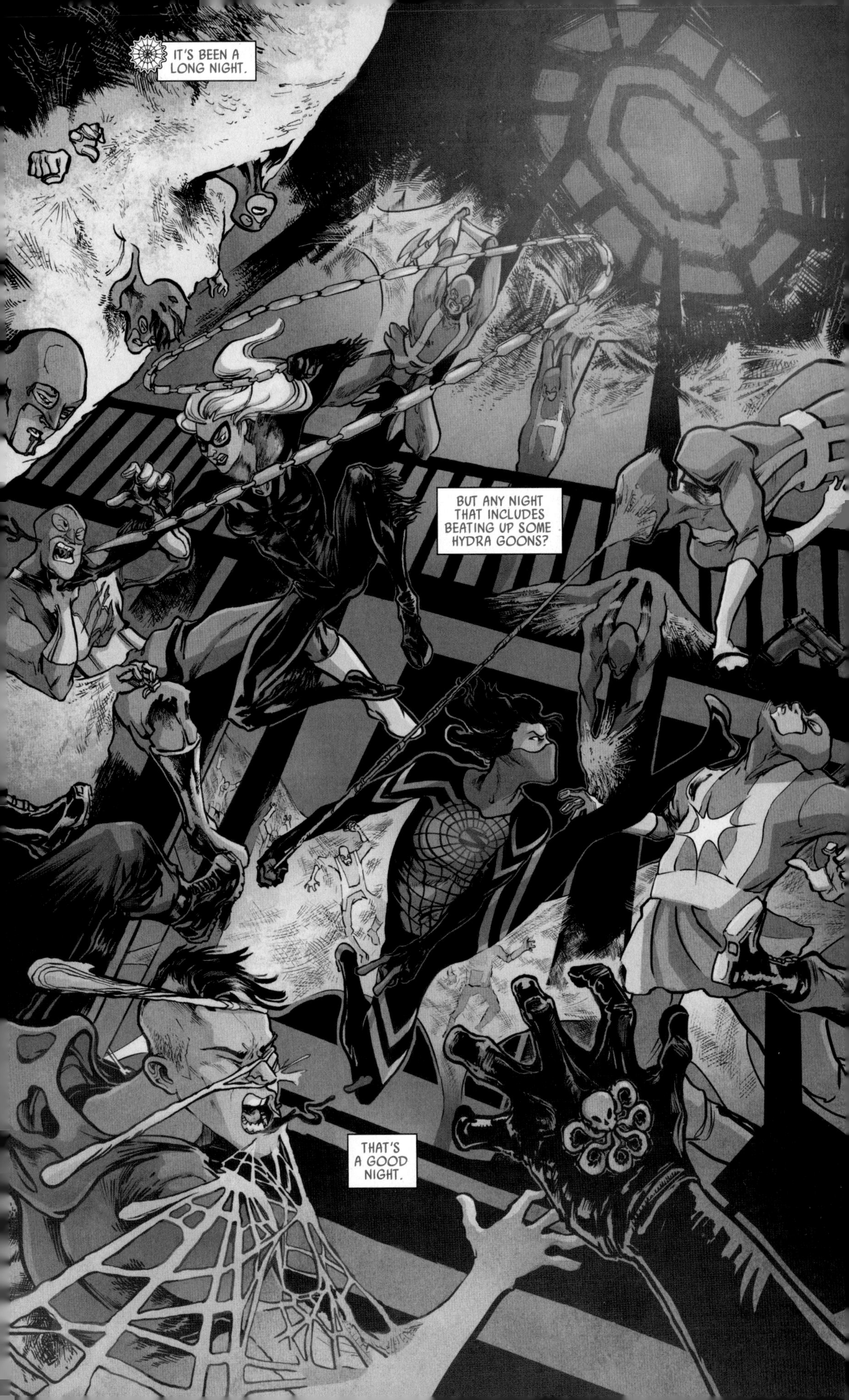
IT'S BEEN A LONG NIGHT.
BUT ANY NIGHT THAT INCLUDES BEATING UP SOME HYDRA GOONS?
THAT'S A GOOD NIGHT.

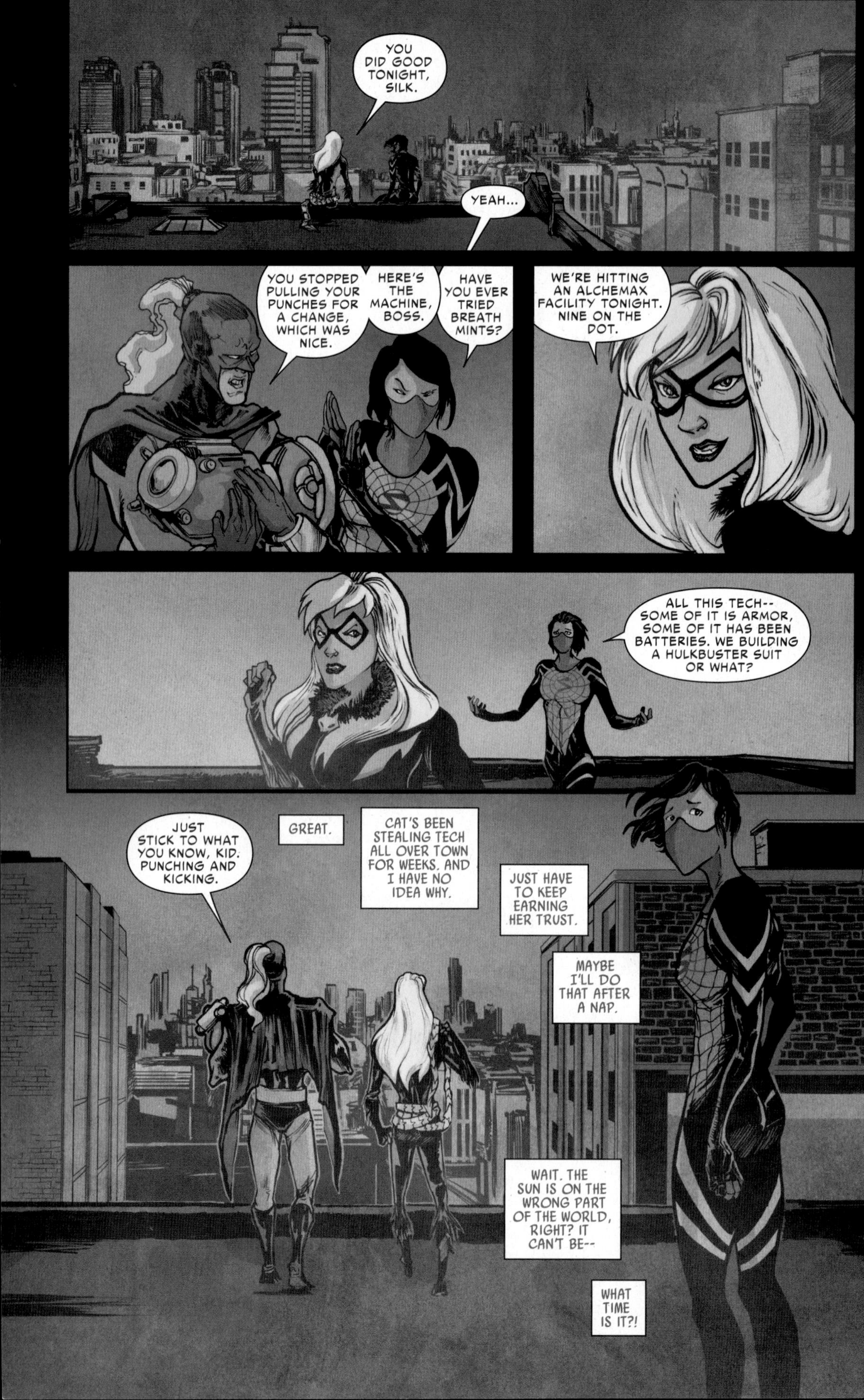
YOU DID GOOD TONIGHT, SILK.
YEAH...
YOU STOPPED PULLING YOUR PUNCHES FOR A CHANGE, WHICH WAS NICE.
HERE'S THE MACHINE, BOSS.
HAVE YOU EVER TRIED BREATH MINTS?
WE'RE HITTING AN ALCHEMAX FACILITY TONIGHT. NINE ON THE DOT.
ALL THIS TECH-- SOME OF IT IS ARMOR, SOME OF IT HAS BEEN BATTERIES. WE BUILDING A HULKBUSTER SUIT OR WHAT?
JUST STICK TO WHAT YOU KNOW, KID. PUNCHING AND KICKING.
GREAT.
CAT'S BEEN STEALING TECH ALL OVER TOWN FOR WEEKS, AND I HAVE NO IDEA WHY.
JUST HAVE TO KEEP EARNING HER TRUST.
MAYBE I'LL DO THAT AFTER A NAP.
WAIT. THE SUN IS ON THE WRONG PART OF THE WORLD, RIGHT? IT CAN'T BE--
WHAT TIME IS IT?!

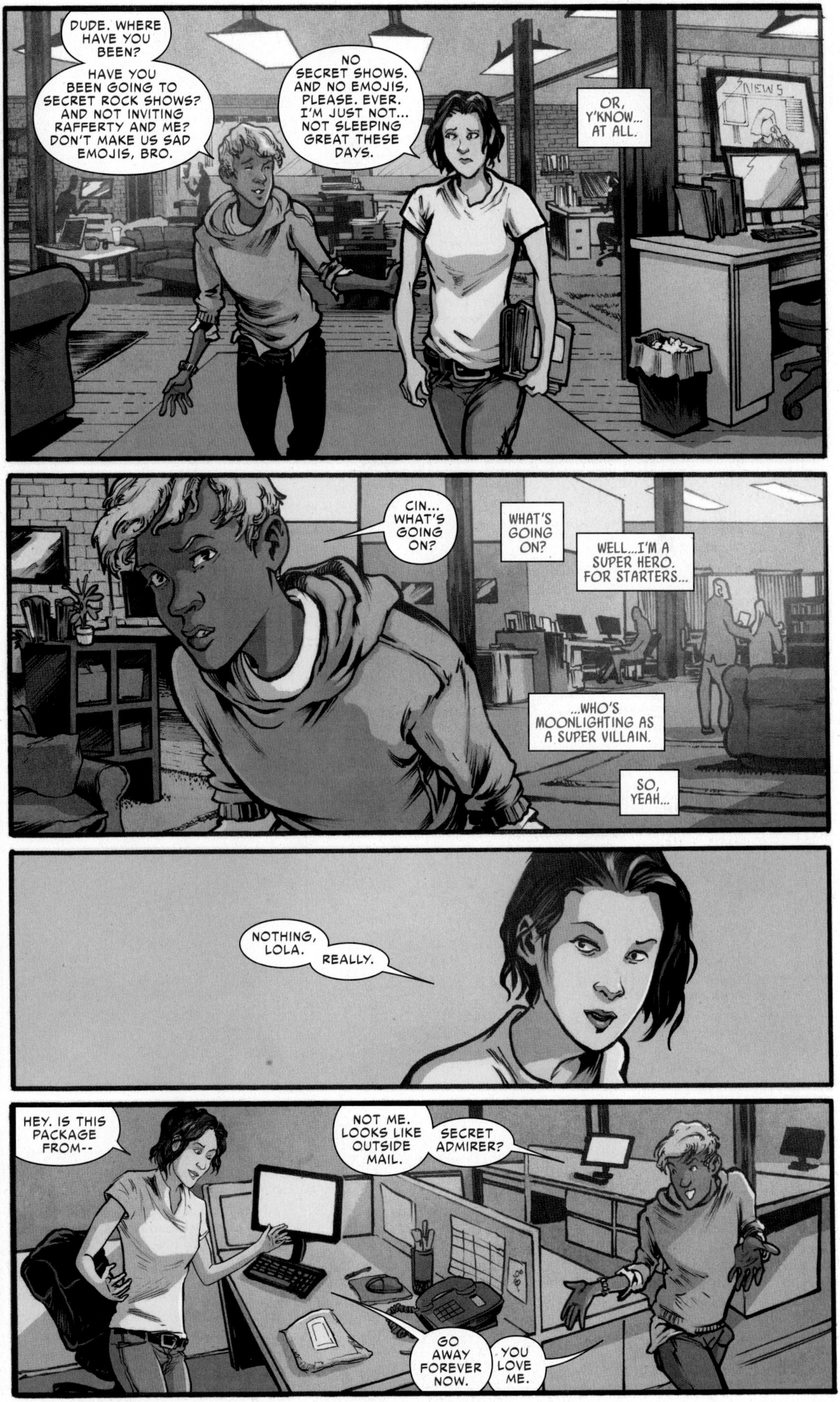
DUDE. WHERE HAVE YOU BEEN?
HAVE YOU BEEN GOING TO SECRET ROCK SHOWS? AND NOT INVITING RAFFERTY AND ME? DON'T MAKE US SAD EMOJIS, BRO.
NO SECRET SHOWS. AND NO EMOJIS, PLEASE. EVER. I'M JUST NOT... NOT SLEEPING GREAT THESE DAYS.
OR, Y'KNOW... AT ALL.
CIN... WHAT'S GOING ON?
WHAT'S GOING ON?
WELL...I'M A SUPER HERO. FOR STARTERS...
...WHO'S MOONLIGHTING AS A SUPER VILLAIN.
SO, YEAH...
NOTHING, LOLA.
REALLY.
HEY. IS THIS PACKAGE FROM--
NOT ME. LOOKS LIKE OUTSIDE MAIL.
SECRET ADMIRER?
GO AWAY FOREVER NOW.
YOU LOVE ME.

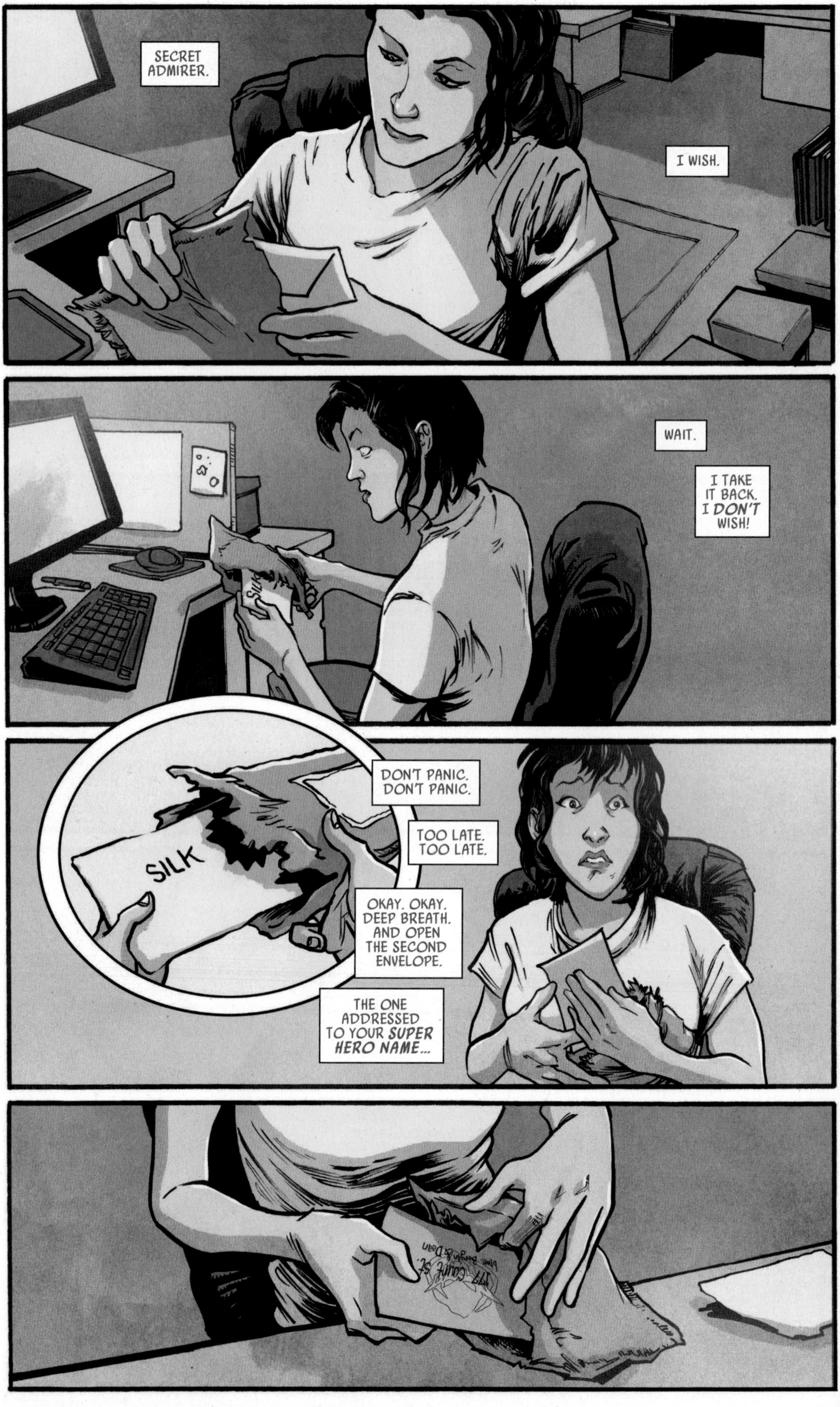
SECRET ADMIRER.
I WISH.
WAIT.
I TAKE IT BACK. I *DON'T* WISH!
SILK
DON'T PANIC. DON'T PANIC.
TOO LATE. TOO LATE.
OKAY. OKAY. DEEP BREATH. AND OPEN THE SECOND ENVELOPE.
THE ONE ADDRESSED TO YOUR *SUPER HERO NAME*...

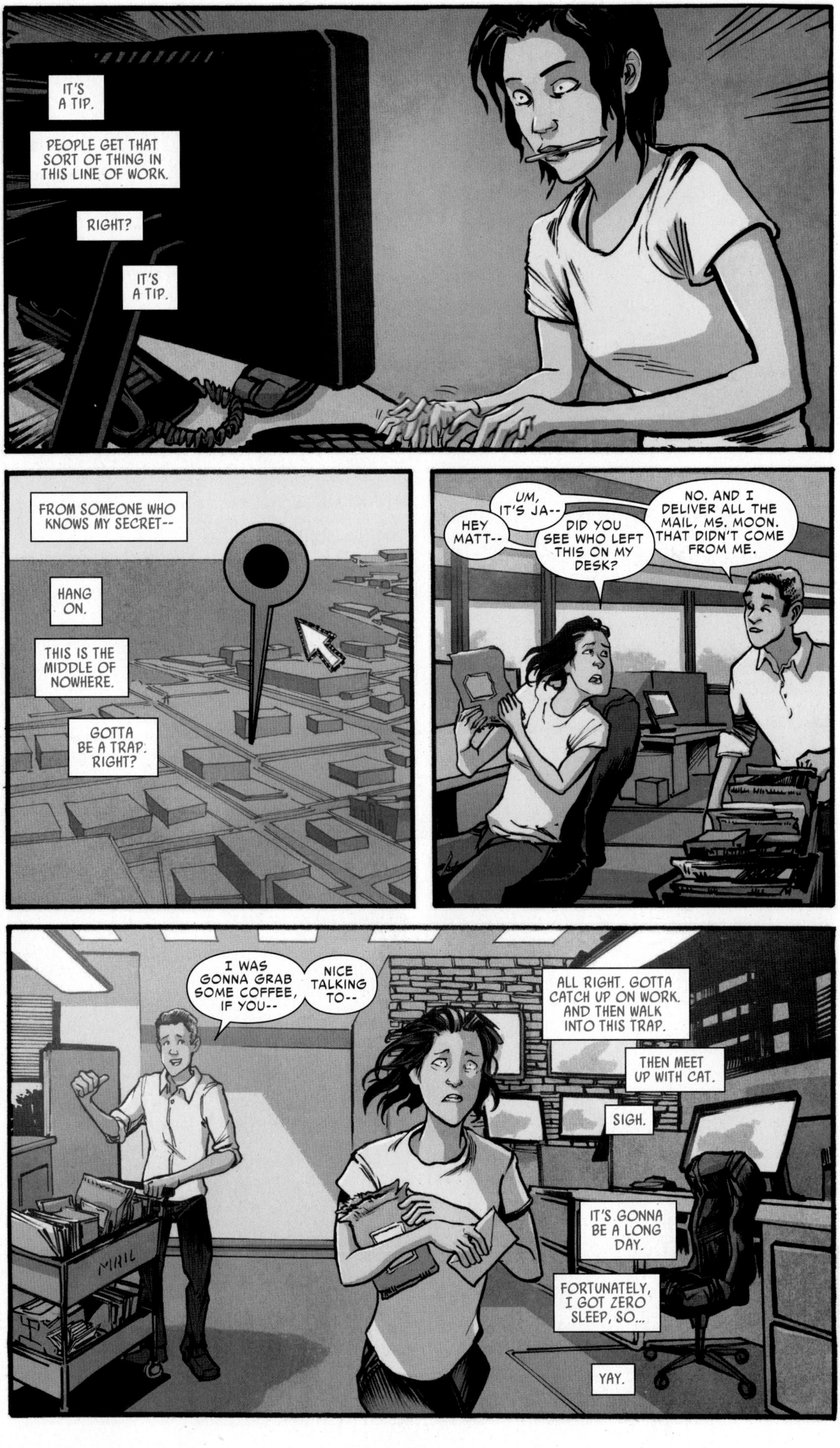
IT'S A TIP.
PEOPLE GET THAT SORT OF THING IN THIS LINE OF WORK.
RIGHT?
IT'S A TIP.
FROM SOMEONE WHO KNOWS MY SECRET--
HANG ON.
THIS IS THE MIDDLE OF NOWHERE.
GOTTA BE A TRAP. RIGHT?
HEY MATT--
UM, IT'S JA--
DID YOU SEE WHO LEFT THIS ON MY DESK?
NO. AND I DELIVER ALL THE MAIL, MS. MOON. THAT DIDN'T COME FROM ME.
I WAS GONNA GRAB SOME COFFEE, IF YOU--
NICE TALKING TO--
ALL RIGHT. GOTTA CATCH UP ON WORK. AND THEN WALK INTO THIS TRAP.
THEN MEET UP WITH CAT.
SIGH.
IT'S GONNA BE A LONG DAY.
FORTUNATELY, I GOT ZERO SLEEP, SO...
YAY.
MAIL

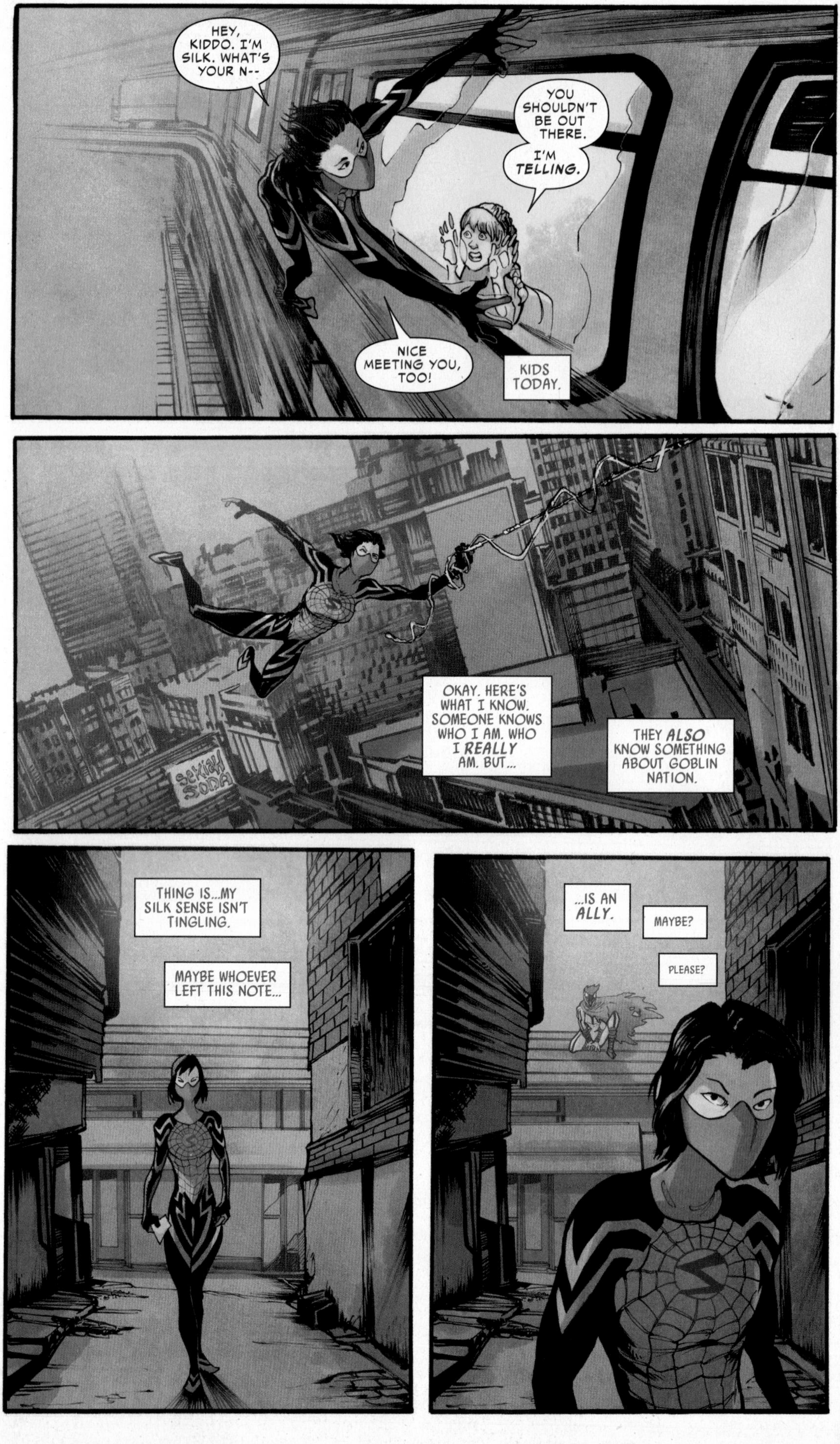
HEY, KIDDO. I'M SILK. WHAT'S YOUR N--
YOU SHOULDN'T BE OUT THERE.
I'M TELLING.
NICE MEETING YOU, TOO!
KIDS TODAY.
OKAY. HERE'S WHAT I KNOW. SOMEONE KNOWS WHO I AM. WHO I REALLY AM. BUT...
THEY ALSO KNOW SOMETHING ABOUT GOBLIN NATION.
THING IS...MY SILK SENSE ISN'T TINGLING.
MAYBE WHOEVER LEFT THIS NOTE...
...IS AN ALLY.
MAYBE?
PLEASE?

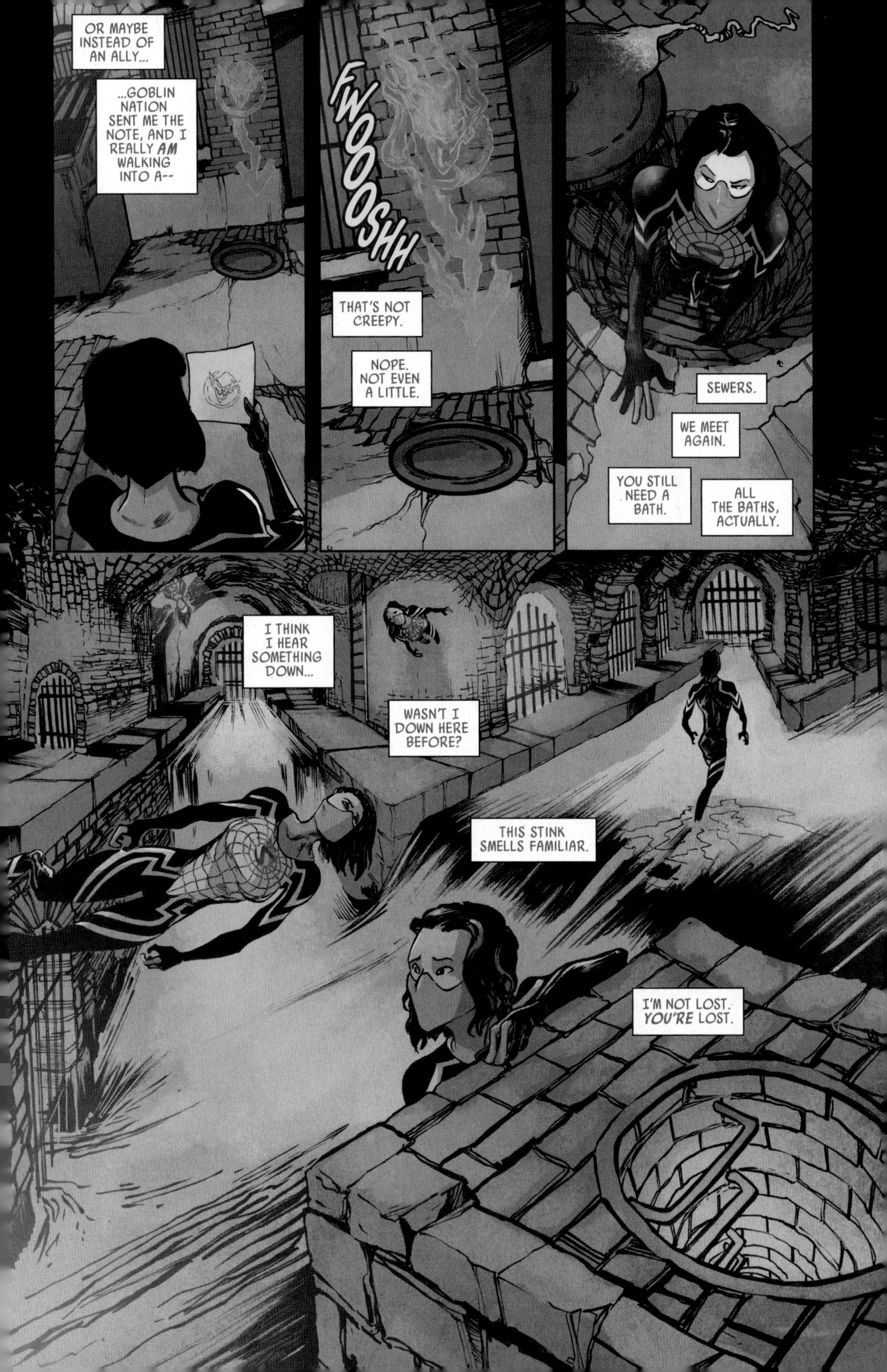
OR MAYBE INSTEAD OF AN ALLY...
...GOBLIN NATION SENT ME THE NOTE, AND I REALLY *AM* WALKING INTO A--
FWOOOOSHH
THAT'S NOT CREEPY.
NOPE. NOT EVEN A LITTLE.
SEWERS.
WE MEET AGAIN.
YOU STILL NEED A BATH.
ALL THE BATHS, ACTUALLY.
I THINK I HEAR SOMETHING DOWN...
WASN'T I DOWN HERE BEFORE?
THIS STINK SMELLS FAMILIAR.
I'M NOT LOST. *YOU'RE* LOST.

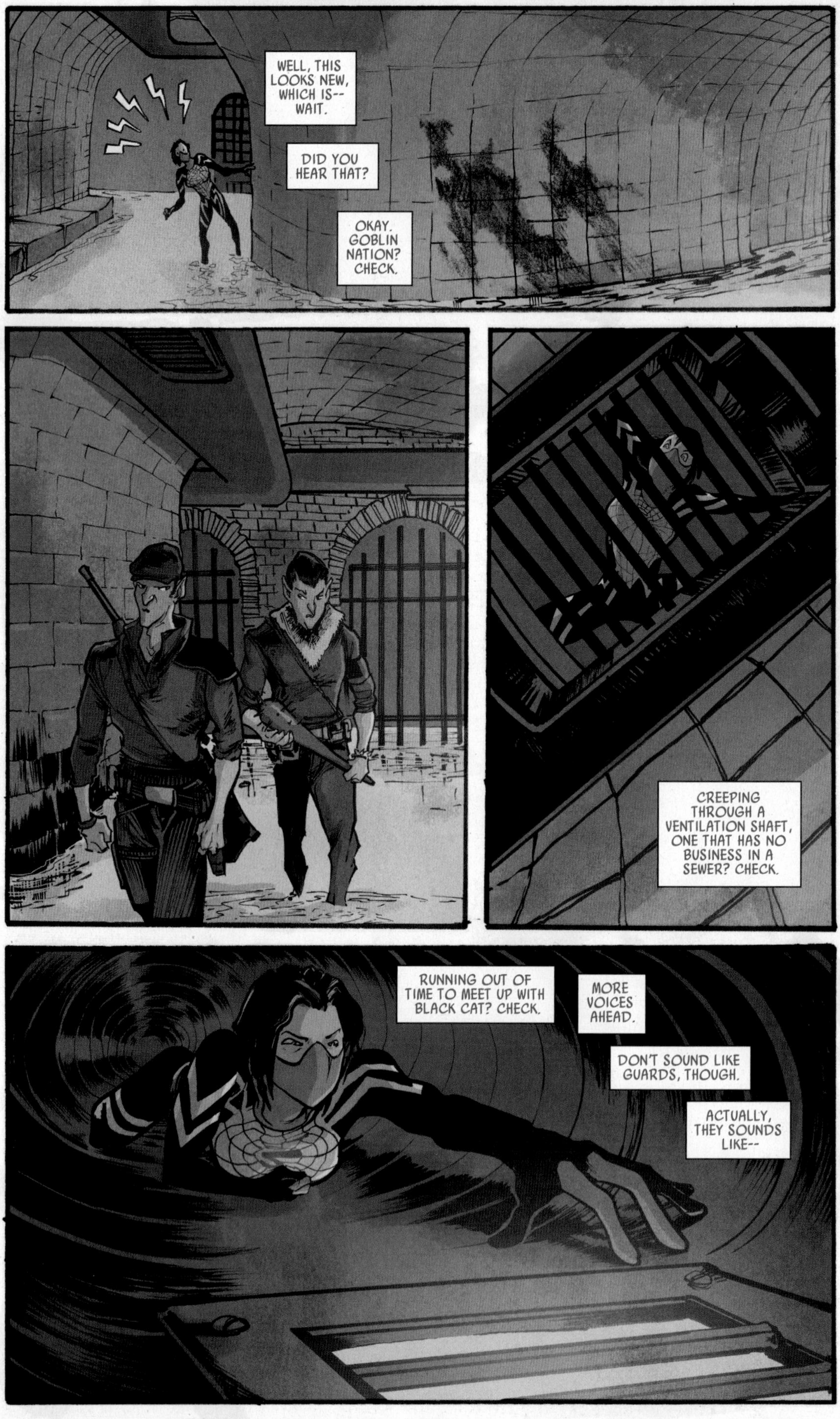
WELL, THIS LOOKS NEW, WHICH IS-- WAIT.
DID YOU HEAR THAT?
OKAY. GOBLIN NATION? CHECK.
CREEPING THROUGH A VENTILATION SHAFT, ONE THAT HAS NO BUSINESS IN A SEWER? CHECK.
RUNNING OUT OF TIME TO MEET UP WITH BLACK CAT? CHECK.
MORE VOICES AHEAD.
DON'T SOUND LIKE GUARDS, THOUGH.
ACTUALLY, THEY SOUNDS LIKE--

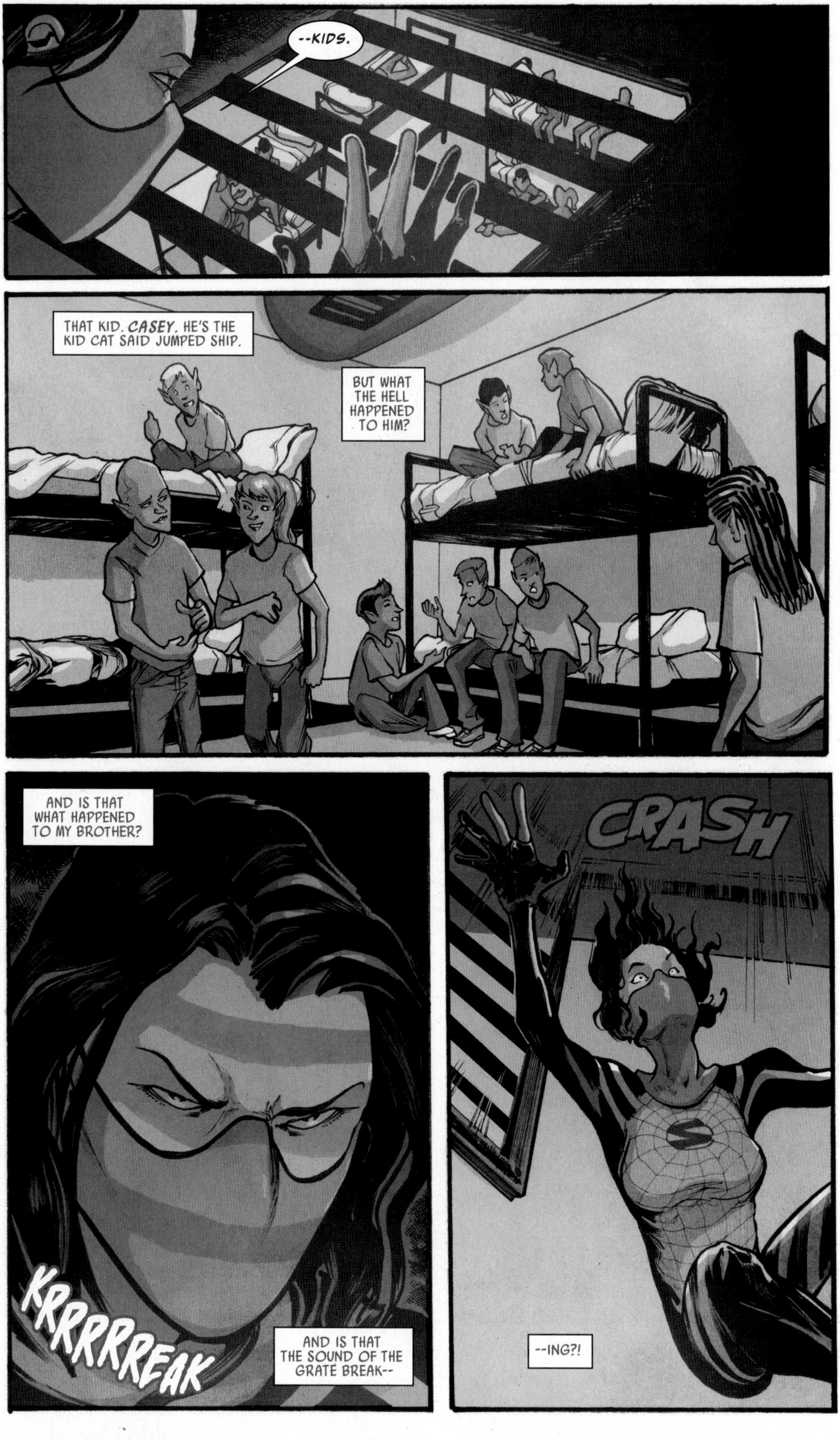
--KIDS.
THAT KID. CASEY. HE'S THE KID CAT SAID JUMPED SHIP.
BUT WHAT THE HELL HAPPENED TO HIM?
AND IS THAT WHAT HAPPENED TO MY BROTHER?
KRRRRREAK
AND IS THAT THE SOUND OF THE GRATE BREAK--
CRASH
--ING?!

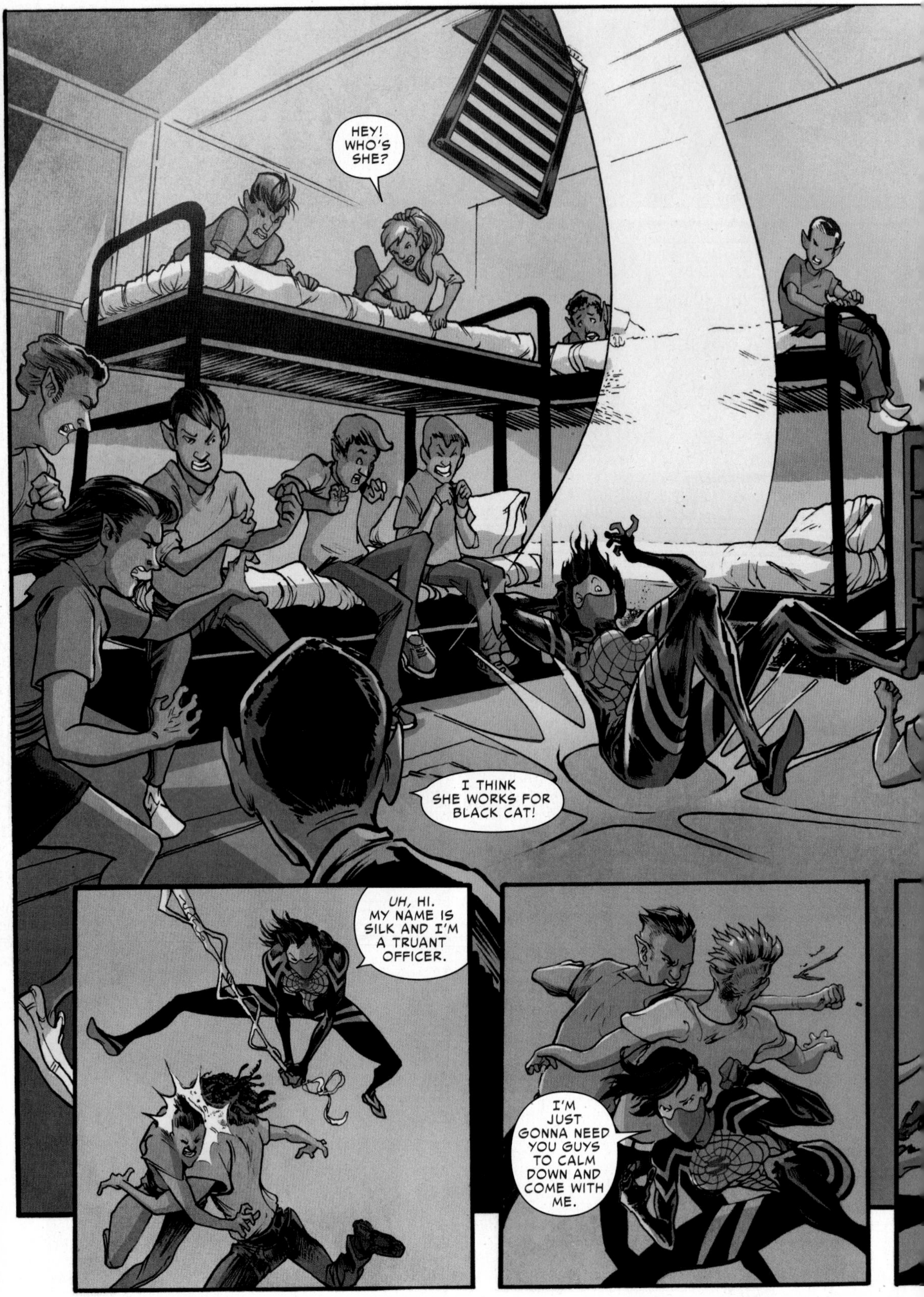
HEY! WHO'S SHE?
I THINK SHE WORKS FOR BLACK CAT!
UH, HI. MY NAME IS SILK AND I'M A TRUANT OFFICER.
I'M JUST GONNA NEED YOU GUYS TO CALM DOWN AND COME WITH ME.

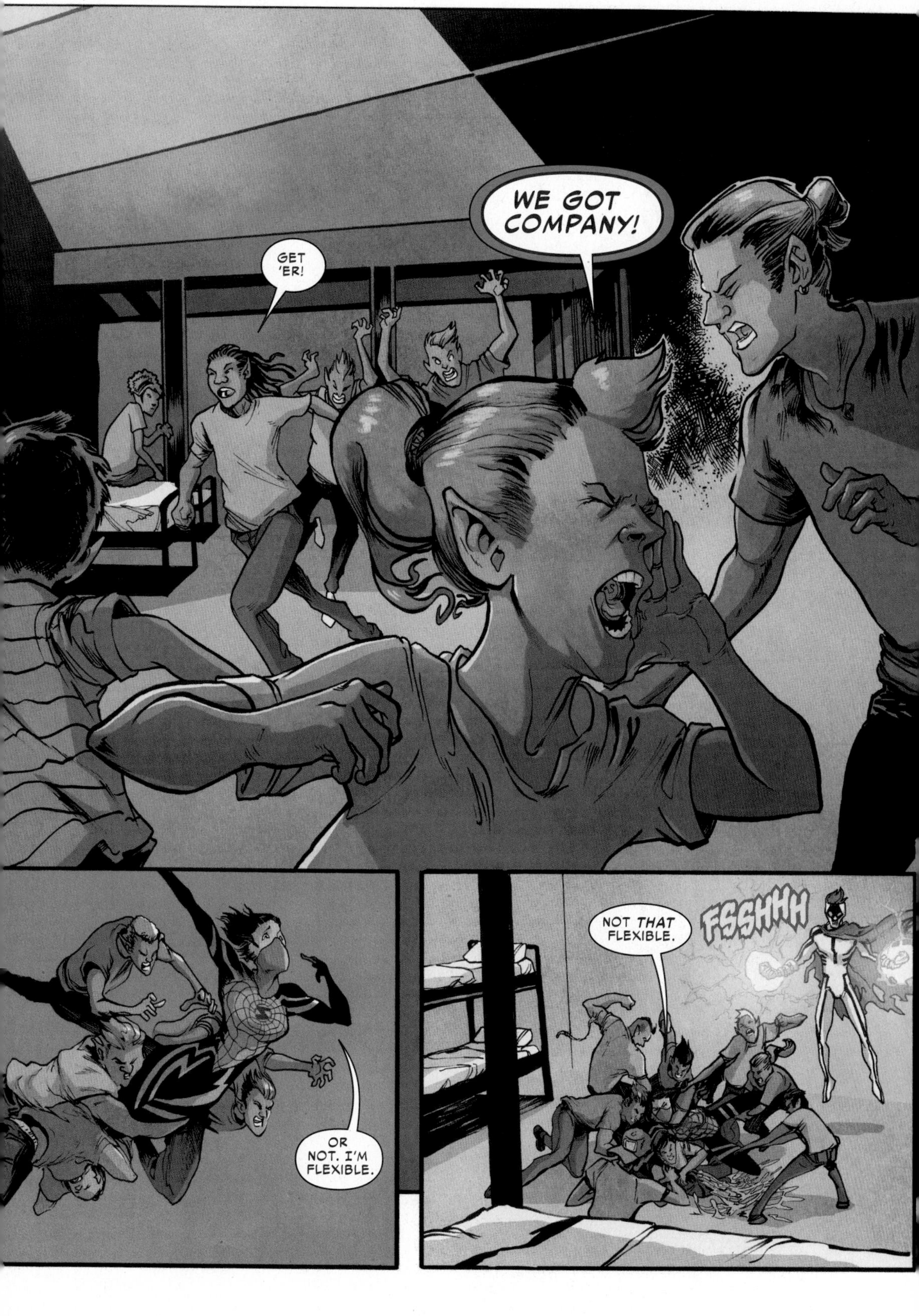
GET 'ER!
WE GOT COMPANY!
OR NOT. I'M FLEXIBLE.
NOT THAT FLEXIBLE.
FSSHHH

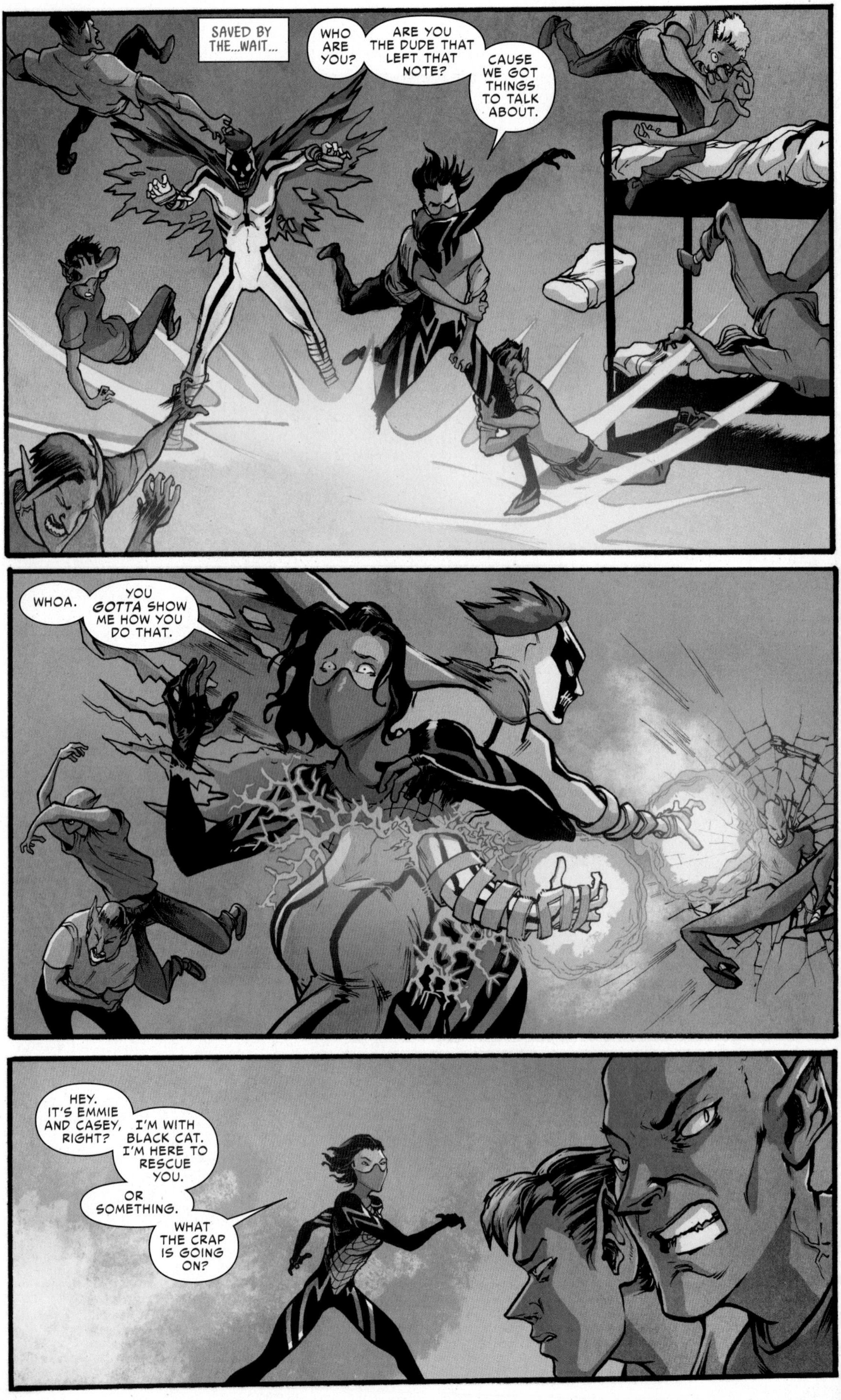
SAVED BY THE...WAIT...
WHO ARE YOU?
ARE YOU THE DUDE THAT LEFT THAT NOTE?
CAUSE WE GOT THINGS TO TALK ABOUT.
WHOA.
YOU GOTTA SHOW ME HOW YOU DO THAT.
HEY. IT'S EMMIE AND CASEY, RIGHT?
I'M WITH BLACK CAT. I'M HERE TO RESCUE YOU.
OR SOMETHING.
WHAT THE CRAP IS GOING ON?

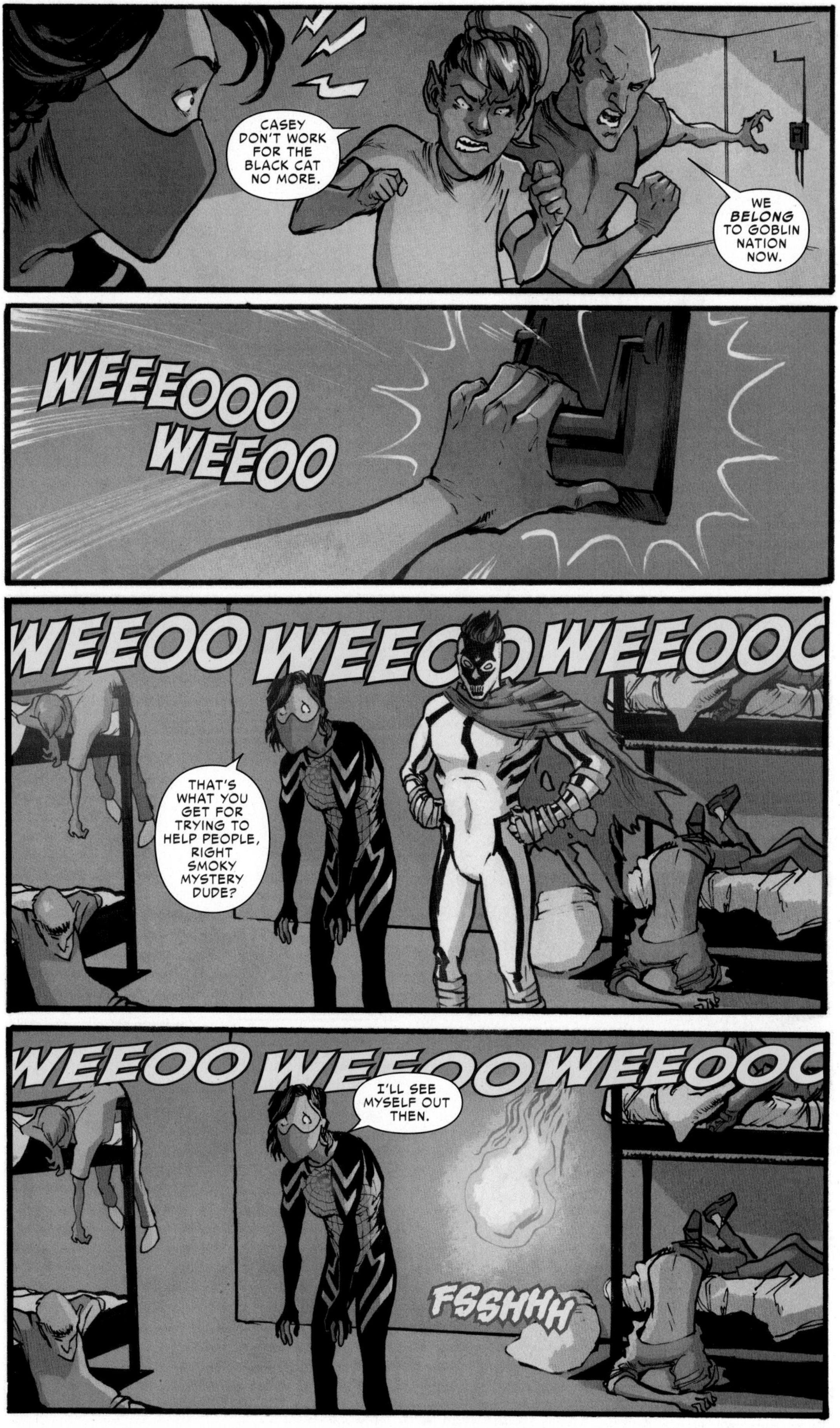
CASEY DON'T WORK FOR THE BLACK CAT NO MORE.
WE *BELONG* TO GOBLIN NATION NOW.
WEEEOOO WEEOO
WEEOO WEEOO WEEOOO
THAT'S WHAT YOU GET FOR TRYING TO HELP PEOPLE, RIGHT SMOKY MYSTERY DUDE?
WEEOO WEEOO WEEOOO
I'LL SEE MYSELF OUT THEN.
FSSHHH

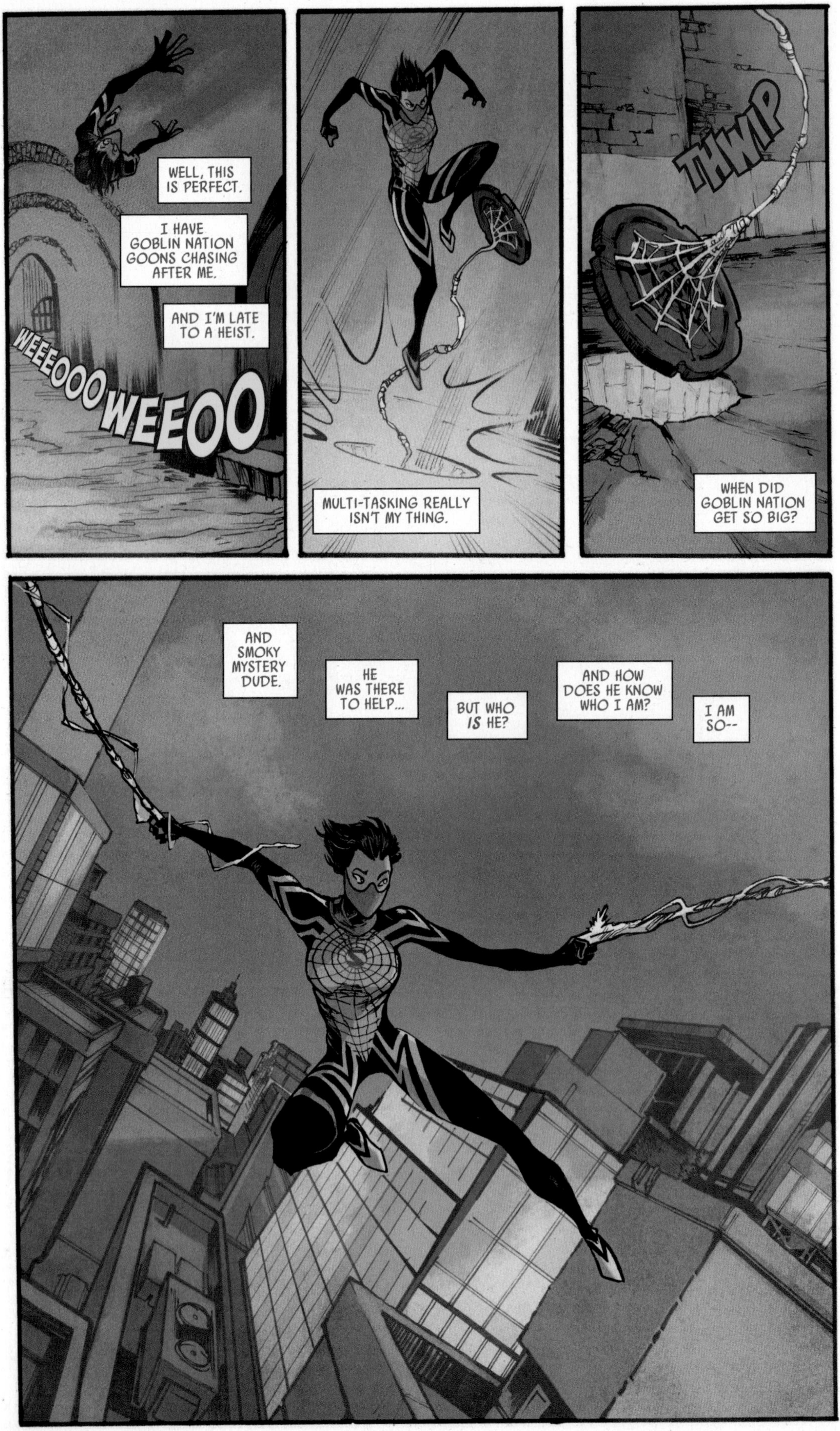
WELL, THIS IS PERFECT.
I HAVE GOBLIN NATION GOONS CHASING AFTER ME.
AND I'M LATE TO A HEIST.
WEEEOOOWEEOO
MULTI-TASKING REALLY ISN'T MY THING.
THWIP
WHEN DID GOBLIN NATION GET SO BIG?
AND SMOKY MYSTERY DUDE.
HE WAS THERE TO HELP...
BUT WHO *IS* HE?
AND HOW DOES HE KNOW WHO I AM?
I AM SO--

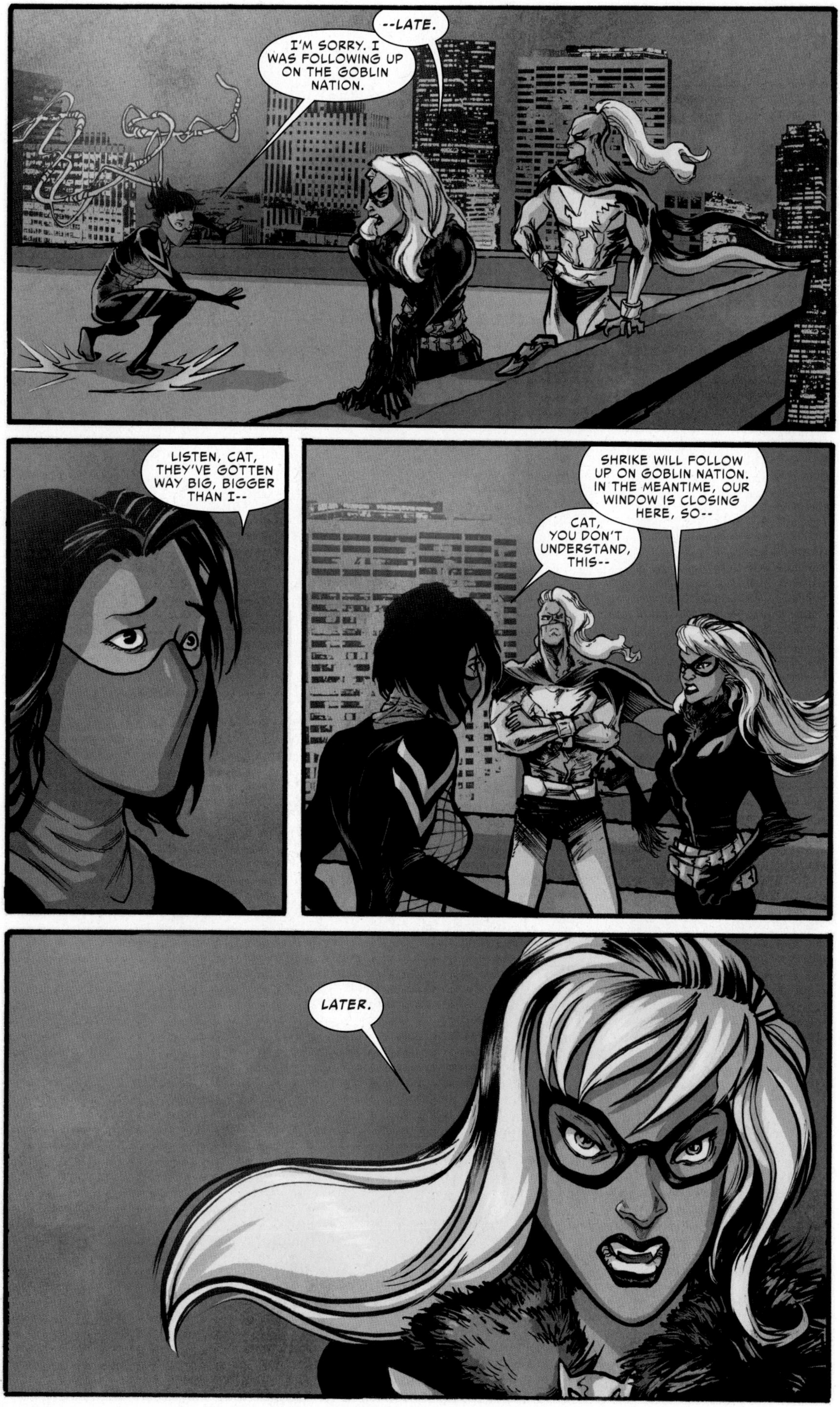
I'M SORRY. I WAS FOLLOWING UP ON THE GOBLIN NATION.
--LATE.
LISTEN, CAT, THEY'VE GOTTEN WAY BIG, BIGGER THAN I--
SHRIKE WILL FOLLOW UP ON GOBLIN NATION. IN THE MEANTIME, OUR WINDOW IS CLOSING HERE, SO--
CAT, YOU DON'T UNDERSTAND, THIS--
LATER.

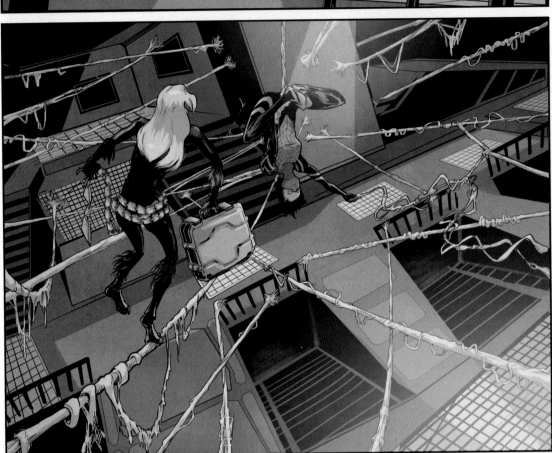

EEEEEEE!

TAKE THEM FOR A RIDE, WE'LL MEET AT THE RENDEZVOUS.

THIS IS ALL KINDS OF BAD.

THAT'S A NEWS CHOPPER, WHICH HELPS MY REP AROUND TOWN...BUT IT ISN'T A FACT CHANNEL CHOPPER, WHICH HURTS MY DAY JOB. STRIKE ONE.

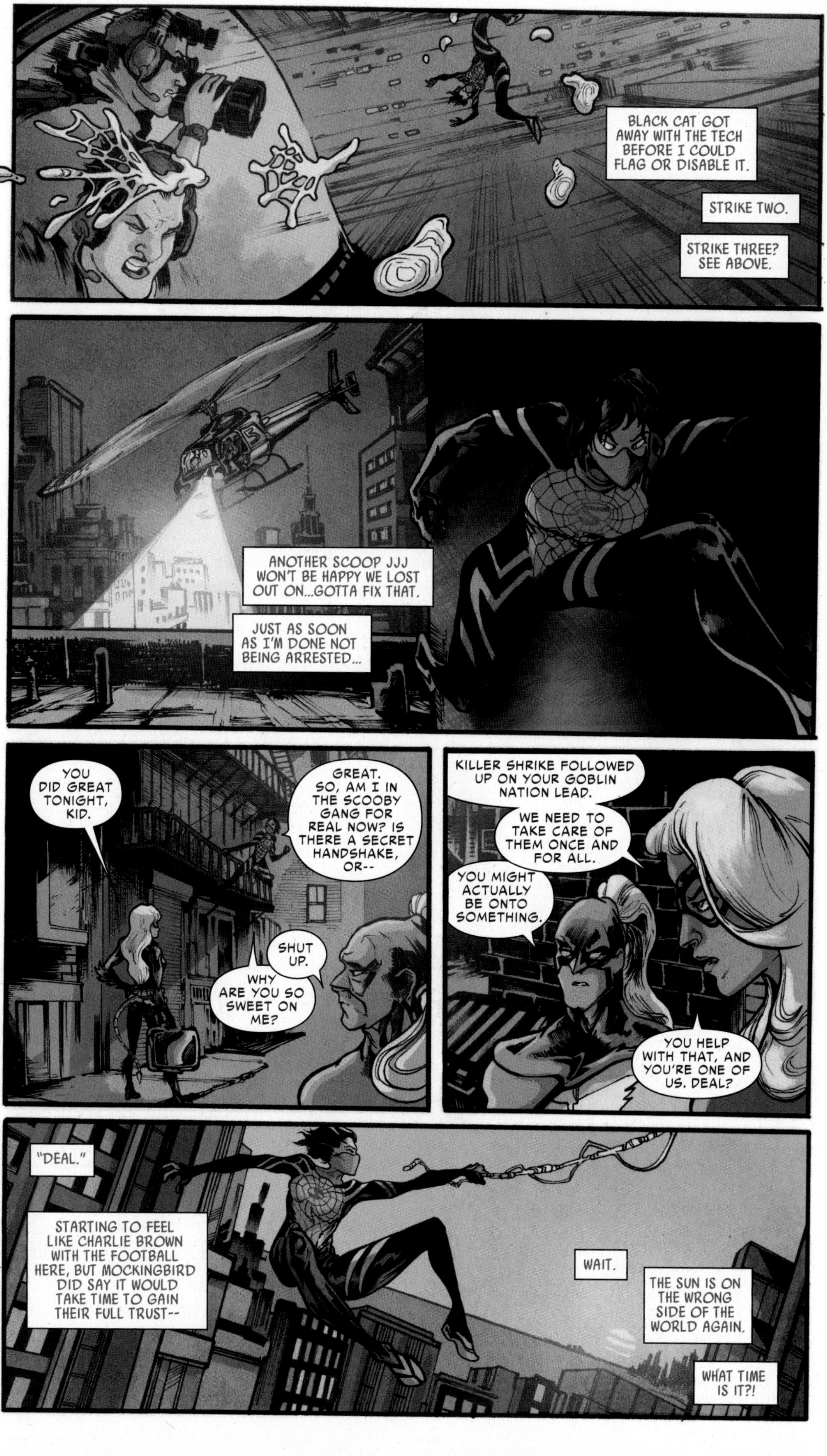
BLACK CAT GOT AWAY WITH THE TECH BEFORE I COULD FLAG OR DISABLE IT.
STRIKE TWO.
STRIKE THREE? SEE ABOVE.
ANOTHER SCOOP JJJ WON'T BE HAPPY WE LOST OUT ON...GOTTA FIX THAT.
JUST AS SOON AS I'M DONE NOT BEING ARRESTED...
YOU DID GREAT TONIGHT, KID.
GREAT. SO, AM I IN THE SCOOBY GANG FOR REAL NOW? IS THERE A SECRET HANDSHAKE, OR--
SHUT UP.
WHY ARE YOU SO SWEET ON ME?
KILLER SHRIKE FOLLOWED UP ON YOUR GOBLIN NATION LEAD.
WE NEED TO TAKE CARE OF THEM ONCE AND FOR ALL.
YOU MIGHT ACTUALLY BE ONTO SOMETHING.
YOU HELP WITH THAT, AND YOU'RE ONE OF US. DEAL?
"DEAL."
STARTING TO FEEL LIKE CHARLIE BROWN WITH THE FOOTBALL HERE, BUT MOCKINGBIRD DID SAY IT WOULD TAKE TIME TO GAIN THEIR FULL TRUST--
WAIT.
THE SUN IS ON THE WRONG SIDE OF THE WORLD AGAIN.
WHAT TIME IS IT?!

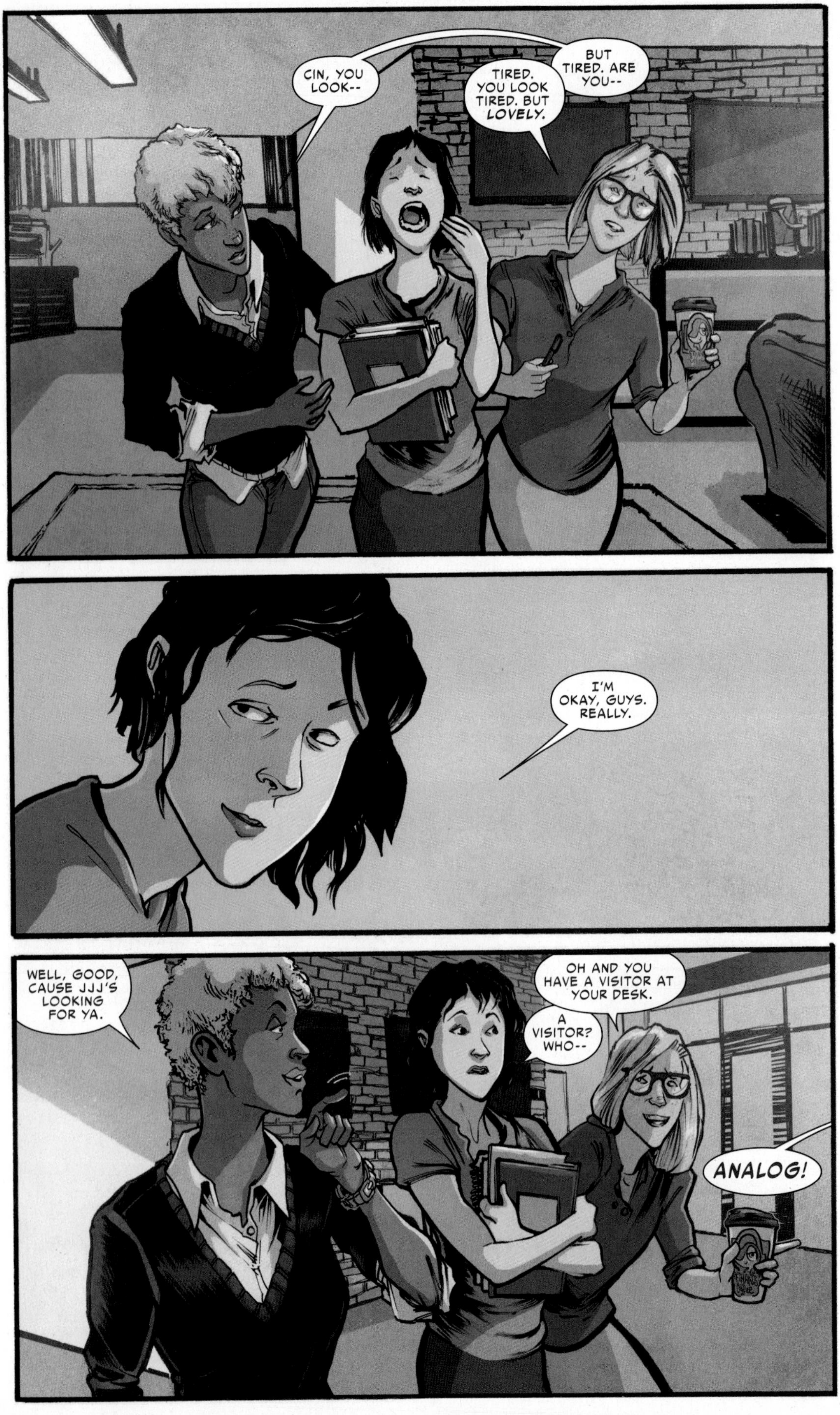
CIN, YOU LOOK--
TIRED. YOU LOOK TIRED. BUT *LOVELY.*
BUT TIRED. ARE YOU--
I'M OKAY, GUYS. REALLY.
WELL, GOOD, CAUSE JJJ'S LOOKING FOR YA.
OH AND YOU HAVE A VISITOR AT YOUR DESK.
A VISITOR? WHO--
ANALOG!

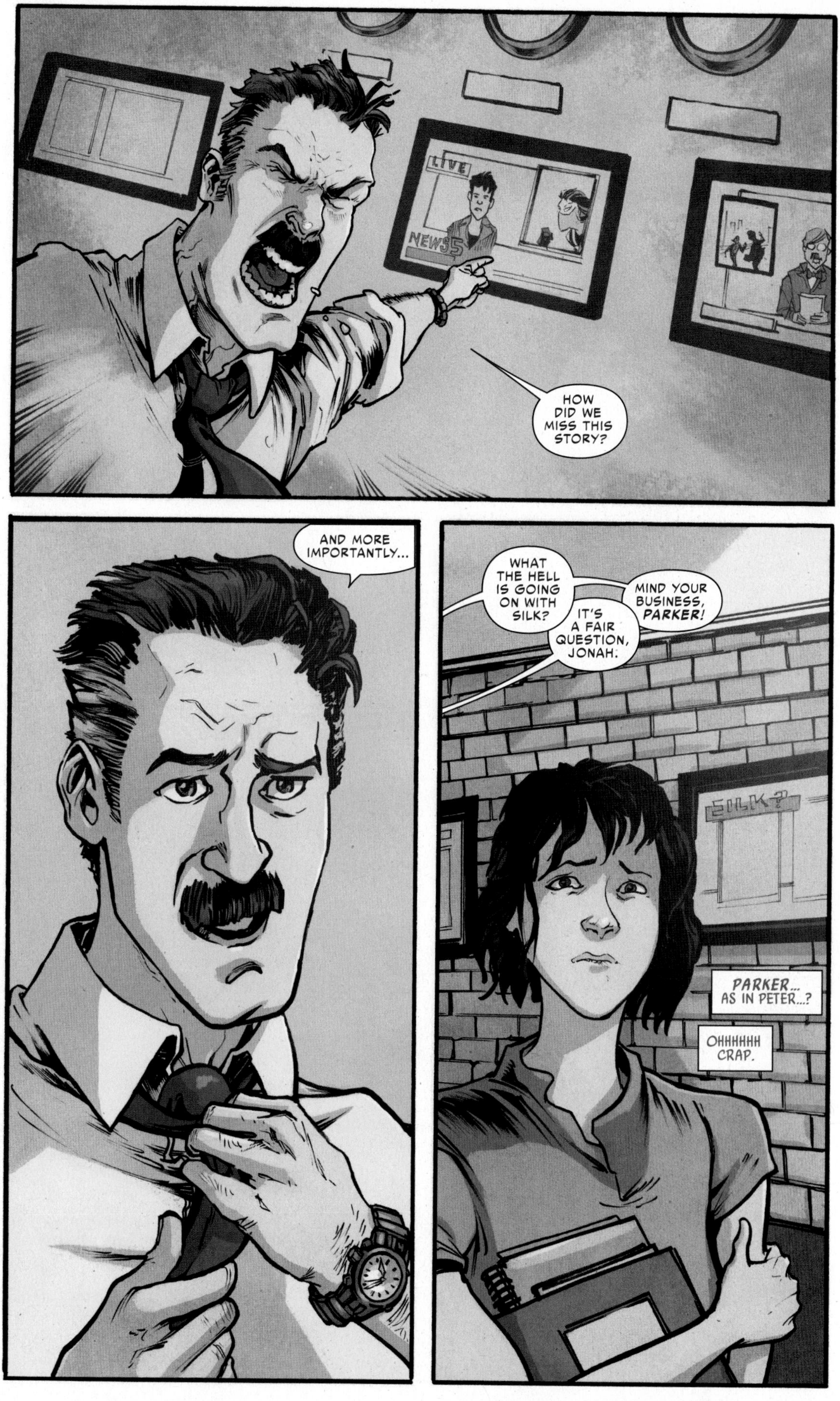
LIVE
NEWS5
HOW DID WE MISS THIS STORY?
AND MORE IMPORTANTLY...
WHAT THE HELL IS GOING ON WITH SILK?
MIND YOUR BUSINESS, PARKER!
IT'S A FAIR QUESTION, JONAH.
SILK?
PARKER... AS IN PETER...?
OHHHHHH CRAP.

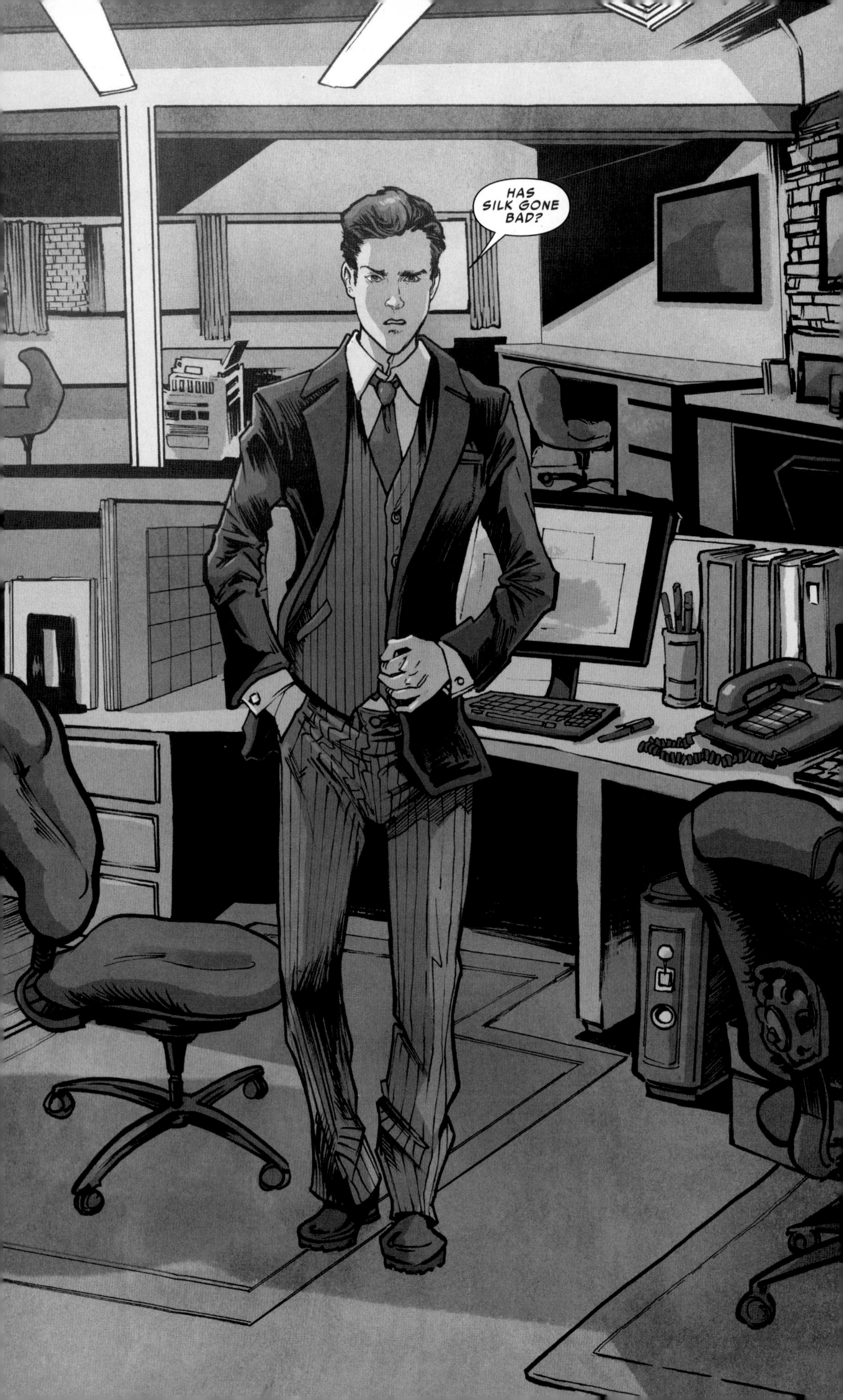
HAS SILK GONE BAD?

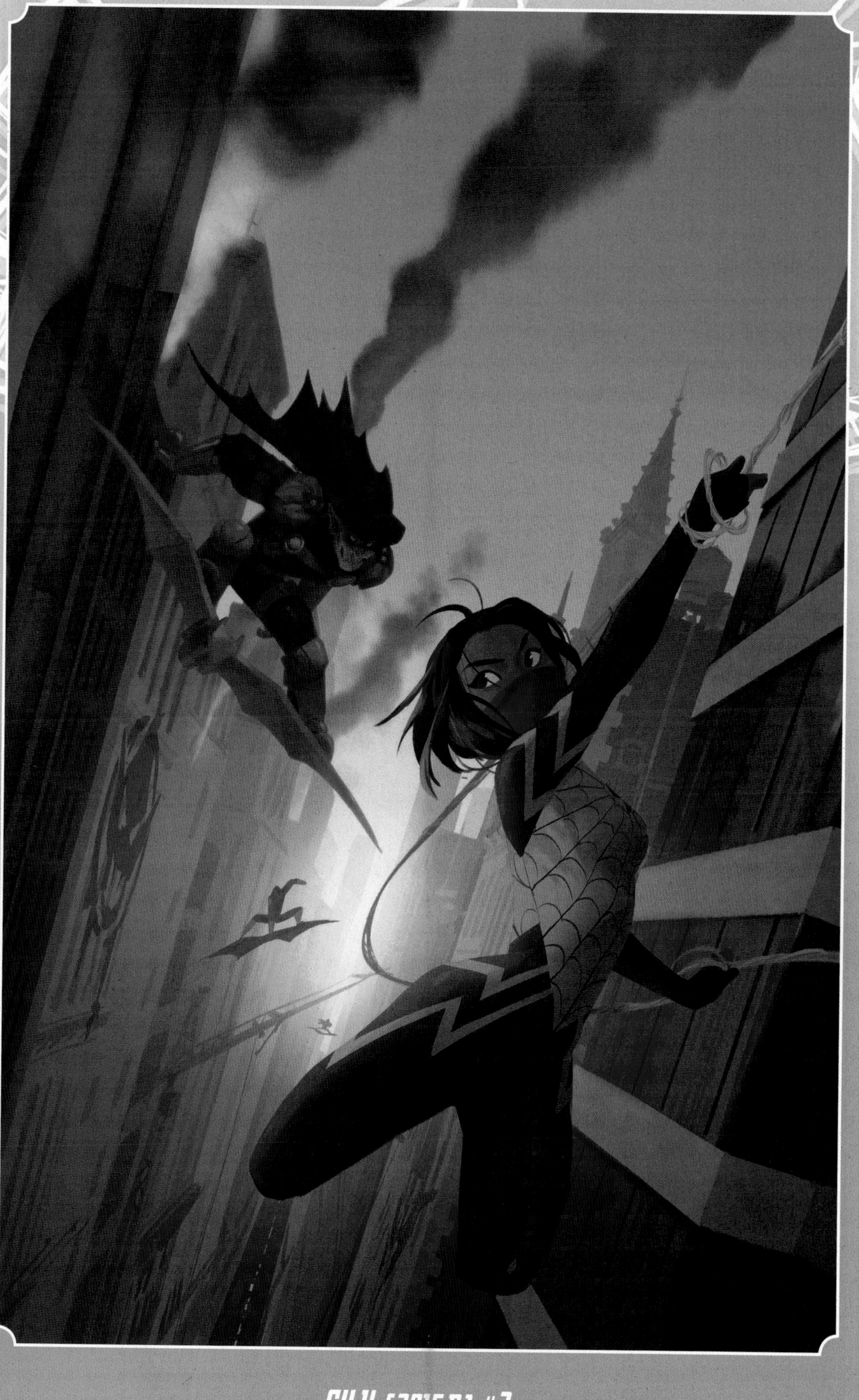

SILK (2015B) #3

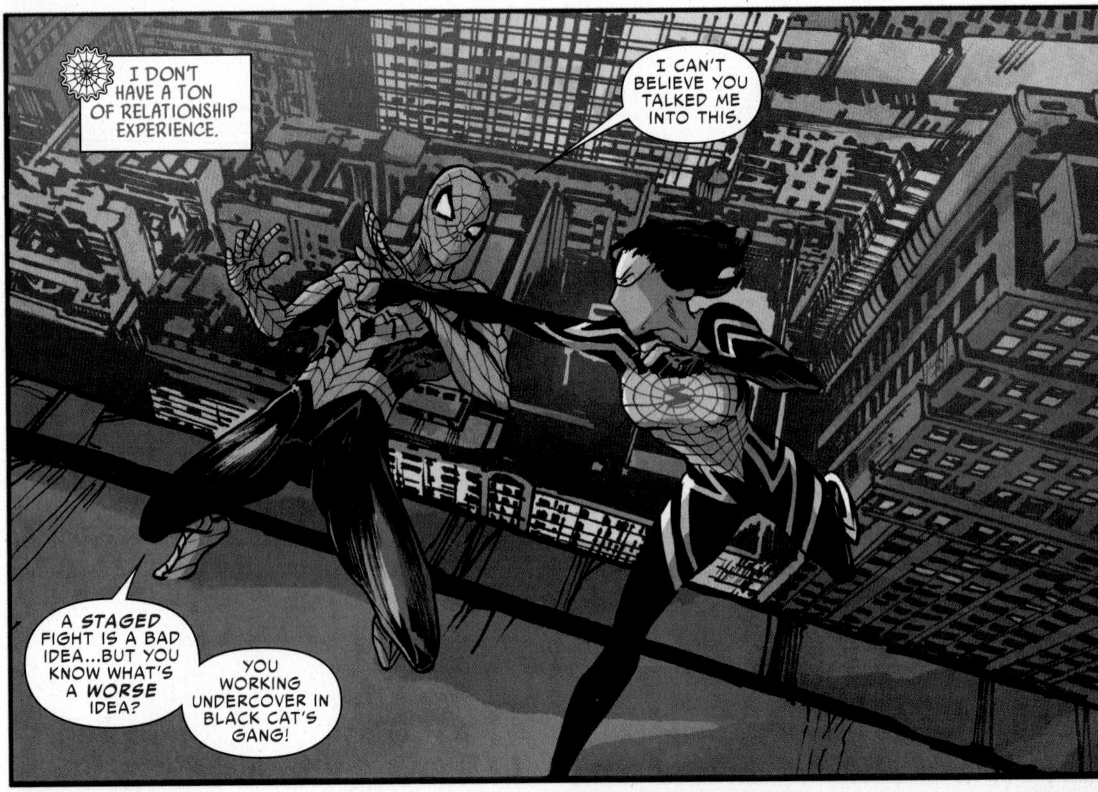
I DON'T HAVE A TON OF RELATIONSHIP EXPERIENCE.
I CAN'T BELIEVE YOU TALKED ME INTO THIS.
A STAGED FIGHT IS A BAD IDEA...BUT YOU KNOW WHAT'S A WORSE IDEA?
YOU WORKING UNDERCOVER IN BLACK CAT'S GANG!

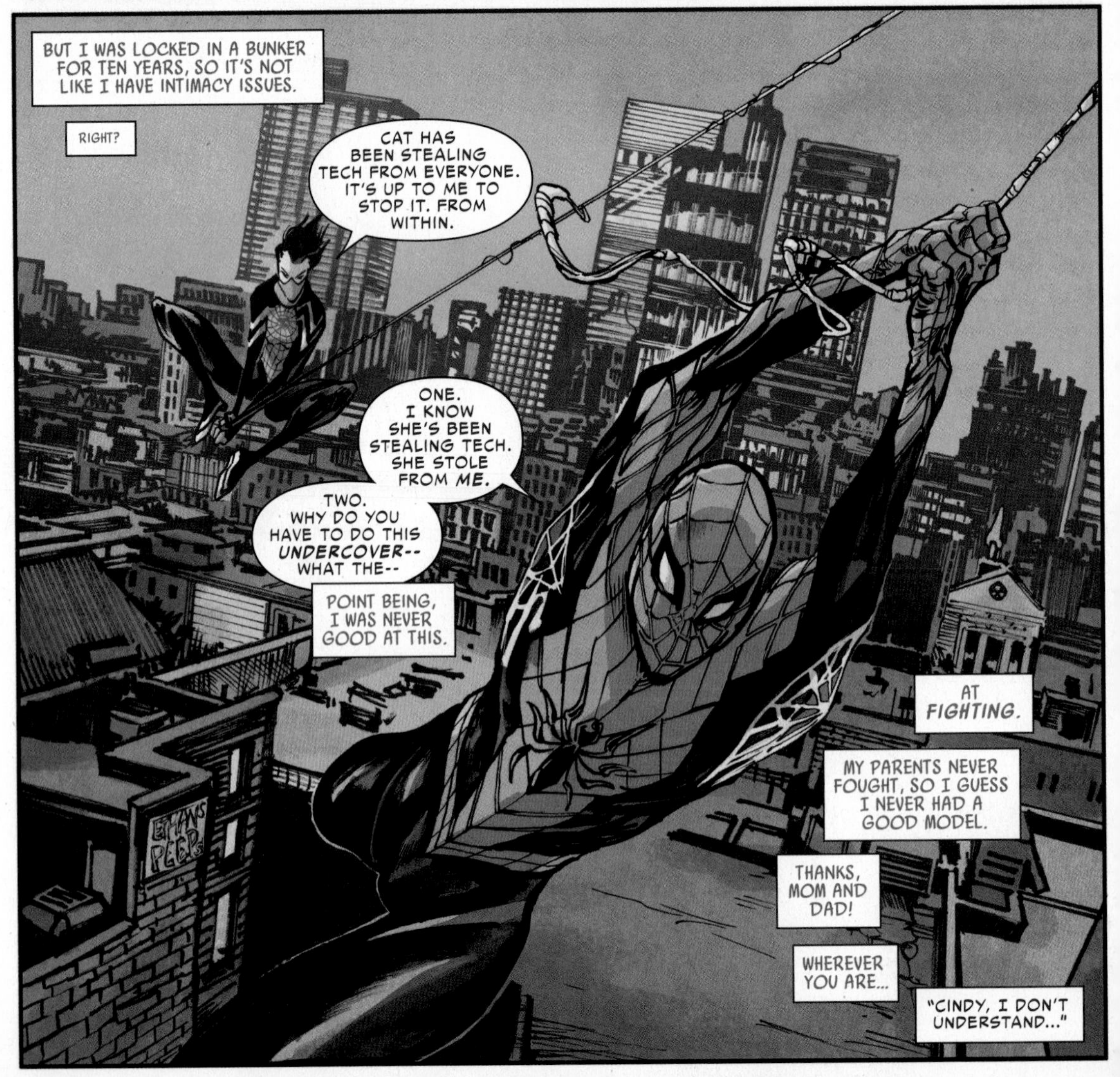
BUT I WAS LOCKED IN A BUNKER FOR TEN YEARS, SO IT'S NOT LIKE I HAVE INTIMACY ISSUES.
RIGHT?
CAT HAS BEEN STEALING TECH FROM EVERYONE. IT'S UP TO ME TO STOP IT. FROM WITHIN.
ONE. I KNOW SHE'S BEEN STEALING TECH. SHE STOLE FROM ME.
TWO. WHY DO YOU HAVE TO DO THIS UNDERCOVER-- WHAT THE--
POINT BEING, I WAS NEVER GOOD AT THIS.
AT FIGHTING.
MY PARENTS NEVER FOUGHT, SO I GUESS I NEVER HAD A GOOD MODEL.
THANKS, MOM AND DAD!
WHEREVER YOU ARE...
"CINDY, I DON'T UNDERSTAND..."

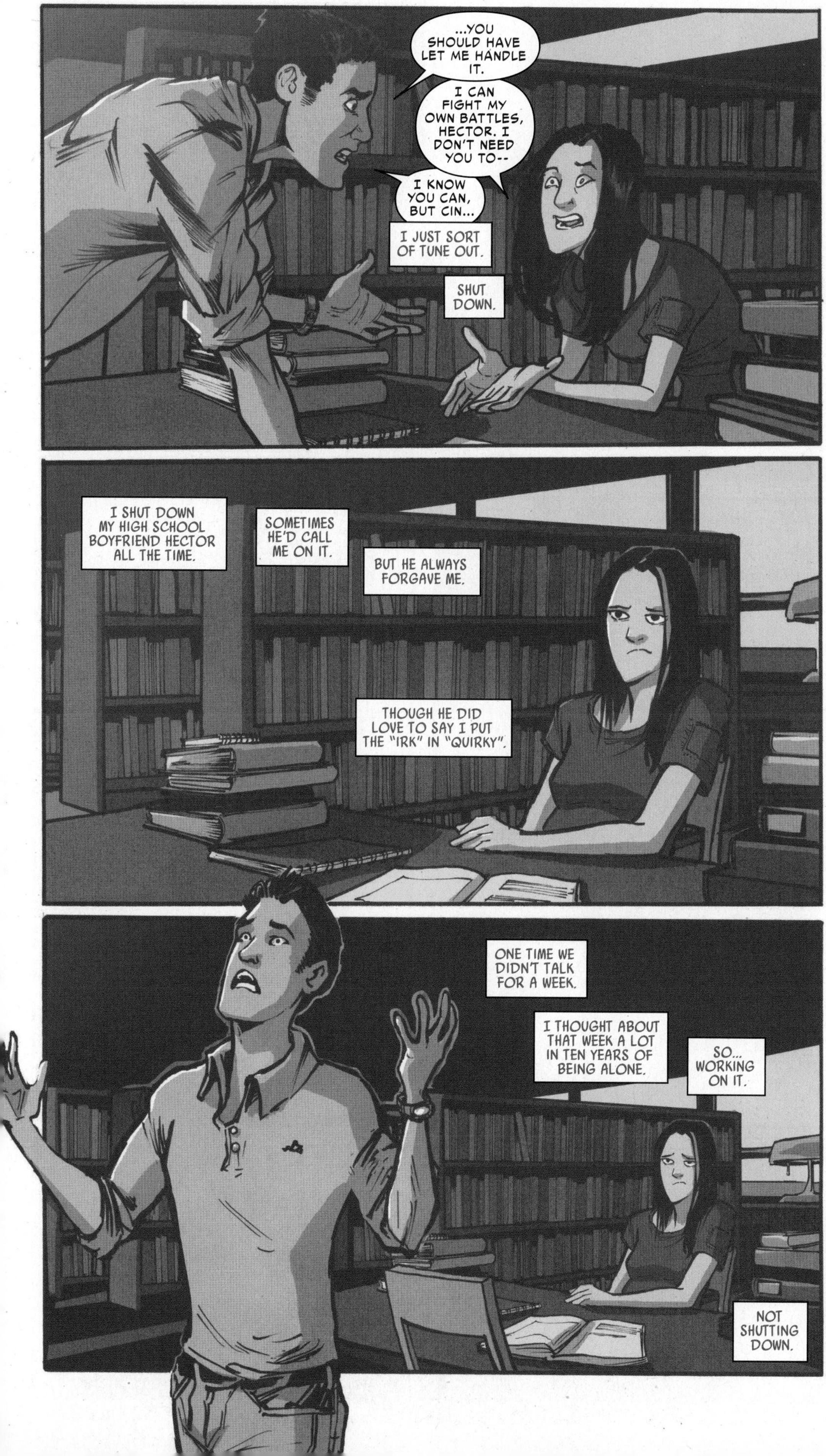
...YOU SHOULD HAVE LET ME HANDLE IT.
I CAN FIGHT MY OWN BATTLES, HECTOR. I DON'T NEED YOU TO--
I KNOW YOU CAN, BUT CIN...
I JUST SORT OF TUNE OUT.
SHUT DOWN.
I SHUT DOWN MY HIGH SCHOOL BOYFRIEND HECTOR ALL THE TIME.
SOMETIMES HE'D CALL ME ON IT.
BUT HE ALWAYS FORGAVE ME.
THOUGH HE DID LOVE TO SAY I PUT THE "IRK" IN "QUIRKY".
ONE TIME WE DIDN'T TALK FOR A WEEK.
I THOUGHT ABOUT THAT WEEK A LOT IN TEN YEARS OF BEING ALONE.
SO... WORKING ON IT.
NOT SHUTTING DOWN.

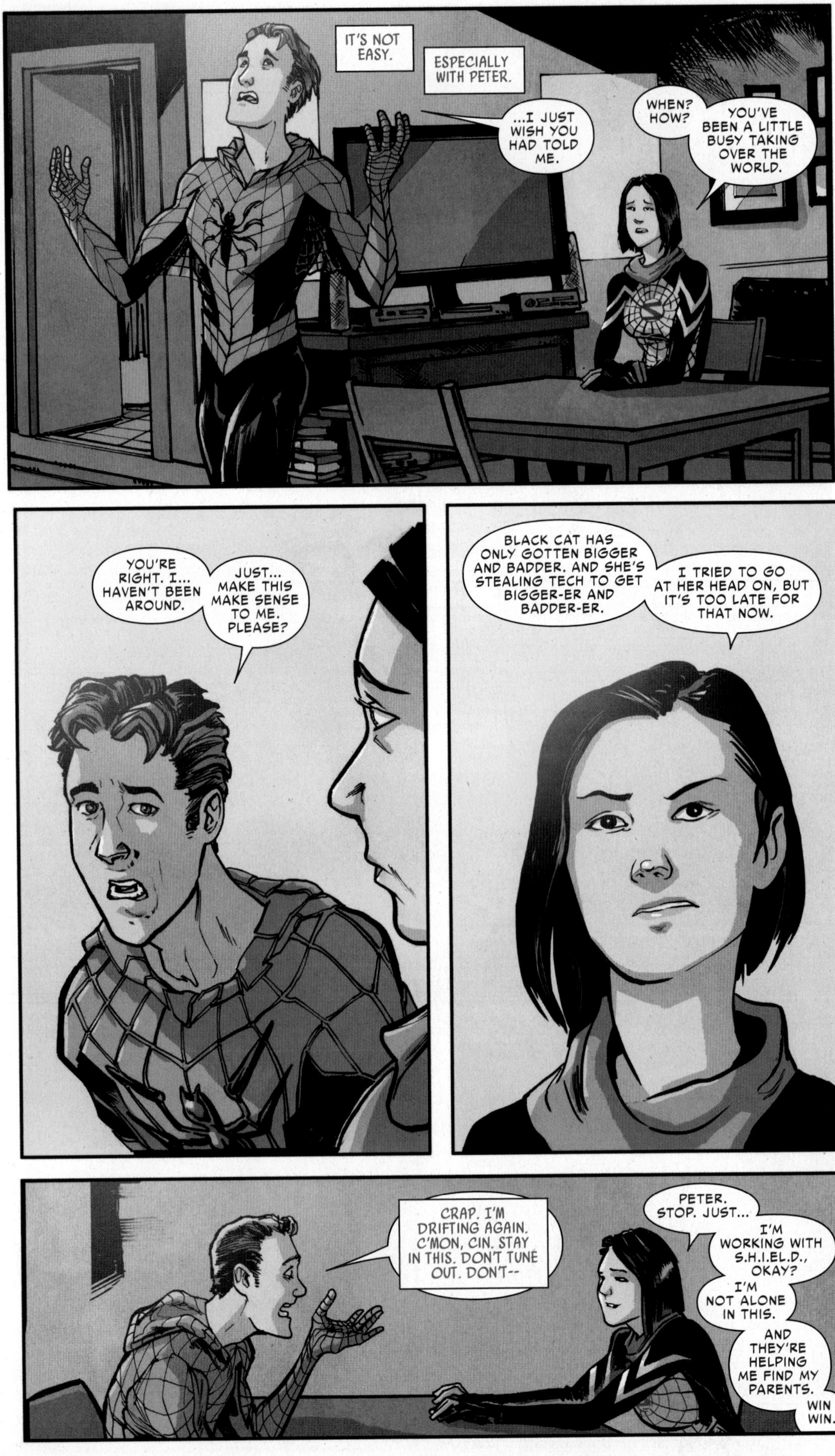
IT'S NOT EASY.
ESPECIALLY WITH PETER.
...I JUST WISH YOU HAD TOLD ME.
WHEN? HOW?
YOU'VE BEEN A LITTLE BUSY TAKING OVER THE WORLD.
YOU'RE RIGHT. I... HAVEN'T BEEN AROUND.
JUST... MAKE THIS MAKE SENSE TO ME. PLEASE?
BLACK CAT HAS ONLY GOTTEN BIGGER AND BADDER. AND SHE'S STEALING TECH TO GET BIGGER-ER AND BADDER-ER.
I TRIED TO GO AT HER HEAD ON, BUT IT'S TOO LATE FOR THAT NOW.
CRAP. I'M DRIFTING AGAIN. C'MON, CIN. STAY IN THIS. DON'T TUNE OUT. DON'T--
PETER. STOP. JUST...
I'M WORKING WITH S.H.I.EL.D., OKAY?
I'M NOT ALONE IN THIS.
AND THEY'RE HELPING ME FIND MY PARENTS.
WIN WIN.

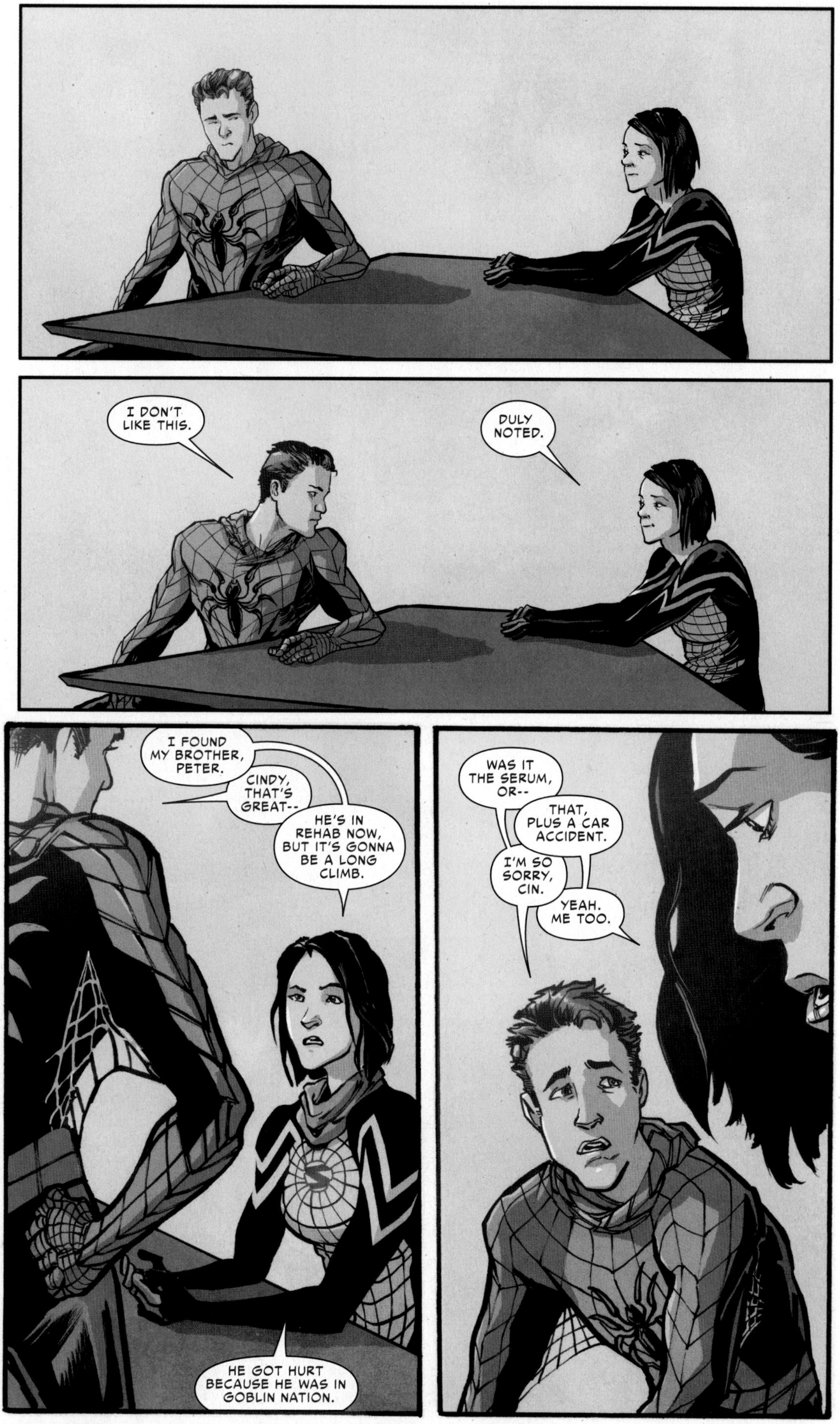
I DON'T LIKE THIS.
DULY NOTED.
I FOUND MY BROTHER, PETER.
CINDY, THAT'S GREAT--
HE'S IN REHAB NOW, BUT IT'S GONNA BE A LONG CLIMB.
HE GOT HURT BECAUSE HE WAS IN GOBLIN NATION.
WAS IT THE SERUM, OR--
THAT, PLUS A CAR ACCIDENT.
I'M SO SORRY, CIN.
YEAH. ME TOO.

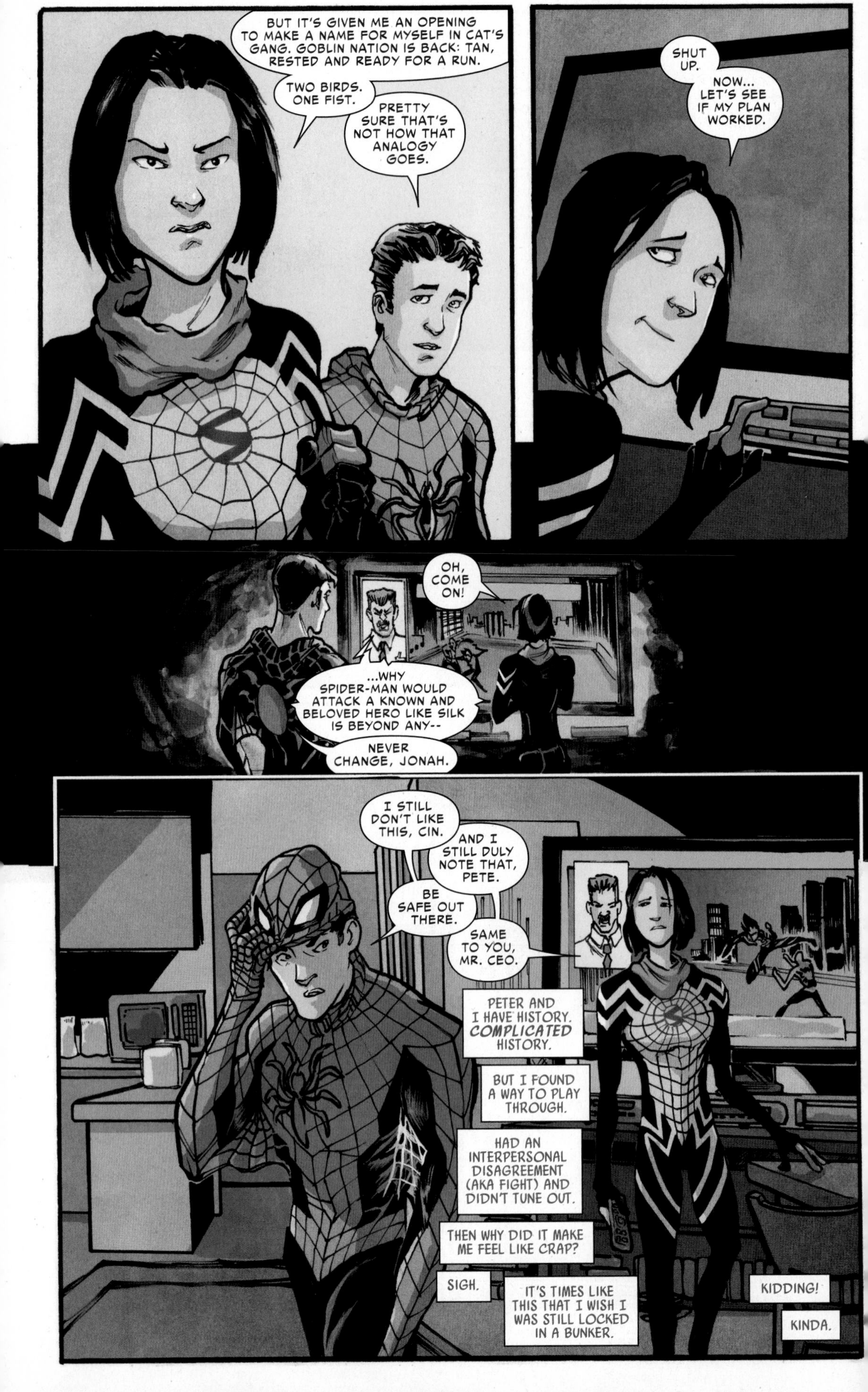
BUT IT'S GIVEN ME AN OPENING TO MAKE A NAME FOR MYSELF IN CAT'S GANG. GOBLIN NATION IS BACK: TAN, RESTED AND READY FOR A RUN.
TWO BIRDS. ONE FIST.
PRETTY SURE THAT'S NOT HOW THAT ANALOGY GOES.
SHUT UP.
NOW... LET'S SEE IF MY PLAN WORKED.
OH, COME ON!
...WHY SPIDER-MAN WOULD ATTACK A KNOWN AND BELOVED HERO LIKE SILK IS BEYOND ANY--
NEVER CHANGE, JONAH.
I STILL DON'T LIKE THIS, CIN.
AND I STILL DULY NOTE THAT, PETE.
BE SAFE OUT THERE.
SAME TO YOU, MR. CEO.
PETER AND I HAVE HISTORY. COMPLICATED HISTORY.
BUT I FOUND A WAY TO PLAY THROUGH.
HAD AN INTERPERSONAL DISAGREEMENT (AKA FIGHT) AND DIDN'T TUNE OUT.
THEN WHY DID IT MAKE ME FEEL LIKE CRAP?
SIGH.
IT'S TIMES LIKE THIS THAT I WISH I WAS STILL LOCKED IN A BUNKER.
KIDDING!
KINDA.

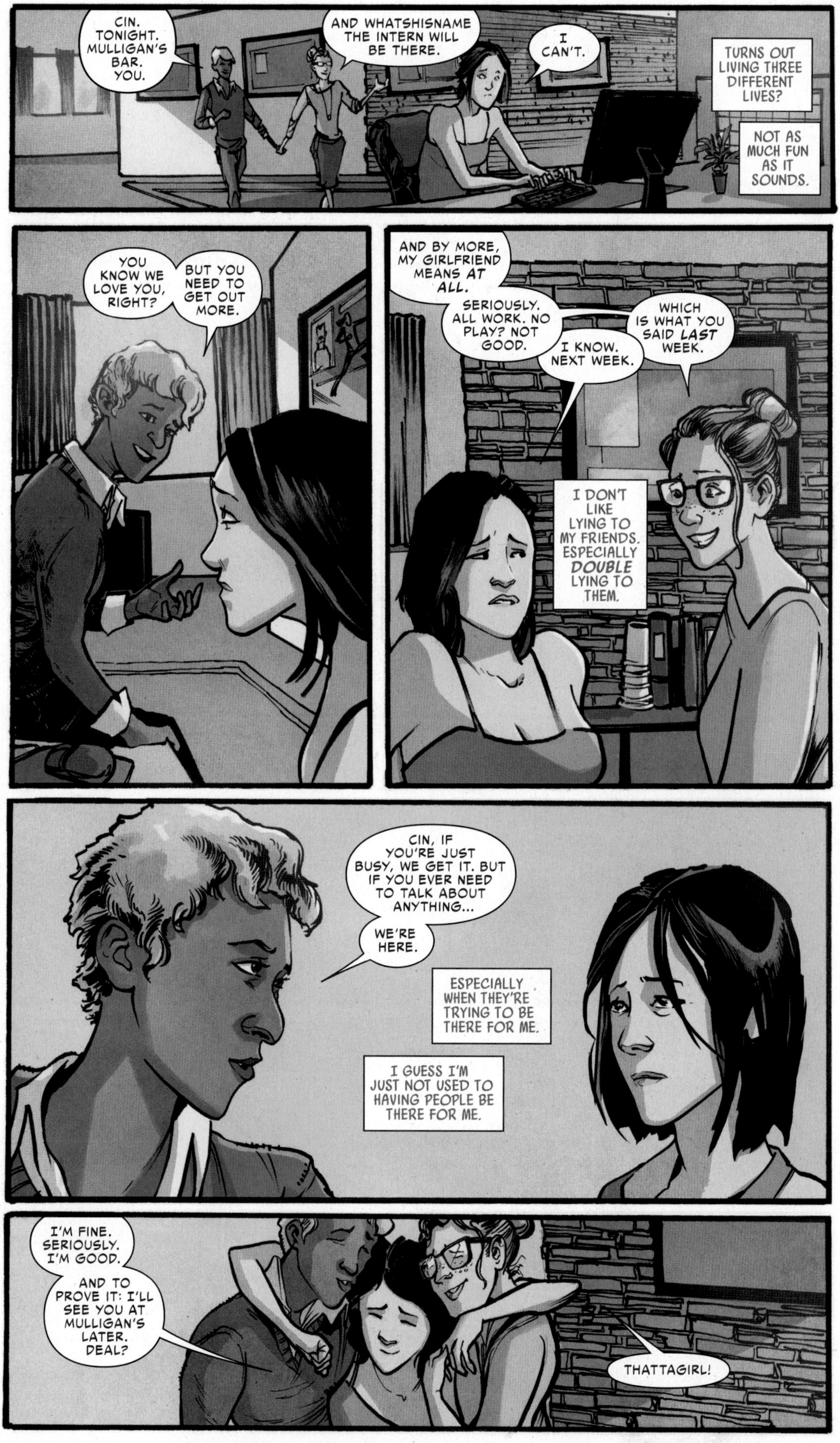
CIN. TONIGHT. MULLIGAN'S BAR. YOU.
AND WHATSHISNAME THE INTERN WILL BE THERE.
I CAN'T.
TURNS OUT LIVING THREE DIFFERENT LIVES?
NOT AS MUCH FUN AS IT SOUNDS.
YOU KNOW WE LOVE YOU, RIGHT?
BUT YOU NEED TO GET OUT MORE.
AND BY MORE, MY GIRLFRIEND MEANS AT ALL.
SERIOUSLY. ALL WORK. NO PLAY? NOT GOOD.
I KNOW. NEXT WEEK.
WHICH IS WHAT YOU SAID LAST WEEK.
I DON'T LIKE LYING TO MY FRIENDS. ESPECIALLY DOUBLE LYING TO THEM.
CIN, IF YOU'RE JUST BUSY, WE GET IT. BUT IF YOU EVER NEED TO TALK ABOUT ANYTHING...
WE'RE HERE.
ESPECIALLY WHEN THEY'RE TRYING TO BE THERE FOR ME.
I GUESS I'M JUST NOT USED TO HAVING PEOPLE BE THERE FOR ME.
I'M FINE. SERIOUSLY. I'M GOOD.
AND TO PROVE IT: I'LL SEE YOU AT MULLIGAN'S LATER. DEAL?
THATTAGIRL!

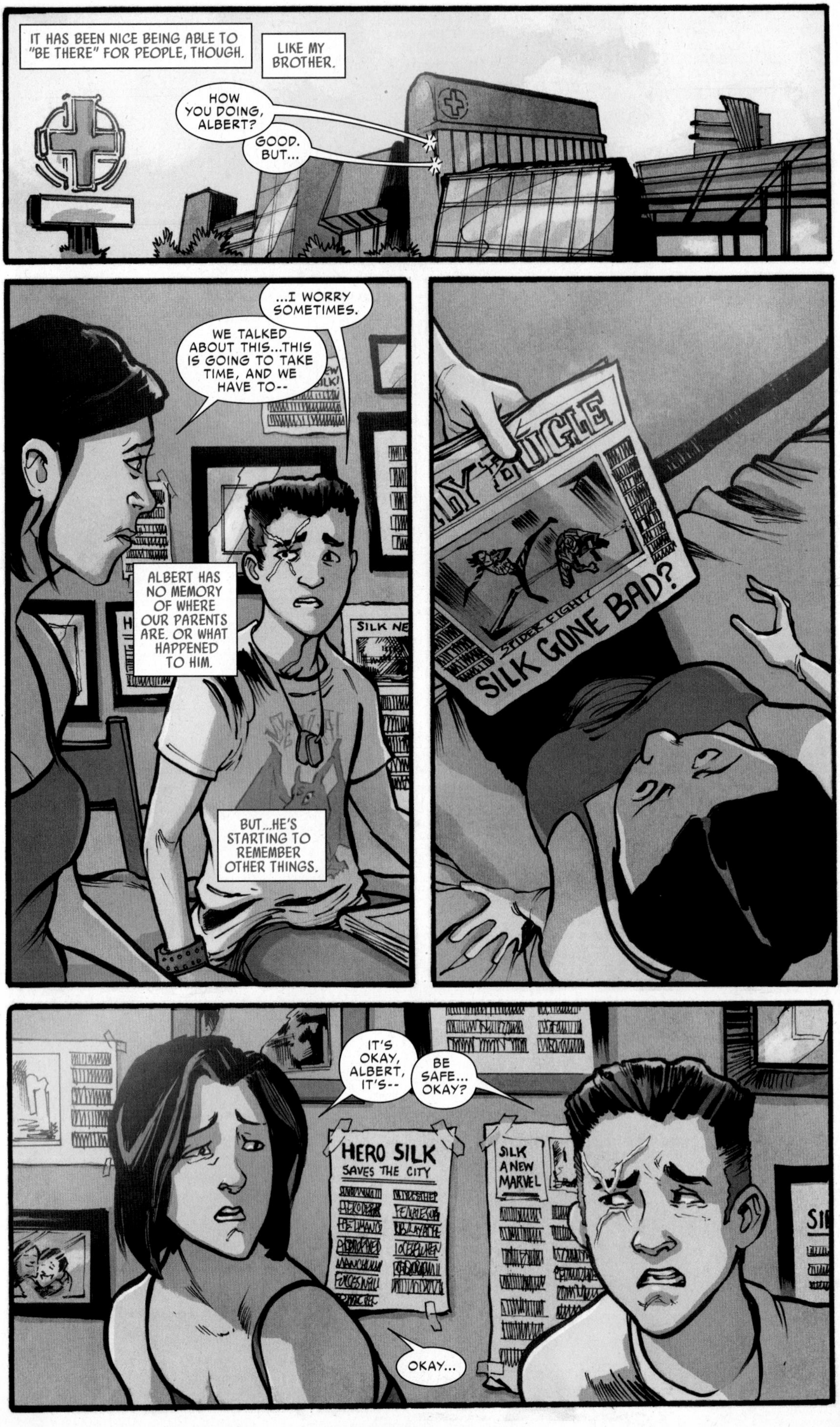
IT HAS BEEN NICE BEING ABLE TO "BE THERE" FOR PEOPLE, THOUGH.
LIKE MY BROTHER.
HOW YOU DOING, ALBERT?
GOOD. BUT...
...I WORRY SOMETIMES.
WE TALKED ABOUT THIS...THIS IS GOING TO TAKE TIME, AND WE HAVE TO--
ALBERT HAS NO MEMORY OF WHERE OUR PARENTS ARE. OR WHAT HAPPENED TO HIM.
BUT...HE'S STARTING TO REMEMBER OTHER THINGS.
SILK GONE BAD?
IT'S OKAY, ALBERT, IT'S--
BE SAFE... OKAY?
HERO SILK
SAVES THE CITY
SILK A NEW MARVEL
OKAY...

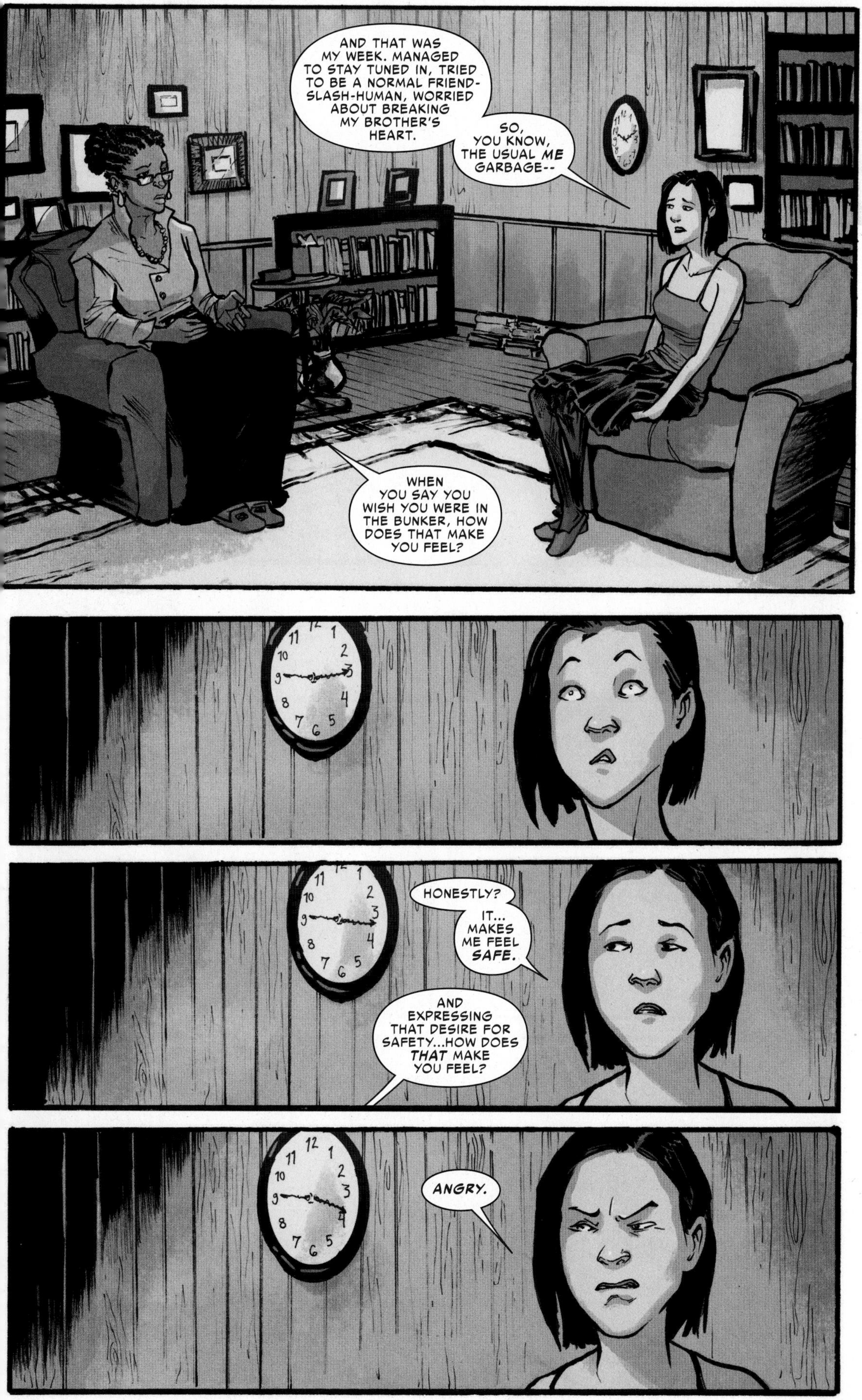
AND THAT WAS MY WEEK. MANAGED TO STAY TUNED IN, TRIED TO BE A NORMAL FRIEND-SLASH-HUMAN, WORRIED ABOUT BREAKING MY BROTHER'S HEART.
SO, YOU KNOW, THE USUAL *ME* GARBAGE--
WHEN YOU SAY YOU WISH YOU WERE IN THE BUNKER, HOW DOES THAT MAKE YOU FEEL?
HONESTLY?
IT... MAKES ME FEEL ***SAFE.***
AND EXPRESSING THAT DESIRE FOR SAFETY...HOW DOES *THAT* MAKE YOU FEEL?
ANGRY.

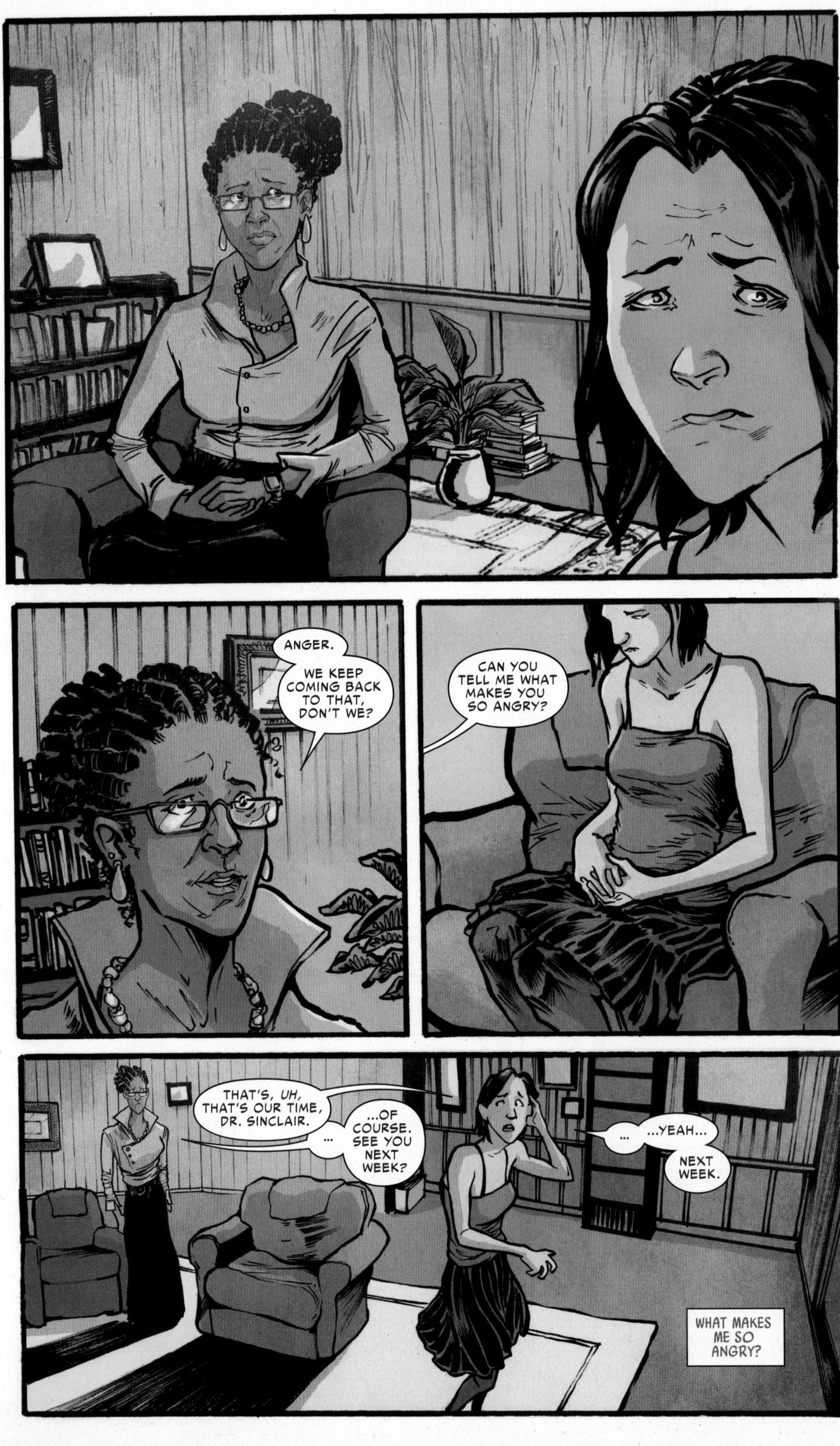
ANGER.
WE KEEP COMING BACK TO THAT, DON'T WE?
CAN YOU TELL ME WHAT MAKES YOU SO ANGRY?
THAT'S, UH, THAT'S OUR TIME, DR. SINCLAIR.
...
...OF COURSE. SEE YOU NEXT WEEK?
...
...YEAH...
NEXT WEEK.
WHAT MAKES ME SO ANGRY?

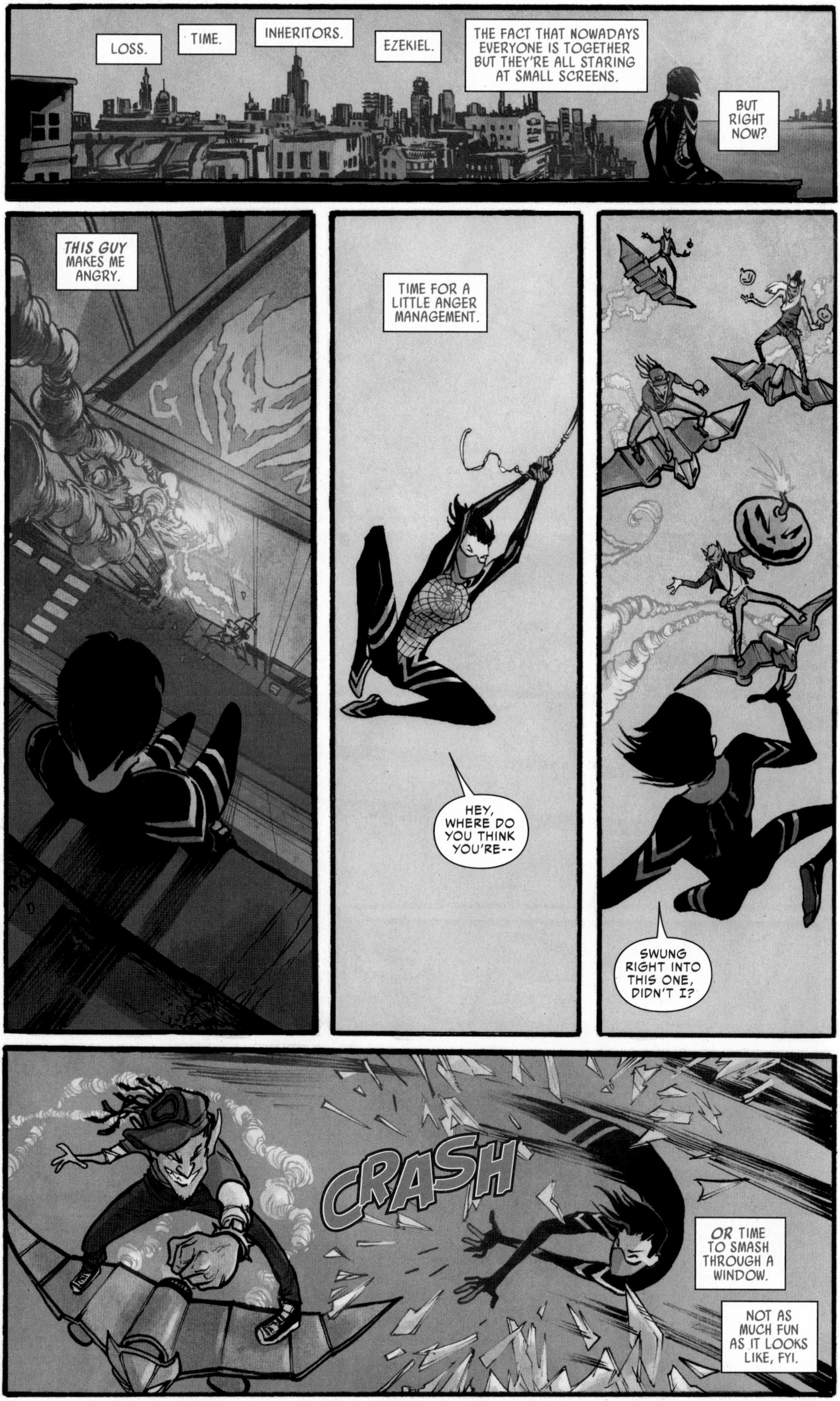
LOSS.
TIME.
INHERITORS.
EZEKIEL.
THE FACT THAT NOWADAYS EVERYONE IS TOGETHER BUT THEY'RE ALL STARING AT SMALL SCREENS.
BUT RIGHT NOW?
THIS GUY MAKES ME ANGRY.
TIME FOR A LITTLE ANGER MANAGEMENT.
HEY, WHERE DO YOU THINK YOU'RE--
SWUNG RIGHT INTO THIS ONE, DIDN'T I?
CRASH
OR TIME TO SMASH THROUGH A WINDOW.
NOT AS MUCH FUN AS IT LOOKS LIKE, FYI.

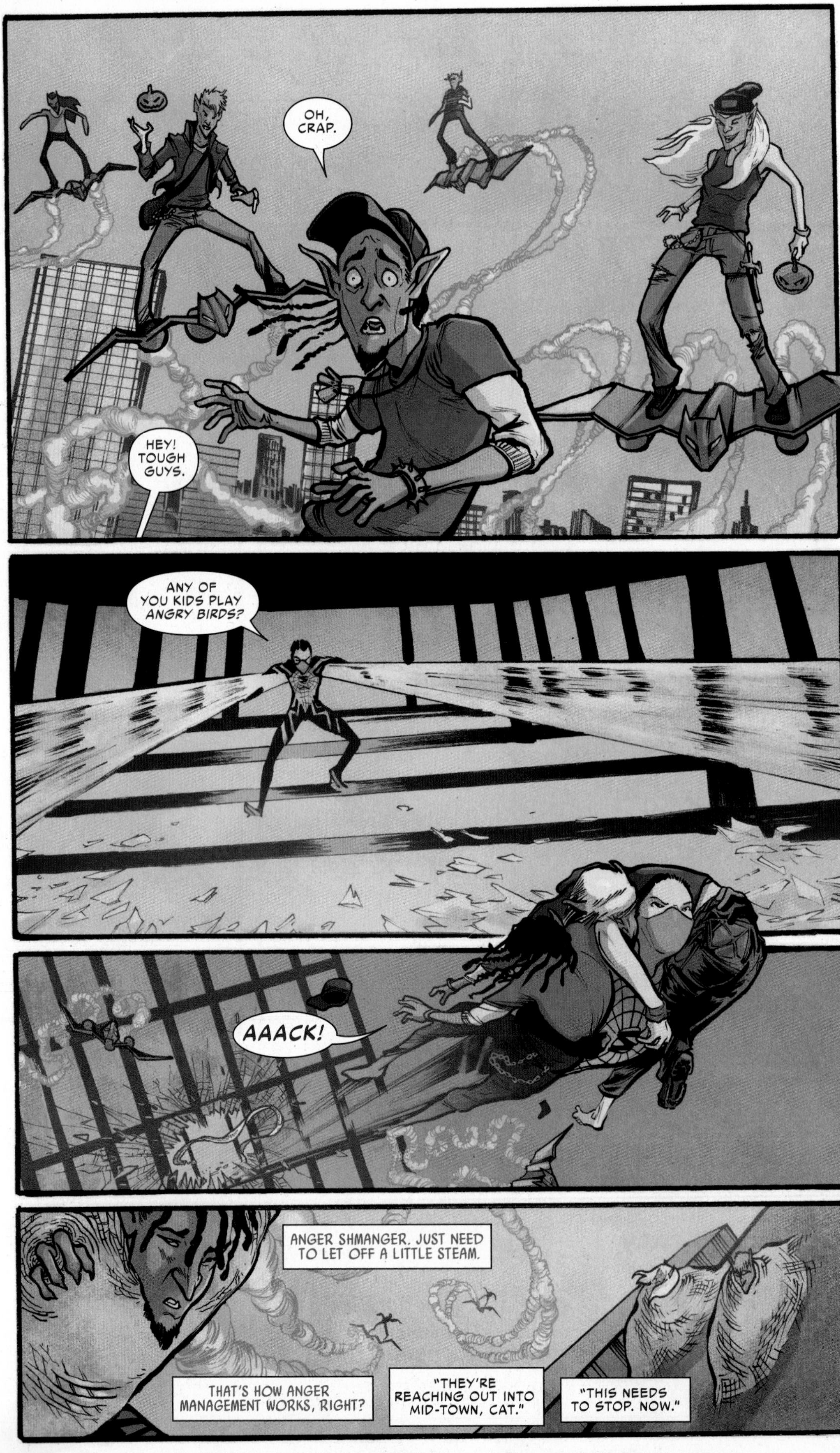
OH, CRAP.
HEY! TOUGH GUYS.
ANY OF YOU KIDS PLAY ANGRY BIRDS?
AAACK!
ANGER SHMANGER. JUST NEED TO LET OFF A LITTLE STEAM.
THAT'S HOW ANGER MANAGEMENT WORKS, RIGHT?
"THEY'RE REACHING OUT INTO MID-TOWN, CAT."
"THIS NEEDS TO STOP. NOW."

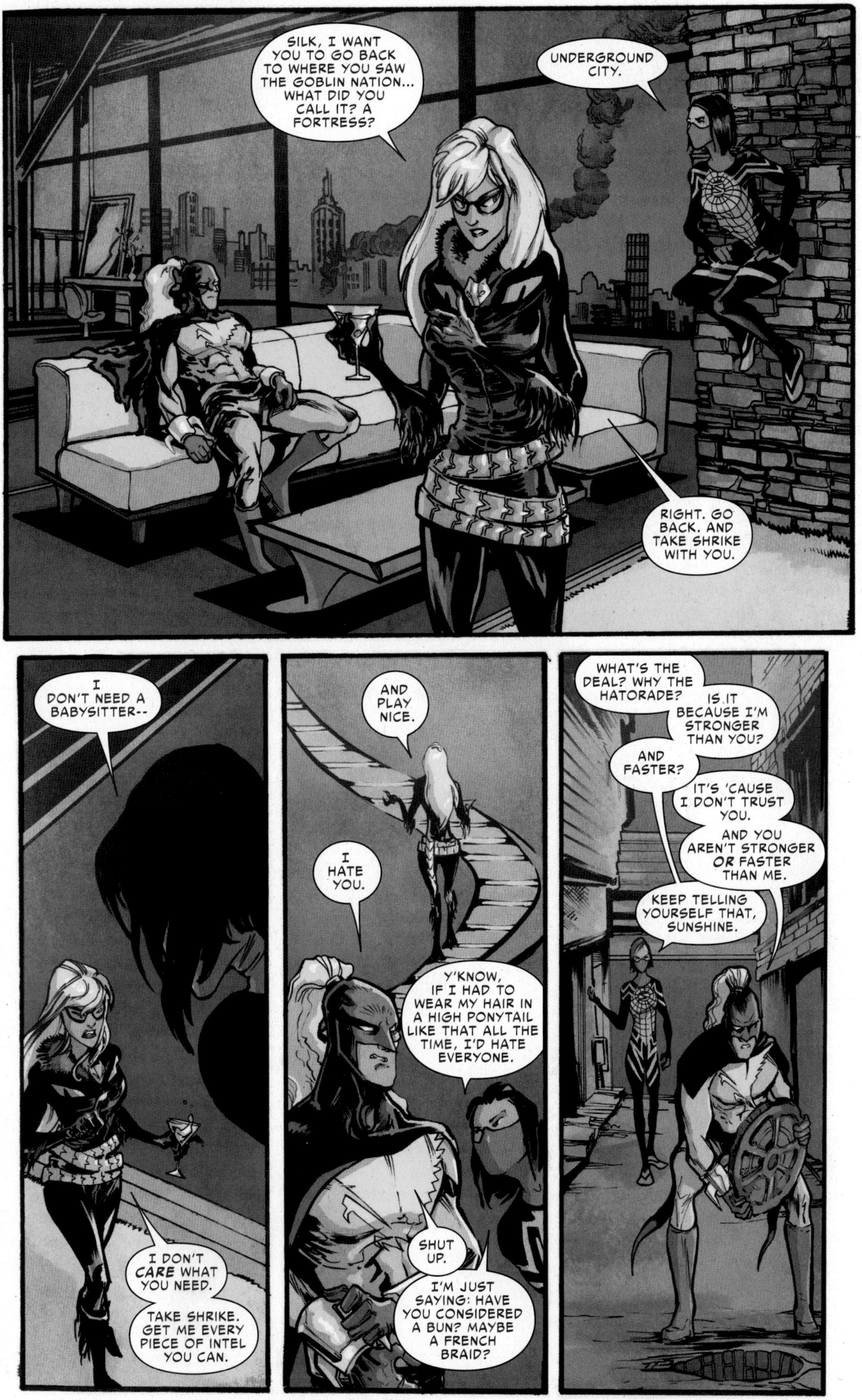

SILK, I WANT YOU TO GO BACK TO WHERE YOU SAW THE GOBLIN NATION... WHAT DID YOU CALL IT? A FORTRESS?
UNDERGROUND CITY.
RIGHT. GO BACK. AND TAKE SHRIKE WITH YOU.
I DON'T NEED A BABYSITTER--
I DON'T CARE WHAT YOU NEED.
TAKE SHRIKE. GET ME EVERY PIECE OF INTEL YOU CAN.
AND PLAY NICE.
I HATE YOU.
Y'KNOW, IF I HAD TO WEAR MY HAIR IN A HIGH PONYTAIL LIKE THAT ALL THE TIME, I'D HATE EVERYONE.
SHUT UP.
I'M JUST SAYING: HAVE YOU CONSIDERED A BUN? MAYBE A FRENCH BRAID?
WHAT'S THE DEAL? WHY THE HATORADE?
IS IT BECAUSE I'M STRONGER THAN YOU?
AND FASTER?
IT'S 'CAUSE I DON'T TRUST YOU.
AND YOU AREN'T STRONGER OR FASTER THAN ME.
KEEP TELLING YOURSELF THAT, SUNSHINE.

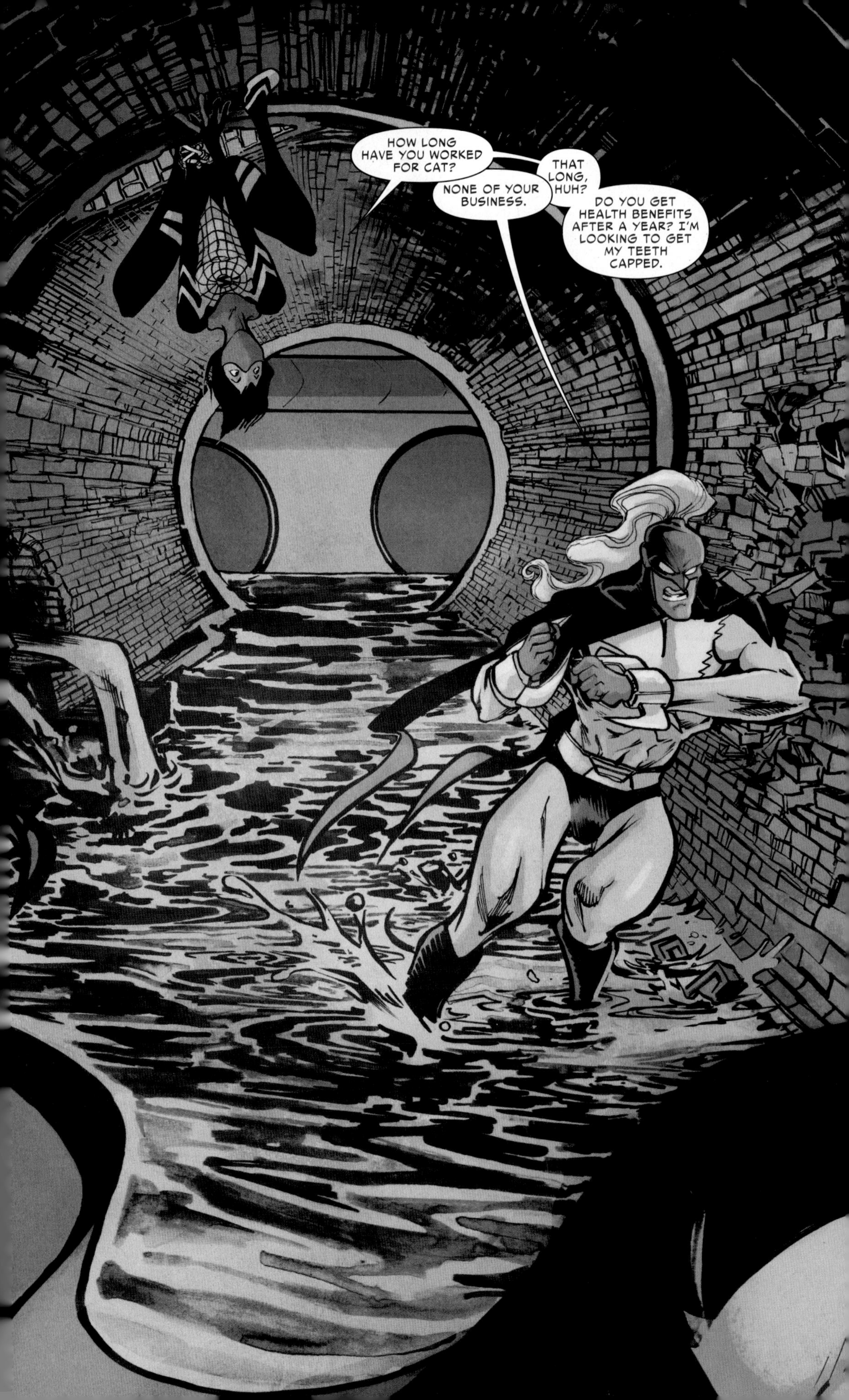
HOW LONG HAVE YOU WORKED FOR CAT?
NONE OF YOUR BUSINESS.
THAT LONG, HUH?
DO YOU GET HEALTH BENEFITS AFTER A YEAR? I'M LOOKING TO GET MY TEETH CAPPED.

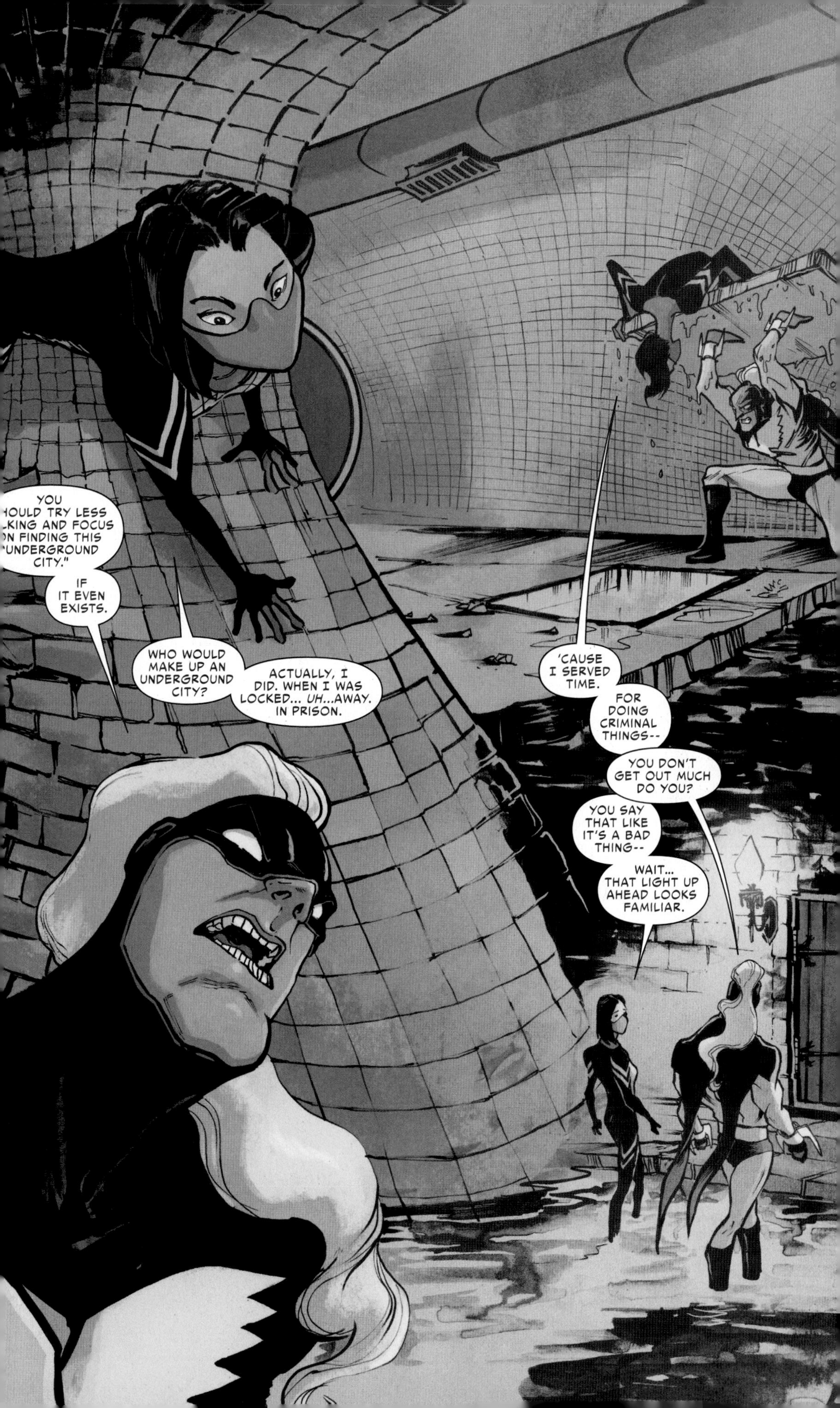

YOU HOULD TRY LESS LKING AND FOCUS ON FINDING THIS "UNDERGROUND CITY."
IF IT EVEN EXISTS.
WHO WOULD MAKE UP AN UNDERGROUND CITY?
ACTUALLY, I DID. WHEN I WAS LOCKED... UH...AWAY. IN PRISON.
'CAUSE I SERVED TIME.
FOR DOING CRIMINAL THINGS--
YOU DON'T GET OUT MUCH DO YOU?
YOU SAY THAT LIKE IT'S A BAD THING--
WAIT... THAT LIGHT UP AHEAD LOOKS FAMILIAR.

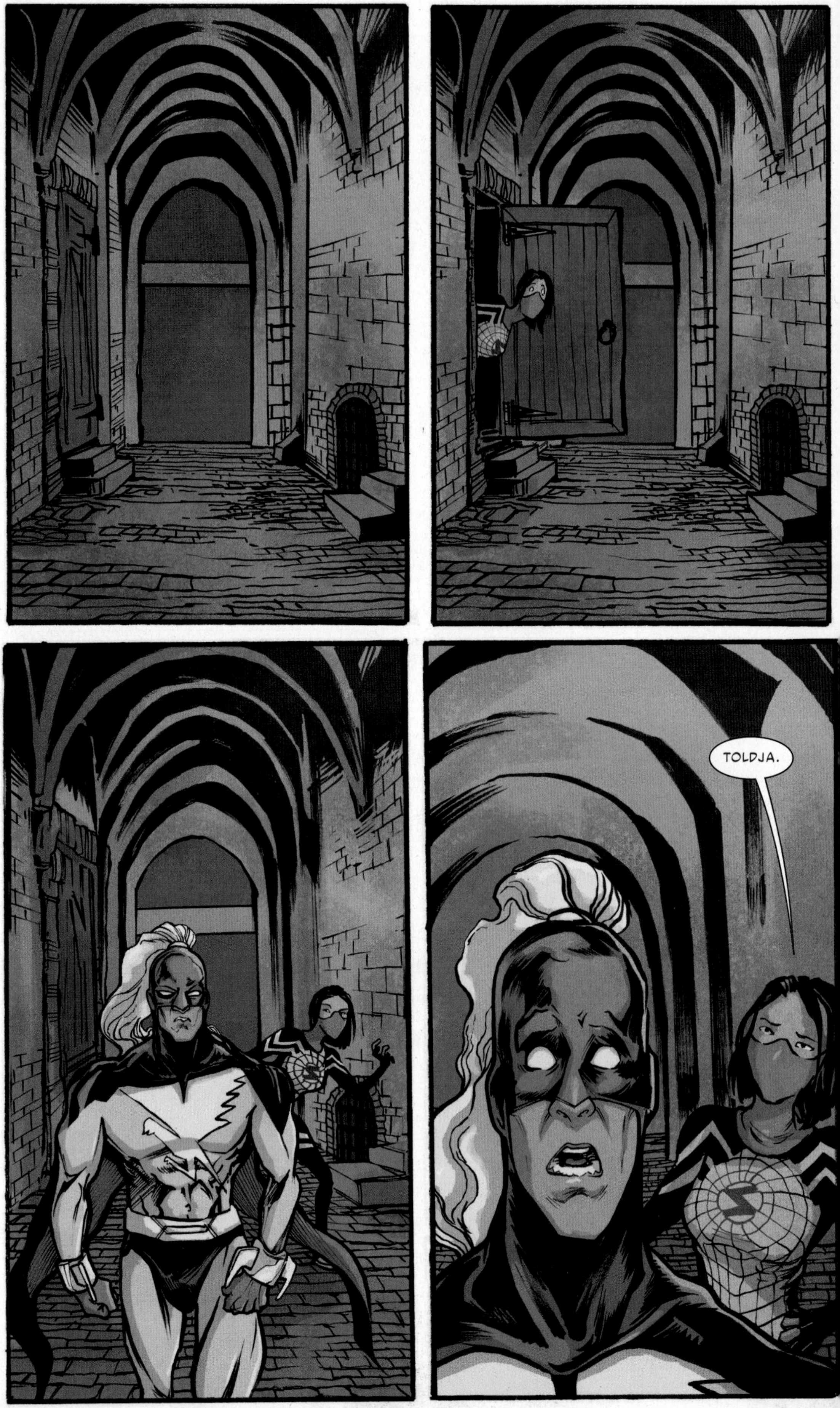
TOLDJA.

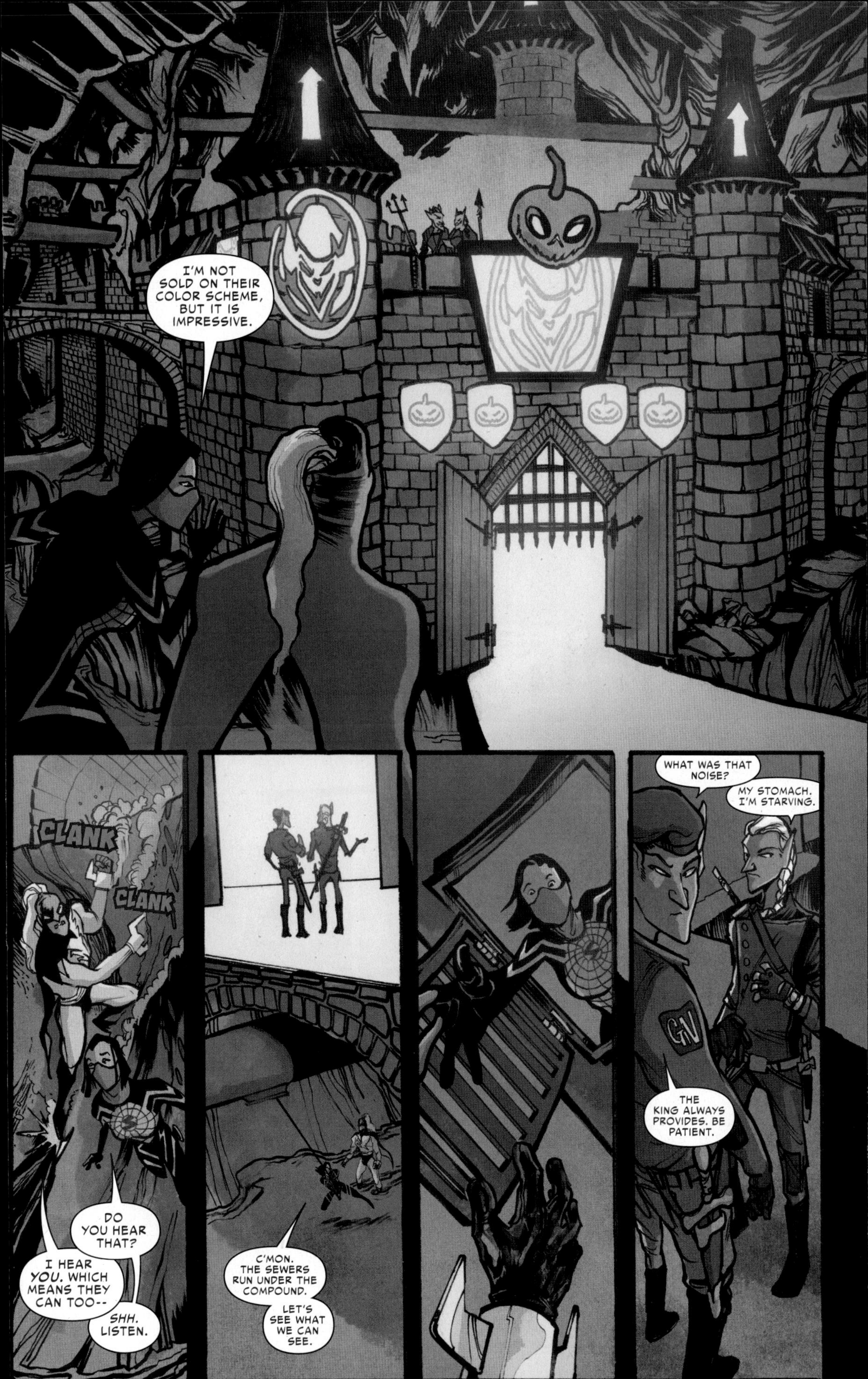
I'M NOT SOLD ON THEIR COLOR SCHEME, BUT IT IS IMPRESSIVE.
CLANK
CLANK
DO YOU HEAR THAT?
I HEAR YOU. WHICH MEANS THEY CAN TOO--
SHH. LISTEN.
C'MON. THE SEWERS RUN UNDER THE COMPOUND.
LET'S SEE WHAT WE CAN SEE.
WHAT WAS THAT NOISE?
MY STOMACH. I'M STARVING.
THE KING ALWAYS PROVIDES. BE PATIENT.

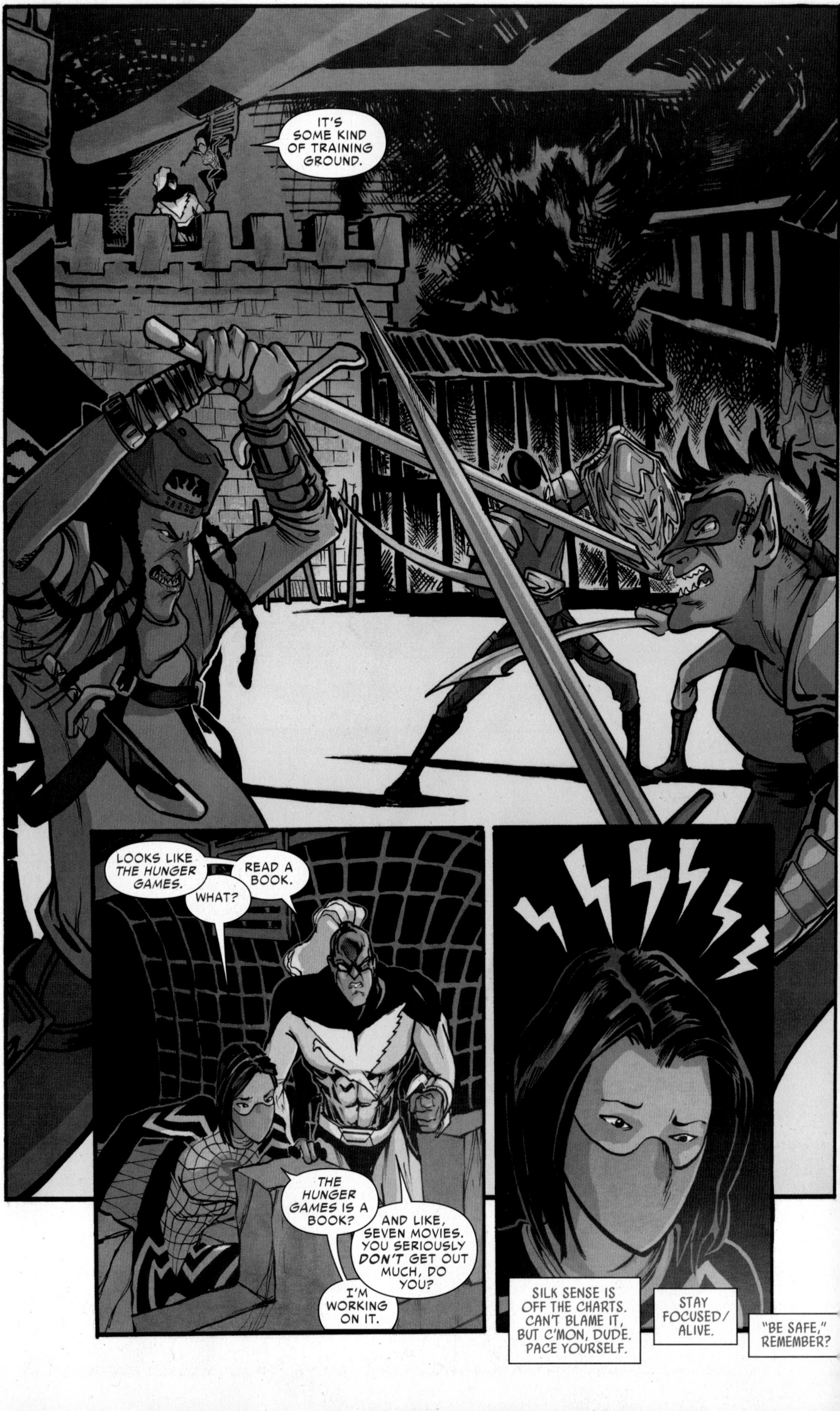
IT'S SOME KIND OF TRAINING GROUND.
LOOKS LIKE THE HUNGER GAMES.
READ A BOOK.
WHAT?
THE HUNGER GAMES IS A BOOK?
AND LIKE, SEVEN MOVIES. YOU SERIOUSLY DON'T GET OUT MUCH, DO YOU?
I'M WORKING ON IT.
SILK SENSE IS OFF THE CHARTS. CAN'T BLAME IT, BUT C'MON, DUDE. PACE YOURSELF.
STAY FOCUSED/ ALIVE.
"BE SAFE," REMEMBER?

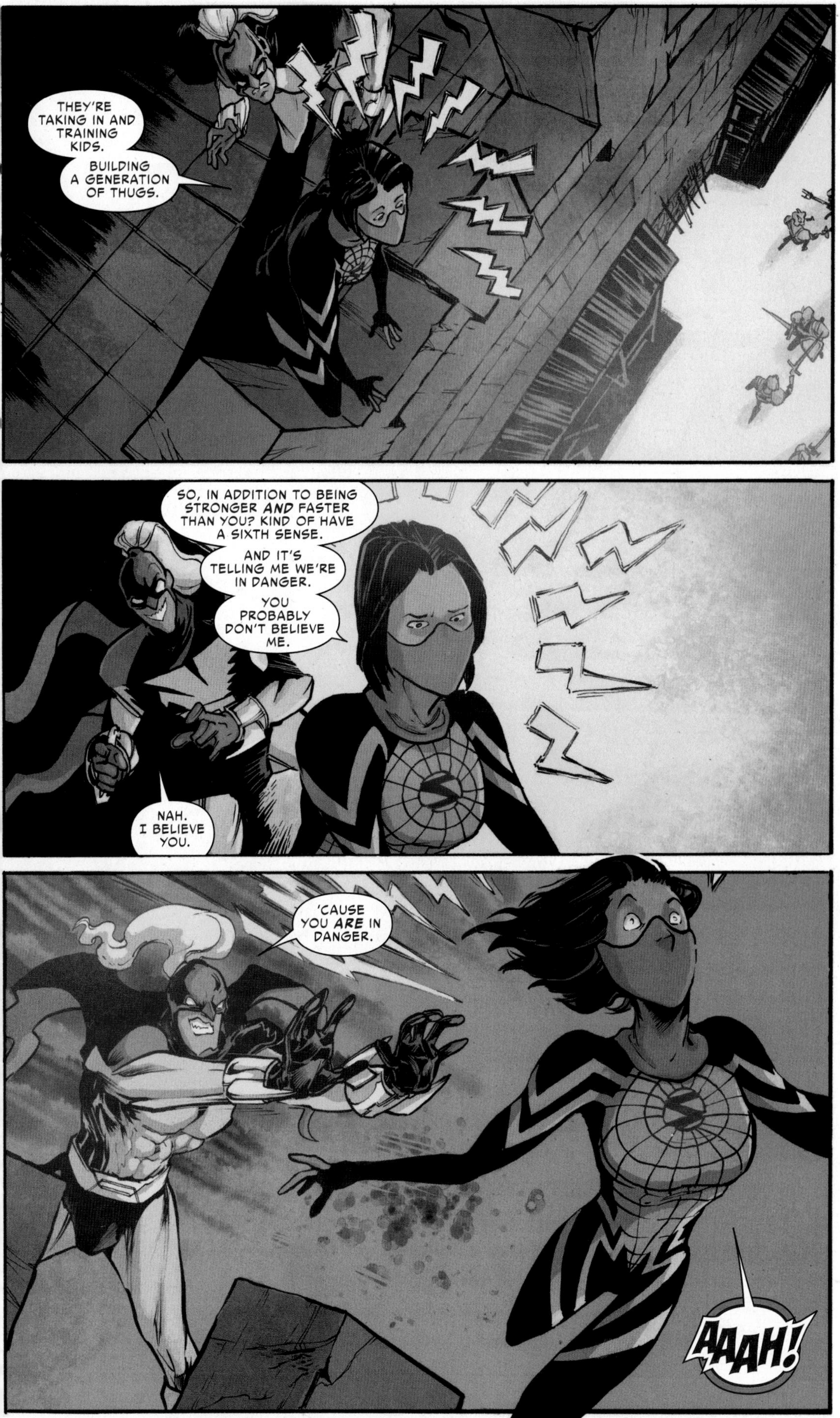
THEY'RE TAKING IN AND TRAINING KIDS.
BUILDING A GENERATION OF THUGS.
SO, IN ADDITION TO BEING STRONGER AND FASTER THAN YOU? KIND OF HAVE A SIXTH SENSE.
AND IT'S TELLING ME WE'RE IN DANGER.
YOU PROBABLY DON'T BELIEVE ME.
NAH. I BELIEVE YOU.
'CAUSE YOU ARE IN DANGER.
AAAH!

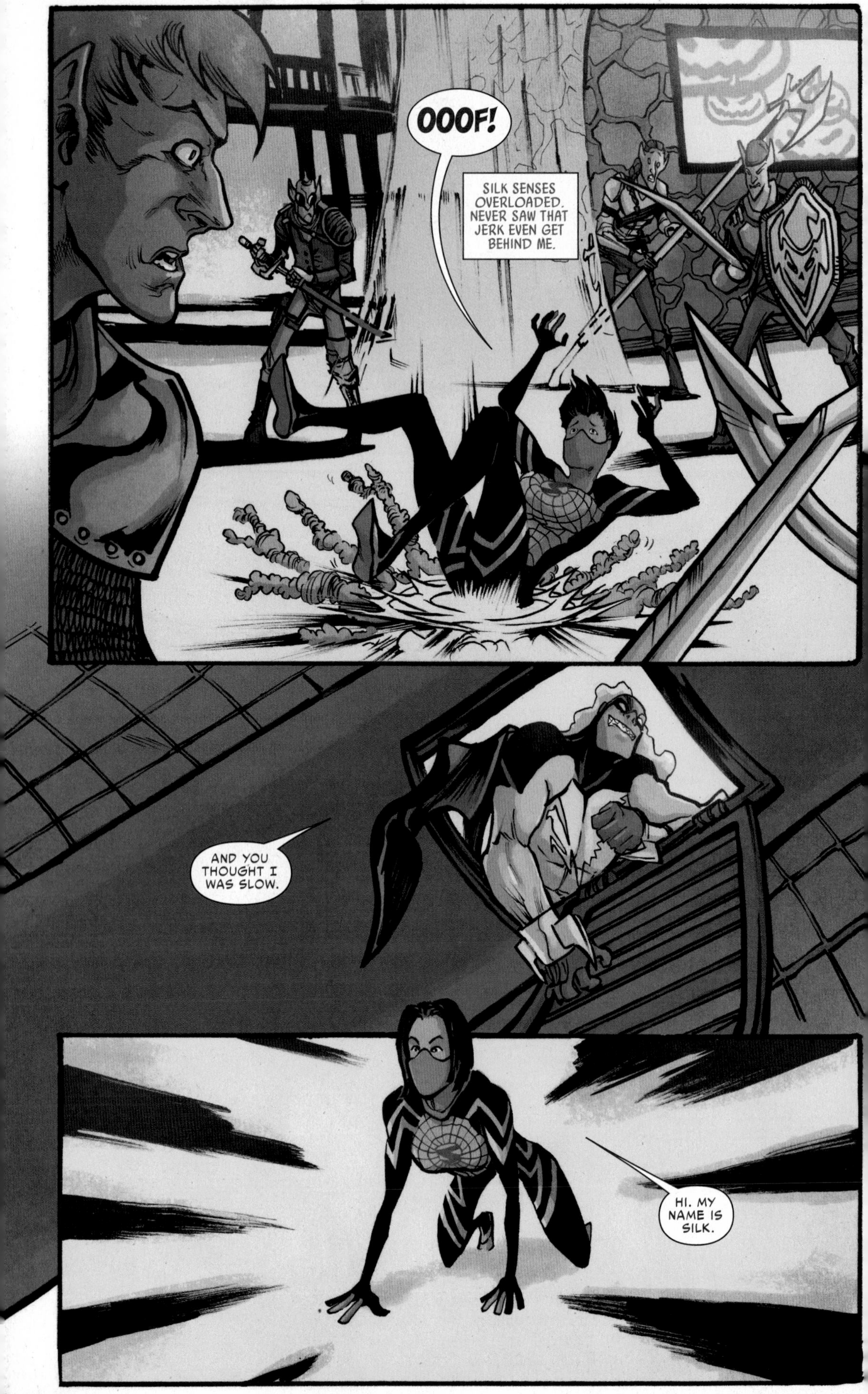
OOOF!
SILK SENSES OVERLOADED. NEVER SAW THAT JERK EVEN GET BEHIND ME.
AND YOU THOUGHT I WAS SLOW.
HI. MY NAME IS SILK.

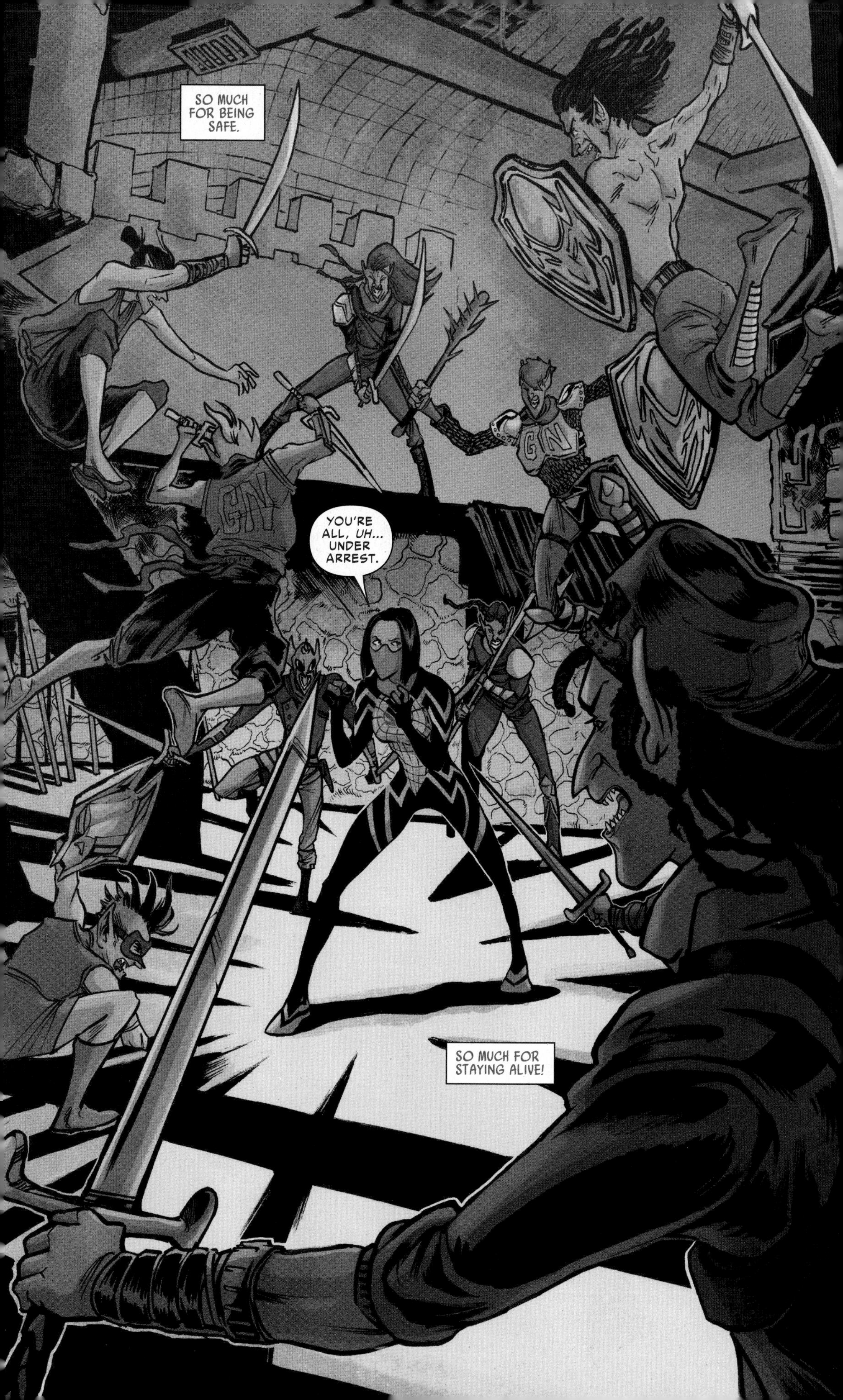
SO MUCH FOR BEING SAFE.
YOU'RE ALL, *UH*... UNDER ARREST.
SO MUCH FOR STAYING ALIVE!

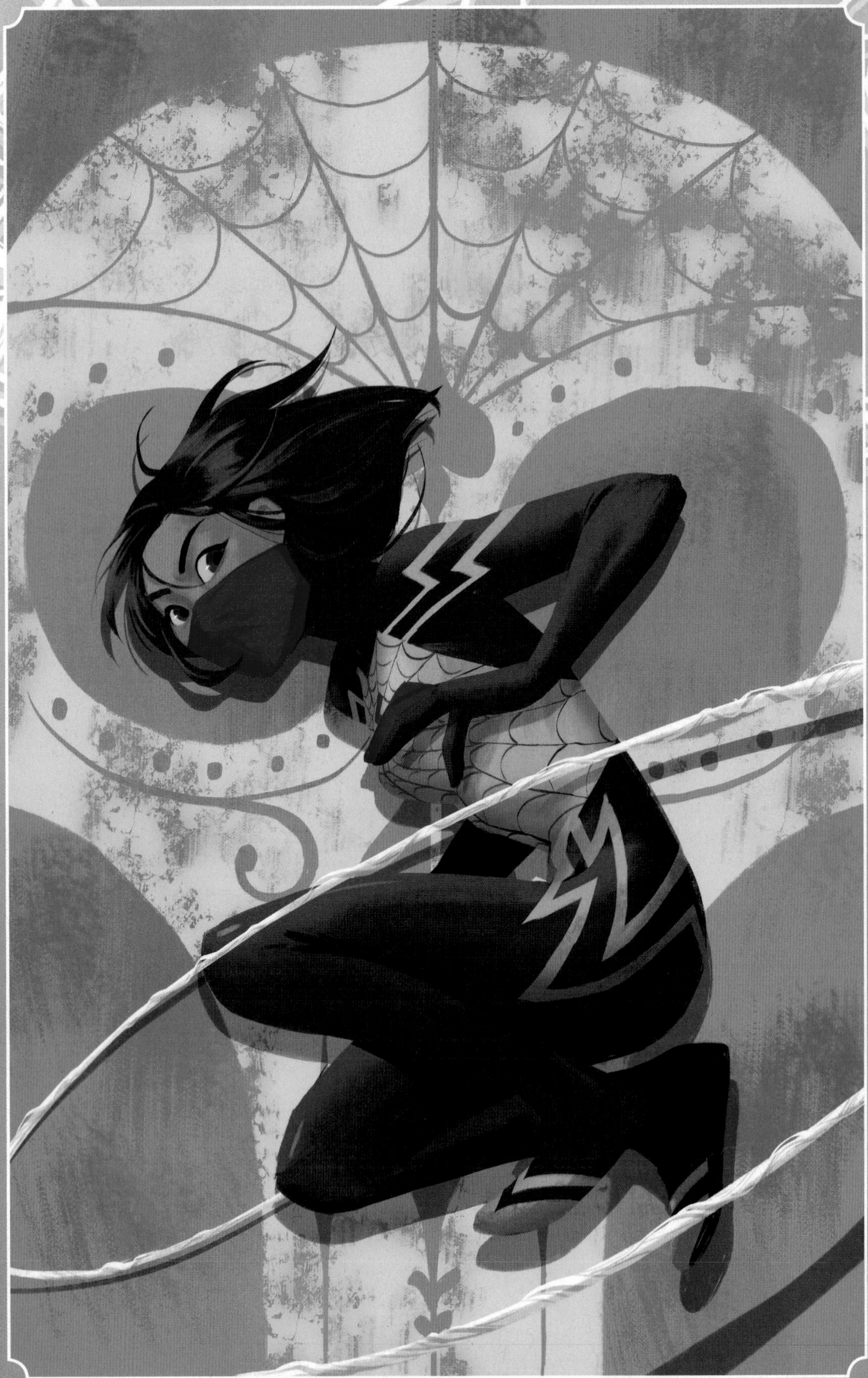

SILK (2015B) #4

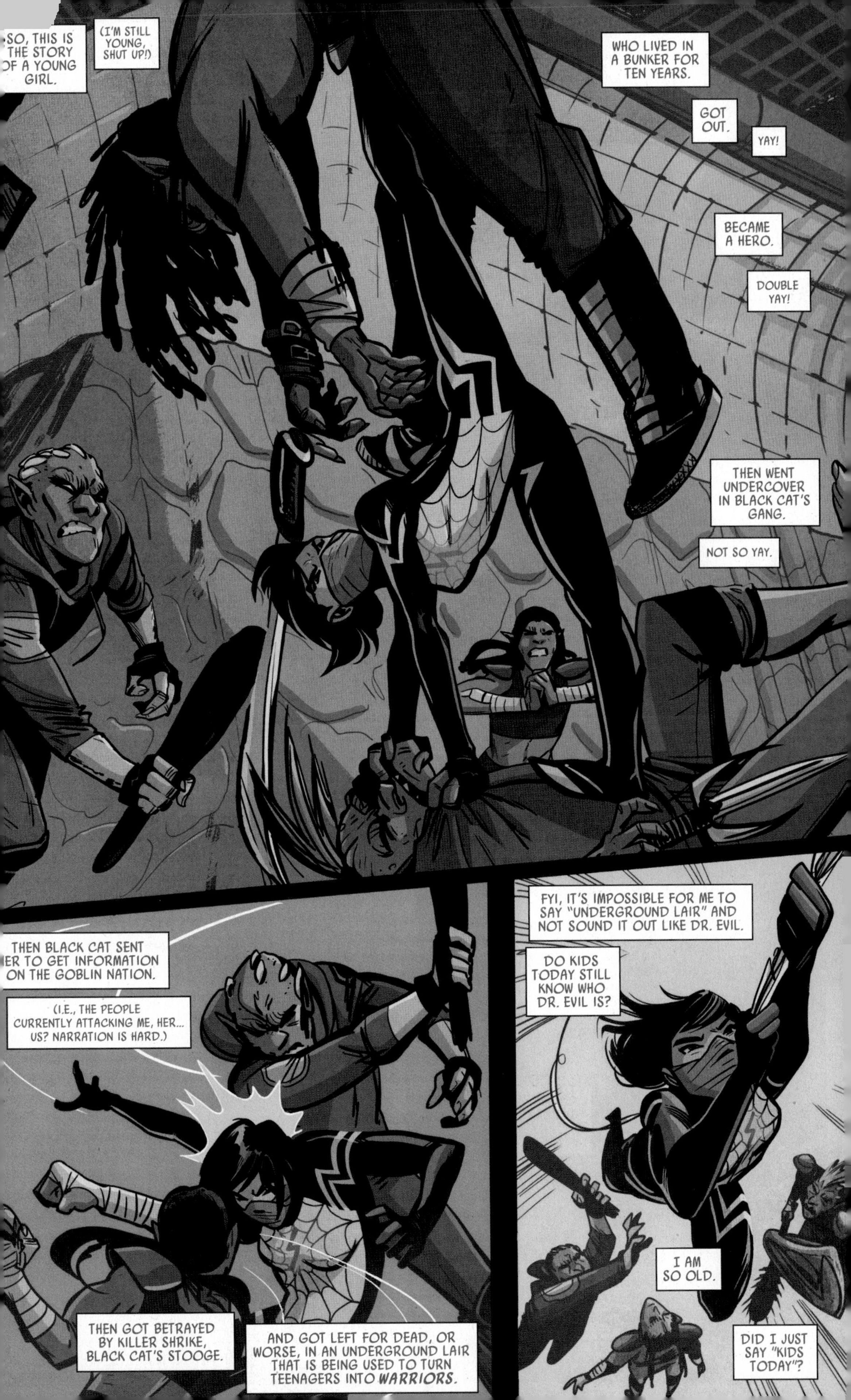
SO, THIS IS THE STORY OF A YOUNG GIRL.
(I'M STILL YOUNG, SHUT UP!)
WHO LIVED IN A BUNKER FOR TEN YEARS.
GOT OUT.
YAY!
BECAME A HERO.
DOUBLE YAY!
THEN WENT UNDERCOVER IN BLACK CAT'S GANG.
NOT SO YAY.
THEN BLACK CAT SENT ER TO GET INFORMATION ON THE GOBLIN NATION.
(I.E., THE PEOPLE CURRENTLY ATTACKING ME, HER... US? NARRATION IS HARD.)
THEN GOT BETRAYED BY KILLER SHRIKE, BLACK CAT'S STOOGE.
AND GOT LEFT FOR DEAD, OR WORSE, IN AN UNDERGROUND LAIR THAT IS BEING USED TO TURN TEENAGERS INTO *WARRIORS*.
FYI, IT'S IMPOSSIBLE FOR ME TO SAY "UNDERGROUND LAIR" AND NOT SOUND IT OUT LIKE DR. EVIL.
DO KIDS TODAY STILL KNOW WHO DR. EVIL IS?
I AM SO OLD.
DID I JUST SAY "KIDS TODAY"?

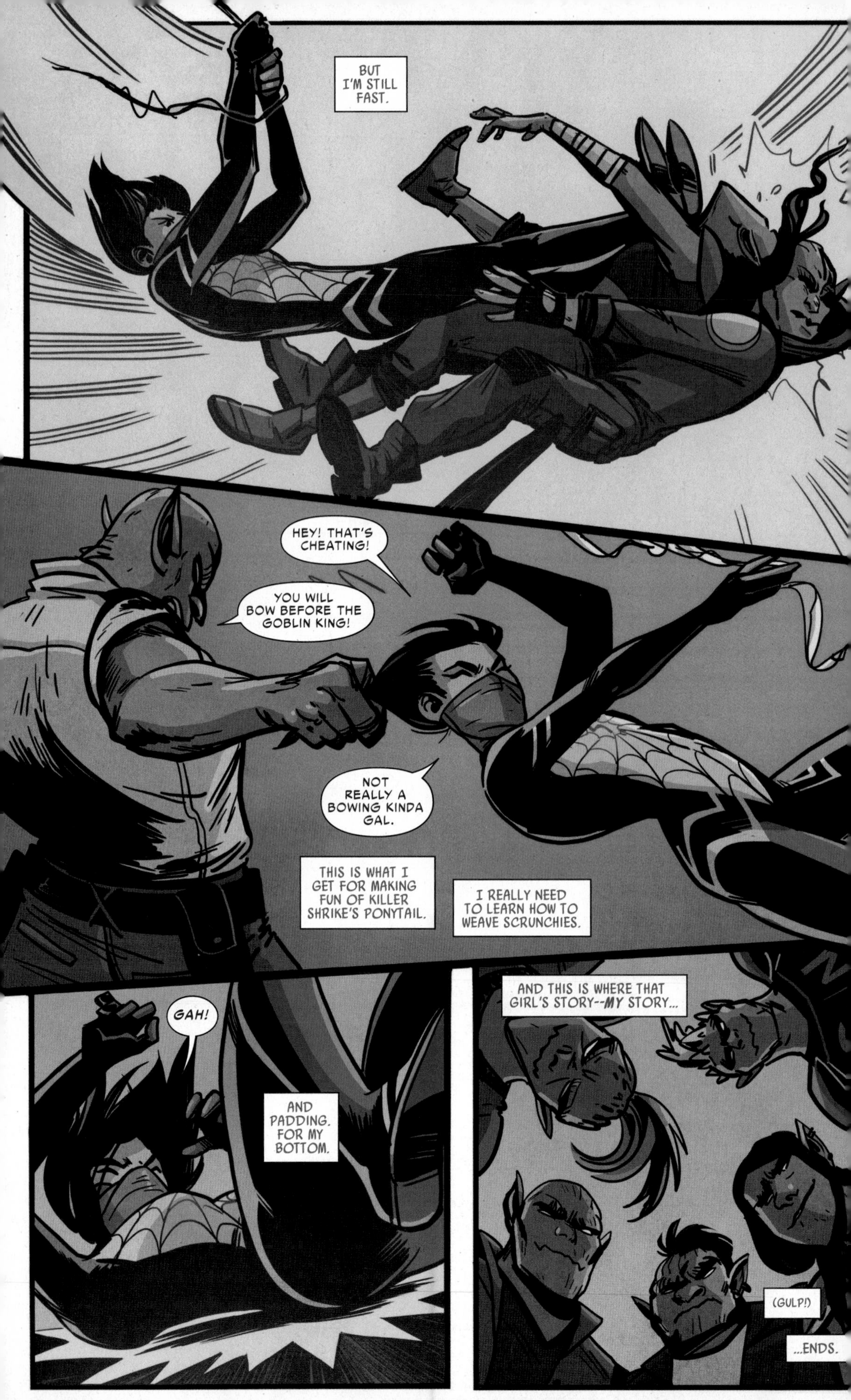
BUT I'M STILL FAST.
HEY! THAT'S CHEATING!
YOU WILL BOW BEFORE THE GOBLIN KING!
NOT REALLY A BOWING KINDA GAL.
THIS IS WHAT I GET FOR MAKING FUN OF KILLER SHRIKE'S PONYTAIL.
I REALLY NEED TO LEARN HOW TO WEAVE SCRUNCHIES.
GAH!
AND PADDING. FOR MY BOTTOM.
AND THIS IS WHERE THAT GIRL'S STORY--MY STORY...
(GULP!)
...ENDS.

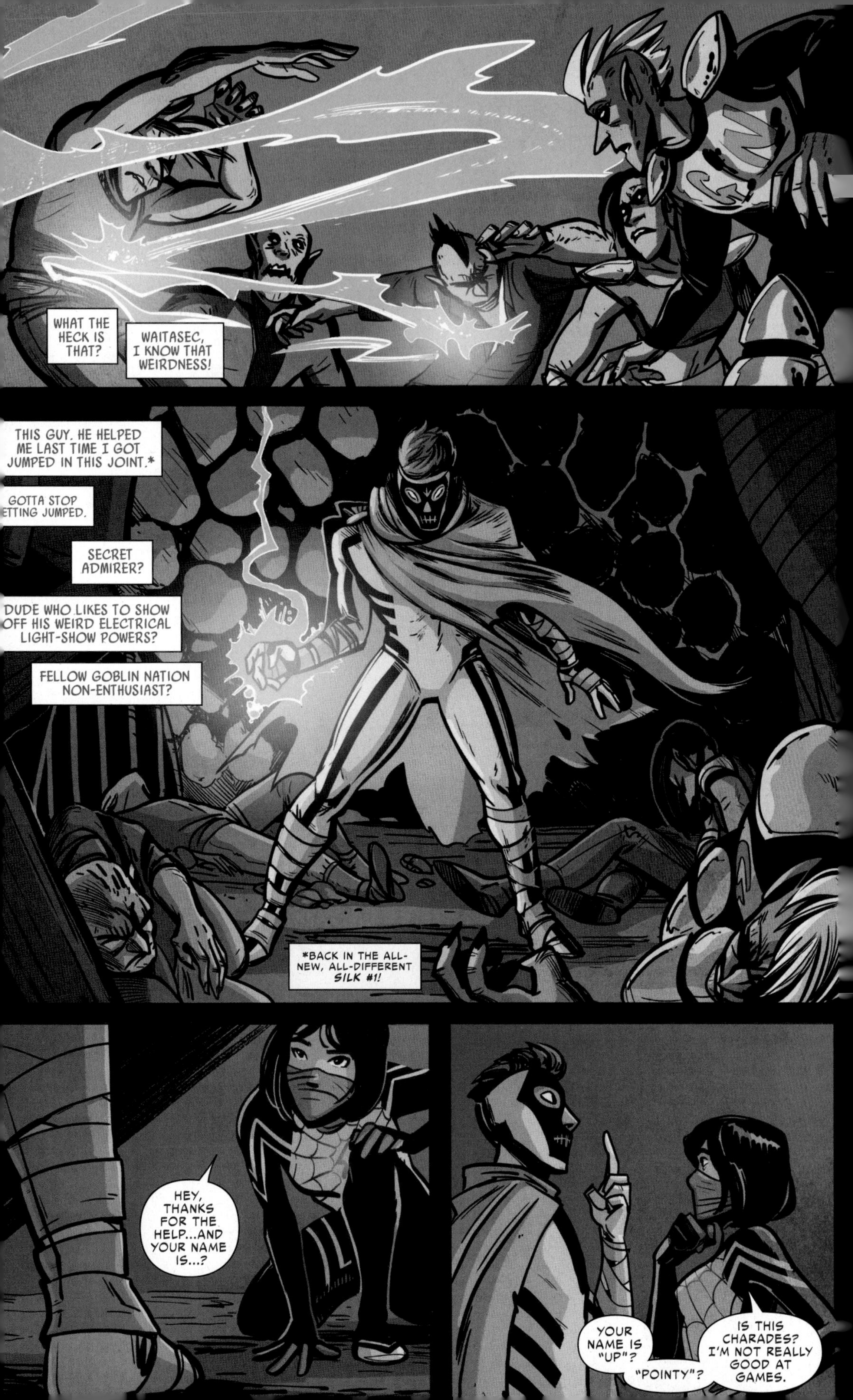
WHAT THE HECK IS THAT?
WAITASEC, I KNOW THAT WEIRDNESS!
THIS GUY. HE HELPED ME LAST TIME I GOT JUMPED IN THIS JOINT.*
GOTTA STOP ETTING JUMPED.
SECRET ADMIRER?
DUDE WHO LIKES TO SHOW OFF HIS WEIRD ELECTRICAL LIGHT-SHOW POWERS?
FELLOW GOBLIN NATION NON-ENTHUSIAST?
*BACK IN THE ALL-NEW, ALL-DIFFERENT SILK #1!
HEY, THANKS FOR THE HELP...AND YOUR NAME IS...?
YOUR NAME IS "UP"?
"POINTY"?
IS THIS CHARADES? I'M NOT REALLY GOOD AT GAMES.

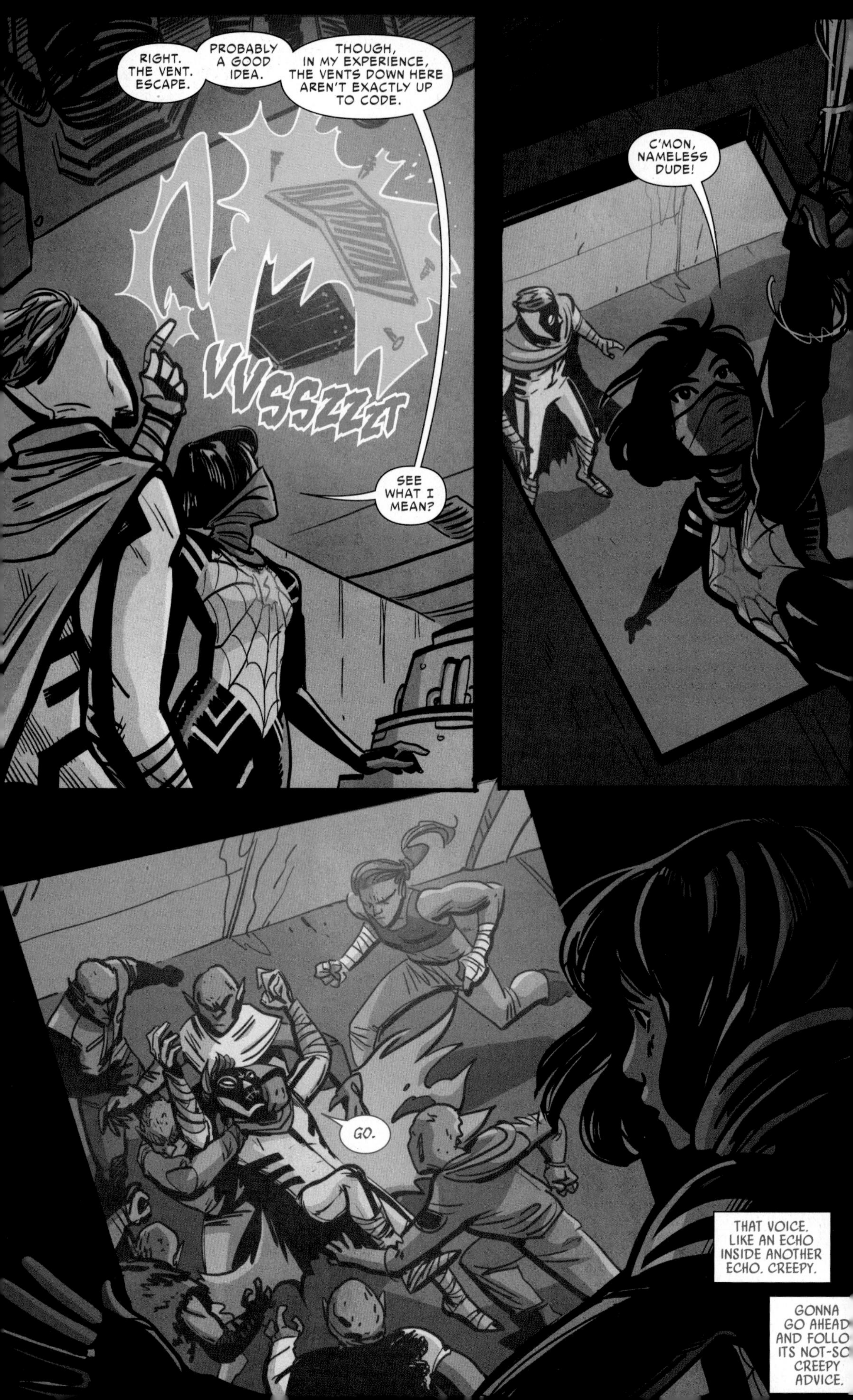

RIGHT. THE VENT. ESCAPE.
PROBABLY A GOOD IDEA.
THOUGH, IN MY EXPERIENCE, THE VENTS DOWN HERE AREN'T EXACTLY UP TO CODE.
VVSSZZZT
SEE WHAT I MEAN?
C'MON, NAMELESS DUDE!
GO.
THAT VOICE. LIKE AN ECHO INSIDE ANOTHER ECHO. CREEPY.
GONNA GO AHEAD AND FOLLO ITS NOT-SO CREEPY ADVICE.

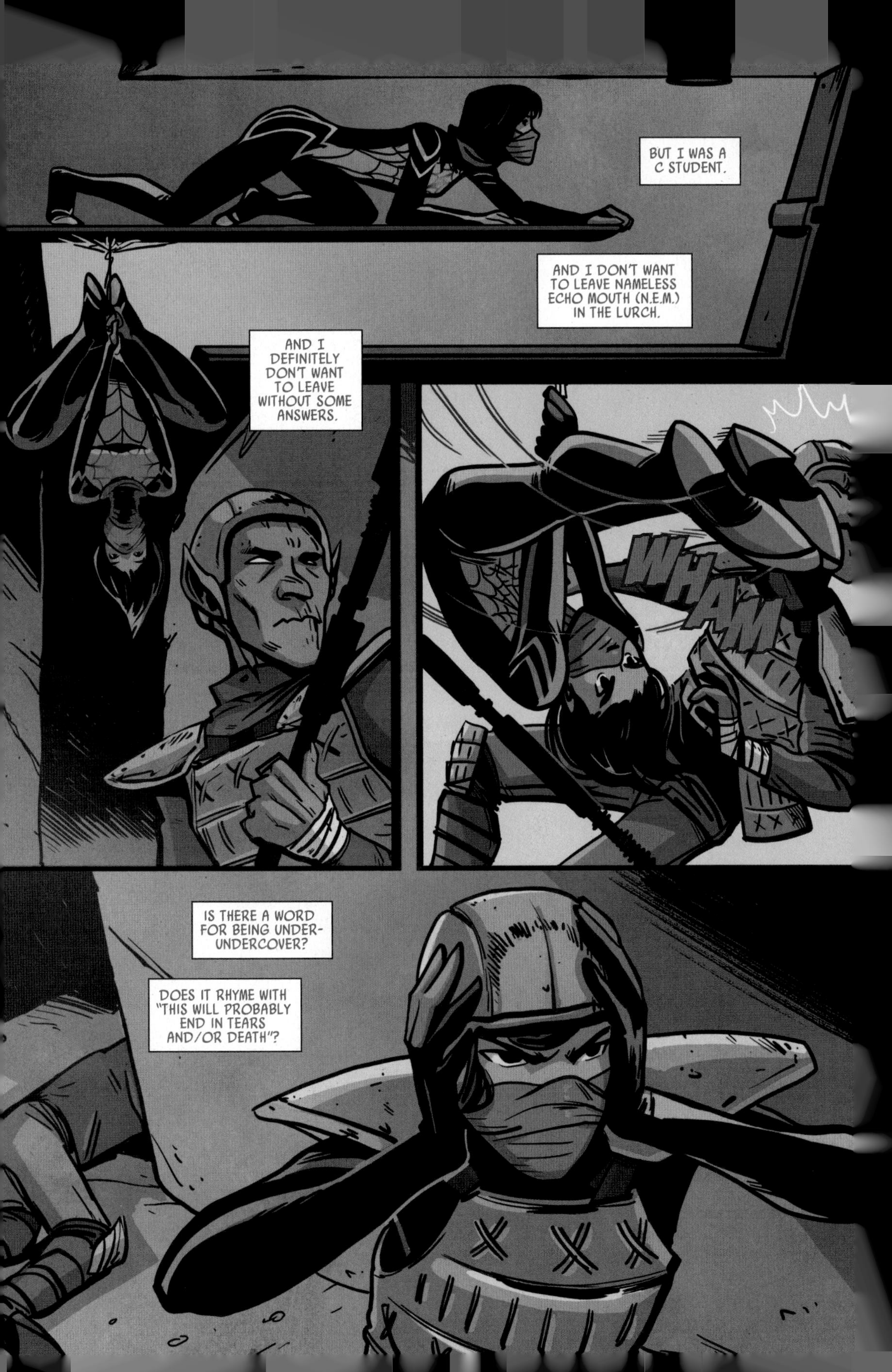

BUT I WAS A C STUDENT.
AND I DON'T WANT TO LEAVE NAMELESS ECHO MOUTH (N.E.M.) IN THE LURCH.
AND I DEFINITELY DON'T WANT TO LEAVE WITHOUT SOME ANSWERS.
WHAM
IS THERE A WORD FOR BEING UNDER-UNDERCOVER?
DOES IT RHYME WITH "THIS WILL PROBABLY END IN TEARS AND/OR DEATH"?

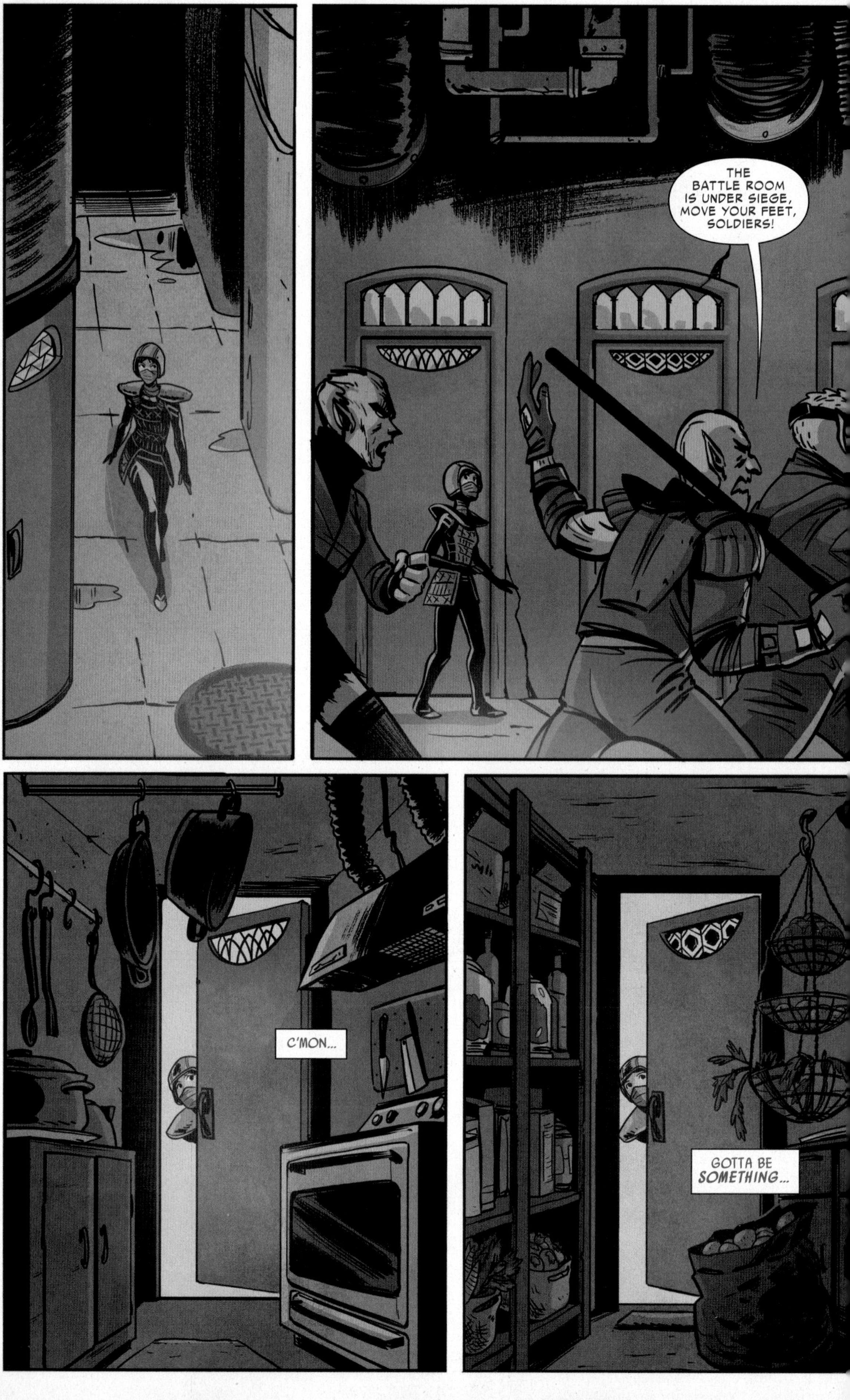

THE BATTLE ROOM IS UNDER SIEGE, MOVE YOUR FEET, SOLDIERS!
C'MON...
GOTTA BE SOMETHING...

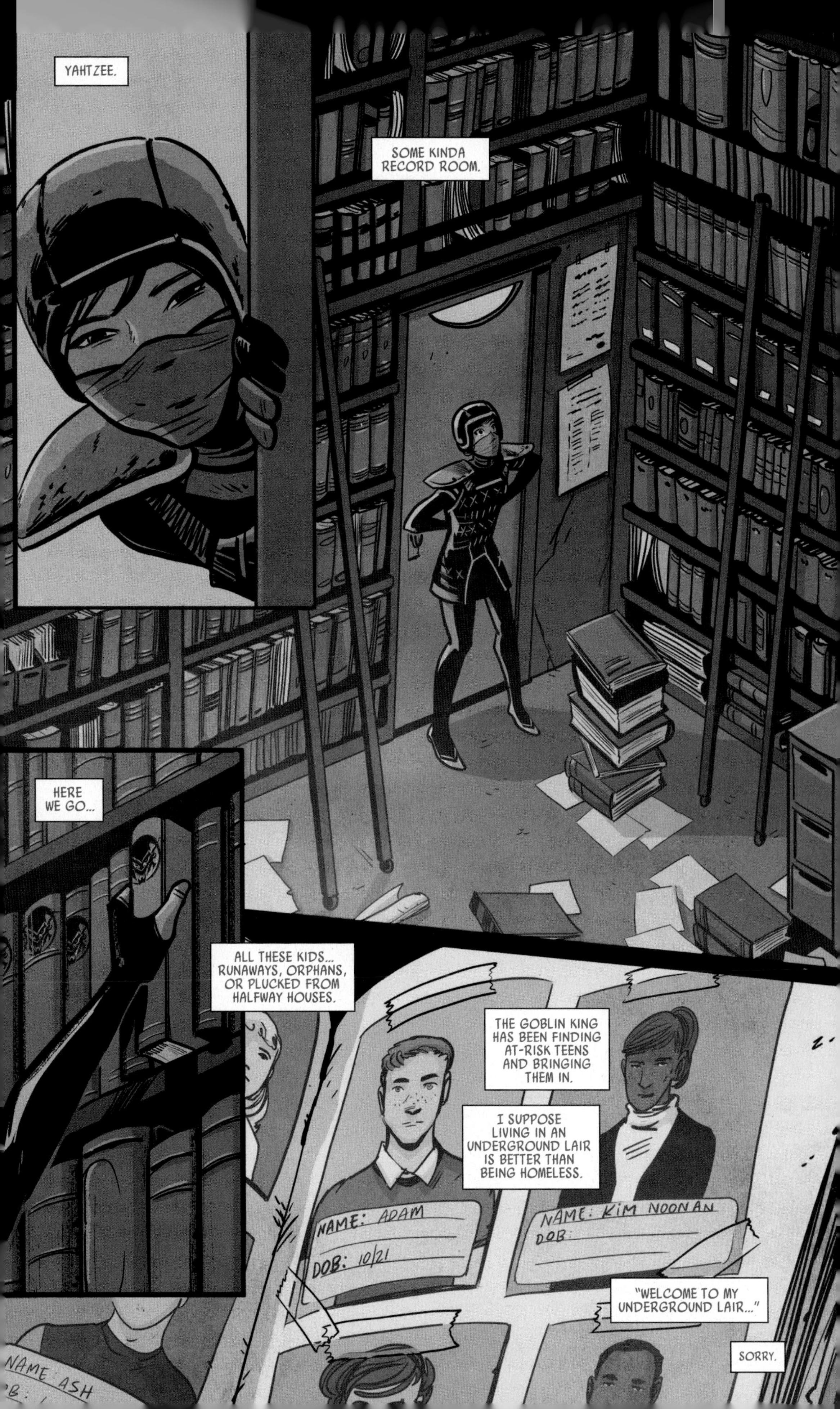
YAHTZEE.
SOME KINDA RECORD ROOM.
HERE WE GO...
ALL THESE KIDS... RUNAWAYS, ORPHANS, OR PLUCKED FROM HALFWAY HOUSES.
THE GOBLIN KING HAS BEEN FINDING AT-RISK TEENS AND BRINGING THEM IN.
I SUPPOSE LIVING IN AN UNDERGROUND LAIR IS BETTER THAN BEING HOMELESS.
NAME: ADAM
DOB: 10/21
NAME: KIM NOONAN
DOB:
NAME: ASH
"WELCOME TO MY UNDERGROUND LAIR..."
SORRY.

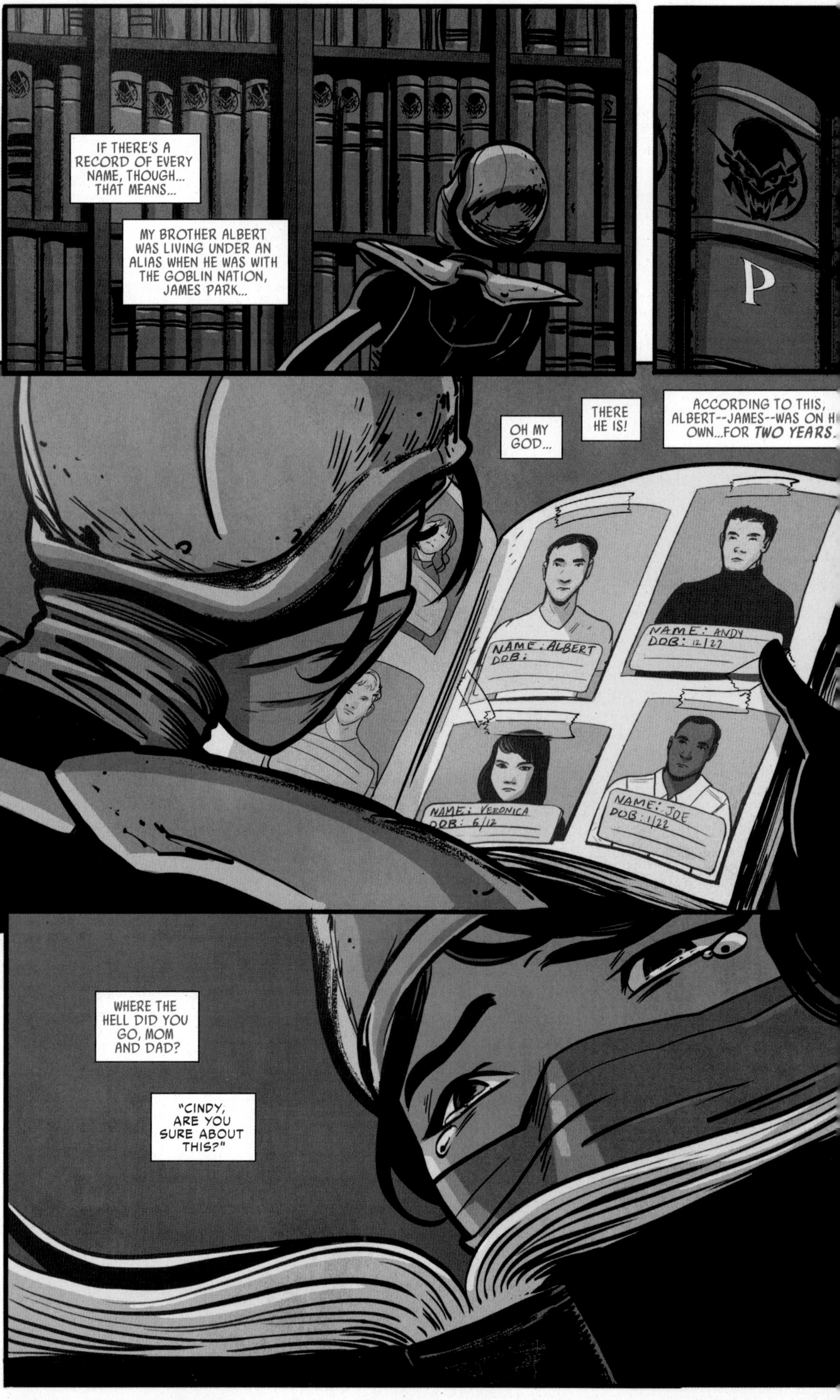
IF THERE'S A RECORD OF EVERY NAME, THOUGH... THAT MEANS...
MY BROTHER ALBERT WAS LIVING UNDER AN ALIAS WHEN HE WAS WITH THE GOBLIN NATION, JAMES PARK...
P
OH MY GOD...
THERE HE IS!
ACCORDING TO THIS, ALBERT--JAMES--WAS ON H OWN...FOR *TWO YEARS.*
NAME: ALBERT DOB:
NAME: ANDY DOB: 12/27
NAME: VERONICA DOB: 6/12
NAME: JOE DOB: 1/22
WHERE THE HELL DID YOU GO, MOM AND DAD?
"CINDY, ARE YOU SURE ABOUT THIS?"

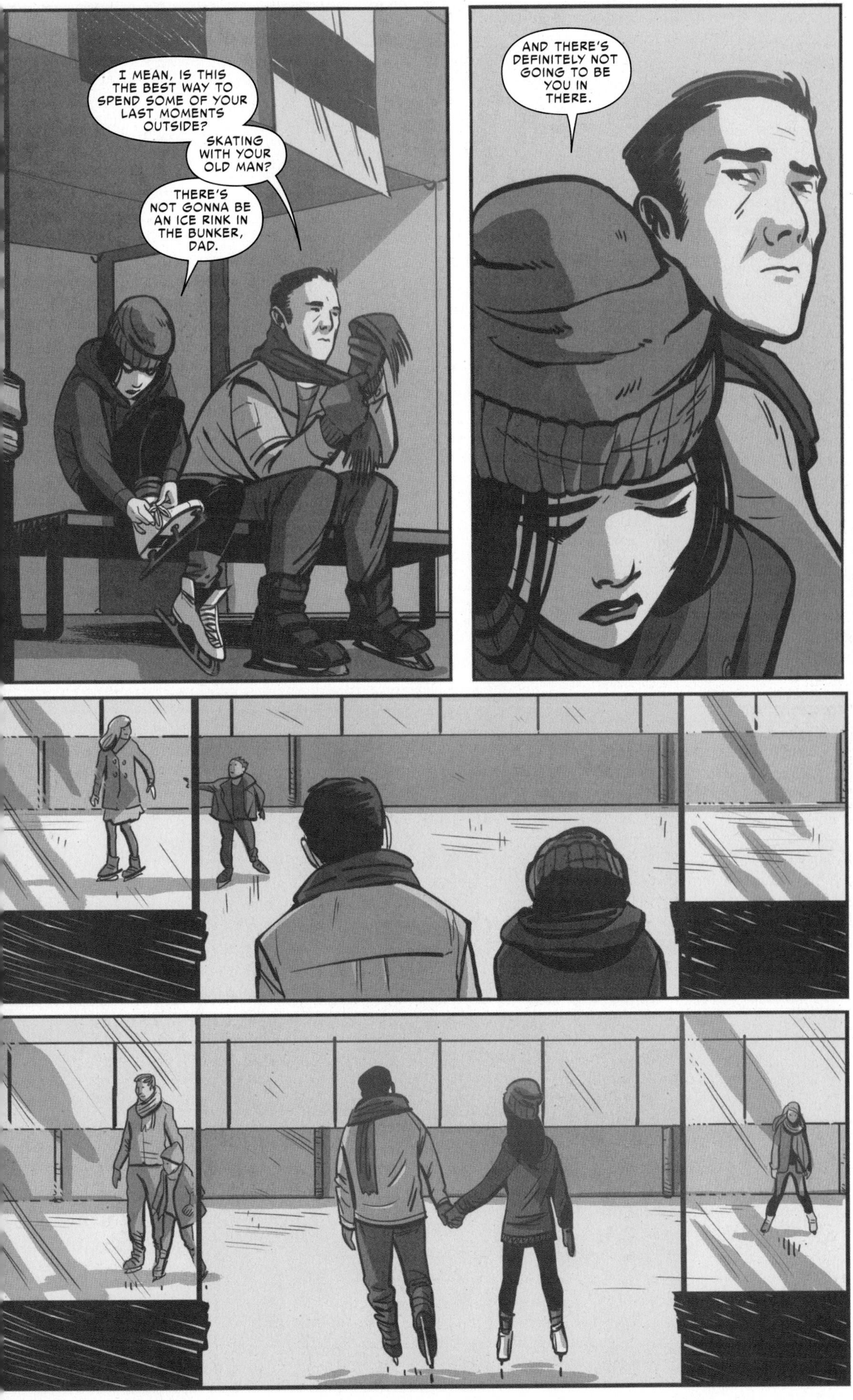
I MEAN, IS THIS THE BEST WAY TO SPEND SOME OF YOUR LAST MOMENTS OUTSIDE?
SKATING WITH YOUR OLD MAN?
THERE'S NOT GONNA BE AN ICE RINK IN THE BUNKER, DAD.
AND THERE'S DEFINITELY NOT GOING TO BE YOU IN THERE.

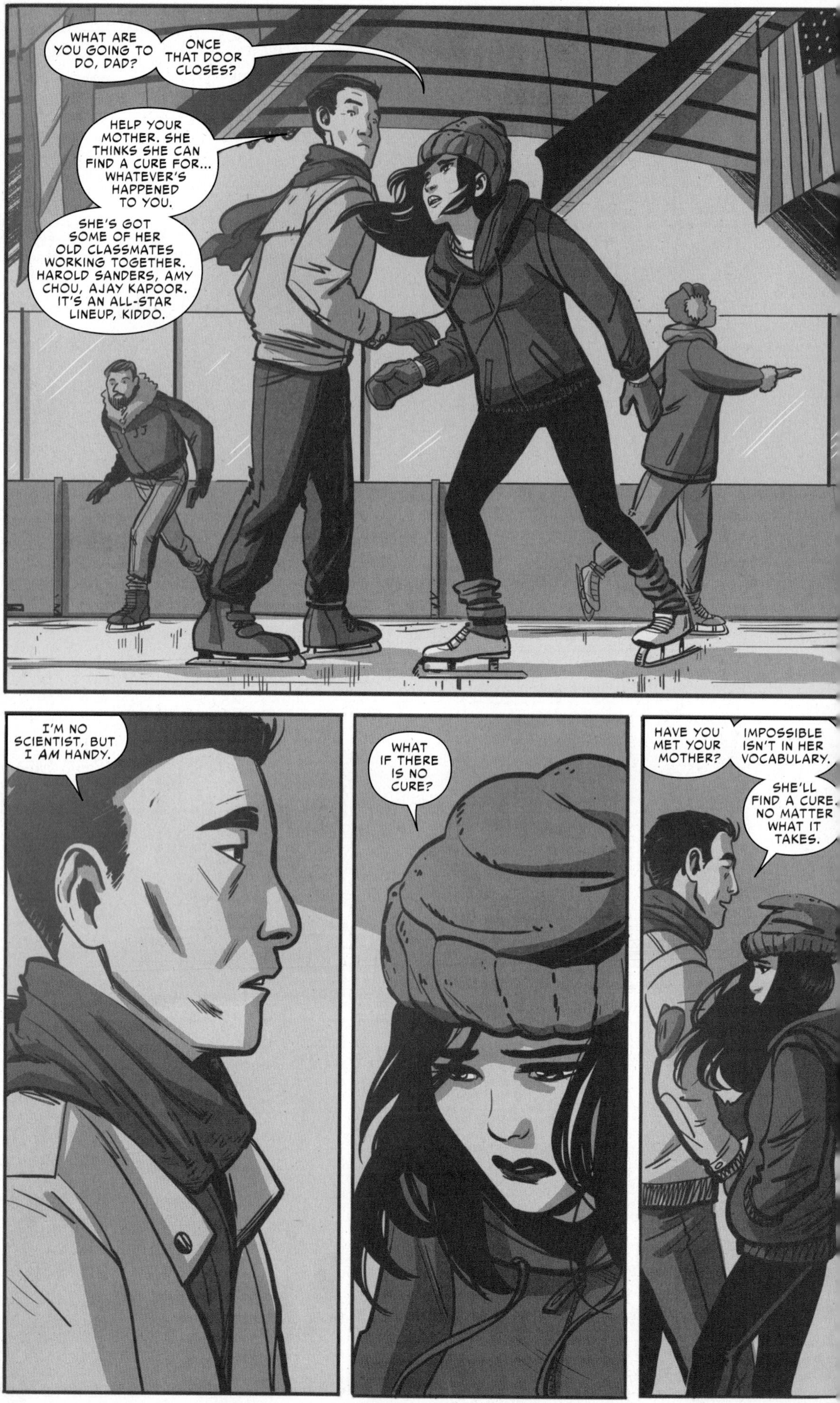
WHAT ARE YOU GOING TO DO, DAD?
ONCE THAT DOOR CLOSES?
HELP YOUR MOTHER. SHE THINKS SHE CAN FIND A CURE FOR... WHATEVER'S HAPPENED TO YOU.
SHE'S GOT SOME OF HER OLD CLASSMATES WORKING TOGETHER. HAROLD SANDERS, AMY CHOU, AJAY KAPOOR. IT'S AN ALL-STAR LINEUP, KIDDO.
I'M NO SCIENTIST, BUT I *AM* HANDY.
WHAT IF THERE IS NO CURE?
HAVE YOU MET YOUR MOTHER?
IMPOSSIBLE ISN'T IN HER VOCABULARY.
SHE'LL FIND A CURE. NO MATTER WHAT IT TAKES.

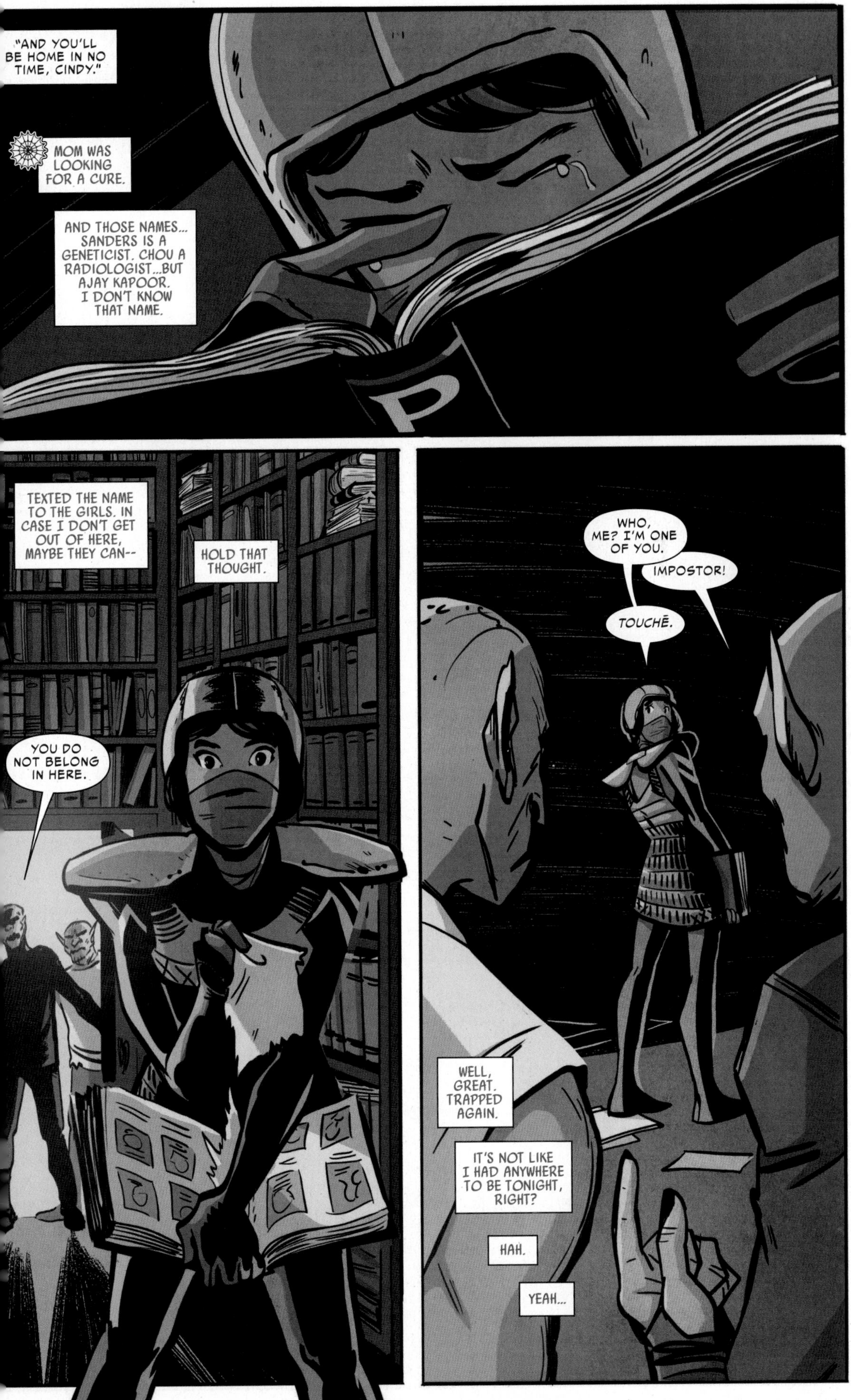
"AND YOU'LL BE HOME IN NO TIME, CINDY."
MOM WAS LOOKING FOR A CURE.
AND THOSE NAMES... SANDERS IS A GENETICIST. CHOU A RADIOLOGIST...BUT AJAY KAPOOR. I DON'T KNOW THAT NAME.
TEXTED THE NAME TO THE GIRLS. IN CASE I DON'T GET OUT OF HERE, MAYBE THEY CAN--
HOLD THAT THOUGHT.
YOU DO NOT BELONG IN HERE.
WHO, ME? I'M ONE OF YOU.
IMPOSTOR!
TOUCHÉ.
WELL, GREAT. TRAPPED AGAIN.
IT'S NOT LIKE I HAD ANYWHERE TO BE TONIGHT, RIGHT?
HAH.
YEAH...

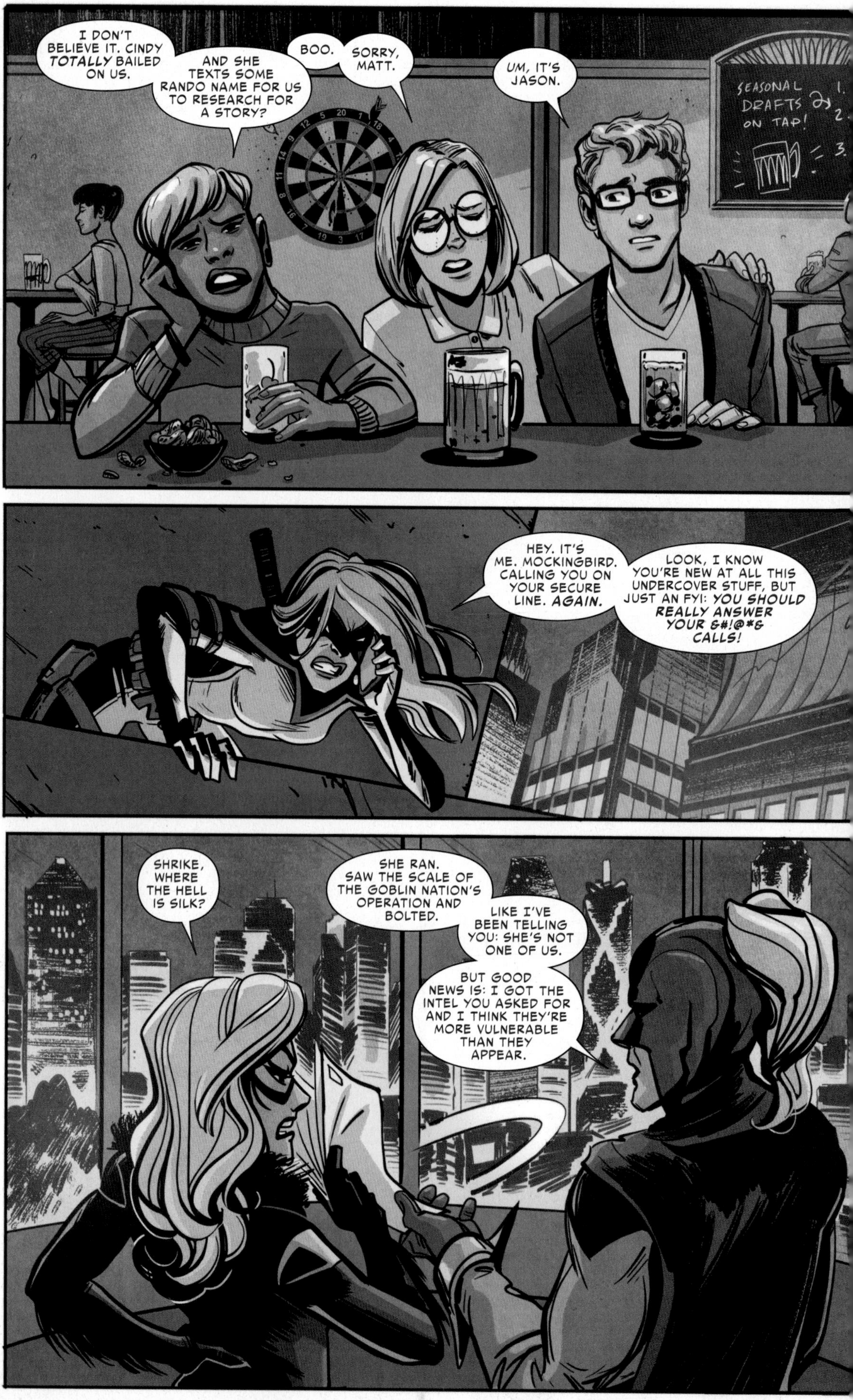
I DON'T BELIEVE IT. CINDY TOTALLY BAILED ON US.
AND SHE TEXTS SOME RANDO NAME FOR US TO RESEARCH FOR A STORY?
BOO.
SORRY, MATT.
UM, IT'S JASON.
SEASONAL DRAFTS ON TAP!
HEY. IT'S ME. MOCKINGBIRD. CALLING YOU ON YOUR SECURE LINE. AGAIN.
LOOK, I KNOW YOU'RE NEW AT ALL THIS UNDERCOVER STUFF, BUT JUST AN FYI: YOU SHOULD REALLY ANSWER YOUR &#!@*& CALLS!
SHRIKE, WHERE THE HELL IS SILK?
SHE RAN. SAW THE SCALE OF THE GOBLIN NATION'S OPERATION AND BOLTED.
LIKE I'VE BEEN TELLING YOU: SHE'S NOT ONE OF US.
BUT GOOD NEWS IS: I GOT THE INTEL YOU ASKED FOR AND I THINK THEY'RE MORE VULNERABLE THAN THEY APPEAR.

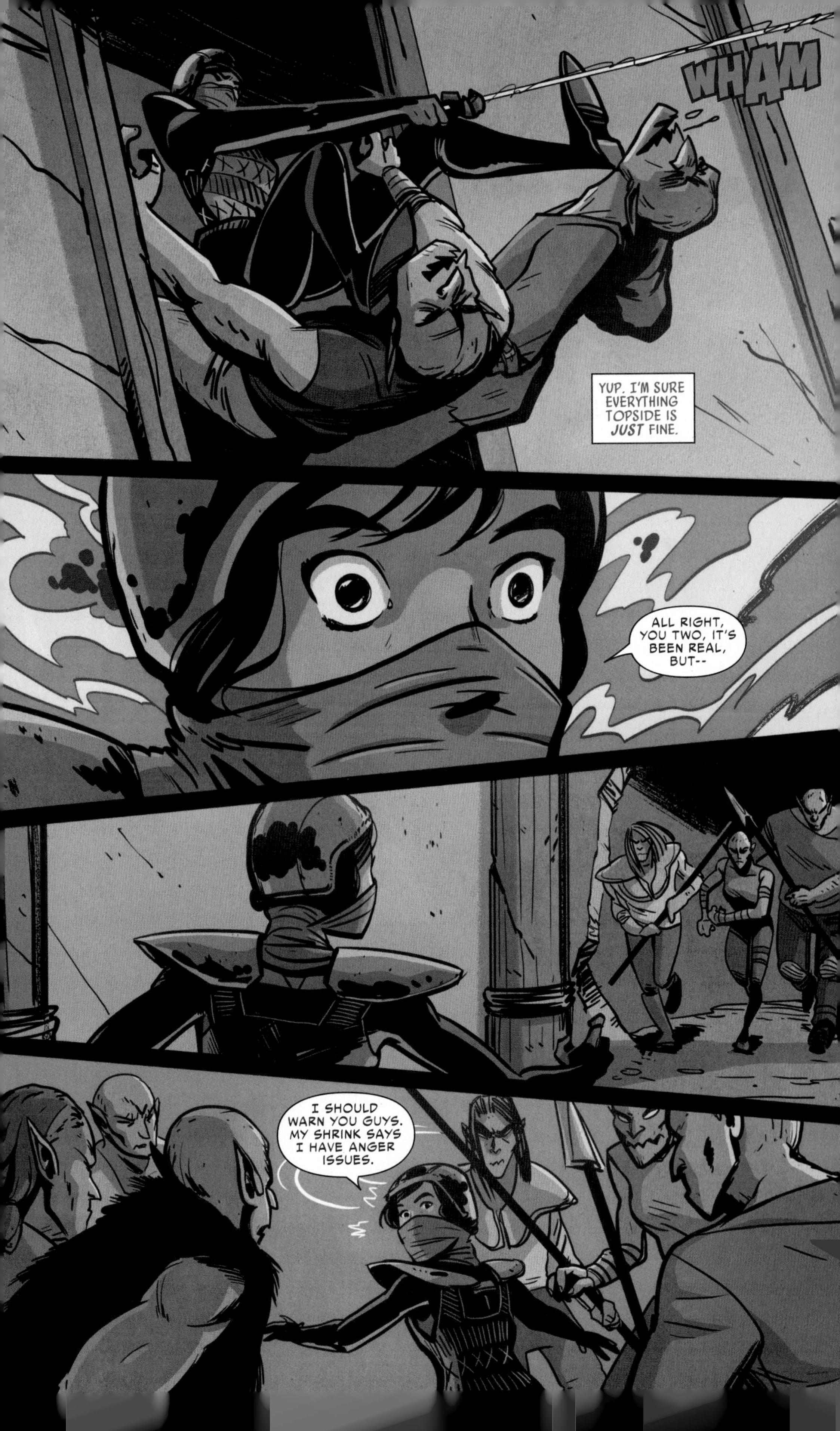
WHAM
YUP. I'M SURE EVERYTHING TOPSIDE IS *JUST* FINE.
ALL RIGHT, YOU TWO, IT'S BEEN REAL, BUT--
I SHOULD WARN YOU GUYS. MY SHRINK SAYS I HAVE ANGER ISSUES.

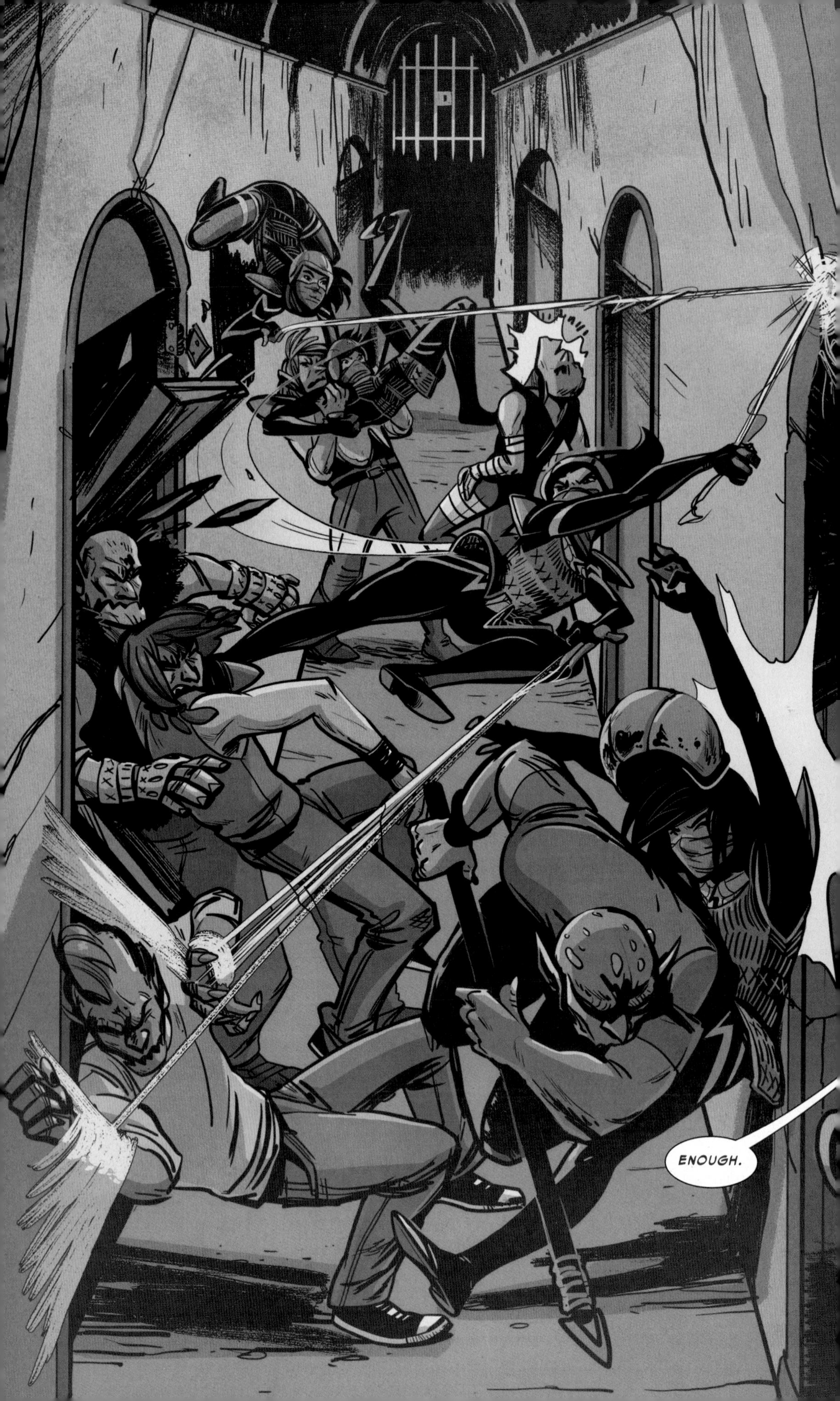
ENOUGH.

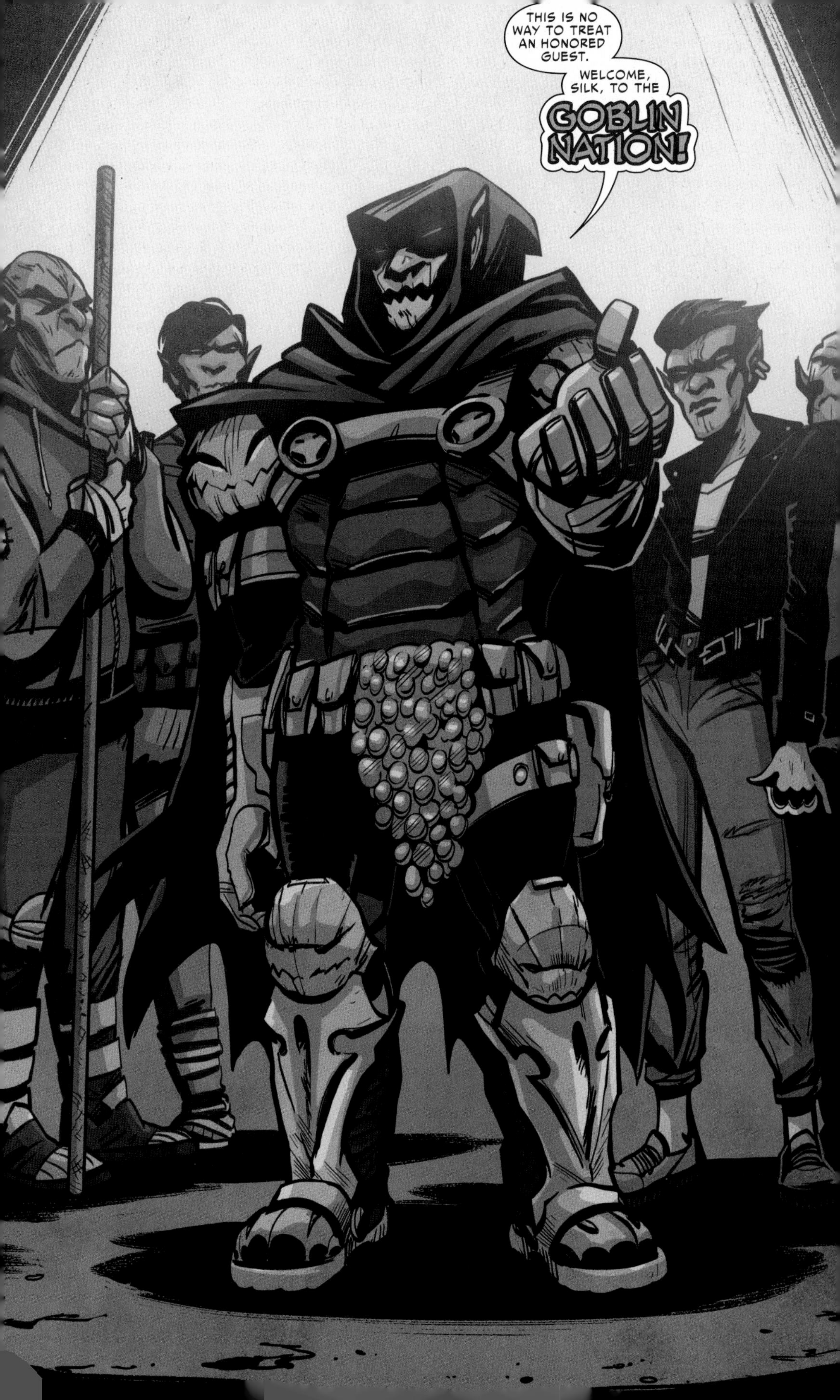
THIS IS NO WAY TO TREAT AN HONORED GUEST.
WELCOME, SILK, TO THE
GOBLIN NATION!

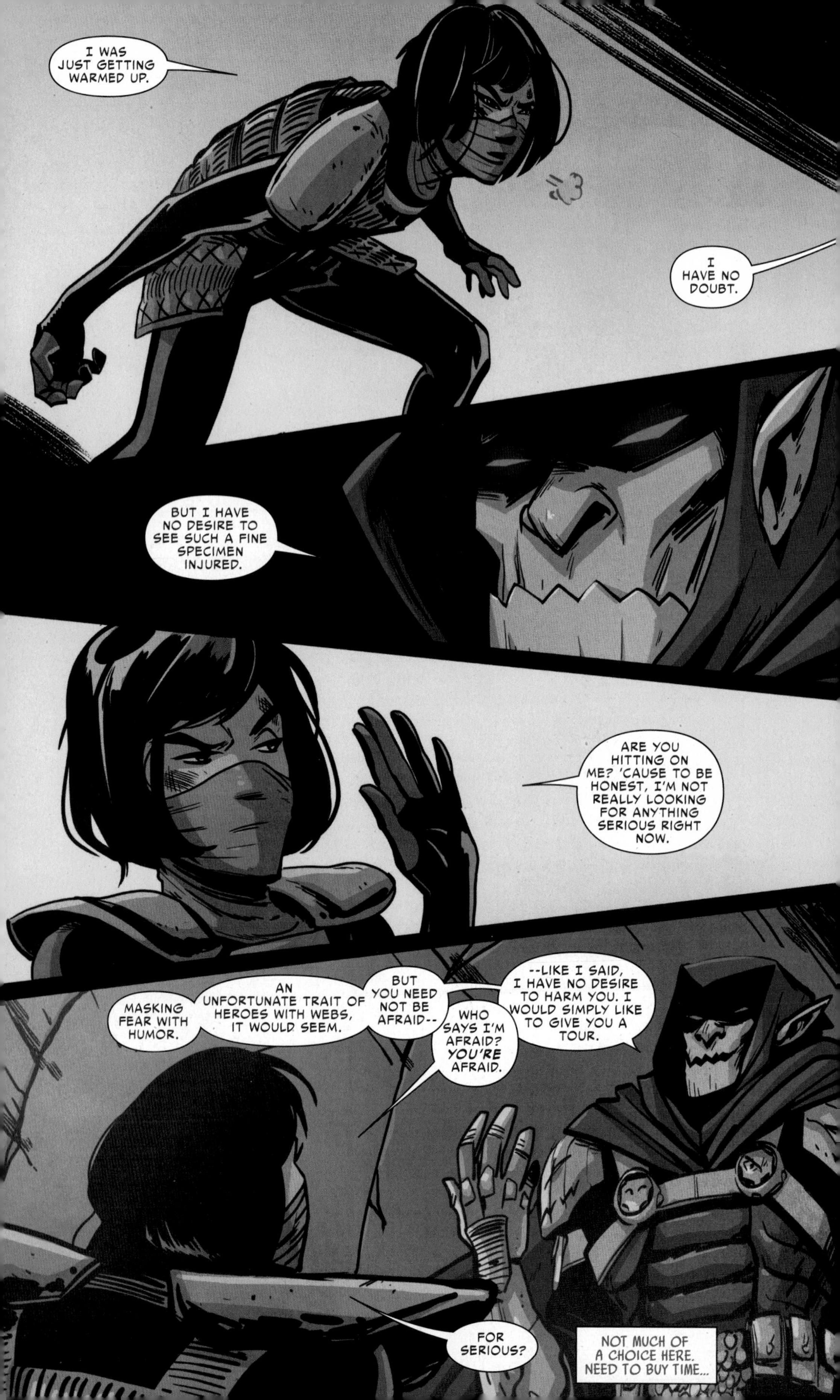
I WAS JUST GETTING WARMED UP.
I HAVE NO DOUBT.
BUT I HAVE NO DESIRE TO SEE SUCH A FINE SPECIMEN INJURED.
ARE YOU HITTING ON ME? 'CAUSE TO BE HONEST, I'M NOT REALLY LOOKING FOR ANYTHING SERIOUS RIGHT NOW.
MASKING FEAR WITH HUMOR.
AN UNFORTUNATE TRAIT OF HEROES WITH WEBS, IT WOULD SEEM.
BUT YOU NEED NOT BE AFRAID--
WHO SAYS I'M AFRAID? *YOU'RE* AFRAID.
--LIKE I SAID, I HAVE NO DESIRE TO HARM YOU. I WOULD SIMPLY LIKE TO GIVE YOU A TOUR.
FOR SERIOUS?
NOT MUCH OF A CHOICE HERE. NEED TO BUY TIME...

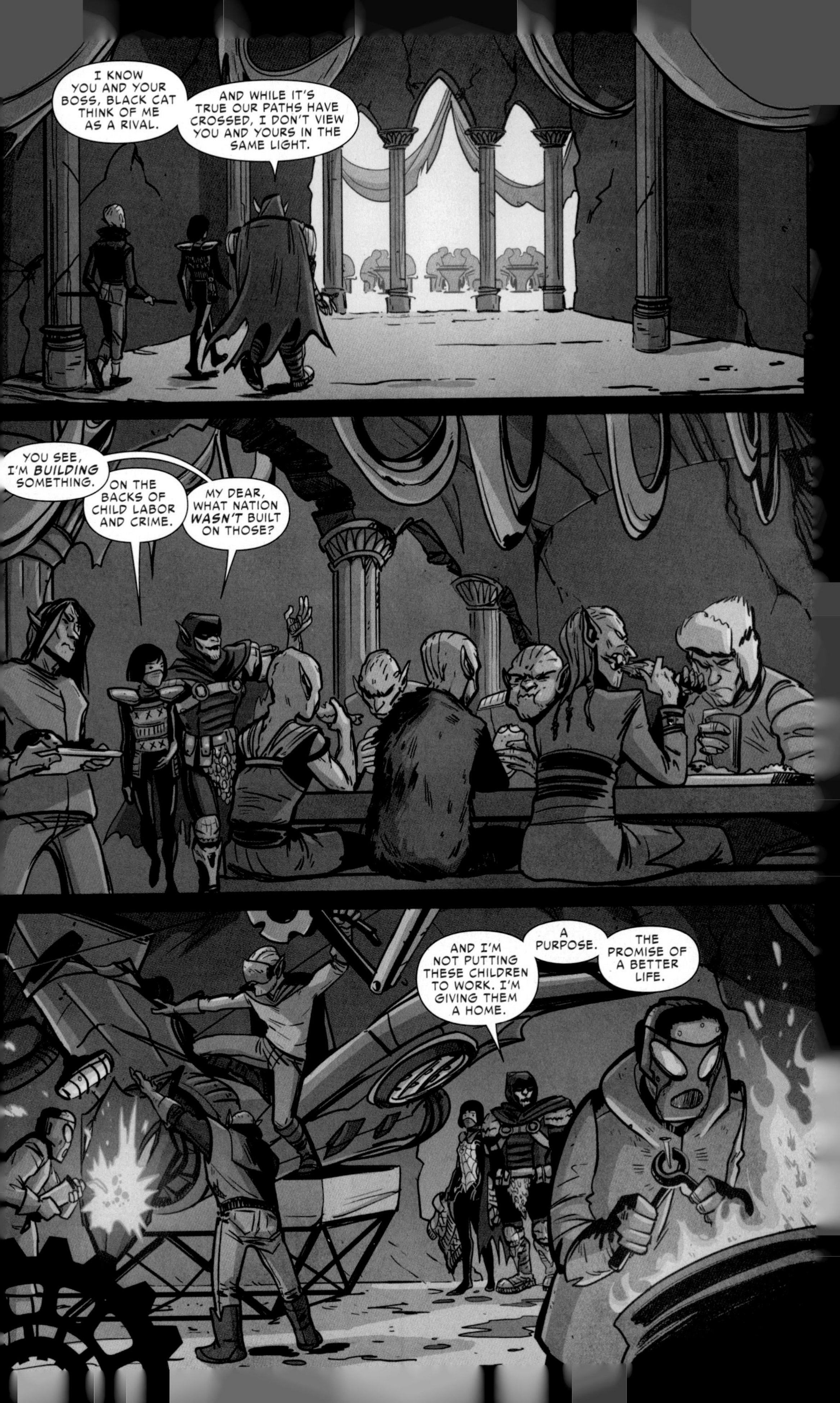
I KNOW YOU AND YOUR BOSS, BLACK CAT THINK OF ME AS A RIVAL.
AND WHILE IT'S TRUE OUR PATHS HAVE CROSSED, I DON'T VIEW YOU AND YOURS IN THE SAME LIGHT.
YOU SEE, I'M BUILDING SOMETHING.
ON THE BACKS OF CHILD LABOR AND CRIME.
MY DEAR, WHAT NATION WASN'T BUILT ON THOSE?
AND I'M NOT PUTTING THESE CHILDREN TO WORK. I'M GIVING THEM A HOME.
A PURPOSE.
THE PROMISE OF A BETTER LIFE.

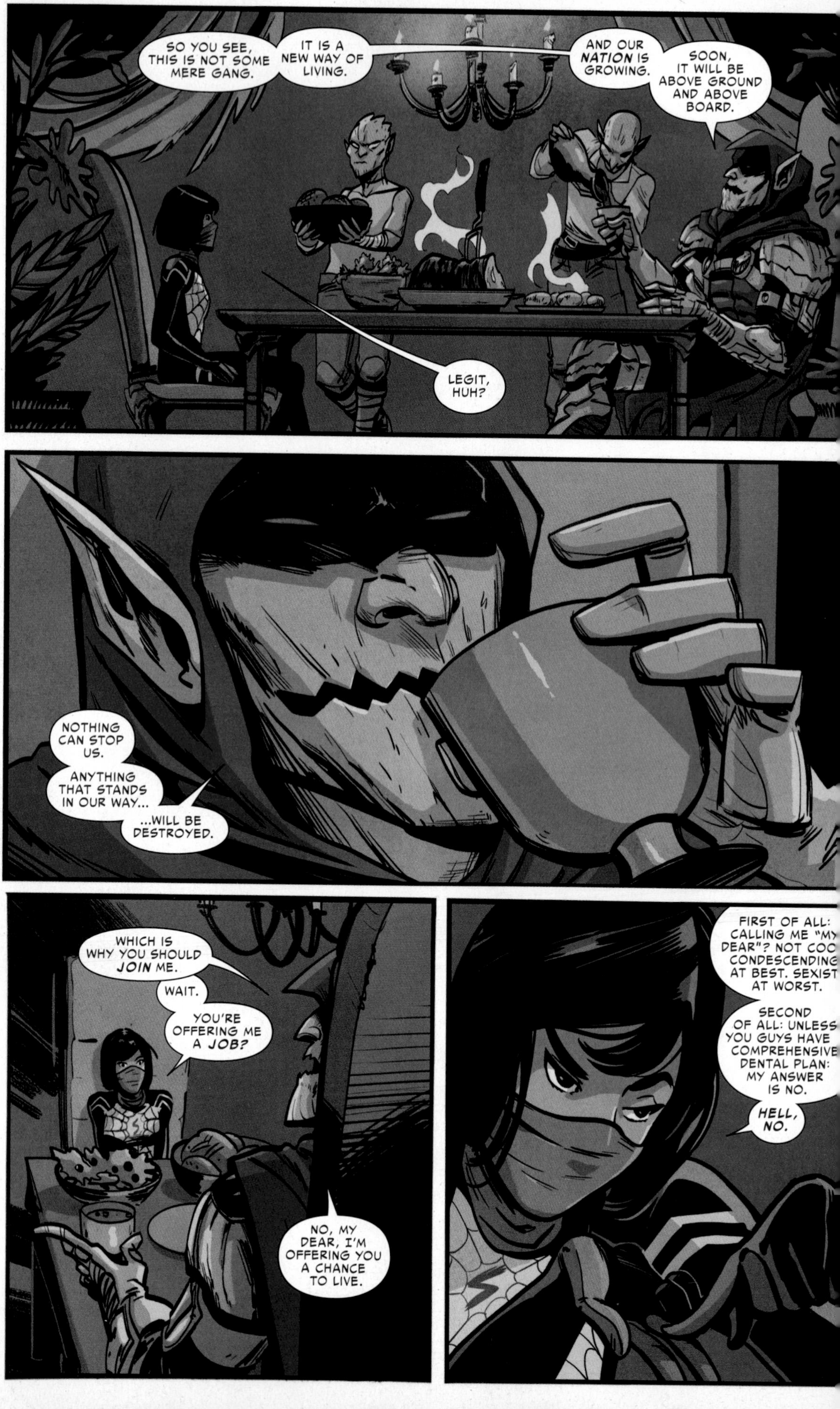

SO YOU SEE, THIS IS NOT SOME MERE GANG.
IT IS A NEW WAY OF LIVING.
AND OUR NATION IS GROWING.
SOON, IT WILL BE ABOVE GROUND AND ABOVE BOARD.
LEGIT, HUH?
NOTHING CAN STOP US.
ANYTHING THAT STANDS IN OUR WAY...
...WILL BE DESTROYED.
WHICH IS WHY YOU SHOULD JOIN ME.
WAIT.
YOU'RE OFFERING ME A JOB?
NO, MY DEAR, I'M OFFERING YOU A CHANCE TO LIVE.
FIRST OF ALL: CALLING ME "MY DEAR"? NOT COO
CONDESCENDING AT BEST. SEXIST AT WORST.
SECOND OF ALL: UNLESS YOU GUYS HAVE COMPREHENSIVE DENTAL PLAN: MY ANSWER IS NO.
HELL, NO.

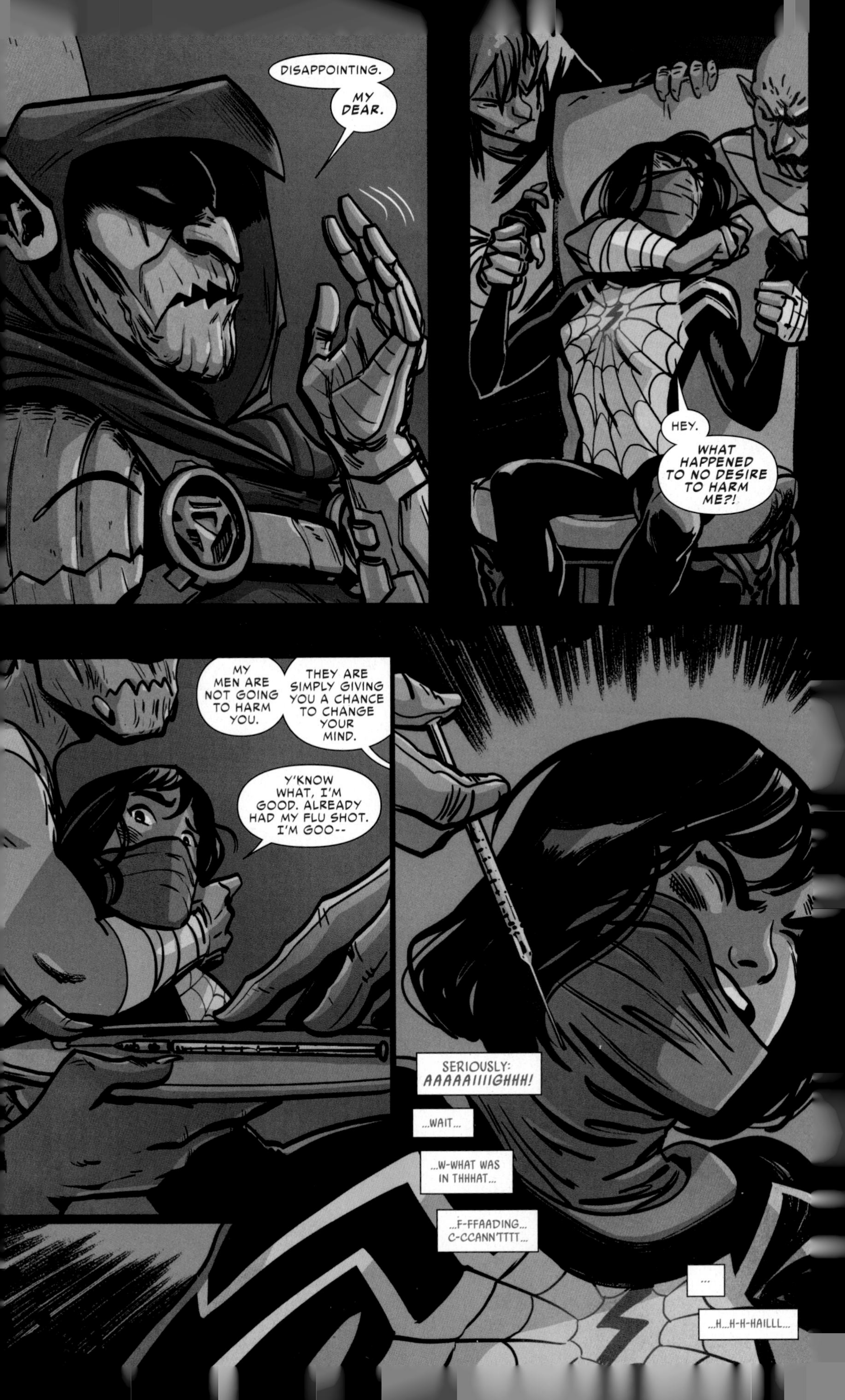
DISAPPOINTING.
MY DEAR.
HEY.
WHAT HAPPENED TO NO DESIRE TO HARM ME?!
MY MEN ARE NOT GOING TO HARM YOU.
THEY ARE SIMPLY GIVING YOU A CHANCE TO CHANGE YOUR MIND.
Y'KNOW WHAT, I'M GOOD. ALREADY HAD MY FLU SHOT. I'M GOO--
SERIOUSLY: AAAAAIIIIGHHH!
...WAIT...
...W-WHAT WAS IN THHHAT...
...F-FFAADING... C-CCANN'TTTT...
...
...H...H-H-HAILLL...

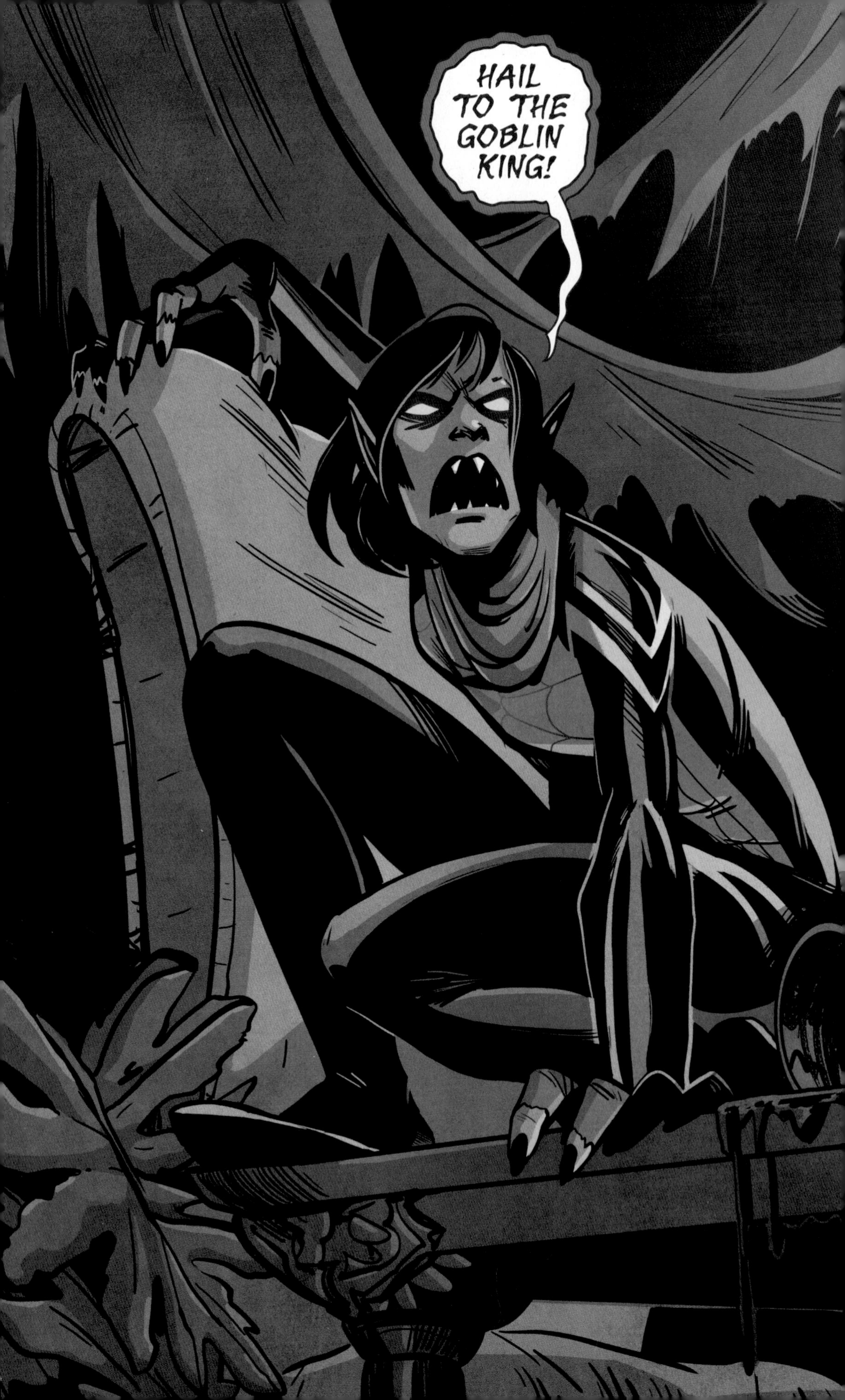
HAIL TO THE GOBLIN KING!

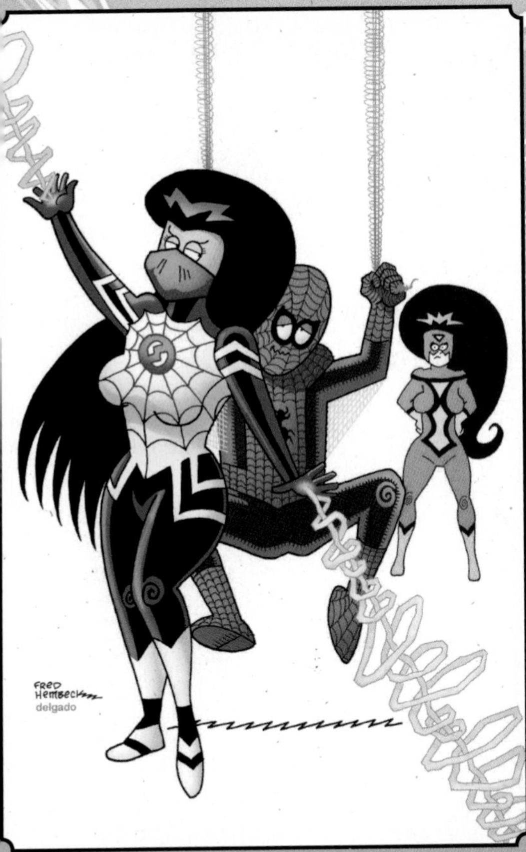
FRED HEMBECK
delgado

Silk (2015B) #2 variant by Fred Hembeck & Edgar Delgado

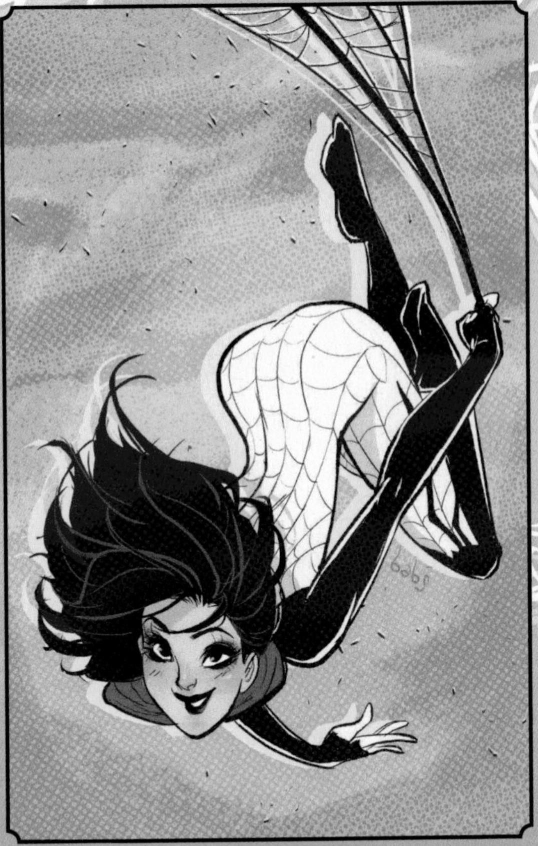

Silk (2015B) #2 variant by Babs Tarr

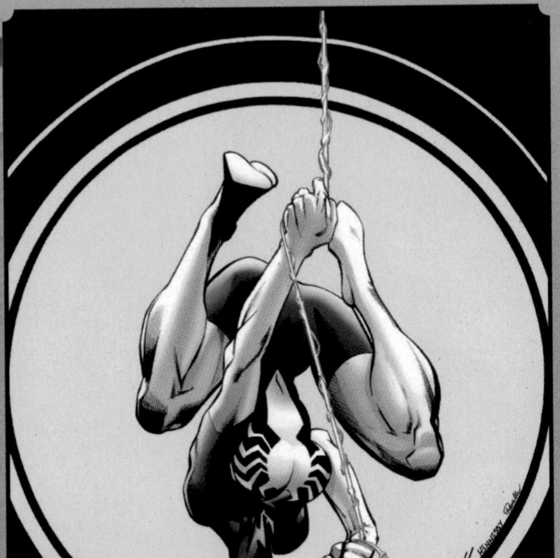

Silk (2015B) #2 Marvel '92 variant by
Mark Bagley, Andrew Hennessy & Rachelle Rosenberg

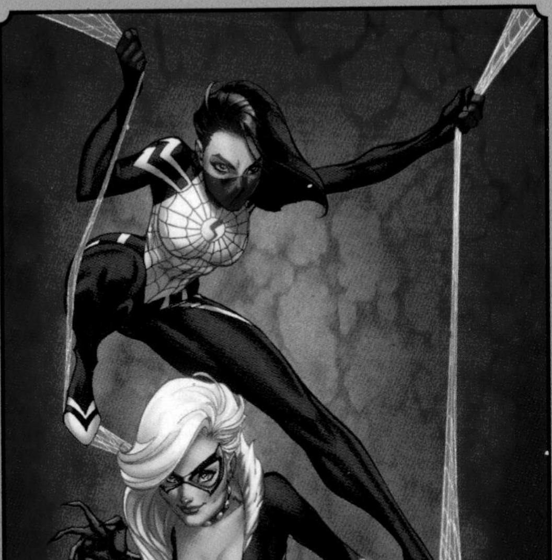

Silk (2015B) #3 variant by J. Scott Campbell & Nei Ruffino

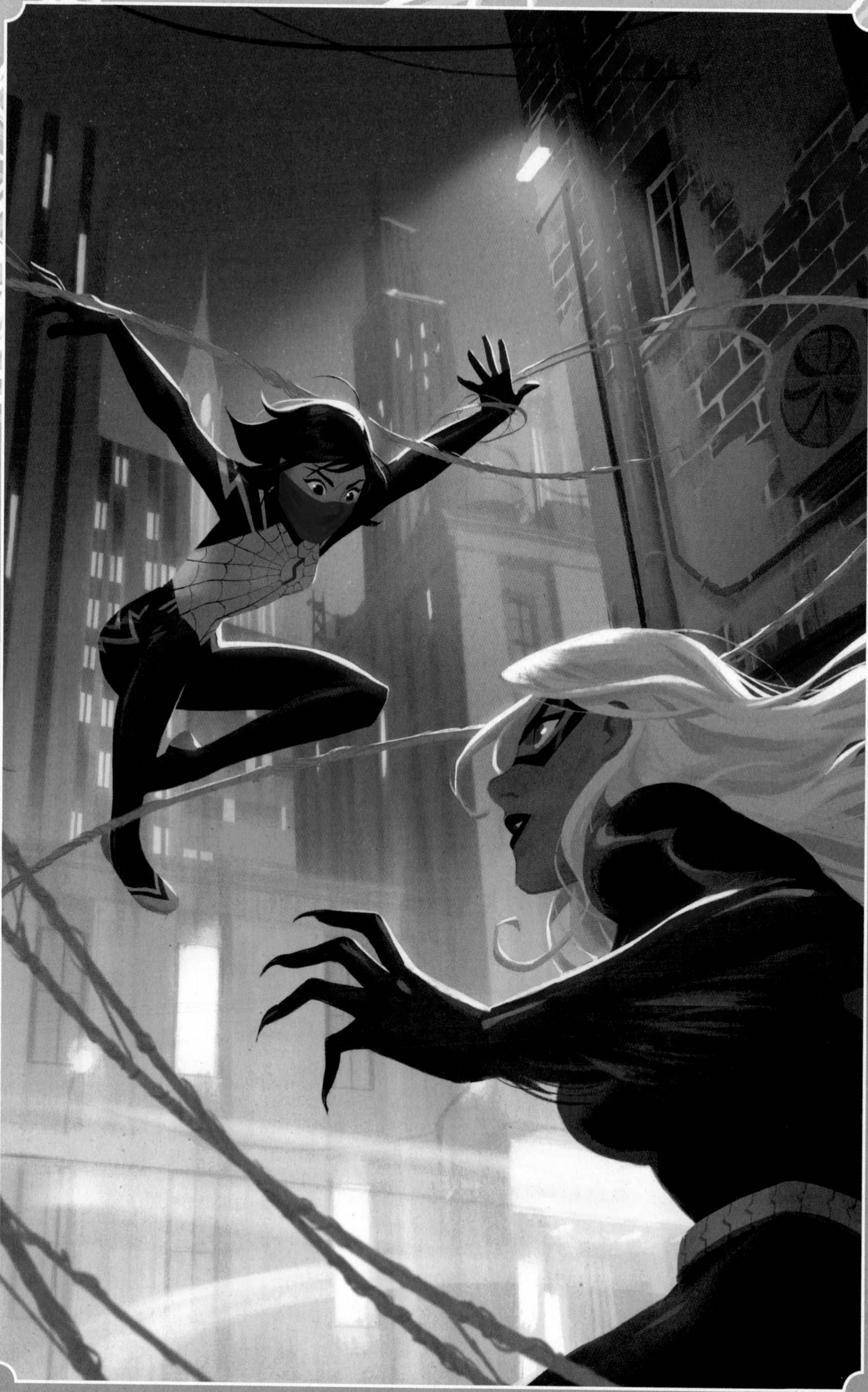

SILK (2015B) #5

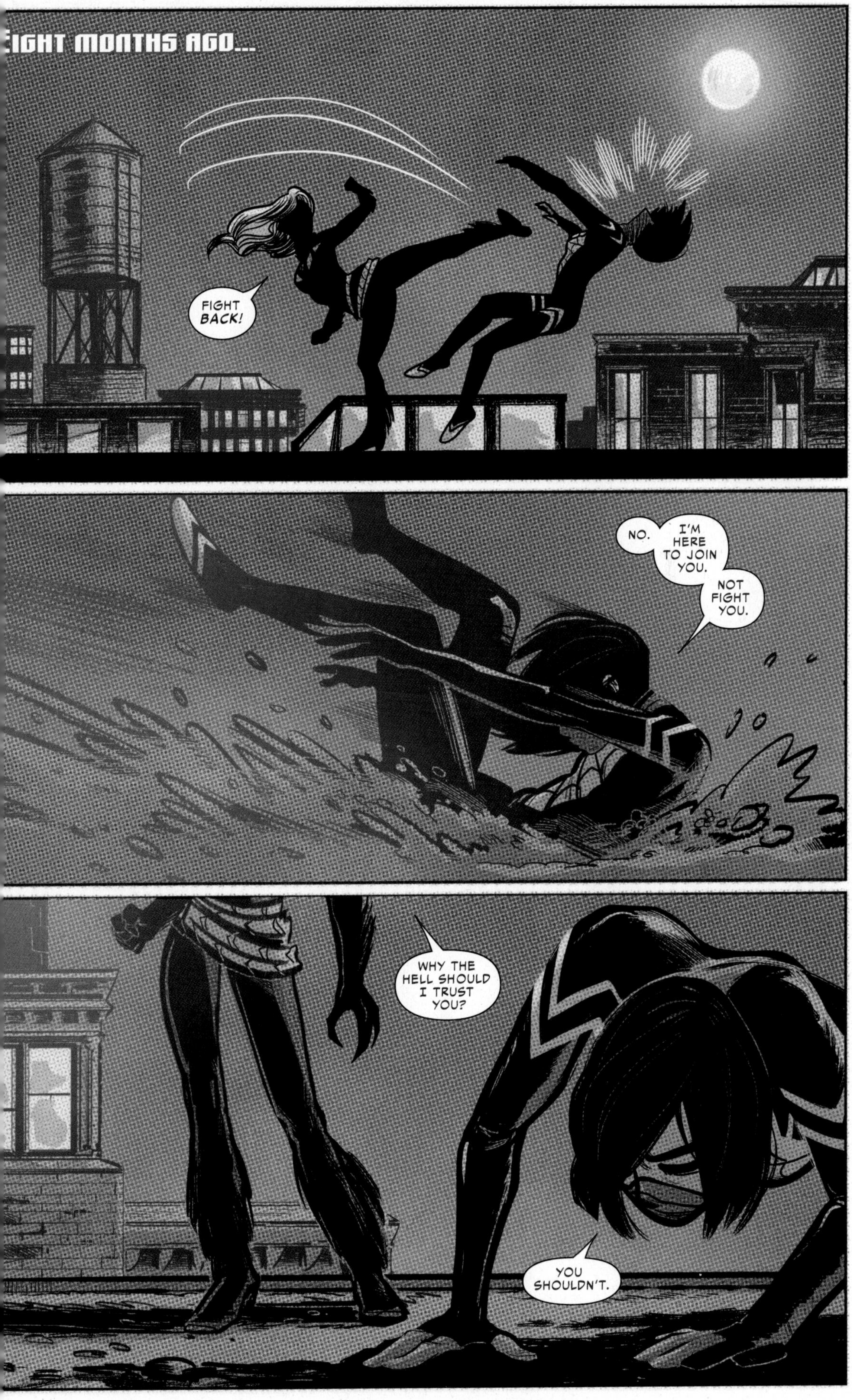
EIGHT MONTHS AGO...
FIGHT BACK!
NO.
I'M HERE TO JOIN YOU.
NOT FIGHT YOU.
WHY THE HELL SHOULD I TRUST YOU?
YOU SHOULDN'T.

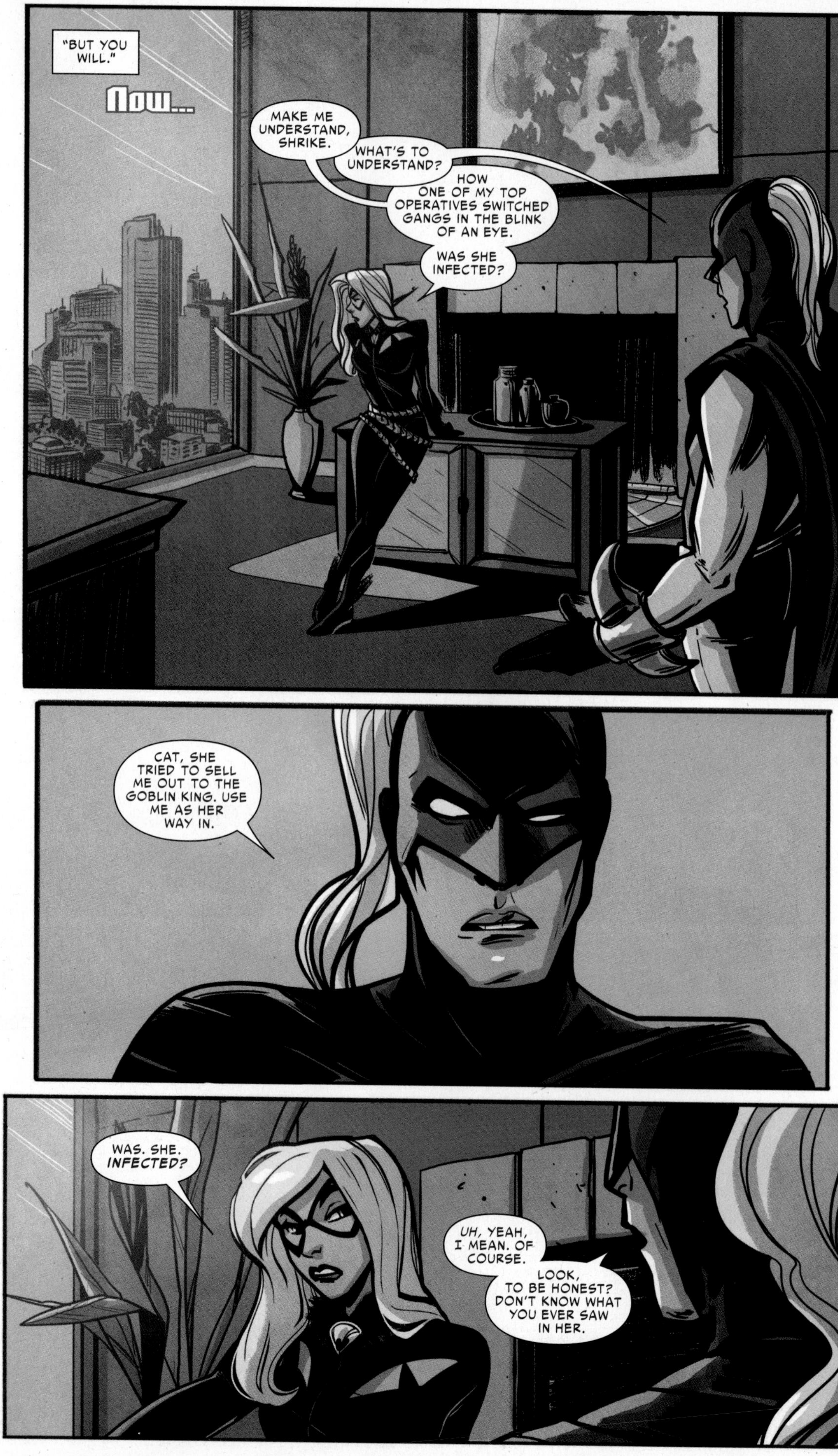
"BUT YOU WILL."
NOW...
MAKE ME UNDERSTAND, SHRIKE.
WHAT'S TO UNDERSTAND?
HOW ONE OF MY TOP OPERATIVES SWITCHED GANGS IN THE BLINK OF AN EYE.
WAS SHE INFECTED?
CAT, SHE TRIED TO SELL ME OUT TO THE GOBLIN KING. USE ME AS HER WAY IN.
WAS. SHE. *INFECTED?*
UH, YEAH, I MEAN. OF COURSE.
LOOK, TO BE HONEST? DON'T KNOW WHAT YOU EVER SAW IN HER.

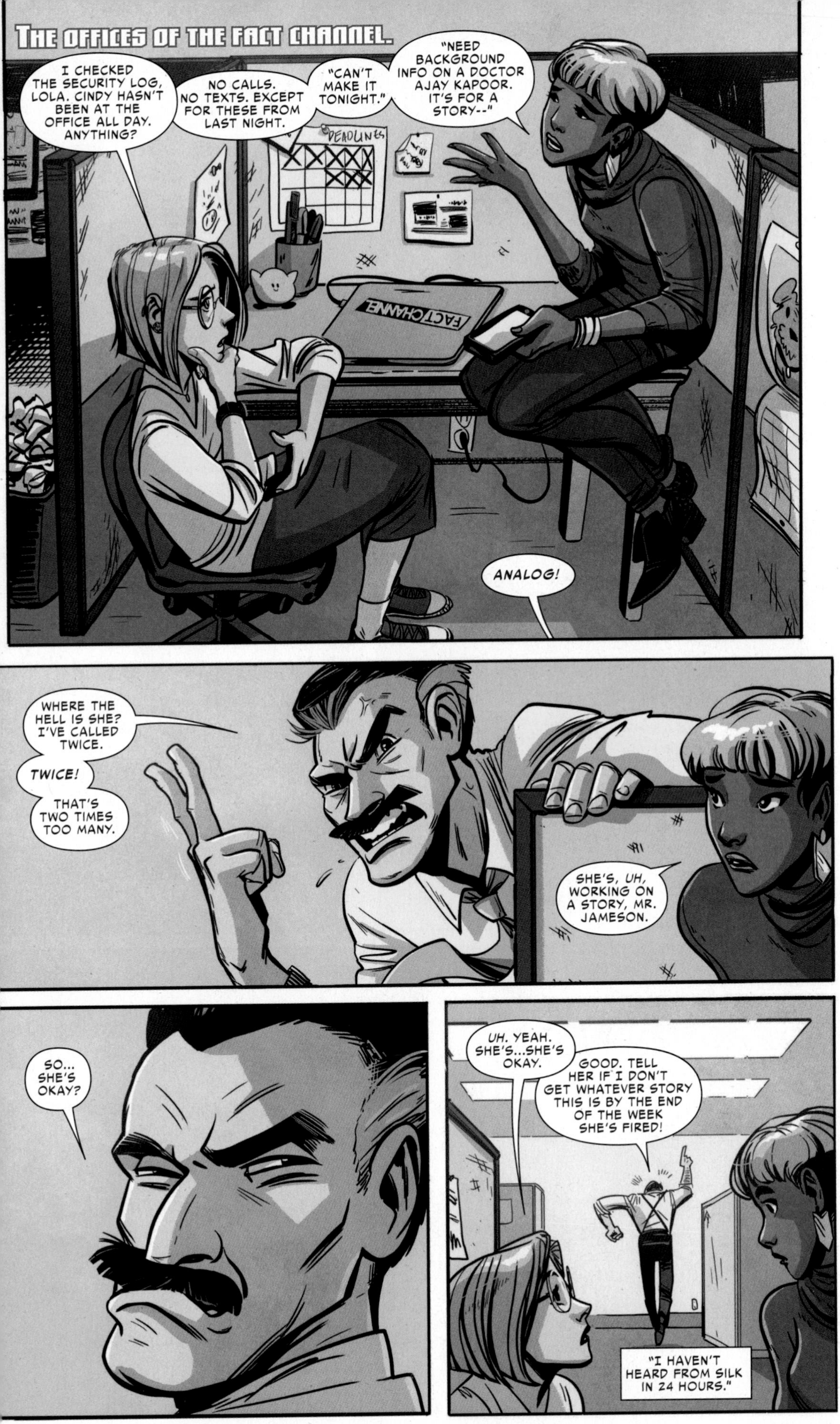
THE OFFICES OF THE FACT CHANNEL.
I CHECKED THE SECURITY LOG, LOLA. CINDY HASN'T BEEN AT THE OFFICE ALL DAY. ANYTHING?
NO CALLS. NO TEXTS. EXCEPT FOR THESE FROM LAST NIGHT.
"CAN'T MAKE IT TONIGHT."
"NEED BACKGROUND INFO ON A DOCTOR AJAY KAPOOR. IT'S FOR A STORY--"
DEADLINES
FACT CHANNEL
ANALOG!
WHERE THE HELL IS SHE? I'VE CALLED TWICE.
TWICE!
THAT'S TWO TIMES TOO MANY.
SHE'S, UH, WORKING ON A STORY, MR. JAMESON.
SO... SHE'S OKAY?
UH. YEAH. SHE'S...SHE'S OKAY.
GOOD. TELL HER IF I DON'T GET WHATEVER STORY THIS IS BY THE END OF THE WEEK SHE'S FIRED!
"I HAVEN'T HEARD FROM SILK IN 24 HOURS."

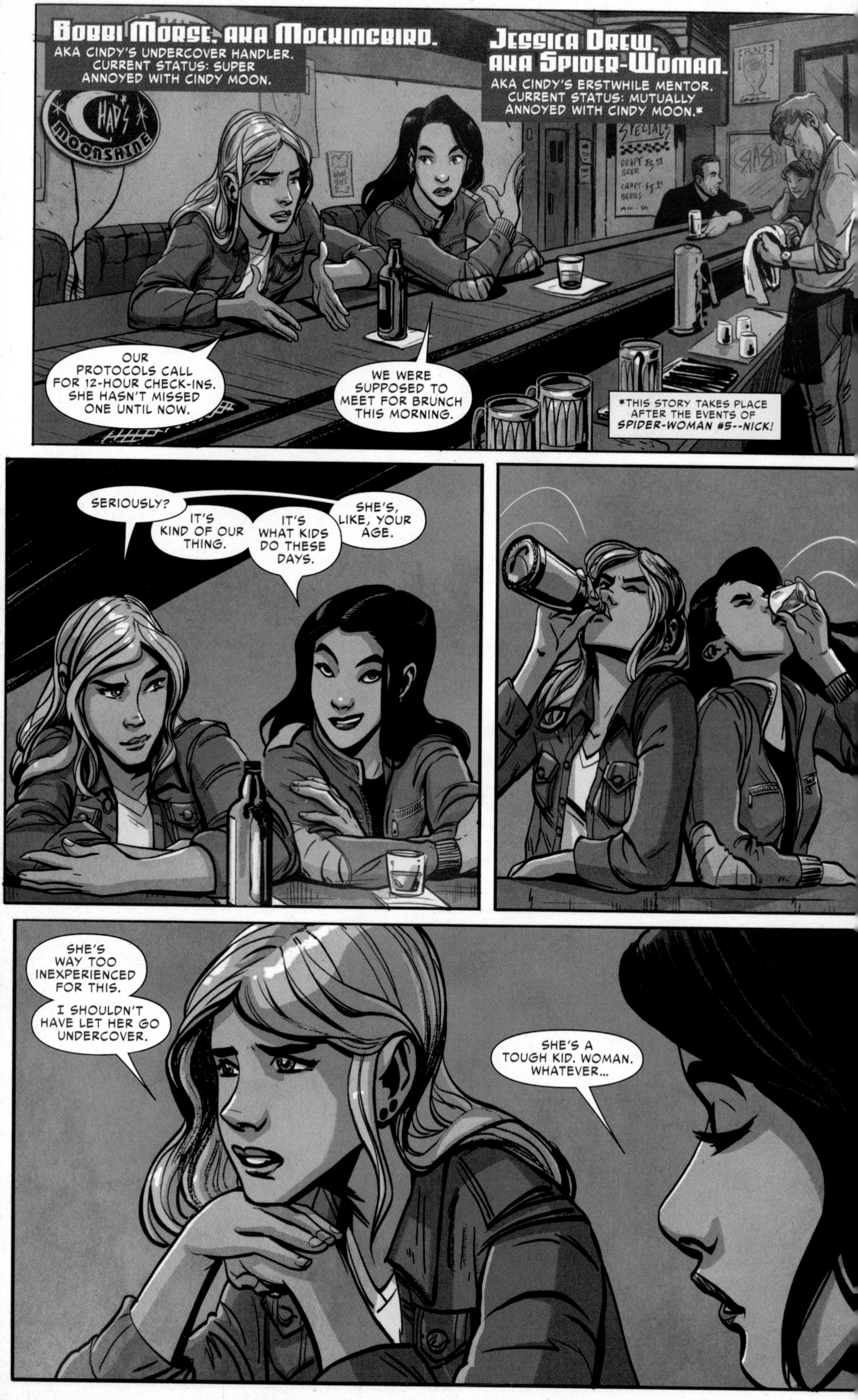

BOBBI MORSE, AKA MOCKINGBIRD.
AKA CINDY'S UNDERCOVER HANDLER. CURRENT STATUS: SUPER ANNOYED WITH CINDY MOON.
JESSICA DREW, AKA SPIDER-WOMAN.
AKA CINDY'S ERSTWHILE MENTOR. CURRENT STATUS: MUTUALLY ANNOYED WITH CINDY MOON.*
OUR PROTOCOLS CALL FOR 12-HOUR CHECK-INS. SHE HASN'T MISSED ONE UNTIL NOW.
WE WERE SUPPOSED TO MEET FOR BRUNCH THIS MORNING.
*THIS STORY TAKES PLACE AFTER THE EVENTS OF SPIDER-WOMAN #5--NICK!
SERIOUSLY?
IT'S KIND OF OUR THING.
IT'S WHAT KIDS DO THESE DAYS.
SHE'S, LIKE, YOUR AGE.
SHE'S WAY TOO INEXPERIENCED FOR THIS.
I SHOULDN'T HAVE LET HER GO UNDERCOVER.
SHE'S A TOUGH KID. WOMAN. WHATEVER...

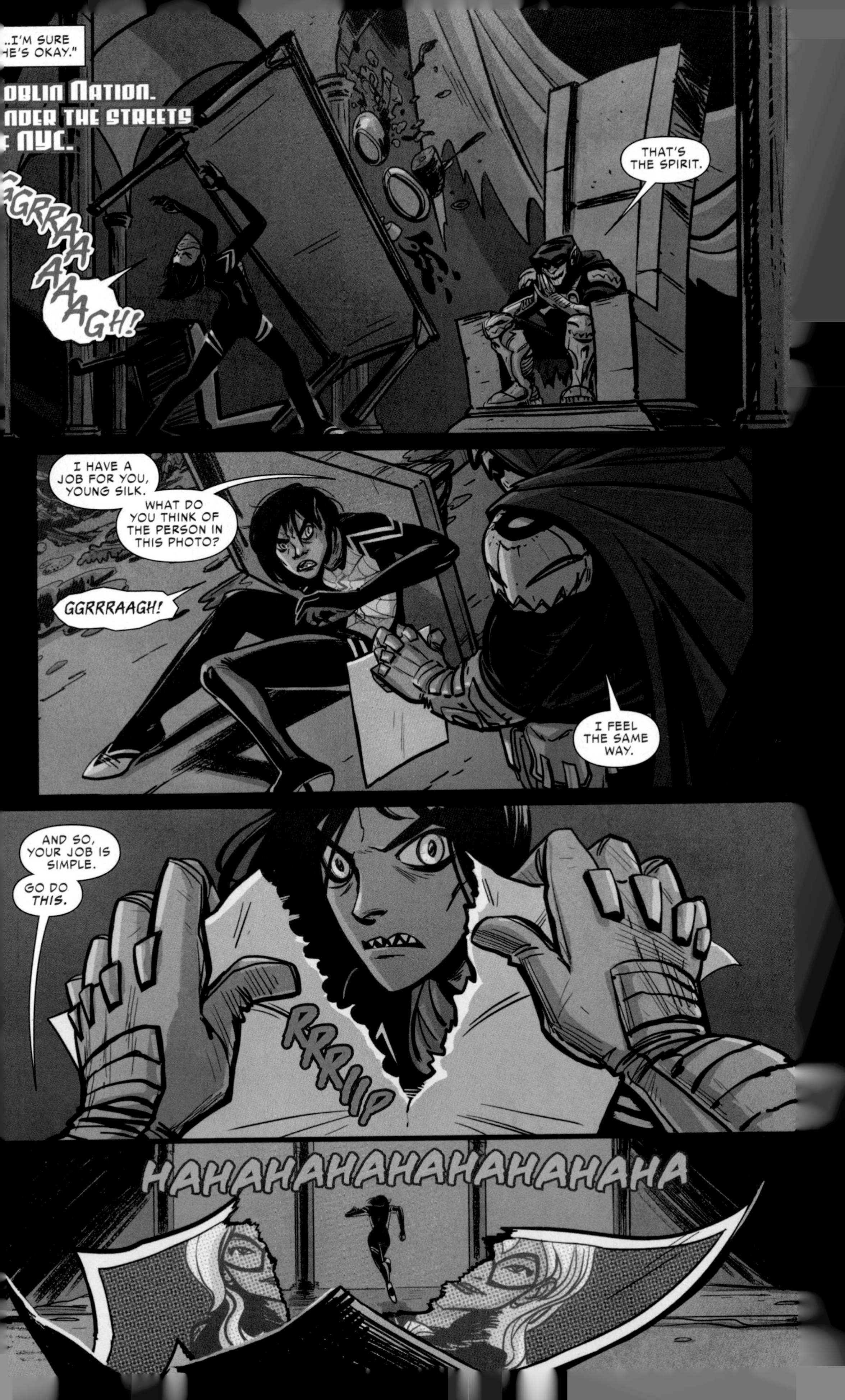
..I'M SURE
HE'S OKAY."
OBLIN NATION.
NDER THE STREETS
NYC.
GRRAAAAAAGH!
THAT'S THE SPIRIT.
I HAVE A JOB FOR YOU, YOUNG SILK.
WHAT DO YOU THINK OF THE PERSON IN THIS PHOTO?
GGRRRAAGH!
I FEEL THE SAME WAY.
AND SO, YOUR JOB IS SIMPLE.
GO DO THIS.
RRRIIIP
HAHAHAHAHAHAHAHAHAHA

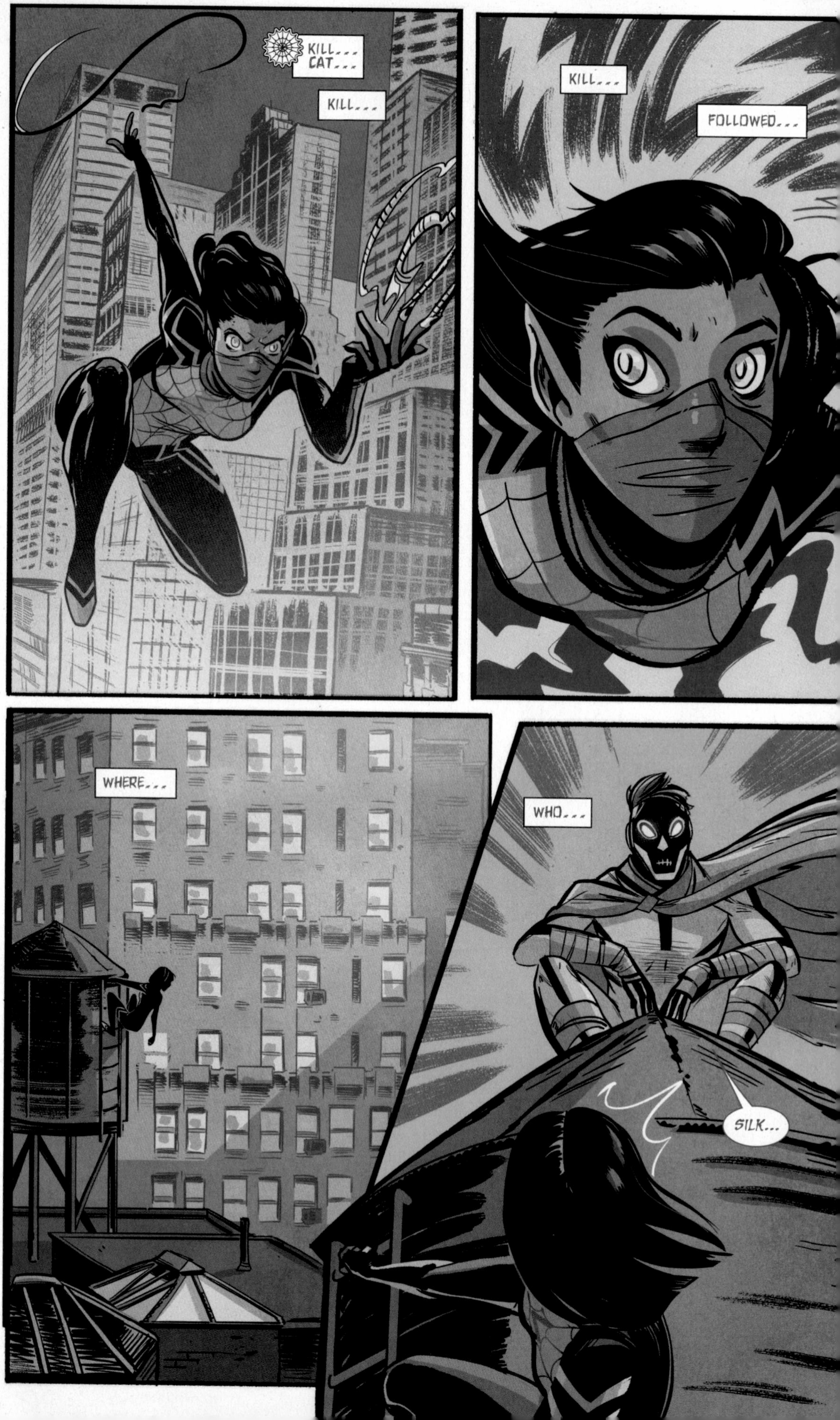
KILL...
CAT...
KILL...
KILL...
FOLLOWED...
WHERE...
WHO...
SILK...

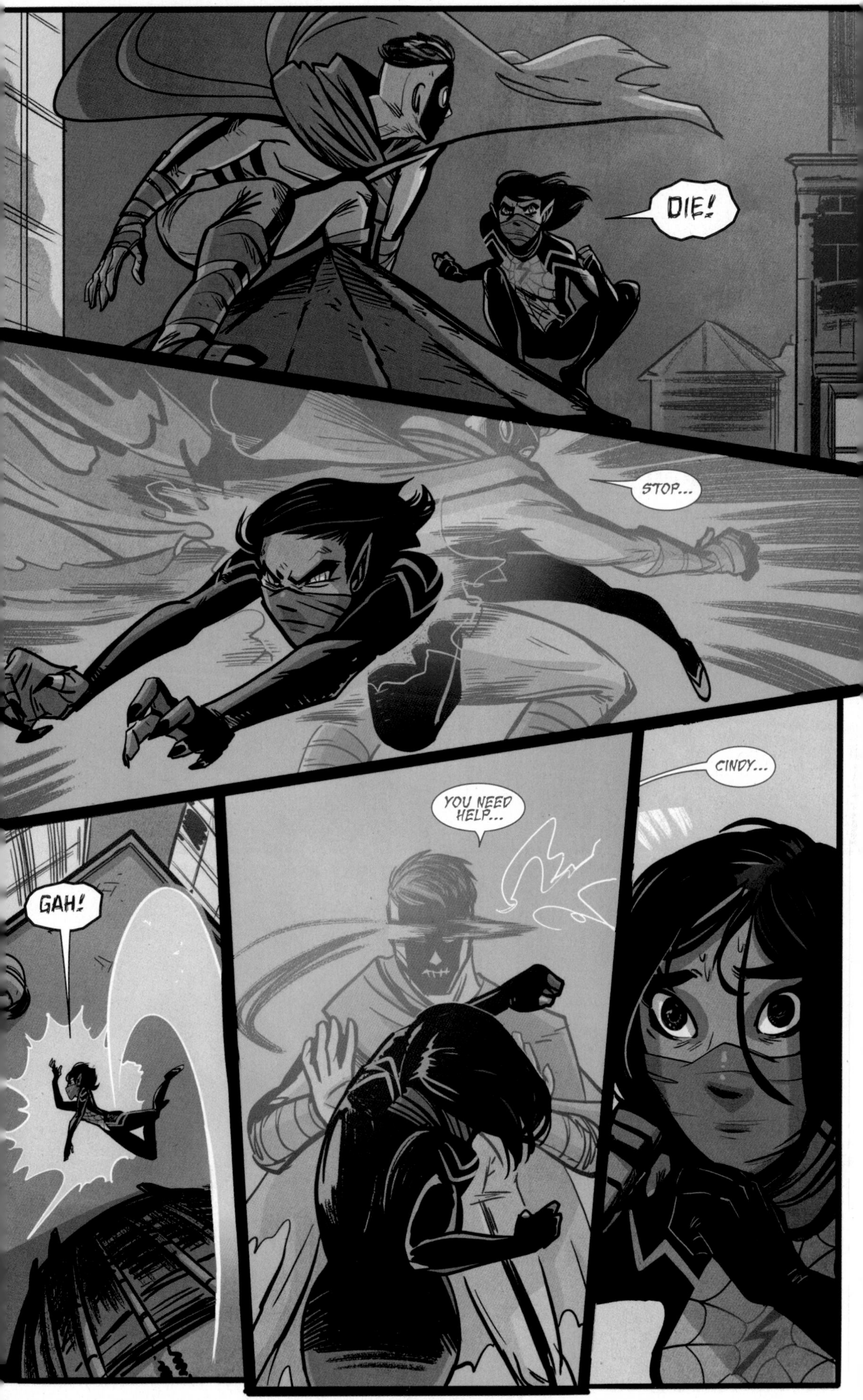

DIE!
STOP...
CINDY...
YOU NEED HELP...
GAH!

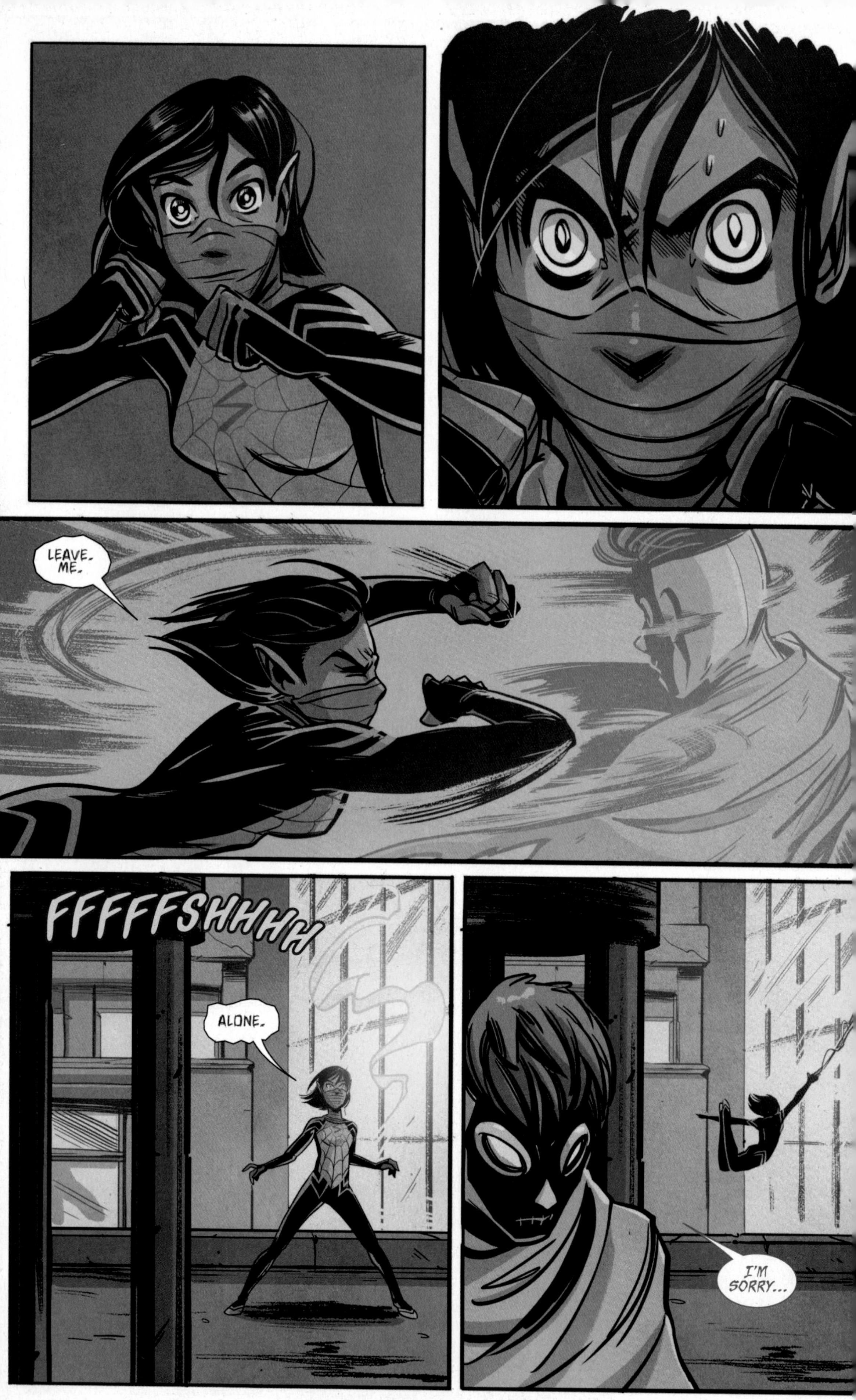

LEAVE. ME.
FFFFFSHHHHH
ALONE.
I'M SORRY...

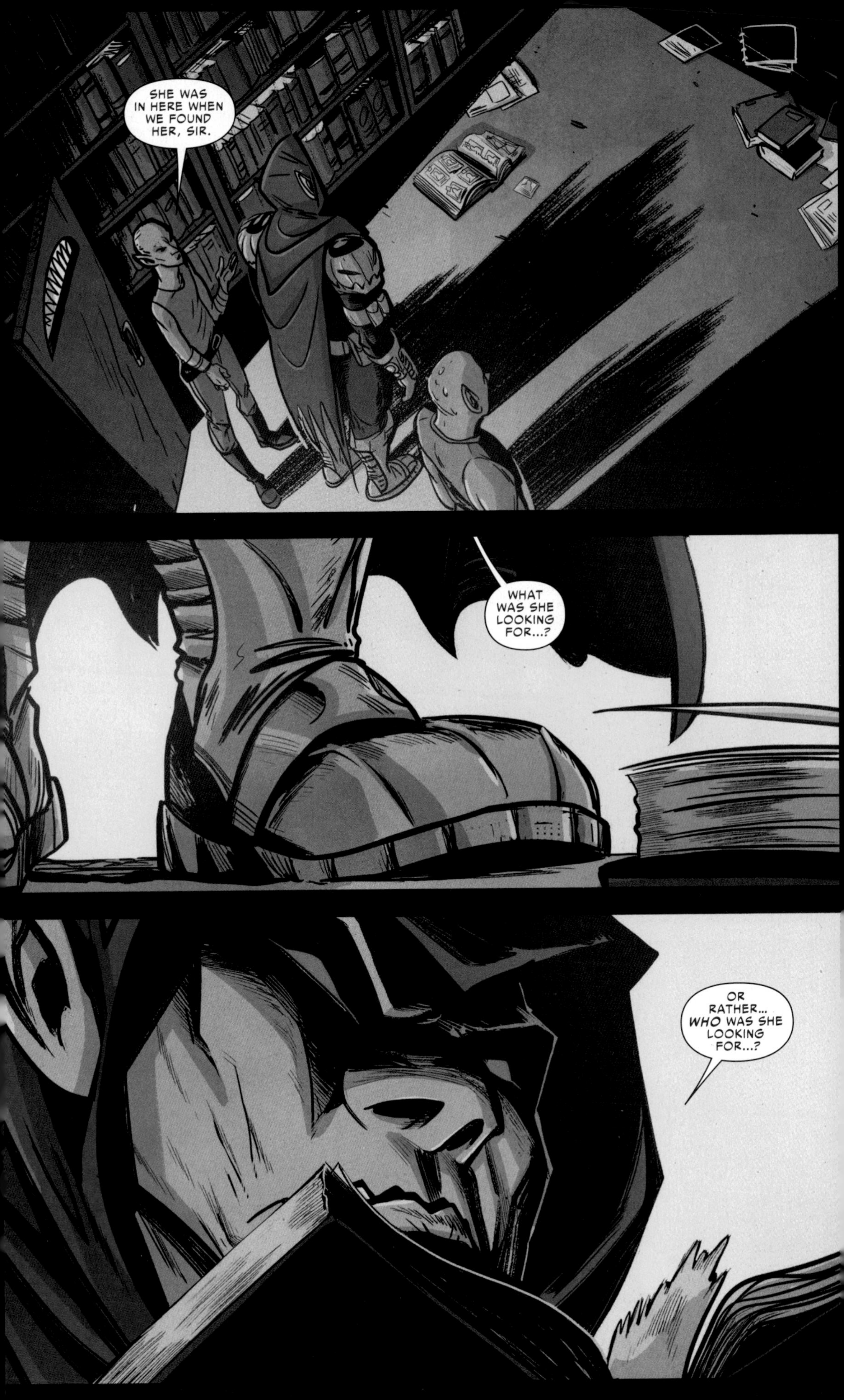
SHE WAS IN HERE WHEN WE FOUND HER, SIR.
WHAT WAS SHE LOOKING FOR...?
OR RATHER... WHO WAS SHE LOOKING FOR...?

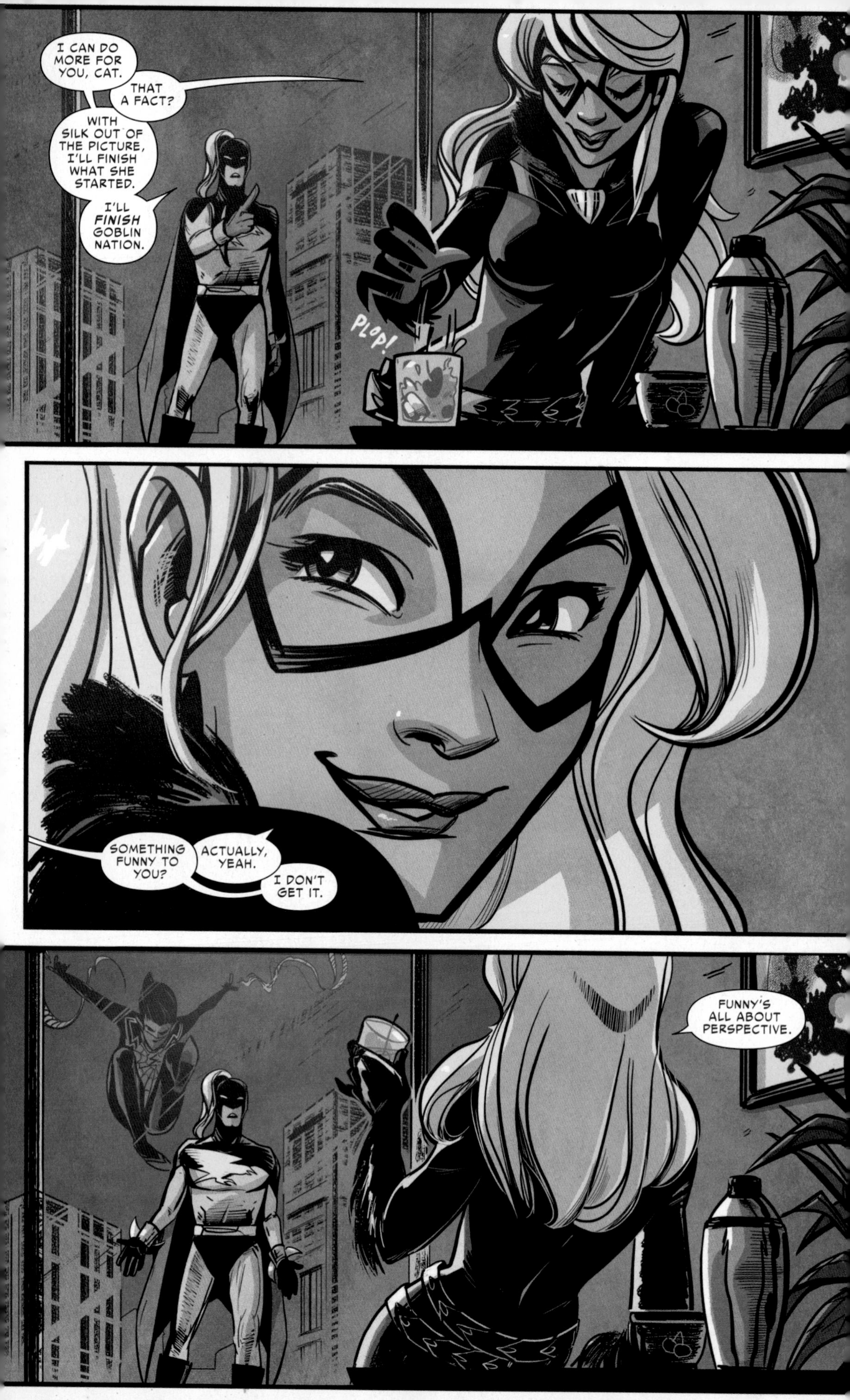
I CAN DO MORE FOR YOU, CAT.
THAT A FACT?
WITH SILK OUT OF THE PICTURE, I'LL FINISH WHAT SHE STARTED.
I'LL FINISH GOBLIN NATION.
PLOP!
SOMETHING FUNNY TO YOU?
ACTUALLY, YEAH.
I DON'T GET IT.
FUNNY'S ALL ABOUT PERSPECTIVE.

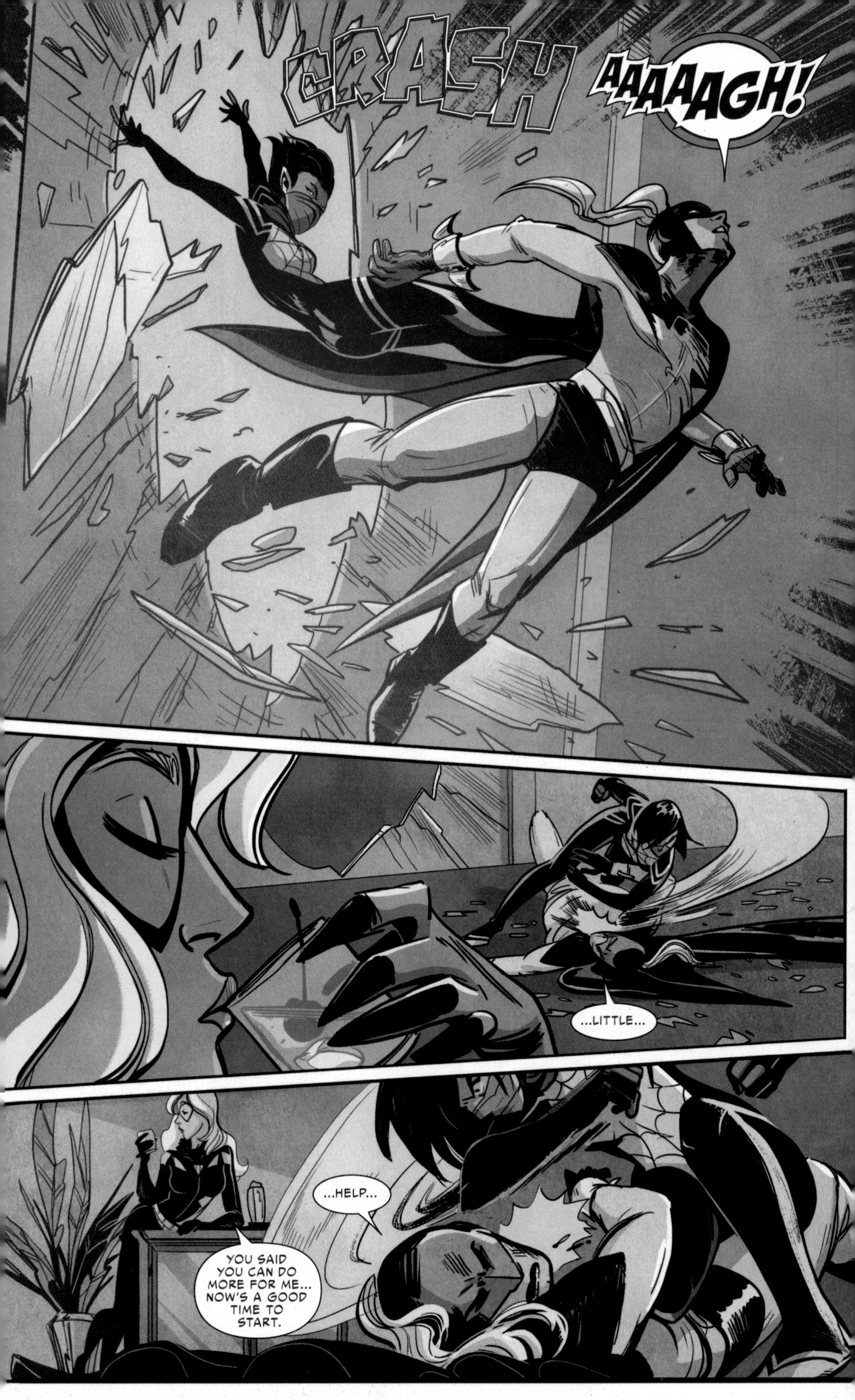
CRASH
AAAAAGH!
...LITTLE...
...HELP...
YOU SAID YOU CAN DO MORE FOR ME... NOW'S A GOOD TIME TO START.

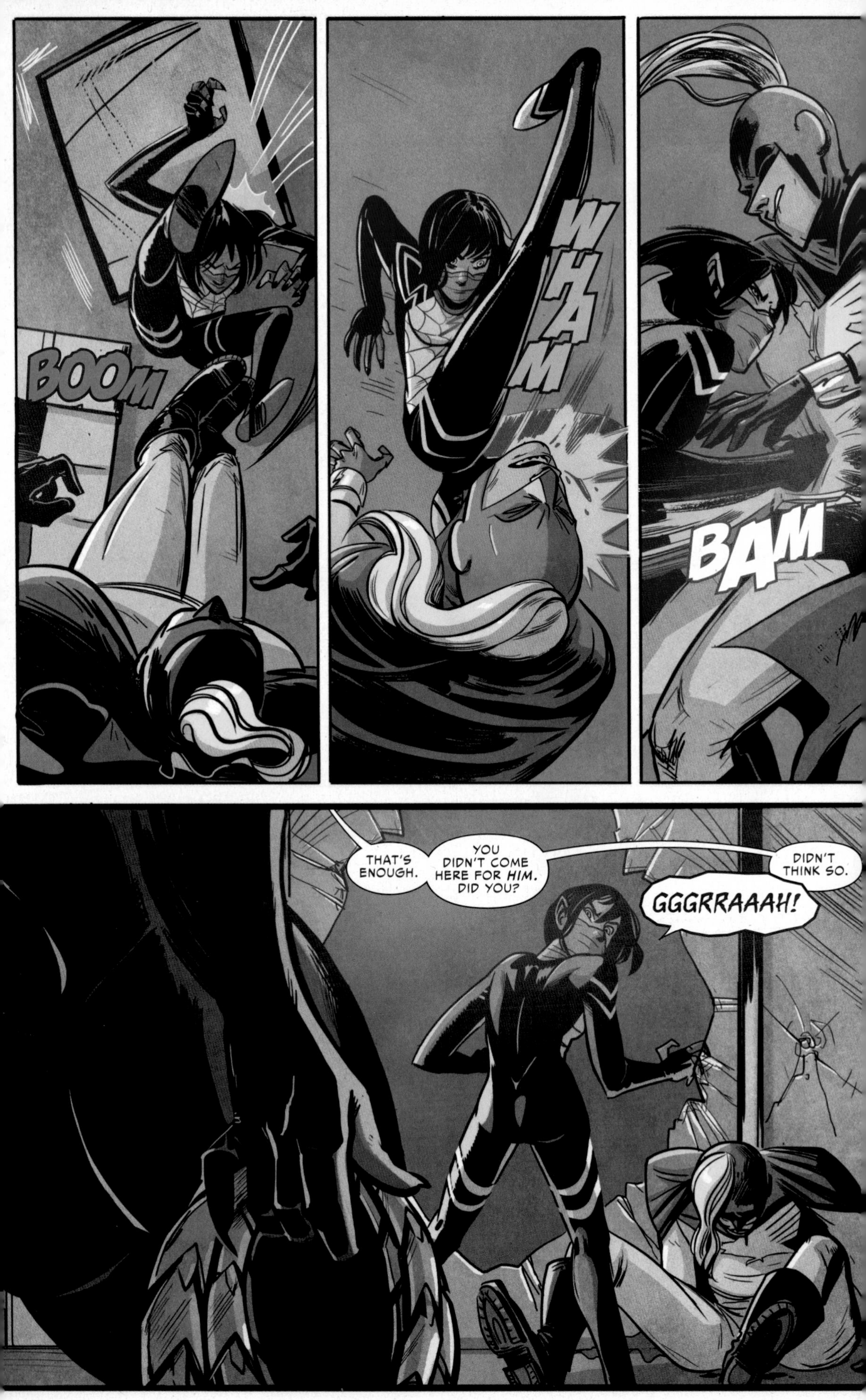
BOOM
WHAM
BAM
THAT'S ENOUGH.
YOU DIDN'T COME HERE FOR *HIM*. DID YOU?
DIDN'T THINK SO.
GGGRRAAAH!

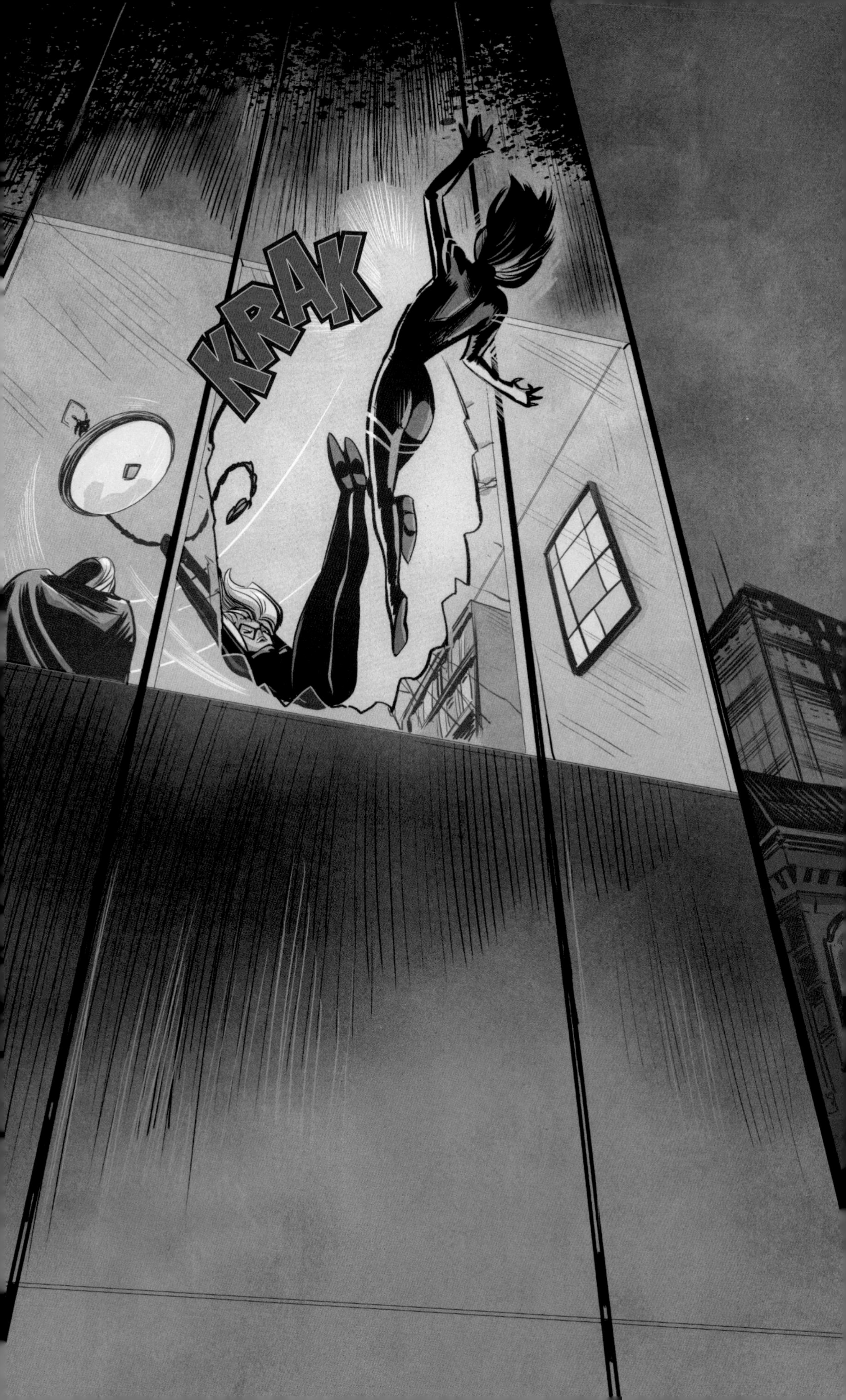
KRAK

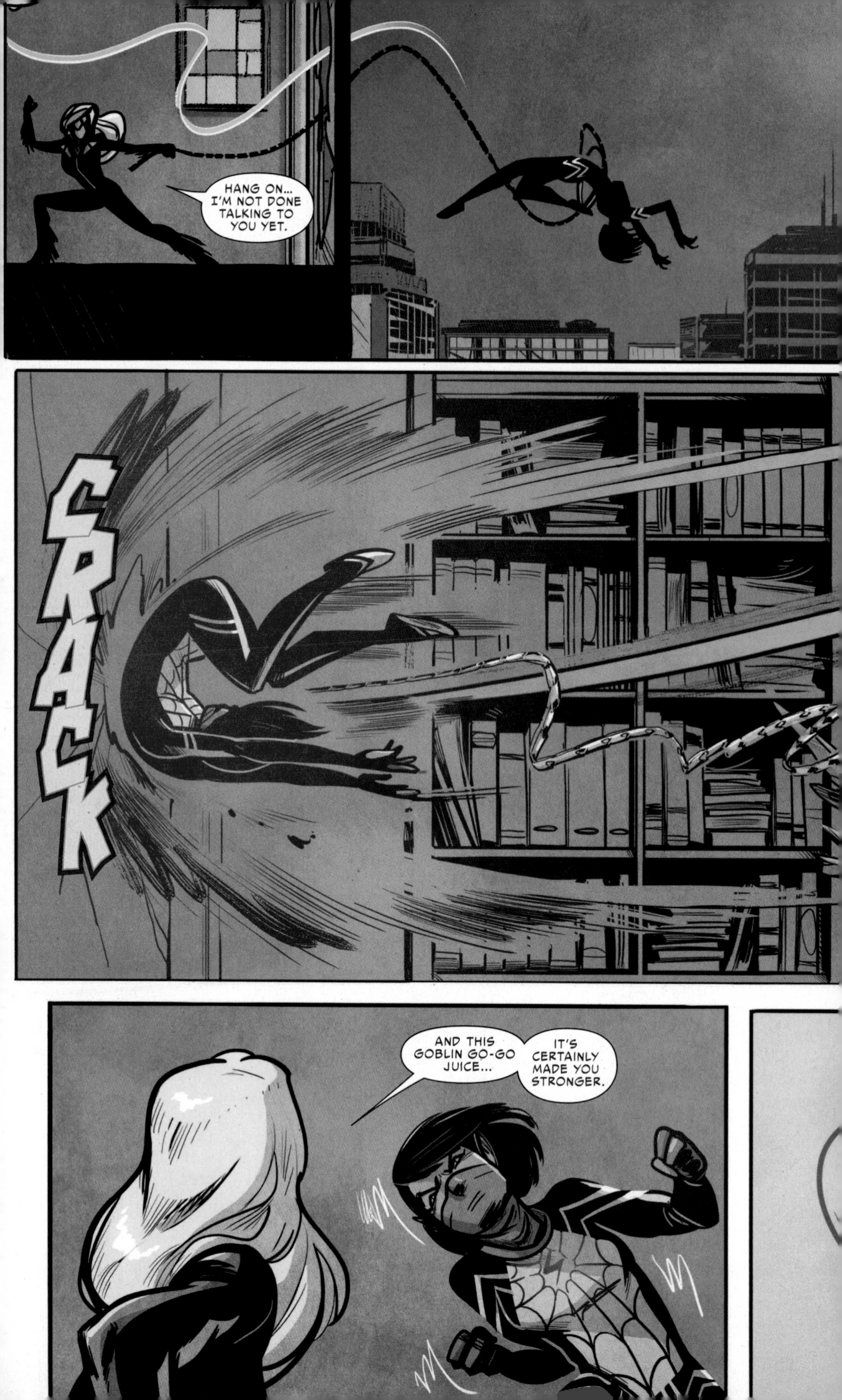
HANG ON... I'M NOT DONE TALKING TO YOU YET.
CRACK
AND THIS GOBLIN GO-GO JUICE...
IT'S CERTAINLY MADE YOU STRONGER.

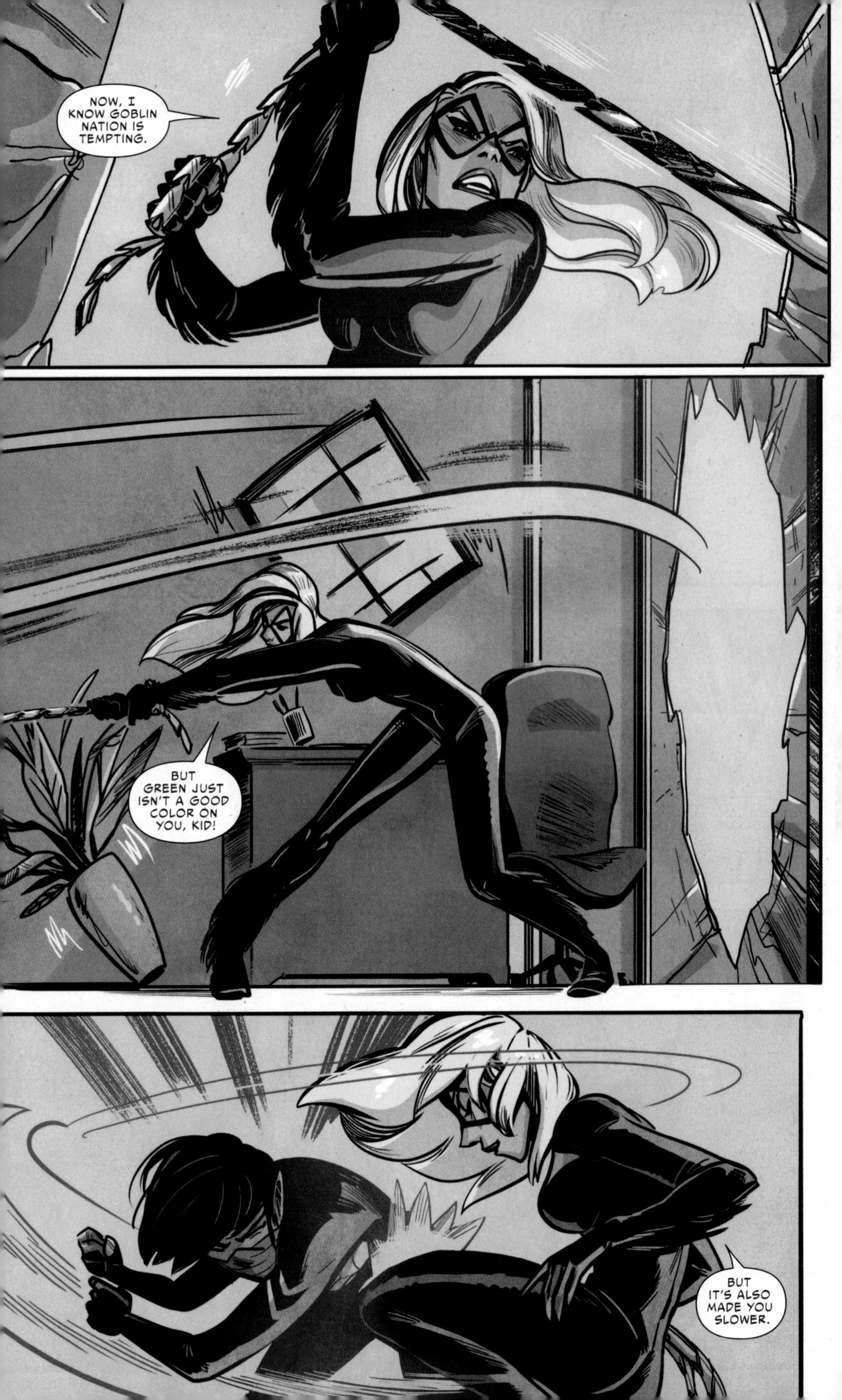
NOW, I KNOW GOBLIN NATION IS TEMPTING.
BUT GREEN JUST ISN'T A GOOD COLOR ON YOU, KID!
BUT IT'S ALSO MADE YOU SLOWER.

BUT I THINK WE CAN WIN YOU BACK. FIRST AND FOREMOST...

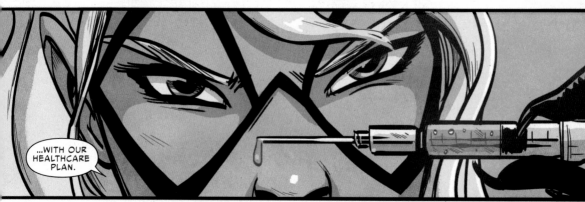

...WITH OUR HEALTHCARE PLAN.

AAAAGHH!

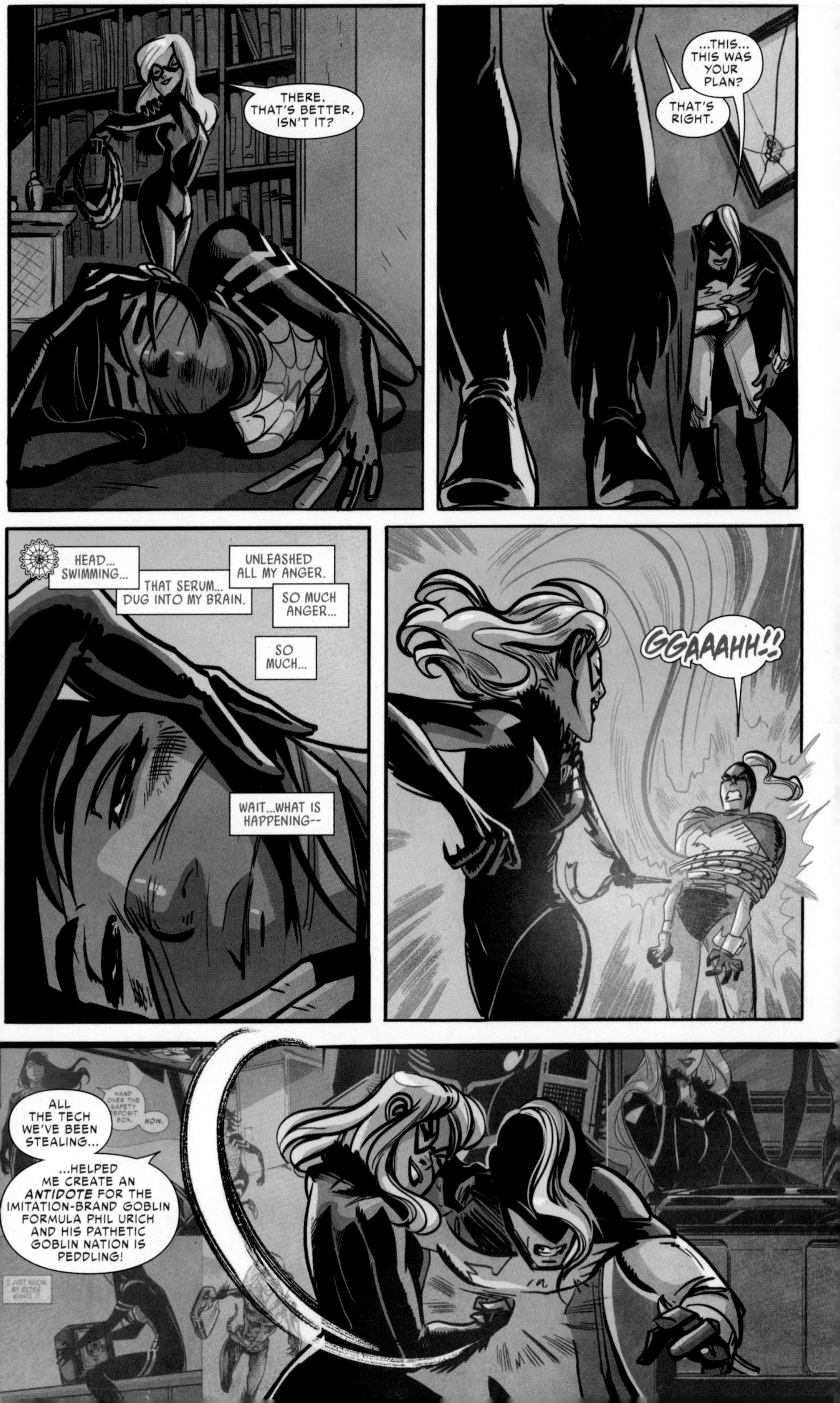
THERE. THAT'S BETTER, ISN'T IT?
...THIS... THIS WAS YOUR PLAN?
THAT'S RIGHT.
HEAD... SWIMMING...
THAT SERUM... DUG INTO MY BRAIN.
UNLEASHED ALL MY ANGER.
SO MUCH ANGER...
SO MUCH...
WAIT...WHAT IS HAPPENING--
GGAAAHH!!
ALL THE TECH WE'VE BEEN STEALING...
HAND OVER THE SAFETY DEPOSIT BOX.
NOW.
...HELPED ME CREATE AN *ANTIDOTE* FOR THE IMITATION-BRAND GOBLIN FORMULA PHIL URICH AND HIS PATHETIC GOBLIN NATION IS PEDDLING!
I JUST KNOW MY BOSS WANTS IT.

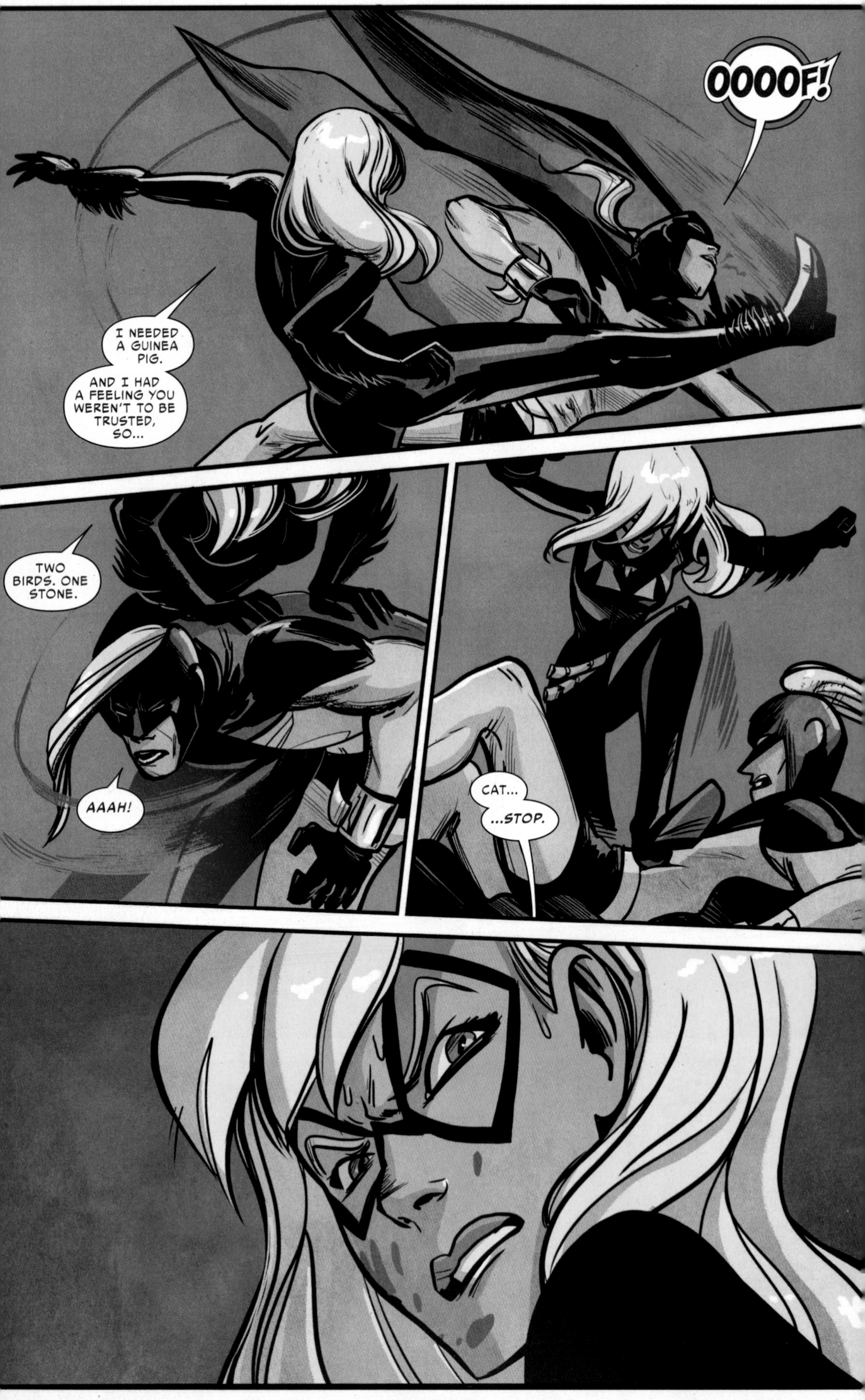
OOOOF!
I NEEDED A GUINEA PIG.
AND I HAD A FEELING YOU WEREN'T TO BE TRUSTED, SO...
TWO BIRDS. ONE STONE.
AAAH!
CAT...
...STOP.

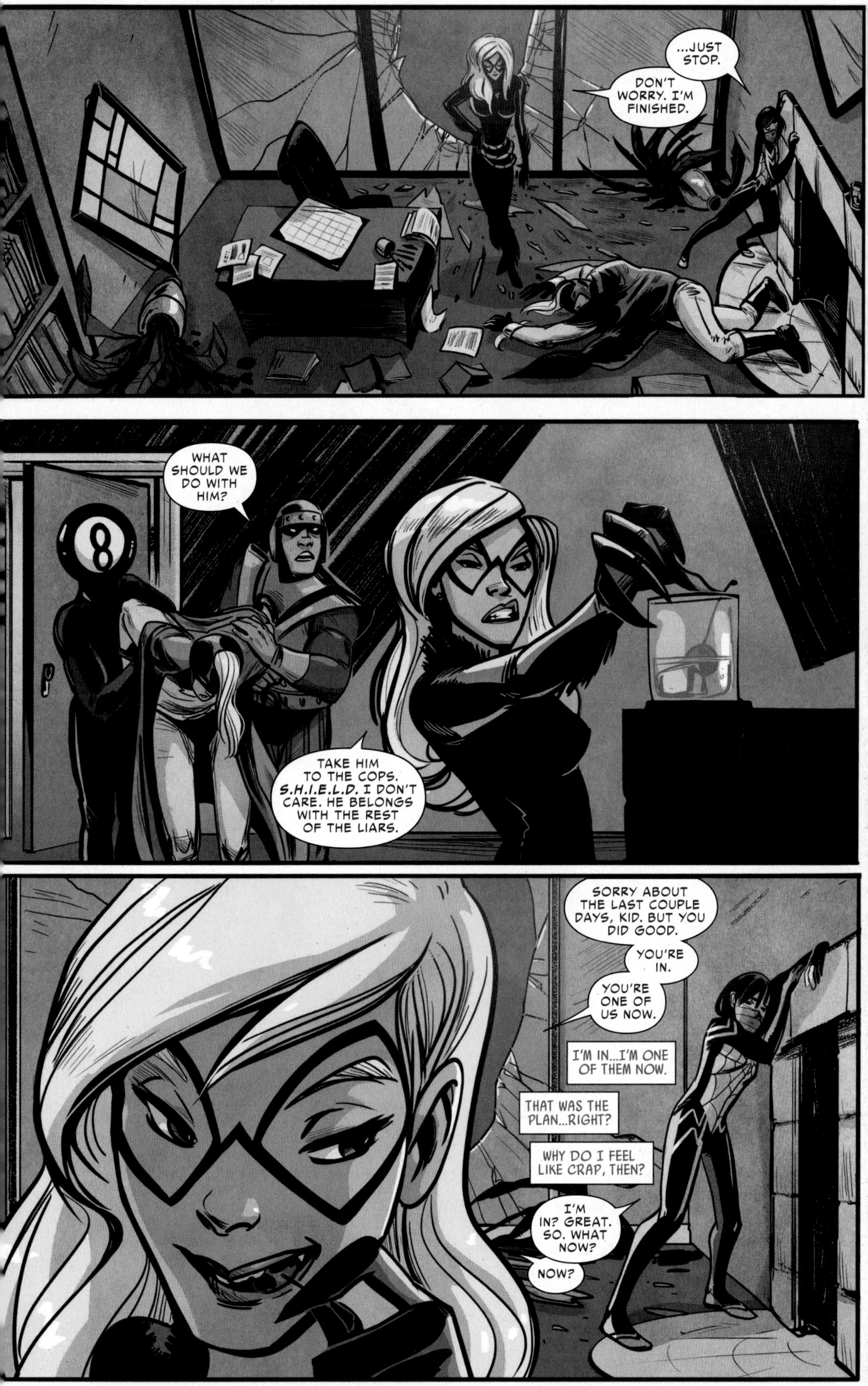
...JUST STOP.
DON'T WORRY. I'M FINISHED.
WHAT SHOULD WE DO WITH HIM?
TAKE HIM TO THE COPS. S.H.I.E.L.D. I DON'T CARE. HE BELONGS WITH THE REST OF THE LIARS.
SORRY ABOUT THE LAST COUPLE DAYS, KID. BUT YOU DID GOOD.
YOU'RE IN.
YOU'RE ONE OF US NOW.
I'M IN...I'M ONE OF THEM NOW.
THAT WAS THE PLAN...RIGHT?
WHY DO I FEEL LIKE CRAP, THEN?
I'M IN? GREAT. SO. WHAT NOW?
NOW?

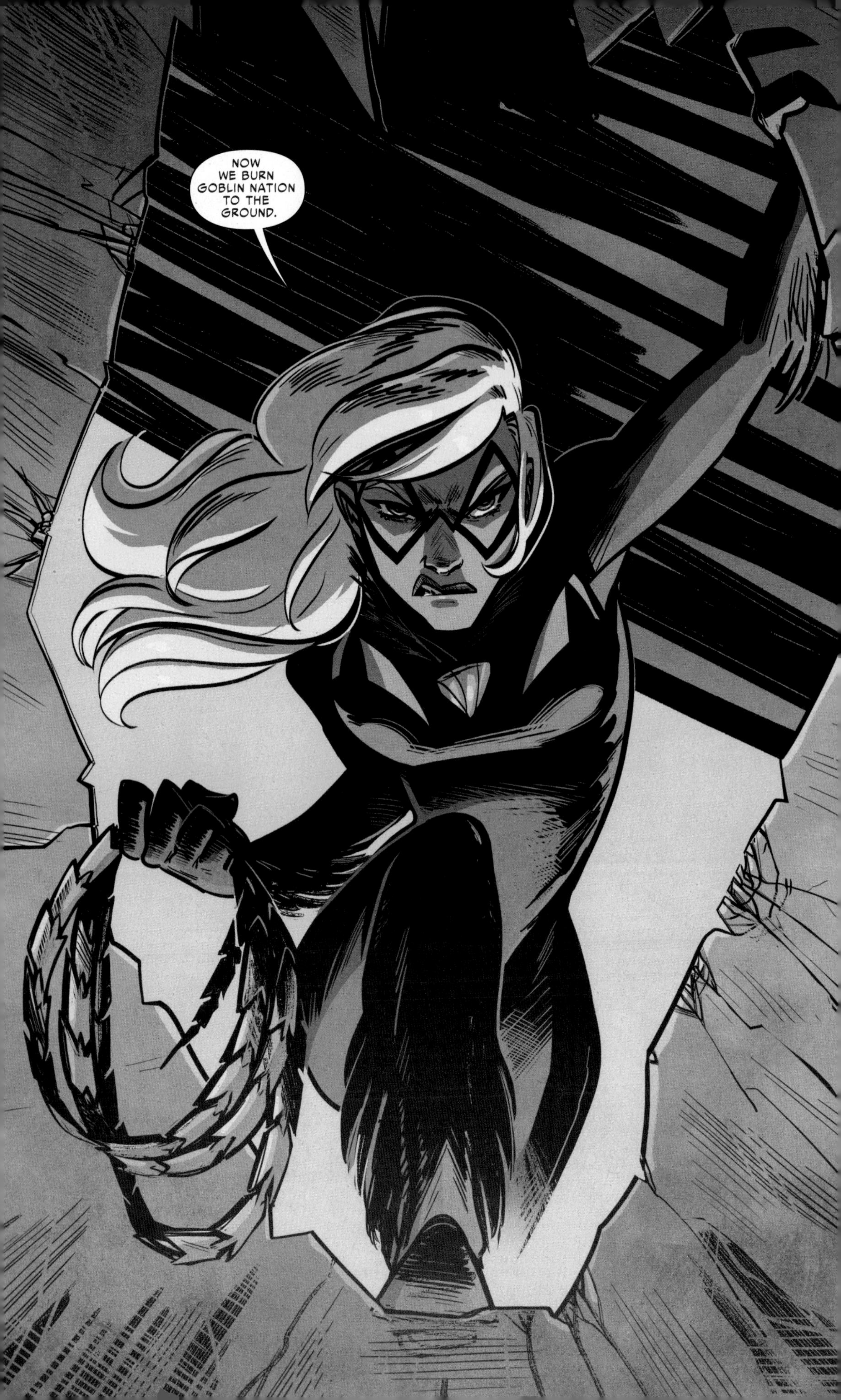
NOW WE BURN GOBLIN NATION TO THE GROUND.

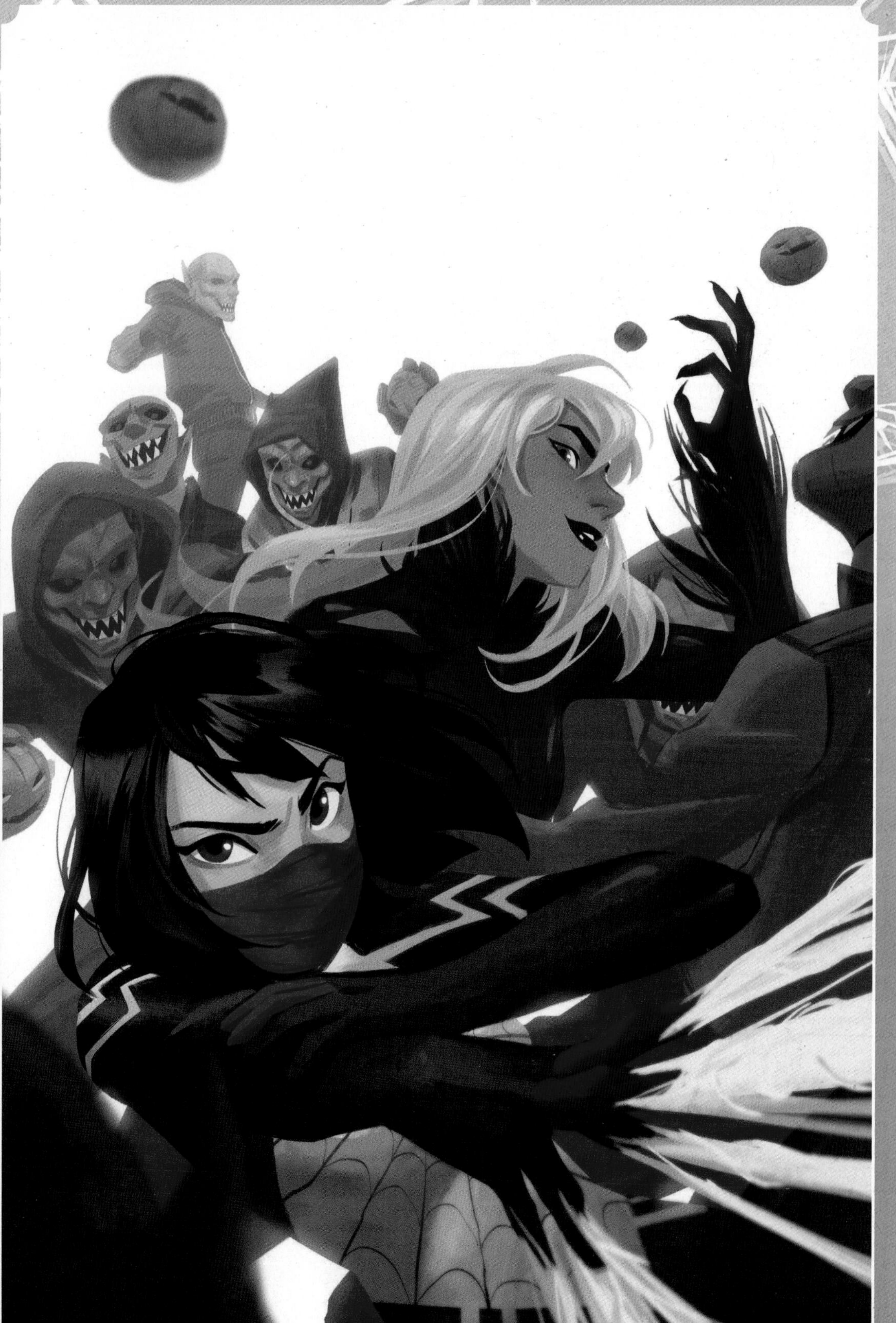

SILK (2015 B) #6

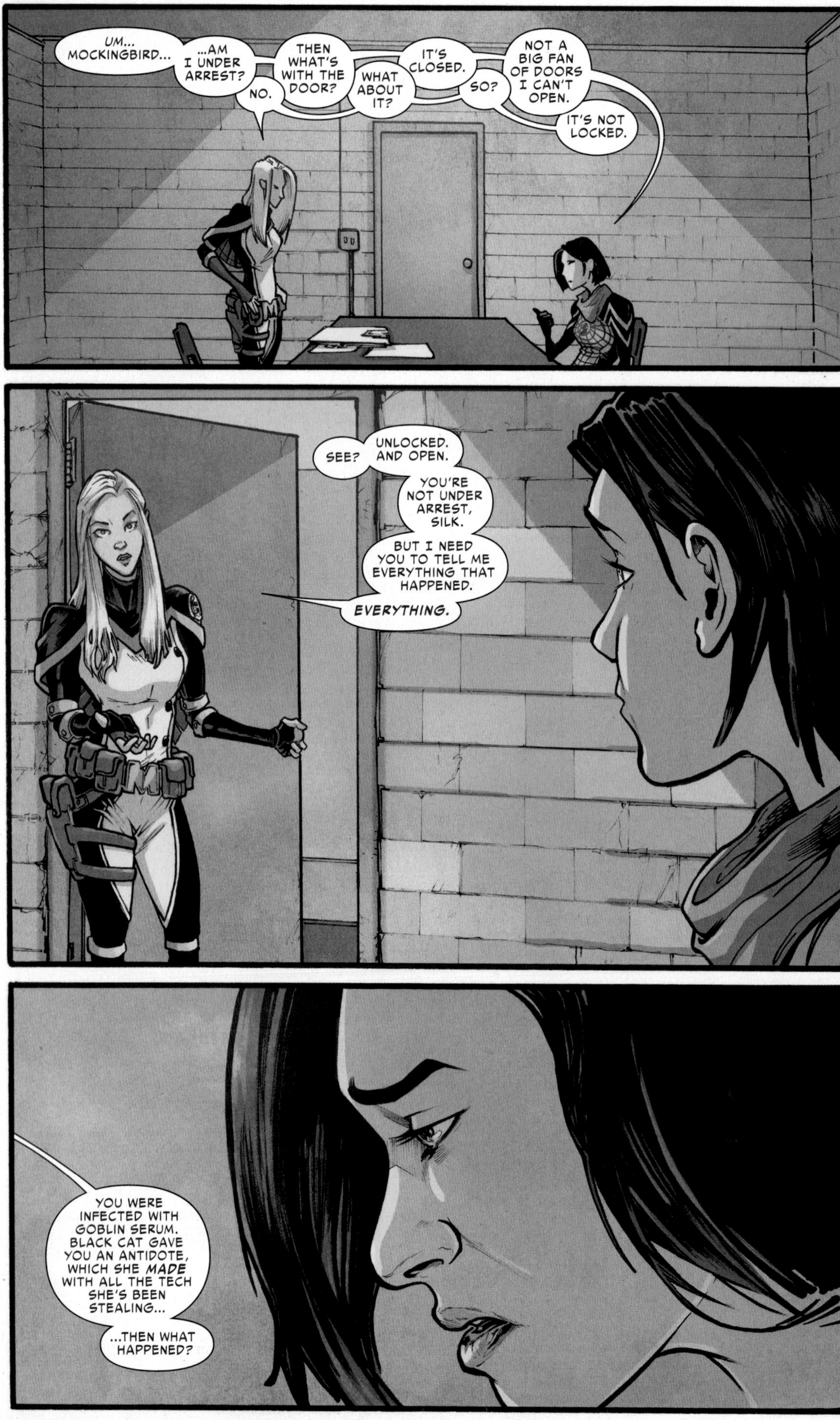
UM... MOCKINGBIRD...
...AM I UNDER ARREST?
NO.
THEN WHAT'S WITH THE DOOR?
WHAT ABOUT IT?
IT'S CLOSED.
SO?
NOT A BIG FAN OF DOORS I CAN'T OPEN.
IT'S NOT LOCKED.
SEE?
UNLOCKED. AND OPEN.
YOU'RE NOT UNDER ARREST, SILK.
BUT I NEED YOU TO TELL ME EVERYTHING THAT HAPPENED.
EVERYTHING.
YOU WERE INFECTED WITH GOBLIN SERUM. BLACK CAT GAVE YOU AN ANTIDOTE, WHICH SHE MADE WITH ALL THE TECH SHE'S BEEN STEALING...
...THEN WHAT HAPPENED?

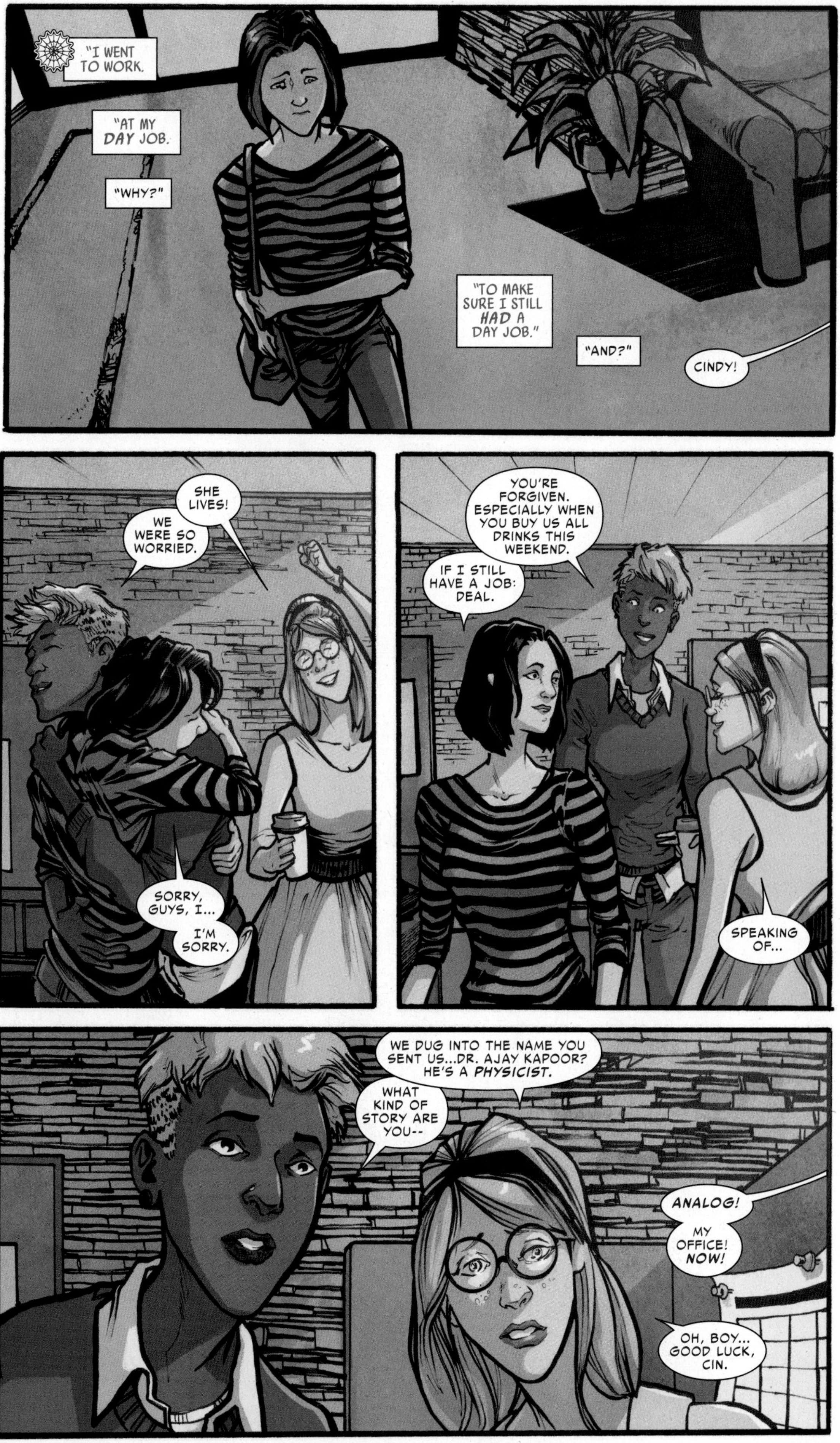
"I WENT TO WORK.
"AT MY DAY JOB.
"WHY?"
"TO MAKE SURE I STILL HAD A DAY JOB."
"AND?"
CINDY!
WE WERE SO WORRIED.
SHE LIVES!
SORRY, GUYS, I...
I'M SORRY.
YOU'RE FORGIVEN. ESPECIALLY WHEN YOU BUY US ALL DRINKS THIS WEEKEND.
IF I STILL HAVE A JOB: DEAL.
SPEAKING OF...
WE DUG INTO THE NAME YOU SENT US...DR. AJAY KAPOOR? HE'S A PHYSICIST.
WHAT KIND OF STORY ARE YOU--
ANALOG!
MY OFFICE! NOW!
OH, BOY... GOOD LUCK, CIN.

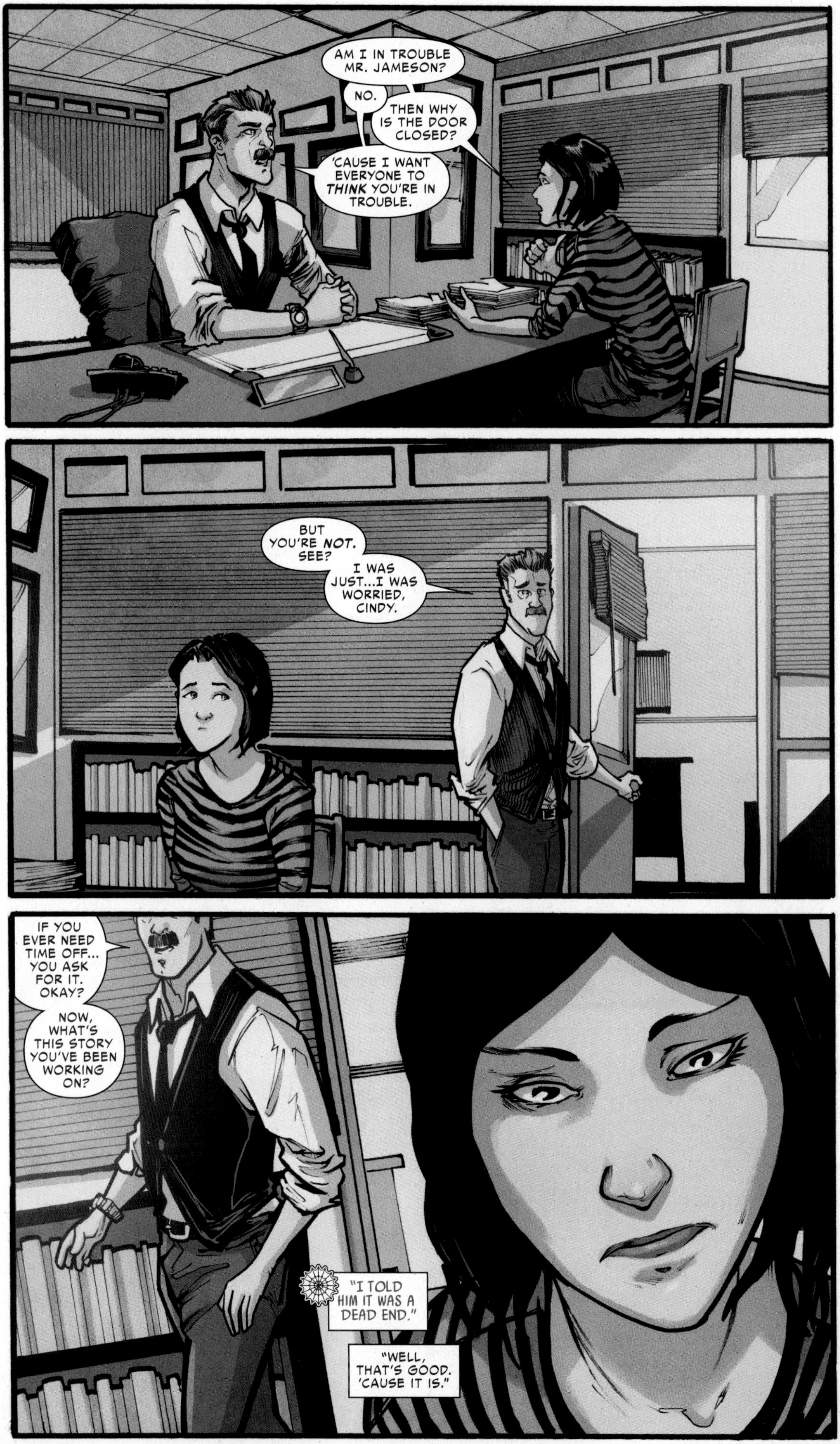

AM I IN TROUBLE MR. JAMESON?
NO.
THEN WHY IS THE DOOR CLOSED?
'CAUSE I WANT EVERYONE TO *THINK* YOU'RE IN TROUBLE.
BUT YOU'RE *NOT.* SEE?
I WAS JUST...I WAS WORRIED, CINDY.
IF YOU EVER NEED TIME OFF... YOU ASK FOR IT. OKAY?
NOW, WHAT'S THIS STORY YOU'VE BEEN WORKING ON?
"I TOLD HIM IT WAS A DEAD END."
"WELL, THAT'S GOOD. 'CAUSE IT IS."

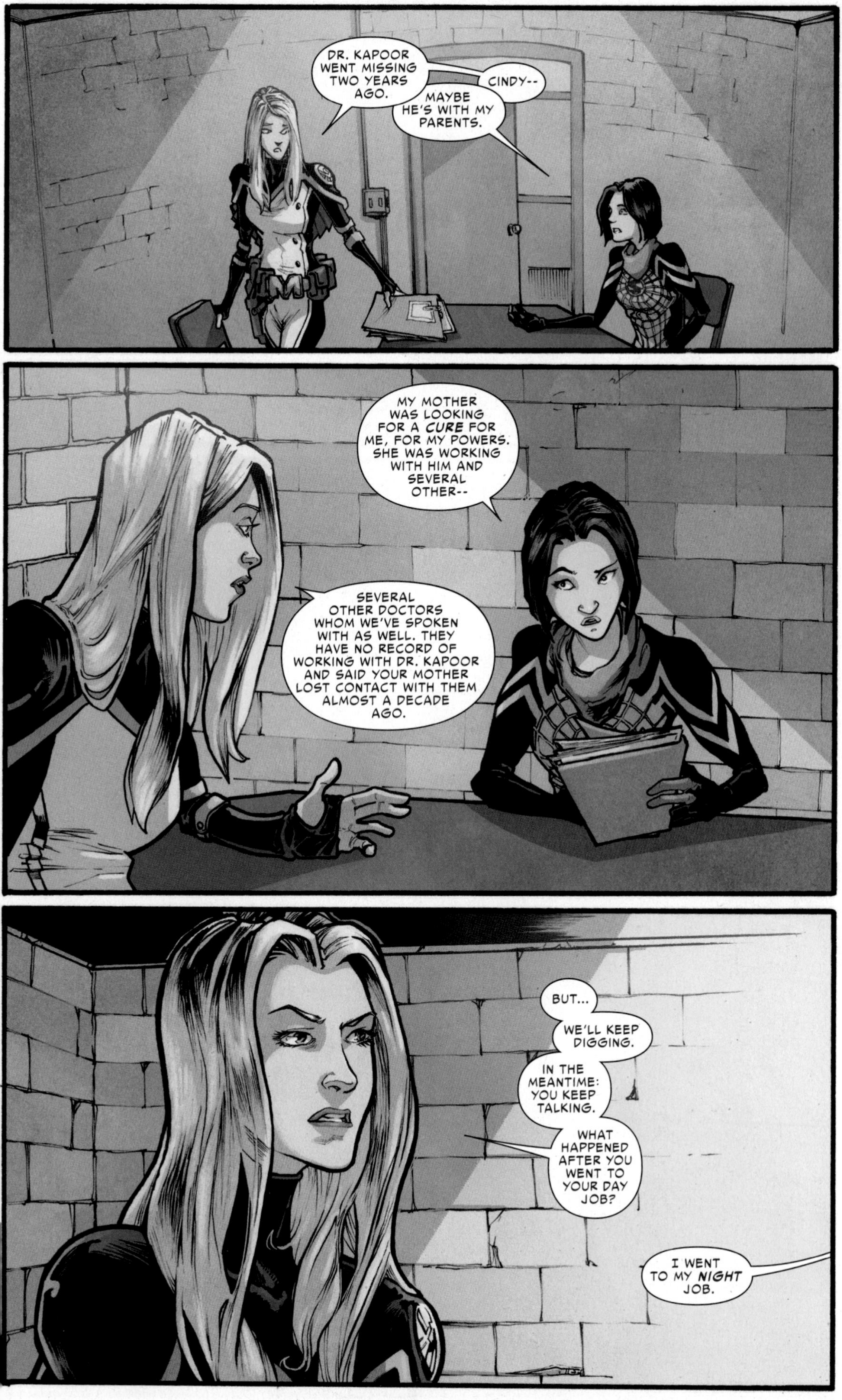

DR. KAPOOR WENT MISSING TWO YEARS AGO.
CINDY--
MAYBE HE'S WITH MY PARENTS.
MY MOTHER WAS LOOKING FOR A *CURE* FOR ME, FOR MY POWERS. SHE WAS WORKING WITH HIM AND SEVERAL OTHER--
SEVERAL OTHER DOCTORS WHOM WE'VE SPOKEN WITH AS WELL. THEY HAVE NO RECORD OF WORKING WITH DR. KAPOOR AND SAID YOUR MOTHER LOST CONTACT WITH THEM ALMOST A DECADE AGO.
BUT...
WE'LL KEEP DIGGING.
IN THE MEANTIME: YOU KEEP TALKING.
WHAT HAPPENED AFTER YOU WENT TO YOUR DAY JOB?
I WENT TO MY ***NIGHT*** JOB.

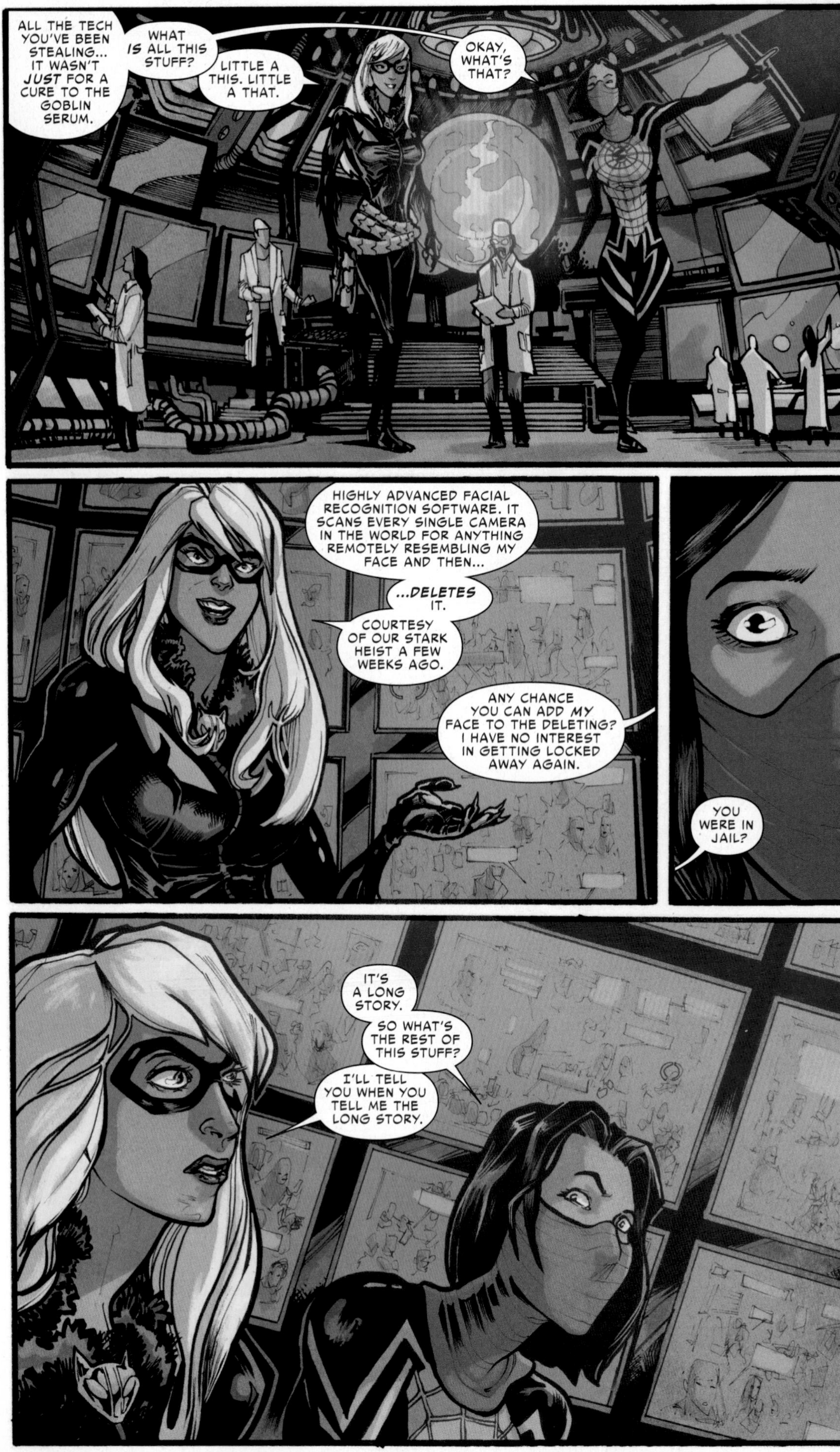

ALL THE TECH YOU'VE BEEN STEALING... IT WASN'T JUST FOR A CURE TO THE GOBLIN SERUM.
WHAT IS ALL THIS STUFF?
LITTLE A THIS. LITTLE A THAT.
OKAY, WHAT'S THAT?
HIGHLY ADVANCED FACIAL RECOGNITION SOFTWARE. IT SCANS EVERY SINGLE CAMERA IN THE WORLD FOR ANYTHING REMOTELY RESEMBLING MY FACE AND THEN...
...DELETES IT.
COURTESY OF OUR STARK HEIST A FEW WEEKS AGO.
ANY CHANCE YOU CAN ADD MY FACE TO THE DELETING? I HAVE NO INTEREST IN GETTING LOCKED AWAY AGAIN.
YOU WERE IN JAIL?
IT'S A LONG STORY.
SO WHAT'S THE REST OF THIS STUFF?
I'LL TELL YOU WHEN YOU TELL ME THE LONG STORY.

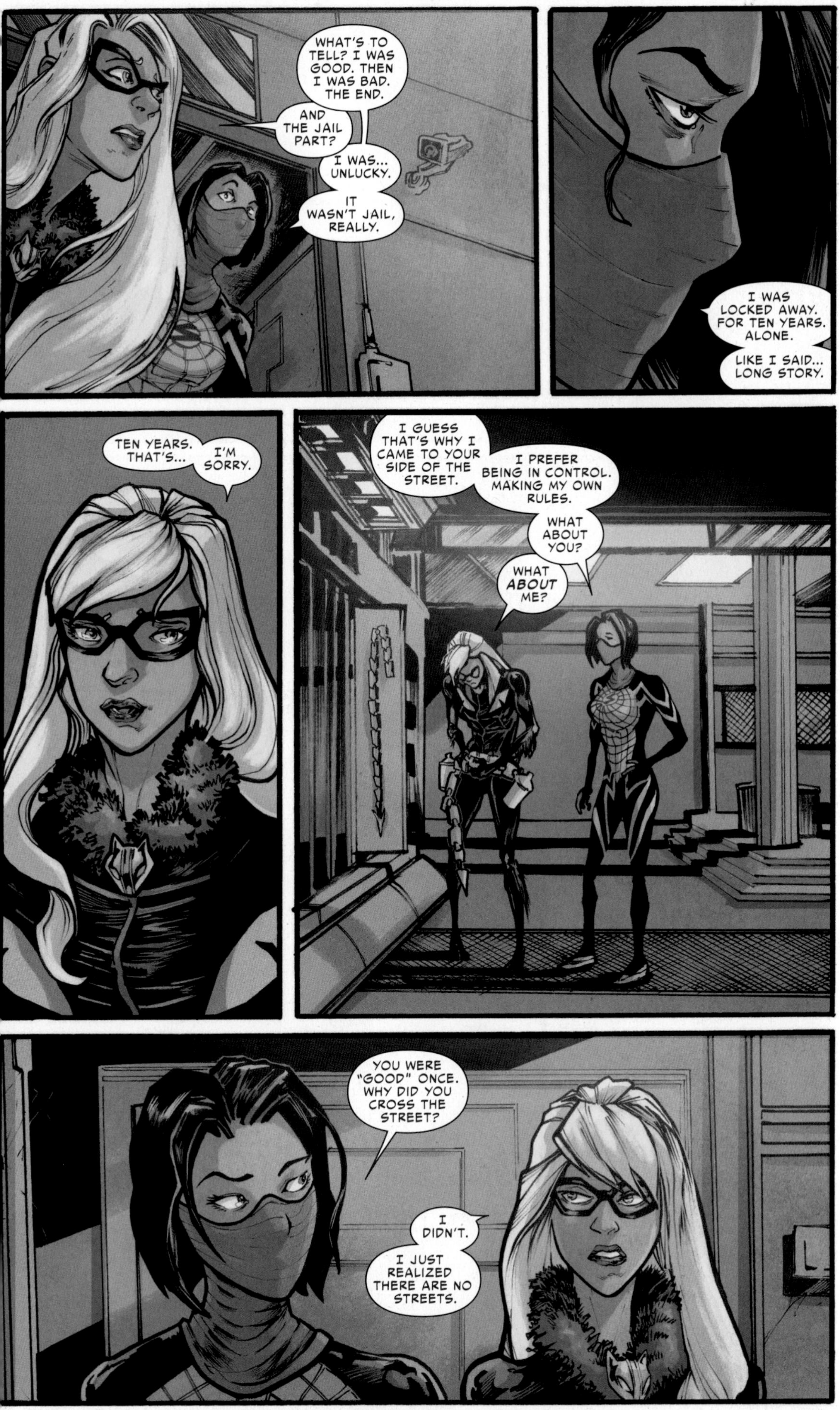
WHAT'S TO TELL? I WAS GOOD. THEN I WAS BAD. THE END.
AND THE JAIL PART?
I WAS... UNLUCKY.
IT WASN'T JAIL, REALLY.
I WAS LOCKED AWAY. FOR TEN YEARS. ALONE.
LIKE I SAID... LONG STORY.
TEN YEARS. THAT'S...
I'M SORRY.
I GUESS THAT'S WHY I CAME TO YOUR SIDE OF THE STREET.
I PREFER BEING IN CONTROL. MAKING MY OWN RULES.
WHAT ABOUT YOU?
WHAT *ABOUT* ME?
YOU WERE "GOOD" ONCE. WHY DID YOU CROSS THE STREET?
I DIDN'T.
I JUST REALIZED THERE ARE NO STREETS.

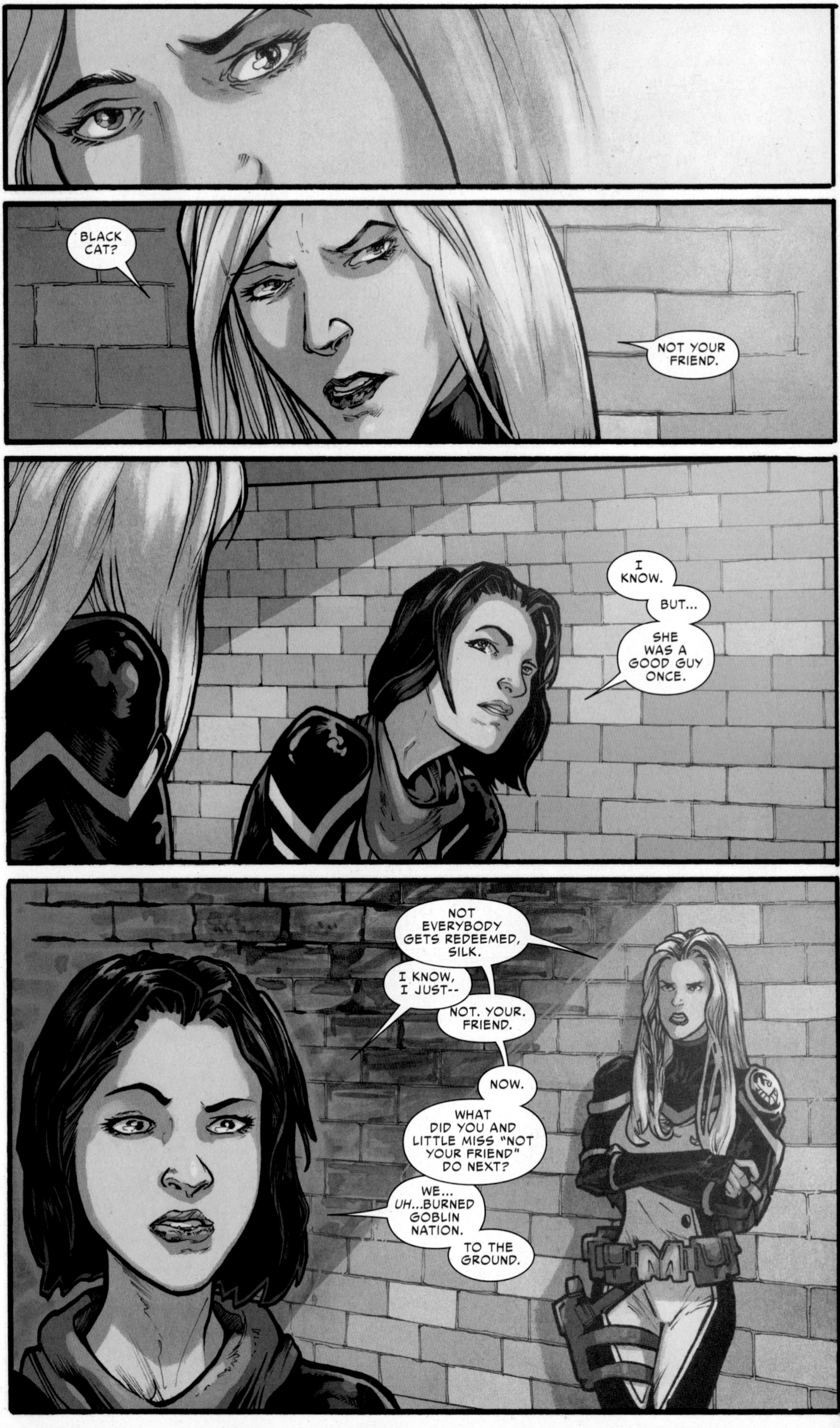
BLACK CAT?
NOT YOUR FRIEND.
I KNOW.
BUT...
SHE WAS A GOOD GUY ONCE.
NOT EVERYBODY GETS REDEEMED, SILK.
I KNOW, I JUST--
NOT. YOUR. FRIEND.
NOW.
WHAT DID YOU AND LITTLE MISS "NOT YOUR FRIEND" DO NEXT?
WE... *UH*...BURNED GOBLIN NATION.
TO THE GROUND.

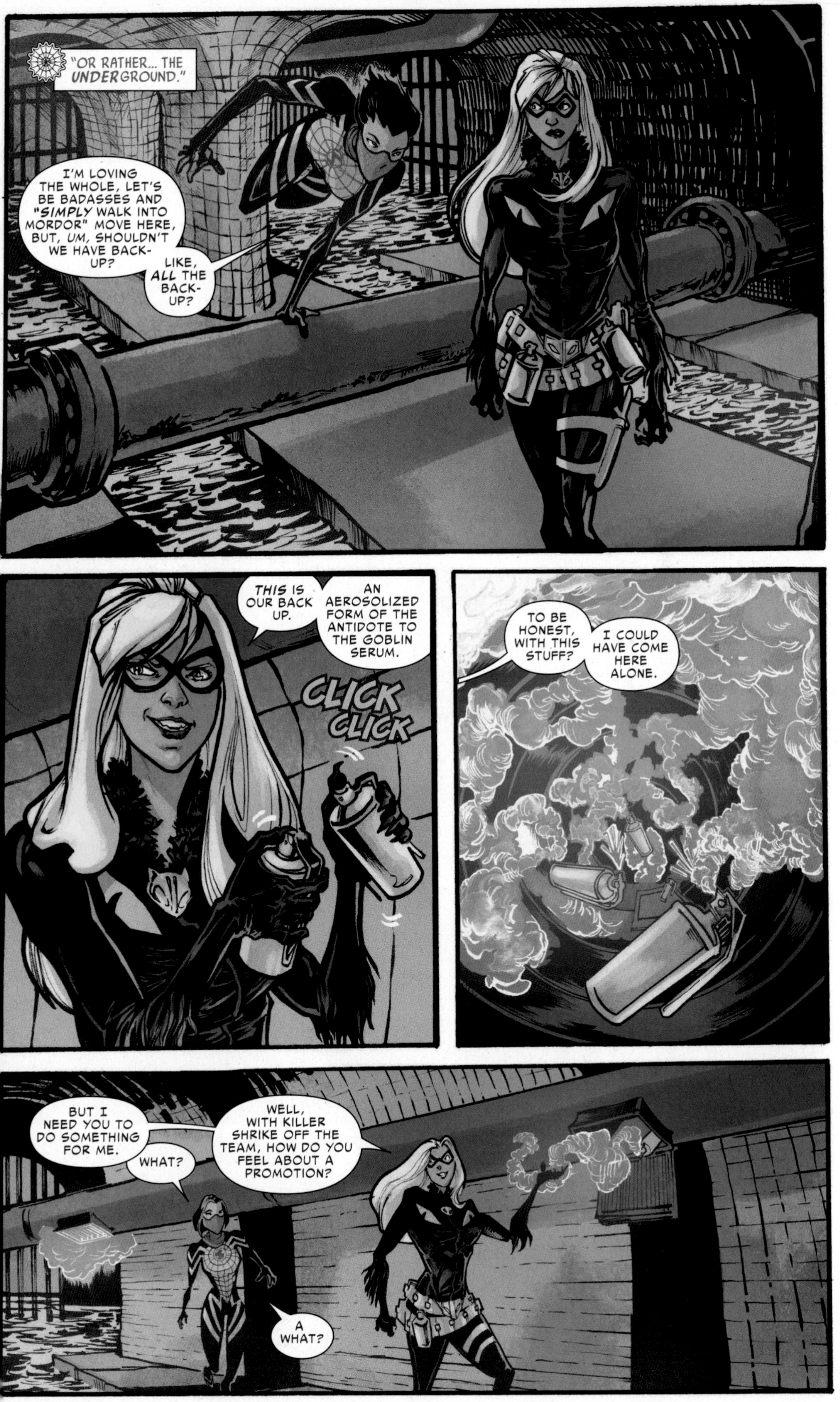
"OR RATHER... THE *UNDER*GROUND."
I'M LOVING THE WHOLE, LET'S BE BADASSES AND *"SIMPLY* WALK INTO MORDOR" MOVE HERE, BUT, *UM*, SHOULDN'T WE HAVE BACK-UP?
LIKE, *ALL* THE BACK-UP?
THIS IS OUR BACK UP.
AN AEROSOLIZED FORM OF THE ANTIDOTE TO THE GOBLIN SERUM.
CLICK CLICK
TO BE HONEST, WITH THIS STUFF?
I COULD HAVE COME HERE ALONE.
BUT I NEED YOU TO DO SOMETHING FOR ME.
WHAT?
WELL, WITH KILLER SHRIKE OFF THE TEAM, HOW DO YOU FEEL ABOUT A PROMOTION?
A WHAT?

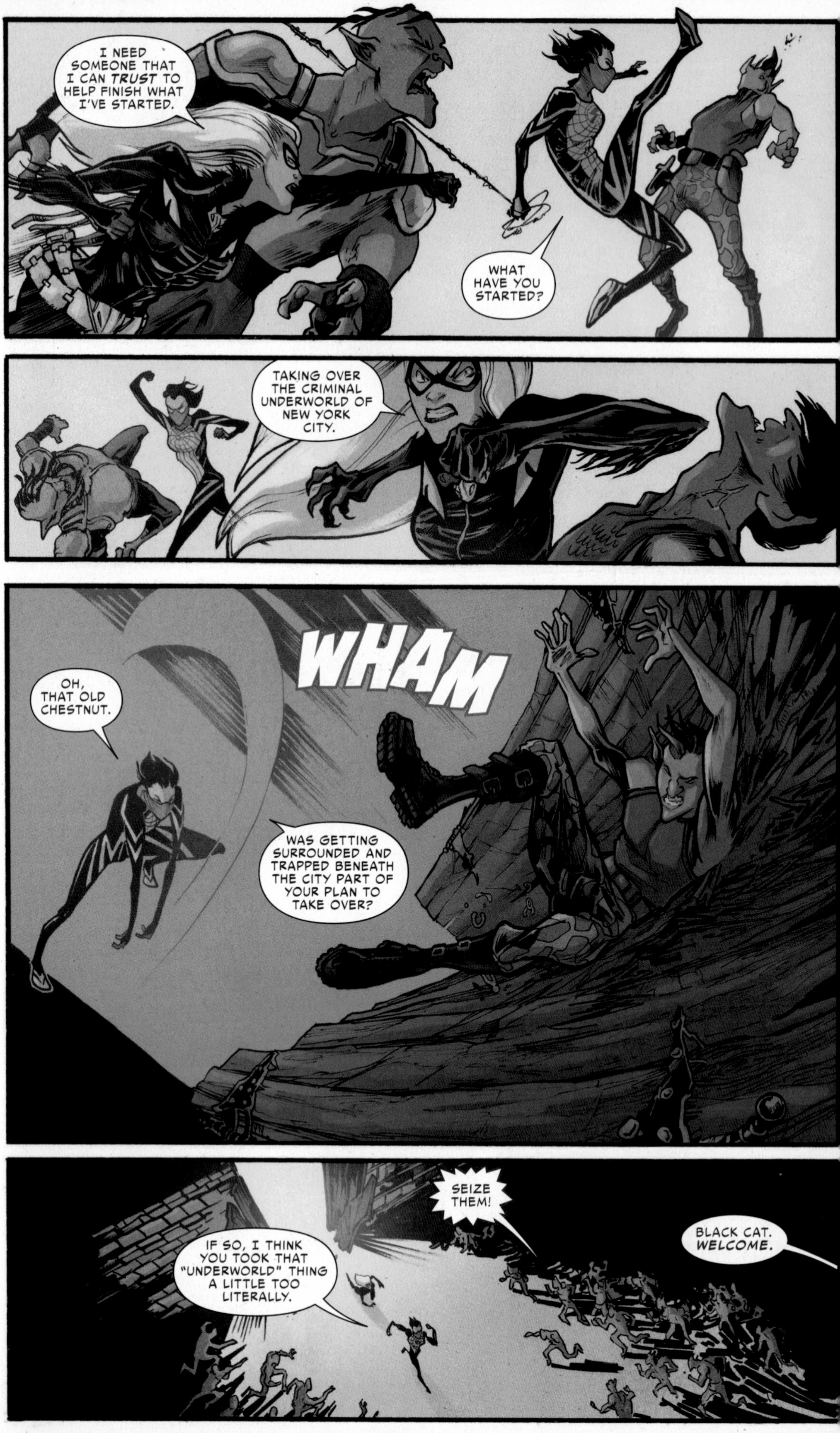
I NEED SOMEONE THAT I CAN *TRUST* TO HELP FINISH WHAT I'VE STARTED.
WHAT HAVE YOU STARTED?
TAKING OVER THE CRIMINAL UNDERWORLD OF NEW YORK CITY.
WHAM
OH, THAT OLD CHESTNUT.
WAS GETTING SURROUNDED AND TRAPPED BENEATH THE CITY PART OF YOUR PLAN TO TAKE OVER?
IF SO, I THINK YOU TOOK THAT "UNDERWORLD" THING A LITTLE TOO LITERALLY.
SEIZE THEM!
BLACK CAT. *WELCOME.*

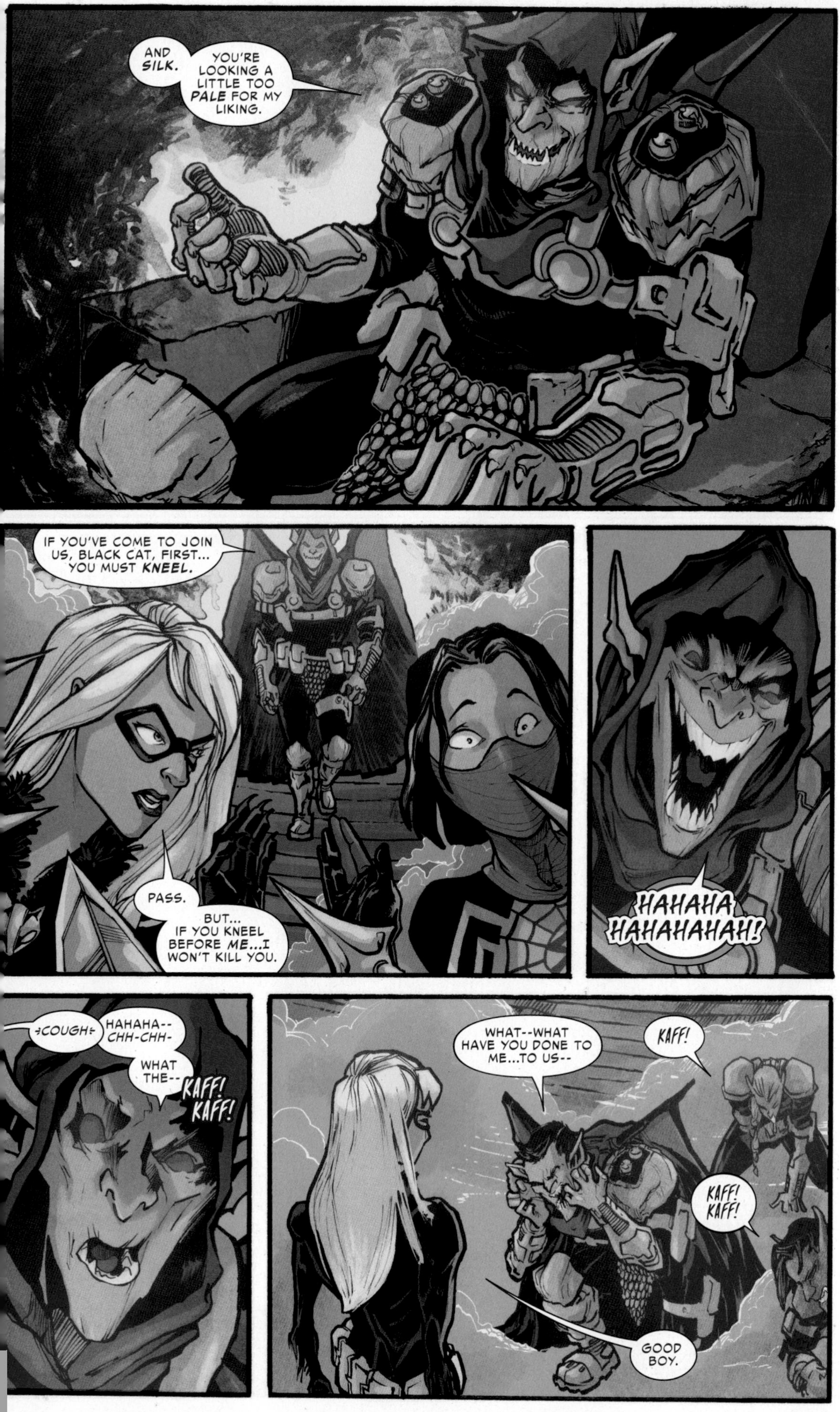
AND SILK.
YOU'RE LOOKING A LITTLE TOO PALE FOR MY LIKING.
IF YOU'VE COME TO JOIN US, BLACK CAT, FIRST... YOU MUST KNEEL.
PASS.
BUT... IF YOU KNEEL BEFORE ME...I WON'T KILL YOU.
HAHAHA HAHAHAHAH!
COUGH
HAHAHA-- CHH-CHH-
WHAT THE--
KAFF! KAFF!
WHAT--WHAT HAVE YOU DONE TO ME...TO US--
KAFF!
KAFF! KAFF!
GOOD BOY.

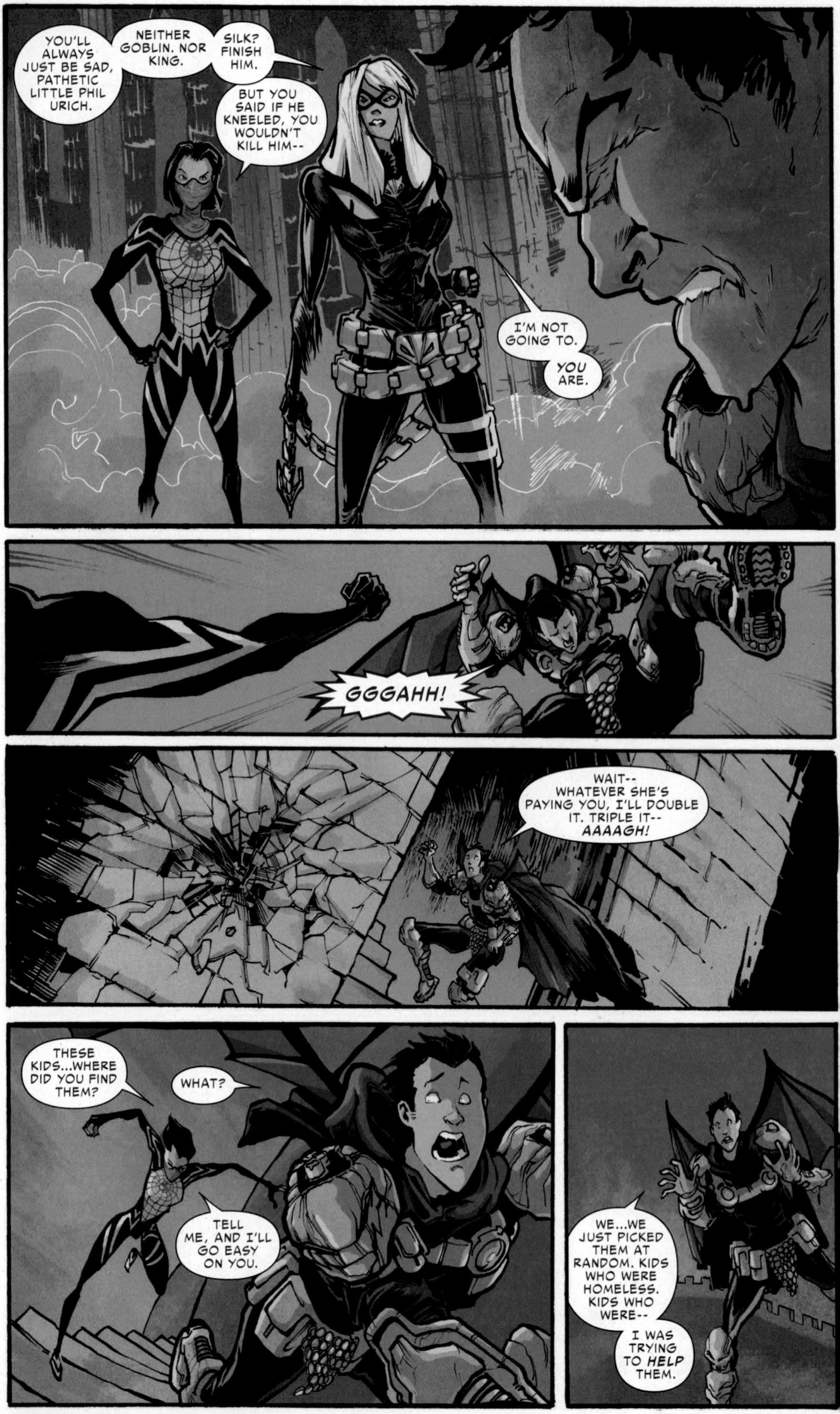
YOU'LL ALWAYS JUST BE SAD, PATHETIC LITTLE PHIL URICH.
NEITHER GOBLIN. NOR KING.
SILK? FINISH HIM.
BUT YOU SAID IF HE KNEELED, YOU WOULDN'T KILL HIM--
I'M NOT GOING TO.
YOU ARE.
GGGAHH!
WAIT-- WHATEVER SHE'S PAYING YOU, I'LL DOUBLE IT. TRIPLE IT-- AAAAGH!
THESE KIDS...WHERE DID YOU FIND THEM?
WHAT?
TELL ME, AND I'LL GO EASY ON YOU.
WE...WE JUST PICKED THEM AT RANDOM. KIDS WHO WERE HOMELESS. KIDS WHO WERE--
I WAS TRYING TO HELP THEM.

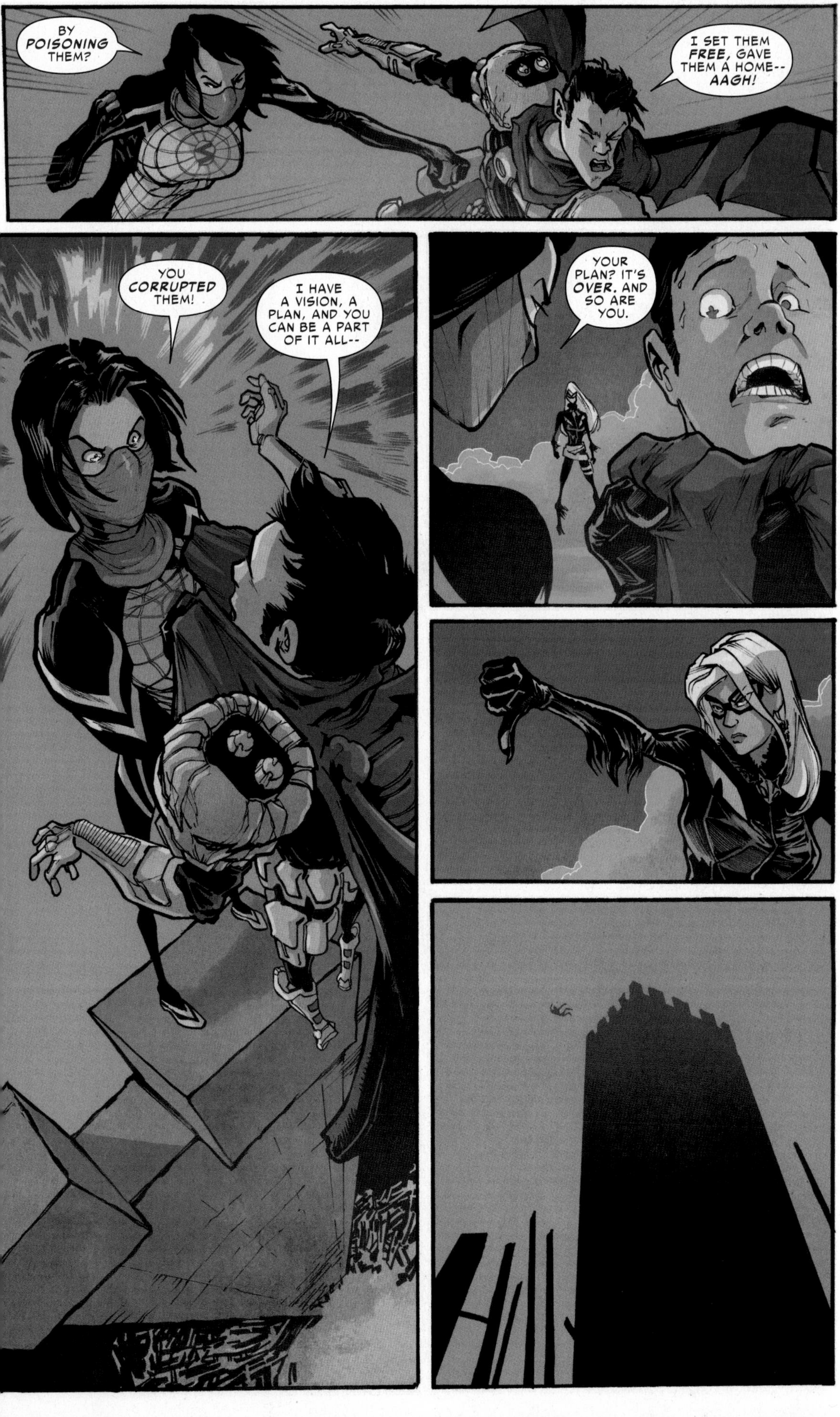

BY POISONING THEM?
I SET THEM FREE, GAVE THEM A HOME-- AAGH!
YOU CORRUPTED THEM!
I HAVE A VISION, A PLAN, AND YOU CAN BE A PART OF IT ALL--
YOUR PLAN? IT'S OVER. AND SO ARE YOU.

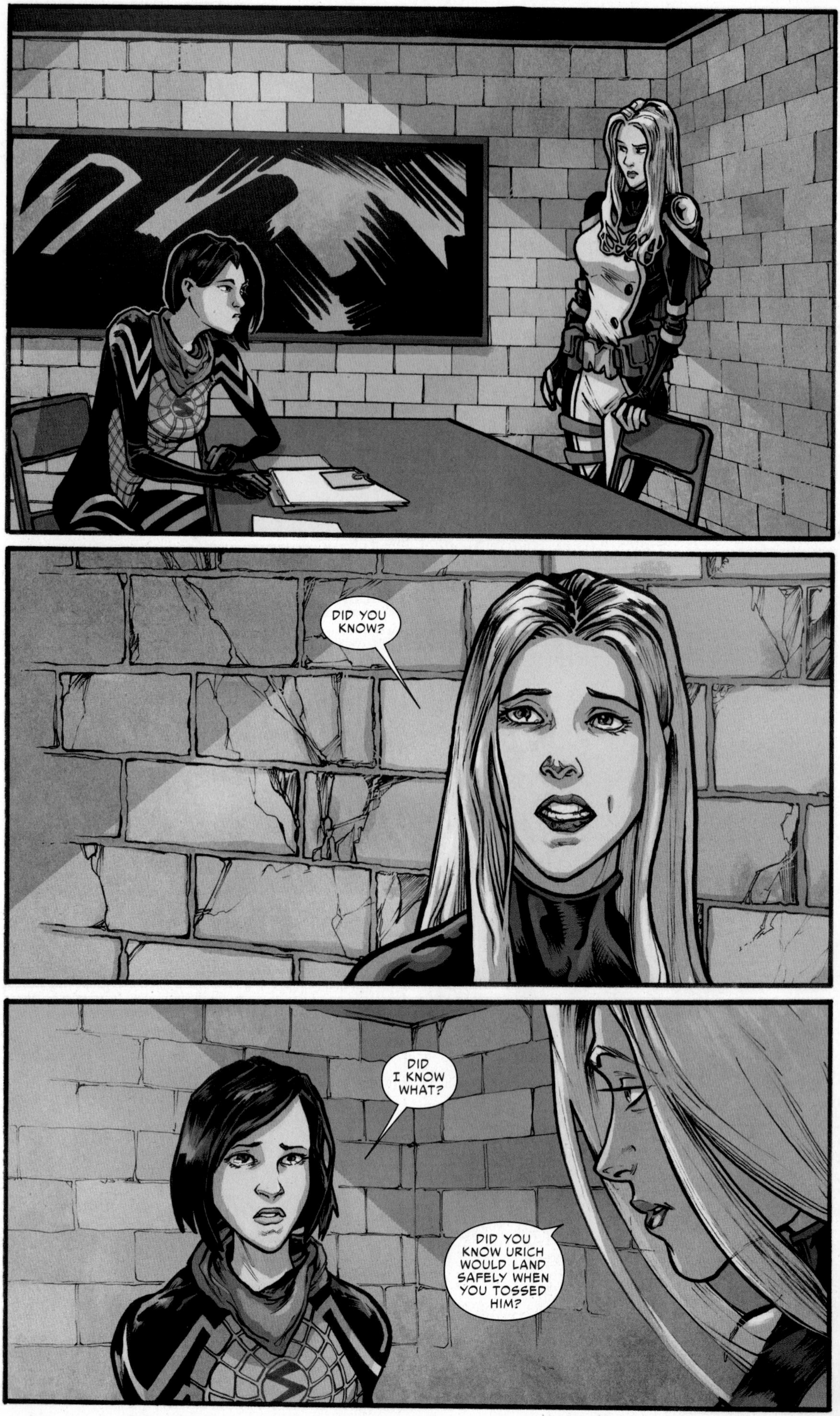
DID YOU KNOW?
DID I KNOW WHAT?
DID YOU KNOW URICH WOULD LAND SAFELY WHEN YOU TOSSED HIM?

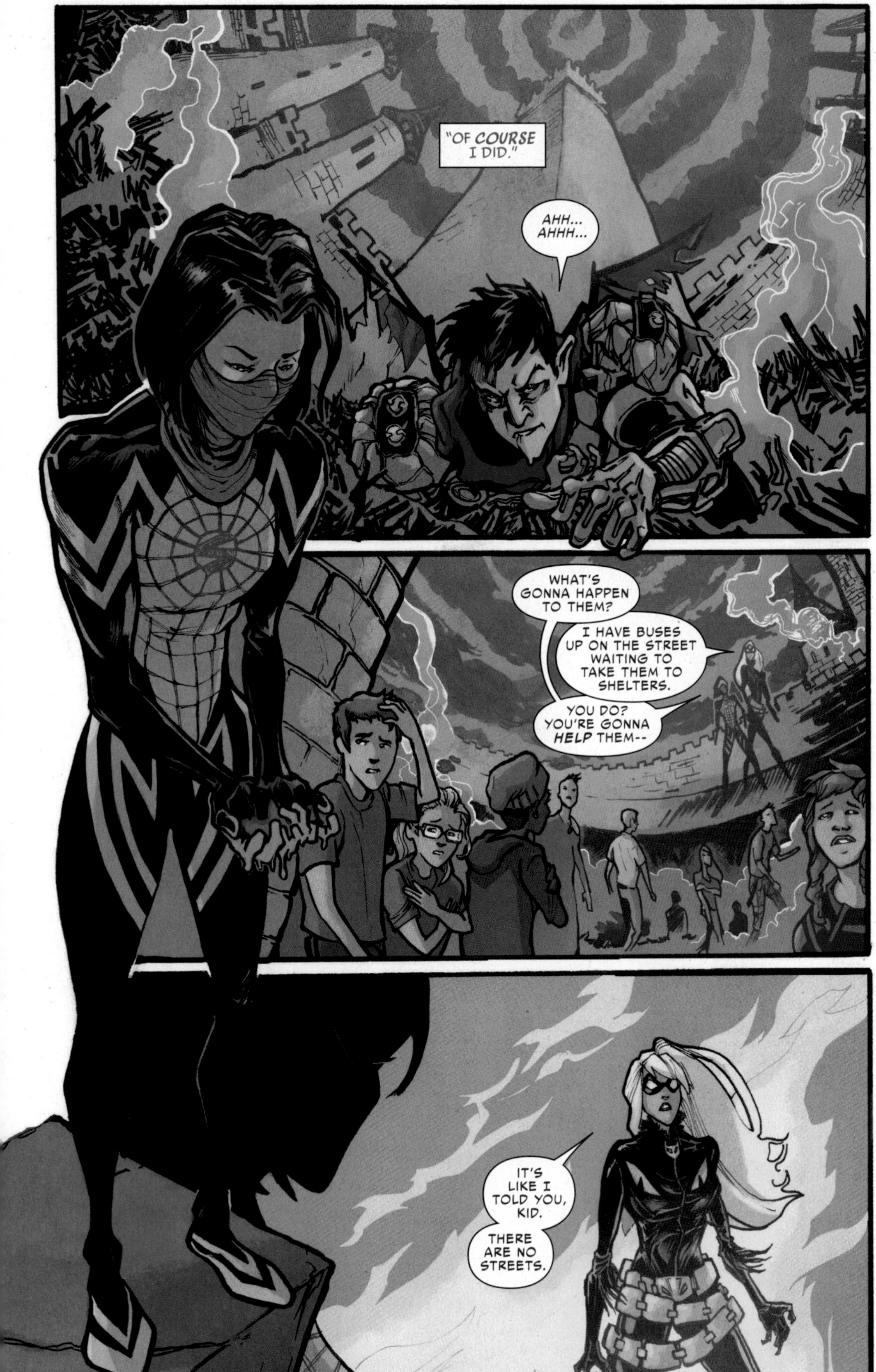
"OF COURSE I DID."
AHH... AHHH...
WHAT'S GONNA HAPPEN TO THEM?
I HAVE BUSES UP ON THE STREET WAITING TO TAKE THEM TO SHELTERS.
YOU DO? YOU'RE GONNA HELP THEM--
IT'S LIKE I TOLD YOU, KID.
THERE ARE NO STREETS.

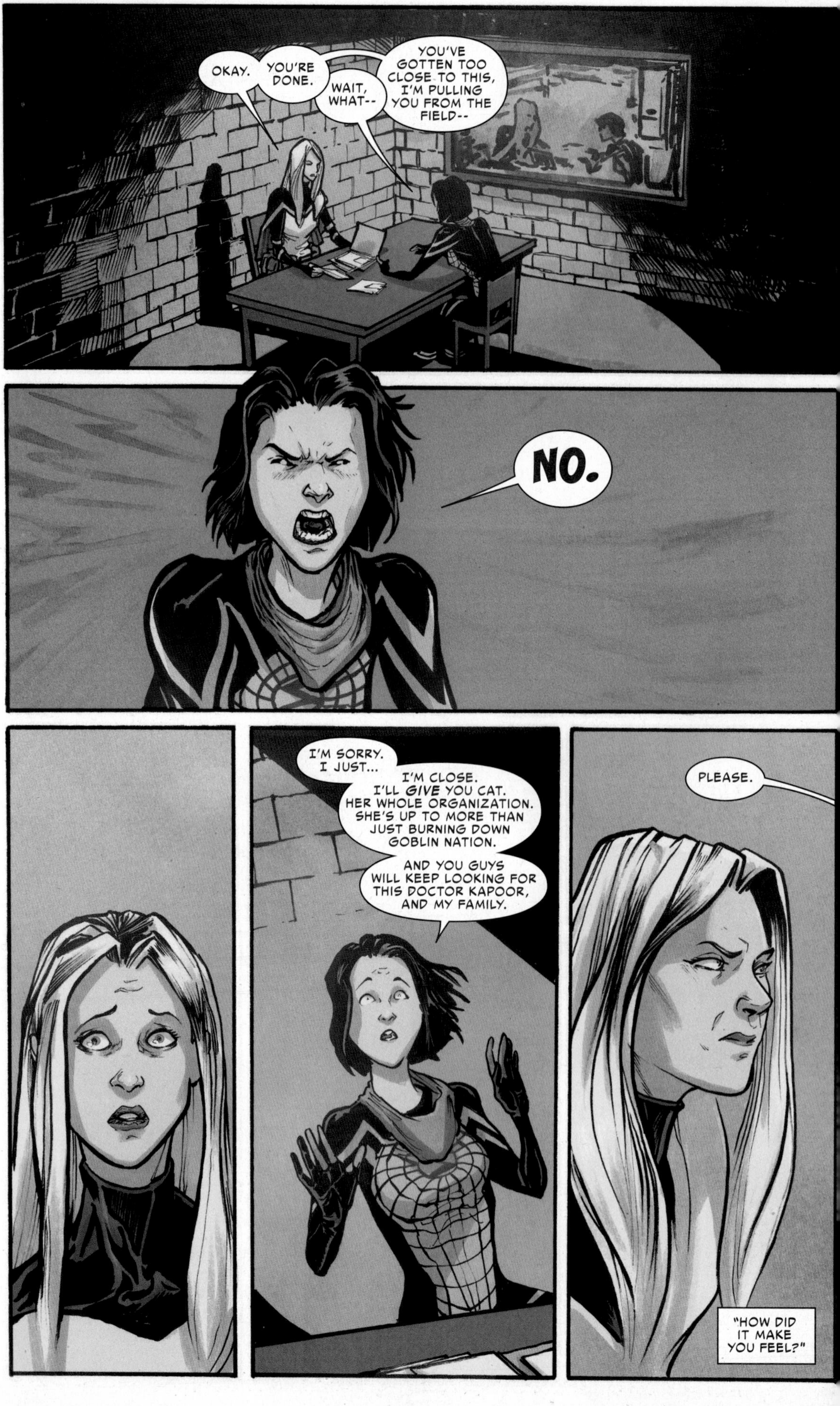
OKAY.
YOU'RE DONE.
YOU'VE GOTTEN TOO CLOSE TO THIS, I'M PULLING YOU FROM THE FIELD--
WAIT, WHAT--
NO.
I'M SORRY. I JUST...
I'M CLOSE. I'LL *GIVE* YOU CAT. HER WHOLE ORGANIZATION. SHE'S UP TO MORE THAN JUST BURNING DOWN GOBLIN NATION.
AND YOU GUYS WILL KEEP LOOKING FOR THIS DOCTOR KAPOOR, AND MY FAMILY.
PLEASE.
"HOW DID IT MAKE YOU FEEL?"

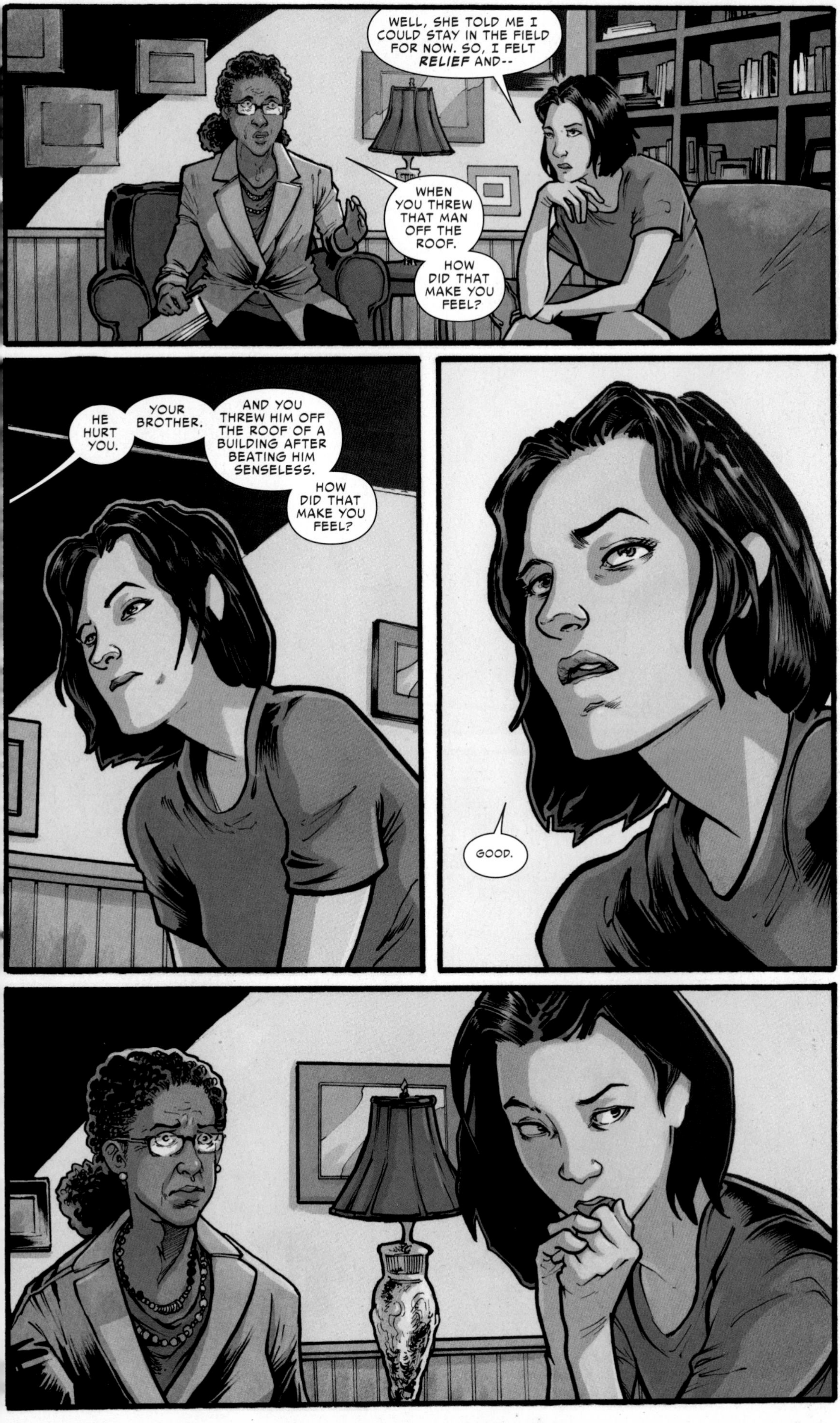

WELL, SHE TOLD ME I COULD STAY IN THE FIELD FOR NOW. SO, I FELT *RELIEF* AND--
WHEN YOU THREW THAT MAN OFF THE ROOF.
HOW DID THAT MAKE YOU FEEL?
HE HURT YOU.
YOUR BROTHER.
AND YOU THREW HIM OFF THE ROOF OF A BUILDING AFTER BEATING HIM SENSELESS.
HOW DID THAT MAKE YOU FEEL?
GOOD.

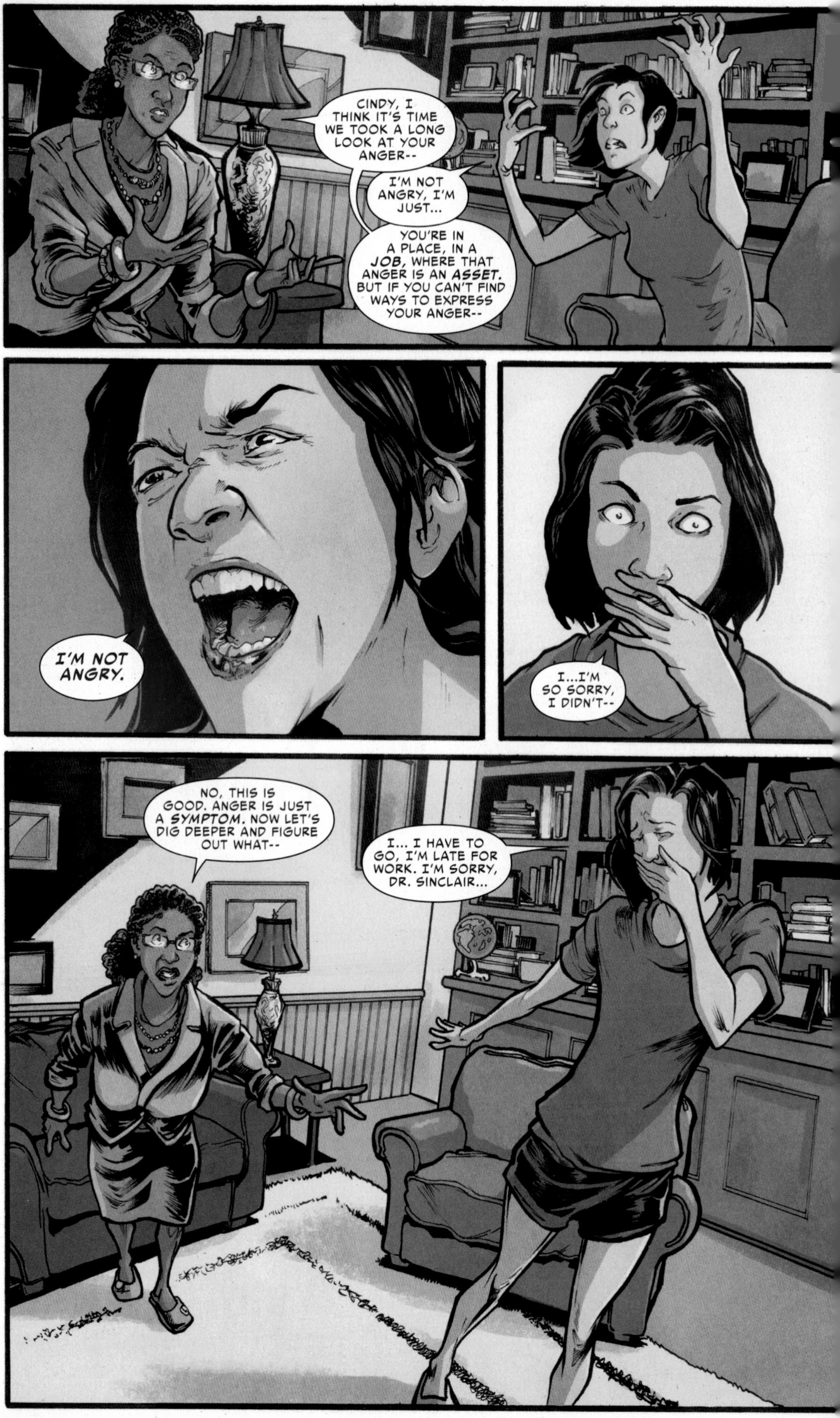
CINDY, I THINK IT'S TIME WE TOOK A LONG LOOK AT YOUR ANGER--
I'M NOT ANGRY, I'M JUST...
YOU'RE IN A PLACE, IN A *JOB*, WHERE THAT ANGER IS AN *ASSET*. BUT IF YOU CAN'T FIND WAYS TO EXPRESS YOUR ANGER--
I'M NOT ANGRY.
I...I'M SO SORRY, I DIDN'T--
NO, THIS IS GOOD. ANGER IS JUST A *SYMPTOM*. NOW LET'S DIG DEEPER AND FIGURE OUT WHAT--
I... I HAVE TO GO, I'M LATE FOR WORK. I'M SORRY, DR. SINCLAIR...

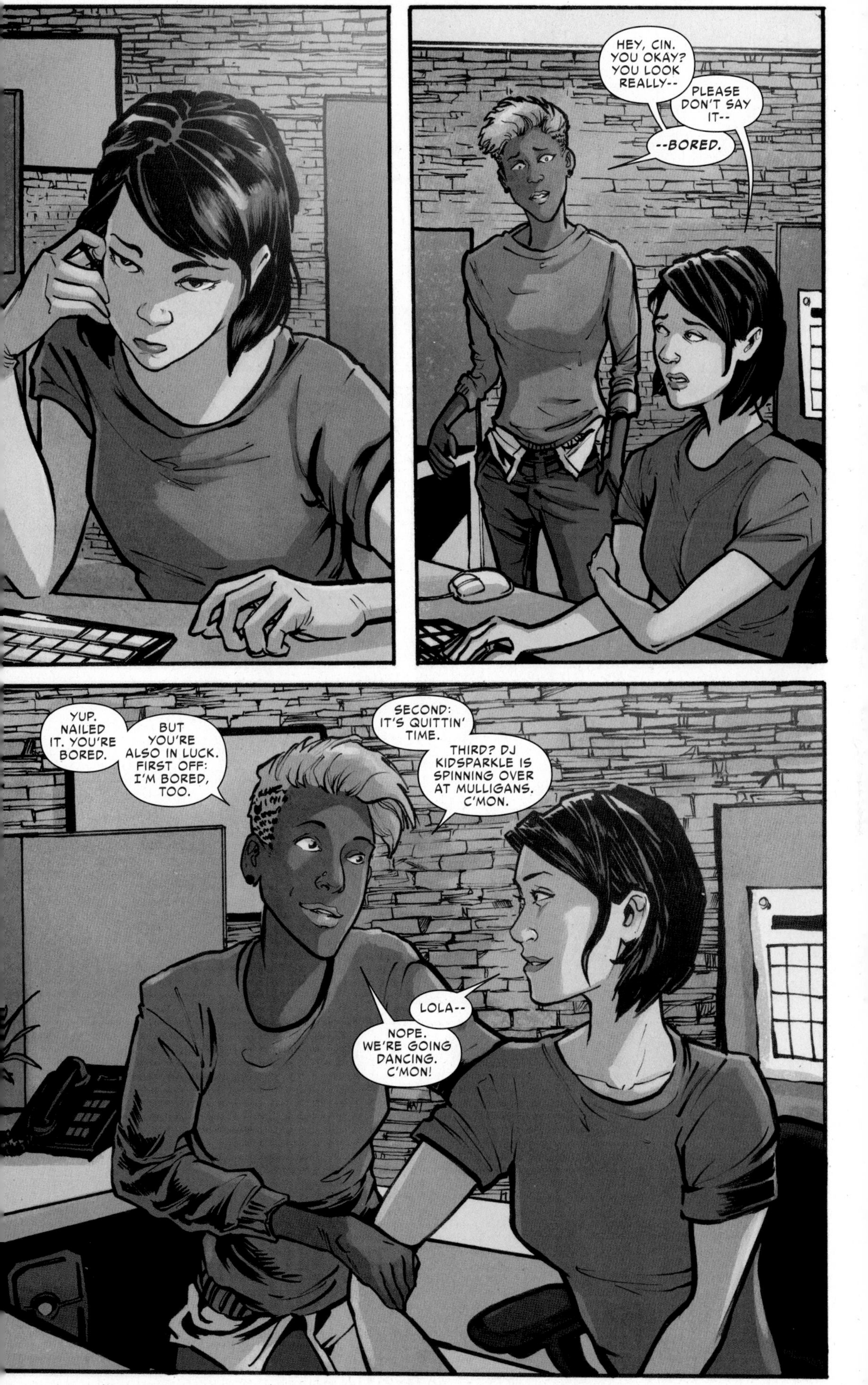
HEY, CIN. YOU OKAY? YOU LOOK REALLY--
PLEASE DON'T SAY IT--
--BORED.
YUP. NAILED IT. YOU'RE BORED.
BUT YOU'RE ALSO IN LUCK. FIRST OFF: I'M BORED, TOO.
SECOND: IT'S QUITTIN' TIME.
THIRD? DJ KIDSPARKLE IS SPINNING OVER AT MULLIGANS. C'MON.
LOLA--
NOPE. WE'RE GOING DANCING. C'MON!

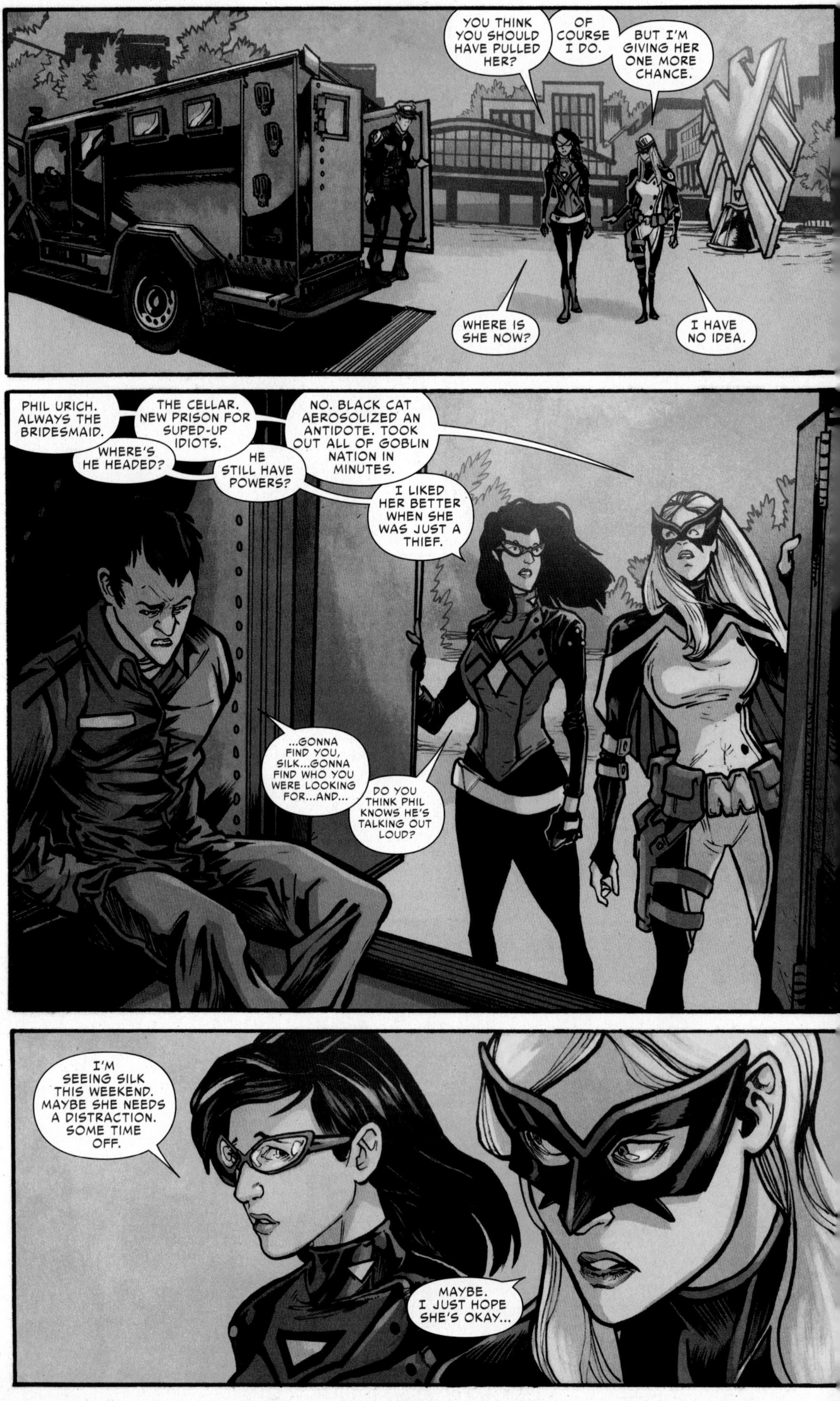
YOU THINK YOU SHOULD HAVE PULLED HER?
OF COURSE I DO.
BUT I'M GIVING HER ONE MORE CHANCE.
WHERE IS SHE NOW?
I HAVE NO IDEA.
PHIL URICH. ALWAYS THE BRIDESMAID.
WHERE'S HE HEADED?
THE CELLAR. NEW PRISON FOR SUPED-UP IDIOTS.
HE STILL HAVE POWERS?
NO. BLACK CAT AEROSOLIZED AN ANTIDOTE. TOOK OUT ALL OF GOBLIN NATION IN MINUTES.
I LIKED HER BETTER WHEN SHE WAS JUST A THIEF.
...GONNA FIND YOU, SILK...GONNA FIND WHO YOU WERE LOOKING FOR...AND...
DO YOU THINK PHIL KNOWS HE'S TALKING OUT LOUD?
I'M SEEING SILK THIS WEEKEND. MAYBE SHE NEEDS A DISTRACTION. SOME TIME OFF.
MAYBE. I JUST HOPE SHE'S OKAY...

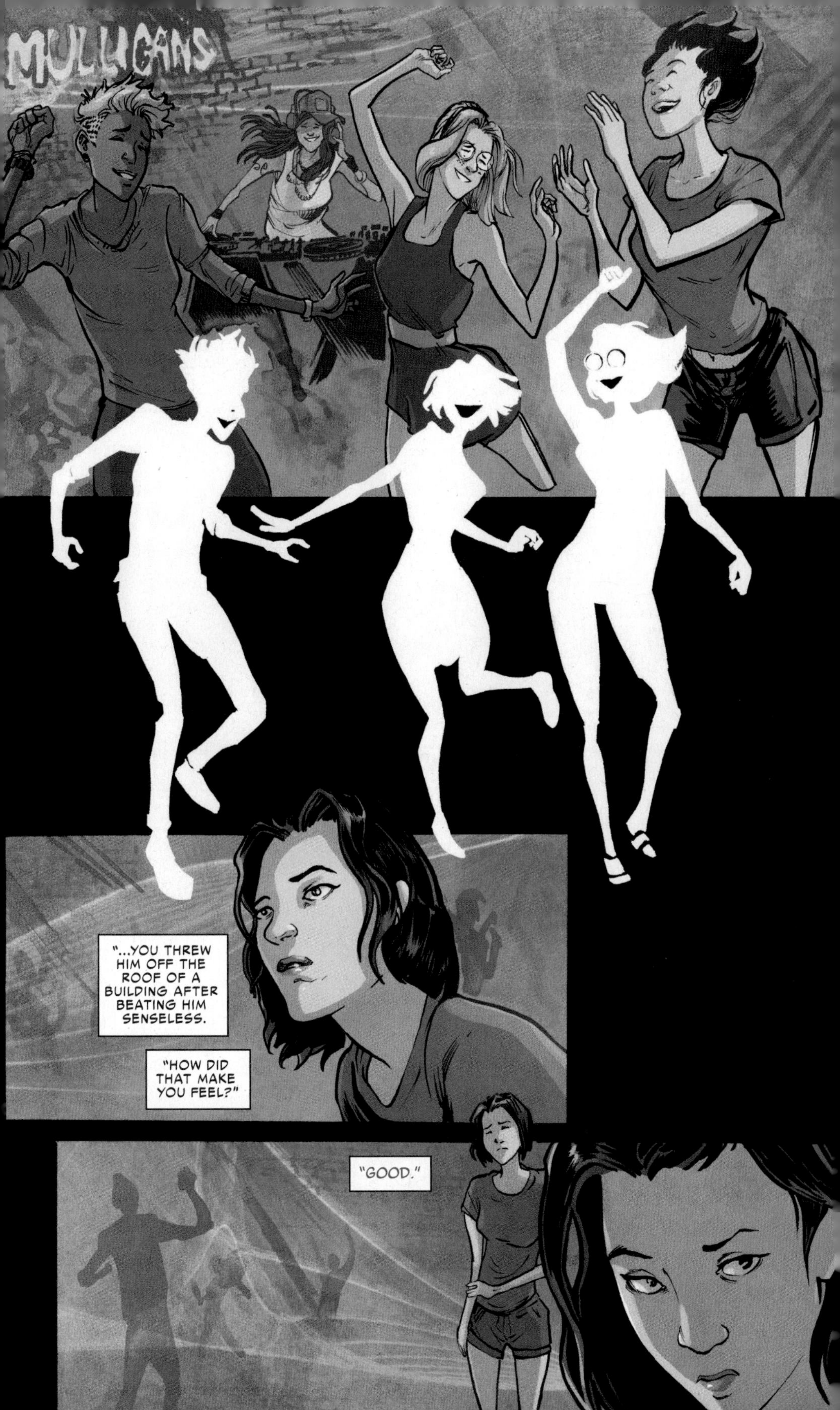
MULLIGANS
"...YOU THREW HIM OFF THE ROOF OF A BUILDING AFTER BEATING HIM SENSELESS.
"HOW DID THAT MAKE YOU FEEL?"
"GOOD."
NEXT: SPIDER-WOMEN!!

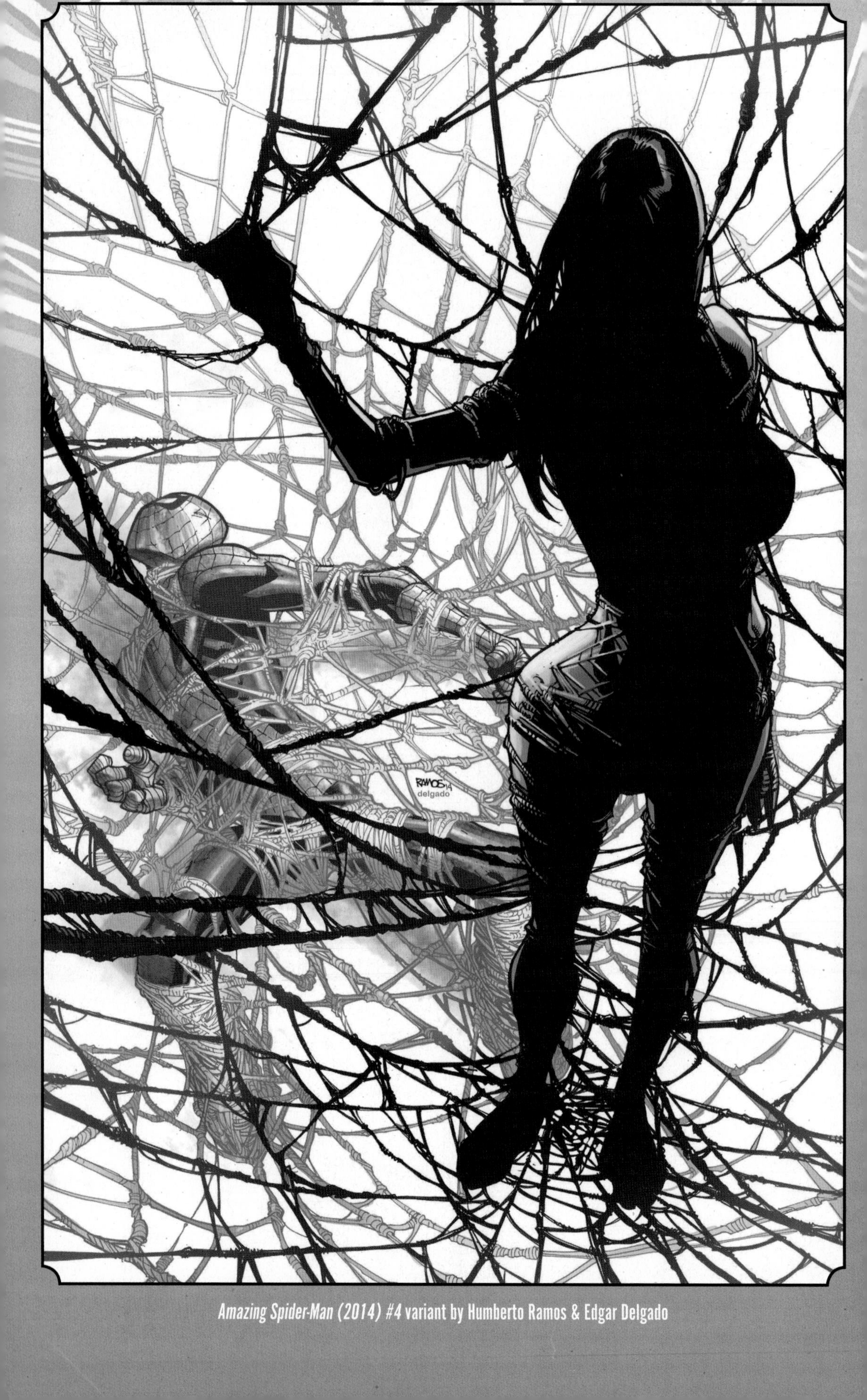
RAMOS 14
delgado

Amazing Spider-Man (2014) #4 variant by Humberto Ramos & Edgar Delgado

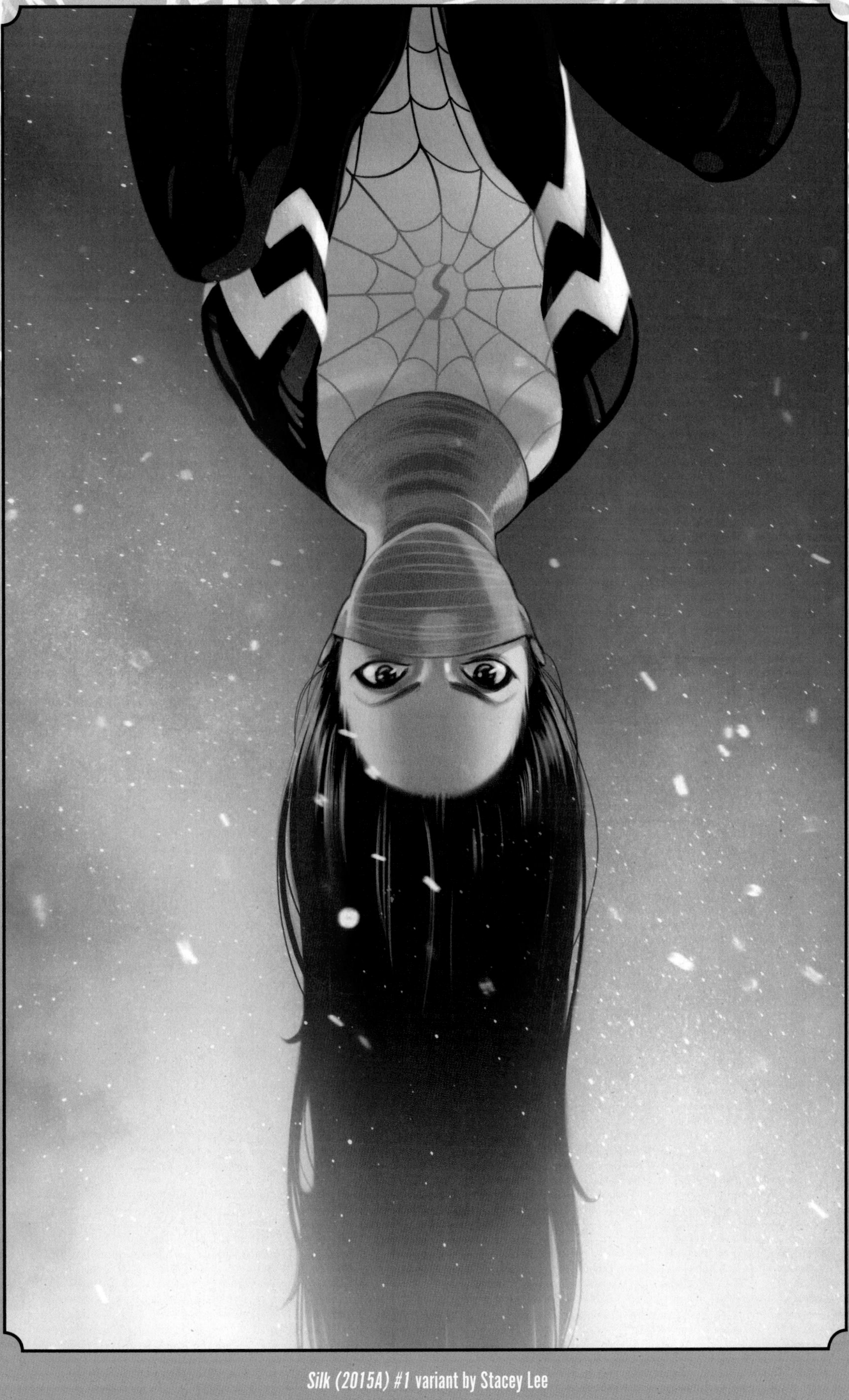

Silk (2015A) #1 variant by Stacey Lee

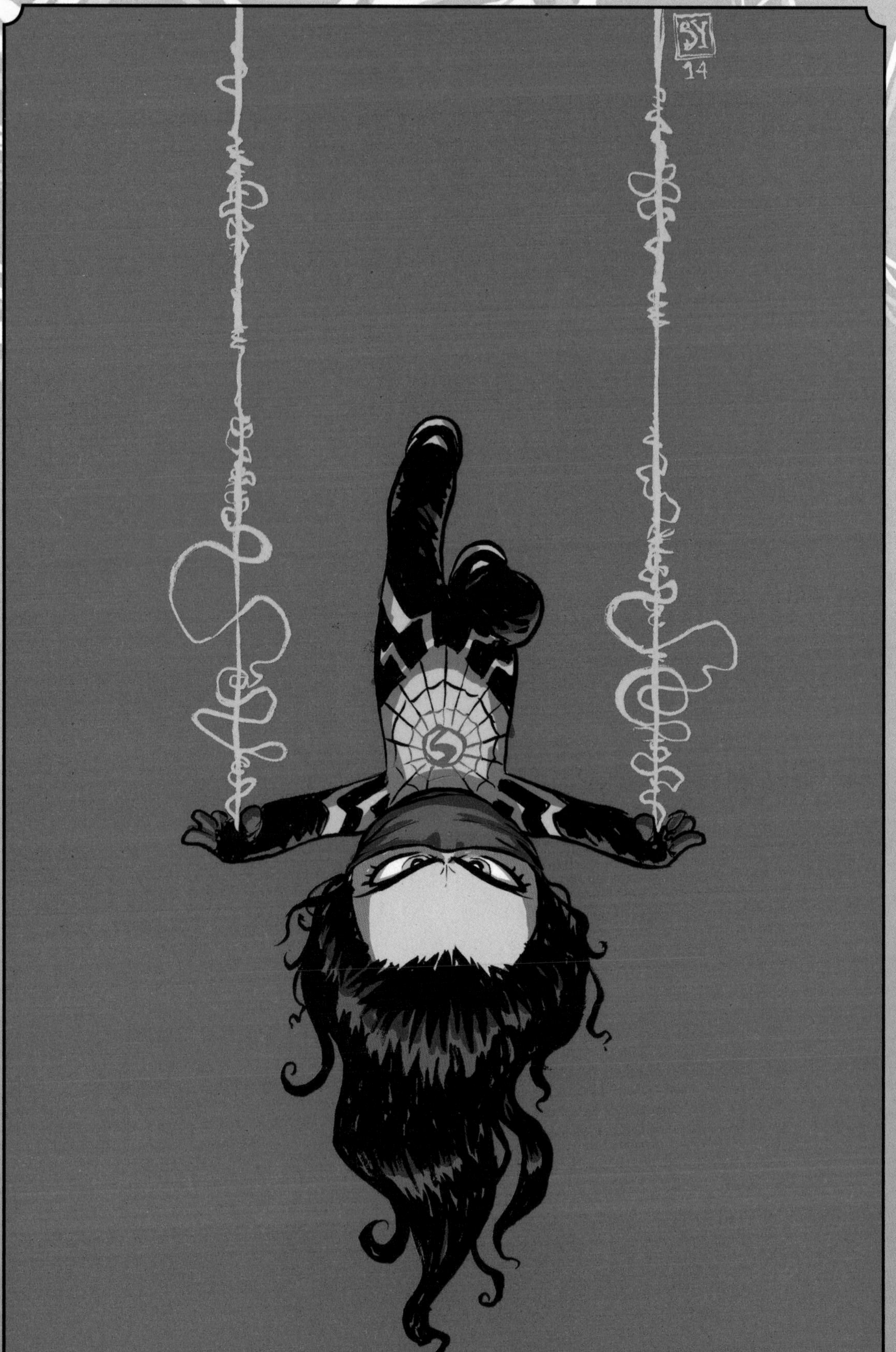
SY
14

Silk (2015A) #1 variant by Skottie Young

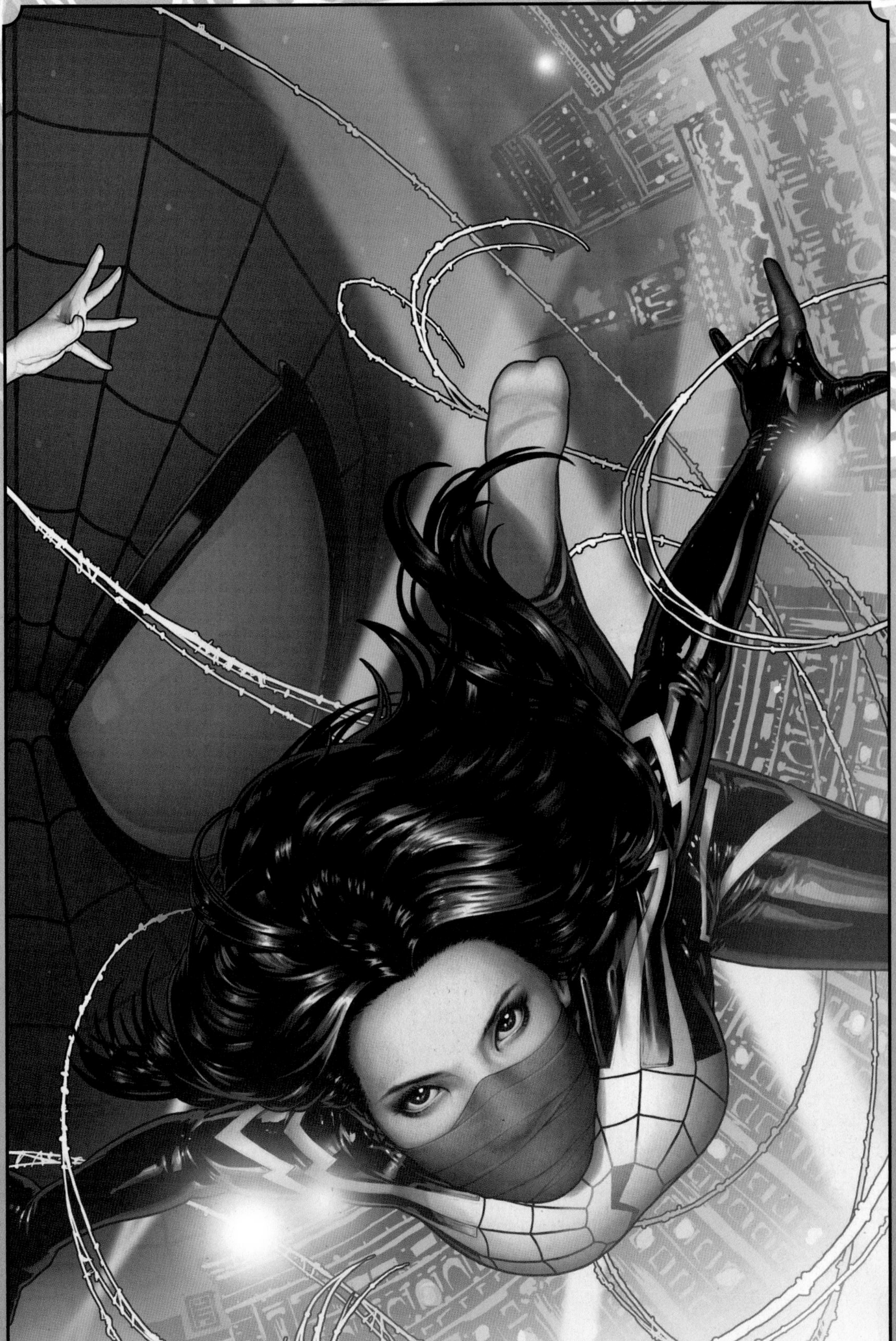

Silk (2015A) #1 variant by John Tyler Christopher

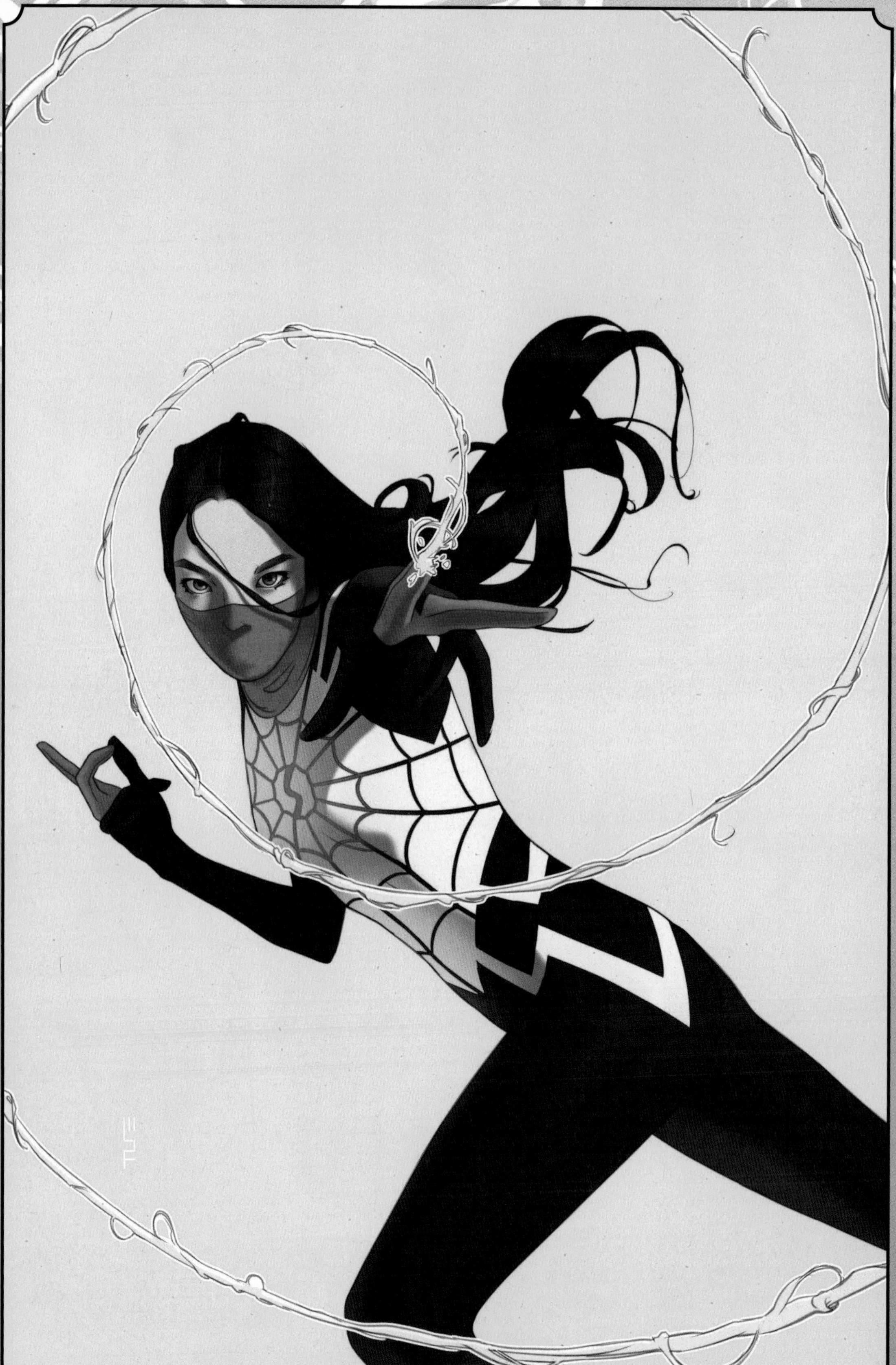

Silk (2015A) #2 variant by W. Scott Forbes

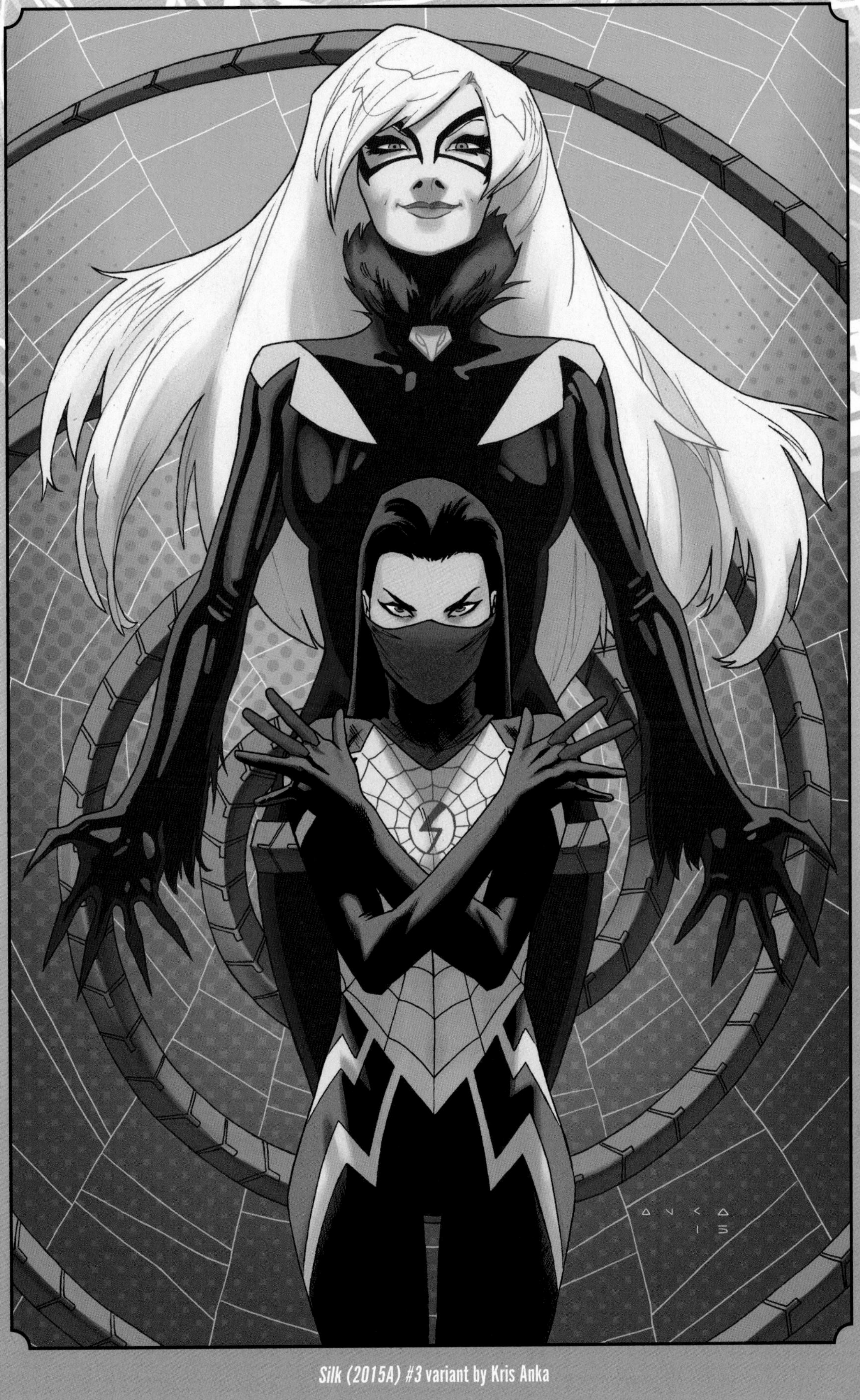
ANKA 15

Silk (2015A) #3 variant by Kris Anka

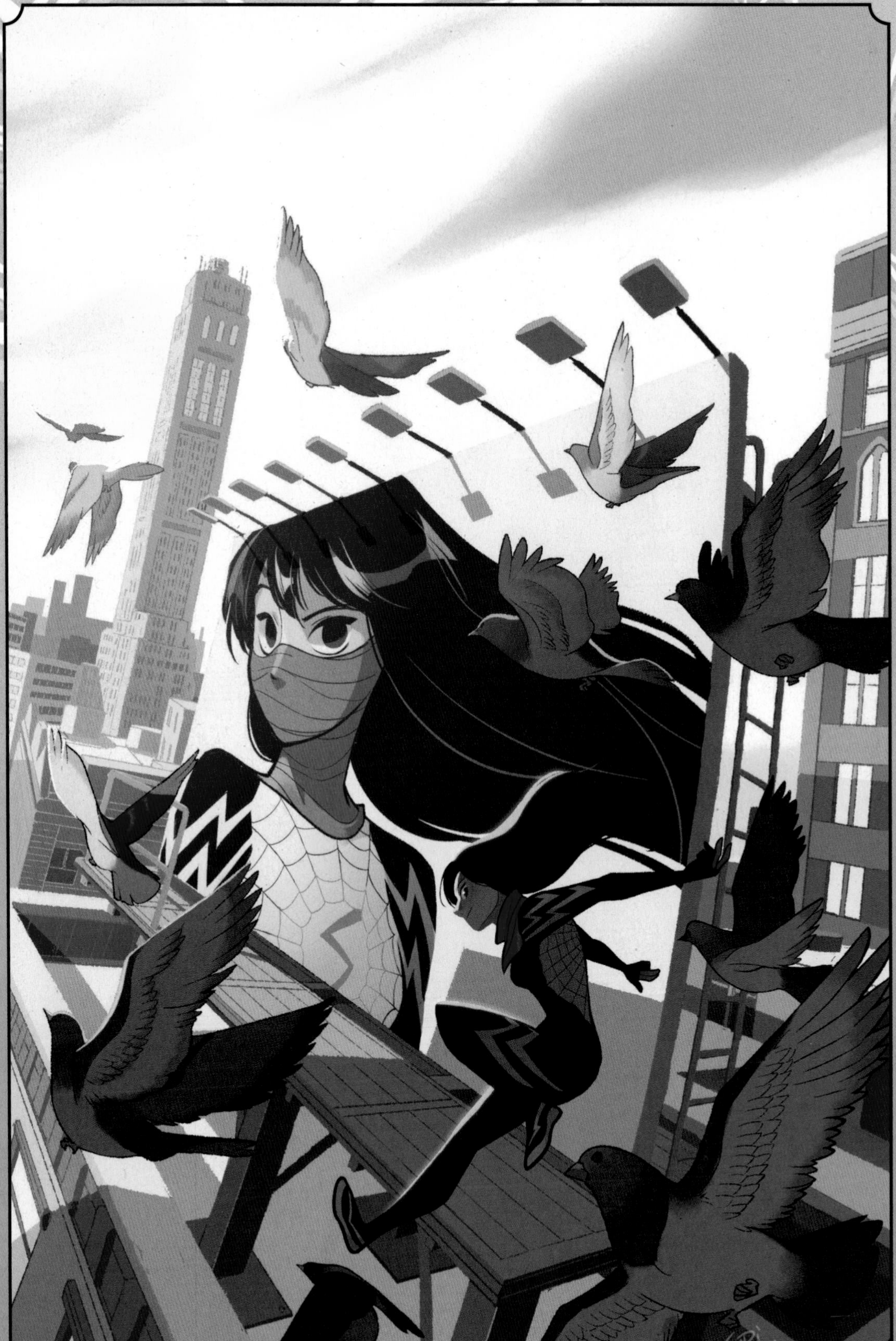
GURIHIRU

Silk (2015A) #7 Manga variant by Gurihiru

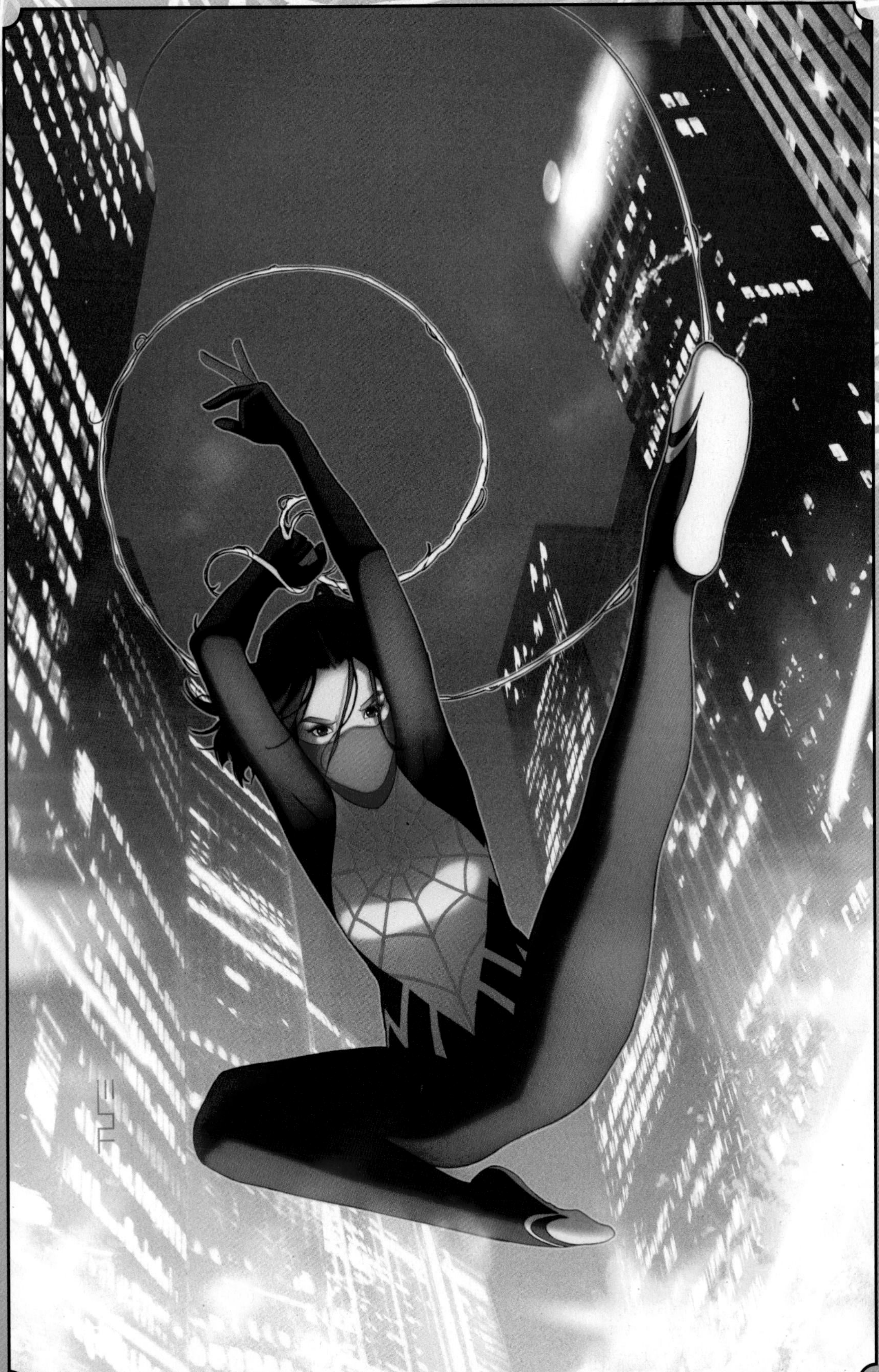

Silk (2015B) #1 variant by W. Scott Forbes

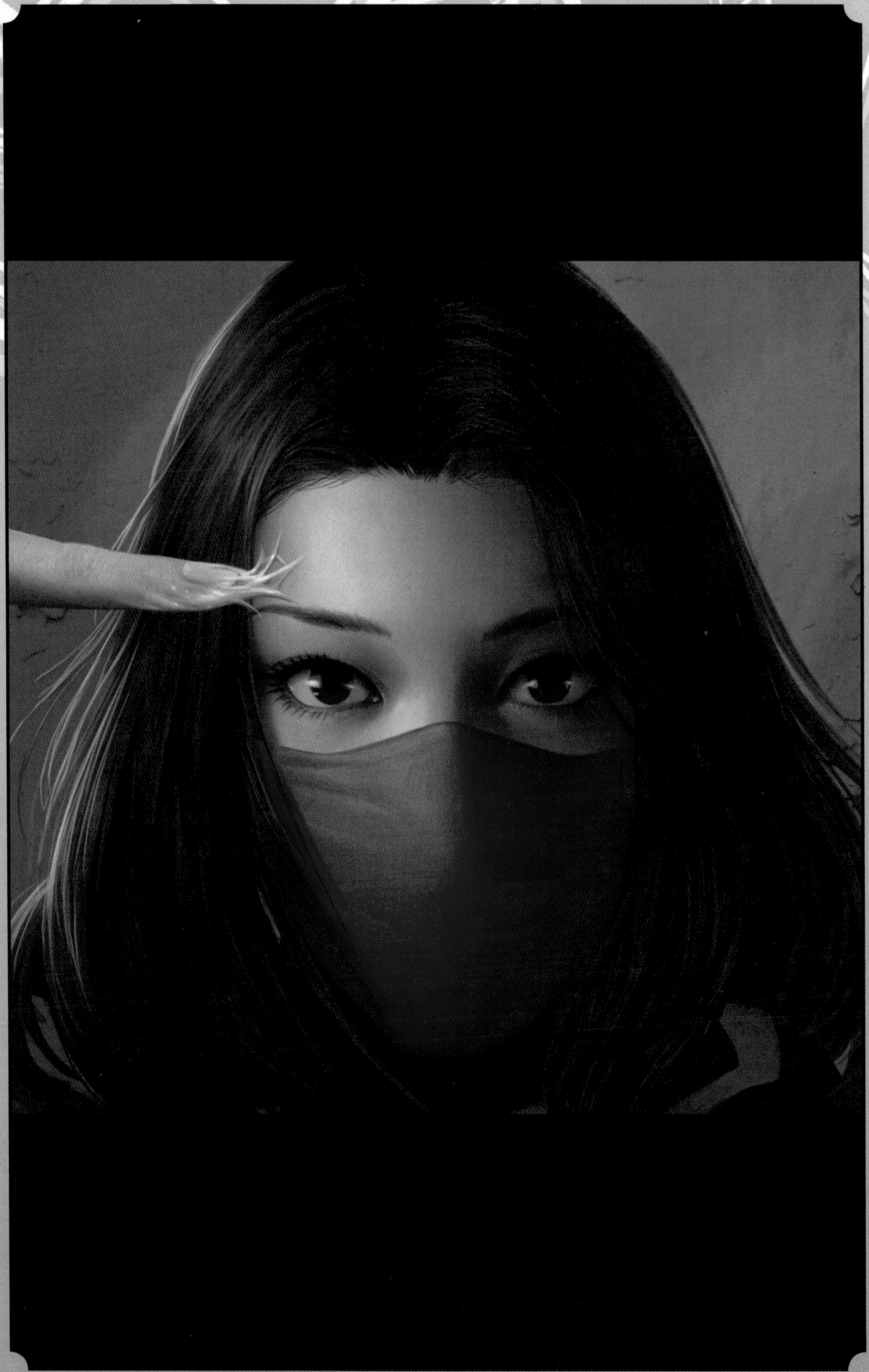

Silk (2015B) #1 Hip-Hop variant by Woo Dae Shim

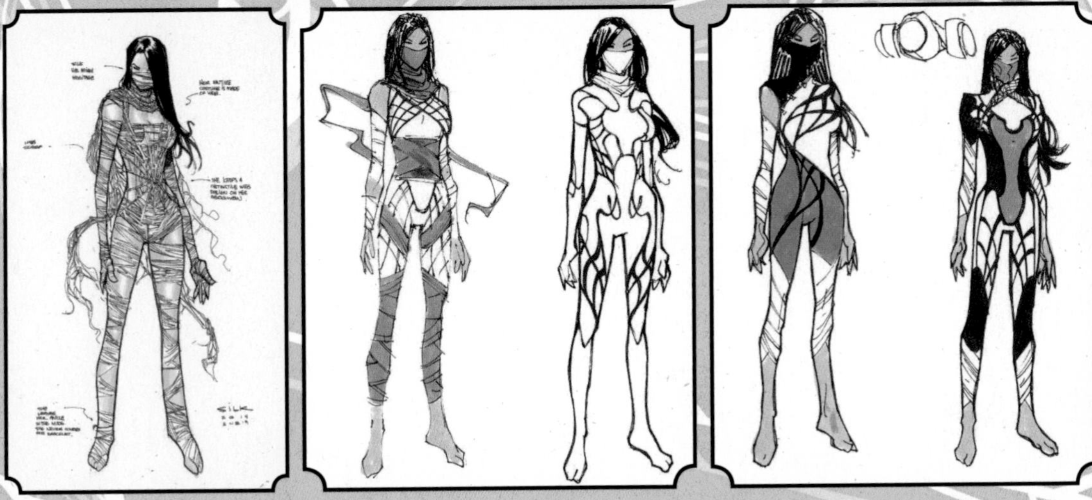

Silk character designs by Humberto Ramos

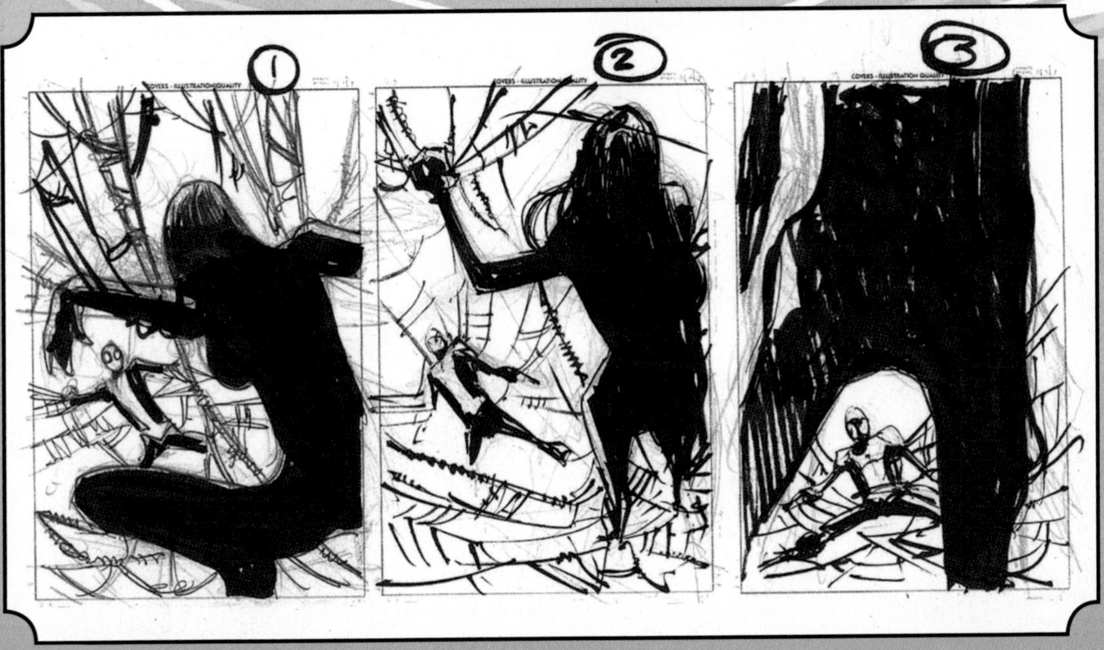

Amazing Spider-Man (2014) #4 variant cover sketches by Humberto Ramos

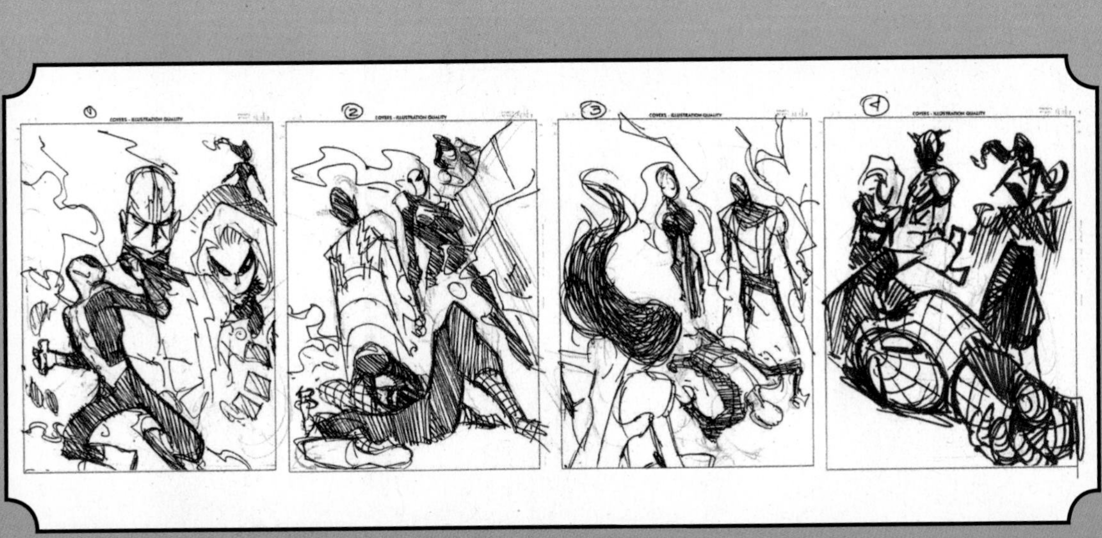

Amazing Spider-Man (2014) #5 cover sketches by Humberto Ramos

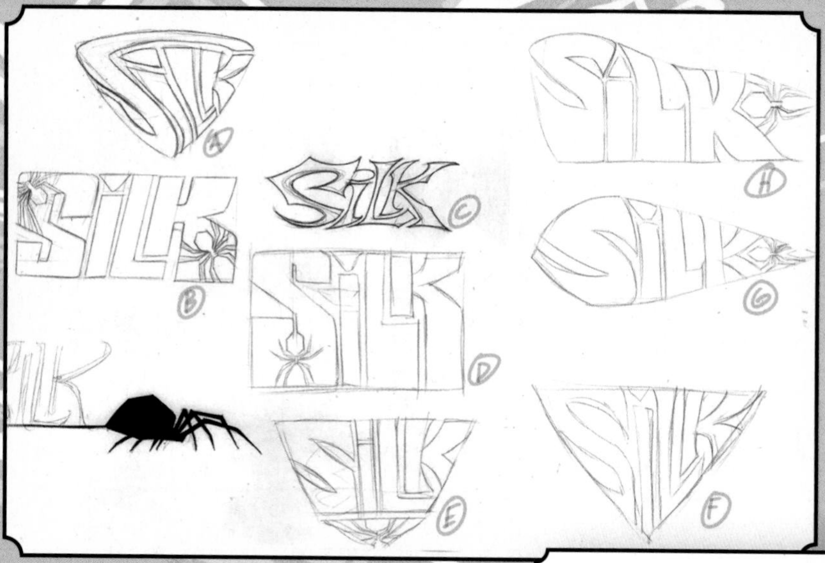

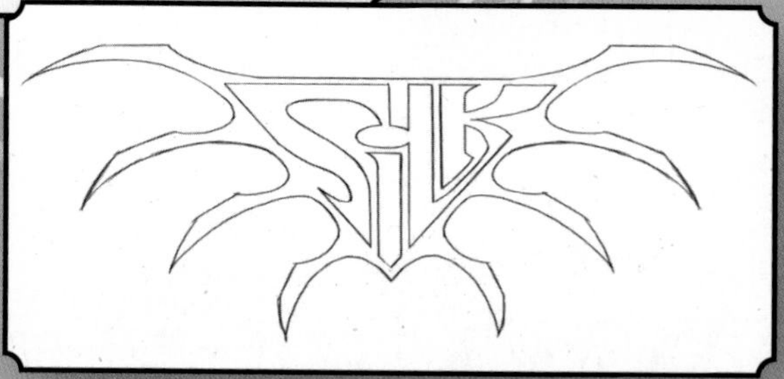

Silk logo sketches by Dave Johnson

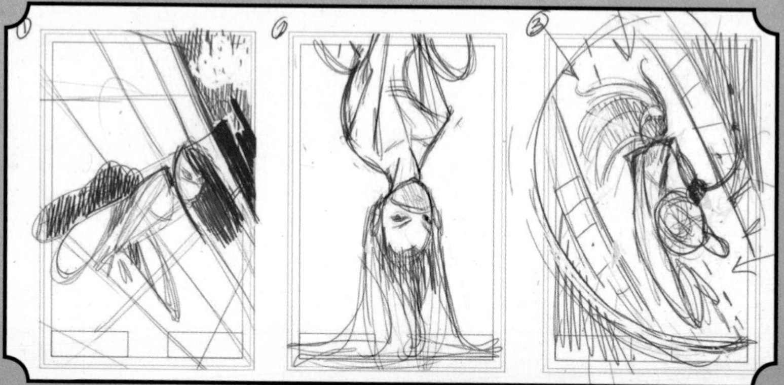

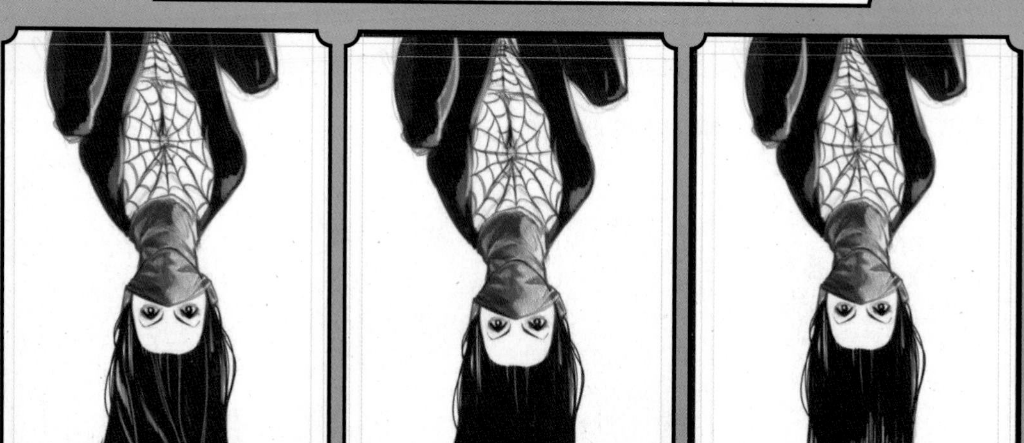

Silk (2015A) #1 variant cover sketches by Stacey Lee

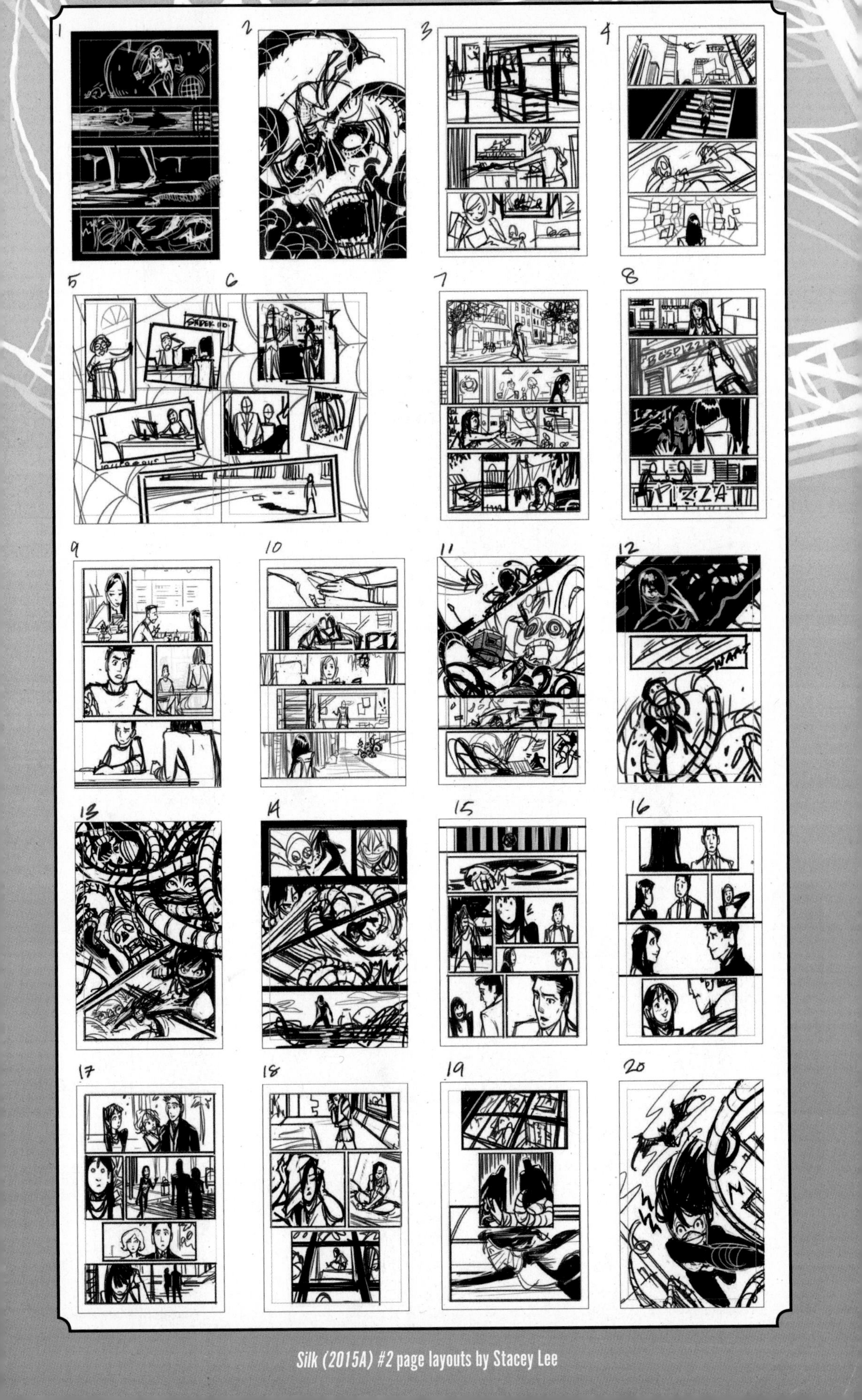
1
2
3
4
5
6
7
8
9
10
11
12
13
14
15
16
17
18
19
20
PIZZA

Silk (2015A) #2 page layouts by Stacey Lee

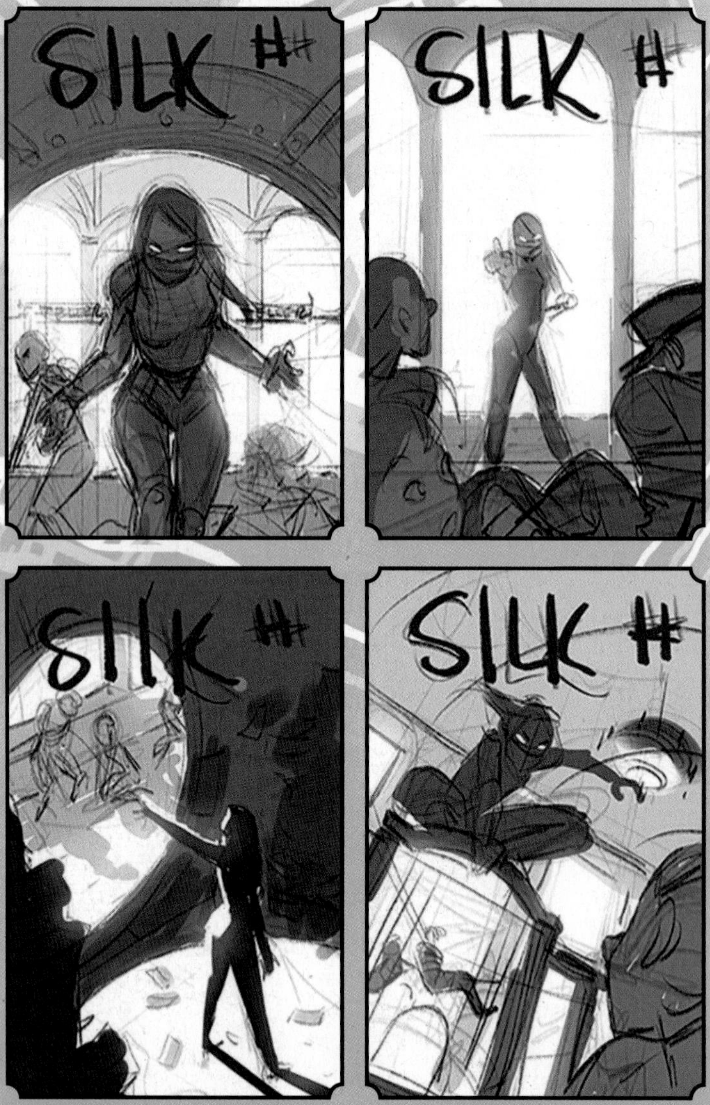
SILK #
SILK #
SILK #
SILK #

Silk (2015B) #1 cover sketches by Helen Chen

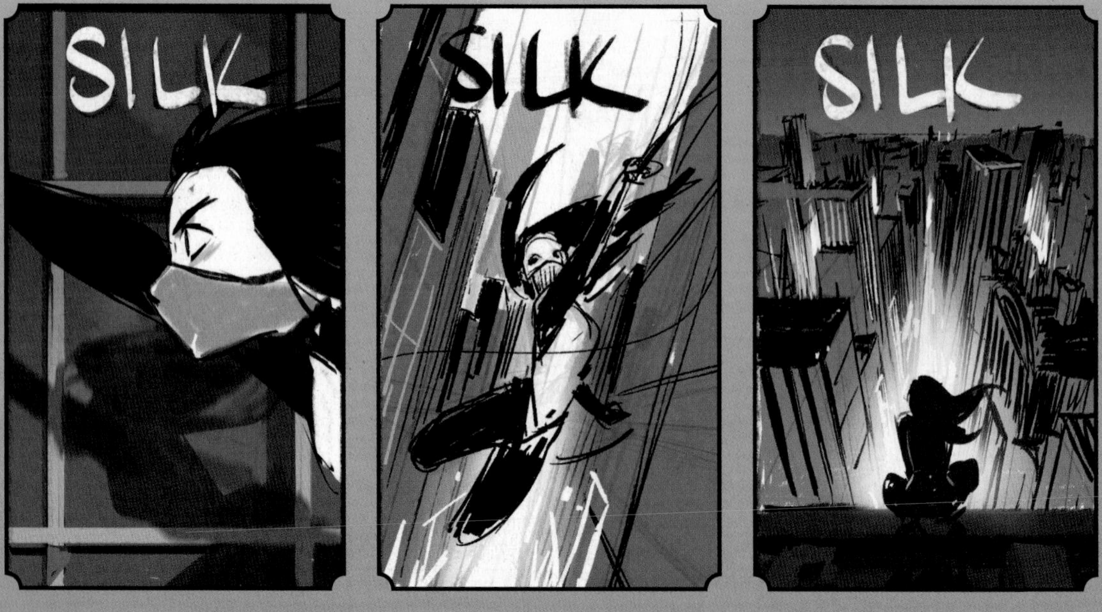
SILK
SILK
SILK

Silk (2015B) #3 cover sketches by Helen Chen

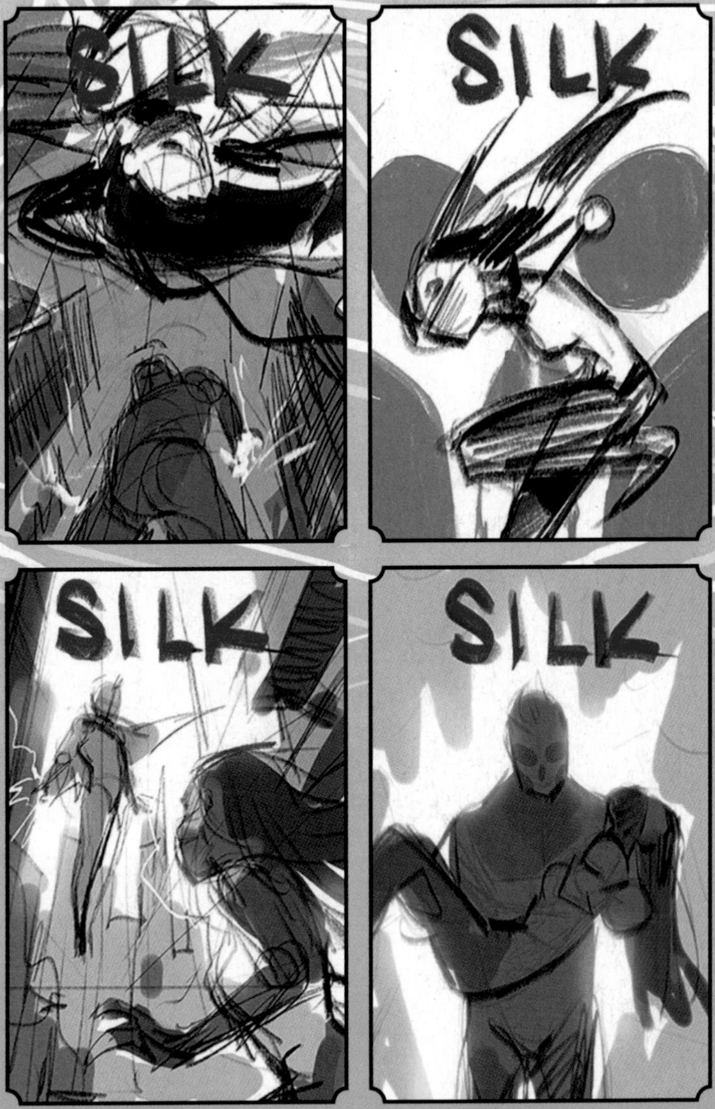
SILK
SILK
SILK
SILK

Silk (2015B) #4 cover sketches by Helen Chen

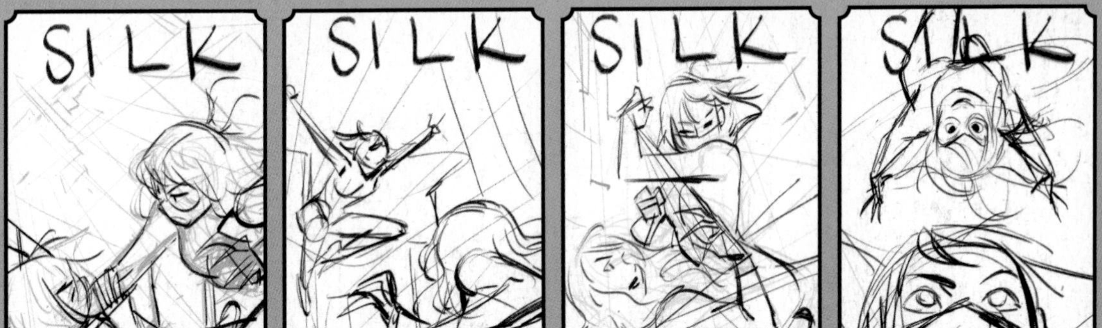
SILK
SILK
SILK
SILK

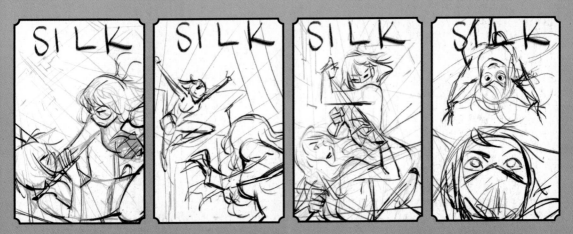

Silk (2015B) #5 cover sketches by Helen Chen

Silk (2015B) #6 cover sketches by Helen Chen

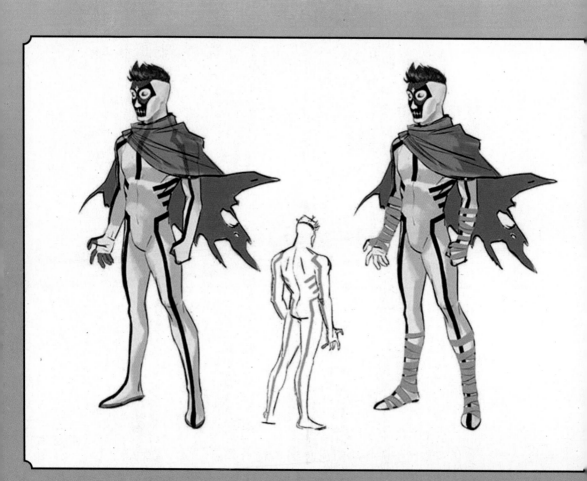

Spectro character designs by Helen Chen